Economic Reform and State-Owned Enterprises in China 1979–1987

Studies on Contemporary China

The Contemporary China Institute, based at the School of Oriental and African Studies (University of London), was established in 1968. Throughout its existence, it has been a national focus for research and publications on twentieth-century China. This new series, which is edited at the Institute, seeks to maintain and extend that tradition by making available the best work of scholars throughout the world. Future volumes will embrace a wide variety of subjects, including China's social, political, and economic change, intellectual and cultural developments, and foreign relations.

Economic Reform and State-Owned Enterprises in China, 1979–1987

DONALD HAY, DEREK MORRIS,
GUY LIU, AND SHUJIE YAO

CLARENDON PRESS · OXFORD

This book has been printed digitally and produced in a standard specification in order to ensure its continuing availability

OXFORD
UNIVERSITY PRESS

Great Clarendon Street, Oxford OX2 6DP

Oxford University Press is a department of the University of Oxford.
It furthers the University's objective of excellence in research, scholarship, and education by publishing worldwide in

Oxford New York

Auckland Bangkok Buenos Aires Cape Town Chennai
Dar es Salaam Delhi Hong Kong Istanbul Karachi Kolkata
Kuala Lumpur Madrid Melbourne Mexico City Mumbai Nairobi
São Paulo Shanghai Singapore Taipei Tokyo Toronto

with an associated company in Berlin

Oxford is a registered trade mark of Oxford University Press in the UK and in certain other countries

Published in the United States
by Oxford University Press Inc., New York

Reprinted 2002

ISBN 0-19-828845-X

Foreword

Reform of the economic system in China has two aspects, operational reform and ownership reform. Operational reform refers to the substitution of the mandatory planning system by a market-orientated system. Ownership reform includes two elements. The first element is to reform the existing ownership structure where public ownership predominates. A multi-ownership system may be established in which the public sector still plays a key role but other forms of ownership are encouraged. The second element is to reform state (public) ownership itself and establish a new form of public ownership in order to stimulate economic growth. The two aspects of economic reform are interdependent. The formation and successful operation of a market system, which depends on other reforms such as price reform to allow the market instead of government to determine prices, should permit state-owned enterprises to operate in the market. So it is necessary to reform their ownership because without reform they are unlikely to become a major force in the market. Of the two aspects of reform, ownership reform, especially in state-owned enterprises, is the more critical. This is because state-owned enterprises still play an important role in the national economy despite the fact that the collective and private sectors have grown rapidly in recent years, and that the share of industrial output produced by such enterprises as a proportion of total industrial output declined from 77.6% in 1978 to 54.6% in 1990 (in current prices).

Reform in state-owned enterprises in China started in October 1978 when six state-owned enterprises in Sichuan were selected for an experiment in increasing enterprise autonomy. Since then, enterprise reform has experienced four different stages: (1) 1978–80, reform was focused on increasing enterprise autonomy; (2) 1981–82, reform was focused on contract profit delivered to the state; (3) 1983–86, reform was focused on the substitution of profit delivery with taxes; and (4) from 1987, reform has been focused on the contract-responsibility system. In 1992, reform in state-owned enterprises has entered a new stage, i.e. the share system. Although there are many different opinions about their reform, it is generally agreed that they should become entirely responsible for their own management, profits, and losses.

State-owned enterprises require reform to become independent. If they are not independent, they cannot participate actively in market activities and respond quickly to market signals. Before reform, they were not independent, being subject to state mandatory-plan control, and being simultaneously dictated to by many government departments.

They also require reform to be made responsible for their own profits and losses. If they are not responsible, they do not care about their own profits and losses, nor do they bear the risks from participation in market competition, or respond to market signals. Before reform, they were not responsible for their own profits or losses. Their profits were entirely or almost entirely delivered to the State. Except for short-term bank loans, their capital was directly allocated by the State. Their losses were entirely covered by budgetary subsidies.

There is no doubt that without reform of state-owned enterprises to enable them to become responsible for their own management, profits, and losses, they will not become a major force in the market and the market system cannot be established. Thus, the problem of their reform has attracted increasing attention. Without reform of state-owned enterprises, reform of the entire economic system is not likely to be successful.

However, reform of state-owned enterprises has been very difficult. Since the experiment in 1978, reform has continued for thirteen years but the target of making them entirely responsible for their own management, profits, and losses is still far from being achieved. Like China's economic system which is still in the process of being transformed from the old to the new system, state-owned enterprises are in a process of transformation. The old and new systems coexist and are reflected in every aspect of enterprise behaviour. They have a certain degree of autonomy but do not have entire autonomy. They are now concerned about profits and losses but not entirely responsible for them. If they make losses, the government still has to help them through direct subsidies, or a reduction in interest payments, or a delay in credit repayments. Thus, they currently depend on both the market and government. This creates various conflicts and makes it impossible for state-owned enterprises to behave like real competitors in the market. Improvements in enterprise performance are therefore limited. In recent years, state-owned enterprises have been making increasing losses. The proportion of loss-making firms has also been rising. How to reform these enterprises further has become an urgent problem for economic development in China.

As mentioned above, reform in state-owned enterprises began with increasing enterprise autonomy which was entirely necessary. Later reforms, including the replacement of profit delivery with taxes and the contract-responsibility system, were all intended to increase enterprise autonomy, to create hard budget constraints, and to make enterprises responsible for their own profits and losses. Although these reform measures have achieved many desirable outcomes, they have not solved all the problems. This is because the reform measures so far have not involved any reform of the property rights in these enterprises. I was the first to raise this issue in China (in September 1978, and published as an article in January 1979 in *Economic Research*). For a long time, the idea was not widely accepted. Most maintained that it was sufficient just to reform management and not necessary to reform the ownership system. After many years of experiments, more people have realized that state-owned enterprises cannot become entirely responsible for their own management, profits, and losses unless the ownership system is reformed. China has experimented with some measures. A few small-scale state-owned enterprises have been sold, or leased to individuals, or changed to collective ownership. However, selling and leasing are not applicable to most state-owned enterprises, especially to large and medium-sized ones. Most people consider the share system to be an effective means to make enterprises responsible for their own management, profits, and losses. Although its applicability to the reform of state-owned enterprises has been fiercely debated, the share system has been accepted by more and more people because the contract-responsibility system has failed to make these enterprises entirely responsible for their own management, profits, and losses. The share system is currently an important experiment in China.

To investigate the progress and outcome of reform in state-owned enterprises and to inform future reforms, the Chinese Academy of Social Sciences (CASS), the University of Oxford, and the University of Michigan (later, the University of California at San Diego) launched a collaborative research project in 1988 to study the performance of state-owned enterprises under economic reforms. The project was financed by the Ford Foundation, the Science Foundation of CASS in China, the Gatsby Foundation, and the Economic and Social Research Council (ESRC) in Britain. In the University of Oxford, research also involved the collaboration of economists from Poland and Hungary. The project has conducted an in-depth investigation of many state-owned enterprises in China. Apart from a field study of over thirty enterprises by the researchers, a sample survey was also conducted through a unified questionnaire sent to over 400 enterprises. Through the questionnaires, data were collected for 246 variables in 1980 and 1983–87. The second phase surveyed 769 enterprises in four provinces. The data-set included 391 variables over 1980–89. In total, the two surveys covered 1,172 enterprises and 3.4 million figures. This data-set is the largest of its type on enterprises in China, if not in the world. The reliability of data collected from the two surveys is very high. Using the data, researchers in this collaborative project produced many papers which were presented in two workshops respectively held in Shenzhen in 1990 and in Guilin in 1992. Because of the enormous amount of information provided by the papers, we have not been able to make full use of them. They need to be further exploited and used. None the less, based on some initial analyses, we have been able to make some new discoveries about the reforms and their outcome in state-owned enterprises in China. The initial research results will be published in several books.

The present book is written by the University of Oxford Research Team based on their studies of the first data-set. They have just begun to conduct research into the second data-set so that research results from it are not included in this book. As one of the project leaders, I am very pleased to see this book published. The materials on which it is based are far superior to those of any previous studies (including the collaborative study between CASS and the World Bank in the early 1980s which investigated twenty-two state-owned enterprises). I trust that the book will greatly help people to understand more about reform in these enterprises, and reform of the entire economic system in China.

Reforms of the economic system in China are still in progress: there is still a long way to go to establish a new economic system. However, the success of the economic reforms has been widely recognized. Although the progress of reform has not been smooth and is still full of difficulties, the great achievements so far suggest that reform will eventually be successful. I think that readers will be able to see this through the research results published in this book.

As one of the project leaders, I would like to thank the authors and other researchers who have made a contribution to the work for their efforts and collaboration over the last several years. I would also like to thank the Chinese economists involved in the project.

The research project has almost finished but the utilization of the research results has just begun. I hope that the authors of the book can conduct further research into the second data-set. I also hope that we will be able to collect data for another five years for the second sample of 800 enterprises. If possible, we would like to continue our collaboration with the authors and other researchers in the project.

Dong Fureng

New York,
5 May 1992

Preface

The end of communist control of the countries of Eastern Europe and the collapse of the Soviet Union dramatically focused attention on the economic reform of socialist economies and their transition to Western-style market economies. However, this has to some extent obscured the process of reform which has been gathering pace in China since the late 1970s. This has embraced large-scale privatization of agriculture, gradual but now very extensive price decontrol, and several phases of enterprise reform which have generated much greater autonomy. In most respects these reforms have been very successful, generating rapid economic growth and large increases in living standards without precipitating insuperable inflationary pressures. Indeed one of the unfortunate features of the transition now occurring in Eastern Europe is that neither governments nor their advisers paid sufficient attention to the reform process in China in the 1980s and the useful lessons which could be learnt from it. Political conditions in the period 1989–92 may in practice have made it difficult or impossible for Eastern Europe to have followed alternative policy programmes, but many of the problems of inflation, of unemployment, and of reductions in output, tax revenue, and expenditure consequent upon the 'big bang' strategies adopted might at least have been attenuated had the Chinese experience been more widely known.

Options for further reform in most Eastern European countries are now heavily constrained. In contrast, China, on the basis of a decade or more of successful gradualist reform, and despite a setback to the reform process arising from the tragic events in Tiananmen Square in June 1989, is now well placed to embark on a further stage of reform. Our purpose is to look at the process of enterprise reform to date, analyse the behaviour and performance of large state-owned industrial enterprises that has resulted, and to draw out some implications for the future. Our hope is that this will be of direct benefit to the continuing discussion on enterprise reform in China, and also of some interest and relevance to the process of transition in other socialist economies.

In 1988 the Chinese Academy of Social Sciences (CASS) organized an extensive exercise to collect detailed questionnaire and quantitative economic data from over 400 of the larger state-owned Chinese enterprises covering most of the years 1980–87. This data-set, comprising 600,000 observations, is the basis of our analysis. We have used it to explore many aspects of enterprise behaviour and performance including production, employment, and investment; costs, profitability, and finance; and autonomy, incentives, and budgetary issues. We have also constructed from this a complete model of a Chinese industrial enterprise, used it for some simulations, and examined prospects for further enterprise reform. We hope that this will add significantly to understanding of Chinese enterprises and the transformation which they are undergoing.

Our debts to others in an undertaking of this nature are immense. First and foremost we wish to express our great gratitude to Professor Dong Fureng, formerly Director of the Economic Research Institute at CASS and a member of the Economics and Finance Committee of the National People's Congress, who was the prime mover for this work and a driving force while it was being carried out. Professor Dong has played a major role in the thinking behind the enterprise reform process and in the analysis of its consequences and it has been very gratifying for us to be associated with him in this work. We thought it was very appropriate that this book should contain a Foreword from him and are very grateful that he readily agreed to provide one. We should stress, however, that neither he nor any others mentioned below necessarily agrees with any of the methods, results, arguments, or inferences contained in this book.

Our next obligation which it is our pleasure to record is to the numerous members of the Institute of Economics in CASS with whom we collaborated, who designed, collected, and provided the data-set, acted as delightful hosts and efficient translators on our visits to China, and contributed so much in ideas, analysis, energy, and enthusiasm to the project. One of the great rewards of the project was the new friendships we made with our Chinese colleagues and we very much hope that we will maintain these links in the future.

In similar vein we are very grateful to the US members of the team with whom we worked, in particular Barry Naughton, John MacMillan, Roger Gordon, and Ted Groves. They have all been excellent and convivial colleagues with whom to work and are a key group at the present time in moving forward understanding of the Chinese economy. We have all gained greatly from Barry Naughton's immense knowledge and appreciation of Chinese society, culture, and language, and the ways in which political and social values interact with economic behaviour in China.

Though few of the many Chinese managers whom we met and interviewed, or the hundreds more who dutifully filled out enormously detailed questionnaires, will ever read this book, we none the less would like to record our great debt and gratitude to them. Without their effort and assistance this book could not have been written. Their enthusiasm and patience as we struggled via translation to come to grips with a quite new world of Chinese accounting procedures, distinctive organizational structures and forms of behaviour, and with a range of recent reforms, many still developing as we watched, impressed us greatly.

There are also several institutions without whose support this work could not have been carried out. The Ford Foundation has been involved in financing research on the Chinese economy for many years and we gratefully acknowledge their support in funding the overseas costs of the work involved in this project. With many competing demands on their resources we very much hope that this contribution will be seen as worth while. We should also like to record our appreciation for the help, advice, and support we received from Peter Geitner and Peter Harris of the Ford Foundation while we were pursuing this work.

Funding of our ongoing research effort in the UK, primarily the employment of our research officers, was provided by the Economic and Social Research Council. The size and nature of our database was such that without the research assistance financed by the ESRC it is doubtful whether we could have completed the research at all and we are very grateful for their support. We also wish to thank the Leverhulme Trust which provided crucial funding for initial research costs at an early stage when the likely scale and scope of the research was still very unclear. We appreciate their confidence and hope it was merited. Derek Morris also wishes to acknowledge the help of the Sir John Hicks Trust which financed a research fellowship for the year 1991–92, and Donald Hay similarly thanks the Institute of Economics and Statistics at Oxford which did likewise. The reduction in heavy teaching loads which these awards permitted was invaluable in creating more time for research and we are most appreciative.

A key role in setting up the project, obtaining finance, and co-ordinating the operation in China, the USA, and the UK was played by Cyril Lin, Director of the Centre for Modern Chinese Studies in Oxford. Under Cyril's direction, this institution has become a focal point for the development of Chinese studies in the UK in recent years. We are very grateful to him for involving us in the analysis of the Chinese economy, providing the infrastructure of support that a large-scale project needs, providing advice and comments on drafts of various chapters, and acting as an excellent sounding-board for ideas, lines of enquiry, etc. We should also like to thank very much Stephen

Bond, Fellow of Nuffield College, Oxford for his help and advice on econometric issues involved in the analysis of panel data, and Adrian Wood of the Institute of Development Studies, University of Sussex for suggestions and comments on our work as it progressed. All errors of fact, analysis, or interpretation none the less remain entirely our responsibility.

Anyone who has tried to carry out large-scale collaborative research with heavy empirical content will know how important are the research facilities available and the people who supply them. In this respect we were, not for the first time, extremely fortunate to be given a base at the Institute of Economics and Statistics at Oxford, directed by Professor Stephen Nickell. We are eternally grateful to the Administrator, Gillian Coates, not only for her seemingly effortless efficiency but for the convivial way in which she handled any and every request we made. Similarly, we were fortunate to have such friendly, helpful, and efficient people as Caroline Wise and Candy Watts to type (several versions of) the whole book. The support of all three contributed much to our enjoyment of this work.

Vivien Foster read through a penultimate draft of the book and made numerous editorial suggestions to improve the presentation of the arguments and the clarity of the text. We are very grateful to her. Any obscurities that remain are entirely our fault.

It is clear from the above that we are indebted to a great many people, but the list would be very far from complete if it did not include our families, Elizabeth, Rebecca, and Mark; Sue, Alastair, and Roderick; Jenny and Xiaowen; and, as the project progressed, Joseph, Jean, and Julia. Our working at all sorts of unsociable hours, our disappearance to China for extended periods of time, and our constant preoccupation with the work involved, all affected our wives and children and we would like to record how much we appreciated their tolerance, love, and support. It made all the difference.

Donald Hay
Derek Morris
Guy Liu
Shujie Yao

Institute of Economics, Oxford
August 1992

Contents

PART I

Economic Reform and State-Owned Manufacturing Enterprises

1

The Enterprise Reform Programme in China since 1979

The events of 4 June 1989 in Tiananmen Square probably marked the end of a ten-year period of economic reform in China, which had affected every aspect of the planned economy built up by the Communist Party since the revolution. In this period agriculture was extensively decollectivized, the complex central planning system effectively dismantled for a wide range of industrial goods, and much greater autonomy given to industrial firms. The purpose of the research reported in this book is to trace the impact of the economic reforms as they affected the larger state-owned industrial enterprises. In particular, the objective is to provide a detailed statement of the external environment of the firm under the reform regime, to model the behaviour of firms in this new environment, and to quantify, as far as possible, the impact of different policy measures.

This research project was made possible by the availability of responses to two questionnaires sent to a sample of nearly 400 state-owned enterprises in 1988. One questionnaire asked for data on production, work-force, and financial accounts for 1980 and 1983–87. This questionnaire is described in detail in Part II of the book. The other questionnaire, which is described in Chapter 2, was addressed to the directors (managers) of the firms. As well as collecting qualitative information about the 'contract' between the firm and its bureaucratic supervisors, the questionnaire elicited information about the motivations and behaviour of the directors, e.g. the basis on which they decided outputs or prices where they had the freedom so to decide.

The focus of the research is entirely on the analysis of these two data-sets. The material in Part I of the book sets the scene for the subsequent analysis. Thus this chapter gives a brief description of the process of reform as it affected state-owned firms. It deals with the *formal* position on the supervision and control of firms, the balance between plan and market, the systems for allocating the factors of production, and the tax system. It should be noted that it is widely reported that the realities of the Chinese economic system do not always accord with the details of the administrative and legal framework. In application, the 'rules' are negotiable between the firm and the bureaucratic supervisors giving rise to the possibility of quite substantial deviations from the prescribed forms of behaviour. Chapter 2 begins to address this issue, with an analysis of the directors' questionnaire. The responses from the managers enable us to describe how the enterprises responded to control by the bureaucratic supervisors, how they made decisions on outputs and prices, employment and wages, and how financial constraints were seen to operate. The sample is also sufficiently large to enable the analysis to differentiate the responses by industrial sector, location, and contract form. The last is particularly interesting, since the majority of the firms operate under either the 'contract-responsibility' system or the 'director-responsibility' system. Prima facie, these systems are sufficiently different that one might expect the directors to respond and to behave in significantly different ways. If such differences do not emerge in the analysis, then it supports the suspicion, noted above, that the precise formal structure is of little consequence in determining firms' behaviour.

Chapter 3 provides evidence on enterprise autonomy and incentives, utilizing the quantitative data for 1980 and 1983–87. (The characteristics of the sample of firms are described in Appendix I, comparing the sample with the total universe of Chinese industrial enterprises. This Appendix also addresses briefly the question of the reliability of the data-set.) The broad objectives of the reform programme were to give firms greater freedom to produce and to sell their products, and greater incentives to production and efficiency; the hope was that these would result in improved performance by the state-owned industrial sector.

Part II builds on the previous chapters to examine the behaviour and performance of the firms. Chapter 4 focuses on the labour market and the employment behaviour of the firms. Chapters 5 and 6 present a complete econometric model of production, cost, and profit behaviour of the firms, and Chapters 7 to 10 model financial and investment behaviour. In Chapter 11 the two models are integrated to generate a complete model of the firm, which is then used to simulate the impact of economic reforms on behaviour and performance. Part III sums up the conclusions from the previous work, and then makes proposals for further reforms, in particular the vexed question of the future ownership of these enterprises in the context of a very uncertain economic future.

The rest of this chapter gives the background for the analysis which follows. In Section 1 there is an overview of the reforms in the period since 1979. Subsequent sections give a more detailed analysis of the development of particular reforms.

1. An Overview of the Economic Reform Programme since 1979

China achieved respectable growth rates in the pre-reform era. The development strategy followed the Soviet model in which heavy industry was given attention at the expense of agriculture and consumer-goods industry. Enterprises were regarded as subsidiaries of the state's administrative system and subjected to direct control and mandatory plans. This traditional socialist system exhibited the following defects:

1. Lack of autonomy and labour incentives. Enterprises were subordinated to their higher authorities on all issues concerning production, employment, investment, and finance. Wages were set accordingly to seniority rather than ability or effort.

2. Enterprises experienced a 'soft' state budget constraint. Superficially, enterprises were defined as separate units of accountability. But financial accounting was only a means by which higher authorities could find out what was going on in each enterprise; it had nothing to do with decisions on whether an enterprise should be shut down or expanded. Since quantity, quality, and prices of inputs and outputs were all entirely under state control, profits or losses in enterprise accounts were not necessarily linked to performance. If enterprises failed to generate sufficient revenue to cover costs, their higher authorities would have to make up the shortfall.

3. In addition there was a lack of price signals and market dynamism. Because prices were artificially set by the state, they rarely reflected costs and demands. The role normally played by markets and prices in resource allocation was absent.

All these defects impinged adversely on economic development. Following the death of Mao and the downfall of the Gang of Four, problems which had accumulated during the Cultural Revolution came to the surface, requiring radical reform. Experimental reforms were initiated in the countryside, beginning in 1978. Experiments with expanded enterprise autonomy also began in October 1978 in Sichuan Province. In May 1979 the State started experiments to expand autonomy in eight large state-owned enterprises, including the Beijing Iron and Steel Complex. By the end of 1979, the number of experimental enterprises in the whole country had increased to 4,200. Reforms to increase enterprise autonomy in these early years included freedom to market some outputs outside the plan, profit retention for investment, welfare and bonus payments, charges for the use of fixed capital and interest charges on circulating capital, and a degree of autonomy in personnel decisions. We now sketch the chronology of reform and the policy debate in four areas. More detail is given in subsequent sections.

1.1 Taxation of profits

By the end of 1982, 80% of the state-owned enterprises covered by the state budget were on some form of profit-delivery system. In general, successful fulfilment of state-set norms (e.g. profit, output volume, quality, variety, and costs) entitled the enterprises to retain profits in excess of the required delivery. From the retained funds, bonuses could be paid and welfare services provided. However, the initial stages of the policy involved some problems in setting the level of delivery. First, relative profitability depended mainly on the price structure set by the state and on the availability of state-allocated inputs. This made it extremely difficult to formulate universal rules for profit delivery. In practice, delivery of profit had to be determined on a firm-by-firm basis, which involved intensive bargaining between the authorities and the enterprises. Second, the system gave rise to uncertain government revenue. Because every enterprise wanted to retain as much profit as possible and because the state still had a 'soft' budget to protect less profitable and loss-making enterprises, government revenue decreased sharply.

To solve these problems, a revised system was introduced in late 1982 and put into effect for all enterprises in July 1983. The new system substituted an income tax for fixed profit delivery. In the first stage, large and medium enterprises were asked to pay a uniform income (profit) tax which was equal to 55% of target profit, and because of different conditions as regards location, resource endowment, and price structure, they were also asked to deliver a quota of after-tax profit. For smaller enterprises, a lower but progressive income tax was imposed.

In the second stage, profit delivery was entirely abandoned. Enterprises were asked to pay income (profit) tax (the basic rate for large and medium-scale enterprises being 55%), value added tax (designed to eliminate unequal opportunities caused by the distorted price system), resource tax (only applied to the extractive industry sectors such as coal, oil, and metallurgical enterprises), local tax for the local authority, and the adjustment tax (designed to eliminate unequal opportunities caused by other conditions such as different capital stocks). The adjustment tax was imposed on net income after payment of profit tax. By the end of 1985 four-fifths of state-owned enterprises were covered by the system.

This tax system still failed to solve the problems of bargaining particularly over the adjustment tax to be paid by the firm. It also failed to eliminate the unequal treatment of enterprises. All these problems were ultimately attributed to the irrational price system and many policy-makers came to the conclusion that price reform was a priority to induce competition and efficiency.

1.2 Price reforms

A preliminary price reform was implemented between 1978 and 1984. It was however a limited 'price adjustment' with the primary objective of changing the terms of trade in favour of agriculture. Proper price reform was not implemented until late 1984 when the profit tax system was getting into difficulty. The most important feature of price reform in this period was the introduction of the dual price system.

Originally, there were two schools of thought about how to reform the price system. One school maintained that the administered price structure must be rationalized by progressive adjustment as in the first period between 1978 and 1984. The other school argued that the history of price reform in the Soviet Union and other East European countries showed that the price structure could never be rationalized by piecemeal adjustment because of inevitable errors in calculating prices. Given change and development of the economy, very frequent price adjustment would be required. The preferred solution would be to allow prices to move freely in response to market conditions. However, because the price system was seriously distorted, it could not be replaced by a market-determined price system in a single step. The alternative was to implement a 'dual price system' in which planned prices would be applied to products covered by state plan quotas and market prices to products outside the quotas.

The principle of the dual price system was to induce enterprises to face market competition without causing a sudden disruption of the planning mechanism. By progressively increasing the share of production outside the state plan, market forces would play an increasingly major role in guiding resource allocation. Under the dual price system, enterprises would be forced to improve efficiency as well as to meet the requirements of the state macroeconomic plan. This would enable the authorities gradually to restructure industries to solve the problem of shortages, and to adjust controlled prices towards their market values. It was also hoped that the dual price system could avert the risk of an inflation spiral induced by price reform as observed in many East European countries.

The dual price system was formally adopted by the State Council in

May 1984 in a document called 'Provisional Regulations for Further Expansion of State-Owned Enterprises' Autonomy', stipulating that outputs and inputs of each enterprise were to be divided into two parts, i.e. planned and non-planned. Mandatory prices set by the State would apply to planned outputs and inputs while non-planned output could be sold to the market at prices with an upper limit not higher than 20% above the mandatory prices. In October 1984 the State Planning Commission issued a number of proposals to reduce the number of products subject to mandatory planning and to allow prices to respond to market conditions. In February 1985, the State Bureaux of Commodity Prices, Goods, and Materials jointly issued a document to eliminate the restriction of the upper price limit on non-planned products.

The number of types of industrial goods and materials subject to mandatory allocation fell from 256 to twenty-three in 1986. The proportion of mandatorily allocated coal, steel, timber, and cement in total output of these products fell to 50%, 50.9%, 30.7%, and 19.4% respectively. The proportion of retail sales subject to a mandatory price in total retail sales fell from 97% in 1979 to 47% in 1986, the proportion of retail sales subject to indicative prices rose from 0.5% to 19%,[1] and the proportion of retail sales at market prices rose from 2.5% to 34%.

This price reform has had a significant impact on almost every aspect of the economy. China has experienced rapid economic growth but also a severe price spiral, and high inflation has had other undesirable consequences, including some social instability, income redistribution, and, for those adversely affected, loss of morale. China has also experienced corruption within the bureaucracy during this period, causing widespread dissatisfaction. Because of these problems, the dual price system has been hotly debated. Its advocates argue that the dual price system had at least three advantages. First it stimulated production and efficiency, and helped to alleviate the pressure of excess demand. Since enterprises were allowed to sell part of their production at market prices, which were much higher than planned prices, they had greater incentive to improve efficiency, increase output, and hence profitability. Second, it encouraged saving of energy and materials. The old system under which inputs were supplied by the state at fixed prices, gave no incentive for the enterprises to save energy and materials. Market-determined prices were normally higher than planned prices giving a greater incentive to economize. Third, the most important advantage of the dual price system was that it could reduce the risks inherent in economic reform, by 'changing a big earthquake into several small tremors', i.e. by permitting gradual change and adjustment over a number of years.

Opponents of the dual price system argued that it had a number of major disadvantages. It failed to eliminate unequal opportunities and treatment of enterprises as in the first period of economic reform (1978–84). Under the dual price system, the determination of output and input quotas subject to state control was based on the past performance of enterprises. Thus, a well-managed enterprise would receive a larger output quota and a smaller input quota, while a less efficient one would receive more favourable treatment. Nor did the system eliminate bargaining over these quotas between enterprises and their higher authorities. Second, the dual price system also helped to create an environment ripe for speculation and bureaucratic corruption. In a fully planned system, speculation and bureaucratic corruption are inevitable, but with the dual price system, the scope for corruption increased and the scale of it became more apparent to the public. Officials in charge of allocating outputs or input quotas could take advantage of the system by extracting the difference between market prices and plan prices because there was no effective monitoring system to supervise their activities. Third, the system induced deceptive behaviour. On the one hand, enterprises tried to hide their production capacity so that they would get lower output quotas, but on the other hand they strove to claim a higher allocation of materials in order to improve profit potential. In some cases firms made profits simply by selling their input quotas rather than producing any products. Fourth, the system did not necessarily improve allocative efficiency. High prices and profitability in the free market attracted investment. Investment was therefore directed to the 'more profitable' industries, frequently to small and inefficient enterprises which had been given greater autonomy in marketing outputs. These enterprises (mainly township enterprises) also competed with the big ones for raw materials and energy. With greater autonomy and hence higher profits they could often bid away these scarce resources. It was not surprising, therefore, that occasionally the best-equipped rolling-mills or steel plants stood idle, while energy-inefficient township mills continued to operate. Finally, the dual price system was also rather chaotic. It failed to create equilibrium market prices; instead, there were multiple market prices for different transactions. Nor was the planned price unique; there were mandatory, indicative, regional, protective, break-even, negotiated prices, etc.

Therefore, although the dual price system permitted strong growth of industrial production, and was successful in providing for gradual transfer from a fully planned system, the reforms none the less were seen as having failed to meet the overall objectives of increased competition and efficiency. The situation was worsened by the rise in inflation from 1987 onwards. In late 1986, economists in China argued that further reforms were needed apart from the responsibility system and price reform. The major obstacles for economic reform were still thought to be that state-owned enterprises had no real autonomy, that budget constraints were soft, and that there were insufficient incentives to productive efficiency. To solve these problems, reform was directed towards establishing a new management mechanism in which economic interests, real autonomy, incentives, and responsibility would be combined, based on the principle of separating ownership from management rights.

1.3 Managerial reforms

Implicit in the reform of taxation and prices described above has been the ceding of much greater authority to the enterprise management to make decisions concerning the allocation of resources by the firm. A number of alternatives have been experimented with, and these are detailed in Section 3. Here we give a brief account of the main chronology of reform.

In the period 1979–83, the profit-delivery system was associated with greater managerial autonomy in an early form of contract responsibility, involving the fulfilment of production targets of various kinds. With the switch to a profits tax in 1983, the contractual guarantee to deliver profit was formally dropped, though in practice it was often retained. A new system of manager (or director) responsibility was gradually introduced from 1984. This confirmed the greater powers ceded to the managers, and also released them from political control within the enterprise. But the lack of any commitment to meet profit targets was subsequently identified as a serious weakness. While some large and medium-sized firms have continued with the system, a new contract-responsibility system was introduced in 1986. This system restored targets for profit delivery, and made more explicit the link between enterprise performance and the payment of bonuses to the workers. The system differs from the profit tax system which preceded it in that it identifies separate rights of the state and the management, whereas the profit tax system had merely specified the distribution of profits between them. Surveys carried out since 1987 suggest that the contract-responsibility system has had a positive effect on state-owned enterprises. The major advantages of the system are that it strengthens the incentive mechanism, gives greater autonomy to enterprises, and strengthens the state budget constraint. But the system is still considered to be far from perfect. Setting the contract requires a complex bargaining procedure between the enterprise and the authorities. It is also suspected that enterprises are likely to maximize short-run profitability at the expense of long-run objectives. Precisely which direction future reforms should take is a matter of debate.

1.4 The control of investment

A consequence of the greater managerial autonomy given to enterprises, and the increased level of retained profits, has been that direct controls on investment have been significantly relaxed since 1979. The authorities have sought to restrain investment by replacing grants by repayable loans, and by charging interest. But these mechanisms have generally proved to be ineffective, because the benefits which decision-takers at all levels can extract from investments substantially exceed the financing costs. In general, the opportunity cost to the firm of internal finance is small because the interest on bank deposits is low. Monetary policy has resulted in the cost of funds being substantially lower than the returns to investment, if funds can be obtained.

In fact real lending rates for a sizeable proportion of investment were negative even after a round of adjustments introduced in the latter part of 1988. An alternative system of quantitative controls designed to limit investment expenditure has proved both distortionary and only partially effective. In addition, repayment provisions continued to be lax. A large proportion of capital investment was exempt from repayment (in 1986, it was 50%). Provisions of the financial system were also altered *ex post facto* to ease repayment conditions for all kinds of loans.

Apart from the low real cost of funds, there are many other factors which help to drive investment demand: the incentive to build an industrial power base and the absence of penalties for commercial failure; the opportunities available to local bureaucracies to appropriate rents by expanding local production of products with high accounting profits; the scope for political leaders to intervene to secure the approval of 'prestige' projects in which they have a personal interest; and the incentives to procure investment funding in order to obtain other scarce resources.

In the hope of controlling investment more effectively, the policy-makers have divided fixed investment into three categories the control of which differs substantially in the degree of rigidity. These categories are capital construction, innovation and replacement, and 'other' investment. This division is made with two separate intentions in mind. First, projects with a major construction component should be controlled more tightly; innovation and replacement investment is less closely monitored because it has less implications for total output and resource requirements and is generally carried out at existing enterprises. Second, 'other' investments are exempt from control either because they fund energy development or because they involve purchases of small-scale machinery in excess supply. In practice, however, these distinctions have had little impact on investment demand. Historically, innovation and replacement investment was simply the name given to investments funded by retained depreciation allowances. In most cases such spending created new capacity. In recent years some 5–7% of total innovation and replacement investment has gone to projects not connected with existing enterprises. In addition, enterprises have strong incentives to 'package' projects, which involves breaking a large project down into smaller parts and obtaining approval for each component as innovation and replacement investment. This reduces screening or may even avoid the need for approval at all if each component is less than the limit for which approval is required. The separation of fixed investment into categories in this way channels investment into less than optimal-size projects with artificially extended completion periods.

Another problem is the insufficient funding of individual projects. The central government purposely underfunds priority projects to stimulate local participation to balance the books. On the other hand, local authorities seek to initiate 'good' projects in order to strengthen the case for investment quotas, and underfund central government projects in favour of their own projects. This can be very disruptive when the process of screening projects is weak. While the central planning apparatus must approve large-scale investments, approval for small-scale investment projects is thoroughly decentralized, with each province, municipality, and county having authority to start projects. During certain periods, such as 1982 to early 1984, the central government imposed a general cap on project starts, the restriction being lifted in late 1984. The result was that the number of projects under construction increased by 27% between 1984 and 1985, and the budgeted volume of all projects increased by over 28%. A similar surge occurred in 1987–88, magnifying the problem of demand management.

These problems have begun to interact with the inflationary environment. Underfunding worsens during the course of the construction period as costs increase. Decision-makers at all levels find themselves in charge of numerous half-finished investment projects that require additional finance. This creates the illusion that the short-run returns are exceptionally high because a little more investment will cause a whole project to be completed. There is enormous pressure on the banking authorities, in particular, to extend credit. Central authorities are then forced to launch campaigns to cut investment projects, and to vet projects under construction. Paradoxically, these campaigns, which have recurred since 1979, and most recently in 1988, create the expectation of further uncertainty in investment allotments, and make it especially advantageous to maintain numerous projects. The manager who can save a project while others are being cut, receives a bigger share of the total in later periods. One outcome is that resources are tied up in incomplete construction projects. In principle, strict discipline exerted through the banking system could counteract these incentives to expand investment. Indeed the independence and professionalism of the banking system have increased significantly and measures proposed in late 1988 should strengthen controls by the central authorities over credit expansion. But it is none the less apparent that nearly every aspect of the investment-management system combines to make investment control difficult. The low cost of funds, the existence of a soft budget constraint, and the common interests of different bureaucracies in the objective of output growth—all these factors tend to swell aggregate investment and lead to macro-economic problems.

2. *The Planning System and the Supervisory Structure*

In China, government administration operates at four levels: central government in Beijing, ministry or province, city or county, and basic organizations. This hierarchical administration also operates in state industrial planning and supervision. Every state-owned enterprise is at the bottom of a hierarchical structure, and is supervised by or is responsible to a relevant 'higher authority'. The higher authority may be a ministry, a provincial government, a local government (city or county), or a specialized industrial bureau. These authorities are in turn directed by a higher authority in the central government.

The central government is defined by Article 85 of the Constitution of 1982: 'The State Council, that is the central People's Government of the People's Republic of China is the executive body of the highest organ of state power; it is the highest organ of state administration.' For state industrial planning as a whole, the State Planning Commission which is a special agency directly under the State Council, is responsible for economic activities (Laaksonen 1988: 133), in charge of long-term (ten years), medium-term (five years), and short-term economic planning.

Ministries and provincial governments are the second level of the planning hierarchy, and they exercise their supervisory role through the agency of their industrial planning bureaux. These bureaux not only are responsible for implementing the central plan, they also have a role in drawing up local plans. For example, a bureau of a provincial government making output plans for its enterprises depends partly on central government plans, and partly on its local government development policy. Thus central government planning will be modified before its implementation in enterprises.

The planning bureaux of city or county governments have a similar function to provincial ones, and they are in turn supervised by provincial planning bureaux. Since economic reform, some of the large cities have been released from provincial government control, and are directly responsible to the central government. These cities are referred to in Chinese as cities with 'planning alone'.

Because a variety of planning bureaux exists, the supervisory auth-

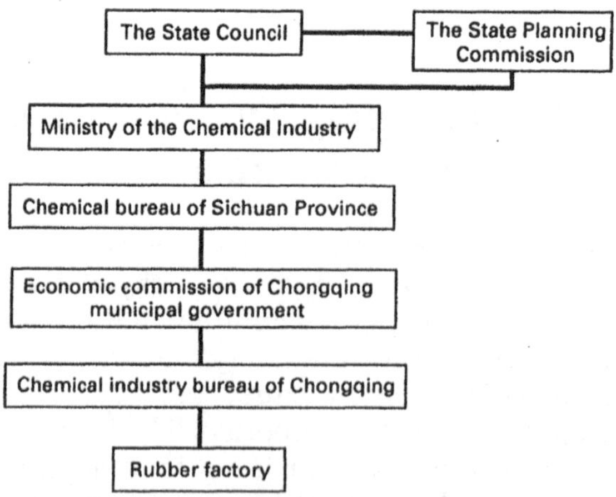

Note: 2,000 employees in December 1986.
Source: Laaksonen (1988), 141.
FIG. 1.1. Administrative control of Chongqing rubber factory

orities that firms are responsible to are correspondingly various. There appears to be no fixed rule as to how a particular higher authority is assigned to a firm, and indeed the identity of the firm's supervisory agency may change over time. But in general, it is a matter of scale. The largest firms, especially in heavy industry and energy, are likely to be required to report directly to the appropriate ministry in Beijing. Medium and small firms are supervised at a level appropriate to markets they serve. This system is illustrated in Fig. 1.1 for an individual firm as an example and in Fig. 1.2 for the state sector as a whole.

The objective of the system is that different higher authorities control their enterprises on behalf of the state, seeking maximization of output, employment, and social benefits, as well as the generation of revenue for the state, and political education for the workers. There was no fundamental change in the formal supervision structure during the reform period, but the supervisory system no longer domi-

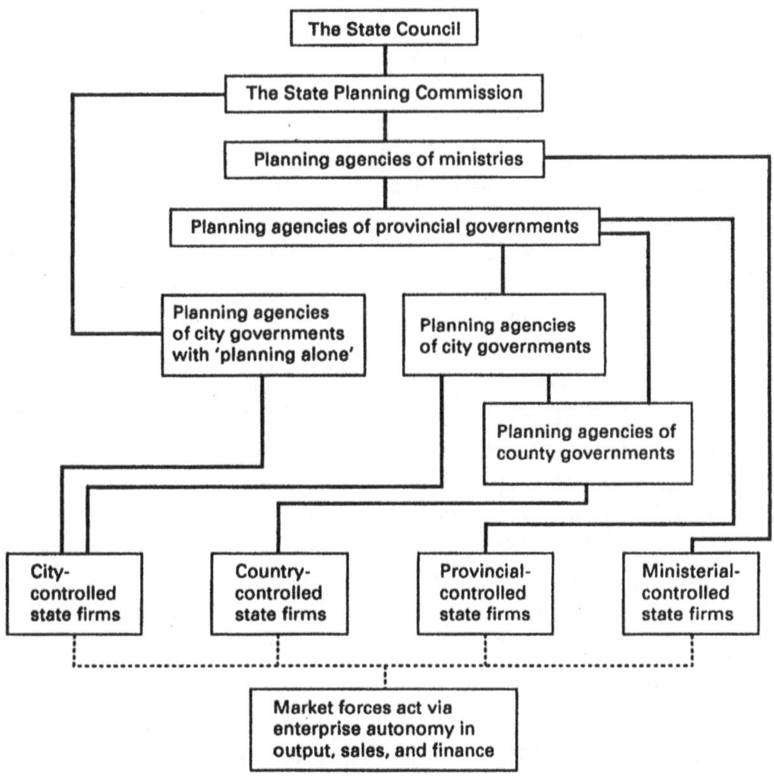

FIG. 1.2. Hierarchical structure of the Chinese planning system for industry after 1980

nated all the activities of the firm. The right to control production in excess of the plan quota has been transferred to the firm from its higher authority, and therefore the firm has some freedom to organize a part of its production largely in response to market conditions. This mixed plan–market system was referred to as 'the two-tier system' by Dong (1992). Market signals therefore act directly on the firm as the basic unit in the hierarchy via managers' own decision-making powers over part of output and sales. This market-orientated planning system requires the firm to respond to dual signals from both market and plan as demonstrated by Fig. 1.2.

The reform has also particularly affected planning procedures. Before the reform, the procedure was that the central planner made plans based on central leadership policies; these plans were then disaggregated into mandatory production quotas for state-owned enterprises (Hsu 1992: 77). The procedure was one-way planning with a presumption of planners having sufficient information about enterprises under their supervision. In contrast, since the reform, the procedure has become two-way:

(i) each individual enterprise submits an initial production plan for the next year to their supervisory authorities;

(ii) the supervisory authorities make initial aggregate production plans at their agency level, based on individual enterprise plans, for submission to higher supervisory authorities;

(iii) higher supervisory authorities make an initial aggregate production plan based on submitted plans and regional development goals, for submission to the central planning committee;

(iv) the State Planning Commission makes an aggregate production plan at national level, based on plans submitted by each agency, and on development goals for the economy as a whole, and then submits the aggregate national state budget to the State Council for approval;

(v) having obtained approval for the budget, the State Planning Committee gives individual mandatory plans to each major agency; and

(vi) having received the central government plan, major agencies give a combination of plans, covering central government targets and the agencies' targets, to lower agencies or to large enterprises; lower agencies repeat the exercise for firms under their control.

The establishment of the new planning system detailed above began in October 1978 when the Sichuan provincial government experimented with increasing enterprise autonomy for six of its state-owned enterprises (Dong 1992). This experiment was the beginning of the industrial economic reform and administrative decentralization. By mid-1980, the number of experimental state enterprises rose to 6,600 (about 16% of the total), accounting for 60% of output value and 70% of profit (Riskin 1987: 344). These enterprises were given a quite significant degree of freedom from government plan control and supervision. They were granted eight rights:

(i) To retain part of the profit. (After fulfilment of the main economic and technical targets set in the state plan the enterprises could retain 3–5% of the profit they had made within the plan. In addition, they could keep, depending on their industry, 15–25% of the profits made outside the state plan.)

(ii) To expand production with funds they themselves had accumulated and to keep the profit derived from it in the first two years.

(iii) To retain 60% of the depreciation fund for fixed assets as against 40% in the past.

(iv) To engage in production outside the state plan, such as processing for other factories and producing more in response to market demand, but only when the state plan had been fulfilled.

(v) To market that part of their output which the commercial and materials departments did not purchase at trade fairs.

(vi) To apply to export their products and to retain part of the foreign exchange earnings for the import of new technology, materials, and key equipment.

(vii) To pay bonuses at the enterprise's own discretion, in the light of its specific circumstances, within a range approved by the state (generally not more than two months' average wages of the workers and staff).

(viii) To penalize those responsible for losses due to negligence at work or other reasons, including workers, party secretaries, and factory directors. In the most serious cases those responsible could be expelled from the factory (Tian 1982: 94–5).

These eight rights underlined a major difference between state firms of the 1970s and the reformed ones of the early 1980s. The former were production units completely subordinate to their higher authorities which provided all details of their production plans. In contrast, the latter had a limited autonomy in determining production, sales, finance, and investment. Although production autonomy remained limited, the reforms were a success: not only did the output of the experimental enterprises grow in 1979 and 1980, but also the total volume of profits they delivered to the state increased by 7.4% (Tian 1982: 93).

In order to consolidate the reform, after more than four years' experiment, and to strengthen the motivation of managers and employees, the State Council promulgated in May 1984 the 'Provisional Regulations on Further Extending the Decision-Making Power of the State Industrial Enterprises' (*Beijing Review* 11 and 18 June 1984). The State Council's announcement was a signal that industrial reform was moving to a new stage: the official abandoning of the 1970s' system of state plans dominating production, and instead the adoption of a system of power-sharing between the planning authorities and the enterprise managers. The Provisional Regulations also introduced the legislative framework to establish a market-orientated planning system in the industrial sector.

The Regulations gave state enterprises ten rights, which are listed in Appendix 1.1. The major points can be summarized as follows. The firm has rights to produce, market, and price products once the state plans and orders have been fulfilled; to choose its material suppliers; to use funds from retained profit, depreciation, and repair funds; to sell unneeded machinery or other fixed assets; to determine investment in existing activities, and to set up new businesses so long as the new activity remains under state ownership and subject to the same supervision; to employ workers under the guidance of the state labour agencies, although the firm can reject forced assignments; and, finally, to determine internal wages.

Associated with the granting of these rights to state-owned firms, there was a fiscal reform which began in late 1984. The firm was required to pay taxes on profits rather than to negotiate the amount of profit delivery with its higher authority. By the end of 1985, 81% of enterprises in China had switched to this tax payment system (Riskin 1987: 347). The tax system was intended to eliminate bargaining over profit distribution between the state and the firm, and thereby to increase incentives for profit maximization. Implementation of these reform measures resulted in a quite substantial decline in state-controlled outputs (Dong 1992).

Methods of supervising fulfilment of the plan were complex, developing from the single method of administrative compulsion to the introduction of indicative guidance and contract-management responsibility. The type of plan could be identified according to the supervision method used, such as 'compulsory plan', 'guidance plan', and 'contract plan'. The adoption of the guidance plan method was very important for implementation of the reform policy. The purpose of this type of plan was to encourage enterprises to take state plans into account when they drafted their own production plans in accordance with market and supply conditions (Dong 1992). The major feature of guidance plans is that the state uses economic instruments (prices, interest rates, taxes, exchange rates, credit allocation, orders for products) to induce the firm to fulfil government plans rather than using administrative means to enforce plan fulfilment (He 1982). Guidance planning rapidly became very significant as the reform progressed: for example, by 1986, the output under guidance planning in the city of Qingdon was 59%, compared with 15% mandatory planning and 26% market sale (Huang 1990). Under the contract plan, compulsory fulfilment is retained but the firm is allowed to participate in formulating its plan. Since the introduction of contract-management responsibility in 1987, plans in contract form have been popularized, and have provided both economic incentives and clarification of responsibilities. The contract provisions are intended to stimulate enterprises to fulfil state planning targets. Contractual plans were introduced not only between state agencies and enterprises, but also between a state agency and its higher supervisory authority. For example, the central government plans may be contracted to the sectors of industry represented by their respective ministries, and, ministerial plans can then be subcontracted to their lower planning agencies, and to their controlled enterprises (Sah 1990). The 1970s' type of compulsory plans hardly existed in the late 1980s since the authorities used the contract system to encourage the firm to realize national plans.

In summary, although the formal structure of the Chinese industrial planning system has remained almost unchanged over the 1980s, a great change in the content of planning took place in terms of (*a*) planning procedures: the top-downwards planning of the 1970s was replaced by procedures involving interaction between the enterprises and the planning authorities; (*b*) the scope of planned production: the situation where the state plan dominated all industrial production was replaced by the state plan directly controlling only a small part; and (*c*) supervision methods to ensure the fulfilment of plans: administrative controls were developed to include economic incentives to influence the behaviour of the firm.

3. The Relationship between the Firm and Higher Authorities

Despite the almost unchanged formal planning structure, new relationships between the firm and its higher authorities had to be developed to match the great changes in the content of planning. Our focus in this section, therefore, is on characterizing the development of the relationship between the state-owned enterprises and their higher authorities, and on the detail of how control was exercised.

Reform was achieved through two programmes which respectively focused on: (*a*) who within the firm should be responsible to its supervisory agency: the enterprise party committee or the director; and (*b*) whether the responsibility should be primarily political or economic; and if economic, then, how it should be specified. These two reform programmes were carried through simultaneously during the 1980s, and both of them had two stages: more tentative in the first half of the 1980s, and more advanced in the second half. We look at the two programmes in turn.

3.1 Who takes responsibility for the firm?

A major aim of the reform programme was to transfer enterprise leadership from the collective group represented by the party committee to the manager or director. The hurdle to be overcome was Mao's principle that the Party should direct and control everything, which did not permit removal from the Party of control over the basic industrial units. This principle induced inefficiency in decision-making, and did not identify who should take responsibility for any losses caused by a mistaken decision. The collective system was criticized by Deng Xiaoping: 'Nominal responsibility of the committee for decision-making means no responsibility, or nobody to be really responsible for decisions' (Zhang 1987: 9).

Reform started with an attempt to reduce the influence of the party committee and to limit its rights to make decisions about production. Regulations issued over 1982 and 1983 were intended to allow a director or manager to take more control over production. The state introduced 'The System of Director Responsibility under the Leadership of the Party Committee' during this period. Under this system, however, the director remained responsible to the party committee which took upon itself the discussion of business and production policies, and the director or manager had no formal authority independent of the party committee (Child 1987: 42). As a result, the reform did not effectively improve decision-taking efficiency. In addition, the announcement by the State Council in 1984 of increased autonomy for enterprises in making decisions about production and business operation generated a requirement to identify who would take responsibility for decisions.

In October 1984, a policy document on 'China's Economic Structure Reform' marked the second stage of reform. This policy stated:

> Modern enterprises have a minute division of labour, a high degree of continuity in production, strict technological requirements, and complex relations of co-operation. It is therefore necessary to establish a unified, authoritative, and highly efficient system to direct production and conduct operations and management. This calls for a system of the director or manager assuming full responsibility. (Child 1987: 43)

Under this new 'director-responsibility system' the director of the firm was identified as the responsible person in charge of business operations, and the party committee or secretary was responsible only for political education of employees. The committee also was required to assist the director to improve the productive performance of the firm. One important feature of this reform was to create some presumption of personal responsibility (Byrd 1991: 7–35); it was the first instance of official acceptance of a unitary management system since the adoption of the Soviet model in the 1950s (Child 1987).

Putting this new arrangement into practice was likely to take time. Experimental adoption of the director-responsibility system started in Changzhou and Dalian in the spring of 1984 (*Beijing Review*, 16 Feb. 1987). By 1987, the system had been introduced in 36,000 state-owned enterprises, and in Beijing, and in Shizhun, Hubei, and Anwei provinces, more than 50% of the state firms were operating this system (*Journal of Enterprise Management* (1987): 6). The system allowed the pay of a director to exceed the average level of workers by 100–300%, but how the director's reward was to be determined was left unclear (Byrd 1991: 11).

The reform programme specified clearly who within the enterprises should exercise decision-making, but the programme failed to address the question of how the director could be made responsible to the supervisory agency. Several important issues were left unresolved by the programme:

1. There was an ambiguity about 'responsibility' (what was the content of responsibility—was it administrative, political, or economic?) and the interpretation of it was flexible.

2. There were few material incentives given to the responsible director by the higher authority, and this weak motivation discouraged directors from doing their best to improve performance. A number of directors of state-owned firms did not want to accept the system because they were not willing to take responsibility (Zhang 1987).

3. Responsibility was 'one-way': the director was responsible to the higher authority, but this did not prevent intervention by the higher authority which did not take any responsibility for the consequences of its interventions.

These major issues called for solutions which were pursued in the parallel programme of development of the economic-responsibility system.

3.2 Developing the system of economic responsibility

Economic responsibility has already been identified with the 'financial accountability' of the firm: the idea was that financial accountability would make enterprises responsible for their own profits and losses (Hsu 1992: 84). The objective in adopting the economic-responsibility system was to build up a new relationship between the agency and the enterprise, which was expected to provide the firm with a strong motivation to improve performance and efficiency in production.

In the first stage, the success in implementing the economic-responsibility system in grain production in rural areas in 1979 encouraged the central government to introduce a similar incentive mechanism to urban state-owned enterprises at the beginning of the 1980s. This was marked by the state issuing two documents: 'Mandatory Rule for Introducing the Retained-Profit Scheme' on 13 July 1979, and 'Information on Implementation of the Economic-Responsibility System in Industrial Production' on 29 October 1981. The reform programme sought to develop a profit-sharing relationship between the state and the firm, and took the form of a contract to secure profit delivery by enterprises. The implementation of the programme was on a trial basis, and about 60% of state-owned firms practised this new relationship with their higher authorities in various forms (Sah 1990). The programme allowed enterprises to retain a quite substantial part of above-quota profits as a reward for the firm exceeding the planned targets: profit, quality of products, quantity of products, and fulfilment of customer contracts. The results of the experiments were initially good, but the *ad hoc* nature of target-setting and the scope for bargaining greatly weakened the supposedly strong incentive effects. A haemorrhage of government revenue also may have occurred since enterprises and supervisory agencies could effectively conspire to cut profit remittances to the public finance system (Byrd 1990). As Naughton (1985) noted, this gave local governments too much financial authority over local enterprises. For example, the state revenue from industrial profits dropped to 398.6 hundred million yuan in 1983 from 415.9 hundred million yuan in 1979 (SYC 1984: 418). In addition, there was no penalty on the enterprise for failing to reach the base profit.

Because of these drawbacks to the profit-sharing form, the reform programme moved to a second stage. A profits tax was introduced with the aim of creating 'distance' between the authorities and the firm, thus eliminating bargaining over profit remittance, and making enterprises more accountable for both profits and losses. In 1983, the State introduced a flat-rate tax of 55% on the profit of large and medium-sized state-owned enterprises, plus an adjustment tax which was determined by local governments on a case-by-case basis (EEPRC 1988: 347). The adjustment tax was imposed mainly to compensate for price distortions which had random effects on profitability. Implementation of the profits tax started in 1980 on a trial basis for ten state-owned enterprises (later expanded to 400), and was introduced gradually to more enterprises over the period between 1983 and 1984. By 1985, the bulk of the enterprises were subject to the tax (Byrd 1991).

Due to the existence of the adjustment tax, bargaining was not entirely eliminated. But it was much weakened in terms of the amount of profit affected when compared with the profit-sharing system. In practice, from the point of view of the firm, the tax system led to lower profit retention, which gave poor incentives to the firm. For example, a report of the economic and development research centre of the State Council showed that the eleven most profitable enterprises in Tientsin only retained about 10% of profit of which 7% was distributed as bonus and only 3% was actually at the disposal of the enterprises (Sah 1990). From the point of view of the authorities, the tax could not guarantee the fulfilment of the planned target of income tax, and the actual revenues fluctuated over time. This was particularly the case in 1986 when the economy was affected by the government austerity policy.

Consequently, the central government was forced to move to a third stage of reform, which was marked by the State Council issuing a 'Decision on Intensifying the Enterprises Reform and Revitalizing

Enterprise' on 5 December 1986. This document suggested two major reforms of the state–enterprise relationship: (*a*) leasing for small enterprises, and for some medium-sized enterprises running at a loss or earning low profits; and (*b*) contract-management responsibility in large and medium-sized enterprises. The adoption of contract responsibility became the mainstream of the reform programme. By the end of 1987, it had been implemented in 78% of state-owned enterprises, and in 90% by 1988 (Sah 1990).

These three stages in development of the economic-responsibility system can be further distinguished by comparing the system before and after 1986. The main distinctions are as follows.

First, the situation was different in terms of responsibility within the firm, and the scope of the autonomy the firm was permitted. Before 1986, the enterprise party committee was responsible and enterprise autonomy was limited. In contrast, after 1986, the director was required to take decision-making responsibility, and autonomy was greatly enhanced.

Secondly, the implications of the responsibility were different. Before 1986, there was no hard financial or fiscal constraint, and responsibility was only relevant in that the level of bonus was linked to profit. There was little emphasis on the obligation to fulfil profit targets, and almost no penalty for failure to deliver the profit quota. After 1986, the firm was obliged to guarantee delivery of the contractual profit regardless of its performance. That is, the firm could retain profit only if the profit exceeded the quota; otherwise, the firm had to make up the quota from its own funds or saving deposits. Evidence on this point was reported by Du (1992):

> [I]n order to fulfil the taxation targets in the contract, many enterprises had to reduce their loan repayments and cut down their retentions. In 1989, 103 state-owned firms under the contract in Shanghai used funds which should have been used for their loan repayments, and retained funds, for the payment of the quota, amounting to 354 million yuan and 950 million yuan, respectively. Similarly, in 1990, firms in the same situation in Tianjin had to use part of their funds allocated to loan repayments to make up the quota, amounting to 243 million yuan.

It is apparent that there was considerable risk for the enterprise in the post-1986 contract form, at least in respect of the profit quota. This explains a fact reported by Du (1992): 80% of directors of state firms were not willing to take contractual responsibility in the second round of the contract.

Thirdly, the contract period was different. Before 1986 the period was one year; after 1986, the period was three years or more. The advantages of multi-year contracts were the lesser incentives for short-term behaviour (e.g. the firm hiding its potential capability in production to get lower targets), and also the reduced scope for bargaining during the process of target-setting. Although the contract targets were fixed for several years, in practice the targets could be revised on a yearly basis to account for some special circumstances such as a sudden change in the macroeconomy. For example, in Zhenjiang province a number of state-owned enterprises reserved the right to revise their basic contract targets in the range plus or minus 5–15%; in Shandong province, this was referred to as 'a long-term contract with a short-term revision' (Du 1992). This suggests that the contract commitment was not a binding constraint.

Fourthly, legal status was accorded to the post-1986 contracts which had not been accorded to the pre-1986 contracts, which focused solely on incentive arrangements and profit (Sah 1990). The later contracts were a formal legal document, and the commitment was imposed not only on the contractee of the firm but also on the contractor of the higher authority. That is, the state agency could be challenged in a civil court if it failed in its contractual duty to the contractee ('The Concept of Economic Responsibility in China's Enterprises' (1986: 107)). This signalled an important step towards a limited separation of the agency from the enterprise.

Fifthly, the forms of the contract were quite different; they were simple and primitive before 1986, but were sophisticated and complex after 1986. The major forms used after 1986 were contract responsibility, assets-management responsibility, and leasing. Their common features were 'contractual guarantees of targets with incentive links'. For example, 'two guarantees and one link' in contract responsibility implied that the enterprise was required to pay taxes and hand over the share of profit due to the state, and to have funds available for investment in technical upgrading, at the same time linking their total wage bill to economic performance. The 'three guarantees and one link' contract additionally required an enterprise to guarantee the growth of the firm's fixed assets, a point particularly stressed under the assets-responsibility contract.

Another important feature in the late 1980s' contracts was 'bidding'. About 65% of the contract enterprises had experimented with bidding for the contract and the majority of these enterprises were successful, which led the Beijing authorities to believe that the introduction of competition was the key to the success of the contract system (Sah 1990). Bidding was applied mainly to small enterprises with leasing contracts, because leaseholders were thought to have the capacity to bear the risks of a small business. Leaseholders selected by bidding were granted full rights in determining their production, sales, and the allocation of net income after payment of leasing fees, ranging from a fixed amount to a flat-rate tax on profits. It has been reported that about 50% of leasing contracts were terminated before the end of their term (*Beijing Review*, 6 July 1987). However, bidding for contracts can introduce stronger incentives for managers.

To summarize, the economic-responsibility system was gradually developed during the 1980s. This development brought a great change to the state–enterprise relationship from the previous hierarchical planning links to fiscal and financial responsibilities governed by an explicit contract. Under the new relationship, enterprises experienced more independence from their supervisory agencies in organizing their production, more risk and tougher constraints in their commitment to contract targets, and incentives to improve productive performance.

As a result, it was widely agreed that the post-1986 contract-responsibility system was successful, and enterprise performance typically improved much more than in firms not using the new system. This encouraged the authorities to continue the practice of the system for the next round of contracts in the 1990s despite the decline in performance in most enterprises in 1989, which resulted from the anti-inflation austerity policy. On 10 April 1989, the state issued an 'Outline of Economic Reform for 1989', announcing further development of the contract form of the economic-responsibility system.

Although the contract-responsibility system is thought generally to have been a success, there remain a number of problems arising from state ownership of the firms. For example, even the use of three-year contracts does not counter effectively the 'short-term' behaviour of the firms, which are reluctant to invest to increase or renew state capital using retained funds. Instead, these funds are expended on bonuses, welfare, and buying luxury goods for the workers. It was reported that in Liaoning province state-owned firms increased welfare expenses by 23.4% in 1987, when their profit only increased by 5.8% (Xiao 1989). In addition, where 'rent-seeking' behaviour (Buchanan *et al.* 1980) exists, the costs of implementation of the contract can greatly increase. For example, it is widely reported that state enterprises commonly reduce their profit or place a limit on their capacity in an attempt to obtain lower targets in the next round of contract. Given these defects, it is questionable how long the contract form of the economic-responsibility system can last.

4. *Factor Allocation*

4.1 Labour supply

Enterprises obtain labour in several ways, the most important of which is the labour quota: this is the permanent work-force of the enterprise, and its size and composition is tightly planned and controlled by the Ministry of Labour via local labour bureaux and by the supervisory authority of enterprises. Changes in the labour quota are generally linked to capacity expansion, changes in output (but with a lag), and changes in ownership, e.g. a shift from collective to state ownership, but they are not related to short-run variations in market conditions. Dismissing permanent employees is extremely difficult, because the link between employment and housing, pensions, and medical and educational benefits makes dismissal or redundancy extremely serious for workers. Resignations and transfers of employees from one unit to another seldom occur. Employees who retire or die may be replaced by their children.

Enterprises may also hire 'seasonal contract' workers: this kind of employment is outside the plan. Since economic reform, state-owned enterprises have been granted the right to employ temporary workers to fulfil the needs arising from fluctuations in markets and production so long as it is done in co-operation with local governments. Most seasonal workers are recruited from rural areas. Mobility of this type of worker is high as they are not entitled to non-wage benefits. The length of seasonal contract could be up to a year depending on the needs of enterprises and the permission of local governments. The size of the contract labour force is affected by the enterprise quota of annual expenditure on total wages which is determined by local labour bureaux. The seasonal contract worker is usually poorly trained and educated.

It should be noted that seasonal contract workers are to be distinguished from ordinary 'contract workers'. Since 1985, as a result of the reforms, all new employees have been described as 'contract workers'. In practice they have the same status as permanent workers, e.g. rights to welfare benefits and housing, and they may eventually be transferred to permanent employment.

Finally, state-owned enterprises are allowed to recruit young employees for subsidiary enterprises. The ability to set up subsidiary collective enterprises depends on local policy. Subsidiary enterprises are not independent accounting units, and they rely on their parent company. Employees of these enterprises are all temporary or seasonal, and most of them are local young people with a good education. The aim of government is to encourage this type of enterprise in order to relieve unemployment in the cities. In practice, parent enterprises may either put this labour into non-plan production to generate new business and new revenue with the parent enterprises providing land, buildings, supplies, administrative support, investment subsidy, and a captive market, or employ them directly in formal (planned) production. All outlays for these subsidiary enterprises or employment would come from the parent enterprises and be accounted under 'costs for non-production business', i.e. not planned production.

The basic wage of workers is determined nationally, with variations by region and industry sector. However, as will be explained in detail in Chapter 4, the firm is able to determine additional wage payments in the form of bonuses, 'floating wages', etc. But the total wage payments of the firm have to be approved by the local labour bureau on an annual basis. This control, which has remained in place throughout the reform period, is intended to curb wage inflation. The annual wage budget is the outcome of negotiations between the firm and the bureau, taking into account the needs of the firm for additional workers, and differentials for different types of work.

4.2 Land

In principle, ownership of land belongs to the state but in practice the power to use land is controlled by village committees in rural areas, and enterprises or institutes in urban ones. There is no charge or land tax for state-owned enterprises and collectives. There is no open market for straightforward land transactions but land can be acquired by firms in several ways. For new plant construction, land is usually allocated by government. Existing enterprises can acquire more land for their production through planned allocations so long as their development is a priority for the authorities concerned. In practice, this is not always easy, so enterprises often inflate their initial request for land when a factory is set up.

Transfers of land between state-owned or collective enterprises are quite common. The process is as follows: one enterprise A wishes to take over some unoccupied land from another enterprise B. Enterprise B negotiates compensation with enterprise A; compensation may take the form of either providing employment for workers displaced by the land transaction, or a monetary payment. Enterprise A submits to the relevant authority a report giving reasons for requiring more land and detailing the agreement between the parties: if the relevant authorities approve the report and the agreement, then enterprise A can acquire the land.

Alternatively, an enterprise can move part of the production process away from the original site to a village or small town where labour and space are available. Because in general the village committee has the right to determine land-use, it welcomes urban enterprises to set up workshops on its land, since it can then receive 'rent' and other land-use charges, and tax revenues. Another solution is a merger or joint venture relationship with another enterprise: this solution is quite common, particularly between urban and rural enterprises. A number of state-owned enterprises have close relationships with rural enterprises for expanding production and increasing factor inputs.

4.3 Capital

The system for determining investment plan quotas, and controlling investment finance is illustrated in Fig. 1.3. The top half of the diagram shows how the plan quotas for individual state-owned enterprises are determined. The system operates in much the same way as the production planning system described in Section 1 above: the parallels are evident from a comparison with Fig. 1.2. The lower half of Fig. 1.3 shows how the banks control the payment of investment subsidies, and the making of loans in line with agreed quotas. It also shows the other sources of finance for investment.

The three categories of investment—in construction, in machinery and plant (innovation and replacement), and in stocks—are handled slightly differently within the system. Investment in buildings is determined by the annual plan quota of construction investment. The plan quota of individual firms is determined by the relevant level of the planning commission based on consideration of (*a*) the annual aggregate plan quota for construction investment in its agency; e.g. ministry agency, provincial agency etc.; (*b*) the amount of construction investment individual firms require; (*c*) how important a firm's project is for the state or local economy, together with (*d*) the amount of self-financing available. For instance, the higher the proportion of self-finance to the total value of investment, the easier it is for individual projects to get approval since less state funds will be required.

Similarly a firm's investment for innovation in production facilities is determined by individual plan quotas approved by the relevant supervisory authority. In practice, particularly in recent years, there has been very little control of this type of investment so long as the

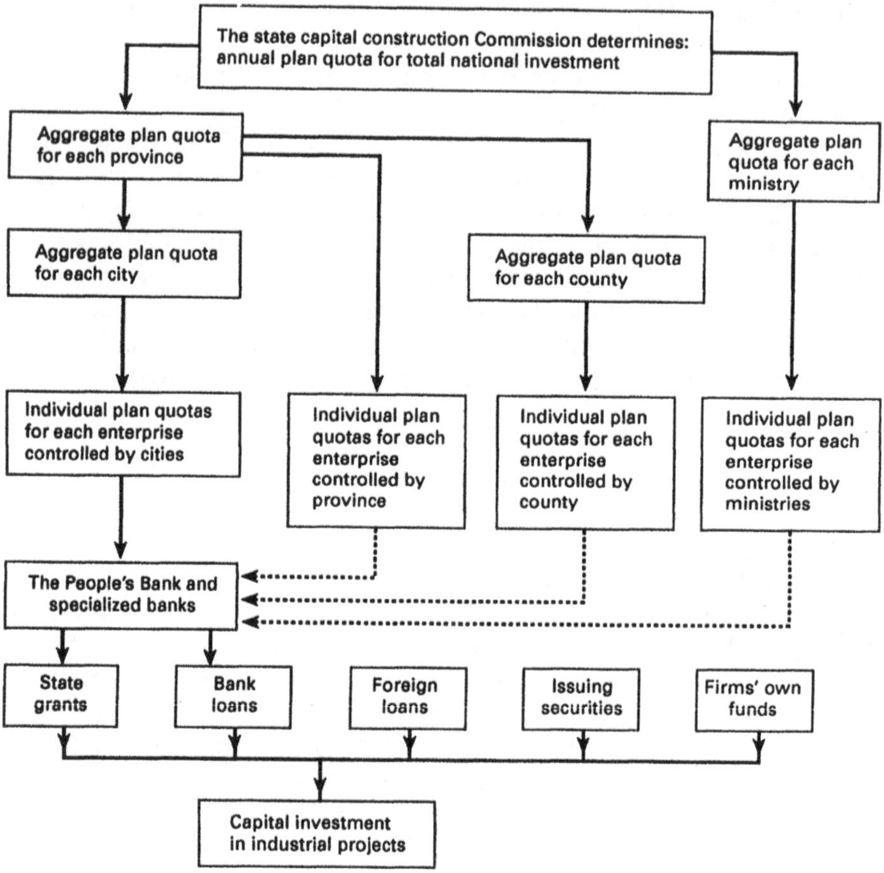

FIG. 1.3. Plan quotas and sources of finance for investment

modernization projects do not rely much on state subsidies. In the period 1981–88, the annual aggregate plan quota for modernization investment at national level was determined by the State Economic Commission, but since the beginning of 1989 control has passed to the State Planning Commission.

Since late 1986, with the implementation of contract responsibility for about 80% of state-owned enterprises, there has been a substantial reduction in state grants for investment, partly offset by the introduction of bank loans and by the release of most of depreciation and part of fulfilled profit to firms. Although the investment planning system remains and the State Planning Commission has still been setting an aggregate plan quota of investment for each administrative agency (province or ministry), an individual firm's long-term investment is hardly affected so long as the investment value of individual projects is not over 30 million yuan, and the aggregate plan quota of its agency is not exceeded. Instead of direct control via plan quotas, the central government is seeking to control aggregate investment at the macro-level by direct control of the finance provided by the People's Bank of China and other specialized banks. In 1989, faced with a high inflation rate, the central government effectively reduced investment by tightening up on bank loans for most investment projects, and by raising interest rates.

The sources of finance for physical investment (construction and/or plant and machinery) are also given in Fig. 1.3. Grants and bank loans will always reflect the plan quota of the firm. The alternative sources of finance are the firm's own sources, foreign loans, and the issuing of securities.

In practice, firms have come to rely more and more on borrowing as grants have been cut back, and as investment demand has exceeded the growth of retained profits. Thus the ratio of liabilities to net worth in the state-owned sector was only 11% in 1978, but increased to 33% in 1984, 60% in 1986, and has continued to increase since. Despite rising profitability, three-quarters of investment in the period 1978–86 was financed by borrowing. There have been a number of interesting experimental developments of capital markets during the reform period. In the state sector, some large and well-known companies, and a few experimental firms, have issued bonds for capital investment. In addition, many state-owned enterprises have issued 'shares' which carry a guaranteed minimum interest rate, and a dividend to be paid if allowed by the enterprise's profit.[2] Secondary markets have been initiated in Guangdong province and Shanghai city for bonds and equities. True equity securities hardly exist although a few enterprises have issued nominal shares experimentally since 1987. The capital market is still in an embryonic stage, and the freedom of state enterprises to use it is limited by the People's Bank (except for a few experimental enterprises). Approval to use the capital market is based on whether or not the project for which the enterprise plans to issue securities is approved by the supervisory authorities or is within the plan quota, and on how necessary is the issuing of securities.

State-owned enterprises can obtain working capital finance for investment in stocks from 'quota circulating funds' and 'non-quota circulating funds'. The former is the amount required by enterprises for maintenance of normal business turnover and is provided within the plan on favourable terms. The latter is the requirement over and above the quota, and it reflects temporary and seasonal needs plus the financing of goods in transit. Funds can be obtained by short-term bank loans with a given interest rate (the so-called 'extra bank loan'), or from the firm's own sources.

5. The Tax System

5.1 Direct taxes

An income tax, levied on the net profit of state-owned enterprises, replaced profit delivery after July 1983. There were two regimes, one a fixed-rate income tax imposed on large and medium-scale enterprises, and the other a progressive income tax imposed on small-scale enterprises. Development of the fixed-rate income tax came in three stages. In 1983, the tax was initiated with a 50% rate on the fulfilled profit of enterprises; the residual profit after income tax was shared between the supervisory authority and the enterprise, so-called 'profit-sharing'. From October 1984, the income tax was levied at a rate of 55% on the fulfilled profit of enterprises, and instead of 'profit-sharing' an adjustment tax was levied at a negotiable rate on profit remaining after the 55% tax. The adjustment tax was introduced to adjust for high profitability of state enterprises, particularly large and medium-scale enterprises, arising from price distortions. In principle, once the adjustment tax had been set up, only 30% of incremental profit would be subject to the tax in subsequent years. But in practice the collection of the tax varied from one enterprise to another. From 1986 onwards, increasing numbers of enterprises were switched to the contract-responsibility system (some 80% of all enterprises by 1988). Under this system, income tax and adjustment tax were replaced by a target quota for the delivery of profit tax, negotiated as part of the contract. The contract specified how much profit was to be delivered in each year of the contract period. The advantages of this system were thought to be the incentives to the firm implicit in the right to retain remaining profits, and that the delivery of profit could be more easily tuned to the precise circumstances of the enterprise.

Industrial and commercial income tax (ICIT) is a tax on collectives, joint ventures, and foreign enterprises. ICIT was created in 1950, and was changed formally into income tax for collective enterprises in 1985. The tax rate is on a progressive scale, ranging from 10% to 55%. It is also levied on rural collective enterprises such as village enterprises, but new firms were exempted in the first two to three years of operation. For joint venture and foreign enterprises, a preferential rate is applied, in the range 3–15% depending on local policy. Since 1989, the exemption for rural enterprises is said to have been eliminated. Individual income tax was instituted in 1980 for self-employed individuals and households engaged in commercial and industrial business, and levied according to a ten-point scale, with rates in the range 7–60%.

Other direct taxes were introduced in the mid-1980s, for the purpose of enhancing government revenue, discouraging investment and consumption, regaining control over expenditure, and influencing decision-making:

1. A tax levied on funds that are under the control of the enterprises themselves, including retained earnings, retained depreciation, and resources borrowed from local governments. Such funds are called 'extra-budgetary funds', since they are outside the control of the state budget. The tax rate was 10% initially and 15% in later years.

2. A construction tax levied on projects financed outside the state budget; but projects constructed by the enterprise itself for energy, transport, medical and school facilities, and projects financed by foreign investors or joint ventures are exempted. The tax rate is 10% of the total value of investment, and is collected by local government.

3. A bonus tax levied on the enterprise in relation to the annual bonus paid to employees, at the rate of 30% for annual bonuses equivalent to four months' basic wages, 100% for bonuses over four months' but less than six months' wages, and 300% for bonuses more than six months' wages. A wage tax is levied on 'floating wages' which are payments over and above state-fixed basic wages paid out of retained earnings and determined by the managers of enterprises. This wage tax is levied on *increases* in annual floating wages: increases over 7% but less than 12% at the rate of 30%, increases between 12% and 20% at the rate of 100%, and over 20% at the rate of 300%.

5.2 *Indirect taxes*

The Consolidated Industrial and Commercial Tax (CICT) was first created in 1958, and was essentially a turnover tax or sales tax imposed on products. In 1984, four separate taxes were distinguished: (*a*) product tax, a turnover tax imposed at a variety of rates on all types of enterprises—there are 400 commodity groups subject to tax at different rates ranging from 3% to 66%; (*b*) value added tax

(VAT), introduced in 1986 for fourteen selected industrial commodities, levied at rates ranging from 6% to 25%, such as agricultural machinery (6%), bicycles (16%), fans (25%), and sewing-machines (12%), a tax credit being allowed on input goods previously taxed; (*c*) business tax, imposed on gross sales of commercial enterprises at rates ranging from 3% to 15% in 1986; and (*d*) urban maintenance and construction tax, a surcharge on the previous three taxes, at rates of 7% in cities, 5% in townships or counties, and 1% elsewhere. This is a local government tax, collected and retained by local governments. Local governments are entitled to levy taxes or surcharges on central government taxes, notably a surcharge on the ICIT at rates of 10–100% for collectives, joint ventures, and foreign enterprises.

6. *Markets, Competition, and Pricing*

Before the reforms, markets had no role in the operations of Chinese state-owned enterprises, except for some transactions in barter form between enterprises mainly to secure materials. Since the economic reforms began in 1979, the role of markets has been gradually increased to weaken central control over inputs and outputs of state enterprises. For instance, before the reform only 3% of output of rolled steel was accounted for by sales outside the state plan, but this figure increased to about 20% in 1981 (Tanhe 1984: 357). The change indicated a shift from the old framework of planned allocation of outputs, to a new framework of mixed market and plan allocations. The new structure is presented in Fig. 1.4.

For state-owned enterprises, the plan quota consists of mandatory targets for output, which firms have to fulfil since the inputs for these outputs are also allocated by planning; and guidance targets, which are frequently linked to special input allocations, prices, or other incentives. The state-owned enterprise may also produce outside the plan: some of this production will be included in the enterprise contract (non-plan contract sales), but much will not (direct sales to markets). All other enterprises are outside the planning system, and operate entirely in the market sector.

Administrative control over the entry of enterprises into new markets has been considerably relaxed since 1983. Entry by urban and rural collective firms has not been restricted, except in a few industrial markets. Entry by joint ventures and foreign firms depends on the type of product; production that substitutes for imports is generally allowed. For a state-owned enterprise, entry into new markets requires the permission of its supervisory authority and of local govern-

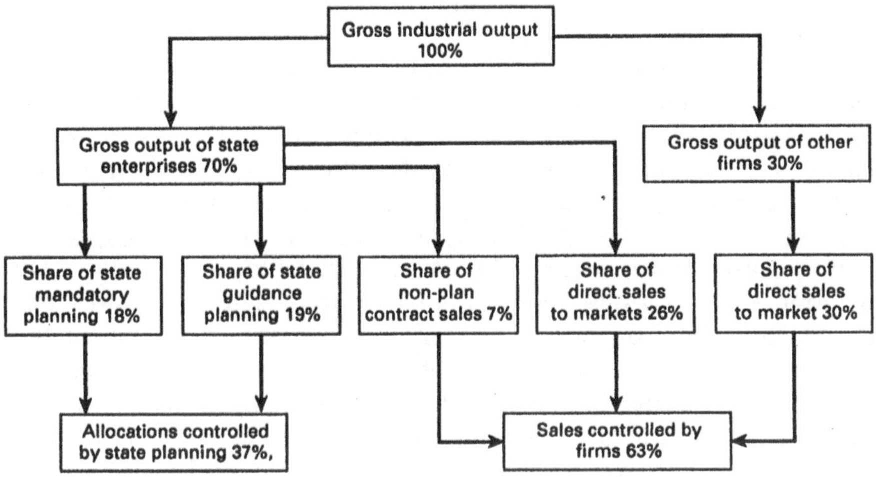

FIG. 1.4. The system of output allocation in 1985

Sources: Figures (all 1984) based on *Statistical Year Book of China* (SYC 1985) and *China: Finance and Investment* (World Bank 1989), 79.

ment. Permission is more likely to be forthcoming where the enterprise can be expected to increase its budgetary contribution to the local authorities.[3]

Since the mid-1980s, the greater freedom of market entry has generated considerable protests from state-owned enterprises that enjoy planned allocation of inputs at low prices. They complain that their production is threatened by a shortage of inputs, even state-allocated inputs, due to competition from non-state enterprises like rural collectives which are prepared to pay higher prices. The authorities have sometimes reacted by instituting a 'product licensing system', particularly at the provincial and local level, if they think that allowing free entry will result in 'excessive competition' to the detriment of existing enterprises.

Within an industry, competition in the domestic market may come from state enterprises in different cities or regions, urban collective enterprises, rural township or village enterprises, or joint venture and foreign enterprises, or imports. State-owned enterprises have some advantages over other enterprises, because the government protects them with state subsidies, allocations of raw materials and other inputs at low prices, long-term loans with low interest rates, and protected markets (guaranteed markets for their output even if poor quality). They also enjoy the advantages of economies of scale and of a trained labour force. Disadvantages *vis-à-vis* other firms arise from administrative interference, resulting in higher unit costs, low mobility of the labour force, and high overheads.

Competition occurs not only in selling output but also in the procurement of inputs since a considerable shortage of materials has directly affected output in most enterprises. This kind of competition leads to price increases for materials sold to enterprises who are willing to pay higher prices; and to local government intervention to prevent local raw materials flowing out to other regional markets.

In the pre-reform period, the prices of the industrial goods were determined by various levels of government. A black market was never significant. For state-owned enterprises, transactions outside the planning system were usually in barter form with negotiated prices. This kind of transaction was called 'co-operative relations'. After the 3rd Plenum of the 11th Party Committee in December 1978, price reform was introduced for state-owned enterprises. In the first period of reform 1980–81, the recommended reforms for pricing were similar to the measures taken by Czechoslovakia in 1967–68, including adjusting factory prices, making them more responsive to market conditions (Reynolds 1988: 21). Alongside the implementation of these recommendations, the State Council set up a 'Price Research Centre' for research into price reform and centralized control over the pricing of industrial goods was further relaxed in the period 1980–83. In May 1984, the State Council permitted industrial goods produced outside the plan quota to be sold at a range of prices within ±20% of state prices. In February 1985, however, the State Price Administration and the State Materials Administration jointly cancelled the 20% limit. Furthermore, the proportion of planned quota goods in the total output of enterprises has been further decreased. Prices for many daily commodities have been totally freed, particularly in the coastal area.

The 'dual pricing system' has grown out of these reforms. Different prices can be charged for identical goods, the main distinction being between goods produced for the plan quota, and goods that are produced outside the plan. Five different types of prices can be distinguished:

1. State prices set by the central government pricing bureau. Industrial goods that are subject to this control are essential production materials like steel and rubber. Only about twenty items have remained subject to direct control by the central government since 1985.

2. Local government prices set by local pricing bureaux for industrial goods, and controlled by their related provincial government. Often, the plan-quota output of an enterprise is in part allocated to

the central government plan and in part to the local government plan. Thus it is not unusual for enterprises to face two different state procurement prices.

3. Quasi-market prices, which are market prices but with a ceiling set by local price bureaux.

4. Negotiated prices between firms as sellers and buyers, based on voluntary contracts. This type of price is used for bulk sales or barter trade, and the goods could be within or outside the state plan. For example the plan quota of consumer goods produced by an enterprise has to be purchased by state commercial bureaux but since 1985 prices have been negotiated.

5. Market prices determined by the firm on the basis of cost and its judgement of what the market will bear.

5. *Conclusion*

This description of the economic reforms as they affected state-owned enterprises illustrates the speed and extent of reform in the period since 1979. In virtually every area of the firm's operations the effect of the reforms has been to increase the autonomy of the firm. However, much of the bureaucratic apparatus of the planned system has remained in place, at both national and local levels. Apparently local bureaux continue to exercise considerable influence in the decision-taking of the enterprises in their local areas. Under the contract system, for example, it will be the city or provincial industrial bureau which negotiates the contract with the firm and monitors performance. Their interest is motivated by the fact that the enterprises are the major source of revenue for the authorities at every level within the bureaucratic system. The experimentation with different forms of relationship between the firm and the authorities, and the chopping and changing of the rules in profit delivery/profit tax suggest that the tensions inherent in the transition from planned to market economy have not yet been satisfactorily resolved institutionally.

The implication is that the behaviour of the enterprises in this period may have been determined more by bargaining and negotiation between the firm and the authorities than by strict application of the 'rules'. Some enterprises may therefore have had more effective autonomy in decision-taking than others. In this respect, the situation is better understood as an evolution from the planned economy which preceded it rather than as a complete break. The rate of evolution and change has to be inferred from the actual behaviour of the enterprises during this period rather than from the institutional progression. This issue is addressed in the following two chapters.

APPENDIX 1.1

*Ten Rights Given to Enterprises in 1984**

In May 1984 the State Council promulgated the '*Provisional Regulations on Further Extending the Decision-Making Power of the State Industrial Enterprises*' giving such enterprises due power in the following ten aspects:

1. *Production*. Businesses have the right to produce whatever is needed or is in short supply, after fulfilling their state plans and orders.
2. *Sales*. With certain exceptions, firms have the right to sell products they retain for themselves, products in excess of state quotas, their own trial-produced or overstocked items, and those refused by state purchasing agencies. They must keep special accounts for the products they sell themselves and pay tax according to regulations.
3. *Pricing*. For the means of industrial production which they sell themselves and the products exceeding state quotas, businesses have the right to set prices within a 20% range of the state price, or to negotiate the prices with buyers. They must abide by the state prices for the means of livelihood and the means of farm production.
4. *Purchase of materials*. Businesses have the right to choose their suppliers when they order state-distributed raw materials. Businesses may also obtain raw materials directly from producers without going through state monopoly suppliers.
5. *Use of funds*. Enterprises have the right to decide whether their share of profits goes into expanding production, trial production of new products, a reserve fund, the workers' welfare fund, or bonuses. They also have the right to sue other funds for the first three items, together with funds for depreciation and large-scale renovation and repair.
6. *Handling of assets*. Businesses have the right to lease or transfer with compensation unneeded machinery or other fixed assets, but the income must be used to upgrade or renew their own facilities.
7. *Structural establishment*. Businesses have the right to decide on the setting-up of organizations and to assign their staff according to their needs as long as they stay within their authorized size.
8. *Personnel and labour*. The factory director or manager has the right to appoint or dismiss cadres under him. His deputies, however, are subject to approval from above. The director or manager and the party secretary are to be appointed by the higher competent departments

* Reproduced from O. Laaksonen (1988), 240–1.

concerned. The factory director has the right to reward or punish his workers and staff, with promotions, wage hikes, or even disciplinary dismissal. Directors have the right to employ workers on the basis of examinations under the guidance of the state labour-recruiting agencies. They also have the right to reject forced assignment from higher agencies or individuals.

9. *Wages and bonuses*. Businesses have the right to adopt any wage system, in line with state standards. Factory directors may promote 3% of their workers each year, with the increased wages counted as a cost of production.
10. *Inter-unit operations*. Enterprises have the right to enter into joint projects which cut across official divisions, as long as they maintain their present system of ownership, finances, and subordinate relationships.

NOTES

1. That is, prices fixed by the authorities which are advisory rather than mandatory to the enterprises.
2. For example a typical issue might have the following characteristics: 'bearer shares' issued at par with 7.2% p.a. guaranteed minimum interest, plus a dividend of up to 7.8% p.a., for a maximum total return of 15% p.a., issued for a term of 1–3 years in the total amount of ¥5 million; sold primarily to the public in units of 1 yuan, 10 yuan, and 100 yuan; negotiable through a bank at a 1.2% fee but without a specific repurchase promise; and with no voting rights for the holder' (*World Bank, 1989*: 314–18). This 'share' should really be termed a bond with profit participation. A true 'equity' would have no guaranteed interest component, no limits on the dividend, voting rights, and a long maturity. This type of enterprise 'share' was sold in over 2,000 issues for a total of 200 million yuan in Shanghai in 1984/85, and some 330 issues for 500 million yuan in Guangdong. Of Guangdong's total, 60% was offered to workers only, and 40% to the public at large (ibid. 317).
3. For instance, the shipping enterprise in Guangzhou, which is owned by the Transport and Communication Ministry, entered the hotel industry with a joint venture. The Guangdong provincial government encouraged the Guangdong trading company, which is locally controlled, to enter the shipping market with high subsidies. They set up the Guangdong shipping company to transport local imports and exports in order to earn foreign currency for the local government budget.

2

The Behaviour of Chinese Manufacturing Enterprises: A Survey of Managers

1. Introduction

This chapter presents findings from the analysis of the Questionnaire for Directors (Managers) of State-Owned Enterprises, which was distributed to a sample of 400 Chinese enterprises in the autumn of 1988. Some 351 questionnaires were returned, a response rate of about 88%. The structure of the questionnaire is shown in Appendix 2.1; it was made up of thirty-two sections, with an average of four responses required for each. Some of the sections were purely factual (e.g. section 31 asked the firm to identify its management system, and sections 1–3 asked questions about the nature of the contract under which it operates), while many others were designed to elicit information about behaviour (thus Section 12 enquires about the basis for production decisions on non-plan outputs, and Section 13 asks about responses to a situation of slack demand).

The analysis aims to describe the behaviour of state-owned enterprises after reform by pooling the results of the survey. As noted in Chapter 1, economic reforms in the 1980s were alleged to have given more autonomy to individual enterprises with the aim of improving productivity and efficiency. On the production side, firms were given a greater degree of autonomy in making decisions on output plans and product prices as well as more freedom to buy inputs from markets. They also experienced substantial gains from profit retention. As regards the labour force, firms were encouraged to give more incentives to their workers by implementing a bonus system and were allowed to establish an internal wage system alongside the existing state wage regulations. In addition, worker participation in management was diminished. Overall, the direction of the policy changes was one of decentralization from the state to the enterprise level, particularly in finance and production.

The issue of whether these changes brought about the desired efficiency outcomes will be addressed later in Chapter 5. Our current concern is to assess the degree of autonomy enjoyed by enterprises after the reform by examining the relationship between enterprises and their supervisors. Thus, we are looking for evidence as to whether enterprises were free to act independently or whether there still existed bureaucratic constraints on decision-making. The results should give some indication of the extent to which economic reform in China has succeeded in giving enterprises greater autonomy in different aspects of their operations.[1]

This chapter divides into two: the first part considers these issues at the level of the whole sample, while the second compares the behaviour of subsamples identified by contract form, industry sector, location, and scale.

2. *Enterprise Autonomy at the Whole-Sample Level*

The analysis which follows reports the group behaviour of enterprises as regards:

(i) enterprise responses to bureaucratic supervisors (principally the local bureaux and banks);
(ii) decision-making on output, inputs, and prices;
(iii) decision-making on employment and employee rewards;
(iv) participation of the work-force in management and policy-making; and
(v) the reformed functioning of the 'soft' budget constraint.

2.1 The relationship between enterprises and their authorities

This section presents a general picture of enterprise autonomy following economic reform. As the data do not cover the period prior to 1980, a *comparative* assessment of the autonomy of enterprises in the pre- and post-reform periods is not possible. The issue of autonomy is investigated by examining responses of directors/managers to the qualitative parts of the questionnaire which covered the following issues. (Details of the questionnaire, and the analysis of responses are detailed in Appendix 2.2. In the rest of this chapter responses

TABLE 2.1. Shares of planned outputs in total outputs in 1985–1987 (*Q24C–Q26C*)

Year		Total	Groups (%)				
			0–50%	50–75%	75–85%	85–95%	95–100%
1985	Frequency	346	166	23	29	32	96
	%	100	48	6.6	8.4	9.2	27.7
1986	Frequency	346	173	24	33	36	80
	%	100	50	6.9	9.5	10.4	23.1
1987	Frequency	187	187	25	28	32	74
	%	100	54	7.2	8.1	9.2	21.4

are referenced Q1 . . . Q124 according to the corresponding question numbers.)

1. *Shares of planned outputs in total outputs 1985–87 (Q24–Q25)*

The responses are summarized in Table 2.1. It should be noted that the share of planned outputs is inversely related to enterprise autonomy. About half the enterprises had less than 50% of their total outputs covered by the state plan, a quarter of them had between 50% and 95% covered, and the remaining quarter had more than 95% covered. Thus many enterprises enjoyed a significant degree of autonomy in the product market but a significant proportion was still tightly controlled by the state. The proportion of enterprises subject to a low level of control (<50%) by the authorities steadily increased over time (from 48% in 1985 to 54% in 1987) and the proportion with a high level of control (95%) steadily decreased (from 28% to 21%).

2. *The role played by enterprise directors in making the production plans (Q27)*

Responses are given in Table 2.2 which tell us that only half the directors said they played an important or very important role: the

TABLE 2.2. Role of director in making production plan, 1987 (*Q27*)

	Total	'Very important' to 'Not important'			
		1	2	3	4
Frequency	273	63	94	75	41
%	100	23.1	34.4	27.5	15.0

TABLE 2.3. The year when enterprises acquired the right to make annual plans (*Q28C–Q33C*) (frequency distribution, %)

Plans for:	1983 and before	1984–5	1986 and after	No response
Output value	12.3	15.4	29.6	42.7
Output volume	11.7	16.0	29.1	43.3
Variety	13.1	15.7	28.5	42.7
Production technique	12.0	14.8	27.4	45.9
Production schedule	13.7	15.1	27.6	43.6
Exports	6.3	7.7	20.8	65.2

other half just act as agents between the higher authority and their firms.

3. *The year when enterprises were granted the right to make various decisions (Q28–Q33)*

Annual plans include output value, output volume, product variety, choice of production technique, production schedule, and exports. Responses to this group of questions are presented in Table 2.3. About 40% of the firms had no right to make any plans in any of the areas listed above. This proportion was 65% when the plan was for exports. For those which were granted the right to make various annual plans the majority acquired the right very recently and the proportion of firms obtaining the right increased markedly over time. Thus the direction of economic reforms has been clearly towards decentralization.

4. *Restrictions imposed by higher authorities on enterprises when they purchase inputs from, and sell products to, the market (Q34–Q40)*

There are four types of restrictions: price, quality, suppliers/buyers, supplier/buyer regions. The questionnaire asked managers to rank these restrictions. The responses are given in Table 2.4 (for the input market) and Table 2.5 (for the product market). Price restrictions were considered to be the most important ones in both input and output markets, with quality restrictions in second place. Enterprises faced much stronger government restrictions in the output market than in the input market. The percentage of firms reporting no restrictions at all was 56% for input purchases, but only 40% for product sale. Furthermore, almost half the firms considered price to be the most important restriction in selling products, whereas only 21% found it to be the most important restriction in purchasing inputs.

TABLE 2.4. Restrictions on firms in purchasing materials from the market (*Q34–Q37*) (no. of responses and frequency distribution)

Priority			Types of restriction					
			0	1	2	3	4	5
First	Frequency	351	198	75	15	22	9	32
	%	100	56.4	21.4	4.3	6.3	2.6	9.1
Second	Frequency	351	274	2	41	13	17	4
	%	100	78.1	0.6	11.7	3.7	4.8	1.1
Third	Frequency	351	309	0	1	18	16	7
	%	100	88.0	0	0.3	5.1	4.6	2.0

Note: 0 = No response; 1 = Price; 2 = Quality; 3 = Suppliers; 4 = Supply regions; 5 = Others.

TABLE 2.5. Restrictions on firms in selling their products (*Q38–Q40*) (no. of responses and frequency distribution)

Priority			Types of restriction					
			0	1	2	3	4	5
First	Frequency	351	126	170	30	10	9	5
	%	100	35.9	48.4	8.5	2.8	2.6	1.7
Second	Frequency	351	168	34	105	15	26	3
	%	100	47.9	9.7	29.9	4.3	7.4	0.9
Third	Frequency	351	205	7	21	40	28	50
	%	100	58.4	2.0	6.0	11.4	8.0	14.2

Note: 0 = No response; 1 = Price; 2 = Quality; 3 = Buyers; 4 = Buyer locations; 5 = Others.

5. *Means by which enterprises may influence decision-making by the authorities (Q68–Q85)*

This group of questions asked directors of firms how they would go about influencing the higher authorities in order to arrange for a supply of raw materials on favourable conditions, to provide various kinds of loan, and to decide contract targets. The methods used can be classified as constructive and less constructive. Constructive steps have included the creation of a well-known product, the earning of foreign exchange through exports, and the improvement of management. Examples of less constructive steps are bargaining with the authority and the use of social contacts. The responses are given in

TABLE 2.6. Means used by firms to influence higher authority on making decisions (*Q68–Q73*; *Q74–Q79*; *Q80–Q85*)

Decisions on		Means used to affect decision-making							
		1	2	3	4	5	6	7	Total
A	Frequency	71	73	45	15	57	15	75	351
	%	20.2	20.8	12.8	4.3	16.2	4.3	21.4	100
B	Frequency	94	75	72	13	31	16	50	351
	%	26.8	21.4	20.5	3.7	8.8	4.6	14.2	100
C	Frequency	27	24	130	61	7	23	79	351
	%	7.7	6.8	37.0	17.4	2.0	6.6	23.5	100

Note: A = Decision-making on supplying raw materials with favourable conditions
B = Decision-making on providing loans
C = Decision-making on determining contract targets
Means: 1 = Creating a well-known product; 2 = Earning foreign exchange; 3 = Improving management; 4 = Bargaining with authority; 5 = Using different social contacts; 6 = Others; 7 = No response.

Table 2.6. Most enterprises took constructive steps in order to win the favour of the higher authority in securing materials, loans, and setting contract targets. However, a sizeable proportion (15–25%) of firms relied on the less constructive approaches (for instance, 16% of firms were reported to use social contacts to secure supplies of raw materials while 17% of firms relied on bargaining directly with higher authorities in setting contract targets).

We conclude that these responses are consistent with an increased autonomy for the majority of firms as the reforms progressed. Nevertheless the evidence also indicates that the authorities continued to have an important impact on the firms, especially in output markets, and that firms devoted considerable energies to influencing the decisions of the authorities.

2.2 *Decision-making on outputs and prices*

The objective of this section is to analyse how firms react to changes in supply and demand in the market. An implicit objective of economic reform has been to introduce markets and competition so that resources are allocated and utilized more efficiently, and market disequilibrium can be more rapidly eliminated. Within the framework of the pre-reform centrally planned economy, marketing activity was dominated by the state planning mechanism. Enterprises were not allowed to make their own decisions and hence did not need to worry about changes in the markets. Thus the behaviour of firms was not influenced by market signals. Since enterprises have been given more autonomy in decision-making since the reforms, we would expect their behaviour to be more sensitive to changes in the market environment.

This issue can be addressed by investigating firms' responses to changes in the market demand and supply situation and finding out how they adjust their output targets and price levels. In particular, analysis in this section concentrates on firms' responses to the following issues (details of the questionnaire are given in Appendix 2.3):

1. *Criteria used to determine production outside the state plan (Q47–Q49)*

Six criteria are commonly used to make such decisions and firms were asked to rank the three most important ones. Responses are summarized in Table 2.7. 'Present orders' and 'market forecast' were ranked by 55% of firms as the first criterion in making production decisions outside the state plan. Only 9.4% of firms considered profit to be the most important factor. This appears to go against a common assertion that Chinese enterprises have been more interested in achieving profit targets since economic reform. That so many firms based their production plans on criteria other than profit may well indicate that output maximization has been the dominant objective.

TABLE 2.7. Criteria used by firms in determining non-plan production (*Q47–Q49*) (no. of responses and frequency distribution)

Priority		Criteria								
		0	1	2	3	4	5	6	7	Total
First	Frequency	48	26	84	109	3.3	4	44	3	351
	%	13.7	7.4	23.9	31.1	9.4	1.1	12.5	0.9	100
Second	Frequency	52	17	57	69	62	25	69	2	351
	%	14.8	4.8	16.2	19.1	17.7	7.1	19.7	0.6	100
Third	Frequency	62	22	25	47	64	26	87	18	351
	%	17.7	6.3	7.1	13.4	18.2	7.4	24.8	5.1	100

Note: First, second, and third identify the ranking of criteria by the firm.
Criteria: 0 = No response; 1 = Past sales; 2 = Present orders; 3 = Forecast market; 4 = Profit maximization; 5 = Supply of energy or electricity; 6 = Supply of raw materials; 7 = Other criteria.

TABLE 2.8. Short-term responses to insufficient demand (*Q50–Q52*) (no. of responses and frequency distribution)

Priority		Responses					
		0	1	2	3	4	Total
First	Frequency	88	61	52	140	10	351
	%	25.1	17.4	14.8	39.9	2.8	100
Second	Frequency	282	1	10	51	7	351
	%	80.3	0.3	2.8	14.5	2.0	100
Third	Frequency	342	0	1	5	3	351
	%	97.4	0	0.3	1.4	0.9	100

Note: First, second, and third identify the ranking of responses.
Responses: 0 = No response; 1 = Cut output; 2 = Cut price; 3 = Promote sales; 4 = Maintain same output.

2. *Short-term response to insufficient demand for the product (Q50–Q52)*

This section was designed to investigate how firms respond to a situation in which they find it difficult to sell their products. There are four possible choices: reducing output, reducing price, promoting sales, and no reaction, i.e. maintaining the same production level. The responses to these questions are given in Table 2.8. Some 32% of firms responded by cutting prices or reducing production as their first choice and 40% by promoting sales. Another 15% made sales promotion their second choice. The fact that more than 30% of the firms responded by cutting prices and reducing output is evidence that enterprises have been sensitive to market signals. This argument is reinforced by the finding that very few firms took no action at all (less than 5% in the fourth column in Table 2.8). Firms on the whole adopted a single strategy when they found it difficult to sell products, as is indicated by the low number of responses to second and third choices.

3. *Reasons for not cutting production when there is insufficient demand (Q53)*

Three major reasons are given: planning constraints; the fact that reducing output would involve greater losses than cutting price; and marketing uncertainty. These responses are presented in Table 2.9. About one-third of firms did not cut production because they thought it was more profitable to cut prices. The rest did not cut production either because they were restricted by the state plan or because

TABLE 2.9. Reasons for maintaining production levels under insufficient demand (*Q53*)

Reasons	1	2	3	4	Total
Frequency	63	79	48	36	226
%	27.9	35.0	21.2	15.9	100

Note: 1 = Plan constraint; 2 = Price cut preferred; 3 = Marketing problem; 4 = Other.

TABLE 2.10. Criteria for setting prices on non-plan products (*Q54*)

Criteria	0	1	2	3	4	Total
Frequency	57	51	132	78	33	351
%	16.2	14.5	37.6	22.2	9.4	100

Note: 0 = No response; 1 = State-planned price; 2 = Production cost of the firm; 3 = Based on average price of similar firms; 4 = According to market condition.

of marketing uncertainty, or for other reasons. This suggests that although a significant proportion of firms behaved rationally in the context of the market, many firms were still unable to do so due to government intervention and imperfections in the market system.

4. *Criteria for setting prices on products outside state plans (Q54)*

There are four criteria used to set prices: state price, production cost, market price, and market conditions. The responses are presented in Table 2.10 which gives rise to the following observations. First, only a small proportion of firms set their prices based on the state price. This indicates that state prices usually differ from market prices, which is after all the basic problem of a planned economy. More than one-third of firms charged a price based on the production cost, indicating that they were price setters and hence able to pass their costs on to consumers. This phenomenon could be explained either by inadequate competition or by chronic supply shortages.

5. *Reasons for pricing below the market level (Q55)*

Three major reasons are listed in the questionnaire: low cost, market penetration, and exchange of output for raw materials and energy (a significant proportion of firms are restricted by the supply of these inputs). The responses are presented in Table 2.11. The results indi-

TABLE 2.11. Reasons for price being below market price (*Q55*)

Reasons	0	1	2	3	Total
Frequency	165	56	96	34	351
%	47.0	16.0	27.4	9.7	100

Note: 0 = No response; 1 = Low cost; 2 = Market penetration; 3 = Exchange output for raw materials and energy.

TABLE 2.12. Reasons for making investments in other enterprises (*Q92*)

Reasons	0	1	2	3	4	5	6	Total
Frequency	182	14	74	22	22	24	13	351
%	51.9	4.0	21.1	6.3	6.3	6.8	3.7	100

Note: 0 = No response; 1 = Promoting sales; 2 = Securing materials supply; 3 = Expanding production capacity; 4 = Increasing profit; 5 = Co-operation with other firms; 6 = Other reasons.

cate that a majority of firms charge lower prices because they are able to reduce costs or they want to expand market share.

6. *Reasons for making investments in other firms (Q92)*

The reasons and responses are given in Table 2.12. The results indicate that only half the firms have investments in other firms. About 40% of these are motivated by the need to secure supplies of material. Inter-plant penetration has not been a common practice; however some firms are beginning to look for opportunities for expansion and integration.

We conclude that firms have become more responsive to market conditions in determining output and prices, but behaviour is still far from competitive. Firms are guided more by rules of thumb than by considerations of efficiency and/or profit maximization.

2.3 Decision-making on employment and employee rewards

This section aims to investigate how much autonomy has been given to enterprises concerning employment and employee rewards. We have found strong evidence that enterprises have been granted a degree of autonomy in output and input markets. However, if manage-

TABLE 2.13. Whether enterprises have ever refused employees assigned by the authority (*Q41*)

Responses	0	1	2	Total
Frequency	49	70	232	351
%	14.0	19.9	66.1	100

Note: 0 = No response; 1 = Have refused; 2 = Never refused.

ment has no power to make its own decisions on employment, its degree of 'autonomy' is limited. There are two distinct dimensions of autonomy in labour management: employee remuneration and employment decisions. In fact, different systems of employee remuneration may have widely differing impact on productivity, even if management does not have the power to make decisions about employment. Autonomy in employment decisions is assessed according to whether enterprises have ever refused to accept employees assigned by the authority and what procedures exist for dismissing employees. The degree of freedom in employee remuneration is given in response to whether enterprises have imposed an internal wage system, whether enterprises have excess supply (demand) of (for) labour, and the types of excess labour. (Details of the questionnaire are given in Appendix 2.4.)

1. *Whether enterprises have ever refused to accept employees assigned by the authority (Q41)*

The responses to this question are given in Table 2.13. Only 20% of the firms gave a positive response, the rest had never refused to accept employees assigned by authority. There was no question asking how many times enterprises had refused to accept employees, but other evidence suggests that the freedom to reject employees assigned by the authorities is very restricted.

TABLE 2.14. Procedures for the dismissal of employees (*Q41*)

Procedures	0	1	2	3	4	Total
Frequency	59	55	176	18	43	351
%	16.8	15.7	50.1	5.1	12.3	100

Note: 0 = No response; 1 = Determined solely by director; 2 = Determined by the director and higher authority; 3 = Nominated by the leadership and determined by the representative committee of the trade union; 4 = Higher authority alone.

2. *Procedures for the dismissal of employees (Q41)*

The responses are presented in Table 2.14. Although in a significant proportion of firms (16%) this decision is made by the directors alone, most of the firms have the decision taken by higher authority (12%) or by the directors on consulting their superiors (50%), suggesting that the higher authority has a strong position. The representative committee of the trade union has little influence.

3. *Whether or not enterprises have imposed an internal wage system (Q44)*

The responses given in Table 2.15 indicate that about one-third of the firms gave a positive response suggesting a radical change in policy on labour rewards.

4. *Whether or not enterprises have excess supply of, or demand for, labour (Q86–Q88)*

The original responses to this question are regrouped into three levels, with level 1 representing firms with excess labour of more than 10%, level 2 with 0–10%, and level 3 with insufficient labour supply. The responses are reported in Table 2.16. There are no responses to level 3 at all, indicating that all firms either have excess labour or have the exact amount of labour they require. One-fifth of the firms have excess labour of more than 10%. The fact that many firms have to

TABLE 2.15. Whether enterprises have introduced an internal wage system (*Q44*)

Procedures	0	1	Total
Frequency	245	106	351
%	69.8	30.2	100

Note: 0 = No internal wage system; 1 = Internal wage system introduced.

TABLE 2.16. Excess supply or demand for labour (*Q86C* (*Q86–Q88*))

Responses	1	2	3	Total
Frequency	71	280	0	351
%	20.2	79.8	0	100

Note: 1 = Excess labour supply >10%; 2 = Excess labour supply 0–10%; 3 = Excess demand for labour.

TABLE 2.17. Types of excess labour (*Q89–Q90*)

First Priority

Responses	0	1	2	3	4	5	6	7	Total
Frequency	112	83	24	67	1	5	45	14	351
%	31.9	23.6	6.8	19.3	0.3	1.4	12.8	4.0	100

Second Priority

Responses	0	1	2	3	4	5	6	7	Total
Frequency	137	0	11	22	3	1	46	131	351
%	39.0	0	3.1	6.3	0.9	0.3	13.1	37.3	100

Note: 0 = No response; 1 = Managerial staff; 2 = Political staff; 3 = Office-workers; 4 = Engineering technical staff; 5 = Skilled workers; 6 = Ordinary workers; 7 = Service workers.

employ unnecessary workers leads to severe inefficiency in the use of labour, but reflects the policy of a socialist economy to guarantee a job to everyone who can work (at least in urban areas). The findings in this subsection are consistent with those discussed above: management has little power to rationalize labour use; and the State ensures job security for the workers at the expense of efficiency.

5. *Which groups within the work-force experience the greatest excess supply? (Q89–Q90)*

The responses to this question are given in Table 2.17. The work-force is classified into seven groups comprising managerial staff, political staff, office-workers, engineering technicians, skilled workers, ordinary workers, and service workers. The majority of firms considered managerial staff (24%), political staff (7%), office-workers (19%), and ordinary workers (13%) to be those in the greatest excess supply. Less than 2% of the firms considered engineering technicians and skilled workers to be in excess.

We conclude that the enterprises had little or no autonomy in deciding on the size of their labour force, and that only a third were able to vary their internal wage structure. Note however that these questions did not include the payment of bonuses, which have a major impact on total wages paid.

2.4 Work-force participation in decision-making

In Section 2.1 we found that enterprise directors have been granted a significant degree of autonomy in making decisions. In this section we ask whether autonomy has been given mainly to the director or whether it is also shared to some degree by the work-force. A 'democratic system' would require management to be supervised by the work-force. Discussion focuses on the following issues (details of the questionnaire are given in Appendix 2.4):

1. *Participation of the work-force in making decisions within enterprises (Q113–Q115)*

In the questionnaire, there are questions asking directors to choose and rank the three most important aspects of work-force participation in decision-making. To simplify, the eleven options were regrouped into three major choices. The responses are presented in Table 2.18. Only 20% of the firms allow the work-force to make decisions on

TABLE 2.18. Staff participation in decision-making (*Q113–Q115*)

First Priority

Responses	0	1	2	3	Total
Frequency	31	72	151	97	351
%	8.8	20.5	43.0	26.7	100

Second Priority

Responses	0	1	2	3	Total
Frequency	35	48	164	104	351
%	9.9	13.7	46.7	29.6	100

Third Priority

Responses	0	1	2	3	Total
Frequency	46	61	126	118	351
%	13.1	17.4	35.9	33.6	100

Note: 0 = No response; 1 = Electing the leadership of firms; 2 = Decisions on wages/bonus, assignment of workers to posts, developing new products, investment, use of retained profit and the production/finance plan; 3 = Allocation of houses and other decisions.

personnel, including the election of their leaders, and the recruitment or dismissal of workers. About 70% of the firms allow workers to participate in other decision-making, including wages/bonuses, assignment of workers to posts, and investment.

2. *Appointment of directors (Q21)*

Responses given in Table 2.19 suggest that the majority of directors are directly appointed by the higher authorities, thus the work-force has little say in this matter. This structure of appointments has important implications for both enterprise behaviour and performance.

3. *How the middle-level cadres of enterprises are appointed (Q43)*

The responses are presented in Table 2.20 which illustrates that the majority of the firms have their middle-level cadres appointed by the directors alone. The work-force has no power in their appointments.

We conclude that the greater autonomy given to the enterprises has not been extended to involve the work-force in any significant decision-taking. The powers of the manager of the firm have thereby been enhanced.

2.5 *Firm inertia and the 'soft' budget constraint*

Most socialist economies have a 'soft' budget constraint, i.e. state-owned enterprises are rescued when they get into financial difficulties.

TABLE 2.19. Appointment of directors (*Q21*)

Responses	0	1	2	3	4	5	Total
Frequency	43	244	14	38	7	5	351
%	12.3	69.5	4.0	10.8	2.0	1.4	100

Note: 0 = No response; 1 = Appointed by higher authorities; 2 = Elected by workers; 3 = Bid; 4 = Nominated by contract body; 5 = Other.

TABLE 2.20. Appointment of middle-level cadres within firms (*Q43*)

Responses	0	1	2	3	4	5	Total
Frequency	29	279	31	0	11	1	351
%	8.3	79.5	8.8	0	3.1	0.3	100

Note: 0 = No response; 1 = Appointed by the director alone; 2 = Appointed by the director on consultation with the higher authority; 3 = Elected by workers; 4 = Bid; 5 = Appointed by higher authority.

In a planned economy, because product prices and resource allocation are tightly controlled by the state, prices may not reflect the market values of the products. This means that on the one hand firms which are highly profitable may not be those that are performing well, whereas those which are making severe losses may not be performing very badly. If the latter get into financial difficulty, the state will come to their aid because they are making 'policy' losses, i.e. losses which are due to price distortion. On the other hand, firms may really perform badly and make losses. However, in order not to dismiss workers the government has to rescue the firm from bankruptcy by giving 'soft' budget support. A 'soft' budget constraint has some positive effects. In the first a 'soft' budget may be considered as a supplementary tool in a planned economy used to adjust the allocation of resources so that resources can be used more efficiently. In the second case, it gives a sense of security to the work-force so that social stability can be maintained. However, the negative effects are both obvious and inevitable. It not only creates inertia in firms which are making losses, but also discourages those firms which are profitable. Loss-making firms need not worry about their performance and make no effort to eliminate or reduce losses because they can receive subsidies from the state. To subsidize less efficient firms, the state has to tax efficient firms more. As a result, more profitable firms may well find it pointless to improve management performance and efficiency.

One objective of economic reform has been to minimize the negative effects of a soft budget constraint by introducing a 'contract'-responsibility system in which loss-making firms come under more pressure and profitable firms are allowed to benefit if they can increase efficiency. However whether this objective can be realized still remains unclear.

This section presents the responses to questions on this aspect. The following questions were asked (details of the questionnaire are given in Appendices 2.2 and 2.3):

1. *Whether higher authorities helped when firms had difficulty repaying loans (Q45)*

The results of this question are given in Table 2.21. About 40% of the firms have experienced difficulty in repaying loans and have been helped by the government.

2. *Means adopted by the authorities to help firms in paying loans (Q46)*

The responses are presented in Table 2.22. For those firms which received help from the government, extending the loan period and

TABLE 2.21. Whether higher authorities assisted when firms had difficulties in repaying loans (*Q45*)

Responses	No help	Help	Total
Frequency	211	140	351
%	60.1	39.9	100

TABLE 2.22. Means to assist repayment of loans by higher authority (*Q46*)

Responses	0	1	2	3	4	5	Total
Frequency	170	53	3	21	89	15	351
%	48.4	15.1	0.9	6.0	25.4	4.3	100

Note: 0 = No response; 1 = Extending loan period; 2 = Writing off the debt; 3 = Granting a new loan to replace the existing one; 4 = Loan repayment before taxation; 5 = Other.

TABLE 2.23. Reasons for delaying repayment of loan (*Q91*)

Responses	0	1	2	3	Total
Frequency	152	12	113	74	351
%	43.3	3.4	32.2	21.1	100

Note: 0 = No response; 1 = Higher authority having agreement with bank; 2 = Firms having agreement with bank; 3 = Unable to pay.

making loan repayments tax-deductible, were the most common form of support.

3. *Reasons for delaying repayment of loans (Q91)*

Results for this question are illustrated in Table 2.23. About 21% of the firms were unable to repay loans, presumably because they were in severe financial difficulty. More than one-third of firms did not repay loans on time because they were supported by the government and banks.

4. *Percentage of firms reporting some loss-making outputs (Q94)*

The results of this question are given in Table 2.24, which indicates that one-third of the firms produced loss-making products.

TABLE 2.24. Percentage of firms reporting some loss-making outputs (*Q94*)

	No losses	Losses	Total
Frequency	233	128	351
%	66.4	33.6	100

TABLE 2.25. Reasons for producing loss-making products (*Q95*)

Reasons	1	2	Total
Frequency	89	46	135
%	65.9	34.1	100

Note: 1 = Compulsory plan, attracting subsidy from State, unwilling to lay off workers: influences by government on soft budget and employment policy; 2 = Unable to use new technology because of its high cost and other reasons: difficulties arising within enterprises themselves.

5. *Reasons for producing loss-making products (Q95)*

The original question included several reasons: adhering to the compulsory plan, attracting a subsidy from the state, being unwilling to lay off workers, or unable to use new technology. We interpret the first three reasons as reflecting the influence of the soft budget, and the fourth reason as reflecting difficulties arising within enterprises themselves. The results are presented in Table 2.25. In about two-thirds of the firms, loss-making activities can be attributed to the policies of the higher authorities.

6. *Problems faced by the enterprise (Q97–Q99)*

Directors were asked to identify the three most important difficulties experienced by their firms. The responses are summarized in Table 2.28. From this we discover that for a majority of firms their most prominent difficulties were the shortage of electricity, raw materials, and funds, as well as the unsuitability of products for the market and the shortage.

These responses indicate the extent to which the industrial sector still experienced resource misallocation, with production being undertaken without regard to market conditions, and subject to physical

TABLE 2.26. Problems faced by enterprises (*Q97–Q99*)

First Priority Problem

Responses	1	2	3	4	5	Total
Frequency	297	15	13	3	23	351
%	84.6	4.3	3.7	0.9	6.6	100

Second Priority Problem

Responses	1	2	3	4	5	Total
Frequency	258	26	19	17	31	351
%	73.5	7.4	5.4	4.8	8.8	100

Third Priority Problem

Responses	1	2	3	4	5	Total
Frequency	170	52	39	29	61	351
%	48.4	14.8	11.1	8.3	17.4	100

Note: 1 = Short of electricity, energy and raw materials, products find no market and short of funds; 2 = Backwardness of technology or shortage of skilled workers and managerial personnel; 3 = Low incentive of workers and too many disputes among staff; 4 = Too much intervention by government; 5 = No specific response.

plan targets or constraints. In particular, production may be initiated without adequate regard for supplies of energy and materials. The soft budget rescues firms from the financial consequences of these problems, but almost certainly with adverse effects on efficiency.

2.6 *Summary of findings*

Findings in the previous sections enable us to describe the nature of the relationships between the enterprise, the bureaux, and the general economic environment in the management system for Chinese state-owned enterprises described in Chapter 1, and illustrated in Fig. 2.1.

The main features of the system can be described as follows:

1. The industrial bureaux determine the appointment of directors who in turn determine the appointment of middle-level cadres. The

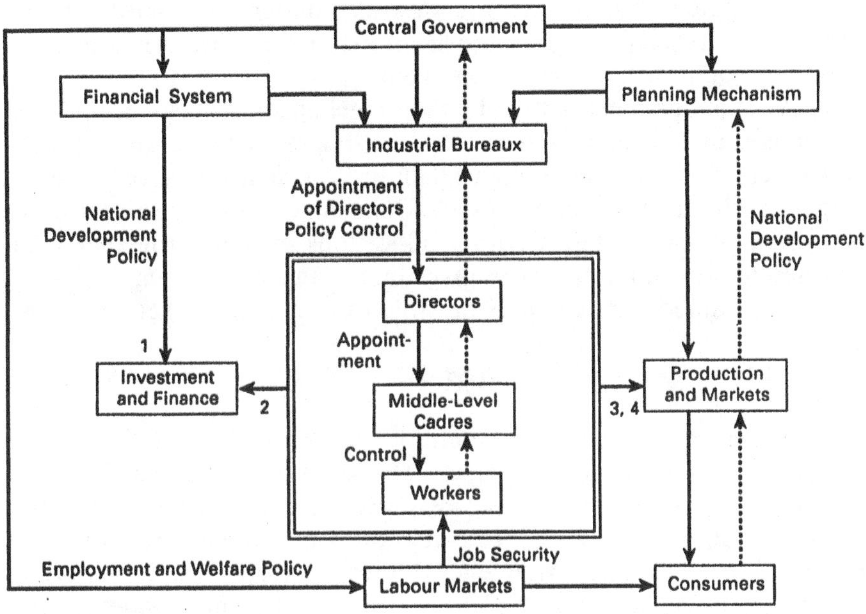

1 'Soft' budget
2 Retained profit for investment
3 Outside state plan
4 Execution of state plan

——— Direct effect
- - - - - Indirect effect
═══ Boundary of the enterprise

FIG. 2.1. Flow chart of the management system of the chinese state-owned enterprises under economic reform

work-force has little to say about the appointment of personnel. The directors are not supervised by anyone but the bureaux.

2. Although directors are allowed some freedom in making decisions *outside* state plans (including procurement of inputs, production planning, price-setting, and sales of products) the government and the higher authorities are still in control of the main activities *within* state plans (especially production, inputs, and prices).

3. The government sets regulations for the industrial bureaux. It also supports the workers in terms of job security, and the firms in terms of the 'soft' budget. The linkage between the firm and the government is weak in the sense that every response from the grass roots must be passed through the higher authority before reaching the government.

4. Investment and finance are basically under the control of the industrial bureaux, though retained profits enable enterprises to do a certain amount of their own investment.

5. As it is difficult for the planning mechanism to respond quickly to changes in consumer preferences, the linkage between the market/consumers and the government/planning mechanism is very weak. The growth of the non-plan sector has made firms responsive to consumer pressures, but arbitrary allocations of inputs together with continuing limited autonomy in investment, finance, and employment, have constrained the degree of possible response to market signals.

3. A Comparison of Enterprise Autonomy between Subsamples

In the rest of this chapter, attention is switched from the whole sample of enterprises to comparison of responses to the questionnaire by the managers of subsamples, identified by contract form, industry sector, location, and scale. The methodology applied was straightforward. We examined frequency tables of responses to different questions: chi-square tests were then used to determine whether responses differed significantly by contract form, industry sector, or scale of enterprise. Due to the nature of the data and of the chi-square tests, rejection of the null hypothesis (of no difference) at the 20% level is noted, and rejection at the 10% level is taken to indicate a significant difference.

Our expectation is that economic reform has proceeded faster in some locations, in some industries, and in larger enterprises. Furthermore some contract forms are designed specifically to give greater autonomy (especially the contract-responsibility system), and we expect this to be reflected in the behaviour and attitudes reported in the questionnaire responses. This raises the further question of the degree to which contract form is itself closely associated with particular locations, industry sectors, or scale of enterprise. We focus briefly on this question before analysing responses.

The questionnaire specifies five types of contract form.[2] Two of these, form 2 (contract-responsibility system) and form 5 (director-responsibility system) respectively account for 49% and 40% of the responses. Given the very few observations of the other contract forms, it is not feasible to analyse them separately. Of these, form 1 (share system), form 3 (leasing system), and form 4 (asset-management system) resemble the contract-responsibility system in that they involve similar responsibilities for the use of assets in production. For the purpose of analysis they have therefore been grouped with form 2

TABLE 2.27. Industry groups

Survey section	Group	Description
1–9	1	Extractive industries
10–13	2	Food, drink, tobacco
14–16	3	Textiles, tailoring, and leather
17–22	4	Light industry and crafts
23–25	5	Energy
26–30	6	Chemicals, medicine, and plastics
31–34	7	Building materials and metals
35–39	8	Engineering and electrical

under the general classification 'contract-responsibility system'. Contract form 5, the director-responsibility system, is thought to be different in its effects on the behaviour of the enterprise, and is retained as a separate category.

In the data, enterprises are assigned to thirty-nine different industries. For the purposes of analysis, it has been necessary to group these into just eight industry groups. These are listed in Table 2.27. Inevitably these groups represent a compromise between the need to

TABLE 2.28. Locations

Code 1	Large coastal cities SHANGHAI, DALIAN, QINGDAO, GUANGZHOU, TIANJIN Population greater than 1 million Economically advanced
Code 2	Large inland cities WUHAN, ANSHAN, TAIYUAN, SHENYANG, CHONGQING, HARBIN Population greater than 1 million Experimental cities: more radical economic reform
Code 3	Medium and small coastal and/or economically advanced cities WUXI, YANTAI, HANGZHOU, CHANGZHOU Population: medium 0.5 to 1 million: small, less than 0.5 million Less central by authorities. WUXI and CHANGZHOU are two of the four 'Little Dragons'—economically progressive cities
Code 4	*Medium-sized inland cities* SHIJIAZHUANG, CHANGSHA, GUIYANG, NANCHANG, HEFEI, ZHENGZHOU Population: 0.5 to 1 million Least economically advanced: least autonomy
Code 5	*Small inland cities* XINING, SIPING, HENYANG, KAIFENG Population: less than 0.5 million Not economically advanced, little control by authorities

have sufficient observations for the various cells of the frequency tables, and a loss of detail through aggregation. For the same reasons, the twenty-five city locations identified in the data have been amalgamated into five location groups, which are listed in Table 2.28. There are three criteria by which cities are assigned to these groups: population size (large (greater than 1 million), medium (0.5 to 1 million), and small (less than 0.5 million)); geographical location (distinguishing the economically more developed coastal region from less progressive inland locations); and the degree of economic dynamism (which particularly characterizes the group of four cities included in group 3). State-owned enterprises are conventionally classified as

TABLE 2.29. Contract form by industry group

Group	Name	No. of firms	% with contract responsibility	% with director responsibility
1	Extractive	19	57.9	42.1
2	Food, Drink, Tobacco	47	53.2	46.8
3	Textiles etc.	34	52.9	47.1
4	Light/Craft	46	62.5	37.5
5	Energy	15	13.3	86.7
6	Chemicals etc.	58	67.2	32.8
7	Building Materials/Metals	52	73.1	26.9
8	Engineering	59	57.6	42.4
ALL		324	59.3	40.7

Note: The null hypothesis of no difference between industry groups in contract types rejected at the 0.5% level by the chi-square test.

TABLE 2.30. Contract form by location

Location	No. of enterprises	Contract responsibility (%)	Director responsibility (%)
1	83	50.6	49.4
2	93	69.9	30.1
3	42	59.5	40.5
4	77	50.7	49.3
5	29	72.4	27.6
ALL	324	59.3	40.7

Note: The null hypothesis of no difference between locations in contract forms is rejected at the 3% level of the chi-square test.

'small, medium, or large'. The criteria for classification differ between industries.

The key finding is that the incidence of contract form is significantly associated with industry group and location, but not with the scale of the enterprise. Industry group 6 (chemicals etc.) and group 7 (building materials and metals) have a higher incidence of the contract-responsibility system, while group 2 (food etc.), group 3 (textiles etc.), and especially group 5 (energy) have a higher incidence of the director-responsibility system (see Table 2.29 for the details). Contract form also varies significantly across location (see Table 2.30). The large inland cities (location 2) and small inland cities (location 5) have a much higher incidence of the contract-responsibility system. This cannot be attributed to differences in the industrial mix of enterprises in different locations, since they appear to be quite similar.

3.1 The relationship between enterprises and their authorities

In Section 2.1 we looked at responses to a number of questions designed to throw light on the relationship between the firm and its bureaucratic supervisors. In this section we return to this issue to see whether we can discern any variation in responses between firms operating under different contract forms, or in different locations, sectors, and scales of operation. (Statistical results are reported in Appendix 2.2.)

(A) By contract form

We begin with a set of questions (Q24–Q38) which relate to the ability of enterprises to make their own decisions about production and sales according to contract form.

1. *Percentage of planned output in total output for the enterprises in 1985–87 (Q24C–Q26C)*

The frequency distribution was given in Table 2.1. Except for 1986, there is no significant difference between contract-responsibility and director-responsibility enterprises. Nor is there any significant difference in the directors' evaluation of their role in determining the annual plan (Q27), more than half believing they had an important role in this process. Looking at the years when enterprises received the discretion to make annual plans for different aspects of production (Q28–Q33), we note that if anything, director-responsibility enterprises had gained discretion in production earlier than contract-responsibility enterprises, but the differences are not statistically significant. The managers indicated the nature of the restrictions on their activities coming from the purchase of raw materials and energy (Q34G), and the sales of their products (Q38G). In both cases, there was a significant difference between contract forms: a greater proportion of the contract-responsibility enterprises made no response. This confirms our expectation that they have relatively more autonomy in selling their products, and in purchasing inputs.

2. *Decisions about the labour force of the enterprise (Q41–Q44C)*

Only 22% of the enterprises have ever refused to accept workers assigned by higher authority, and that does not vary between contract forms (Q41). One-third of the enterprises imposed their own internal wage system, and this was more common under the contract-responsibility system (Q44C).

3. *Help with loan repayment (Q45)*

Only 43% of the enterprises had sought help with loan repayments in recent years, and there was no significant difference in the incidence according to contract form.

4. *Means by which the enterprises sought to influence higher authority in (a) the supply of raw materials under favourable conditions (Q68G), (b) the provision of loans (Q74G), and (c) the determination of the contract targets (Q80G)*

Only for (*b*) was there any difference in respect of contract form: in particular, director-responsibility enterprises relied more on contacts to persuade the authorities to lend to them.

In general, enterprises which are under the contract-responsibility system tend to have more decision-making power (or autonomy), and are less influenced by the higher authorities than those operating under the director-responsibility system. However, the differences are not generally very pronounced. One significant difference was in the means used to secure loans for the enterprise: contract-responsibility enterprises relied more on making a well-known brand, or the quality of their management, director-responsibility enterprises were more likely to use their social contacts.

(B) By industrial sector

In this section, we look briefly at the relationship between industry sectors and the responses to the questionnaire. (The statistical results are given in Appendix, Table 2.A2.) Quite a number of the questions show significant differences in responses between our eight industry groups (defined in Table 2.27). Here we summarize the major differences that are present in the data.

1. *The shares of planned output in the total output values in 1985–87 (Q24C–Q26C)*
These are closely associated with industrial sector. The role of the production plan is greatest in industry 1 (extractive) in all three years, followed by industry 2 (food), 5 (energy), and 3 (textiles). Industry 4 (light/craft) experiences least planning in all three years, followed by 6 (chemicals), 7 (building materials and metals), and 8 (engineering and electrical). In addition, the role played by enterprises in making decisions on production plans of those products directly controlled by the authorities (Q27C) varies between industries. Industries 2 (food) and 5 (energy) tend to play a greater role, despite the importance of the plan in these industries. The year when enterprises had the right to plan for varieties of product and exports (Q28–Q33) is closely associated with industrial groups. Enterprises in industry groups 1 (extractive), 2 (food), and 5 (energy) in which planning has remained most important none the less generally had the right to plan varieties of products earlier than others. The same was true of exports. Enterprises in industry groups 3 (textiles) and 8 (engineering) tended to get these rights rather later than average. The degree of intervention by the government when enterprises sell their products to the market (Q38G) varies among industries. The types of intervention by the government are also closely associated with the types of industry. Industry 1 (extractive) is more likely to be controlled on prices and buyers when it sells products. Industries 2 (food), 3 (textiles), and 4 (light/craft) are more likely to be controlled on price and quality than other industries when they sell products to the market. Industry 5 (energy) is more likely to be controlled on quality and buying regions. Industries 6 (chemicals), 7 (building materials and metals), and 8 (engineering) are more likely to be controlled on buying regions and buyers.

2. *Decision procedures to reject employees allocated by the state (Q42)*
These are closely associated with types of industry. More than 50% of the enterprises under investigation use the second procedure, i.e. a decision made by the director and the higher authority, to dismiss employees allocated to the enterprise. Industries 1 (extractive), 4 (light/craft), 6 (chemicals), and 8 (engineering) are particularly more likely

to use such a procedure. Compared with other industries, industry 7 (building materials and metals) is more likely to use the third procedure (nominated by the leadership and determined by the representative committee of the trade union) to dismiss employees. Industries 7 (building materials and metals) and 8 (engineering) are relatively more likely to introduce internal wage systems than the others (Q44C).

3. *Help with loan repayment (Q45C)*

This is closely associated with industries. Enterprises in industries 2 (food) and 8 (engineering) were more likely to be helped by the higher authorities.

4. *The means used by enterprises to influence their higher authorities in order to obtain supplies of raw materials under favourable conditions (Q68G) and to secure loans from various sources (Q74G)*

These are also closely associated with types of industry. To achieve the same objectives, industry 2 (food) is relatively more likely to produce a well-known product; industries 3 (textiles), 4 (light/craft), and 8 (engineering) are more likely to increase exports; industry 5 (energy) is more likely to improve management; and industries 1 (extractive) and 6 (chemicals) are more likely to use different kinds of social contacts.

Overall we are not able to generate a consistent picture as to whether enterprises in some industries generally have more decision-making power or autonomy than in others. Industries which have more autonomy in some aspects appear to have less autonomy in other aspects; this is not unexpected, given the very different nature of the industrial groupings.

(C) By scale of enterprise

The association of enterprise scale and directors' responses to the questionnaire is discussed in this section. Enterprises are allocated to categories—large, medium, and small—on a basis which varies between industries. We have no prior expectations as to how scale will affect autonomy. On the one hand, large scale gives the director additional power in relation to the bureaucratic authorities; on the other hand, large scale of enterprise will make it all the more important for bureaucratic supervision to be exercised.

1. *Discretion given to the enterprise in decisions about production and sales*

Large-scale enterprises are more likely to play an important part in drawing up the production plan for products controlled by the authorities (Q27C), and large and medium-scale enterprises were given the right to make annual plans of product value (Q28C), outputs (Q29C), varieties of product (Q30C), and production schedules (Q32C) at an earlier stage. The types of restriction and/or the degrees of restriction imposed upon enterprises by the higher authorities when enterprises purchase raw materials from the market (Q34G) and sell their products (Q38G) are closely associated with industrial scale. In particular, larger-scale enterprises are likely to face more restrictions than smaller-scale ones.

2. *Decisions about the labour force (Q43)*

The choice of different procedures to appoint and fire middle-level cadres is associated with scale. In virtually all the large-scale enterprises this was the responsibility of the directors, who were more likely to have the freedom to appoint and fire middle-level cadres than their counterparts in smaller-scale enterprises.

3. *Help with loan repayment (Q45C)*

Large-scale enterprises are more likely to be assisted.

4. *Means used by enterprises to influence higher authorities in order to obtain raw materials supplied under favourable conditions (Q68G) and secure loans from various sources (Q74G)*

These are associated with industrial scale. Large-scale enterprises are more likely to increase marketing effort and improve product quality in order to achieve their goals. Small-scale enterprises are more likely to improve management or use various kinds of social contacts in order to achieve the same objectives. This may be because larger-scale enterprises are more able to carry out effective marketing or improve quality.

We conclude that larger-scale enterprises may face more restrictions from the higher authorities in terms of production, demand, and supply of raw materials, in comparison with those of smaller scale. However, directors in these larger-scale enterprises have more power in making administrative decisions within the firms, such as appointing or firing the middle-level cadres. They may also have more freedom to negotiate with their superiors on issues such as output plans, varieties of product, etc. When they need to influence their higher authority in order to get favourable treatment to obtain raw materials or secure loans, larger-scale enterprises are more likely to emphasize the marketing of their products than those of smaller scale. This may be because larger-scale enterprises have greater capacity or more advanced technologies than smaller firms. In order to get the same treatment, smaller firms are more likely to have to improve management or make use of contacts.

(D) By location

Finally we examine the relationship between location and the degree of autonomy in decision-taking enjoyed by the enterprise. The five location codes are defined in Table 2.28. We would anticipate that location does have a significant effect on the degree of autonomy.

1. *Percentage of planned output in total output (Q26C)*

The 1987 frequency distribution by location is given in Table 2.31. It is evident that enterprises in location 2 (large inland cities) have considerably more autonomy in production than enterprises elsewhere. This finding is not surprising: these cities include Wuhan, Shenyang, and Chongqing, where many experiments in radical economic reforms have been tried. A set of questions (Q28C and Q33C) record the years when enterprises received the discretion to make annual plans for different aspects of their business. The same pattern is evident across all the questions (except perhaps that which relates to exports): enterprises in location 1 (large coastal cities) were given discretion earlier than enterprises in other locations. By contrast restrictions on purchases and sales are not significantly differentiated by location, though if anything it is enterprises in large cities (locations 1 and 2) that suffer restrictions on raw materials and energy, and on sales of their products.

2. *Decisions about the work-force (Q41 to Q44C)*

Significant differences appear with respect both to refusal to accept workers assigned by the authorities and to decision-making about

TABLE 2.31. % of Planned output in total output (1987) by location

Location	% of enterprises reporting				
	0–50%	50–75%	75–85%	85–95%	95–100%
1	9.8	14.8	16.4	16.4	42.6
2	42.2	14.1	6.3	10.9	26.6
3	34.6	7.7	3.9	23.1	30.8
4	23.9	6.5	17.4	13.0	39.1
5	25.0	10.0	25.0	15.0	25.0
ALL	26.7	11.5	12.9	14.8	34.1

Note: Derived from Q26C. The null hypothesis of no association is rejected at the 5% level; rows sum to 100% except for rounding.

appointments to the management staff. Large city enterprises were more likely to take decisions on managerial staff, but small and medium city enterprises (locations 4 and 5) had exercised more discretion in refusing workers allocated by the authorities.

3. *Means used by the enterprise to affect the decisions of higher authorities on the supply of raw materials, the provisions of loans, and the determination of the contract (Q68G, Q74G, and Q80G)*

There was no significant association with location.

To conclude, the pattern of responses across locations confirmed our expectation of significant differences. But no single pattern emerges: large city enterprises (especially those located in the experimental economic reform cities in location 2) were given more autonomy in production, and at an earlier date, but they also report restrictions on their behaviour in purchasing materials, selling output, and taking on labour.

3.2 Decision-making on output and prices

In Section 3.1 we considered the responses to questions which dealt with the relationship of the enterprises to bureaucratic supervision in the area of production. In this section we apply the same methodology to a series of questions (Q47–Q55 and Q92–Q96), which seek to elicit information about how the enterprises make their decisions, given the constraints under which they operate. (The different questions are described in Appendix 2.3, and the formal statistical results are also presented there.) In the following exposition we will look first at the general responses, and then discuss where these responses are significantly associated with contract form, industry group, scale of enterprise, or location. The questions cover four areas of decision-taking.

1. *Criteria for non-plan outputs and prices (Q47G, Q54–Q55)*

Just over a quarter of the enterprises relied on their forecasts of market demand: slightly less weight was given to supply constraints on inputs, the level of current orders, and the principle of profit maximization. With respect to the contract form, it is evident that director-responsibility enterprises give greater weight to past sales, and less weight to supply constraints. There is no association of responses with location or scale: but the association with industry group is very strong. Industry groups 4 (light/craft), 5 (energy), and 6 (chemicals) are apparently more influenced by supply conditions

TABLE 2.32. Criteria for setting prices of non-plan outputs

Industry	% of enterprises reporting				
	No. of enterprises	State prices	Production cost	Market price	Sales conditions
1 Extractive	15	33.3	13.3	33.3	20.0
2 Food etc.	36	38.9	47.2	5.6	8.3
3 Textiles etc.	31	12.9	64.5	16.1	6.5
4 Light/craft	38	21.1	31.6	39.5	7.9
5 Energy	12	16.7	41.7	25.0	16.7
6 Chemicals etc.	54	11.1	51.9	29.6	7.4
7 Building materials/ metals	53	15.1	34.0	30.2	20.8
8 Engineering etc.	55	7.3	54.6	29.1	9.1
TOTAL	294	17.4	44.9	26.5	11.2

Note: Derived from Q54; rows sum to 100% except for rounding errors.

for raw materials, while industry 1 (extractive), 3 (textiles), and 8 (engineering) are more concerned about demand.

About 45% of the enterprises based prices on production costs, 27% looked at prices charged by other enterprises, and only 17% relied on state-fixed prices. Rather more than half the enterprises set prices below those of the market, and the major reason given was market penetration. There is therefore plenty of evidence of incipient market behaviour by those enterprises. Curiously, the responses were not associated at all with either contract form or scale of enterprise, but were strongly associated with industry group. The relevant frequencies are set out in Table 2.32. Responses also varied across locations in an interesting manner. Enterprises in the large coastal cities (location 1) based their prices for non-plan outputs on their production costs, while those in locations 4 and 5 (small and medium-sized cities) more frequently looked at the level of the market price. Enterprises in coastal cities (locations 1 and 3) attributed their lower prices to lower costs, whereas enterprises in medium and small inland cities (locations 4 and 5) used pricing to expand their market share.

2. *Responses to insufficient demand (Q50G)*

The most interesting feature of these responses was that more than half the enterprises said that they would respond by sales promotion, with price and quantity reduction much less likely. Enterprises in industry 5 (energy) and industry 7 (building materials/metals) were somewhat different: they were more likely to cut output, and less likely to use sales promotion.

3. *Incidence of, and reasons for, loss-making products (Q94–Q96)*
About one-third of the enterprises reported that they were producing loss-making products, and the incidence was higher among director-responsibility enterprises. Such enterprises were more likely to be found in the large inland cities (location 2), but less likely in the coastal and economically advanced medium cities (location 3). Two-thirds of the enterprises gave reasons indicating that they were required to make the products by higher authorities. These reasons were observed particularly in enterprises from industry groups 1 (extractive), 2 (food), 3 (textiles), and 5 (energy). More of these enterprises were located in the large cities (locations 1 and 2) than elsewhere.

4. *Reasons for making investments in other enterprises (Q92)*
About half the enterprises responded to this question, which gives a rough index of the degree to which trade investments are made. Not surprisingly, the main reason given (44% of the responses) was concern for securing supplies. Increasing production capacity and joint ventures were also given as reasons. Some differences between industry groups are noted: industry group 6 (chemicals) is particularly concerned with securing supplies, while enterprises in group 3 (textiles) and group 8 (engineering) put more emphasis on increasing their production capacity.

In Section 3.1 above, we noted the responses to questions concerning restrictions on the market behaviour of enterprises with respect to securing inputs and making sales (Q34C and Q38C). A significant difference between contract forms was that a greater proportion of the contract-responsibility enterprises made no response, which was interpreted to mean that they experienced no restrictions. It is therefore a little surprising that when it comes to actual decision-making on output and prices we have been unable to detect differences between contract forms. There is however evidence of differences between industry groups, though no clear picture emerges.

3.3 Decision-making on employment and employee rewards

This section follows the pattern of the last one, but focuses on a group of questions relative to employment and wages: excess labour in the enterprises (Q86–Q90), worker participation in decisions (Q113–Q115), and non-pecuniary rewards (Q116–Q118). The analysis suggests that the level of bureaucratic intervention remains high, though director-responsibility enterprises have more autonomy in fixing their own wage systems (Q41–Q44). There are some industry differences: industry 7 (building materials/metals) is more likely to use internal procedures to discard workers, while large-scale enterprises appear to have greater autonomy.

1. *Excess labour force (Q86–Q90)*

Overall about a quarter of the enterprises report an excess of labour of more than 10%. There were significant differences between contract forms in both the incidence and type of excess employees. Fewer contract-responsibility enterprises had excess labour of more than 10%, and those were more likely to be office personnel. For director-responsibility enterprises, excess of ordinary workers was more prevalent. Excess workers were particularly problematic for industry groups 1 (extractive) and industry 8 (engineering). The incidence of excess workers however was much lower among small-scale enterprises than larger ones. Enterprises in the coastal and economically advanced medium and small cities (location 3) are less likely to have excess labour (less than one in ten enterprises reported excess labour of greater than 10% of their labour force, compared to one in five enterprises for the whole sample). However in the large inland cities (location 2), three out of ten enterprises reported excess labour greater than 10%.

2. *Degree of worker participation in decision-making (Q113–Q115)*

Nearly half the responses indicate involvement in decisions affecting production, finance, and worker rewards. Once again, enterprise scale differences are very pronounced: in large-scale enterprises, workers are more likely to participate in decisions on housing. Worker participation in decision-taking apparently does not vary with location.

3. *Non-pecuniary rewards to good workers (Q116–Q118)*

One-third of the enterprises gave 'public praise' as an important means of giving non-pecuniary rewards followed by promotion, educational opportunities, and priority in housing allocations. As between the latter two methods of reward, contract-responsibility enterprises were more likely to use educational opportunities, while director-responsibility enterprises relied more on priority in housing. Enterprises in large inland cities (location 2) and medium inland cities (location 4) were significantly more likely to use political promotion as incentives for workers. By contrast coastal cities (locations 1 and 3) were more likely to provide education or training opportunities, or to favour good workers in the allocation of housing.

The statistical analysis reported in Appendix 2.4 suggests a degree of success in distinguishing the response to these questions from enterprises of different contract forms and scales, but not with respect to industry group. However, more detailed inspection suggests that they do not represent major differences in behaviour. Our suspicion is that this area of the activity of enterprises has been relatively little affected by economic reforms, with bureaucratic intervention and worker participation still very important for all enterprises, regardless of their contract form, scale, or industry group. The most interesting finding with respect to different locations is the greater degree of excess labour supply in the inland cities, and the relatively better position of the enterprises in the coastal and economically more advanced medium and small cities.

3.4 Summary of findings

We may summarize our conclusions as follows:

1. In Section 3 we examined the incidence of different contract forms in different industry groups: we found that contract responsibility is more common in chemicals etc. and in building materials/metals, while director responsibility has a higher incidence in food etc., textiles, and energy. The large inland cities (location 2) and small inland cities (location 5) have a much higher incidence of the contract-responsibility system. This cannot be explained by industrial mix, which does not vary significantly across location.

2. In Section 3.1 we analysed questions relating to the autonomy of enterprises as indicated by the objective characteristics of the contract. All enterprises gave responses indicating considerable autonomy, though more on prices and outputs than on labour and wages. Contract-responsibility enterprises reported more autonomy than director-responsibility enterprises, but the differences were not great. Various indicators of enterprise autonomy varied significantly across industry groups, but there are no groups that consistently have more or less autonomy across all indicators. Large-scale enterprises reported significantly more bureaucratic intervention on prices, outputs, and raw materials, but less on decisions about the labour force and wages. They also reported that they could exercise more bargaining power to persuade the authorities. Large city enterprises (particularly those located in the inland experimental economic-reforms cities)

were given more autonomy in production, and decision-taking powers at an earlier date than those located elsewhere; but it is the same enterprises that report a significantly higher incidence of restrictions on their behaviour in purchasing raw materials, selling output, and taking on workers.

3. Sections 3.2 and 3.3 analysed the responses to questions about enterprise decision-taking in the areas of output and prices, and employment and wages. A puzzling pattern emerged. For output and prices, there was no difference between contract forms, but there was considerable variation across industries. For employment and wages, this pattern was reversed, though the differences between contract forms are not major. Enterprises in large cities (locations 1 and 2) were more likely to price non-plan output on the basis of cost, and were more likely to be required to produce loss-making products by the authorities (especially the large inland cities). Large inland city enterprises reported a higher than average incidence of excessive labour, those in location 3 (medium and small-sized coastal or economically advanced cities) reported below average incidence. There was some evidence that enterprises in coastal cities were more ready to reward good workers with tangible incentives such as education or training, or the allocation of superior housing.

We admit to being somewhat disappointed with these results. We had expected to see clearer differences emerging between contract forms in their responses to the questionnaire. In fact, the greatest degree of diversity occurs between industry groups: this diversity needs careful interpretation, though we probably have too few responses per industry group for a satisfactory statistical analysis. Scale of enterprise emerged as a significant correlate of autonomy in terms of objective characteristics of the contracts faced by the enterprises, but it did not figure when actual decision-making was the question addressed. The findings on effects of location cannot be easily summarized. It seems that the large inland cities and medium inland cities had a significantly higher incidence of the contract-responsibility form. One would therefore expect them to have had more autonomy. But greater autonomy in production (and at an earlier date) went to enterprises in the large coastal cities; the fact that those enterprises were more likely to be operating with the director-responsibility system may explain why they reported a greater incidence of bureaucratic intervention in purchases of materials, sales, and taking on workers. It may also explain why they relied on production costs to determine the prices of non-plan output. The more dynamic performance of enterprises in location 3 (small and medium-sized coastal and/or economically advanced cities) does show up in the responses: they had a lower incidence of excess workers, a lower incidence of loss-making products, and were prepared to use intangible incentives to reward good workers.

4. Conclusions

The progress of the enterprise reform programme in the 1980s was described in Chapter 1. The major themes of the reforms were the granting of greater autonomy to the enterprises in respect of production, and the increased responsibility put on the managers for ensuring the success of the operations. The greater autonomy came in the form of a decreased role for the plan, with a corresponding increase in economic activity responding to market pressures. The increased responsibility of the enterprise, and especially the managers, was brought about by the changes in the relationship between the enterprise and higher authorities, especially the director-responsibility and contract-responsibility forms. The purpose of this chapter has been to assess, by means of a questionnaire addressed to managers in 1988, how far the institutional changes affected the perceptions and behaviour of the managers.

The responses to the questionnaire definitely indicate that the managers of the enterprises experienced greater autonomy, though within a framework where relationships with their higher authorities remained very important. Most autonomy was experienced in the area of output, where the firms became more responsive to market signals, though the response was more in terms of developing heuristic rules rather than any pursuit of profit maximization. There was less autonomy in terms of the size of the labour force and the wage structure, though the scope for paying profit-related bonus made the latter less important. The dependence of the firms on the authorities was evident in their response to questions about the 'soft' budget constraint: many of them either had been helped out, or expected to be, if the enterprise faced financial difficulties. The responses to the questionnaire also reflected the increased responsibilities and powers of the enterprise managers, and the diminished role for the party committee.

Variation of responses across firm characteristics were less varied than expected. In particular, there seemed to be only minor differences in responses between firms operating the contract-responsibility system, and those still under the director-responsibility system. Large-scale enterprises reported greater control from the authorities, probably because they remained such important sources of tax revenue. Large city enterprises had more formal autonomy, but also, paradoxically, greater interference from the authorities. The contract-responsibility system was more prevalent in heavy industries than in light industries; but there was no consistent pattern of some industries experiencing more autonomy in all areas of their activities than others.

To sum up, by 1988, the year in which the questionnaire was administered to the enterprises, managers were clearly still learning how to operate as independent units outside the controls of the plan. Links to their higher authority remained important for them, perhaps giving them some security as they developed new skills relevant to operating in the market. And, of course, the local authorities retained a keen interest in their activities, not only because they were the major source of tax revenues, but also because of the significance of their activities for the local community in terms of employment and economic development.

APPENDIX 2.1

Structure of Qualitative Questionnaire

Identification of the Enterprise: A, B, B1, B2
Contract and Appointment of Director
  Sections 1–4: variables Q1–Q23
Relationship of the Enterprise to Bureaucratic Supervisors
  Sections 5–11: variables Q24–Q46
Role of the Enterprise in Decisions: Behaviour in Short Run and Long Run
  Sections 12–24: variables Q47–Q99
Incentives within Firms
  Sections 25–28: variables Q100–Q118
Characteristics of Director
  Sections 29–30: variables Q119–Q122
Management System after Reform
  Section 31: variables Q123–Q124

APPENDIX 2.2

Enterprise Relationships with the Bureaucratic Supervisors

Description of Variables

Q24–Q26. The shares of planned outputs in total outputs in 1985, 1986, and 1987 respectively. The original range of shares of planned outputs spreads from 0.0 to 100%. For convenience they are regrouped as follows with zero values omitted.

Original variables Q24–Q26		New variables Q24C–Q26C
>0.0 and <50.0	⇒	1
>50.0 and <75.0	⇒	2
>75.0 and <85.0	⇒	3
>85.0 and <95.0	⇒	4
>95.0	⇒	5

It is obvious that the higher the shares of planned outputs, the less autonomy enterprises will have:

Q27: The role played by the enterprises in making annual production plans: ranking from 'very important', to 'not important'. There are four levels in Q27 and the zero observations are dropped in the analysis.

Q28–Q33: The year when enterprises had the right for annual planning concerning: (1) output value, (2) product volume or physical outputs, (3) varieties of products, (4) production techniques, (5) production schedules, and (6) exports.

For convenience, these variables are regrouped into four levels as follows:

Original variables Q28–Q33		New variables Q28C–Q33C	
≤1983	⇒	1	Before 1983
1984 +1985	⇒	2	1984 + 1985
≥ 1986	⇒	3	After 1986
=0	⇒	4	No right at all

If enterprises give zero responses, it is assumed that they do not have any right to plan at all. It is also assumed that the earlier enterprises were given the right to plan their activities, the more autonomy they would have had.

Q34–Q37: According to their priorities, directors were asked to choose four from five restrictions the higher authorities impose when they purchase raw materials, fuel, and other energy from the market-place. These five restrictions are: (1) prices, (2) quality, (3) suppliers, (4) supply regions, and (5) others. All the nil responses in these four questions are deleted.

Q38–Q40: According to their priorities, directors were asked to choose three out of the five restrictions that the higher authorities impose upon enterprises when they sell their products to the market. These five restrictions are the same in Q34 to Q37. Again, nil responses are dropped in the analysis.

Q41: This question asks whether the enterprises have ever refused to accept employees assigned by the authorities. There are two responses in this question: 1 means that enterprises have refused to accept employees assigned by the state while 2 means that they have not refused. Nil observations are dropped from the analysis.

TABLE 2.A1. Tests of association between enterprise responses to the questionnaire, and contract form, industry group, enterprise scale, and location

Question no.	Contract form	Industry group	Scale	Location
24C	—	0.087*	0.955	0.123*
25C	0.060*	0.196*	0.882	0.033*
26C	0.914	0.010*	0.985	0.033*
27C	0.300	0.208	0.491	0.874
28C	0.262	0.715	0.419	0.181*
29C	0.243	0.665	0.331	0.222
30C	0.341	0.474	0.222	0.295
31C	0.231	0.637	0.671	0.205
32C	0.180*	0.645	0.324	0.043*
33C	0.848	0.004*	0.340	0.446
34	0.099*	—	—	0.398
35	0.135*	—	—	—
36	0.277	—	—	—
37	0.426	—	—	—
38	0.192*	—	—	0.310
39	0.294	—	—	—
40	0.067*	—	—	—
41	0.687	0.483	0.363	0.008*
42	0.353	0.061*	0.568	0.286
43	0.325	0.294	0.430	0.045*
44C	0.212	0.404	0.057*	0.344
45C	0.500	0.070*	0.462	0.422
34G (34/35)	0.113*	0.960	0.471	—
38G (38/40)	0.046*	0.000*	0.161*	—
68G (68–73)	0.838	0.226	0.620	0.455
74G (74–79)	0.706	0.026*	0.284	0.803
80G (80–85)	0.343	0.932	0.833	0.800

Note: 1. The test statistics are probabilities for acceptance of the null hypothesis of no association: we tentatively reject the null hypothesis when probability is less than 0.2. These cases are starred in the table.

2. A C by a question number indicates that responses have been recoded before analysis: a G indicates grouping of responses to a number of related questions (these are given in parentheses).

Q42: There are four different procedures to fire employees: (1) determined by the director alone, (2) determined by the director and higher authorities, (3) suggested by the leadership and determined by the representative committee of the trade union, and (4) determined by higher authority alone. Nil responses are dropped from the analysis.

Q43: There are five different means of appointing the management staff of an enterprise: (1) by director alone, (2) by higher authorities on nomination from director, (3) by staff election, (4) by bidding in the enterprise, and (5) by the higher authority directly.

Q44: This question asks whether and when enterprises imposed an internal wage system. The original answers actually give the years when enterprises started imposing internal wage systems. For convenience, the question is redefined so that it only has two responses: 1 means that enterprises do not impose an internal wage system while 2 means that enterprises do impose an internal wage system regardless of when they started imposing it.

Q45: This concerns whether and when the higher authority came to help the enterprises when they faced difficulties in repaying loans. Like Q44, Q45 is regrouped into two responses regardless of when the higher authority came to help.

Q46: There are five different means to help the enterprises in repaying loans: (1) extending loan periods, (2) writing off the debt, (3) granting a new loan to replace the old, (4) loan repayment before taxation, and (5) others.

Q68–Q73, Q74–Q79, Q80–Q85: There are six options to influence the higher authorities by the enterprises in three aspects of decision-making. The options are ordered according to their priority by the director. These three aspects are respectively: (1) supplying raw materials under favourable conditions (Q68–Q73), (2) providing all kinds of loans (Q74–Q79), and (3) determining the contract targets (Q80–Q85).

The six options include: (1) creating a famous product, (2) earning foreign exchange through exports, (3) improving management, (4) bargaining with the higher authority, (5) using various kinds of social relationship, and (6) others.

Regrouping some Variables

The responses to Q68–Q73, Q74–Q79, and Q80–Q85 are actually three homogeneous variable groups answering three distinct questions, and it is meaningless to analyse the relationship between contract form and each of these variables independently. As an alternative, these three groups of variables are aggregated into three new variables, with each representing six original questions. For example, a new variable called Q68G represents Q68–Q73, Q74G represents Q74–Q79, and Q80G represents Q80–Q85.

For similar reasons, Q34–Q35, Q38–Q40 are also aggregated into two single variables Q34G and Q38G.

APPENDIX 2.3

Enterprise Decision-Taking: Output and Prices

Questions and variables

Q47–Q49: The question concerns the criteria used by the enterprises in determining non-plan production. Six possibilities are listed: past sales, current sales, market forecasts, profit maximization, and supply constraints (raw materials or energy). Enterprises were allowed to tick three options. The data have been aggregated to give Q47G.

Q50–Q52: These give short-term responses to insufficient demand. There are four possible responses: production down, price down, promote sales, and no response. The data are grouped to give Q50G.

Q53: This gives reasons for not cutting production when insufficient demand; there are four options: production plan constraints, price-cutting preferred, marketing problems, and other.

Q54: This question asks the criteria for setting prices on non-plan products. There are four options: state prices, production costs, market prices, and sales conditions.

Q55: This concerns the reasons for prices being below market prices. There are three responses: lower cost, market penetration, and to exchange for raw materials and energy.

Q92, Q93: As regards the reasons for making investments in other enterprises. There are six choices: promote sales, secure supplies, expand produc-

TABLE 2.A2. Tests of association between enterprises on decision-taking (output and prices), and contract form, industry group, enterprise scale, and location

Question no.	Contract form	Industry group	Scale	Location
47G (47–49)	0.135*	0.079*	0.821	0.417
50G (50–52)	0.806	0.144*	0.222	0.583
53C	0.802	0.187*	0.917	0.027*
54C	0.811	0.001*	0.265	0.112*
55C	0.752	0.009*	0.074	0.079
92G (92–93)	0.980	0.132*	0.309	0.245
94C	0.909	0.247	0.517	0.195*
95G (95–96)	0.353	0.015*	0.830	0.084*

Note: The test statistics are probabilities for acceptance of the null hypothesis of no association. We tentatively reject the null hypothesis when probability is less than 0.2: these cases are starred in the table.

A C by a question number indicates that responses have been recoded before analysis: a G indicates grouping of responses to a number of related questions (these are given in parentheses).

tion capacity, increase profits, co-operation, and other. Responses aggregated to give Q92C.

Q94: The percentage of loss-making output in value of total output has responses coded as follows: zero = 1, greater than zero = 2.

Q95, Q96: These concern the reasons for producing loss-making products. There are five choices: (1) compulsory plan, (2) high-cost technology, (3) attracts subsidy, (4) unwilling to lay off workers, and (5) other. The responses have been coded as follows to give Q95G:

1, 3, 4 ⇒ 1 all reflect influence by higher authority
2, 5 ⇒ 2 both reflect enterprise specific reasons.

APPENDIX 2.4

Enterprise Decision-Taking: Employment and Wages

Questions and Variables

Q86–Q88: For excess supply or demand for labour the data are grouped to give the following classification (Q86G):

Excess labour > 10% of labour force ⇒ 1
Otherwise ⇒ 2

Q89–Q90: For the types of excess labour: managerial, political, office, technicians, skilled, ordinary, rear-service workers the responses are aggregated to give Q89G.

Q113–Q115: As regards staff participation in decisions the eleven options are grouped as follows to give Q113G:

TABLE 2.A3. Tests of association between enterprise responses on decision-taking (employment and wages), and contract form, industry group, enterprise scale, and location

Question	Contract form	Industry group	Scale	Location
86G (86–88)	0.168*	0.024*	0.145*	0.040*
89G (89–90)	0.160*	0.679	0.425	0.074*
113G (113–115)	0.185*	0.985	0.018*	0.680
116G (116–118)	0.185*	0.780	0.005*	0.121*

Note: The test statistics are probabilities for acceptance of the null hypothesis of no association. We tentatively reject the null hypothesis when the probability is less than 0.2. These cases are starred in the table.

A G by a question number indicates grouping of responses to a number of related questions (these are given in parentheses).

1, 2, 3	⇒	1	politics and administration
4–9	⇒	2	production, finance, rewards
10, 11	⇒	3	housing, others

Q116–Q118: For non-pecuniary rewards to workers there are six options: promotion, praise, access to educational opportunities, housing priority, employment for family, and others. Responses grouped to give Q116G.

NOTES

1. Quantitative measures of autonomy are the subject of Ch. 3.
2. The different contract forms were discussed in Ch. 1, Sect. 2, with a brief description of the sequence of their introduction.

3

Enterprise Autonomy and Incentives

1. Introduction

One objective of economic reform in China since 1979 has been to increase the degree of autonomy of the enterprises in making decisions. Under the planning system the enterprise was, in principle, given instructions by the planning apparatus in respect of all aspects of production and sales. Since 1979 these constraints have been relaxed, and Chapter 1 documents this process from official Chinese sources. The purpose of Section 2 of this chapter is to describe the evolution of greater autonomy over time, differentiated by sector, location, and other characteristics of the enterprise. This is done by analysing the quantitative data provided by the enterprises for the period since 1980.

A second objective was to strengthen incentives. The economic rationale is straightforward: if rewards are more closely linked to results, then economic actors are likely to put in more effort. In Section 3, the degree to which the reforms increased incentives for the whole firm is explored. Prior to reform, not only were the operations of the firm planned by the bureaucracy, but also the whole of any surplus had to be handed over to the authorities, and any deficit was automatically made up. Incentives, in so far as they existed at all, were indirect: the manager of a firm which was performing moderately well (meeting plan quotas, remitting the plan surplus, and not making great demands for new investment) would have the benefit of a 'quiet life' and the prospect of promotion in due course. Giving the firm greater autonomy would, in these circumstances, give the firm more room to manœuvre in meeting the expectations of the higher authorities, but it would not in itself give any encouragement to improve the efficiency of operations.

Incentives to more efficient use of the firm's resources require that at least some of the returns to greater effort can be retained by the firm to be used for its own purposes. There is, for example, no point in reacting to new profit opportunities (as greater autonomy would allow) if none of the gains can be shared by the firm. There is, of course, the further issue of exactly how the benefits from the gains are appropriated. One obvious route, which is discussed in Chapter 4, is the payment of profit-related bonuses to the work-force. An alternative route, which is absent from the Chinese enterprise, but typical in a Western firm, is that additional profits are paid to the shareholders. A third route is that the managers of the firm succeed in appropriating the gains for their own purposes—higher salaries, greater perquisites, and the opportunity to enhance their own position and prestige by building up the enterprise.

There is, of course, the obverse situation, where the firm is making losses. The operation of an incentive scheme will be blunted if there is a soft budget constraint, implying that losses can be written off or offset by subsidies, without affecting the situation of the managers or workers. In the West, the eventual sanctions are insolvency, bankruptcy, and/or take-over, with implied costs for shareholders, managers, and possibly the labour force. Despite the formal existence of bankruptcy laws in China, as part of the reform programme, there is a widespread belief that they are non-operative. There is a full discussion of these issues in Chapter 10.

In Section 3 we explore the existence of profit-retention incentives for the whole enterprise, and their development over the reform period. We attach considerable importance to quantitative indicators, because the formal situation in terms of law and administrative regulations is often a poor guide to what happens in practice in China. Regulations are seldom applied in a manner which is cut and dried: often they will be shaped and amended to fit the particular situation of the enterprise, as the outcome of bargaining between the firm and the bureaucratic authorities.

2. *Indicators of Autonomy*

A variety of indicators of enterprise autonomy, drawn from the quantitative and qualitative survey data, are used:

(i) The share of raw materials bought from the market (*IS*): variable 156 in the quantitative data.

(ii) The share of total outputs controlled by the state plan (*PS*): variables Q24–Q26 in the qualitative database (note that these only cover the years 1985–87).

(iii) The proportion of new workers recruited by the firms themselves (*D*): the ratio of variables 55 and 52 in quantitative survey.

(iv) The ratio of contract employees to total employment (*CE*): the ratio of variable 33 to variable 31 in the quantitative survey.

(v) The share of total product sales (by value) accounted for by 'own sales' by the enterprise (*OS*): the ratio of variables 133 and 130 in the quantitative survey. 'Own sales' are sales made by the firm on its own initiative rather than deliveries required by the plan.

(vi) The share of state subsidies, own funds, and borrowing in the finance of investment by the firm.

The method adopted is to explore the variations in these indicators over time, and in relation to locations, sectors, and other enterprise characteristics, by use of the general linear model. This is equivalent to a multiple regression in which time and characteristics are entered as dummy variables. The number of dummy variables entered is always one less than the number of characteristics in each group. For example, we have five location codes for the enterprises: dummy variables are therefore entered for locations 1 to 4 inclusive, and the effect of location 5 is subsumed in the regression constant. It is appropriate therefore to interpret the fitted coefficients on other location code dummies as deviations from the case of location 5.

The following characteristics are included in the regression:

1. *Year* (*YR*): 1980 and 1983–87 (except for the dependent variable *PS* where data are available only for 1985–87 and the financial variables only for 1983–87). Separate regressions were attempted for all six years together, for the first four years (1980 and 1983–85), and for the last two years (1986–87). The reason for examining these time-periods separately is to try to identify the differences arising from the introduction of the contract-responsibility system later in the period under consideration.

2. *Location* (*LOC*): five location codes were assigned to the twenty-five cities identified in the sample of enterprises. Cities were grouped on the basis of geographical location, city size, and degree of participation in economic reform as explained in Chapter 2.

3. *Scale* (*SC*): all Chinese state-owned enterprises are categorized as large, medium, or small on a basis that differs between sectors. The significance of scale is thought to be the degree of interest that is shown by the authorities. Large enterprises are monitored more closely than small ones.

4. *Contract forms* (*CF*): the original data identified five types of contract form between the enterprise and the authorities. Two of these, the contract-responsibility system and the director-responsibility

system, account respectively for 49% and 40% of the enterprises. As was explained in Chapter 2, given the very few observations for other types of contract, we have grouped them with the contract-responsibility system with which they have more in common. This grouping is contract form 1 in the analysis: contract form 2 comprises those enterprises operating with the director-responsibility system.

5. *Industry group* (*IND*): for analysis it has been necessary to group enterprises in just eight industries (see Chapter 2). These groupings represent a trade-off between the need to have sufficient observations in each grouping for statistical purposes, and the loss of detail through aggregation.

The results of the regressions are given in Tables 3.1 to 3.6.

1. The share of raw materials bought from the market (IS)

Results are presented in Table 3.1. The shares of materials purchased from markets increased steadily and consistently: the change is of the order of 19 percentage points over the period. It reflects the reduced role for the authorities and the planning mechanism in the supply of materials as the reforms progressed. The results for the location codes suggest that autonomy in the purchase of materials is inversely related to the size of the city in which the enterprise is located. Thus the difference between the smallest cities (location 5) and the largest (location 1) was of the order of 17 percentage points, if anything increasing in the last 2 years. A similar result is obtained for small-scale enterprises relative to larger ones: they are given considerably greater freedom. As expected, the pattern across industries is quite varied. The ranking of industries suggests that industries 1 (construction), 5 (energy), and 8 (engineering) enjoyed considerably less autonomy than all the light industries, but also less than 6 (chemicals) and 7 (building materials/metals). There is little change in the ranking over time.

The evidence on contract form is mixed. The results suggest that the contract-responsibility system was associated with significantly less autonomy in raw material procurement, in 1986 and 1987. However, this result is not borne out by a comparison of means. The interactive variable *ID*CF* suggests a reason for the ambiguity: the effect of contract form is by no means uniform across industry and scale. For example, contract-responsibility enterprises gave significantly greater autonomy in industry 5 (energy), but significantly less autonomy in industries 3 (textiles) and 7 (chemicals); contract responsibility was associated with less freedom for small-scale enterprises, but not for medium or large enterprises.

TABLE 3.1. Results for the share of inputs purchased from the markets (*IS*)

Independent variables		1980–87 (n = 878)		1980–85 (n = 523)		1986–87 (n = 354)	
		Coeff.	Prob.	Coeff.	Prob.	Coeff.	Prob.
Intercept		0.6994	0.0001	0.4229	0.0001	0.8613	0.0001
YR	1	−0.1877	0.0001	−0.0841	0.0137	—	—
	2	−0.1731	0.0001	−0.0664	0.0438	—	—
	3	−0.1494	0.0001	−0.0449	0.1628	—	—
	4	−0.1026	0.0004	0.0000	—	—	—
	5	−0.0559	0.4730	—	—	−0.0553	0.0404
	6	0.000	—	—	—	0.000	—
LOC	1	−0.1702	0.0100	−0.1237	0.1579	−0.2205	0.0297
	2	−0.1655	0.0136	−0.2021	0.0217	−0.1214	0.2422
	3	−0.1316	0.0562	−0.1100	0.2334	−0.1523	0.1445
	4	−0.1484	0.0211	−0.1099	0.1916	−0.1960	0.0499
	5	0.0000	—	0.0000	—	0.0000	—
SC	1	−0.1583	0.0141	−0.0024	0.9791	−0.2896	0.0018
	2	−0.1565	0.0055	−0.0554	0.4685	−0.2554	0.0028
	3	0.0000	—	0.0000	—	0.0000	—
CF	1	−0.1466	0.1095	0.0089	0.9430	−0.2773	0.0433
	2	0.0000	—	0.0000	—	0.0000	—
IND	1	−0.0640	0.4301	−0.0211	0.8494	−0.0965	0.4116
	2	0.2183	0.0001	0.1628	0.0248	0.2939	0.0002
	3	0.3336	0.0001	0.5100	0.0001	0.2105	0.0321
	4	0.3577	0.0001	0.4953	0.0001	0.2309	0.0077
	5	−0.1303	0.0374	−0.0659	0.4423	−0.2225	0.0148
	6	0.1307	0.0047	0.1874	0.0027	0.0585	0.3965
	7	0.2668	0.0001	0.3623	0.0001	0.1938	0.0125
	8	0.0000	—	0.0000	—	0.0000	—
*IND*CF*		—	0.0001	—	0.0024	—	0.0107
*SC*CF*		—	0.0014	—	0.0197	—	0.0182
*LOC*CF*		—	0.1475	—	0.1300	—	0.2202
Statistics	*F*-test	$F = 10.22$	0.0	$F = 5.82$	0.0001	$F = 4.99$	0.0001
	R^2	—	0.2787	—	0.2614	—	0.3002

2. *The share of total outputs determined by the state plan (PS)*

This variable is only available for 1985 to 1987. Results are presented in Table 3.2. The results suggest that the share fell about 6 percentage points over the period, that enterprises located in large and medium-sized inland cities had significantly less planned output than coastal and small cities, and that proportions of planned outputs were higher in the light industries and energy industry than in heavy industry. For contract form the results are not straightforward. The results indicate that interactive terms between contract form and both industry and

TABLE 3.2. Results for *PS*, share of planned outputs

Independent variables		1985–87 (n = 640)	
		Coeff.	Prob.
Intercept		0.8342	0.0001
YR	1		
	2		
	3	—	—
	4	0.0572	0.0334
	5	0.0307	0.2516
	6	0.0000	—
LOC	1	−0.1370	0.1913
	2	−0.2960	0.0055
	3	−0.1726	0.1140
	4	−0.1941	0.0674
	5	0.0000	—
SC	1	0.0462	0.5006
	2	0.0361	0.5997
	3	0.0000	—
CF	1	−0.2173	0.1194
	2	0.0000	—
IND	1	0.1603	0.0294
	2	0.1280	0.0278
	3	0.1425	0.0919
	4	−0.0449	0.5408
	5	0.1422	0.0180
	6	−0.0472	0.4456
	7	−0.0956	0.1563
	8	0.0000	—
*IND***CF*		—	0.0780
*SC***CF*		—	0.2893
*LOC***CF*		—	0.0039
Statistics	*F*-test	$F = 5.98$	0.0001
	R^2	—	0.2131

location are statistically significant. Differences in mean values suggest that enterprises with contract responsibility had more autonomy if located in medium and small coastal cities (location 3), or in small inland cities (location 5), but less autonomy if located in medium-sized inland cities (location 4). Similarly contract responsibility gave significantly greater autonomy in industry 4 (light/craft), but less in industry 7 (building materials and metals).

TABLE 3.3. Results for *D*: employment autonomy

Independent variables		1980–87 (n = 1705)		YR = 4 (n = 1118)		YR = 2 (n = 586)	
		Coeff.	Prob.	Coeff.	Prob.	Coeff.	Prob.
Intercept		0.1212	0.0477	0.1352	0.0701	0.0923	0.3675
YR	1	0.0721	0.0040	0.0735	0.0038	—	—
	2	−0.0281	0.2601	−0.0262	0.2991	—	—
	3	−0.0132	0.5959	−0.0111	0.6586	—	—
	4	−0.0016	0.9476	0.0000	—	—	—
	5	0.0231	0.3470	—	—	0.0243	0.3229
	6	0.000	—	—	—	0.000	—
LOC	1	−0.0483	0.3365	−0.0364	0.5575	−0.0713	0.4103
	2	−0.1046	0.0472	−0.1197	0.0677	−0.0750	0.4035
	3	−0.0753	0.1630	−0.1033	0.1208	−0.0189	0.8392
	4	−0.1354	0.0078	−0.1487	0.0177	−0.1108	0.2080
	5	0.0009	—	0.0000	—	0.0000	—
SC	1	0.1573	0.0001	0.1410	0.0040	0.1862	0.0046
	2	0.1659	0.0001	0.1707	0.0001	0.1554	0.0113
	3	0.0000	—	0.0000	—	0.0000	—
CF	1	0.2395	0.0007	0.2596	0.0030	0.1925	0.1153
	2	0.0000	—	0.0000	—	0.0000	—
IND	1	−0.0501	0.3325	−0.0909	0.1620	0.0173	0.8411
	2	0.0758	0.0428	0.0710	0.1240	0.0831	0.1983
	3	0.1978	0.0001	0.1647	0.0024	0.2618	0.0005
	4	0.1176	0.0084	0.1092	0.0485	0.1322	0.0820
	5	−0.0635	0.1852	−0.0643	0.2758	−0.0618	0.4572
	6	0.0665	0.1032	0.0505	0.3176	0.0964	0.1672
	7	−0.0371	0.3805	−0.0435	0.4044	−0.0245	0.7367
	8	0.0000	—	0.0000	—	0.0000	—
*IND*CF*		—	0.0023	—	0.0089	—	0.3682
*SC*CF*		—	0.0001	—	0.0001	—	0.0046
*LOC*CF*		—	0.0622	—	0.0769	—	0.5252
Statistics	*F*-test	$F = 6.67$	0.0001	$F = 4.69$	−0.0001	$F = 1.99$	0.0024
	R^2	—	0.0949	—	0.1110	—	0.0875

3. *The proportion of new workers recruited by the firms themselves (D)*

A key result in Table 3.3 is that this indicator of autonomy has not apparently changed over time, with the exception that it was 7 percentage points higher in 1980 than over the rest of the period. For the period 1980–85, enterprises located in large and medium-sized inland cities (locations 2 and 4) had significantly less autonomy, but this difference no longer applied in 1986 and 1987. Throughout the period large and medium-sized enterprises exhibited considerably more freedom to recruit workers than small enterprises. The same is true for enterprises in industries 3 (textiles) and 4 (light/craft). Contract form is significant on its own in the period 1980–85, with those enterprises that subsequently operated under the contract-responsibility system enjoying greater autonomy in hiring workers. However this difference is no longer statistically significant in 1986 and 1987, when the contract-responsibility system began to be introduced. Once again the interactive terms are important. The contract-responsibility system was associated with greater autonomy in industry 7 (building materials/metals), and with less autonomy in industry 4 (light/craft); much greater autonomy in small-scale enterprises; and with greater autonomy for enterprises located in medium and small coastal cities (location 3) and medium-sized inland cities (location 4).

4. The ratio of contract employees to total employment (CE)

The results are given in Table 3.4. The ratio is a significant indicator of autonomy in that the enterprise has much greater flexibility in both hiring and dispensing with contract employees than permanent employees. It also has greater flexibility in allocating contract employees to different activities both within and outside the firm. The results suggest that the ratio has increased by 7% since 1983–84. Contract employees are clearly a more important feature of labour markets in coastal regions (locations 1 and 3), of food and metals industries (industries 2 and 7), and of medium-scale enterprises.

5. The proportion of 'own sales' in total sales (OS)

Since 'own sales' are sales which the enterprise arranges itself, this variable may be interpreted as an indicator of both autonomy and responsibility for the enterprise. The general feature of these results is that this indicator of enterprise autonomy has not changed over the period 1980–87, but that the variation across other characteristics of enterprises—location, scale, contract form of industry—is substantial (Table 3.5). For the location variable, the benchmark value is for enterprises in small inland cities (location 5). All other locations had lower proportions of 'own sales', the size of the differential being larger in 1986–87 than in the previous period. Large-scale enterprises had less autonomy in this area than small and medium-sized enterprises, and so did enterprises under the contract-responsibility system. A lower proportion of 'own sales' was recorded throughout the period by enterprises in textiles (industry 3), chemicals (industry 6), building materials and metals (industry 7), and especially energy (industry 5).

TABLE 3.4. Results for ratio of contract workers to total employees (*CE*) (5-year data, *n* = 1186)

Independent variables		1983–87 (*n* = 1186)	
		Coeff.	*t*-test
Intercept		0.160	8.81
YR	1	−0.103	−12.1
	2	−0.081	−9.6
	3	−0.054	−6.4
	4	−0.023	−2.7
	5	0.000	—
LOC	1	−0.013	−1.0
	2	−0.038	−2.9
	3	0.041	2.9
	4	−0.003	−0.3
	5	0.000	—
SC	1	−0.016	−2.0
	2	−0.009	−0.1
	3	0.000	—
CF	1	−0.001	−0.1
	2	0.000	—
IND	1	0.052	2.9
	2	0.030	2.3
	3	0.030	2.3
	4	0.009	0.7
	5	−0.009	−0.2
	6	0.033	3.0
	7	−0.036	3.4
	8	0.000	—
Contract form		−0.001	−0.1
		0.000	—
Wage system	N	−0.017	−1.6
	Y	0.000	—
City	N	−0.033	−4.3
	Y	0.000	—
Statistics	R^2	0.223	
	F	10.70	

Notes: Interactive terms *IND*CF* and *LOC*CF* included but results not reported.

Wage system = firm has autonomy in determining internal wage structure.

City: cities with special autonomy in planning.

TABLE 3.5. Results for 'own sales'

Independent variables		1980–87 (n = 179)		1980–85 (n = 723)		1986–87 (n = 455)	
		Coeff.	Prob.	Coeff.	Prob.	Coeff.	Prob.
Intercept		1.0736	0.0001	1.0214	0.0001	1.1071	0.0001
YR	1	0.0131	0.7067	0.0333	0.3621	—	—
	2	−0.0025	0.9405	0.0175	0.6226	—	—
	3	−0.0284	0.3865	−0.0070	0.8385	—	—
	4	−0.0210	0.5088	0.0000	—	—	—
	5	−0.0195	0.5320	—	—	−0.0189	0.5278
	6	0.000	—	—	—	0.000	—
LOC	1	−0.2184	0.0007	−0.1636	0.0496	−0.2947	0.0041
	2	−0.2412	0.0003	−0.1971	0.0222	−0.3017	0.0059
	3	−0.0732	0.3030	0.0342	0.7150	−0.2087	0.0615
	4	−0.1029	0.1196	−0.0405	0.6386	−0.1796	0.0872
	5	0.0000	—	0.0000	—	0.0000	—
SC	1	−0.1862	0.0040	−0.2397	0.0006	−0.1068	0.1942
	2	−0.0494	0.2943	−0.0679	0.2727	−0.0183	0.8021
	3	0.0000	—	0.0000	—	0.0000	—
CF	1	−0.2013	0.0271	−0.2050	0.0819	−0.1828	0.2087
	2	0.0000	—	0.0000	—	0.0000	—
IND	1	0.1366	0.0743	0.1781	0.0713	0.0684	0.5765
	2	−0.0864	0.1177	−0.0586	0.4180	−0.1180	0.1711
	3	−0.2787	0.0001	−0.2703	0.0006	−0.2927	0.0014
	4	−0.0661	0.2887	−0.0822	0.3184	−0.0440	0.6453
	5	−0.4472	0.0001	−0.4159	0.0001	−0.4969	0.0001
	6	−0.1365	0.0259	−0.0528	0.5280	−0.2225	0.0138
	7	−0.2627	0.0001	−0.2828	0.0005	−0.2370	0.0115
	8	0.0000	—	0.0000	—	0.0000	—
*IND*CF*		—	0.0002	—	0.0168	—	0.0060
*SC*CF*		—	0.0519	—	0.0773	—	0.3195
*LOC*CF*		—	0.0011	—	0.0493	—	0.0422
Statistics	*F*-test	$F = 9.43$	0.0	$F = 5.61$	0.0001	$F = 5.55$	0.0001
	R^2	—	0.2083	—	0.1954	—	0.2667

6. *Subsidies, borrowing, and own funds in long-term finance*

An increase in autonomy is thought to be associated with a decline in state subsidies for investment, and a corresponding increase in loan finance and especially own sources. While investment plans may still require approval by higher authorities, the bargaining position of the firm is greatly improved if it can supply some of the financial resources internally. Owing to data limitations, we are able to look only at these indicators for 1984 to 1987. Because the ratios of state subsidies,

TABLE 3.6. Subsidies, borrowing and firms' own sources in long-term finance (5 years' data: n = 1186)

Independent variables		Subsidies Coeff. (t-test)	Bank borrowing Coeff. (t-test)	Own sources Coeff. (t-test)
Intercept		0.104 (1.9)	0.455 (6.5)	0.562 (7.9)
YR	1	0.085 (3.3)	−0.109 (−3.3)	0.039 (1.2)
	2	0.069 (2.7)	−0.100 (−3.1)	0.010 (0.33)
	3	0.051 (2.0)	−0.024 (−0.7)	−0.038 (−1.1)
	4	−0.002 (−0.1)	−0.022 (−0.7)	0.011 (0.3)
	5	0.000	0.000	0.000
LOC	1	0.094 (2.3)	−0.051 (−1.0)	−0.066 (−1.3)
	2	0.128 (3.0)	−0.028 (−0.6)	−0.113 (−2.2)
	3	0.069 (1.6)	−0.199 (3.6)	0.037 (0.7)
	4	0.013 (0.4)	0.016 (0.3)	−0.034 (−0.7)
	5	0.000	0.000	0.000
SC	1	−0.049 (−2.0)	−0.049 (−1.6)	0.033 (1.0)
	2	−0.102 (−4.5)	0.017 (0.6)	0.039 (1.2)
	3	0.000	0.000	0.000
CF	1	0.219 (3.1)	−0.070 (−0.8)	−0.208 (−2.3)
	2	0.000	0.000	0.000
IND	1	0.313 (5.9)	−0.322 (−4.7)	−0.029 (−0.4)
	2	−0.162 (−4.0)	0.088 (1.7)	−0.095 (−1.8)
	3	−0.090 (−2.5)	0.028 (0.5)	−0.074 (−1.4)
	4	0.061 (1.7)	−0.122 (−2.6)	0.043 (0.9)
	5	−0.072 (−0.6)	0.019 (0.1)	0.049 (0.3)
	6	0.015 (0.4)	−0.088 (−2.1)	0.011 (0.3)
	7	0.001 (0.1)	−0.125 (−3.0)	0.058 (1.4)
	8	0.000	0.000	0.000
City	Y	0.066 (2.8)	−0.001 (−0.1)	−0.091 (−3.0)
	N	0.000	0.000	0.000
Statistics	R^2	0.147	0.09	0.06
	F	6.44	3.96	2.45

Notes: Interactive terms *IND*CF* and *LOC*CF* included in regression, but results not reported.

Contract form: 1 = contract-responsibility system and 2 = director-responsibility system.

firms' own funds, and bank loans to total long-term investment finance are clearly interrelated (together the ratios should sum to unity), the three equations are run as a system rather than independently. The results are given in Table 3.6. It is clear that over time, the firms have become less reliant on state subsidies, with the gap being made up by bank loans and, to a lesser extent, own sources. There are some significant differences between industries: industry 1 (extractive) is much more reliant on state subsidies than other industries, but industries 2 (food, drink, and tobacco) and 6 (chemicals, medicines, and plastics) are less reliant. Industries 5 (energy) and 7 (metals and building materials) generate more funds internally and borrow less. Neither location nor scale emerge as significant determinants of the pattern of long-term financing. Although particular coefficients are statistically significant, the overall explanation, as measured by R^2, is very low. The external characteristics of the enterprise—location, industry, scale etc.—are much less important than the particular circumstances of each enterprise. A similar analysis for short-term finance produced insignificant coefficients for characteristic variables.

The key results may be summarized as follows. With the exception of the share of inputs purchased from the market (*IS*), there has not been a statistically significant change in the degree of autonomy in production exercised by the enterprises. For *IS* the change is of the order of 19 percentage points over time. It appears that 'own sales' (*OS*) were a very high proportion of total sales throughout the period, so little change in the direction of greater autonomy could have been expected. Firms have made increasing use of contract labour (*CE*) since 1983–84, and they have come to rely less on subsidies, and more on own funds or borrowing, for investment.

Generally speaking, enterprises in location 5 (small inland cities), and to a lesser extent in location 3 (medium and small coastal cities) had greater autonomy in production than enterprises in large cities. The differences are most marked for the share of inputs purchased from markets (*IS*), and the proportion of own sales (*OS*). However when the share of total output controlled by the state plan is considered (*PS*), the situation is reversed, with relatively greater autonomy (in 1985–87 only) for enterprises in large inland cities (location 2) and medium-sized inland cities (location 4). Coastal cities made more use of contract labour (*CE*).

Large and medium-scale enterprises had less freedom of action than small-scale enterprises for all indicators except for the recruitment of new labour. Between large and medium-scale enterprises a significant difference appeared with 'own sales': medium-sized enterprises were closer in their experience to small enterprises.

The pattern across industries is difficult to summarize as industry groups do not show a consistent pattern across all four indicators of autonomy. One exception is industry 5 (energy), where on virtually every indicator the enterprises had less freedom in their operations. Industries 2, 3, and 4 (food, textiles, light/craft) and industries 6 and 7 (chemicals, building materials/metal) illustrate the mixed pattern clearly: they generally had a greater share of inputs purchased from the market (*IS*) and recruited directly higher proportions of their new workers than other industries (*D*); but they also had lower proportions of 'own sales' (*OS*). As far as planning outputs are concerned, industries 2 and 3 experienced a higher proportion of planned outputs in 1985–87.

The results for contract form are very interesting. Recall that control via contracts was introduced generally only in 1987 or 1988. The contract-responsibility system is thought to give greater autonomy to the enterprises than the director-responsibility system. The interesting point is that contract form is a significant 'determinant' of many of the indicators either on its own, or more frequently in interaction with other variables such as location or industry, and not only in the 1986–87 period but over the entire period since 1980. The pattern is complicated by interaction of contract form with other variables. For example, the share of inputs purchased in markets is much lower for contract-responsibility enterprises in industries 3, 4, and 7 (textiles, light/craft, building materials/metals), for enterprises located in location 5 (small inland cities), and for small-scale enterprises. It is difficult to discern any particular logic in the results for interaction variables. The interpretation of these results for the contract-form variable is taken up in Section 4.

3. Enterprise Incentives

In this section we look at the degree to which the firm can retain profits. While our main analysis of behaviour and performance is given in the chapters of Part II, there will be a brief discussion of behavioural issues, where this is necessary to assess the incentive effects. The analysis needs to consider not just the time-dimension—the evolution of profit retention over time—but also to show how the incentive varied by sector and location. It will be seen that the progress of reform was by no means uniform in its effects on all firms: some sectors and locations were more progressive than others.

The division of profit between a Chinese state-owned enterprise and its bureaucratic supervisors is the outcome of a bargaining process. This is quite different from the operation of the tax system in the West, where it is acknowledged that profit taxes are determined by the application of rules. Any scope for discussion is solely about the appropriate application of these rules, given the circumstances of the firm. In China, the rules of the tax system constitute at best a starting-point for discussions between the enterprise and its bureaucratic supervisors. The actual outcome, in terms of the shares of profits paid over to the authorities, and retained by the enterprises, depends on the interests of the two parties and their relative bargaining strength.

It is not too difficult to identify the interests of the enterprise and the authorities. The enterprise wishes to retain as much profit as possible: it will then be able to pay out larger bonuses to the workforce, and spend more on investment, both for production and welfare. In brief, the retention of profit gives the director greater freedom of action and greater security, and probably lessens the degree of effort that he has to put in. The authorities rely on enterprise profits to fulfil their obligation to remit to provincial authorities (and hence ultimately to central government), and to finance their own local expenditure. However they will also be aware that their own position depends on thriving local enterprises both politically and financially. Hence they will, if prudent, curb their desire to use enterprises as a source of cash to be milked.

It is more difficult to identify the determinants of the bargaining strengths of the enterprise and the authorities. It is likely that the local authorities have the formal power to order the enterprise to hand over whatever cash sums they may require. Furthermore, the director of the enterprise is a member of the bureaucratic group that constitutes the local authorities. He was probably appointed by them, and will be seeking to return to the bureaucracy by promotion from the enterprise. But this does not mean that he will necessarily acquiesce in all demands, however unreasonable. To begin with he needs to succeed in his job if he is to get promotion. That means making a success of running the enterprise, and, in particular, keeping the workers happy. His strongest bargaining counter is probably the power of the workers to take political action, via the local Party, if they feel that the enterprise is being treated unfairly. This will particularly be the case for a large-scale enterprise.

Unfortunately there is insufficient evidence about the circumstances of the discussions between enterprises and local authorities to be able to model their interaction empirically by reference to explicit factors affecting their interests and bargaining strength. Instead, the assumption is that location, contract form, scale of enterprise, and industry sector are sufficient to proxy these factors indirectly. The objective is to explain the variance in the profit-retention rate across enterprises by such variables, as well as by variables relating to the financial circumstances of the enterprise. Estimates of such empirical functions are discussed below. But first we note the formal features of the profit tax or profit-remittance systems, though our belief is that these do not represent anything more than a signal of the general intentions of the Chinese authorities as to how the enterprise profit is to be divided up.

There were two systems operating, either of which may have affected a particular enterprise, but not both. The first involved the enterprise in delivering to the authorities a quota of profits. The quota was determined in advance by negotiation between the enterprise and the authorities, but was supposed to take into account previous profit performance. The second system was a standard profit tax system. Except for relatively small enterprises, which do not feature in our sample, the tax rate was 55% of fulfilled profit. However there may be a further adjustment tax, designed to limit the profit retention to a level considered appropriate. This adjustment was determined by the local authorities, and was the subject of negotiation between them and the enterprise. Despite the formal differences between these two systems, we believe that in practice they both amount to a procedure where the profit ultimately retained by the enterprise is the outcome of bargaining between the enterprise and the local authorities.

The official formulas for determining retentions by the enterprise are apparently quite complicated. Consider for example the rules determined by the State Council and the Ministry of Finance in 1983 (*Economic Events in the People's Republic of China* (henceforth *EEPRC*), p. 347): these rules apply to the profit tax system described above, and in principle determine the retention rate of the enterprise. The rules are best understood by considering their application step by step:

1. Define FP, fulfilled profit after accounting adjustments. Profit tax is given by k_1FP, where the rate k_1 is 55%. So profit after tax is $FP(1 - k_1)$. Further rules then determine how much of this after-tax profit can be retained by the enterprise.

2. The enterprise is entitled to a basic retained profit; calculated as r_1FP, where r_1 is determined as follows:

$$r_1 = \frac{A + B + C + D}{FP},$$

where A = annual appropriation from total fulfilled profit for expenditure on development of products,
B = annual appropriation for training,
C = annual appropriation for welfare (approximately 11% of wage costs),
D = annual appropriation to bonus fund.

r_1 is based on the ratio in the year before the profits tax system was applied to the enterprise.

3. The enterprise is also entitled to retain a proportion, r_2, of incremental profits over the profit level achieved in the previous year: $r_2 \cdot \Delta FP$. The proportion r_2 varies across industries: in 1983 it was fixed at 10% in oil and electric power industries, 20% in metal-processing, engineering, and 30% for coalmining, postal services, and agricultural engineering (EEPRC, 376).

4. Suppose however that the entitlement to retained profit in (2) and (3) is less than the after-tax profit of step (1). Then a further tax is applied to this residual profit: this adjustment tax is levied at a rate k_2 which is determined on a case-by-case basis, and is therefore the subject of negotiation between the enterprise and the local authorities.

The additional retained profit is given by:

$$(1 - k_2)[FP(1 - k_1) - r_1 FP - r_2 \Delta FP],$$

if

$$FP(1 - k_1) > r_1 FP + r_2 \Delta FP.$$

However for $FP(1 - k_1) \leqslant r_1 FP + r_2 \Delta FP$, there is no adjustment tax, and retentions are given by

$$FP(1 - k_1).$$

5. Total retentions (RP) are the sum of the elements in (2), (3), and (4): if the enterprise is liable for adjustment tax, then:

$$RP = r_1 FP + r_2 \Delta FP + (1 - k_2)[FP(1 - k_1) - r_1 FP - r_2 \Delta FP]$$

or the retention ratio, r,

$$r = \frac{RP}{FP} = (1 - k_2)(1 - k_1) + k_2 r_1 + k_2 r_2 \frac{\Delta FP}{FP}.$$

If the enterprise is *not* liable for adjustment tax, then:

$$r = \frac{RP}{FP} = (1 - k_1).$$

However our impression is that the actual experience of Chinese enterprises is nothing like as predictable as these rules would suggest. At best, we believe that the profit tax rate determines a starting-point for bargaining by the enterprise and the authorities: the enterprise potentially can hope to retain 45% of its profits, and the question at issue is how far it can defend that retention against the predations of the authorities.

The empirical model suggests that the outcome of the bargaining over profits between the enterprise and the authorities is determined partly by the characteristics of the enterprise, and partly by the financial circumstances of the enterprise in the year under consideration. The characteristics of the enterprise are location, scale, and contract form as in Section 2.

The financial circumstances of the enterprise are captured by the following variables: in the empirical equation for the retention ratio each is divided by current fulfilled profits, *FP*.

1. Fulfilled profit in the previous period, FP_{-1}. This could affect retentions in two ways. First, we note that the formal tax system entitles the enterprise to retain a proportion of the growth in profits since the previous year. Hence low profits last year, *ceteris paribus*, push up the current retention ratio. Second, an enterprise that has had high profits over a number of periods will find it difficult to argue that high current profits are due to special features, and hence avoid the imposition of adjustment taxes. We therefore expect FP_{-1} to have a negative sign.

2. Lagged tax payments, T_{-1}. If there is some element of continuity in the bargaining over tax payments, an enterprise that has accepted a high tax bill in the previous period may be a soft target for the authorities in the current period. We expect a negative sign.

3. Loan repayments in the current period, *L*. The repayment of loans is an alternative to delivering profits to the authorities. This could affect tax payment in two ways. If the enterprise is doing well, then ability to repay loans will be correlated with ability to pay taxes. Hence one would expect *L* to have a negative sign. On the other hand, an enterprise might use the fact of loan repayments falling due to argue for a lower tax bill: in that case *L* would enter with a positive coefficient.

4. Investment in current and previous periods, *I* and I_{-1}. Investment is an alternative use of funds to tax payment: so the enterprise may try to use its investment programme as a reason for avoiding tax payment. The authorities may see the matter differently: if the enterprise can afford to invest, it can also afford to pay more taxes. The first argument would give a positive sign, the second a negative sign in the determination of the retention ratio.

5. The price change variable, *CP*, is a measure of the incremental profit earned by the enterprise due to favourable changes in the prices of its products and/or reductions in the prices of its inputs. The existence of such profits will attract the attention of the authorities: it can be argued that they have arisen as a 'windfall' to the enterprise, and do not reflect any increased effort by the enterprise that needs to be rewarded by higher retentions. We therefore export *CP* to have a negative effect on retentions.

In the empirical results reported in the next section, the dependent variable is the retained profit ratio: *RP/FP*. The independent variables are dummy variables for year (*YR*), industry (*IND*), contract form (*CF*), location (*LOC*), scale (*SC*), and the financial variables discussed above (each normalized by dividing by current fulfilled profits), giving the following regression equation:

$$\frac{RP}{FP} = f\left(\frac{FP_{t-1}}{FP}, \frac{L}{FP}, \frac{CP}{FP}, \frac{I}{FP}, \frac{I_{t-1}}{FP}, \frac{T_{t-1}}{FP}, YR, IND, LOC, SC, CF\right).$$

The strategy was to apply this equation in linear form to significant subsets of the data according to the characteristics of the enterprises.

1. Evolution of retention rates over time

Because of the introduction of lagged financial variables we can consider only the years 1984–87 inclusive. Results are given in Table 3.7. The constants in the equations are to be interpreted as the retention ratios in sector 8 (engineering and electrical), location 5 (small inland cities) scale 3 (small), and enterprises with contract form 2 (director-responsibility system). All other coefficients give the 'deviations' from that standard case. It will be noted that virtually all the other characteristics dummy variables have negative signs. The 'standard' therefore reflects enterprises with relatively the highest retention ratios. A number of features of the results are worthy of note:

(*a*) The average retention ratio rose over the period 1984–87 by 10 percentage points.

(*b*) Comparing the equation for 1984–85 with that for 1986–87 it is evident that the latter is much more successful than the former in explaining variance of retention ratios. One possibility is that the tax system was applied less arbitrarily in the later period, perhaps an indicator of some success in the reform process in creating 'autonomy within rules' for the enterprises.

(*c*) Industries 2 (food etc.), 3 (textiles etc.), and 6 (chemicals etc.) had significantly lower retention ratios throughout the period, though it appears that industry differentials narrowed in the last 2 years.

(*d*) Contract form is not a significant determinant of the level of retentions.

(*e*) Location was a significant determinant of retention ratios in the 1984–85 period (but not in 1986–87): notably enterprises in the coastal zone (locations 1 and 3) had significantly lower ratios.

(*f*) As anticipated, large-scale and medium-scale enterprises had significantly lower retention ratios than small enterprises: the differences averaged 12 and 8 percentage points over the period.

TABLE 3.7. Profit-retention bargaining model by time-periods

Independent variables		RP					
		1984–85		1986–87		1984–87	
Intercept		0.533	(13.5)	0.59	(10.6)	0.63	(17.2)
YR	84	−0.044	(−2.9)			−0.10	(−5.4)
	85	0.000	—			−0.05	(−2.5)
	86			−0.018	(−0.86)	−0.007	(−0.4)
	87			0.000	—	0.000	—
IND	1	−0.029	(−0.78)	−0.097	(−1.7)	−0.072	(−2.0)
	2	−0.109	(−4.11)	−0.036	(−0.9)	−0.079	(−3.2)
	3	−0.115	(−3.9)	−0.069	(−1.7)	−0.098	(−3.7)
	4	−0.044	(−1.6)	−0.007	(−0.2)	−0.027	(−1.1)
	5	−0.066	(−1.5)	−0.104	(−1.8)	−0.009	(−0.2)
	6	−0.074	(−2.9)	−0.093	(−2.7)	−0.092	(−4.1)
	7	−0.030	(−1.2)	−0.031	(−0.9)	−0.029	(−1.3)
	8	0.000	—	0.000	—	0.000	—
CF	1	−0.015	(−0.9)	−0.024	(−1.1)	−0.014	(−0.9)
	2	0.000	—	0.000	—	0.000	—
LOC	1	−0.058	(−1.7)	−0.007	(−0.2)	−0.038	(−1.3)
	2	0.002	(0.08)	0.018	(0.4)	0.009	(0.32)
	3	−0.072	(−2.03)	−0.032	(−0.7)	−0.063	(−1.9)
	4	−0.047	(−1.4)	0.004	(0.09)	−0.039	(−1.3)
	5	0.000	—	0.000	—	0.000	—
SC	1	−0.111	(−4.6)	−0.113	(−3.3)	−0.125	(−5.6)
	2	−0.060	(−2.6)	−0.099	(−3.1)	−0.087	(−4.2)
	3	0.000	—	0.000	—	0.000	—
FP_{t-1}		−0.021	(−2.9)	−0.034	(−5.9)	−0.045	(−9.8)
L		−0.069	(−2.9)	0.005	(0.32)	−0.011	(−0.9)
CP		0.021	(3.9)	−0.009	(−2.2)	−0.006	(−1.9)
I		0.004	(1.9)	−0.023	(−17.6)	−0.020	(−19.9)
I_{t-1}		0.009	(2.7)	0.017	(9.1)	0.017	(10.5)
T_{t-1}		−0.112	(−4.1)	−0.075	(−1.8)	−0.115	(−4.4)
R^2		0.27		0.81		0.70	
N		525		507		1033	
F-value		8.92		99.4		105	

(*g*) The financial variables were generally significant, though the *size* of the parameters does not suggest large effects on the retention ratio. FP_{-1} and T_{-1} are always negative: FP_{-1} presumably is a signal of ability to pay higher taxes, T_{-1} is an indicator of weakness by the enterprise in bargaining with the authorities (a high tax bill last year suggests a high starting-point for this year's tax discussions with the authorities). The signs on L (loan repayments) and I (current investment) are not stable between the two subperiods. Investment is a substitute for tax payments in 1984–85, but is positively correlated with those payments in the later period. Finally, we note that *CP*, the variable measuring profits arising from price changes, has an unexpected positive sign in the earlier period (1984–85). Taken as a group, it is evident that these financial variables do have a significant effect on the retention ratio, thus confirming our hypothesis that there is a degree of bargaining between the enterprise and the authorities in which the financial circumstances of the enterprise do affect the outcome.

2. *Location and profit-retention ratios*

The results for each location type are given in Table 3.8. We note first that the equation explains less of the variance in location 1 (large coastal cities), and particularly in location 2 (large inland cities). The cities in location 2 were the locations for giant state enterprises created by investments from the 1950s. Although some of the cities were targeted for economic reform experiments, the behaviour of the large state enterprises remained conservative. They are very important enterprises, both in relation to the planning system and their contribution to state revenues. Economic reform was therefore directed to improving internal efficiency rather than giving them greater discretion over their profits. Hence the variance of the retention ratio not explained by the equation reflects the greater incidence of *ad hoc* exactions by the authorities rather than the application of the rules of the tax system. This point can be seen clearly by a comparison of the coefficients on the scale variables across all five location types. It is evident that in the large and medium-sized cities (locations 1 to 3) large and medium-scale enterprises had much lower retention ratios than small enterprises, suggesting that the authorities were using these enterprises as sources of revenue. This is not so evident in the small and medium-sized cities.

3. *Industry and profit-retention ratios*

Results for each industry group are given in Table 3.9. An interesting feature here is that the quality of the results (as indicated by R^2) is inversely correlated with the level of labour productivity in each industry group (if we ignore industry 1 and industry 5 where there are too few observations to give any confidence in the equations). The distinction is between primarily consumer-goods sectors (2, 3, 4), and producer-goods sectors (6, 7, 8). One explanation is that the latter have been regarded as being of greater importance for control of

TABLE 3.8. Profit-retention bargaining model by location

Independent variables		loc = 1		loc = 2		loc = 3		loc = 4		loc = 5	
Intercept		0.57	(10.71)	0.662	(11.7)	0.607	(10.6)	0.357	(6.14)	0.654	(6.1)
YR	84	−0.142	(−4.9)	−0.087	(−2.7)	−0.117	(−3.7)	−0.077	(−2.1)	−0.008	(−0.1)
	85	−0.076	(−2.7)	−0.025	(−0.7)	−0.061	(−1.98)	−0.025	(−0.7)	−0.007	(−0.1)
	86	−0.041	(−1.4)	−0.033	(−0.95)	0.0099	(0.33)	0.021	(0.6)	0.023	(0.5)
	87	0.000	—	0.000	—	0.000	—	0.000	—	0.000	—
	86			−0.018	(−0.86)	−0.007	(−0.4)				
	87			0.000	—	0.000	—				
CF	1	0.021	(0.92)	−0.030	(−1.1)	−0.009	(−0.36)	0.018	(0.7)	−0.069	(−1.4)
	2	0.000	—	0.000	—	0.000	—	0.000	—	0.000	—
SC	1	−0.199	(−4.4)	−0.169	(−4.1)	−0.180	(−4.4)	0.0298	(0.7)	−0.093	(−1.5)
	2	−0.143	(−3.2)	−0.129	(−3.2)	−0.067	(−1.7)	0.022	(0.6)	−0.122	(−2.2)
	3	0.000	—	0.000	—	0.000	—	0.000	—	0.000	—
IND	1	0.043	(0.5)	−0.137	(−2.6)	−0.043	(−0.7)	0.034	(0.5)		
	2	0.003	(0.1)	−0.147	(−3.3)	−0.033	(−0.7)	−0.119	(−2.2)	−0.145	(−2.1)
	3	−0.107	(−2.7)	−0.147	(−2.6)	−0.008	(−0.2)	0.003	(−0.1)	−0.036	(−0.4)
	4	−0.057	(−1.4)	−0.045	(−0.9)	−0.092	(−2.3)	0.016	(0.3)	0.133	(1.1)
	5	−0.111	(−1.9)	−0.175	(−2.7)	0.347	(4.4)	0.023	(0.4)		
	6	−0.067	(−2.0)	−0.164	(−3.7)	−0.082	(−2.2)	−0.014	(−0.3)	0.002	(0.3)
	7	0.016	(0.4)	−0.075	(−1.8)	−0.050	(−0.9)	0.011	(0.3)	−0.067	(−1.0)
	8	0.000	—	0.000	—	0.000	—	0.000	—	0.000	—
FP_{t-1}		−0.013	(−1.8)	−0.016	(−2.4)	0.008	(0.2)	0.005	(0.4)	−0.066	(−1.4)
L		−0.034	(−1.3)	−0.043	(−1.8)	−0.365	(−6.3)	−0.0197	(−0.7)	−0.365	(−3.1)
CP		0.022	(3.2)	0.006	(1.3)	0.023	(1.8)	−0.026	(−2.9)	−0.006	(−0.3)
I		−0.009	(−1.2)	0.003	(1.1)	−0.0003	(−0.03)	−0.029	(−10.6)	0.0002	(0.03)
I_{t-1}		0.012	(3.9)	0.002	(0.9)	−0.014	(−0.9)	0.069	(10.7)	0.018	(1.4)
T_{t-1}		−0.070	(−1.9)	−0.036	(−0.8)	−0.220	(−4.2)				
R^2		0.317		0.188		0.648		0.927		0.721	
N		278		284		144		254		69	
F-value		6.3		3.24		12.09		157.15		7.90	

TABLE 3.9. Profit-retention bargaining model by industry

Independent variables		RP							
		ind = 1		ind = 2		ind = 3		ind = 4	
Intercept		0.66	(5.45)	0.43	(4.9)	0.52	(6.9)	0.74	(6.2)
YR	84	−0.022	(−0.28)	−0.157	(−3.2)	−0.175	(−3.9)	−0.083	(−1.6)
	85	0.027	(0.3)	−0.061	(−1.3)	−0.139	(−3.3)	−0.065	(−1.4)
	86	0.004	(0.1)	0.017	(0.3)	−0.039	(−0.9)	−0.029	(−0.6)
	87	0.000	—	0.000	—	0.00	—	0.00	—
LOC	1	0.106	(0.8)	0.131	(1.9)	−0.088	(−1.2)	−0.357	(−3.1)
	2	−0.013	(−0.2)	0.082	(1.3)	0.006	(0.1)	−0.216	(−1.9)
	3	−0.197	(−1.6)	0.022	(0.3)	−0.023	(−0.3)	−0.437	(−3.6)
	4	0.000	—	0.016	(0.2)	−0.084	(−1.2)	−0.303	(−2.6)
	5			0.000	—	0.00	—	0.00	—
CF	1	−0.098	(−1.1)	0.038	(1.2)	−0.047	(−1.4)	−0.086	(−2.3)
	2	0.000	—	0.000	—	0.00	—	0.00	—
SC	1	−0.240	(−2.7)	−0.188	(−4.2)	−0.164	(−3.5)	−0.068	(−1.1)
	2	−0.058	(−0.6)	−0.124	(−2.6)	−0.160	(−3.8)	0.043	(0.8)
	3	0.000	—	0.000	—	0.00	—	0.00	—
FP_{t-1}		−0.016	(−0.3)	−0.003	(−0.06)	0.039	(1.0)	−0.038	(−1.2)
L		0.152	(0.7)	−0.161	(−2.80)	−0.002	(−0.1)	−0.063	(−1.3)
CP		−0.036	(−1.2)	0.003	(0.4)	0.005	(0.4)	0.016	(0.9)
I		−0.024	(−2.0)	−0.0003	(−0.3)	−0.008	(−0.6)	−0.004	(−0.5)
I_{t-1}		0.019	(1.6)	0.039	(3.9)	−0.017	(−0.8)	0.024	(1.8)
T_{t-1}		−0.256	(−2.5)	−0.073	(−0.9)	−0.042	(0.7)	0.016	(0.2)
R^2		0.99		0.40		0.37		0.54	
N		46		125		118		121	
F-value		246		4.6		3.8		7.6	

TABLE 3.9 (*cont.*)

Independent variables		*RP*							
		ind = 5		ind = 6		ind = 7		ind = 8	
Intercept		−0.39	(−0.15)	0.46	(7.79)	0.40	(5.68)	0.52	
YR	84	−0.155	(−2.6)	−0.100	(−3.0)	−0.102	(−2.7)	−0.09	(−2.1)
	85	−0.118	(−1.9)	−0.015	(−0.5)	−0.051	(−1.4)	−0.036	(−0.9)
	86	−0.029	(−0.5)	−0.046	(−1.4)	−0.017	(−0.5)	0.016	(0.3)
	87	0.000	—	0.00	—	0.00	—	0.00	—
LOC	1	−0.266	(−3.4)	−0.102	(−2.2)	0.033	(0.6)	0.028	(0.4)
	2	−0.248	(−2.9)	0.089	(1.9)	0.060	(1.1)	0.148	(2.1)
	3	0.282	(3.1)	−0.105	(−2.2)	0.121	(1.6)	0.024	(0.3)
	4	0.000	—	−0.054	(−1.1)	0.041	(0.7)	0.047	(0.7)
	5	—		0.000	—	0.00	—	0.00	—
CF	1	0.176	(2.0)	0.023	(0.9)	−0.006	(−0.2)	0.030	(1.1)
	2	0.000	—	0.000	—	0.00	—	0.00	—
SC	1	0.730	(0.3)	−0.053	(−1.3)	0.017	(0.3)	−0.082	(−1.1)
	2	0.711	(0.3)	−0.074	(−1.8)	0.044	(0.8)	−0.046	(−0.7)
	3	0.000	—	0.000	—	0.00	—	0.00	—
FP_{t-1}		0.319	(2.6)	−0.026	(−1.3)	−0.017	(−0.6)	−0.101	(−1.9)
L		−0.192	(−2.3)	−0.007	(−0.4)	−0.171	(−3.9)	−0.197	(−4.1)
CP		−0.013	(−0.7)	0.000	(0.1)	0.024	(1.3)	−0.007	(−0.55)
I		0.016	(0.5)	0.008	(1.8)	−0.002	(−0.03)	0.004	(0.46)
I_{t-1}		0.011	(0.3)	0.005	(1.4)	0.009	(2.5)	−0.018	(−0.7)
T_{t-1}		−0.281	(−1.9)	−0.039	(−0.9)	−0.148	(−2.9)	−0.123	(−1.9)
R^2		0.86		0.21		0.22		0.21	
N		39		186		182		200	
F-value		10.2		2.8		3.0		3.1	

the economy via the planning mechanism. There is therefore more bureaucratic intervention by the authorities in enterprises in these sectors. Another feature of the results is that scale is not a significant determinant of retention ratio in the producer-goods sectors.

The financial variables do not perform well in these equations by sector, probably due to small sample size. The pattern of signs on location variables is not consistent across sectors, suggesting that we should be cautious about interpreting the results reported above.

4. *Scale of enterprise*

Results for subsamples defined by the three scale characteristics are tabulated in Table 3.10. One striking feature is the low R^2 for the equations for large and medium-sized enterprises relative to small scale. Another is the size of the intercept: 0.30 for large scale, 0.43 for medium scale, and 0.90 for small scale. Inspection of the year dummy coefficients suggests that retention ratios increased more rapidly over time for small-scale enterprises. For small-scale enterprises, contract form is significant (contract-responsibility enterprises have much lower retention ratios—some 14 percentage points): but industry is not. For large and medium-scale enterprises the position is the reverse. The financial variables display much the same pattern of signs and significance irrespective of scale. The overall impression is that large and medium-scale enterprises are much more subject to bureaucratic intervention with random effects on profit retention when the whole sample is considered.

5. *Contract form*

Table 3.11 gives the results for the sample divided according to the contract form under which the enterprise operated in 1988: these contract forms would *not*, of course, have been operative in the early years of the sample, since the contract-responsibility form (CF1) was only introduced in 1987. The interesting feature of the results is that although the intercepts are *not* statistically significantly different, some of the coefficients on independent variables are quite different. Thus the location variables are generally significant for director-responsibility enterprises (CF2) but not for contract-responsibility enterprises (CF1). One explanation is that the former group of enterprises work more closely with the local authorities: so the attitudes of the local authorities towards enterprises as a source of revenue is likely to be more important in determining the retention ratio. When it comes to industry variables, the situation is reversed: they are significant generally for contract-responsibility enterprises, but not for director-

TABLE 3.10. Profit-retention bargaining model by scale of firms

Independent variables		RP					
		Scale = 1		Scale = 2		Scale = 3	
Intercept		0.295	(5.8)	0.43	(9.12)	0.896	(8.0)
YR	84	−0.09	(−3.9)	−0.08	(−3.2)	−0.14	(−2.5)
	85	−0.03	(−1.5)	−0.02	(−0.8)	−0.17	(−3.1)
	86	0.01	(0.6)	−0.025	(−0.96)	−0.04	(−0.7)
	87	0.000	—	0.000	—	0.000	—
LOC	1	0.05	(1.0)	−0.006	(−0.2)	−0.09	(−1.1)
	2	0.089	(1.9)	0.02	(0.5)	−0.06	(−0.85)
	3	0.05	(0.96)	−0.04	(−0.8)	0.018	(0.2)
	4	0.12	(2.5)	−0.021	(−0.44)	−0.22	(−3.5)
	5	−0.000	—	0.000	—	0.000	—
CF	1	0.02	(1.2)	−0.01	(−0.6)	−0.14	(−2.7)
	2	0.000	—	0.000	—	0.000	—
IND	1	−0.08	(−1.8)	0.01	(0.25)	0.15	(1.1)
	2	−0.09	(−3.3)	−0.05	(−1.3)	−0.01	(−0.1)
	3	−0.08	(−2.1)	−0.11	(−2.95)	0.063	(0.7)
	4	−0.12	(−3.5)	0.01	(0.3)	0.05	(0.5)
	5	−0.03	(−0.8)	−0.004	(−0.04)	−0.06	(−0.2)
	6	−0.07	(−2.7)	−0.09	(−2.6)	0.03	(0.3)
	7	−0.009	(−0.4)	0.009	(0.29)	−0.05	(−0.5)
	8	0.000	—	0.000	—	0.000	—
FP_{t-1}		−0.014	(−2.7)	−0.009	(−1.1)	−0.17	(−7.3)
L		0.02	(3.5)	0.001	(0.3)	(0.5)	(0.01)
CP		−0.02	(−0.9)	−0.03	(−2.0)	−0.08	(−1.6)
I		0.004	(0.5)	−0.003	(−2.0)	−0.00099	(−0.2)
I_{t-1}		0.013	(2.53)	0.005	(2.5)	0.004	(0.6)
T_{t-1}		−0.07	(−2.3)	−0.07	(−1.96)	−0.29	(−3.2)
R^2		0.199		0.155		0.939	
N		459		413		159	
F-value		5.9		3.42		101.71	

responsibility enterprises. The same is true for the financial variables, where coefficients are much better determined for the contract-responsibility enterprises. This suggests that for the contract-responsibility group of enterprises, the retention ratio is more closely linked to industry performance and enterprise performance according to the application of some predictable process or rules. This suggestion is borne out by a comparison of the degree to which the equation explains the variance of the dependent variable: $R^2 = 0.78$ for the contract-responsibility enterprises compared with $R^2 = 0.30$ for the others.

TABLE 3.11. Profit-retention bargaining model by contract form

Independent variables		RP			
		CF1		CF2	
Intercept		0.567	(11.8)	0.643	(11.66)
YR	84	−0.099	(−3.7)	−0.106	(−4.4)
	85	−0.044	(−1.6)	−0.044	(−1.78)
	86	−0.003	(−0.1)	−0.017	(−0.7)
	87	0.000	—	0.000	—
LOC	1	0.032	(0.80)	−0.108	(−2.3)
	2	0.073	(1.91)	−0.034	(−0.7)
	3	−0.001	(−0.1)	−0.104	(−2.1)
	4	0.036	(0.9)	−0.097	(−2.1)
	5	−0.000	(1.0)	0.000	—
SC	1	−0.106	(−3.5)	−0.150	(−4.8)
	2	−0.064	(−2.2)	−0.128	(−4.4)
	3	0.000	—	0.000	—
IND	1	−0.162	(−3.1)	0.029	(0.66)
	2	−0.087	(−2.4)	−0.061	(−1.99)
	3	−0.129	(−3.4)	−0.043	(−1.3)
	4	−0.111	(−3.1)	0.042	(1.2)
	5	−0.012	(−0.1)	0.010	(0.3)
	6	−0.087	(−3.1)	−0.060	(−1.9)
	7	−0.049	(−1.6)	−0.010	(−0.3)
	8	0.000	—	0.000	—
FP_{t-1}		−0.036	(−6.7)	−0.019	(−1.5)
L		−0.039	(−1.9)	−0.053	(−3.4)
CP		−0.018	(−3.8)	0.006	(1.4)
I		−0.020	(−16.97)	0.015	(2.1)
I_{t-1}		0.019	(10.03)	0.001	(0.2)
T_{t-1}		−0.111	(−3.0)	−0.124	(−3.8)
R^2		0.78		0.30	
N		603		429	
F-value		97.5		7.76	

The hypothesis explored in this section is that the division of profit between the enterprise and the local authorities is better explained by a process of bargaining between the parties than by the application of the rules of an admittedly complex tax system. To examine this hypothesis, we suggested that under a bargaining model the retentions/profit ratio for an enterprise would be a function of the characteristics of the enterprise—industry, location, scale, and contract form—and of the financial situation of the enterprise. The 'rules' of the tax system would be at best the starting-point for the bargaining process.

The detailed results give modest support to this approach. One key set of results concerns the lower explanatory power of our empirical equations for large and medium-scale enterprises, for large city locations, and for producer-goods sectors, compared to small-scale enterprises, smaller city locations, and consumer-goods sectors. Our interpretation is that profit retention for enterprises with the former characteristics is determined by a procedure involving *ad hoc* negotiations between the enterprise and the authorities. The procedure is not modelled accurately by the variables in our equation. A second interesting result is the improvement of the performance of the equation in 1986–87 compared to 1984–85. This suggests that the process of taxation of profits by the authorities became more predictable over time. When this is linked to the fact that the level of retentions rose by some 10 percentage points on average over 1984–87, the implications for incentives to the enterprise are evident. Not only would the enterprise expect to retain more of its profit, it could also be more certain that it would be permitted to do so. That represents an important increase in the incentives to make profits by reducing costs or seeking new markets for goods produced.

4. The Determination of Contract Form

In the previous two sections, the contract-form variable has emerged as a significant 'determinant' of enterprise autonomy in the reform period. Since the distinction between contract responsibility and director responsibility only applied at the very end of the period under analysis, it is puzzling that the variable appears to be significant over the whole period. Since the puzzle recurs in Chapter 5, where productive efficiency is analysed, it is appropriate to consider the interpretation of the contract-form variable more closely in this section.

The interpretation proposed here is that the distinction between the two contract forms formalized a distinction in control regime (and behaviour) which had existed throughout the reform period. In particular, the analyses of sections 2 and 3 suggest that the contract-responsibility group of firms had experienced more autonomy in retention of profits (in the sense that profit retention was subject to less arbitrary interference by the authorities) and in the labour market, but less autonomy in procurement of materials and in sales.

This interpretation poses the further question of whether the alloca-

TABLE 3.12. Probit analysis of determinants of contract forms of firms

Independent variables		Coefficient (standard error)	
Intercept		−0.560	(0.61)
IND	1	0.044	(0.58)
	2	0.243	(0.43)
	3	−0.477	(0.47)
	4	−0.489	(0.43)
	5	1.772*	(0.72)
	6	−0.195	(0.36)
	7	−0.549**	(0.35)
	8	0.000	—
LOC	1	1.414*	(0.56)
	2	0.592	(0.54)
	3	1.409*	(0.58)
	4	1.034**	(0.55)
	5	0.000	
VW		−0.595**	(0.33)
Z_0		−4.896	(4.94)
χ^2		200.99**	
Log likelihood		−100.49	
DF		160	
N		174	
CF = 1		110 (63.2%)	

Notes: The equation is predicting the probability that a firm will have the contract responsibility form (CFI).

VW is average output per worker (units: 10,000 yuan) in the firm 1983–87: Z_0 is ratio of workers with higher education and senior schooling to total work-force.

* significant at 5% level (χ^2 test).

** significant at 10% level.

tion of firms to the two groups was arbitrary, or whether it can be traced to particular characteristics of the enterprise. This was explored via a probit analysis, which is reported in Table 3.12. The equation seeks to predict the allocation of firms to the contract-responsibility form. A sample of 174 firms was chosen where the contract form was unambiguously indicated in the questionnaire responses: 63% of this sample had the contract-responsibility form. The explanatory variables were taken to be industry and location, to which were added average value added per worker and an indicator of labour quality. The coefficients reported in Table 3.12 are to be interpreted as the contributions of each explanatory variable to the probability that a firm was assigned to the contract-responsibility form. The intercept gives this probability (56%) for a firm in location 5 (small inland cities) and industry 8 (engineering and electrical) with mean value added per worker and labour quality. Two of the industry coefficients and three of the location coefficients are statistically significant. The contract-responsibility form is more likely in industry 5 (energy) and in the coastal cities (locations 1 and 3). But the coefficients are not large. The coefficient of value added per worker is significant at the 0.7% level. But the size of the coefficient does not indicate a strong effect. Value added per worker is measured in units of 10,000 yuan per worker: the average for the sample is approximately 0.658 with standard deviation 0.377. The coefficient therefore implies that an increase in value added per worker equivalent to one standard deviation *reduces* the probability that the firm will be a contract-responsibility firm by about 2.2%. The implication is that, *ceteris paribus*, less efficient firms were more likely to be assigned to the contract-responsibility system, perhaps in the hope that their efficiency would be improved thereby.

But none of these effects is particularly strong. Our conclusion is that the allocation of firms to contract forms is only endogenous to a limited extent in terms of objective characteristics of the firms. However, it appears that the allocation did reflect relationships between the firm and the authorities that existed prior to the introduction of the formal differentiation of contracts. In particular, the contract-responsibility group of firms had less autonomy on virtually all the quantitative indicators than the director-responsibility group throughout the period from 1980. They also relied more on subsidies to finance long-term expenditures, and less on own sources (Table 3.6). By contrast, profit retention for this group appears to be more predictable than for the director-responsibility group.

5. Conclusions

The objective of this chapter was to examine certain quantitative indicators of firm autonomy and incentives over the period since 1980. One set of indicators is a measure of the extent to which the operations of the firm were market rather than plan. The other indicator is the behaviour of the retained profit ratio.

A variety of indicators of autonomy were explored using the general linear model with year, location, scale, industry, and contract form as the regressors. With respect to changes over time two indicators show substantial changes: the share of material inputs purchased in the market rather than allocated under the plan rose by some 19 percentage points, and the share of contract workers to total employment also rose. The proportion of sales accounted for by 'own sales' (that is, not allocated under the plan) did not vary greatly. The results with respect to scale and location generally confirm those of the qualitative analysis of Chapter 2. On many of the indicators, enterprises located in small inland cities (and to a lesser extent those located in small and medium-sized coastal cities) had more autonomy. But when it came to the share of output under the state plan (in 1985–87 only), it was enterprises in the large and medium-sized inland cities that had the most autonomy. That is, of course, only a measure of formal autonomy; it cannot pick up the extent of administrative interference. As expected, large-scale enterprises appeared to have less autonomy, except perhaps in respect of the labour force.

Profit retention was a key feature of the reforms, and it is an indicator not only of autonomy (it gave the enterprise a degree of financial independence which had not been ceded to it previously), but also of incentives. The discussion in Chapter 1 described the evolution of the tax and profit-retention system over the reform period, and indicated that the formal system left substantial scope for bargaining between the enterprises and their local authorities over the level of 'profit delivery' or tax. In Section 3.3, a model of profit retention was specified, based on an analysis of the actual tax rules in operation, but with variables for firm characteristic variables and financial variables added. The empirical results suggest that the retention ratio increased by 10 percentage points over the period 1984–87, as expected. A more interesting result was that the fitted equations were less satisfactory for large and medium-scale enterprises, for enterprises in large cities, and for enterprises in producer-goods industries, which suggests that profit retention for these firms was determined in a more arbitrary fashion, e.g. bargaining between the firms and the authorities. However, a further feature of the results was that the predictive power of the equations improved over time, suggesting that the taxation system became more rule-based as the reforms progressed.

A final section of the chapter addressed a puzzle which arose from the previous empirical result: although the distinction between contract responsibility and director responsibility was introduced only in 1987, contract form was frequently a significant variable in explaining differences between firms. This raised the question whether the assignment of particular contract forms to enterprises could be explained by the characteristics of the enterprises. The probit results gave some support to the hypothesis that less efficient firms in the coastal cities were slightly more likely to be assigned the contract-responsibility form. But the effects are not quantitatively very great. What is evident however is that the contract-responsibility enterprises had less autonomy on virtually all the quantitative indicators. They also appear to have enjoyed a more predictable profit-retention regime.

PART II

Modelling the Behaviour of the Chinese State-Owned Enterprises during the Reform Period, 1980–1987

The Structure of Part II: An Explanatory Note

Chapters 4 to 10 report a series of econometric analyses of various aspects of enterprise behaviour during the reform period, which are then combined in a single model of the enterprise in Chapter 11, which is used for policy simulations. The structure of Part II can be discerned most easily from Fig. 4.1, a flow chart of the complete model which is detailed in Chapter 11. The analysis begins in the bottom left-hand corner of the chart with an examination of employment, wages, and bonus payments which is the subject of Chapter 4. Chapter 5 is concerned with productive efficiency and costs in relation to the use of capital and labour. (These relationships are indicated in the centre of the chart.) Chapter 6 continues the themes of Chapter 5, but now concentrating on the determinants of profits (and profit margins), indicated by the heading 'profits' in the chart. In Chapters 7 to 9 a financial model of the firm is developed. Chapter 7 focuses on the flow of funds, both internal (including profit retention and depreciation payments) and external (loans and grants). Chapters 8 and 9 examine investment behaviour (additions to capital stock) and the interaction of financial and expenditure decisions. Chapter 10 begins to address policy issues, and in particular financial discipline for the firms. The issue is whether firms which make losses are subsequently rescued by subsidies from the authorities: the 'soft' budget constraint.

Chapter 11 integrates all the previous analyses in a single simultaneous-equation model of the enterprise. This model permits the identification of significant linkages and feedbacks between different aspects of the firms' activities. These linkages are important not only for their behavioural interpretation, but also because they enable a complete evaluation of all the consequences of different policy variables. To quote just one example which is explored in Chapter 11: a change in the bonus rate will affect employment, output, and profits directly, with further indirect effects on the flow of funds, expenditures on capital stock, and hence further impacts on efficiency and output.

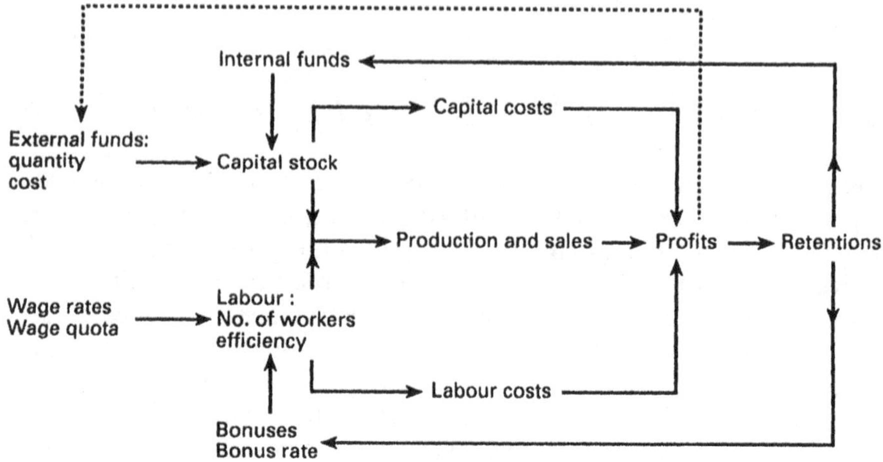

FIG. 4.1. Flow chart of complete model of the firm

4

Employment and Wages

1. Introduction

In this chapter, we turn our attention to incentives for the labour force. Three areas are explored. The first is the relationship between the contribution of the workers to the value added of the firm, and the wage that they may expect to receive. 'Wages' are defined here to include not only time-wages, but also piece-work wages, bonuses related to cost reduction, and payments in kind (represented by the current cost of welfare provision, such as housing, health, and pensions). The expectation is that we would expect output and worker rewards to be more closely related as the reforms developed.

The second area is the relation of bonus payments to the profits of the enterprise. This aspect of the reform has been considered particularly significant, because it links returns to the work-force directly to the retained profits of the firm. Large retained profits make it easier for the managers to keep the work-force happy. However, it is an incentive to efficiency only if the generation of profits is directly linked to the performance of the firm. If profits are the outcome of an administrative process, e.g. costs and prices fixed without relation to economic costs, then the bonus incentive will fail: workers have to be able to trace a direct link between their efforts and the bonus they receive.

The third area is the existence of wage and salary differentials. The pre-reform Chinese enterprise was highly egalitarian in terms of wages paid to different categories of workers. In so far as the firms began to take a more economic approach with reform, one would expect differentials, e.g. between skilled and unskilled workers, to become more marked. In parallel with the absence of the sanction of bankruptcy for the whole firm, there is no real fear of dismissal should things go badly for the firm. A soft budget constraint ensures that employment is secure for the whole work-force, and even individuals are unlikely to be dismissed for poor work. We surmise that the weakness of sanctions for poor performance, both for the enterprise and for the individual workers, is the Achilles' heel of the attempts in the reform programme to give greater incentives.

2. *Wages, Bonuses, and Employment*

The economic reform programme since 1979 has brought four major changes in wages policy. First, wages have been substantially increased compared to the pre-reform period. The nominal average industrial wage rose from 632 yuan in 1977 to 1,071 yuan in 1984: a real increase when adjusted by the official inflation rate of 40% (Walder 1987). Second, the reintroduction of piece-rates and efficiency bonuses (abolished in 1966) has meant that more of workers' pay is related directly to the performance of the work-force and/or the firm. Third, by 1984 most firms were permitted to retain part of their profits, and to pay profit-related bonuses for these retentions. Fourth, the managers of firms now have considerably greater freedom to introduce wage differentials within the constraints of a given total wage bill. The impact of these changes, in principle at least, has been to introduce a more rational wage system, in which the wages paid and received by groups of workers are much more closely related to their productive effort. The role of wages as an incentive has been restored, at least to some extent.

2.1 A description of the system

The formal mechanisms for the control of wage payments are quite complex, and as we have observed before, there is likely to be some bargaining between the enterprise and the local Labour Bureau on the application of the 'rules' to each enterprise. However an understanding of the basic control mechanisms is an essential starting-point for analysis. The three institutions involved are the Central Labour Bureau in Beijing, the local Labour Bureau, and the firm. The Central Labour Bureau determines labour policy at the macro-level. It fixes the total plan quota of the wage bill, the level of employment in the state-owned industrial sector, and the level of industrial wages. The plan quotas of wages and employment are then allocated between lower-level labour bureaux, whose task is to implement the macro-policy locally in the enterprises under their jurisdictions. Thus for each firm, they will determine the wage bill and the level of employment, as well as ensuring that individual wage payments follow the national guidelines.

Our focus is on the interaction between the firm and the Labour Bureau, in the context of local conditions. In principle, the Labour Bureau ensures implementation of the national wage policy. The total wage received by a worker is made up of a basic wage and an

TABLE 4.1. Composition of basic wage

Wage category	Description	Code in data-set
Aggregate	Total wage bill	017
Basic	Total wages in production-cost account	013
Time	Wages based on time worked	018
Piece-work	Wages based on outputs achieved	019
Bonus from cost	Efficiency bonus related to production-cost account	120–175
Welfare	Welfare expenses included in the production-cost account	014
Non-basic	Total wages less basic wages	017–013

Note: Basic wages equals time-wages, plus piece-work wages, plus bonus from cost, but excludes welfare.

incentive wage (see Table 4.1). The basic wage formally includes wage scales (time-rates or piece-rates) which are uniform across all firms, and a wage allowance, which is in part a general uprating for inflation, but mainly consists of supplements to the scales, to reflect working conditions and labour markets. The formal make-up of the wage is probably not of great significance: the key fact is that the basic wage is differentiated by industry and region. Although the differentials are supposed to be determined nationally, in practice the local Labour Bureau will use its discretion to introduce local variations.

It is convenient to include a further element in our definition of the basic wage. This is bonus payments for efficiency in production related to cost savings on the use of materials and energy, economizing on stocks and work in progress, and cost savings on fixed assets. The level of these bonus payments, which like wage-scale payments and allowances are included in the production-cost account of the firm, is strictly regulated by the Central Labour Bureau in Beijing. We also note that current expenditures on welfare are also included in the production account as a cost: the level of expenditure is strictly regulated. It is appropriate to treat this as being distinct from the money wages received by individual workers.

The incidence of different types of basic wage payments is indicated in Table 4.2. Virtually every firm pays at least some workers on a time-basis: about 52% pay bonuses related to cost savings and 31% operate piece-work rates for at least some of their workers. Cost-saving bonuses are apparently evenly spread across locations and industries, but piece-rate pay is clearly a particular feature of large cities and of the textile industry.

TABLE 4.2. Incidence of piecework wages and cost-saving bonuses by location and industries

		No. of observations				Total
		Cost-saving bonus	%	Piecework wages	%	
Location	1	104	46	106	46	226
	2	128	56	112	49	227
	3	73	54	32	23	135
	4	132	58	39	17	227
	5	55	70	7	8	78
Industry	1	22	51	10	23	43
	2	40	39	35	34	102
	3	43	43	47	50	98
	4	58	48	40	33	120
	5	15	40	4	11	37
	6	104	61	30	17	171
	7	106	57	54	29	184
	8	104	55	74	39	188

Notes: Location codes: 1, large coastal cities; 2, large inland cities; 3, medium and small coastal and/or economically advanced cities; 4, medium-sized inland cities; 5, small inland cities (see Ch. 3 for full listing).

Industry codes: 1, extractive; 2, food, drink, tobacco; 3, textiles etc.; 4, light industry and crafts; 5, energy; 6, chemicals, medicine etc.; 7, building materials and metals; 8, engineering and electrical.

The incentive or non-basic wage consists of the bonus (and other minor allowances), which is paid from retained profit. The firm can pay the equivalent of four months' basic wage as a bonus without attracting penalties. For higher payments, it is taxed on the additional bonus at an increasing marginal rate (30% tax for four to five months, 100% for five to six months, and 300% for bonus payments exceeding six months' basic salary).

Both basic wage and incentive wage payments are subject to a further constraint. The total wage bill of the firm must not exceed the plan quota approved by the local Labour Bureau. This specifies not only total wage payments, but also the level of payments for the production-cost account, and hence the total level of bonus payments from retained profits.

The objective of the constraint from the standpoint of national policy is to control aggregate wage payments, and thus the share of national income going to consumption. At the level of the firm it effectively limits the number of workers that the firm can employ:

given the quota of wages from the production-costs account, and the level of basic wages (scale payments and allowance), the maximum number of workers is determined.

The issue of how the plan quota of wages for each firm is arrived at is therefore of great importance. In practice, it is the outcome of negotiation between the enterprise and the labour bureau. The objectives of the two parties are reasonably clear. The labour bureau is concerned to allocate the wage quota between the enterprises without exceeding its total limit, and to meet employment targets. It will also be anxious to avoid too much inequality in wage payments between firms under its jurisdiction. 'Wage tension' (Kornai 1980: 401) arises when firms in the same locality pay different wages, leading to demands for improved wages from the lower paid, pressure from workers wishing to transfer, and/or poor labour morale among the lower paid. A successful enterprise will be reluctant to take on additional workers for which it has no use, but would like a large total wage quota to satisfy the aspirations of its workers, by paying larger bonuses. An enterprise which is performing badly is probably not greatly concerned about the outcome of negotiations over the wage quota. It knows that the soft budget constraint will enable it to pay at least the basic wages to its workers, and maybe some bonus as well. The deficit is met by subsidies. Walder (1987: 35) observes: 'even enterprises whose profit figures fall, or that run a temporary financial deficit are still entitled to four months' wage bonus if the losses are due to "objective factors" like price changes, rises in material costs, and changes in exchange rates or overseas markets.' If widespread, such practices will greatly weaken the effects of the incentive wage element as a stimulant to greater productive efficiency and performance in markets.

A further issue is how the wage quota, once agreed, is implemented. The system is that the local People's Bank will monitor the account of the firm for withdrawals to pay wages, and could, in principle, block excessive drawings. In practice, again, there are likely to be discussions involving the firm and the Labour Bureau in circumstances where a firm is making excessive withdrawals. So at the end of the financial year there may be discrepancies between the actual wage bill and the plan quota. However, these discrepancies should be understood as forecasting errors rather than wholesale breach of policy. The Labour Bureau is itself subject to monitoring, and the officials' careers may be adversely affected by failure to meet their aggregate targets.

In the light of this discussion, we may conclude that the degree to which the wage-quota policy is a real constraint on the firm depends on the commitment of the authorities to restrictive policy. At its weakest, the policy is a mixture of wage-fixing norms, and forecasts of labour costs. At its most rigorous, the firm would have little or no room for manœuvre on wages and employment. It is not easy to translate this description of the wage–employment system into a framework for analysis. The following should be regarded as illustrative, rather than definitive, in its attempt to capture the main features of the situation. We consider the behaviour of the firm in its demand for labour, and the role of the Labour Bureau in acting as a quasi-market for labour, reconciling supply and demand as far as it can, and putting a dampener on wage pressures. To illustrate the points, we consider the local labour market for a particular type of labour working in a particular industry.

We assume, conventionally, that the demand for labour by the firm is a decreasing function of the real wage. In Western economies, the explanation is that the rational cost-minimizing/profit-maximizing firm, operating in a competitive labour market, will hire labour up to the point where the value of the marginal product equals the real wage. In the Chinese context it is not appropriate to assume full economic rationality, though deviations from it are likely to be random, reflecting the impact of other considerations on the enterprise's demand for labour. For example, an output-maximizing firm will certainly demand more labour at any given wage rate, while a cautious management may reduce its demand for labour to reflect its fear that it will be difficult if not impossible to shed labour if the firm runs into financial difficulties. For these reasons we expect the residual variance of any demand-for-labour equation to be quite large reflecting other factors. We might also expect the residual variance to fall over time as the economic reform programme progressed, and greater rationality crept in.

The supply-of-labour situation is complicated. Those who are already state employees are allocated to specific firms, and cannot easily be removed. They are also guaranteed the basic wage. Typically then the labour bureau will be responsible for a fixed number of state employees with given skills in a given industry, the allocation of those employees across firms being relatively immutable. Flexibility in labour supply comes from new entrants to the labour force. The Labour Bureau controls the total number of new entrants to be taken on to the state payroll, and in principle new entrants are subject to a degree of direction by the Labour Bureau, if they are to become full state employees. In practice, the new entrants have some freedom to choose where they will work. Industries with poor working conditions and/or low wages will find it difficult to attract new workers. This is the primary reason for the differentials introduced by the wage allowances described above.

The control on the number of entrants is designed to protect the employment of local urban residents. The effect is often to restrict the local state labour supply, so that firms may face shortages of particular categories of workers, especially skilled workers. To some extent, the firm can circumvent the restriction by taking on contract workers, either school-leavers or migrants. These workers are not taken on to the state payroll, and only have employment protection for the period of their contract. While their employment has to be authorized by the labour bureau, and their wage payments have to come from the agreed wage quota, there is little doubt that in practice the employment of contract workers gives the firm a degree of flexibility.

We consider first a situation where there is an excess supply of state employees in a particular sector, so that each firm is also required to carry excess labour. The firm, given that excess labour cannot be easily shed, has two options. One is to shift its demand-for-labour curve via increased capacity, improved productivity, or marketing of its product (presumably non-plan outputs). The incentive is that gross profit will increase, and hence the ability to pay bonuses to the workers. The second option is to put the excess labour to work on activities which are distinct from the productive activities of the firm, e.g. contracts for services such as construction and maintenance of buildings, and outside the plan quotas. In the long run, the labour market will adjust by, for example, retirements, and the authorities may also reduce allowances relative to other employment. The alternative is a situation where there is excess demand for labour which is shared out between the firms. The firm may try to solve its problem by taking on contract workers, if the Labour Bureau will permit. In the market as a whole there will be pressure on the Bureau to allow the recruitment of more permanent workers, and, if the existing wage is too low to attract new entrants, to increase the wage.

It is apparent that the outcome in the labour markets will depend on the degree to which the plan-quota constraints on wages and wage bills impinge on the operations of the firm. Except in the unlikely circumstance that the bureau achieves equilibria in the local labour market via its administrative procedures, we must generally see the activities of the bureau as increasing wage-stickiness and inflexibility in labour supply, if the firms are indeed controlled by them. But if the formal framework is something which firms can easily circumvent, by direct negotiations with the Bureau, and by employment outside the plan quotas, then there is more scope for economic rationality to prevail. The impression is that the period of reform has seen a progressive weakening of the powers of the Bureau, and a downgrading of the plan. Firms have taken the opportunity afforded to adjust their employment and wages, given the incentive of being able to retain a part of the profits which result from more economic operations. With this interpretation, the plan quota for the wage bill of each enterprise is less a constraint on the operations of the firm, and more a forecast of wage costs agreed with the Bureau.

2.2 *A formal specification of the system*

Our main focus in this chapter is incentives for workers. Hence we are particularly interested in the determinants of wages and bonuses received by the workers, and the degree to which they reflect the circumstances of the firms. To explore this issue effectively, however, we need to consider the impact of the wage-bill constraint, and the effect of wage rates on the demand for labour by the firm. The complete wage–employment model includes behavioural equations for the following four elements at the level of the firm: employment, the basic wage rate, the bonus rate, and the wage bill or quota. The system takes output as given, but productivity is determined endogenously by the ratio of given output to the employment determined by the system. All the variables used in the subsequent sections are listed and defined in the note to Table 4.3.

1. The employment function

We will show, in Chapter 6, that the relations between productive inputs and outputs in the firm can be adequately described by the Cobb–Douglas production function:

$$V = AK^{\alpha}N^{\beta},$$

where V is output measured as value added, K is the capital stock, N is the labour force, and α and β respectively the output elasticities of capital and labour. If the firms optimize by setting the real wage $W = \partial V/\partial N$, the employment function is given by

$$N = \beta \frac{V}{W}, \tag{4.1}$$

that is, the demand for labour is related positively to the elasticity of output with respect to labour, the desired production (V), and inversely to the real wage.

TABLE 4.3. OLS tests of the equations in wage-employment model

Employment equation	Aggregate sample (OLS)	Disaggregated sample (OLS)			
		1984	1985	1986	1987
Intercept	−0.229 (−34.7)	−0.225 (−16.9)	−0.223 (−16.0)	−0.214 (−15.5)	−0.239 (−17.7)
$(v_t - w_t)$	0.477 (34.7)	0.469 (16.9)	0.464 (16.0)	0.446 (15.4)	0.499 (17.6)
y_t	0.649 (30.3)	0.669 (15.3)	0.662 (14.8)	0.699 (16.4)	0.623 (14.5)
ϕ_{t-1}	−0.963 (−5.1)	−0.600 (−1.4)	−0.419 (−1.1)	−0.708 (−1.8)	−1.164 (−3.4)
WSYS	−0.037 (−0.9)	0.066 (0.5)	−0.018 (−0.2)	−0.039 (−0.5)	−0.025 (−0.4)
YR85	0.073 (2.2)				
YR86	0.064 (2.0)				
YR87	0.041 (1.2)				
$\bar{R}^2$	0.84	0.83	0.84	0.83	0.84
F	723.6	356	362	352	366
N	847	212	212	209	211

Wage-bill equation	Aggregate sample (OLS)	Disaggregated sample (OLS)				Alternative specification*
		1984	1985	1986	1987	
Intercept	−0.880 (−7.2)	−1.328 (−6.0)	−0.639 (−1.9)	−0.462 (−1.3)	−0.235 (−0.8)	−0.802 (−6.8)
$(v_t - v_{t-1})$	0.164 (5.9)	0.134 (2.5)	0.264 (4.9)	0.109 (2.0)	0.166 (2.8)	0.134 (5.0)
n_{t-1}	1.019 (136)	1.034 (72)	1.032 (78)	1.015 (63)	0.994 (61)	1.019 (6.4)
$\bar{\phi}_{t-1}$	1.400 (8.4)	1.588 (4.6)	1.437 (4.6)	0.973 (2.9)	1.580 (4.4)	0.987 (10.4)
$(\phi_{t-1} - \bar{\phi}_{t-1})$	0.591 (5.6)	0.636 (2.7)	0.567 (2.9)	0.380 (1.7)	0.750 (3.6)	0.677 (18.0)
$\bar{w}_{t-1}$	0.667 (17)	0.546 (8.5)	0.813 (6.5)	0.775 (5.9)	0.867 (7.9)	0.692 (25.6)
$(w_{t-1} - \bar{w}_{t-1})$	0.541 (23)	0.465 (9.3)	0.514 (12)	0.489 (10.7)	0.656 (13.6)	0.563 (25.0)
YR85	−0.010 (−0.6)					0.011 (0.6)
YR86	0.071 (3.9)					0.082 (4.7)
YR87	0.017 (0.8)					0.027 (1.4)
$\bar{R}^2$	0.96	0.96	0.97	0.96	0.95	0.96
F	2347	946	1109	761	761	2558
N	847	212	212	209	211	847

TABLE 4.3 (*cont.*)

Bonus rate equation	Aggregate sample	Disaggregated sample			
		1984	1985	1986	1987
Intercept	0.175 (0.9)	0.949 (2.5)	−0.777 (−1.1)	1.374 (2.9)	0.382 (0.8)
q_t	0.157 (57)	0.051 (0.9)	0.183 (3.3)	0.158 (2.6)	0.152 (2.8)
$y_t - n_t$	0.646 (9.8)	0.938 (6.8)	0.744 (5.4)	0.726 (5.3)	0.399 (3.5)
b_{t-1}	0.467 (19.6)	0.441 (9.6)	0.433 (9.3)	0.512 (9.7)	0.611 (12.5)
$\bar{b}_t$	0.166 (3.6)	0.227 (3.5)	−0.069 (−0.4)	0.419 (3.6)	0.222 (1.8)
ind1	0.089 (1.5)	0.061 (0.5)	0.091 (0.7)	0.136 (1.1)	0.053 (0.5)
YR85	−0.116 (−3.5)				
$\bar{R}^2$	0.63	0.59	0.57	0.61	0.68
F	240	60.7	55.7	66.1	94.0
N	847	212	212	209	211

Basic-wage equation	Aggregate sample	Disaggregated sample			
		1984	1985	1986	1987
Intercept	−0.038 (−6.3)	−0.043 (−3.6)	−0.059 (−4.4)	−0.014 (−1.2)	−0.037 (−3.1)
q_t	0.079 (6.3)	0.090 (3.7)	0.124 (4.4)	0.029 (1.2)	0.077 (3.1)
w_{t-1}	0.653 (27.1)	0.712 (17.7)	0.531 (9.0)	0.629 (13.3)	0.676 (13.9)
$\bar{w}_{st}$	0.300 (17.0)	0.232 (5.7)	0.401 (6.6)	0.332 (6.9)	0.254 (5.0)
YR85	0.014 (0.7)				
YR86	0.052 (2.8)				
YR87	0.009 (0.3)				
$\bar{R}^2$	0.54	0.44	0.40	0.54	0.62
F	202.7	83.8	69.6	124.9	166.3
N	840	213	203	207	206

Note: q_t, which is labour productivity, is defined by $[v_t - n_t]$, where v_t is exogenous, and n_t endogenous.

NOTE TO TABLE 4.3. List of Variables

Variable	Brief definition	Corresponding code and calculation formula
Q_t	Real value added per worker	d011/[*idx**d030]
V_t	Real value added	d011/*idx*
N_t	Average number of workers concerned with production during a year	d030
W_t	Real basic wage rate	d013/[*idx**d030]
B_t	Real annual bonus rate	d020/[*idx**d030]
Y_t	Real annual wage bill of a firm	d017/*idx*
π	Real gross profits	
$\bar{B}_t$	Average bonus rate in a locality in year *t*	$\left[\left(\sum_i^n B_{ti}\right)\Big/ n\right]_k$ $i = 1, 2, \ldots n$ firms in a locality k
$\bar{W}_t$	Average basic wage rate in a locality in year *t*	$\left[\left(\sum_i^n W_{ti}\right)\Big/ n\right]_k$
$\bar{W}_{st}$	Average basic wage rate in a sector in year *t*	$\left[\left(\sum_j^m W_{tj}\right)\Big/ n\right]_S$ $j = 1, 2, \ldots n$ firms in a sector S
ϕ_t	Ratio of bonus to basic wage in year *t*	d020/d013
$\bar{\phi}_t$	Average ratio of bonus to basic wage in a locality	$\left(\sum_i^n \phi_{ti}\right)/n$
idx	A firm-level price index of output in terms of 1980 prices	$\frac{\text{d002}}{\text{d001}}$
WSYS	Dummy variable indicating internal wage system = 1, zero otherwise	q44
YR_t	Year dummy	
β	Elasticity of output with respect to labour	

Note: 'dxxx' is code number in the quantitative data-set; 'qxx' is code in the qualitative data-set.

This specification runs counter to the general argument advanced by Kornai (1980) that employment policy is determined outside the firm by the planners in a socialist economy, and the specific argument of Granick (1990) with respect to Chinese enterprises that the state labour bureau controls the size of the labour force. However, one of the objectives of economic reform has been to give the firms greater autonomy in deciding how much labour to recruit and retain. The 'Provisional Regulations on Extending further the Decision-Making Powers of the State Industrial Enterprise' stated that 'Directors have the right to employ workers on the basis of examinations under the guidance of the state labour-recruiting agencies. They also have the right to reject forced assignment from higher agencies or individuals' (*Beijing Review*, 11 and 18 June 1984). Furthermore the State Council issued new regulations to implement reform of the labour system for implementation in October 1986. These regulations covered (*a*) the labour contract system, (*b*) the dismissal of workers who had violated work rules, (*c*) recruitment of workers, and (*d*) insurance for the unemployed (Laaksonen 1988: 246). These reforms imply that, in principle, firms have a certain autonomy in employment decisions. The firm's managers can determine both an increase in employment and the length of new contracts. But, as noted above, their decisions are subject to approval by the local labour bureau which (*a*) controls the wage bill or quota and (*b*) arranges for new employees. So there is likely to be an element of bargaining between the firm and the bureau, and therefore some constraint on the freedom of the firms.

This discussion of the institutional background suggests that we should add variables reflecting the constraints placed on the firm by the policies of the labour bureau to the basic labour demand equation (4.1). It then becomes an empirical matter to what extent economic rationality determines employment rather than the constraints imposed by the labour bureau. The main constraint is undoubtedly the wage bill, the quota of payments that may be made to its workers by the firm within a specified period. This quota is the subject of fairly stringent control by the local labour bureau, which is in turn controlled by a wage quota, for all the firms under its control, imposed by a higher authority. If the wage rate is also fixed outside the firm (more on this below), then the firm's demand for labour is more or less given, once the wage bill is determined.

Does the firm therefore have no room for manœuvre? A firm is not allowed to use other funds, e.g. profit retentions, to hire more workers: the quota is a fixed amount, regardless of the sources of funds. It can only reduce its labour force by cutting the number of temporary workers, but this freedom does not extend to long-term workers. Effectively, then, if the firm wishes to change its employment, it either has to negotiate with the labour bureau for a change in its wage quota, or it has to alter the effective payment per worker. Whether the quota is in practice a constraint on the firm depends on how it is negotiated. But given that the aggregate wage quota is an important policy instrument for employment and aggregate consumption, it is unlikely that the outcome of negotiations with the labour bureau will be completely accommodating of what the firm would like to do.

On the level of payments to each worker, the firm has a bit more flexibility. With the development of the economic reforms, firms have been given more autonomy in distribution of the wage quota: wage differentials can be introduced via the 'incentive-wages' and 'position-wage' systems (Laaksonen 1988: 255–56), so long as the wage quota is not breached (Enterprise Management 1987). It has been suggested that some firms have been able to raise the bonus paid to active workers, by encouraging some long-term workers to take 'leave' on basic wages only. The part of the wage quota which was notionally allocated to pay their bonus of three months' wages is thereby released to pay more to the workers actually in work, who will naturally have to work harder.

All this suggests that the firm *will* have some limited control over employment, within the constraint imposed by the wage-bill quota (Y). We therefore amend equation (4.1) to:

$$N_t = \left(\beta \frac{V_t}{W_t + B_t}\right)^{a_1} Y_t^{a_2} e^{\Sigma a_t YR_t + u_t}.$$

We may rewrite $W_t + B_t$ as $W_t\left(1 + \frac{B_t}{W_t}\right) = W_t(1 + \phi)$ where ϕ is the bonus/wage ratio. In considering how much labour to employ, the firm takes into account not only the basic wage, but also the 'obligation' to pay a bonus equivalent to 3 or 4 months' salary. However, because the bonus is paid from retained profits, the firm will not be absolutely certain, in advance, what bonus level it will actually pay. It seems plausible that the expected bonus/wage ratio on which the firm bases its decisions is the ratio which applied *ex post facto* in the previous period. So we hypothesize that ϕ_{t-1} is the appropriate variable.

Taking natural logarithms, and recalling that $\ln(1 + x) \approx x$, we have:

$$n_t = a_0 + a_1(v_t - w_t) - a_1\phi_{t-1} + a_2 y_t + a_3 n_{t-1} + \sum_t a_t YR_t + u_t,$$

where $a_0 = a_1 \ln\beta$, the YR_t are year dummies (to pick up cyclical effects), and n_{t-1} is the lagged dependent variable (to pick up adjustment effects). Previous work suggested a value of β in the range 0.56–0.63: we adopted the value 0.61 for estimation purposes.

The negative sign on ϕ_{t-1} is worthy of additional comment. The obvious explanation is that a higher bonus/wage ratio, given both output and the basic wage, is a disincentive to employment. We should note that although the bonus rate is officially capped at the level of 4 months' wages, the bonus is not paid to workers who are sick or on leave. However these absent workers are included when the wage bill or quota is calculated, so their bonus allocation is available to pay more to workers at work.

2. *The bonus-rate function*

Bonuses are paid by the firm from retained profit; the determinants of the retention ratio were discussed in Chapter 4. The profit-related bonus (B) may therefore be specified as a fraction θ of gross profits per worker; gross profit is given by value added output minus basic wage costs:

$$\Pi = V - WN.$$

So

$$B = \theta\frac{\Pi}{N} = \theta\left(\frac{V}{N} - W\right). \tag{4.2}$$

Using (4.2), $W = \beta\frac{V}{N}$, or $W = \beta Q$ where Q is value added output per worker $\left(\frac{V}{N}\right)$, we have:

$$B = \theta(1 - \beta)\frac{V}{N}.$$

To this basic formulation we need to add the variables previously identified as significant in determining the bonus: the lagged bonus (B_{t-1}), the average bonus rate in the location, ($\bar{B}_t$), and the wage-bill quota per worker (Y_t/N_t) which acts as a constraint:

$$B_t = e^{b_0} Q_t^{b_1} B_{t-1}^{b_2} \bar{B}_t^{b_3} (Y_t/N_t)^{b_4} e^{u_t},$$

or, once again using lower-case symbols to indicate natural logarithms:

$$b_t = b_0 + b_1 q_t + b_2 b_{t-1} + b_3 \bar{b}_t + b_4(y_t - n_t) + u_t. \tag{4.3}$$

The coefficient b_3 on the local average bonus variable ($\bar{B}$) can be interpreted in two ways: (*a*) it may reflect the impact of policy decisions at either the national or local level to use bonus payments to create regional/local differentials in payments to workers reflecting local conditions in the labour market and differential efficiency; Granick (1990: 191) believes that a national policy of regional differentials has developed; or (*b*) it may reflect the desire of a firm not to be out-of-line on bonus payments with other employers in the same locality. To fall behind in bonus payments will create discontent in the work-force, loss of skilled workers to other enterprises (though formal mechanisms for this do not exist), and inability to recruit good new entrants to the labour force.

The wage-bill variable is included for the reasons adduced previously. If the wage-bill quota is truly a constraint on the behaviour of the firm, then the firm cannot pay a higher bonus to the workers, even if its profit position could justify it, unless it keeps within the predetermined quota. In practice, the quota will normally permit the payment of a bonus of four months' wages, and it is doubtful whether the firm would wish to pay more given the adverse tax consequences of so doing. Moreover, as noted above, if the quota is fixed by negotiation between the firm and the bureau, the firm may be able to obtain sufficient quota to avoid any effective constraints on its bonus behaviour.

3. *Determinants of the basic wage rate*

The neoclassical theory has the firm equating the real wage to the marginal product of labour to maximize profits. In a competitive labour market, or in a planned economy with fixed wages, the firm accepts the wage as given and adjusts employment. At the other extreme, one could imagine a situation in which employment is fixed, and the firm adjusts the real wage accordingly.

Basic wages include: (*a*) the standard wage which varies according to grades determined by skill, age, education, and responsibility of the worker; and (*b*) allowances and subsidies, which include payments to compensate workers for difficult working conditions, and features induced by policy changes.

There exist nationally determined rates for different grades of workers, including any special factors as in (*b*). These are the 'basic wage rates'. Any revision in these rates is promulgated by the authorities: it is not determined by the firm. However, the local labour bureau will be made aware of any difficulties faced by the firm, and it is therefore quite likely that local adjustments will be made. (For example, state-owned shipping companies have been forced to increase their seagoing allowance to ships' officers, because collectives and joint ventures are paying more to officers, who since the reforms have been allowed to resign from state-owned firms if they wished to move.)

The basic wage-rate function is therefore specified as follows:

$$W_t = (\beta Q_t)^{c_1} W_{t-1}^{c_2} \bar{W}_t^{c_3} e^{\Sigma c_t YR_t + u_t},$$

or in log-linear form

$$w_t = c_0 + c_1 q_t + c_2 w_{t-1} + c_3 \bar{w}_t + \sum_t c_t YR_t + u_t, \qquad (4.4)$$

where $c_0 = c_1 \ln \beta$, and β is taken to have the value 0.61 as before; $\bar{W}_t$ is the average wage rate in the locality in the sector to which the firm belongs; and YR_t are year dummies. The variable $\bar{W}_t$ reflects the average wage level set by the labour bureau for the local labour market, and may to some extent reflect supply conditions in the market. The lagged wage rate W_{t-1} is introduced not only to pick up wage inertia, but also to proxy for unobserved factors such as education and skill level of the labour force.

4. *The wage-bill quota*

The wage-bill quota is an instrument within the Chinese planned system to control the level of payments to workers, and hence to restrict aggregate consumption. It is determined, at the level of the firm, by an essentially bureaucratic process, involving negotiations between the firm and the labour bureau. As noted above, the bureau is itself allocated a quota, which it then distributes between the firms under its control.

We have no direct evidence on the bureaucratic process. Our hypothesis is that the starting-point in negotiations for each firm is the number of workers in the previous period, and the expected local average consumption (wage plus bonus) rate. This will then be adjusted for firm-specific factors, e.g. an increase in the labour force, or a rise in basic wages or bonus ratio to retain or motivate workers.

With Y standing for wage bill we may write more formally:

$$\begin{aligned} Y &= N(W + B) \\ &= NW(1 + \phi). \end{aligned}$$

In fixing the wage bill for period t, the firm and the bureau must agree on notional targets for N, W, and ϕ, which we will indicate by the superscript ε.

So $$Y_t = N^{\varepsilon} W^{\varepsilon} (1 + \phi^{\varepsilon}).$$

It remains to indicate how these target values might be arrived at. We consider each in turn:

$$N^{\varepsilon} = N_{t-1}^{g_2}\left(\frac{V_t}{V_{t-1}}\right)^{g_1}.$$

Expected demand for labour is determined by employment in the previous period adjusted by the planned growth rate of output (V_t/V_{t-1}). The assumption is that plans will be fulfilled, so that the realized V_t/V_{t-1} represents the prior expectation (subject to a random error).

$$W_t^{\varepsilon} = \bar{W}_{t-1}^{g_3}\left(\frac{W_{t-1}}{\bar{W}_{t-1}}\right)^{g_4}.$$

The expected wage is based on the previous average wage in the locality, adjusted by the wage differential previously enjoyed by the firm.

The third term is captured by

$$(1 + \phi_t^{\varepsilon}) = (1 + \bar{\phi}_{t-1})^{g_5}\left(\frac{1 + \phi_{t-1}}{1 + \bar{\phi}_{t-1}}\right)^{g_6},$$

where $\bar{\phi}$ is the average ratio of bonus to basic wage in the local labour market, which is the rate which will be applied in the absence of special factors affecting the firm. The second element picks up the special factors by assuming that differentials are carried over between periods.

The specification therefore becomes:

$$Y_t = \left(\frac{V_t}{V_{t-1}}\right)^{g_1} N_{t-1}^{g_2}\bar{W}_{t-1}^{g_3}\left(\frac{W_{t-1}}{\bar{W}_{t-1}}\right)^{g_4}(1 + \bar{\phi}_{t-1})^{g_5}\left(\frac{1 + \phi_{t-1}}{1 + \bar{\phi}_{t-1}}\right)^{g_6} e^{u_t},$$

or, in log-linear form with a constant and year dummies added,

$$y_t = g_0 + g_1(v_t - v_{t-1}) + g_2 n_{t-1} + g_3\bar{w}_{t-1} + g_4(w_{t-1} - \bar{w}_{t-1})$$

$$+ g_5(\bar{\phi}_{t-1}) + g_6(\phi_{t-1} - \bar{\phi}_{t-1}) + \sum_t g_t \cdot YR_t + u_t.$$

The expectation is that g_0 and the year dummies will pick up time-specific shocks arising from policy changes.

Putting together the above components the complete system is as follows (in log-linear form):

Employment

$$n_t = a_0 + a_1(v_t - w_t) - a_1\phi_{t-1} + a_2 y_t + a_3 n_{t-1} + \sum_t a_t YR_t + u_{nt}.$$

Bonus

$$b_t = b_0 + b_1(v_t - n_t) + b_2 b_{t-1} + b_3 \bar{b}_t + b_4(y_t - n_t) + u_{bt}.$$

Basic wage

$$w_t = c_0 + c_1(v_t - n_t) + c_2 w_{t-1} + c_3 \bar{w}_t + \sum_t c_t YR_t + u_{wt}.$$

Wage bill

$$y_t = g_0 + g_1(v_t - v_{t-1}) + g_2 n_{t-1} + g_3 \bar{w}_t + g_4(w_{t-1} - \bar{w}_{t-1})$$
$$+ g_5(\bar{\phi}_{t-1}) + g_6(\phi_{t-1} - \bar{\phi}_{t-1}) + \sum_t g_t YR_t + u_y.$$

To track the performance of the system, given that v_t is taken to be exogenous, we also calculated productivity, $q_t = v_t - n_t$, where n_t is endogenous.

The variable ϕ_{t-1} in the employment equation has a coefficient of about -0.81 when the equation is tested on its own. However, when the whole system is considered, it gives better results to replace it with the level of bonuses, lagged one period (b_{t-1}). In the bonus equation econometric considerations led us to replace the wage-bill variable by the growth of the wage bill.

The endogenous variables in the system are the dependent variables in each equation. The main exogenous variables are lagged dependent variables, average values for other firms in the same location (and sometimes the same sector), and value added output. The assumed exogeneity of value added needs further explanation. The justification is that the firm plans output in advance (the plan may be given to it): but we need the further assumption that these plans are always realized, and not constrained by either labour supply or labour efficiency. The assumption is probably correct in that most Chinese firms report that they have experienced no shortage of labour (except perhaps in some skilled categories).

2.3 Results and interpretation

Some 208 firms had the required data for the full five years, 1983–87. The initial year was 'lost' for estimation purposes by the inclusion of lagged variables in the system. The equations were run independently initially to filter out redundant variables and to obtain appropriate specifications. The results are given in Table 4.3.

Employment

The equation is well determined with the expected signs on the independent variables. The size of the coefficients is generally stable across all four years. In the aggregate sample equation, the year-dummy coefficients are significant, and presumably pick up the cyclical shocks which affected the firms. The coefficient on $(v_t - w_t)$ is between 0.45 and 0.50, whereas theory suggests that in long-run equilibrium the coefficient should be unity. The adjustment of employment to output and basic wage costs is not complete. The coefficient on the lagged bonus/wage ratio is −0.96 for the aggregate sample, and statistically well determined (but the size of the coefficient is not stable across the different years). The implication is that the firm is significantly more sensitive to the costs of paying bonuses than to basic wages in determining its employment. The firms view the bonus as a wage cost which the firm will have to find, at least when it is considering its employment decision *ex ante*. Finally, we note that the wage-bill variable is significant, and the coefficient suggests an elasticity of about 0.5: this is consistent with the wage bill being a constraint on the employment of the firm.

Basic wage

The equation includes three significant variables: productivity, the average wage in the industrial sector, and the lagged dependent variable. The coefficient on productivity is significant but quite small (0.08). The average wage in the sector has a coefficient of 0.3, and the lagged dependent variable 0.65. The implications are that there is substantial inertia in the basic wage paid by the firm, and adjustments are related more to sectoral wage adjustments outside the control of the firm than to the circumstances of the firm itself, e.g. productivity. Among the year dummies, only that for 1986 is significant: examination of the equation for 1986 alone reveals that in that year the productivity coefficient is smaller and not statistically significant. This suggests that the authorities permitted real wage increases in that year, not related to productivity improvements.

Bonus

In the equation, the link to productivity is stronger with a coefficient of 0.16 for the aggregate sample over all four years. The equations for separate years give weaker effects in 1984, but rather stronger ones in 1985. But in general, as might be expected given the institutional background, there is a link between bonus and current efficiency. The coefficient on lagged bonus is of the order of 0.47 (compared to 0.65 for basic wages), indicating substantial inertia. The coefficient of 0.17 (compared to 0.3 for basic wages) on local average bonus payments reflects the impact of local effects on the firms' behaviour, possibly the constraints imposed by the labour bureau to prevent bonus payments that might cause resentment in other local firms. Finally, we note that growth in the wage bill per worker has a significant and positive coefficient of about 0.65. The implication is that the wage-bill quota does act as a constraint in the payment of wages.

Wage bill

The equation fits the data well. The coefficient on previous-period employment is slightly greater than unity, suggesting that an allowance for growth is built into the system of fixing the wage bill generally. But the coefficient on the firms' own output growth is only 0.16 suggesting little adjustment to the expected growth of the individual firm. The coefficient on the previous-period bonus/wage ratio is 1.4, suggesting that an expectation of rapid growth in the bonus/wage ratio generally was built into the system. But once again the adjustment for special factors affecting the firm is less than complete (coefficient 0.59 on $(\phi_{t-1} - \bar{\phi}_{t-1})$). (However, if the firm-specific adjustment factor for the bonus/wage ratio is made current $(\phi_t - \bar{\phi}_t)$ instead of lagged one period $(\phi_{t-1} - \bar{\phi}_{t-1})$, then the coefficient is close to unity.) By contrast, the coefficient on average basic wages in the previous period is significantly less than unity (0.67), and so is the coefficient on the firm-specific factor (0.54). The implication is that the labour bureau is expecting the basic wage to be squeezed as the bonus/wage ratio rises, at least in their determination of the wage quota.

Table 4.4 gives the results for the simultaneous estimation of the equation system. The basic wage, the wage bill, employment, and the bonus rate are now endogenous.

Employment

In the equation the signs of the coefficients remain as expected, but there is some change in their respective magnitudes. Note that in this equation ϕ_{t-1} has been replaced by lagged bonus rate (b_{t-1}): the instability of the coefficient on ϕ_{t-1}, previously reported for the OLS equations, meant that it had to be abandoned in the simultaneous model. This change may account for the change in coefficient values. However, we note that employment is now less responsive to value added/wage, and more responsive to the wage-bill quota. The impli-

TABLE 4.4. Simultaneous tests of the wage-employment model

	Aggregate sample 2SLS AUTO1	Disaggregated sample (2SLS AUTO1)				Alternative specification* 2SLS AUTO1
		1984–85	1986–87	heavy	light	
Employment equation						
Intercept	−0.101	−0.109	−0.703	−0.089	−0.122	−0.099
$(v_t - w_t)$, end	0.211 (18.3)	0.228 (13.5)	0.223 (14.2)	0.186 (11.6)	0.255 (15.1)	0.206 (17.6)
y_t, end	0.818 (51.2)	0.812 (34.2)	0.808 (36.9)	0.870 (37.7)	0.740 (32.4)	0.826 (51.2)
b_{t-1}	−0.298 (−33.3)	−0.284 (−21.6)	−0.303 (−24.2)	−0.292 (−22.3)	−0.295 (−23.7)	−0.299 (−33.3)
WSYS	0.012 (0.5)	0.059 (1.2)	0.002 (0.1)	−0.031 (−0.9)	0.039 (0.9)	0.011 (0.4)
YR85	0.102 (4.4)			0.100 (2.9)	0.112 (3.2)	0.104 (4.4)
YR86	0.059 (2.6)			0.060 (1.8)	0.069 (2.0)	0.059 (2.5)
YR87	0.068 (2.9)			0.049 (2.6)	0.094 (2.6)	0.067 (2.9)
ρ	0.081 (2.3)	0.154 (3.2)	0.018 (0.4)	0.134 (2.8)	0.148 (2.9)	0.081 (2.4)
$\bar{R}^2$	0.93	0.93	0.93	0.92	0.92	0.96
DW	2.00	2.01	2.00	1.99	2.02	1.97
N	839	420	416	430	400	837
Bonus equation						
Intercept	−0.363 (1.8)	−0.069 (−0.2)	0.399 (0.1)	−0.763 (−2.5)	0.014 (0.1)	−0.244 (−1.1)
$(v_t - n_t)$, end	0.216 (7.2)	0.142 (3.3)	0.221 (5.0)	0.205 (5.5)	0.214 (4.7)	0.202 (6.7)
$(y_t - n_t)$, end	0.173 (1.7)	0.520 (3.1)	0.120 (0.9)	0.019 (0.1)	0.380 (2.8)	0.277 (2.6)
b_{t-1}	0.528 (19.9)	0.419 (12.1)	0.608 (15.7)	0.503 (13.4)	0.526 (13.8)	0.515 (19.3)
$\bar{b}_t$	0.219 (4.5)	0.239 (3.7)	0.385 (4.8)	0.244 (3.8)	0.207 (2.7)	0.208 (4.3)
YR85	−0.142 (−4.1)			−0.095 (−2.0)	−0.185 (−3.6)	−0.135 (−4.0)
indI	0.136 (2.2)	0.113 (1.3)	0.150 (1.8)			0.125 (2.1)
$\bar{R}^2$	0.61	0.54	0.64	0.53	0.66	0.62
DW	1.8	1.66	1.94	1.72	1.77	1.77
N	840	419	415	432	402	840

TABLE 4.4 (*cont.*)

	Aggregate sample 2SLS AUTO1	Disaggregated sample (2SLS AUTO1)				Alternative specification* 2SLS AUTO1
		1984–85	1986–87	heavy	light	
Wage-bill equation						
Intercept	−0.879 (−7.2)	−1.176 (−7.8)	−0.513 (−2.3)	−0.741 (−4.4)	−1.154 (−6.5)	−0.776 (−6.3)
$(v_t - v_{t-1})$	0.164 (5.9)	0.189 (5.0)	0.119 (3.0)	0.115 (2.9)	0.222 (5.9)	0.099 (3.4)
n_{t-1}	1.019 (136)	1.032 (106)	1.006 (87.5)	1.000 (94.5)	1.052 (95.2)	1.021 (135)
$\bar{\phi}_{t-1}$	1.395 (8.4)	1.504 (6.6)	1.120 (4.7)	1.112 (4.6)	1.629 (7.3)	0.801 (4.8)
$(\phi_{t-1} - \bar{\phi}_{t-1})$	0.589 (5.6)	0.597 (4.2)	0.591 (3.9)	0.599 (3.8)	0.599 (4.3)	1.332* (10.8)
$\bar{w}_{t-1}$	0.668 (17.3)	0.597 (13.1)	0.741 (9.2)	0.659 (12.2)	0.650 (11.8)	0.707 (18.0)
$(w_{t-1} - \bar{w}_{t-1})$	0.541 (23.6)	0.500 (16.0)	0.553 (16.6)	0.496 (14.9)	0.576 (18.5)	0.579 (24.7)
YR5	−0.009 (−0.5)			0.021 (0.8)	−0.048 (−2.0)	0.015 (0.9)
YR6	0.072 (3.9)			0.071 (2.8)	0.071 (2.8)	0.080 (4.4)
YR7	0.017 (0.9)			0.045 (1.6)	−0.009 (−0.3)	0.075 (1.3)
$\bar{R}^2$	0.96	0.96	0.95	0.96	0.96	0.96
DW	1.9	1.98	1.76	1.91	1.96	1.97
N	837	418	414	428	398	837
Basic-wage equation						
Intercept	−0.033	−0.044	−0.022	−0.025	−0.043	−0.033
$(v_t - n_t)$, end	0.069 (5.7)	0.091 (5.1)	0.046 (2.8)	0.053 (3.2)	0.089 (4.9)	0.069 (5.7)
w_{t-1}	0.672 (28.3)	0.659 (19.6)	0.686 (20.4)	0.669 (18.4)	0.682 (21.1)	0.672 (28.2)
$\bar{w}_{st}$	0.284 (11.6)	0.284 (8.4)	0.271 (8.0)	0.302 (8.3)	0.254 (7.5)	0.284 (11.6)
YR85	0.012 (0.6)			0.053 (2.0)	−0.036 (−1.3)	0.012 (0.6)
YR86	0.044 (2.4)			0.066 (2.6)	0.016 (0.6)	0.046 (2.4)
YR87	0.003 (0.2)			0.019 (0.8)	−0.019 (−0.6)	0.003 (0.1)
$\bar{R}^2$	0.57	0.44	0.60	0.57	0.57	0.57
DW	1.99	1.97	1.81	2.05	1.94	1.97
N	841	418	418	432	402	841

Notes: 2SLS AUTO1 = 2SLS plus first-order autoregressive correction (Pindyck and Rubinfeld, 1981: 377).
heavy = heavy sector of industries; light = light sector of industries.
ρ = indirect estimate of coefficient of n_{t-1} through Hildreth–Lu procedure (Maddala, 1988: 194–5).
end = variable is endogenous.

NOTE TO TABLE 4.4. The Hildreth–Lu Solution for Autocorrelation

Assuming the model is

$y_t = \alpha + \beta\chi_t + u_t$ where $u_t = \rho u_{t-1} + \varepsilon_t$, where ρ is the first-order autocorrelation:
lagging y_t and multiplying by ρ we get

$$\rho y_{t-1} = \rho\alpha + \rho\beta\chi_{t-1} + \rho u_{t-1}$$

$$\therefore \quad y_t - \rho y_{t-1} = \alpha - \rho\alpha + \beta\chi_t - \rho\beta\chi_{t-1} + u_t - \rho u_{t-1}$$

transforming

$$y_t - \rho y_{t-1} = y_t^*$$

$$\Rightarrow y_t^* = \alpha(1 - P) + \beta\chi_t^* + [u_t - \rho u_{t-1}]$$

$$\chi_t - \rho\chi_{t-1} = \chi_t.$$

Regressing y_t^* on χ_t^* gives $\hat{\beta}^*$ and $\hat{\alpha}^*$, which are unbiased estimates with elimination of autocorrelation ρ.
How to estimate ρ?

(1) Cochrane–Orcutt procedure [iterative procedure] (1949)

$$\rho \approx \hat{\rho} = \Sigma\hat{u}_t\hat{u}_t/\Sigma\hat{u}_t^2$$

i.e. regress y_t on y_{t-1}, χ_t and χ_{t-1} and take the estimated coefficient of y_{t-1} as ρ.

(2) Hildreth–Lu [grid-search procedure] (1960)

Calculate y_t^* and χ_t^*, based on $y_t^* = y_t - \rho y_{t-1}$ and $\chi_t^* = \chi_t - \rho\chi_t$, for different values of ρ at intervals of 0.1 in the range $-1 \leqslant \rho \leqslant 1$. Loop this calculation to obtain minimum of RSS (residual sum of square) of y_t^*regressed on χ_t^*.

Repeat this procedure for smaller intervals of ρ around this value to find minimum of the RSS.

cation of the coefficient in the latter is that a 1% increase in wage bill is taken up by a 0.82% increase in employment (the remainder appearing as increased bonus—see below). The coefficient on lagged bonus is stable at about −0.3. The autocorrelation coefficient, ρ, given by the Hildreth–Lu method, can be interpreted as the impact of lagged employment on current employment. The low value of this coefficient (<0.1) is surprising: one might have expected greater inertia in employment to show up in the equations.

Bonus

We note some substantial changes in this equation. The bonus is now more responsive to output per worker, but the coefficient on wage bill per worker is much smaller (0.17 compared to 0.65 previously) and not even statistically significant with the pooled data-set. The lagged-bonus level and the average bonus paid in the locality become slightly more important in determining the bonus.

Basic wage

This equation, by contrast, changes very little when set within the system, confirming the view that it is determined effectively outside the firm. So an increase in firm productivity only increases the basic wage with an elasticity of 0.1. The current wage is essentially the product of lagged wages and outside wages with coefficients 0.67 and 0.28 respectively.

Wage bill

This equation is essentially outside the simultaneous system, and is included in the system only because we expect error terms to be correlated across the equations. The coefficients, not surprisingly, remain close to those estimated with OLS.

The stability of the system was explored by splitting the sample in two ways: first by time-period (1984–85 and 1986–87) and second by type of industry (heavy/light). The coefficients are surprisingly stable across those subsamples: given the progress of the reform over this period, and the very different conditions in the two types of industry, more variation in coefficient values might have been expected. Furthermore, simulations of the model give very stable predictions for each of the endogenous variables, when applied to subsamples of the data.

A key question is whether the wage-bill quota is a predetermined constraint on the employment and bonus decisions of the firm. The system presented suggests that (*a*) the wage bill is adequately described by predetermined variables reflecting both average wages, bonus etc.

in the locality and the special features of the firm and (*b*) an increase in the wage bill leads the firm to increase both its employment and its bonus. There remains however a suspicion that this result may be misleading, and is giving greater significance to the wage-bill quota than it has in reality. Thus it might be argued that since the wage bill is fixed by a bureaucratic process, then if it begins to constrain the firm the process can be reopened, even during the year. This possibility will be reinforced if it is known that the bureau keeps back a part of its allocatable quota as a contingency for such additional calls. One approach to testing this possibility is to make the wage-bill equation at least partially endogenous, by introducing the current bonus/wage ratio in place of the lagged ratio. This is the basis for the 'alternative specification' in Table 4.4. The direct effect is to increase the weight given to the firm-specific bonus/wage ratio, and to decrease that of the (lagged) average ratio. The indirect effect is to increase the coefficient on wage-bill quota per worker in the bonus equation, but not that on the wage-bill quota in the employment equation. The rest of the system is more or less unchanged. These results are not entirely surprising—an estimate of the wage-bill quota which has the current bonus/wage ratio as one of its arguments is highly likely to be a more effective variable for predicting the actual bonus paid. A rather more powerful test is needed to determine whether the wage bill *is* a constraint. At best the results do not contradict that hypothesis.

The most surprising feature of the results is how well the standard neoclassical model seems to fit these firms, even though imperfect adjustment and/or lags are clearly evident. In respect of basic wages, the firm seems to have very little discretion over the rates paid which are quite sticky over time and tied quite closely to the average wage in the locality (presumably wage fixing by the bureau). Bonuses, on the other hand, are quite responsive to firms' efficiency, but probably within the constraints of the wage quota set by the bureau. Employment is sensitive to wage costs—more so to bonus than to basic wages—which is puzzling given the lack of autonomy in employment decisions that the Chinese state-owned firm is reported to have. The results are certainly consistent with the firms being able to control the size of their labour force, at least in the long run, and subject to the probable constraint of the wage-bill quota.

3. Wage Differentials within the Firm

Despite labour market reform and even attempts by some enterprises to pursue the so-called 'optimization of labour' approach (whereby each level in the enterprise selects the people it requires at the next level down, starting at the top) few enterprises appear to have had much discretion to reduce their labour force. Total wage payments on the other hand became much more discretionary as we have noted above, with local wage levels exhibiting some degree of flexibility, and bonuses related to measures of real or financial performance becoming a significant proportion of monthly incomes. Wage and bonus levels, and changes in them, remained constrained by numerous rules determining maxima in various categories but these, at least superficially, appeared to give considerable scope for managerial discretion to vary remuneration as between different types of employee and over time. It would be surprising therefore if we were not to find substantial changes in the pattern of wage differentials developing through time, as a function of the performance of different enterprises and of other characteristics.

This section first examines the data on the remuneration of different types of worker over the period 1980–87, both in absolute terms, and in relation to each other. It measures the extent of changes in differentials, both absolutely and as a ratio, and then explores the extent to which wage levels and differentials are or are not correlated with enterprise performance.

Table 4.5 shows the average wage for various groupings of em-

TABLE 4.5. Remuneration and change in remuneration of different groups of employees (10,000 yuan p.a.)

	1980	1983	1984	1985	1986	1987
Worker	0.083	0.084 4%	0.104 24%	0.117 15%	0.140 19%	0.161 17%
Technical staff	0.098	0.098 3%	0.118 24%	0.132 13%	0.155 19%	0.177 15%
Welfare staff	0.086	0.086 3%	0.103 22%	0.114 15%	0.133 19%	0.152 15%
Others	0.069	0.069 11%	0.080 34%	0.090 19%	0.106 29%	0.123 22%
Junior management staff	0.092	0.098 8%	0.115 23%	0.126 13%	0.147 18%	0.170 15%
Senior admin. staff	0.130	0.113 4%	0.124 14%	0.144 21%	0.168 17%	0.189 15%
Top manager	0.125	0.135 9%	0.145 9%	0.162 18%	0.188 17%	0.219 17%

ployees, 1980 and 1983–87. The data are taken only from enterprises where (*a*) the total wage-bill figure equals the sum of the component groups' wage bills, *and* (*b*) the figure for the total number of employees equals the sum of employees in component groups. Some extreme values are also deleted. Figures are yuan per month in nominal terms and under each is the percentage change from the previous year (except 1980).

Two main points emerge. First, the period 1980–83 sees relatively little change in nominal wages in any group, though there is a significant possibility that data for 1980 are based on 1983 data where 1980 figures are missing in enterprise records. In contrast there are increases typically from 70% to approaching 100% in the period 1983–87, with particularly strong rises in 1983–84. The increase in purchasing power will of course be considerably smaller but is likely to be very sizeable none the less. The second noticeable characteristic of the data is the relatively small changes in differentials over the period. Senior managers, including the top manager, clearly suffered a compression of differentials in 1984 but the shrinkage in the differentials does not continue after that date to any great extent. Some measures of the stability of differentials can be obtained from Table 4.6 which gives absolute differences and ratio differentials in wage per person as between various groups. In all categories apart from welfare workers and 'others', primarily ancillary staff such as cleaners, the ratio measures of wage differentials in these cases have become narrower, though the effect is not very strong after 1984. For welfare and

TABLE 4.6. Absolute wage differential between various groups and production workers (yuan per month)

	1980	1983	1984	1985	1986	1987
Technical	15	14	14	15	15	16
Welfare	3	2	−1	−3	−7	−9
Other	−14	−14	−24	−27	−34	−38
Junior managers	9	14	11	9	7	9
Senior managers	47	29	20	27	28	28
Top manager	42	51	41	45	48	58
Ratio of average wage of various groups to that of production workers						
Technical	1.28	1.17	1.13	1.13	1.11	1.10
Welfare	1.04	1.02	0.99	0.97	0.95	0.94
Other	0.83	0.82	0.77	0.77	0.76	0.76
Junior managers	1.11	1.17	1.11	1.08	1.05	1.05
Senior managers	1.57	1.36	1.19	1.23	1.20	1.17
Top manager	1.51	1.61	1.39	1.38	1.34	1.36

other workers the differential has increased as their ratios have fallen further below 1.

These basic figures are of some interest, even though they do not fit our initial expectations. First, it should be noted that the rather dramatic changes in 1983–84 are largely due to a substantial jump in the remuneration of production workers and junior managers, i.e. the main bulk of the work-force, not fully matched or subsequently attained by other groups. Possible explanations for this are reviewed below.

The second and more general finding is that, in a period of major decentralization and liberalization of decision-taking and, moreover, a period of very rapid change in enterprise performance and overall economic growth, differentials in wages changed very little and actually reduced in percentage terms for all groups except welfare workers and 'other' workers.

Three main factors are likely to be involved. First a centrally planned economy is unlikely to exhibit a set of wage levels which reflect marginal products. A switch to much greater enterprise autonomy on wages (but not on employment) might be expected to bring wage levels more into line with marginal products and, given a highly egalitarian distribution of wages to start with, we would expect this effect to increase differentials. That this has not happened suggests that this rather simple approach is not very appropriate.

A version of this however is more plausible. Reform of the market led to substantial increases in the marginal product of production workers, and decentralization of decision-taking permitted high wage rises to production workers in line with those increases. Similar, and perhaps larger, increases in marginal products were achieved by technical workers and managers but (*a*) these were inherently much less measurable and (*b*) given absolute shortages of both types of skilled employee—shortages which could not be alleviated through the payment of higher wages and the operation of the labour market—there was no profit-based incentive to try to match the higher marginal product of such employees and little to guide any attempt to do so. In this situation it would be unsurprising if wage increases to such groups were largely tied to the wage increases received by production workers, and this could account for the stability of the absolute differentials shown in Table 4.6.

The second factor relates to the use of greater managerial discretion. While one might have expected this to lead to an increase in the differentials between managers and workers, this has not in fact happened. In part this is due to restrictions on the bonuses payable at different levels and the need to link managerial bonuses to those paid to production workers in order to have a quantitative criterion for determining them. None the less the narrow differentials between managers and other workers (by Western standards) and the further compression of the absolute and percentage differentials in recent years is striking given the greater managerial autonomy introduced in the same period.

The third element concerns what might be termed the norms of fairness that arise from a particular social and cultural setting. For a long period of time, remuneration structures within Chinese enterprises have been highly egalitarian, and there are indications that individuals within an enterprise feel a strong sense of common identity irrespective of their position within the enterprise. While this might be partly a cultural characteristic it may also follow from the heavy dependence of all individuals in an enterprise and their families on the enterprise, not only for income but for many other services such as housing, education, and job security which are typically provided quite separately in Western economies. Such norms may have a powerful effect in determining the pattern of bonuses and increases in remuneration. In particular it may lead enterprises to pay general bonuses to all in the light of general performance rather than individual bonuses for individual effort; and it may be an important factor in explaining similar absolute increases in income over the period 1983–87, with the resulting tendency for percentage differentials to narrow.

So far we have been concerned merely to note the average pattern of differentials through time as between production workers and other types of worker, and possible explanations for some narrowing of differentials in a period of substantial liberalization of decision-taking concerning remuneration. We now go on to take a preliminary look at whether the differentials can be correlated in cross-sectional analysis with various performance characteristics of enterprises.

The basic procedure followed is to regress wage levels, absolute differentials, and percentage differentials for the different employment groups on profitability, growth, and productivity and various dummies to see if there are any significant relationships that might throw further light on the pattern of differentials observed. Tables 4.7, 4.8, and 4.9 give the results of this exercise. Table 4.7 regresses absolute total annual wage income per employee for seven different groups (manual, technician, senior technician, welfare, manager, senior manager, and top manager) on the return on capital employed, growth of sales revenue, and value added per worker, as well as industry and location dummies; and on three other dummies which indicate the degree of autonomy in wage-setting in the enterprise, whether the contract-responsibility or manager-responsibility system was operating, and whether the enterprise faced financial difficulty, as indicated by whether it had difficulty in repaying loans on time. In each case the wage is deflated by an index of prices set by the enterprise in question. This is because individual enterprises potentially face very different market conditions and have different opportunities to raise prices. To some extent nominal wage changes through time will reflect no more than the enterprise's ability to pass on these cost increases in the form of price rises. As we are interested in the extent, if any, to which wages respond to various measures of efficiency, independent of market conditions, we need to allow for the latter by deflating nominal wages by the price index of the enterprise's output which is available in the data-set. Table 4.8 repeats the analyses for the six absolute differentials with manual workers and Table 4.9 for percentage differentials. As we are here looking at wage differentials no price-index deflation is required.

Our main interest is in Tables 4.8 and 4.9, but we first look briefly at Table 4.7 to see what information it conveys. First, for all employee groups price-adjusted remuneration per employee is with but one exception positively and significantly related to all three enterprise performance measures. The exception being that senior-management remuneration is positively but not significantly associated with growth of sales revenue. The correlations with productivity are the most significant but given the way the variables are constructed this says little more than that the database is reasonably reliable.

Inspection of the dummies reveals that there are some significant industrial and locational variations in price-adjusted wages; that the latter have been rising exogenously since 1985; and that neither autonomy in wage-setting, type of responsibility system, nor existence of financial difficulty has any significant effect, though the signs as far as autonomy and financial difficulty are concerned are as expected (higher wages with more autonomy, lower wages where financial difficulty exists).

Turning to Tables 4.8 and 4.9 a number of interesting results emerge. First, higher productivity is associated with larger absolute wage differentials for technicians, senior managers, and the managing director and large negative differentials for welfare workers. Higher profitability is also associated with larger absolute wage differentials for management staff and the managing director. These however are

TABLE 4.7. General relation of wage payments to performance by different groups of employees (absolute levels)

		WWK	*WTT*	*WTM*	*WD*	*WWF*	*WST*	*WSM*	*WTL*
Intercept		0.117 (19.1)	0.117 (12.6)	0.117 (15.4)	0.168 (12.8)	0.107 (15.8)	0.2007 (13.5)	0.224 (10.8)	0.1201 (20.5)
FPK		0.011 (2.2)	0.014 (1.8)	0.017 (2.7)	0.032 (2.9)	0.0105 (1.8)	0.0238 (1.8)	0.034 (1.8)	0.0112 (2.2)
GRT		0.013 (2.8)	0.020 (2.7)	0.019 (3.2)	0.019 (1.9)	0.0166 (3.2)	0.0148 (1.2)	0.013 (0.8)	0.0182 (3.9)
VW		0.017 (8.6)	0.017 (5.7)	0.016 (6.3)	0.022 (5.3)	0.0132 (6.0)	0.0215 (4.2)	0.012 (1.7)	0.0191 (9.6)
Dummies									
FW	0	−0.006 (−1.9)	−0.005 (−0.9)	−0.004 (−0.9)	−0.015 (−2.0)	0.003 (0.8)	0.001 (0.1)	0.009 (0.9)	−0.0076 (−2.2)
	1	0.00	0.00	0.00	0.00	0.00	0.00	0.00	0.00
FTB	0	0.003 (0.9)	0.007 (1.2)	0.003 (0.6)	0.004 (0.5)	0.005 (1.3)	−0.005 (−0.6)	−0.006 (0.6)	0.004 (1.2)
	1	0.00	0.00	0.00	0.00	0.00	0.00	0.00	0.00
CF	1	−0.001 (−0.2)	0.002 (0.5)	0.005 (11.7)	0.002 (0.5)	0.0027 (1.1)	0.008 (1.5)	−0.0001 (−0.1)	0.002 (0.7)
	2	0.00	0.00	0.00	0.00	0.00	0.00	0.00	0.00
IND	1	0.001 (0.2)	−0.006 (−0.8)	−0.015 (−2.5)	−0.006 (−0.6)	−0.0047 (−0.9)	−0.0019 (−0.2)	−0.0148 (−0.9)	−0.0005 (−0.1)
	2	−0.025 (−6.1)	−0.019 (−3.0)	−0.033 (−6.3)	−0.046 (5.2)	−0.0349 (−7.5)	−0.0278 (−2.6)	−0.0173 (−1.1)	−0.0309 (−7.5)
	3	0.005 (1.2)	0.027 (4.3)	0.0186 (3.5)	0.006 (0.7)	0.0057 (1.3)	0.0216 (1.8)	0.0539 (3.2)	0.0037 (0.9)
	4	−0.014 (−3.7)	−0.008 (−1.4)	−0.173 (−3.6)	−0.007 (−0.9)	−0.0174 (−4.2)	−0.267 (−2.7)	−0.0296 (−2.1)	−0.0174 (−4.8)
	5	−0.026 (−4.3)	−0.021 (−2.2)	−0.025 (−3.4)	−0.011 (−0.9)	−0.256 (3.9)	−0.0431 (−2.5)	−0.0476 (−1.9)	−0.0281 (−4.8)
	6	0.004 (1.3)	0.015 (2.8)	0.004 (1.01)	0.011 (1.5)	0.004 (1.0)	−0.0117 (−1.3)	−0.0089 (−0.7)	0.003 (0.9)
	7	−0.011 (−3.4)	−0.001 (−0.1)	−0.013 (−3.1)	0.001 (0.1)	−0.010 (−2.8)	−0.0145 (−2.1)	−0.0082 (−0.8)	−0.0118 (−3.7)
	8	0.00	0.00	0.00	0.00	0.00	0.00	0.00	0.00
LOC	1	0.019 (4.3)	0.014 (2.1)	0.021 (3.8)	0.0168 (1.8)	0.0137 (2.8)	−0.0647 (−4.8)	−0.0632 (−3.3)	0.0173 (4.1)
	2	0.007 (1.8)	0.005 (0.8)	0.012 (3.4)	0.0267 (3.1)	0.0017 (0.4)	−0.0634 (−5.0)	−0.00619 (−3.5)	0.0061 (1.5)
	3	0.003 (0.7)	0.001 (0.1)	0.003 (0.5)	0.0096 (0.9)	−0.0004 (−0.1)	−0.0605 (−3.9)	−0.0705 (−3.2)	0.0067 (1.4)
	4	−0.001 (−0.1)	−0.005 (−0.7)	0.003 (0.6)	0.0108 (1.2)	−0.0017 (−0.4)	−0.0508 (−3.9)	−0.0606 (−3.3)	0.0001 (0.1)
	5	0.00	0.00	0.00	0.00	0.00	0.00	0.00	0.00
YR	*84*	−0.028 (−9.1)	−0.020 (−4.4)	−0.023 (−6.0)	−0.036 (−5.5)	−0.0237 (−6.8)	−0.025 (−3.4)	−0.0418 (−3.9)	−0.0280 (−9.3)
	85	−0.025 (−8.7)	−0.022 (−4.8)	−0.024 (−6.5)	−0.034 (−5.4)	−0.0208 (−6.4)	−0.026 (−3.7)	−0.038 (−3.8)	−0.0261 (−9.0)
	86	−0.010 (−3.6)	−0.005 (−1.2)	−0.009 (−2.4)	−0.015 (−2.4)	−0.008 (−2.6)	−0.0114 (−1.7)	−0.023 (−2.4)	−0.0102 (−3.6)
	87	0.00	0.00	0.00	0.00	0.00	0.00	0.00	0.00
R^2		0.35	0.21	0.29	0.19	0.27	0.26	0.19	0.39
N		755	755	755	755	755	317	317	755

TABLE 4.8. Relation of wage differentials to performance by different groups of employees (absolute differentials)

		DWTT	*DWTM*	*DWD*	*DWWF*	*DWSTT*	*DWSM*
Intercept		0.008 (0.9)	0.009 (1.2)	0.009 (0.5)	−0.0005 (−0.1)	0.0414 (3.2)	0.0306 (1.6)
FPK		−0.009 (−1.0)	0.0149 (2.1)	0.046 (2.9)	0.0094 (1.4)		
GRT		−0.001 (−0.2)	−0.0001 (−0.1)	−0.008 (−0.7)	0.0013 (0.3)	−0.0071 (−0.5)	0.0092 (0.4)
VW		0.016 (2.0)	−0.004 (−0.6)	0.049 (3.3)	−0.0142 (−2.2)	0.0004 (0.1)	0.0011 (0.1)
Dummies							
FW	0	−0.001 (−0.1)	−0.0044 (1.0)	−0.006 (−0.7)	0.005 (1.5)		
	1	0.00	0.00	0.00	0.00	0.0121 (1.9)	0.0178 (1.9)
FTB	0	0.002 (0.4)	−0.006 (−1.4)	−0.004 (−0.5)	−0.0001 (−0.1)	0.00	0.00
	1	0.00	0.00	0.00	0.00	−0.0111 (−1.4)	0.0007 (0.1)
CF	1	0.001 (0.2)	0.005 (2.1)	0.0003 (0.1)	0.0016 (0.7)	0.00	0.00
	2	0.00	0.00	0.00	0.00	0.0144 (3.1)	−0.0004 (−0.1)
IND	1	−0.007 (−1.0)	−0.014 (−2.7)	0.0128 (1.1)	−0.0082 (−1.6)	0.00	0.00
	2	−0.005 (−0.8)	−0.015 (−3.2)	−0.0178 (−1.6)	−0.0152 (−3.3)	−0.0236 (−2.6)	−0.0170 (−1.3)
	3	0.003 (0.5)	0.009 (2.2)	−0.0083 (−0.8)	0.0027 (0.6)	−0.0149 (−1.6)	0.0286 (2.1)
	4	−0.003 (0.7)	−0.002 (−0.4)	−0.0264 (2.9)	−0.0037 (−0.9)	0.0199 (2.1)	0.0054 (0.4)
	5	−0.011 (−0.9)	−0.003 (−0.3)	0.0514 (2.2)	−0.0028 (−0.3)	−0.0175 (−2.3)	−0.0121 (−1.1)
	6	0.006 (1.2)	−0.003 (−0.8)	0.0028 (0.3)	−0.0019 (−0.5)	−0.0256 (−3.1)	−0.0216 (−1.8)
	7	0.008 (1.8)	−0.001 (−0.1)	−0.0089 (1.1)	0.002 (0.6)	−0.0070 (−1.2)	−0.003 (−0.4)
	8	0.00	0.00	0.00	0.00	0.00	0.00
LOC	1	−0.0178 (−2.9)	−0.006 (−1.3)	−0.007 (−0.7)	−0.113 (−2.5)	−0.0483 (−4.6)	−0.0313 (−2.0)
	2	−0.0124 (−2.3)	0.001 (0.3)	0.028 (2.9)	−0.0054 (−1.3)	−0.0260 (−2.6)	−0.0085 (−0.6)
	3	−0.006 (−0.9)	−0.005 (−0.9)	−0.014 (−1.1)	0.0059 (−1.2)	0.0006 (0.1)	−0.0352 (−2.0)
	4	−0.008 (−1.4)	−0.001 (−0.3)	0.029 (2.9)	−0.0043 (−1.0)	−0.0124 (−1.1)	−0.0104 (−0.7)
	5	0.00	0.00	0.00	0.00	0.00	0.00
YR	*84*	0.009 (1.9)	0.002 (0.6)	−0.0105 (−1.3)	0.0037 (1.1)	−0.0006 (−1.0)	−0.01672 (−1.7)
	85	0.006 (1.4)	0.001 (0.3)	−0.0101 (−1.3)	0.0034 (1.1)	−0.0014 (−0.2)	−0.0101 (−1.1)
	86	0.005 (1.3)	−0.0001 (−0.1)	−0.0073 (−0.9)	0.0004 (0.2)	0.0011 (0.2)	−0.0073 (−0.8)
	87	0.00	0.00	0.00	0.00	0.00	0.00
R^2		0.05	0.07	0.11	0.06	0.27	0.13
N		743	743	743	743	299	299

TABLE 4.9. Relation of wage differentials to performance by different groups of employees (ratio differentials)

		RWTT	*RWTM*	*RWD*	*RWWF*	*RWST*	*RWSM*
Intercept		0.0692 (0.9)	0.116 (1.9)	0.242 (1.7)	−0.0286 (−0.5)	0.26887 (2.2)	0.1648 (1.0)
FPK		−0.1446 (−1.8)	0.0590 (1.0)	0.4835 (3.4)	0.0623 (1.1)	−0.0948 (−0.7)	0.2072 (1.1)
GRT		−0.0394 (−0.7)	−0.0581 (−1.3)	−0.0993 (−0.9)	0.0182 (0.4)	−0.0481 (0.4)	0.0728 (−0.6)
VW		0.0991 (1.4)	−0.0075 (−0.1)	0.1057 (0.8)	−0.0618 (−1.1)	0.0184 (0.2)	0.290 (1.9)
Dummies							
FW	0	−0.0094 (−0.2)	0.0367 (1.0)	−0.0884 (−1.1)	0.0529 (1.6)	0.1432 (2.5)	0.192 (2.4)
	1	0.00	0.00	0.00	0.00	0.0121 (1.9)	0.0178 (1.9)
FTB	0	0.0513 (1.1)	−0.0644 (−1.8)	−0.0902 (−1.1)	0.0206 (0.6)	−0.0798 (−1.1)	0.0144 (0.1)
	1	0.00	0.00	0.00	0.00	−0.0111 (−1.4)	0.0007 (0.1)
CF	1	0.0284 (1.1)	0.0481 (2.3)	−0.0114 (−0.2)	0.0101 (0.5)	0.1492 (3.4)	0.0390 (0.6)
	2	0.00	0.00	0.00	0.00	0.00	0.00
IND	1	0.0697 (−1.2)	−0.1129 (−2.5)	0.0691 (0.7)	−0.0637 (−1.5)	−0.2715 (−3.3)	−0.1584 (−1.4)
	2	−0.0338 (−0.6)	−0.1016 (−2.5)	−0.0403 (−0.4)	−0.1354 (−3.5)	−0.0354 (−0.4)	−0.3374 (2.8)
	3	0.0132 (0.3)	0.0412 (1.1)	−0.1076 (−1.2)	−0.0011 (−0.1)	−0.1942 (2.2)	0.0861 (0.7)
	4	0.0731 (1.6)	−0.01541 (−0.4)	0.1661 (2.1)	−0.0323 (−1.0)	−0.0784 (−1.1)	−0.0328 (−0.3)
	5	−0.1008 (−0.9)	−0.0107 (−0.1)	0.709 (3.5)	−0.0574 (−0.7)	−0.2314 (−3.1)	−0.2035 (−1.9)
	6	0.0688 (1.6)	−0.0102 (−0.3)	0.081 (1.0)	−0.0178 (−0.5)	−0.0467 (−0.8)	−0.0576 (0.7)
	7	0.0635 (1.6)	0.0138 (0.5)	0.1192 (1.7)	0.0221 (0.8)	0.00	0.00
	8	0.00	0.00	0.00	0.00	−0.3997 (−3.9)	−0.2698 (−2.0)
LOC	1	−0.1703 (−3.3)	−0.0918 (−2.3)	−0.057 (−0.6)	−0.103 (−2.7)	−0.1495 (−1.6)	−0.0141 (−0.1)
	2	−0.1284 (−2.7)	−0.0192 (−0.5)	0.191 (2.3)	−0.0418 (−1.2)	0.1305 (1.2)	−0.1996 (−1.3)
	3	−0.0569 (−1.0)	−0.0632 (−1.4)	−0.087 (−0.9)	−0.0471 (−1.1)	−0.0474 (0.5)	−0.1996 (−1.3)
	4	−0.0635 (−1.3)	−0.0603 (−1.6)	0.286 (3.3)	−0.0651 (−1.8)	0.00	0.00
	5	0.00	0.00	0.00	0.00	−0.0455 (−0.8)	−0.140 (−1.7)
YR	*84*	0.0798 (2.1)	0.0291 (0.9)	0.003 (0.4)	0.0163 (0.6)	0.0404 (0.7)	−0.0123 (−0.1)
	85	0.0915 (2.4)	0.0382 (1.3)	0.004 (0.07)	0.0352 (1.3)	0.0265 (0.5)	−0.0469 (−0.6)
	86	0.0648 (1.8)	0.004 (0.1)	−0.0189 (−0.3)	0.008 (0.3)	0.00	0.00
	87	0.00	0.00	0.00	0.00		
R^2		0.06	0.06	0.10	0.06	0.29	0.13
N		725	725	725	725	291	291

Notes to Tables 4.7–4.9: Definition of variables

Variable	Definition	Formula
Dependent variables		
WWK	Total annual wage-income per annual worker. Wages are deflated by a price index of output on a firm basis.	d021/(d036 *idx*)
WTT	Total annual wage-income per technician. Wages are deflated by a price index of output on a firm basis.	d022/(d039 *idx*)
WTM	Total annual wage-income per management staff. Wages are deflated by a price index of output on a firm basis.	d024/(d041 *idx*)
WD	Total annual wage-income of top director or top manager of a firm. Wages are deflated by a price index of output on a firm basis.	d026/*idx*
WWF	Total annual wage-income per welfare staff such as cooks, doctors, etc. Wages are deflated by a price index of output on a firm basis.	d027/(d043 *idx*)
WST	Total annual wage-income per senior technician. Wages are deflated by a price index of output on a firm basis.	d023/(d040 *idx*)
WSM	Total annual wage-income per senior management staff. Wages are deflated by a price index of output on a firm basis.	d025/(d042 *idx*)
DWTT	Differential between wage per technician and wage per worker.	
DWTM	Differential between wage per management staff and wage per worker.	
DWD	Differential between wage of director and wage per worker.	
DWWF	Differential between wage per welfare staff and wage per worker.	
DWSM	Differential between wage per senior management staff and wage per worker.	

RWTT	Wage differential ratio of technician against worker.
RWTM	Wage differential ratio of management staff against worker.
RWD	Wage differential ratio of director against worker.
RWWF	Wage differential ratio of senior technician against worker.
RWSM	Wage differential ratio of senior management staff against worker.
Independent variables	
FPK	fulfilled profit/capital stock.
GRT	growth rate of sale revenue.
VW	value added per worker.
Dummies	
FW	0 – less autonomy relating to wage distribution of firm.
	1 – greater autonomy relating to wage distribution of a firm.
FTB	0 – no financial trouble concerning repayment of loans.
	1 – financial trouble concerning repayment of loans.
CF	1 Contract-responsibility system
	2 Manager-responsibility system
Industry dummies	
1	Extractive
2	Food and drink
3	Textiles
4	Light and craft
5	Energy
6	Chemical
7	Building materials
8	Engineering
Locational dummies	
1	large coastal cities
2	large inland cities
3	medium coastal cities
4	medium inland cities
5	small cities

the only statistically significant links between wage differentials and performance.

Second, wage differentials are almost entirely unrelated to contract form, financial difficulty, or degree of autonomy in wage-setting. There are indications that management and senior technicians' differentials are higher under the contract system and senior technician and senior-management differentials are higher where there is *less* autonomy over wage payments but that is all. Few industry dummies are significant, but rather more locational dummies are, suggesting in particular that large coastal cities and to a lesser extent, large inland cities exhibit *smaller* differentials than small cities, except for the managing directors of enterprises where large and medium-sized inland cities see larger differentials.

Third, almost all the year dummies are significant, though it is interesting to note that, whether positive or negative, the size of each differential tends steadily to reduce through the period 1984–87. $\bar{R}^2$ are, unsurprisingly, low except perhaps for senior technicians' differentials where almost all industry dummies are significant.

Table 4.9 showing the results of regressions for percentage differentials throws very little if any extra light on the picture. Fewer variables and dummies are significant, though where they are they confirm the results of Table 4.8. The perverse (negative) correlation between technician differential and profitability which is insignificant in Table 4.8 now becomes significant. Correlation coefficients are again generally very low.

Overall three observations may be made. First, there are some signs that absolute differentials for some groups are higher in more efficient enterprises. Though this could be an indication that bigger differentials provide bigger incentives, which in turn improve performance, we shall argue below that this is not the most likely explanation. Second, taking the descriptive results at the beginning of this section together with the regression results, it seems highly likely that increases in wages and bonuses are largely decided in terms of absolute yuan increases rather than percentage increases and, for the most part, are applied in a fairly collective fashion. A good year financially tends to result in most employees being paid a certain number of yuan more rather than percentage increases for all or different increases for different groups. Technicians and managers, in particular the managing director, may do somewhat better than this but to only a very limited extent.

Third, what evidence there is suggests that the growing autonomy of decision-taking by enterprises in the period was not associated with significantly higher-percentage wage differentials but, if anything, lower ones. This is consistent with the pattern of annual dummies and those on wage-setting autonomy.

A tendency towards similar absolute increases across groups of employees and the use of discretion towards narrower percentage differentials improve performance. But it is probably more plausible to see the causality the other way round. Where performance is particularly strong, and most if not all employee groups have received wage and/or bonus increases as a result, there may be some scope for more specific bonuses to particular senior groups in a manner not thought appropriate in cases where general improvements in remuneration have been much smaller. The desire for higher remuneration may still act as an incentive to better performance on the part of the enterprise as a whole but this would largely be a collective incentive rather than individual. It is also possible that some workers are partly paid by piece-rates, creating some differentials *within* an employees' group, but with remuneration of other groups explicitly or implicitly linked to the remuneration of the group containing the piece-rate workers as a whole.

Collective incentives are typically thought in the West to face the free-rider problem of shirking, but this, as is well known, depends in part on monitoring systems and may to some extent be culture-specific, depending as it does on norms of social behaviour and trust. These in turn depend on nature of the organization concerned as a social entity, which is not unalterable but may be rooted in the industry and culture of society as a whole. The broadest notions of responsibility—to whom and for what—are involved and to some extent reflect ownership patterns and their perceived legitimacy. How substantial changes in the perceived responsibilities of Chinese enterprise and how changes in ownership would alter matters are issues which need to be addressed. It appears that the reforms of recent years while being associated with substantial improvements in enterprise performance have so far been associated with slightly more egalitarian wage distributions within enterprises than before.

4. Conclusions

The focus of this chapter has been on incentives for workers in Chinese enterprises during the reform period, and particularly on basic wages, bonuses, and wage differentials. A key feature of the wage-employment system is the role played by the labour bureau in transmitting national wage policy, and in controlling the wage bill of the firm via the quota system. An important question is the degree of control exercised by the bureau, given that the fixing of the wage bill is the outcome of a negotiation between the firm and the bureau. At one extreme, the bureau might be able to control every aspect of the firm's employment and wage policy: at the other, the wage-bill quota might be no more than a forecast of wage costs supplied by the firm and ratified by the bureau.

To sort out this interaction, the employment, wage, and bonus behaviour of the firm was modelled in Sections 2 and 3. The basic framework adopted was the neoclassical theory of production and labour demand: somewhat to our surprise, we found that this fitted the data reasonably well. Our econometric results indicate that basic wages continued during the reform period to be set primarily outside the firm with reference to national and local norms, and that the wage bill is largely determined by rule of thumb with only partial allowance for the conditions within the firm. As expected, the bonus paid by the firms is quite strongly linked to productivity (and hence the profitability) of the firm. The wage bill is apparently a constraint on the firm with a 1% increase in wage bill giving rise to a 0.8% increase in employment and a 0.2% increase in bonus. The result also indicates that employment is quite responsive to the level of bonus paid, but not to the basic wage. The explanation is more probably to be sought in the wage-bill constraint than in any cost-minimizing behaviour by the firm: that is, a higher bonus inevitably involves lower employment given the wage bill. Our conclusion is that, while the labour bureau continued to exercise a strong influence, especially via the national wages policy and the wage-bill quota, firms made full use of the new freedom to pay bonuses with the result that higher productivity was rewarded. In Chapter 7, we will examine the feedback from bonus to productive efficiency. The wage-bill quota had its effect via the implied trade-off between employment and higher bonus.

In Section 4 wage differentials within the firm were examined. Our main finding is that despite the greater discretion given to firms to determine the allocation of labour within the enterprise, differentials narrowed over the reform period. One explanation offered is that increased productivity of production workers was easily identified and rewarded by the management of the enterprise, whereas the higher productivity of non-production workers could not be so identified. A further explanation is the strong egalitarian tradition in the state-owned sector, leading to payment of the same absolute level of bonus to all participants in the enterprise.

5

Productive Efficiency and Costs

1. Introduction

A major objective of the economic reform programme as it affected state-owned enterprises was to improve productive efficiency. The policy measures adopted as a means to this end were described in Part I. They included a reduction in the role of the plan, giving enterprises greater autonomy in making decisions; an increase in enterprise incentives, especially increased profit retention; and the introduction of incentives for workers, most notably the payment of profit-related bonuses. In this chapter we evaluate the impact of these reforms, by examining the productive efficiency of the sample of state-owned firms, the changes in their efficiency over time, and the impact on costs. The evaluation is conducted largely within the framework of the Cobb–Douglas production function: experimentation with more sophisticated specifications did not give better econometric results, and the Cobb–Douglas form has the particular virtue of giving rise to straightforward interpretations of the parameters of the function.

2. Productive Efficiency

2.1 Specification of the production function model

Our approach is to employ a production function, e.g. a Cobb–Douglas function or a CES function, to describe the production behaviour of the enterprises under investigation. In estimating a production function, we have the following objectives in mind:

(*a*) *To investigate the changes of productive efficiency over time.* There have been widespread criticisms that state-owned enterprises have been very inefficient in absorbing capital and new technology. Expansion of industrial output has relied heavily on investment and labour inputs rather than on technical progress. The reforms introduced in the 1980s aimed to increase productive efficiency and to improve technical progress. Whether the objective of the reforms has been achieved may be verified by estimating a production function and examining the change of technical coefficients over time. The Chinese media publish an efficiency indicator by quoting the annual growth of output per worker and ignore the effect of capital. Using a production function to include the combined effect of capital and labour inputs, we will be able to assess the changes of productivity over time on a much more accurate basis.

(*b*) *To investigate the impact of incentives, such as bonuses, piece-work wages, and welfare support on labour efficiency*. One major feature of the Chinese industrial reform was the introduction of retained profit for the enterprise and bonuses for the labour force. The hypothesis is that retained profit and bonuses may increase the incentives of the enterprises and workers and thereby increase total productivity. Since bonus payments for the workers are directly linked to retained profit for the enterprise, we only incorporated bonus to workers as an explanatory variable in the production function. Another change in the enterprise-remuneration system was the introduction of an internal wage system dominated by piece-work wages. As was seen in Chapter 2 about one-third of the enterprises in the database introduced piece-work wages, so a variable representing piece-work wages is incorporated in the function. Welfare expenditures may also be an incentive element for the labour force, but since they are given almost equally to all workers and are not associated directly with individual performance, they may not have had any positive impact on efficiency. To examine this argument, welfare is incorporated into the function.

Two types of production function were estimated, the Cobb–Douglas (CD) function, and a CES function by the Kmenta approximation approach. Since the estimated results from using a CD function are consistent with our database, and since the estimated results from the CES function do not show much significant difference from the results of the CD function, attention is focused on the results generated by the CD function.

(A) CD functions

Suppose total production in terms of real value added of the firm is a function of the net assets or capital stock, the average number of workers, and the quality of workers in the firm, and assume the basic production function takes a CD form, then:

$$V = A_0 A_j A_t A_r K^{\alpha} N^{\beta} Z_0^{\theta_0} Z_1^{\theta_1} Z_2^{\theta_2} Z_3^{\theta_3}, \tag{5.1}$$

where V = value added deflated by a product price index IDX;

$A_0 = e^{a_0}$ is a firm-specific constant term, indicating the total input productivity on a firm basis;

$A_j = e^{a_j ID_j}$ ID_j are industrial dummies $j = 1, 2, \ldots, 8$, indicating eight individual sectors;

$A_t = e^{a_t YR_t}$ YR_t are year dummies, $t = 1, 2, \ldots, 6$, i.e. 1980 ($t = 1$), 1983 ($t = 2$) . . . , and 1987 ($t = 6$);

$A_r = e^{a_r LC_r}$ LC_r are location dummies, $r = 1, 2, \ldots, 5$, indicating five locations;

K = total capital stock in terms of real net assets in each firm;

N = total average number of workers during the corresponding year;

Z_0 = the ratio of workers with higher education and senior middle schooling to the total number of workers in each firm (a measure of labour quality);

Z_1 = share of piece-work wages in total wages which include basic wages, bonus, and welfare;

Z_2 = share of bonus in total wages;

Z_3 = share of welfare in total wages;

α, β, θ_0, θ_1, θ_2, and θ_3 are respectively the coefficients of capital, labour, labour quality, and wage-incentive elements.

If we divide V and K by N, equation (5.1) can be written as:

$$Q = A_0 A_j A_t A_r (K/N)^{\alpha} N^{\psi} Z_0^{\theta_0} Z_1^{\theta_1} Z_2^{\theta_2} Z_3^{\theta_3} e^{\varepsilon}, \tag{5.2}$$

where Q = V/N = value added per worker,
K/N = capital per worker,
ψ = $\alpha + \beta - 1$.

Taking logarithms this gives (where lower-case symbols indicate natural logarithms):

$$q = a_0 + \sum_j a_j ID_j + \sum_t a_t YR_t + \sum_r a_r LC_r + \alpha(k - n) + \psi n + \theta_0 z_0 + \theta_1 z_1 + \theta_2 z_2 + \theta_3 z_3 + \varepsilon. \tag{5.3}$$

There are three types of elasticities embodied in equation (5.3): (*a*) elasticities of output with respect to particular inputs, including α, the elasticity for capital, and β, the elasticity for labour; (*b*) the elasticity of scale ($\gamma = \alpha + \beta$) (in equation (5.3) $\gamma = \psi + 1$), or the elasticity of output with respect to a proportional change in all inputs; and, (*c*) the elasticity of substitution (σ) between labour and capital. In the two-inputs case, the elasticity of substitution is defined as follows:

$$\sigma = \frac{\frac{x_2}{x_1} \mathrm{d}\left(\frac{x_1}{x_2}\right)}{\frac{f_2}{f_1} \mathrm{d}\left(\frac{f_1}{f_2}\right)} \quad \text{(with output constant),}$$

where $f_i = \mathrm{d}f/\mathrm{d}x_i$, is the marginal productivity of the *i*th factor. The elasticity of substitution gives the percentage change in, say, the ratio of capital to labour in response to a 1% change in the marginal rate of substitution between them, holding output constant. By imposing a CD function, we implicitly assume that the elasticity of substitution (σ) is unity and this assumption may be untrue. To test whether such a restrictive form is appropriate, a CES function is also estimated (see below).

The data-set in the present study covers some 386 state-owned manufacturing enterprises in six different years, 1980, 1983–87, distributed among eight different sectors. (No data were available for 1981–82.) Since the degree of capital intensity and the level of technologies may well vary across different industrial sectors, firms in different sectors may have different values for coefficients α and β, i.e. the elasticity of capital and the elasticity of labour input. Although such a hypothesis can be tested by estimating equation (5.3) sector by sector, it is worth while to estimate the same equation by using all the pooled data but allowing α and β to vary across industries. We incorporate this idea by introducing sectoral dummy variables in α and β; they may be expressed as follows:

$$\alpha = \alpha_0 + \Sigma\alpha_j ID_j \quad j = 1, \ldots, 8 \tag{5.4}$$
$$\beta = \beta_0 + \Sigma\beta_j ID_j \quad j = 1, \ldots, 8 \tag{5.5}$$

where α_0 and β_0 are constant elements for α and β respectively. α_j and β_j are supplementary coefficients representing the differences of capital and labour elasticities in a particular industrial sector j from the common terms of elasticities α_0 and β_0. ID_j ($j = 1, \ldots, 8$) are sectoral dummy variables.

If (5.4) and (5.5) are incorporated into equation (5.3), then:

$$q = a + \alpha_0(k - n) + \Sigma\alpha_j ID_j(k - n) + \psi_0 n + \Sigma(\alpha_j + \beta_j)ID_j n + \theta_0 z_0 + \theta_1 z_1 + \theta_2 z_2 + \theta_3 z_3 + \phi,$$

or

$$q = a + \alpha_0(k - n) + \Sigma\alpha_j k_j + \psi_0 n + \Sigma\beta_j n_j + \theta_0 z_0 + \theta_1 z_1 + \theta_2 z_2 + \theta_3 z_3 + \phi. \tag{5.6}$$

where $k_j = ID_j((k - n) + n)$,
$n_j = ID_j n$,
$\psi_0 = \alpha_0 + \beta_0 - 1$,
$a = a_0 + \sum_j a_j ID_j + \sum_t a_t YR_t + \sum_\gamma a_r LC_r$.

If equation (5.6) is estimated to obtain unbiased estimates of α_0, α_j, h_0, β_0, and β_j, then the three types of elasticities can be calculated as follows:

(i) Scale elasticity ε_j for all j:

$$\hat{\varepsilon}_j = \hat{\psi}_0 + 1 = \hat{\beta}_j + \hat{\alpha}_j, \text{ for all } j.$$

(ii) Elasticities of different inputs:

Capital elasticity: $\hat{\alpha}_j = \hat{\alpha}_0 + \hat{\alpha}_j$
Labour elasticity: $\hat{\beta}_j = \hat{\beta}_0 + \hat{\beta}_j$

(iii) Elasticity of substitution $\sigma = 1$.

(B) A combined CD and CES function

To test whether the CD function is appropriate for the data, a combined function form of CES and CD function is introduced as follows:

$$V = e^a Z_0^{\theta_0} Z_1^{\theta_1} Z_2^{\theta_2} Z_3^{\theta_3} [\delta K^{-\rho} + (1 - \delta) N^{-\rho}]^{-\mu/\rho}, \tag{5.7}$$

where K, N, and Z_0 are capital, labour, and labour quality, and V is real value added; a is defined in equation (5.6); Z_1 to Z_3 are incentive elements.

If V and K are divided by N, we obtain:

$$Q = e^a Z_0^{\theta_0} Z_1^{\theta_1} Z_2^{\theta_2} Z_3^{\theta_3} N^{\psi} [\delta + (1 - \delta)(K/N)^{-\rho}]^{-\mu/\rho}, \tag{5.8}$$

where $\psi = \mu - 1$ and $Q = V/N$.

Since the mixed CD and CES function cannot be transformed to a function linear in the parameters and is therefore rather inconvenient to estimate, it is usual to substitute an approximation based on a Taylor series expansion of the logarithm of the function around $\rho = 0$ (this approximation is due to Kmenta (1967) and was implied by Griliches (1971)). Taking the logarithm of equation (5.8) we get:

$$q = a + \theta_0 z_0 + \theta_1 z_1 + \theta_2 z_2 + \theta_3 z_3 + \psi n - (\mu/\rho) f(\rho), \tag{5.9}$$

where q, z_0 to z_3, $(k - n)$, n and a are defined in equation (5.6) and $f(\rho) = \ln[\delta + (1 - \delta)(K/N)^{-\rho}]$.

Expanding $f(\rho)$ around the value $\rho = 0$ and excluding terms of third order and higher we have the approximation:

$$f(\rho) \simeq f(0) + f'(0)\rho + \tfrac{1}{2}f''(0)\rho^2, \tag{5.10}$$

where $f(0) = 0$; $f'(0) = -(1-\delta)(k-n)$;
and $f''(0) = \delta(1-\delta)(k-n)^2$.

Hence:

$$f(\rho) \simeq -\rho(1-\delta)(k-n) + \tfrac{1}{2}\rho^2\delta(1-\delta)(k-n)^2. \tag{5.11}$$

Combining (5.11) with (5.9) we obtain

$$q = a + \theta_0 z_0 + \theta_1 z_1 + \theta_2 z_2 + \theta_3 z_3 + \psi n + \psi_1(k-n) + \psi_2(k-n)^2, \tag{5.12}$$

where $\psi = \mu - 1$, $\psi_1 = \mu(1-\delta)$, and $\psi_2 = -\tfrac{1}{2}\rho\mu\delta(1-\delta)$.

This approximation is better the closer the elasticity of substitution is to unity, and it reduces to the CD form when the elasticity of substitution is exactly equal to unity ($\rho = 0$). The deterioration of the quality of this approximation as σ departs from unity reduces its usefulness as a way of estimating σ, but it does provide us with a direct test of the CD form. If ψ_2 is not significantly different from zero, the CD function need not be rejected. But because of the approximation we expect the ignored higher-order terms to be of increasing importance the farther we get away from the CD case. This may have unpredictable effects on ψ_2 and on the power of the test. If the CD form is rejected we would not have to accept the hypothesis of a CES form with ρ significantly different from zero. A ψ_2 that is significantly different from zero could also be the result of a more general production function, since the alternative hypotheses are not limited to the CES class of production functions.

Suppose (5.12) is estimated to obtain $\hat{\psi}_1$, $\hat{\psi}_2$, $\hat{\psi}$, then because $\hat{\psi}_2 = -\tfrac{1}{2}\hat{\rho}\hat{\mu}\hat{\delta}(1-\hat{\delta})$ leads to $\hat{\rho}\hat{\mu}\hat{\delta}(1-\hat{\delta}) = -2\hat{\psi}_2$, and because $\hat{\psi}_1 = \hat{\mu}(1-\hat{\delta})$ leads to $\hat{\delta} = (\hat{\mu} - \hat{\psi}_1)/\hat{\mu}$, linking these two relations we obtain:

$$\hat{\rho}\hat{\mu}\cdot\frac{\hat{\mu}-\hat{\psi}_1}{\hat{\mu}}\left(1 - \frac{\hat{\mu}-\hat{\psi}_1}{\hat{\mu}}\right) = -2\hat{\psi}_2.$$

Manipulating, we have

$$\hat{\rho} = -2\hat{\mu}\hat{\psi}_2/(\hat{\mu} - \hat{\psi}_1)\hat{\psi}_1.$$

Since $\hat{\psi} = \hat{\mu} - 1$ leads to $\hat{\mu} = \hat{\psi} + 1$, we get

$$\hat{\rho} = -2\hat{\psi}_2(1+\hat{\psi})/\hat{\psi}_1(1+\hat{\psi}-\hat{\psi}_1)$$

and

$$\hat{\sigma} = 1/(1 + \hat{\rho}).$$

In the next section, we will first present the estimated results generated by equation (5.6) to see how the elasticities of α and β vary across different industries by pooling all the 6 years' data. Then we will turn to analysing results generated by equations (5.3) and (5.12) testing various hypotheses suggested at the beginning, and testing whether the CD function is appropriate for our data-set.

2.2 Results and policy implications

Computation results generated by equations (5.6), (5.3), and (5.12) will be discussed in this section. The data are discussed in Appendix 10.1. We present first the results generated by equation (5.6) in which z_0 and z_2 are included. After many experiments, the piece-work variable (z_1) and welfare variable (z_3) were found to have no important impact on the estimated results. Thus these two variables are not included when we carry out a general analysis in this section. Second, we discuss our findings using equations (5.3) and (5.12). We give results not only for aggregated data but also for disaggregated data to examine the outcomes across industries, years, locations, and contract forms. Thirdly, we evaluate results for variables such as z_1 (piece-work wages), z_3 (welfare), and z_4 (proportion of shut-down hours in logs). Because these variables are not as important as z_0 and z_2, we only provide estimates using pooled data.

1. Results for equation (5.6): Cobb–Douglas with varying elasticities across industries

The purpose of estimating (5.6) is to look at how elasticities of capital (α) and labour (β) vary across industries and to see whether such variations affect the magnitude and/or significance of other coefficients or elasticities such as the elasticities for labour quality, bonuses, etc. If the introduction of industrial dummies to capture the variations of α and β does not affect other coefficients, then we can focus our analysis on the simpler equation (5.3) to test hypotheses.

The estimated results are presented in Table 5.1. We have two versions of the model, one incorporating a direct-bonus variable (z_2) and labour quality (z_0) and the other only labour quality. The results on piece-work wages and welfare are discussed below.

The reason why equation (5.6) was estimated with and without a

TABLE 5.1. Results from equation (5.6) (dependent variable q)

Independent variable	Coefficient	Prob > ITI	Coefficient	Prob > ITI
Intercept	0.1294	0.7617	0.7905	0.0742
ID1	−0.5566	0.3697	−0.6279	0.3115
ID2	−3.6355	0.0001	−3.3952	0.0001
ID3	−1.7172	0.0118	−1.8591	0.0063
ID4	−1.6379	0.0142	−1.6165	0.0199
ID5	0.3363	0.7498	0.3788	0.7134
ID6	−1.5768	0.0062	−1.1006	0.0613
ID7	−1.6467	0.0021	−1.6361	0.0025
YR1	−0.0417	0.5097	0.1437	0.0280
YR2	−0.0615	0.3435	0.0927	0.1605
YR3	−0.0012	0.9834	0.0760	0.2170
YR4	0.0685	0.2577	0.1485	0.0146
YR5	0.0106	0.8580	0.0673	0.2606
LC1	0.4994	0.0001	0.3642	0.0001
LC2	0.1538	0.0259	0.0813	0.2503
LC3	0.4455	0.0001	0.2615	0.0011
LC4	0.1847	0.0095	0.1104	0.1252
$k - n$	0.7329	0.0001	0.6605	0.0001
k1	−0.6780	0.0001	−0.7451	0.0001
k2	−0.4323	0.0003	−0.3408	0.0043
k3	−0.3899	0.0016	−0.3324	0.0075
k4	−0.5874	0.0001	−0.5295	0.0001
k5	0.2949	0.0616	0.3610	0.0201
k6	−0.5580	0.0001	−0.5104	0.0001
k7	−0.5908	0.0001	−0.5462	0.0001
n	−0.0991	0.0585	−0.1018	0.0610
n1	−0.0624	0.4218	−0.0458	0.5571
n2	0.5989	0.0001	0.5680	0.0001
n3	0.2247	0.0100	0.2589	0.0030
n4	0.1648	0.0711	0.1700	0.0735
n5	−0.0137	0.9218	−0.0292	0.8306
n6	0.2211	0.0032	0.1517	0.0485
n7	0.1750	0.0084	0.1703	0.0113
z0	0.0502	0.1095	0.2690	0.4031
z2	—	—	0.3665	0.0001
$ADJ\ R^2$	0.4254	—	0.4687	—
N	1532	—	1437	—

Note: the intercept is for industry 8, year 6, location 5. Coefficients of $(k - n)$ and n are for industry 8.

bonus element (z_2) is that there exists a strong multicollinearity between the time-trend and the bonus element. Average bonus increased over time and so did the share of bonus in total wage income. If bonus does not play a positive role in stimulating factor productivity, its inclusion in the production function will just absorb the residual productivity created by technical changes, the effect of which is usually represented by a time-trend element in the production function. In this case, including a bonus variable will underestimate technical changes and thereby total factor productivity over time. On the other hand, if bonus really has a positive impact on productivity as we suspect, its exclusion from the production function will induce an overestimation of technical change and factor productivity and reduce the goodness of fit for the estimated results. There are two ways to overcome this difficulty. One is to estimate the same function by using cross-sectional yearly data which will be discussed later. The other is to compare the results from different specifications of the same function, as in this section. Bearing this in mind, the results in Table 5.1 are interpreted as follows:

When the bonus variable (z_2) is not included in the function, total factor productivity (the exogenous technical level) does not show significant differences among years. The coefficients suggest that total factor productivity improved slightly between 1980 and 1985 and then experienced a setback after 1985. If the bonus variable (z_2) is included, total factor productivity has two peaks in 1980 and 1985 but fell to its lowest level in 1987. The adjusted R^2 is 4.3% higher with the bonus variable than without.

Firms in location 5, the small inland city group, have the lowest labour productivity while firms in location 1, the large coastal cities, and 3, the medium-sized coastal and more advanced cities, tend to have relatively higher labour productivity than firms in any other location.

The elasticities of capital and labour show variations across industries as expected. In particular, the elasticity of capital for industry 5 is unreasonably high and that for industry 1 is unreasonably low. This may be due to the following reasons: the number of observations in both industries 1 and 5 are too small; and the variances of the important variables are high. The unusually high variances may arise from the non-randomness and inconsistency of the very scattered observations. However, when the observations are included in the total data-set, the extreme effects disappear. This suggests that industries 1 and 5 have to be treated with care.

Although the coefficient for labour quality is positive, it is found to be not significantly different from zero. The coefficient for bonus z_2 is significantly and positively different from zero. The value of the coefficient is very stable and significant whether year dummies are included or not.

2. *Results for equations (5.3) and (5.12) with complete sample: Cobb–Douglas and CES*

In this subsection, the dummy variables for α and β are dropped. Thus factor elasticities are constrained to be the same across industries, so the fitted values of α and β will represent the averages of all industries. Intercept dummies are introduced to pick up industry differences. Estimated results generated by both equations (5.3) and (5.12) with the complete sample data are presented in Table 5.2. Comparing the results of Tables 5.1 and 5.2, we have the following findings.

Much of the variance of α and β across industries is absorbed by the intercept dummies. Thus it is important to include industrial dummies in subsequent estimations. According to the coefficients, industry 1 has the lowest productivity level while industries 3, 5, and 6 have the highest. Productivity differences across years are more or less the same as in the previous version. Once again we focus on the version of the model with the bonus variable included. Examining the values of the coefficients associated with the year dummy variables, total factor productivity was at its highest in 1980 and 1985. Between 1983 and 1987, total factor productivity traced an inverted 'V' path. However the 1985 peak is only slightly above the level for 1980. Leaving out 1985, it is hard to avoid the conclusion that total factor productivity due to exogenous technical level fell over the entire reform period. The fact that real factor productivity dropped by about 14% between 1980 and 1987 looks really disappointing if no explanation can be found. However Table 5.3 suggests the following: there was a sharp rise in capital per worker between 1980 and 1983; there was also a significant jump in average number of workers during the same period; value added per worker was only slightly higher in 1983 than in 1980; and mean total value added was much higher in 1983 than in 1980.

These four findings lead to the conclusion that the slide in real factor productivity estimated by the production function was due to two effects: the rapid increase of capital per worker and the sudden jump in total employment. The rapid expansion of investment between 1980 and 1983 was just like other periods but the rapid expansion of total employment was very unusual. It is commonly thought that state enterprises were forced to absorb many educated youths coming back from the countryside who were sent to be 're-educated' by the farmers during the Cultural Revolution. Taking this unusual expansion of employment into account, the slide in real factor pro-

TABLE 5.2. Results from equations (5.3) and (5.12) based upon total aggregated data (dependent variable q)

Independent variables	CD function (1)		CD function (2)		CES Kmenta approximation	
	Coefficients	Prob > ITI	Coefficients	Prob > ITI	Coefficients	Prob > ITI
Intercept	−1.5249	0.0001	−0.5442	0.0068	−0.5538	0.0061
ID1	−0.7986	0.0001	−0.8356	0.0001	−0.8418	0.0001
ID2	0.9515	0.0001	0.8564	0.0001	0.8538	0.0001
ID3	0.1947	0.0065	0.2212	0.0023	0.2141	0.0038
ID4	−0.0437	0.5185	−0.0578	0.4186	−0.0593	0.4069
ID5	0.9990	0.0001	0.9350	0.0001	0.9145	0.0001
ID6	0.4251	0.0001	0.2862	0.0001	0.2849	0.0001
ID7	−0.0328	0.5854	−0.0808	0.1797	−0.0830	0.1695
YR1	−0.0467	0.4629	0.1216	0.0723	0.1185	0.0812
YR2	−0.0660	0.3611	0.0766	0.2640	0.0757	0.2697
YR3	−0.0028	0.9646	0.0570	0.3733	0.0566	0.3763
YR4	0.0643	0.3082	0.1284	0.0422	0.1283	0.0423
YR5	−0.0069	0.9111	0.0478	0.4430	0.0475	0.4460
LC1	0.5468	0.0001	0.3199	0.0001	0.3218	0.0001
LC2	0.1651	0.0186	0.0417	0.5645	0.0452	0.5349
LC3	0.4393	0.0001	0.2237	0.0060	0.2288	0.0053
LC4	0.2415	0.0007	0.0282	0.7023	0.0306	0.6784
$(k - n)$	0.3444	0.0001	0.2759	0.0001	0.2849	0.0001
$(k - n)^2$	—	—	—	—	0.0117	0.6165
n	0.0777	0.0004	0.0584	0.0094	0.0590	0.0088
z_0	—	—	0.0560	0.0916	0.0557	0.0936
z_2	—	—	0.3536	0.0001	0.3525	0.0001
$ADJ = R^2$	0.3753		0.4213		0.4210	
N	1 633		1 437		1 437	

TABLE 5.3. Mean comparisons and annual growth rates of value added per worker, capital stock per worker, and total number of workers, 1980 and 1983–87

Variables		1980	1983	1984	1985	1986	1987
Capital per worker	mean	0.4951	0.5942	0.6370	0.7064	0.7791	0.9103
(*K*/*N*)	ratio	—	1.2002	1.0720	1.1089	1.1029	1.1683
Value added per worker	mean	0.4881	0.4951	0.5635	0.6213	0.5867	0.6368
(*V*/*N*)	ratio	—	1.0143	1.1382	1.1026	1.9443	1.0854
Average total no. of workers	mean	1 434	1 642	1 580	1 661	1 669	1 707
(*N*)	ratio	—	1.2226	0.9622	1.0513	1.005	1.0227
Total value	mean	655.5	812.9	890.3	1031.9	979.2	1087.0
added (*V*)	ratio	—	1.2401	1.0952	1.1590	0.9489	1.1101

Note: 'ratio' is ratio of value in period t to period $t - 1$.

ductivity between 1980 and 1983 is explicable. However, we cannot find a similar explanation for the decline of real factor productivity in 1986 and 1987 except that the growth rate of capital per worker in 1987 was relatively higher than average. Thus it may be concluded that the decline in real factor productivity after 1986 was due to other forces.

The variation of real productivity across different locations is very similar to that found in Table 5.1. The general patterns can be described as follows. Firms in coastal regions tend to have much higher productivity than those in inland regions, while those in smaller cities tend to have lower productivity. Firms in location 3 (the coastal and economically more advanced small and medium cities) have a higher productivity than in location 2 (the large inland cities), which suggests that geographical location is more important than the size of cities in productive efficiency. There are many explanations why coastal regions are more efficient than inland regions. Historically, Shanghai and other large coastal cities have been the centres of industry and commerce since the end of the last century. The dominant position of these cities in industry, technology, trade, and education declined relatively during Mao's rule when efforts were made to develop the inland areas and reduce the gap between the coastal and the inland regions. The rapid development of small and medium cities as represented by location 3 may be largely due to their closeness to large cities such as Shanghai and Tianjian and to the freer and more open policies during the last decade. Being in a more favourable economic and technological environment, and enjoying less control by the central authorities, makes the small and medium cities along the coast strong challengers not only to the large inland cities, but also to the large coastal cities like Shanghai and Tianjian themselves.

The coefficient for $(k - n)^2$ is found to be not significantly different from zero. This suggests that a CD function is appropriate for the data-set at an aggregated level. The coefficient of n is positive and significantly different from zero, indicating economies of scale of about 6%.

The coefficient of bonus variable z_2 is positive and highly significant, suggesting that it has a strong impact on factor productivity. There is however an alternative interpretation of this variable, which cannot be ruled out on the basis of the single-equation estimates in this chapter. The alternative involves reverse causation with high productivity inducing a high ratio of bonus to total wages. The reasoning is that a more productive firm will, *ceteris paribus*, have higher profits, retain more, and pay higher bonuses, giving a higher ratio. This possibility is analysed at the beginning of the next chapter. It is sufficient to note here that the analysis does nothing to weaken the interpretation adopted throughout this chapter—that the bonus incentive does have a major impact on productive efficiency.

3. *Results for equations (5.3) and (5.12) by sector, year, location, and contract form*

As discussed above, differences in the elasticities of capital and labour inputs are highly significant across industrial sectors and indeed elasticities of some particular industries such as industries 1 and 5 are very unusual. We tried regrouping the original eight industrial sectors into two major ones, one representing the more labour-intensive sectors ('light industry'), and the other the more capital-intensive sectors ('heavy industry'). 'Light' industry includes food, drink, and tobacco (2), textiles (3), and light and craft (4), while the 'heavy' industry includes the extractive (1), energy (5), chemicals (6), building materials and metals (7), and engineering (8). Estimated results for both the 'light' (DD1), and the 'heavy' (DD2) industries are presented in Table 5.4. In general, capital plays a more important role in the 'light'-industry sector than in the 'heavy'-industry sector as reflected by the difference of the capital elasticities. The coefficient of labour quality z_0 in heavy industry is large and highly significant, but in light industry it is not different from zero. This leads to the suggestion that labour quality is very important when the firm is capital-intensive but not important if the firm is labour-intensive. The elasticities of scale for

TABLE 5.4. Estimated results from equations (5.3) and (5.12) by major industry groupings (DD = 1, 2) (dependent variable q)

Industries DD	Independent variables	CD		CES	
		Coefficients	Prob > ITI	Coefficients	Prob > ITI
DD = 1 light industry with year dummies	Intercept	−1.5924	0.0001	−1.7155	0.0001
	$(k - n)$	0.4263	0.0001	0.5417	0.0001
	$(k - n)^2$	—	—	0.0748	0.1555
	n	0.2911	0.0001	0.3037	0.0001
	z_0	−0.0043	0.9411	−0.0084	0.8852
	z_2	0.4774	0.0001	0.4655	0.0001
	n	505	—	505	—
	$A - R^2$	0.2808	—	0.2496	—
	$\hat{\sigma}$	1	—	1.8953	—
DD = 2 heavy industry with year dummies	Intercept	0.9270	0.0001	0.8123	0.0004
	$(k - n)$	0.3790	0.0001	0.3895	0.0001
	$(k - n)^2$	—	—	−0.0007	0.9936
	n	−0.0663	0.0123	−0.0580	0.0278
	z_0	0.1503	0.0011	0.1379	0.0027
	z_2	0.4780	0.0001	0.4824	0.0001
	n	932	—	932	—
	$A - R^2$	0.2461	—	0.2566	—
	$\hat{\sigma}$	1	—	1	—

both sectors are calculated: 1.29 for DD1, 0.93 for DD2. It is obvious that the light sector has large and positive economies of scale while the heavy sector has diseconomies of scale. This may be due to the fact that light industry has a much lower capital/labour ratio and this in turn may suggest that capital is likely to be used more efficiently in light industry than in heavy industry.

Coefficients for $(k - n)^2$ (the squared term of capital per worker) for both sectors are not significantly different from zero, although the coefficient for the light-industry sector is greater than that for the heavy-industry sector. Following the formulae for $\hat{\psi}$, $\hat{\rho}$, and $\hat{\sigma}$ defined above, we have $\hat{\sigma} = 1.8953$ for light industry if the coefficient for $(k - n)^2$ is assumed to be correct. This leads to the weak conclusion that factors in light industry are more substitutable than in heavy industry. The elasticity of substitution for heavy industry is found to be very close to unity.

Cross-sectional data for each year are used to estimate equations (5.3) and (5.12) and the results are presented in Table 5.5 for all 6 years. The elasticity of capital increased over time suggesting that capital played a more and more important role in raising output. The elasticity of labour quality is found to be not significantly different from zero for every year. Economies of scale decreased over time suggesting that rapid expansion of investment may have introduced diseconomies or inefficiency in capital utilization. The coefficients in both the CD and CES function for every year are very close and it is thus difficult to reject the CD form. The coefficients for the bonus variable z_2 are highly significant for all years and the values are very consistent over time. This rules out the possibility that including a bonus variable just absorbs the residual productivity created by technical change.

TABLE 5.5. Estimated results from equations (5.3) and (5.12) by years (dependent variable q)

Industries	Independent variables	CD		CES	
		Coefficients	Prob > ITI	Coefficients	Prob > ITI
YR = 1 (1980)	Intercept	−1.2829	0.0211	−1.2730	0.0225
	$(k-n)$	0.1315	0.1150	0.0981	0.3928
	$(k-n)^2$	—	—	−0.0230	0.6733
With industry	n	0.1529	0.0112	0.1515	0.0122
dummies	z_0	0.0267	0.6967	0.0298	0.6652
	z_2	0.4227	0.0001	0.4237	0.0001
	n	247	—	247	—
	$A-R^2$	0.3730	—	0.3708	—
	$\hat{\sigma}$	1	—	≃0.6615	—
YR = 2 (1983)	Intercept	−0.8059	0.1152	−0.8080	0.1152
	$(k-n)$	0.2717	0.0016	0.2875	0.0087
	$(k-n)^2$	—	—	0.0165	0.8151
With industry	n	0.0942	0.1004	0.0945	0.1005
dummies	z_0	0.0189	0.8014	0.0185	0.8060
	z_2	0.3414	0.0001	0.3413	0.0001
	n	206	—	206	—
	$A-R^2$	0.3988	—	0.3958	—
	$\hat{\sigma}$	0.3988	—	≃1.1844	—
YR = 3 (1984)	Intercept	−0.7105	0.1278	−0.7113	0.1282
	$(k-n)$	0.3010	0.0003	0.3045	0.0021
	$(k-n)^2$	—	—	0.0041	0.9480
With industry	n	0.0786	0.1476	0.0787	0.1481
dummies	z_0	−0.0265	0.7454	−0.0260	0.7524
	z_2	0.2855	0.0003	0.2851	0.0004
	n	245	—	245	—
	$A-R^2$	0.3742	—	0.3716	—
	$\hat{\sigma}$	1	—	≃1.0389	—
YR = 4 (1985)	Intercept	0.3707	0.3984	0.4020	0.3631
	$(k-n)$	0.4391	0.0001	0.4079	0.0001
	$(k-n)^2$	—	—	−0.0430	0.4937
With industry	n	0.0071	0.8871	0.0045	0.9285
dummies	z_0	−0.0623	0.4688	−0.0680	0.4316
	z_2	0.4686	0.0001	0.4767	0.0001
	n	250	—	250	—
	$A-R^2$	0.3986	—	0.3973	—
	$\hat{\sigma}$	1	—	≃0.7382	—

TABLE 5.5 (*cont.*)

Industries	Independent variables	CD		CES	
		Coefficients	Prob > ITI	Coefficients	Prob > ITI
YR = 5 (1986)	Intercept	0.3162	0.4630	0.3320	0.4437
	$(k-n)$	0.2824	0.0002	0.2758	0.0005
	$(k-n)^2$	—	—	−0.0223	0.6899
With industry	n	0.0121	0.8104	0.0101	0.8417
dummies	z_0	0.0446	0.5963	0.0413	0.6257
	z_2	0.4423	0.0001	0.4421	0.0001
	n	255	—	255	—
	$A-R^2$	0.4017	—	0.3997	—
	$\hat{\sigma}$	1	—	≈0.8181	—
YR = 6 (1987)	Intercept	−0.0464	0.9175	−0.0417	0.9259
	$(k-n)$	0.4470	0.0001	0.4410	0.0001
	$(k-n)^2$	—	—	−0.0583	0.4380
With industry	n	0.0575	0.2662	0.0575	0.2670
dummies	z_0	0.1388	0.1548	0.1419	0.1465
	z_2	0.4135	0.0001	0.4098	0.0001
	n	234	—	234	—
	$A-R^2$	0.4477	—	0.4467	—
	$\hat{\sigma}$	1	—	≈0.6879	—

Estimated results using equations (5.3) and (5.12) are presented in Table 5.6 for each individual location. Although the coefficients for year dummies are generally not statistically significant, labour productivity over time shows an inverted 'V' shape as found in the previous section. None of the locations has a significant labour-quality elasticity but every locality has a significant coefficient for the bonus variable. Location 5 has very large economies of scale (15%), followed

TABLE 5.6. Estimated results from equations (5.3) and (5.12) for individual locations (dependent variable q)

Locations	Independent variables	CD		CES	
		Coefficients	Prob > ITI	Coefficients	Prob > ITI
LCC = 1	Intercept	−0.4520	0.3284	−0.5554	0.2318
with ID	*YR1*	0.2020	0.1372	0.1968	0.1464
dummies	*YR2*	0.0972	0.4794	0.0983	0.4727
6 years' data	*YR3*	0.0912	0.4710	0.0962	0.4455
	YR4	0.1881	0.1328	0.1971	0.1144
	YR5	0.0439	0.7161	0.0517	0.6675
$n = 364$	$(k-n)$	0.1687	0.0140	0.2748	0.0022
$A-R^2 = 0.4185$	$(k-n)^2$	—	—	0.0952	0.0659
$A-R^2 = 0.4225$	n	0.1303	0.0100	0.1392	0.0102
	z_0	0.0209	0.7324	0.0219	0.7188
	z_2	0.5554	0.0001	0.5352	0.0001

TABLE 5.6 (*cont.*)

Locations	Independent variables	CD		CES	
		Coefficients	Prob > ITI	Coefficients	Prob > ITI
LCC = 2	Intercept	−0.2586	0.4234	−0.3178	0.3260
with ID	*YR1*	0.1628	0.1694	0.1571	0.1826
dummies	*YR2*	0.1512	0.2068	0.1401	0.2411
6 years' data	*YR3*	0.1628	0.1570	0.1546	0.1778
	YR4	0.1671	0.1349	0.1580	0.1564
	YR5	0.0513	0.6480	0.0483	0.6663
$n = 407$	$(k-n)$	0.3044	0.0001	0.2418	0.0007
$A-R^2 = 0.4956$	$(k-n)^2$	—	—	−0.1037	0.0589
$A-R^2 = 0.4989$	n	−0.0247	0.4801	−0.0231	0.5064
	z_0	0.0327	0.5514	−0.0049	0.9326
	z_2	0.2733	0.0001	0.2729	0.0001
LCC = 3	Intercept	−0.1506	0.8186	−0.1633	0.8040
with ID	*YR1*	0.1545	0.4104	0.1803	0.3479
dummies	*YR2*	0.0388	0.8296	0.0547	0.2640
6 years' data	*YR3*	0.0431	0.7889	0.0495	0.7592
	YR4	0.1614	0.3147	0.1650	0.3051
	YR5	−0.0418	0.7803	−0.0345	0.8189
$n = 188$	$(k-n)$	0.4528	0.0001	0.4425	0.0001
$A-R^2 = 0.4239$	$(k-n)^2$	—	—	−0.0668	0.5116
$A-R^2 = 0.4220$	n	0.0775	0.3830	0.0810	0.3633
	z_0	0.1165	0.2310	0.1202	0.2182
	z_2	0.3324	0.0013	0.3375	0.0012
LCC = 4	Intercept	−1.0105	0.0044	−0.9699	0.0067
with ID	*YR1*	0.0249	0.8344	0.0378	0.7534
dummies	*YR2*	−0.0286	0.8133	−0.0244	0.8406
6 years' data	*YR3*	−0.0383	0.7343	−0.0365	0.7469
	YR4	0.0391	0.7270	0.0406	0.7170
	YR5	0.0422	0.7045	0.0428	0.7003
$n = 351$	$(k-n)$	0.2279	0.0001	0.1824	0.0202
$A-R^2 = 0.5097$	$(k-n)^2$	—	—	−0.0429	0.3913
$A-R^2 = 0.5094$	n	0.1278	0.0011	0.1236	0.0017
	z_0	−0.0199	0.8240	−0.0097	0.9145
	z_2	0.3964	0.0001	0.3988	0.0001
LCC = 5	Intercept	−1.2367	0.1141	−1.4067	0.0651
with ID	*YR1*	0.0848	0.7424	−0.1408	0.5912
dummies	*YR2*	0.0021	0.9936	−0.1054	0.6898
6 years' data	*YR3*	0.0386	0.8734	0.0036	0.9876
	YR4	0.0574	0.8163	0.0277	0.9078
	YR5	0.1465	0.5485	0.1388	0.5574
$n = 127$	$(k-n)$	0.4113	0.0001	0.4708	0.0001
$A-R^2 = 0.1884$	$(k-n)^2$	—	—	0.1576	0.0042
$A-R^2 = 0.2375$	n	0.1508	0.1090	0.1426	0.1180
	z_0	0.0532	0.6899	−0.0925	0.5052
	z_2	0.2083	0.0757	0.2275	0.0461

by locations 4 and 1. It seems that location 2 has exploited its economies of scale and has constant returns. Coefficients for the squared term of capital per worker, $(k-n)^2$, are not significantly different from zero for locations 1, 3, and 4. The coefficient for location 2 is significantly negative and it is significantly positive for location 5. This may well indicate that capital is used very inefficiently in location 2 but efficiently in location 5. This finding is consistent with the conclusion from aggregated data in the previous section: capital-scarce regions tend to use capital more efficiently.

Results for different contract forms are given in Table 5.7. Equations for firms subsequently operating under the contract-responsibility

TABLE 5.7. Estimated results from equations (5.3) and (5.12) for each contract form (dependent variable q)

Contract form	Independent variables	CD		CES	
		Coefficients	Prob > ITI	Coefficients	Prob > ITI
CF = 2	Intercept	−0.0710	0.8391	−0.1243	0.7278
with ID	*YR1*	0.3150	0.0050	0.3016	0.0080
YR and LCC	*YR2*	0.2056	0.0688	0.1994	0.0785
dummies	*YR3*	0.1138	0.2668	0.1092	0.2878
6 years' data	*YR4*	0.1632	0.1136	0.1590	0.1238
8 industries	*YR5*	0.0956	0.3441	0.0937	0.3552
	LC1	0.4173	0.0017	0.4329	0.0013
	LC2	0.3189	0.0219	0.3417	0.0167
	LC3	0.4750	0.0015	0.5005	0.0011
	LC4	0.2250	0.0946	0.2455	0.0744
	$k - n$	0.4260	0.0001	0.4422	0.0001
	$(k - n)^2$	—	—	0.0259	0.4648
	n	0.0139	0.7111	0.0162	0.6672
	z_0	0.1676	0.0064	0.1616	0.0091
	z_2	0.4247	0.0001	0.4295	0.0001
	n	584	—	584	—
	$A - R^2$	0.5030	—	0.5026	—
	$\hat{\sigma}$	1	—	≃1.2616	—
CF = 1	Intercept	−0.4696	0.0682	−0.4704	0.0678
with ID,	*YR1*	—	—	—	—
YR, and LCC	*YR2*	0.0179	0.8273	0.0185	0.8214
dummies but	*YR3*	0.0487	0.5318	0.0487	0.5319
YR = 1 and	*YR4*	0.1144	0.1301	0.1138	0.1323
ID = 5 are	*YR5*	0.0284	0.7028	0.0293	0.6944
deleted	*LC1*	0.3359	0.0004	0.3400	0.0004
	LC2	−0.0507	0.5705	−0.0435	0.6280
	LC3	0.1252	0.2166	0.1273	0.2094
	LC4	−0.0345	0.7150	−0.0255	0.7890
	$k - n$	0.2606	0.0001	0.2401	0.0001
	$(k - n)^2$	—	—	−0.0298	0.4710
	n	0.0401	0.1798	0.0392	0.1906
	z_0	0.0436	0.3518	0.0382	0.4216
	z_2	0.2733	0.0001	0.2743	0.0001
	n	695	—	695	—
	$A - R^2$	0.3612	—	0.3607	—
	$\hat{\sigma}$	1	—	≃0.7597	—

system (CFI) and the director-responsibility system (CF2) are estimated separately to see whether they differ in terms of real productivity and how they perform differently over time and in different locations. The contract-responsibility system was only introduced at the end of the period for which we have data. So the contract form cannot be interpreted as a cause of productivity differences: rather the hypothesis is that contract responsibility was introduced for a set of firms that had performed indifferently in the early stage of reform.

The mean value of value added in contract-responsibility firms is much lower than in director-responsibility firms (CF1 = 0.5127, CF2 = 0.6310, Table A5.1) and it has a lower variance. Firms under contract-responsibility may be those which are relatively inferior in labour productivity compared with their counterparts under director-responsibility either because they are in a less favourable economic environment or because they had a history of poor performance. However, if we examine the coefficients for the year dummies in Table 5.7 for both contract forms, it is clear that real productivity in director-responsibility firms declined over the period under investigation and experienced a sudden slump in 1986 and 1987, but productivity in contract-responsibility firms remained stable over time. The sudden slump in productivity in director-responsibility firms after 1986 reflected the tightening of policy by the government at the macro-level. However, the fact that contract-responsibility firms did not have the same setback suggests that these firms may have had more autonomy so that they were less influenced by the macroeconomic policy of the government, and that managers and workers may have had more incentive to improve performance.

The relatively better performance of contract-responsibility firms can also be demonstrated by the changes in three important indicators (capital per worker, value added per worker, and total number of workers) over time and the ratios of these indicators between the two contracts as shown in Table 5.8. In general, although director-responsibility firms had a slightly higher growth rate of capital per worker (86% over six years) than contract-responsibility firms (83% over six years), value added per worker and total number of workers experienced a much lower growth (Q 28%, N 16% over six years) than in contract-responsibility firms (Q 33%, N 36% over six years). Thus, total value added of contract-responsibility firms on the average experienced a much higher growth rate between 1980 and 1987 than director-responsibility firms (81% versus 49%).

The information provided in Tables 5.7 and 5.8, and our analysis above, leads us to the following conclusions. First, although contract-

TABLE 5.8. Changes of $(k - n)$, n, and q over time and comparison between CF1 and CF2

YR		CF1			CF2		
		$(k - n)$	n	q	$(k - n)$	n	q
YR = 1	Mean	−0.7339	7.1751	−0.8191	−0.6475	7.2752	−0.5943
	N	(184)	(184)	(179)	(128)	(130)	(126)
	EXP	0.4800	1306	0.4408	0.5234	1444	0.5519
YR = 2	Mean	−0.5555	7.3553	−0.7900	−0.4399	7.4916	−0.5541
	N	(148)	(148)	(148)	(97)	(97)	(95)
	EXP	0.5738	1564	0.4538	0.6441	1793	0.5746
YR = 3	Mean	−0.4944	7.3803	−0.6562	−0.3878	7.3812	−0.4634
	N	(156)	(156)	(156)	(121)	(121)	(121)
	EXP	0.6099	1604	0.5188	0.6785	1606	0.6291
YR = 4	Mean	−0.3720	7.4146	−0.5560	−0.2973	7.4490	−0.3660
	N	(162)	(162)	(162)	(111)	(112)	(111)
	EXP	0.6894	1660	0.5735	0.7428	1718	0.6935
YR = 5	Mean	−0.2769	7.4335	−0.6087	−0.1926	7.4308	−0.4259
	N	(170)	(170)	(169)	(114)	(115)	(113)
	EXP	0.7581	1692	0.5441	0.8248	1687	0.6532
YR = 6	Mean	−0.1305	7.4805	−0.5306	−0.02596	7.4267	−0.33438
	N	(158)	(159)	(151)	(111)	(114)	(110)
	EXP	0.8777	1773	0.5883	0.9744	1680	0.7090
Growth rates	YR 2/1	1.1954	1.1975	1.0295	1.2306	1.2417	1.0411
	YR 3/2	1.0629	1.0256	1.1432	1.0534	0.8957	1.0948
	YR 4/3	1.1303	1.0349	1.1054	1.0948	1.0697	1.1024
	YR 5/4	1.0997	1.0193	0.9487	1.1104	0.9820	0.9418
	YR 6/5	1.1578	1.0479	1.0812	1.1814	0.9959	1.0854
Ratios CF2/CF1	YR1	1.0904	1.1057	1.2520			
	YR2	1.1225	1.1464	1.2662			
	YR3	1.1125	1.0012	1.2126			
	YR4	1.0775	1.0349	1.2092			
	YR5	1.0880	0.9970	1.2005			
	YR6	1.1102	0.9475	1.2052			

Note: Mean = mean values of $(k - n)$, n, q.
N = number of observations.
EXP = exponents of $(k - n)$, n, and q to give K/N, N and Q measured in constant 1980 prices (10,000 yuan).

responsibility firms started from a relatively inferior condition, they experienced relatively more rapid expansion in terms of capital formation, employment, and total output. Second, factor productivity of contract-responsibility firms had been stable but experienced some improvement between 1983 and 1985. However, director-responsibility firms not only had a declining trend in factor productivity but also experienced a sudden slump in 1986 and 1987, reflecting the influence of macroeconomic policy.

Except in region 1 (the large coastal cities) contract-responsibility firms have very similar real productivity across all regions. However, director-responsibility firms have significantly lower real productivity in locations 4 and 5 than in other locations. The variation in their productivity across different locations reflects the general variation already found on an aggregated basis except that firms in location 3 seem to have outperformed firms in location 1. Thus, the pattern for director-responsibility firms may still be determined by the two factors mentioned above: geographical location and the size of the cities. The fact that contract-responsibility firms had similar productivity in locations 2, 4, and 5 (and even 3) suggests that they may follow a slightly different pattern of variation in productivity.

The coefficient of labour quality, z_0, for director-responsibility firms is highly significant but the coefficient is found not to be different from zero for contract-responsibility firms. This suggests that director-responsibility firms have relatively higher labour quality and may partly explain why contract-responsibility firms have lower productivity.

4. *Results for some miscellaneous variables*

In this subsection general results for z_1, z_3, and z_4 will be presented in comparison with results for z_0 and z_2. The definitions of z_0 to z_3 were given above. The definition of z_4 is (shut-down hours/total working hours) in natural logarithms. We introduce this variable because we suspect that capacity utilization may have some effect on productivity.

Summary statistics for all these variables are given in Table 5.9. Table 5.10 presents the estimated results using equation (5.3). The coefficients are generated separately by using the same common terms which include industry dummies, location dummies, year dummies, $(k - n)$, and n. The coefficients for z_0 and z_2 are consistent with previous findings. The results for z_4 suggest that shut-down hours do not have any significant impact on production efficiency. This may be due to the fact that the average shut-down hours did not vary significantly over time in the period under investigation (Table 5.9). The results for z_1 and z_3 are very interesting. They suggest that piece-work wages have a quite significant and positive impact on productivity although only one-third of firms have this wage system. Welfare has a negative impact on productivity although the coefficient is not statistically significant. This strongly supports our suggestion at the beginning of the chapter that welfare expenditure is not an incentive.

2.3 *Conclusions on productive efficiency*

Industrial growth was very impressive during the period under investigation, but relied very much on the expansion of capital and em-

TABLE 5.9. Summary statistics for miscellaneous variables

Data	Variables	*N*	Mean	Standard deviation
All years	Z_1	508	0.2454	0.1935
	Z_3	1549	0.1653	0.1387
	Z_4	1646	0.1427	0.1766
YR = 1	Z_1	70	0.2006	0.1880
	Z_3	281	0.0897	0.1057
	Z_4	314	0.1291	0.1790
YR = 2	Z_1	85	0.2715	0.1864
	Z_3	234	0.1528	0.0755
	Z_4	243	0.1262	0.1663
YR = 3	Z_1	99	0.2576	0.1898
	Z_3	269	0.1950	0.0967
	Z_4	275	0.1412	0.1796
YR = 4	Z_1	86	0.2483	0.1990
	Z_3	260	0.1913	0.1331
	Z_4	272	0.1394	0.1729
YR = 5	Z_1	84	0.2362	0.1992
	Z_3	264	0.1917	0.1912
	Z_4	281	0.1559	0.1761
YR = 6	Z_1	84	0.2483	0.1967
	Z_3	241	0.1756	0.1626
	Z_4	261	0.1652	0.1822

Note: Z_1 and Z_3 are respectively the shares of piece-work wages and welfare in total wage income; Z_4 is the share of shut-down hours in total working hours.

TABLE 5.10. Statistical tests for miscellaneous variables

Variables	*N*	Coefficients	Prob > ITI	$A - R^2$
z_0	1559	0.0837	0.0089	0.3781
z_1	508	0.0660	0.0101	0.4452
z_2	1563	0.3724	0.0001	0.4225
z_3	1567	−0.0867	0.1076	0.3836
z_4	1437	−0.0027	0.3958	0.3752

Note: Variables common to all equations were: industry dummies, location dummies, year dummies, $(k - n)$ and n. The results of all common terms are not presented in this table. They are consistent with the results presented in the previous section.

z_0 to z_4 are the log forms of Z_0 to Z_4 which are defined in Table 5.9. The coefficients for z_0 to z_4 are estimated separately, using the same common terms.

ployment. Total factor-productivity change was negative over the period 1980–87 as alleged by Lin (1988). In detail, factor productivity shows a fluctuating pattern. Enterprises experienced a slight fall in total factor productivity in the period 1980–83, an improvement in 1983–85, but suffered a severe setback after 1986.[1] This may be explained as follows: in the early 1980s when retained profit and bonus were first introduced to stimulate the firms and their employees, the initial impact was a sudden improvement in productivity; more autonomy to the firms in both input and output markets also helped to increase the incentives of managers and workers to improve productivity and profitability; lessening the control over local bureaucracies and enterprises in the early years induced rapid expansion of investment and employment and created financial crises for the central government who found it more and more difficult to get things under control. The result was overheating of the economy and wasted investment. The situation reached a critical point in late 1985 and early 1986 when the government decided to tighten its control over the economy by cutting credit and instituting more rigid regulation of local government and enterprises. This led to a very serious crisis in 1986 and after. The conflict between the interests of the central authority which is more concerned with control of the economy at the macro-level and the interests of local authorities and enterprises whose major objective is profit and bonus has been a recurring theme in the centrally planned economies. A relaxation of central control often leads to sudden but unbalanced growth while a tightening up of control often leads to slow growth and recession. The Chinese economy has experienced a number of such cycles since the founding of the socialist system. Thus the uneven pattern of growth demonstrated in our study is not exceptional. It simply reflects a basic problem of a centrally controlled economy with public ownership of assets. In terms of productive efficiency, the reform programme is not an outstanding success but it is not a total failure either.

There are positive economies of scale ranging from 5% to 10%. For some sectors (such as light industry), economies of scale could be greater than 18%. The CD function works consistently well in different estimations: there is no necessity to use CES functions. In most cases, labour quality plays a less significant role although it is found to be significant and important for director-responsibility firms and those with a higher capital intensity. It seems likely that firms subsequently implementing a more radical reform programme such as contract responsibility were those in a poorer shape initially in terms of productivity and economies of scale, but they demonstrated a relatively better performance in the sense that they had stable factor productivity and experienced rapid expansion in both capital and employment. They also had a much faster growth rate of total output than their counterparts under the director-responsibility system.

Location plays a dominant role in explaining variations in productive efficiency. Coastal regions tend to have much higher efficiency than their inland counterparts. The size of city is also important but not as dominant as locational advantage. For firms under contract responsibility, the effect of city size is not significant except that the large coastal cities experienced higher productivity. Firms in light-industrial sectors tend to have a higher elasticity of capital and much greater economies of scale than firms in the heavy-industrial sector. This may suggest that labour-intensive industries tend to use capital more efficiently than capital-intensive industries.

Welfare does not play a positive role in stimulating productivity in state-owned enterprises. If workers are guaranteed housing benefits and health care, they will feel more secure and will not worry about the productivity of the firms. On the other hand, a bonus or piece-work wage which is directly linked to performance should have a strong and positive impact on productivity. Our results give strong support for this hypothesis. How far bonus payments can go in stimulating productivity remains unanswered. We have not been able to detect an optimal upper bound of the bonus/wage ratio from available data. However, the setback in productivity after 1985 may be an indication that bonus was playing a diminishing role. In addition, some firms may end up giving bonuses to workers regardless of their actual performance. In that case, bonuses may well become part of the basic salary and may not have much further effect on efficiency.

3. Growth of Output and Productivity

3.1 Specification of the model

The objective of the research reported in this section was to describe the change over time in the output of the panel of state-owned enterprises, in terms of productive inputs and the efficiency with which they were transformed. Following the analysis of the previous section on productive efficiency, we have based the study on the Cobb–Douglas production function. Several of the variables that were found to be significant in the static analyses are also found to be important in the explanation of changes over time.

The theoretical base of the study is the standard form derived by differentiation of the logarithmic form of the production function with respect to time. This gives components of growth of output in terms of the contributions of growth of capital, labour, and materials. Improvements in efficiency are captured by time-trends, by focusing on variables that are thought to be significant determinants of worker effort, such as bonus payments and labour quality, and by variables reflecting the age of the capital stock. Equations are derived for annual changes, two-year and three-year changes. The dependent variables are value added (net output), value added per worker, gross output, and gross output per worker.

The basic Cobb–Douglas function is:

$$S = AK^{\alpha}N^{\beta}M^{\gamma}Z_0^{\theta_0}Z_2^{\theta_2}, \tag{5.13}$$

where S = gross output at 1980 prices of the firm,
A = constant, which varies across year, location, and industry in a manner to be described below,
K = real capital stock,
N = average number of workers,
M = real material inputs,
Z_0 = ratio of workers with either higher education or senior and middle schooling to total labour force in the firm,
Z_2 = share of bonus in total wages,
α, β, γ, θ_0, and θ_2 are coefficients.

For net output (value added, denoted by V), equation (5.13) is amended by the deletion of the term in M.

Taking logarithms and differentiating with respect to time gives (where lower-case symbols with the dot notation indicate the rate of change of the relevant variables):

$$\dot{s} = \dot{a} + \alpha\dot{k} + \beta\dot{n} + \gamma\dot{m} + \theta_0\dot{z}_0 + \theta_2\dot{z}_2 \tag{5.14}$$

and

$$\dot{v} = \dot{a} + \alpha\dot{k} + \beta\dot{n} + \theta_0\dot{z}_0 + \theta_2\dot{z}_2. \qquad (5.14)$$

Alternatively, these equations can be written in terms of growth per worker,

$$\dot{s} - \dot{n} = \dot{a} + \alpha(\dot{k} - \dot{n}) + (\alpha + \beta + \gamma - 1)\dot{n} + \gamma(\dot{m} - \dot{n}) + \theta_0\dot{z}_0 + \theta_2\dot{z}_2 \tag{5.16}$$

or

$$\dot{v} - \dot{n} = a + \alpha(\dot{k} - \dot{n}) + (\alpha + \beta - 1)\dot{n} + \theta_0\dot{z}_0 + \theta_2\dot{z}_2. \tag{5.17}$$

We note that the coefficient on growth of the labour force is an indicator of economies of scale in the firm. The coefficients α, β, and γ

give the elasticities of output with respect to capital, labour, and materials.

The constant a is presumed to vary across year, industry, location, and age of capital stock:

$$a = a_0 + \sum_j a_j ID_j + \sum_t a_t YR_t + \sum_r a_r LC_r + a_m AGE,$$

where ID_j is an industry dummy for industries 1 . . . 8,
YR_t is a year dummy for years 1 . . . 6 (1980 and 1983–87): where the analysis concerns growth over more than one year then the dummy YR_t indicates the final year of the period being considered,
LC_r is a location dummy for locations 1 . . . 5,
AGE is a dummy variable which takes the value 1 in those cases where a firm indicated that most of their capital equipment was installed before 1980; zero otherwise.

For regression analysis a white-noise error term is added to equations (5.14) to (5.17).

3.2 Results and discussion

The basic data are available for 1980 and 1983–87. We therefore choose three different time-spans for analysis:

(i) annual: year on year between 1983 and 1987 giving four observations for each firm;
(ii) 2-year: 1983–85 and 1985–87: previous analysis had suggested that 1985 marked a cyclical peak, and that behaviour might be different in the two periods;
(iii) 3-year: 1980–83 and 1984–87, which separates the early period of reform from the later period of consolidation of reforms.

Each enterprise gives the value of output in each year at 1980 prices. It is therefore possible to derive an implicit price index for each firm. This price index was used to deflate value of output, value added, and materials to obtain 'real' series: this procedure will introduce bias if there are movements in relative prices between inputs and outputs. Labour input is measured in terms of the average number of workers during the year. The measurement of the net capital stock generated considerable difficulties. These are outlined in Appendix 5.2. However, we note that the data on net capital stock are likely to be the least reliable.

Equations (5.14) to (5.17) were run using OLS regression. The full results are given in Tables 5.11–14, and coefficients are collected in Table 5.15 for comparative purposes (with summary statistics for all major variables in Table 5.16). The equations for output performed much better than those for value added. The difference is accounted for almost entirely by the growth of material inputs. The strong coefficient on materials and the dramatic improvement in the fit (as indicated by R^2) are entirely consistent with the observation that the firms were frequently constrained in what they could supply in this period by lack of materials. We also note that introducing the growth of material inputs 'robbed' the capital-growth measure of any statistical significance, suggesting that these two measures are collinear. For this reason, it is better to assess the utilization of capital

TABLE 5.11. Growth of value added ($\dot{v}$)

Variables	Annual	Two-year	Three-year
Intercept	0.114 (4.1)	0.095 (1.8)	0.078
$\dot{k}$	0.092 (2.2)	0.121 (2.3)	0.146 (3.2)
$\dot{n}$	0.419 (3.2)	0.375 (2.2)	0.583 (6.5)
$\dot{z}_2$	0.060 (2.0)	0.114 (2.7)	0.148 (3.4)
$\dot{z}_0$	−0.051 (−0.8)	0.093 (1.2)	0.167 (2.7)
YR83	—	—	−0.086 (−2.1)
84	0.068 (2.8)	—	—
85	0.059 (2.6)	0.206 (6.0)	—
86	−0.026 (−1.2)	—	—
87	0.00	0.00	0.00
IND1	−0.103 (−2.6)	−0.154 (−2.1)	−0.143 (−1.6)
2	−0.079 (−2.6)	−0.137 (−2.2)	−0.093 (−1.4)
3	−0.095 (−2.9)	−0.153 (−2.4)	−0.108 (−1.4)
4	−0.081 (−2.5)	−0.113 (−1.8)	−0.096 (−1.4)
5	−0.085 (−2.4)	−0.041 (−0.6)	−0.003 (−0.1)
6	−0.077 (−2.9)	−0.115 (−2.1)	−0.078 (−1.31)
7	−0.063 (−2.3)	−0.081 (−1.5)	0.031 (0.5)
8	0.00	0.00	0.00
AGE1	−0.045 (−2.4)	−0.080 (−2.0)	−0.012 (−0.2)
2	0.00	0.00	0.00
R^2	0.088	0.14	0.27
F	4.1	4.6	10.6
N	775	368	385
	Mean (SD)	Mean (SD)	Mean (SD)
$\dot{v}$	0.055 (0.23)	0.096 (0.32)	0.064 (0.41)
$\dot{k}$	0.046 (0.20)	0.130 (0.32)	0.154 (0.44)
$\dot{n}$	0.027 (0.06)	0.056 (0.10)	0.064 (0.23)
$\dot{z}_2$	0.052 (0.27)	0.130 (0.38)	0.072 (0.42)
$\dot{z}_0$	0.061 (0.13)	0.126 (0.21)	0.126 (0.31)

TABLE 5.12. Growth of value added per worker ($\dot{v} - \dot{n}$)

Variables	Annual	Two-year	Three-year
Intercept	0.089 (3.2)	0.072 (1.4)	0.037
$\dot{k} - \dot{n}$	0.073 (1.8)	0.106 (2.1)	0.121 (2.5)
$\dot{n}$	−0.235 (−2.0)	−0.226 (−1.5)	0.005 (0.1)
$\dot{z}_2$	0.074 (2.5)	0.127 (3.1)	0.144 (3.3)
$\dot{z}_0$	−0.068 (−1.1)	0.059 (0.8)	0.146 (2.4)
YR83	—	—	−0.045 (−1.2)
84	0.074 (3.1)	—	—
85	0.078 (3.4)	0.211 (6.3)	—
86	−0.017 (−0.8)	—	—
87	0.00	0.00	0.00
IND1	−0.087 (−2.2)	−0.143 (−2.0)	−0.146 (−1.8)
2	−0.079 (−2.6)	−0.100 (−1.7)	−0.099 (−1.6)
3	−0.078 (−2.4)	−0.123 (−2.0)	−0.089 (−1.2)
4	−0.064 (−2.4)	−0.076 (−1.2)	−0.045 (−0.6)
5	−0.074 (−2.1)	−0.008 (−0.1)	−0.015 (−0.2)
6	−0.063 (−2.4)	−0.105 (−2.0)	−0.016 (−0.3)
7	−0.064 (−2.4)	−0.068 (−1.3)	0.007 (0.1)
8	0.00	0.00	0.00
AGE1	−0.035 (−1.9)	−0.072 (−1.8)	−0.006 (−0.1)
2	0.00	0.00	0.00
R^2	0.07	0.154	0.10
F	3.8	5.1	3.1
N	812	374	387
	Mean (SD)	Mean (SD)	Mean (SD)
$\dot{v} - \dot{n}$	0.032 (0.232)	0.057 (0.318)	0.015 (0.36)
$\dot{k} - \dot{n}$	0.032 (0.208)	0.086 (0.306)	0.094 (0.38)
$\dot{n}$	0.029 (0.070)	0.059 (0.105)	0.074 (0.22)
$\dot{z}_2$	0.055 (0.281)	0.133 (0.379)	0.061 (0.41)
$\dot{z}_0$	0.065 (0.138)	0.126 (0.217)	0.112 (0.30)

from the value added equations. As computed, it made little difference whether the equations were run with output or with output per worker as the dependent variable.

In commenting on the results, we will consider first the contributions of the different independent variables, before addressing the question of the overall interpretation.

(*a*) *Capital*

A 1% change in the growth of capital stock raised the growth rate of value added by about 0.1% on an annual basis and by up to 0.14% over three years. This marginal contribution to growth is less than that indicated by the cross-section production function. One hypothesis is

TABLE 5.13. Growth of gross output ($\dot{s}$)

Variables	Annual	Two-year	Three-year
Intercept	0.044 (3.5)	0.073 (2.6)	−0.011 (−0.3)
$\dot{m}$	0.595 (30.4)	0.608 (18.9)	0.622 (17.8)
$\dot{k}$	−0.013 (−0.7)	0.025 (0.9)	0.067 (2.4)
$\dot{n}$	0.250 (4.5)	0.194 (2.2)	0.256 (4.8)
$\dot{z}_2$	0.037 (2.8)	0.086 (3.8)	0.074 (2.9)
$\dot{z}_0$	−0.021 (−0.8)	−0.031 (−0.7)	0.086 (2.4)
YR83	—	—	−0.023 (−1.0)
84	0.037 (3.4)	—	—
85	0.037 (3.5)	0.063 (3.7)	—
86	−0.004 (−0.4)	—	—
87	0.00	0.00	0.00
IND1	−0.034 (−2.0)	−0.079 (−2.3)	−0.024 (−0.5)
2	−0.049 (−3.6)	−0.052 (−1.6)	−0.014 (−0.4)
3	−0.025 (−1.8)	−0.041 (−1.3)	−0.004 (−0.1)
4	−0.033 (−2.3)	−0.043 (−1.4)	−0.009 (−0.2)
5	−0.038 (−2.4)	−0.041 (−1.2)	−0.039 (−0.8)
6	−0.034 (−2.9)	−0.041 (−1.5)	−0.033 (1.0)
7	−0.023 (−1.9)	−0.033 (−1.2)	0.055 (1.6)
8	0.00	0.00	0.00
AGE1	−0.017 (−1.9)	−0.040 (−2.0)	−0.002 (−0.1)
2	0.00	0.00	0.00
R^2	0.60	0.60	0.69
F	76	35	58
N	825	340	385
	Mean (SD)	Mean (SD)	Mean (SD)
$\dot{s}$	0.079 (0.16)	0.144 (0.22)	0.703 (0.35)
$\dot{m}$	0.086 (0.19)	0.155 (0.25)	0.122 (0.37)
$\dot{k}$	0.049 (0.20)	0.116 (0.29)	0.151 (0.44)
$\dot{n}$	0.029 (0.20)	0.055 (0.09)	0.058 (0.23)
$\dot{z}_2$	0.056 (0.28)	0.092 (0.35)	0.059 (0.41)
$\dot{z}_0$	0.062 (0.13)	0.120 (0.19)	0.117 (0.30)

that as the reform relaxed constraints on capital expenditure by enterprises, so they took the opportunity to expand capital stock very rapidly, fearing that controls would be reintroduced later. A good deal of unproductive investment was the result. Furthermore the gestation period for new capital projects was notoriously long in this period.

(*b*) *Labour force*

The contribution of the labour force to growth has three aspects: growth of the labour force, growth of effective labour due to bonus

TABLE 5.14. Growth of gross output per worker ($\dot{s} - \dot{n}$)

Variables	Annual	Two-year	Three-year
Intercept	0.035 (2.8)	0.071 (2.8)	0.014 (0.4)
$\dot{m} - \dot{n}$	0.604 (−0.7)	0.654 (21.6)	0.636 (19.0)
$\dot{k} - \dot{n}$	−0.010 (−0.5)	0.006 (0.2)	0.067 (2.4)
$\dot{n}$	−0.065 (−1.1)	−0.048 (−0.6)	0.085 (2.0)
$\dot{z}_2$	0.034 (2.5)	0.082 (3.9)	0.097 (3.9)
$\dot{z}_0$	−0.004 (−0.2)	−0.031 (−0.8)	0.063 (1.9)
YR83	—	—	−0.027 (−1.1)
84	0.043 (3.9)	—	—
85	0.045 (4.2)	0.065 (4.1)	—
86	0.001 (0.1)	—	—
87	0.00	0.00	0.00
IND1	−0.019 (−1.1)	−0.081 (−2.4)	−0.056 (−1.2)
2	−0.048 (−3.6)	−0.060 (−2.0)	−0.014 (−0.3)
3	−0.024 (−1.7)	−0.049 (−1.6)	−0.016 (−0.4)
4	−0.032 (−2.3)	−0.043 (−1.5)	−0.055 (−1.3)
5	−0.038 (−2.4)	−0.041 (−1.4)	−0.065 (−1.4)
6	−0.032 (−2.7)	−0.032 (−1.3)	−0.015 (0.4)
7	−0.020 (−1.7)	−0.031 (−1.2)	0.014 (0.4)
8	0.00	0.00	0.00
AGE1	−0.019 (−2.0)	−0.047 (−2.5)	−0.006 (−0.2)
2	0.00	0.00	0.00
R^2	0.59	0.64	0.60
F	72	45	43
N	816	370	420
	Mean (SD)	Mean (SD)	Mean (SD)
$\dot{s} - \dot{n}$	0.051 (0.15)	0.111 (0.26)	0.067 (0.32)
$\dot{m} - \dot{n}$	0.057 (0.18)	0.124 (0.29)	0.082 (0.34)
$\dot{k} - \dot{n}$	0.026 (0.20)	0.084 (0.10)	0.125 (0.39)
$\dot{k}$	0.029 (0.06)	0.061 (0.35)	0.095 (0.25)
$\dot{z}_2$	0.049 (0.27)	0.107 (0.20)	0.079 (0.42)
$\dot{z}_0$	0.063 (0.13)	0.117 (0.11)	0.118 (0.31)

incentives, and growth in the quality of labour. The elasticity of value added growth with respect to growth in the labour force is about 0.40 for annual growth and two-year growth, and 0.58 for three-year growth (which includes the earlier period 1980–83, so the results are not directly comparable). These elasticities are somewhat lower, as expected, for growth in output. Once again, the marginal growth elasticities are lower than those derived from cross-section production functions. Growth in the bonus ratio has a very marked statistical effect on output. For output measured by value added the elasticity is 0.06 on an annual basis and 0.15 over three years. Given that

TABLE 5.15. Comparison of coefficients and regression results (dummy variables omitted)

	Constant	$\dot{m}-\dot{n}$	$\dot{k}-\dot{n}$	$\dot{m}$	$\dot{k}$	$\dot{n}$	$\dot{z}_2$	$\dot{z}_0$	R^2	N
$\dot{s}$	0.019			0.613	−0.016	0.223	0.034	−0.009	0.58	825
annual	(4.0)			(31.5)	(−0.97)	(4.0)	(2.6)	(−0.3)		
$\dot{s}$	0.033			0.613	0.028	0.152	0.074	−0.023	0.58	340
Two-year	(2.8)			(19.0)	(0.9)	(1.8)	(3.2)	(−0.5)		
$\dot{s}$	−0.013			0.642	0.056	0.252	0.073	0.091	0.68	385
Three-year	(−1.1)			(19.4)	(2.0)	(4.8)	(2.8)	(2.6)		
$\dot{s}-\dot{n}$	0.016	0.621	−0.016			−0.078	0.029	0.009	0.56	816
annual	(3.4)	(31.7)	(−0.8)			(−1.4)	(2.2)	(0.32)		
$\dot{s}-\dot{n}$	0.026	0.669	0.012			−0.073	0.072	−0.019	0.61	370
Two-year	(2.2)	(22.2)	(0.45)			(−0.9)	(3.4)	(−0.5)		
$\dot{q}-\dot{n}$	−0.018	0.652	0.064			0.085	0.101	0.066	0.58	430
Three-year	(−1.5)	(20.4)	(2.3)			(2.1)	(4.0)	(1.9)		
$\dot{v}$	0.039				0.098	0.389	0.057	−0.032	0.03	775
Annual	(3.7)				(2.3)	(2.9)	(1.9)	(−0.5)		
$\dot{v}$	0.038				0.115	0.293	0.088	0.125	0.04	368
Two-year	(1.7)				(2.2)	(1.7)	(2.0)	(1.6)		
$\dot{v}$	−0.031				0.135	0.583	0.169	0.194	0.24	385
Three-year	(−1.4)				(2.9)	(6.6)	(3.9)	(3.3)		
$\dot{v}-\dot{n}$	0.039		0.075			−0.271	0.065	−0.039	0.02	812
Annual	(3.7)					(2.2)	(2.2)	(−0.6)		
$\dot{v}-\dot{n}$	0.041		0.105			−0.304	0.098	0.100	0.05	374
Two-year	(1.8)		(2.0)			(−1.9)	(2.3)	(1.2)		
$\dot{v}-\dot{n}$	−0.021		0.116			−0.015	0.151	0.156	0.07	387
Three-year	(−1.0)		(2.5)			(−0.2)	(3.5)	(2.6)		

Note: t-values given in parentheses.

TABLE 5.16. Summary statistics of major variables

Year	Variables	Means	Standard deviation
Total	$\hat{c}$	6.2422	1.0750
$n = 1029$	p_k	−1.5419	0.9966
	v	6.8868	1.0006
	w	−2.1091	0.2899
	z_2	−1.6697	0.5104
YR = 1983	$\hat{c}$	6.0570	1.0496
$n = 183$	p_k	−1.5629	1.0207
	v	6.7743	1.0246
	w	−2.3448	0.2324
	z_2	−1.9212	0.5455
YR = 1984	$\hat{c}$	6.0881	1.0909
$n = 214$	p_k	−1.5972	1.0722
	v	6.8031	1.0502
	w	−2.1756	0.2400
	z_2	−1.5962	0.4687
YR = 1985	$\hat{c}$	6.2180	1.0849
$n = 210$	p_k	−1.5529	1.0571
	v	6.8631	1.0045
	w	−2.1250	0.2499
	z_2	−1.6584	0.5053
YR = 1986	$\hat{c}$	6.3803	1.0770
$n = 210$	p_k	−1.5075	0.9566
	v	6.9664	0.9547
	w	−1.9894	0.2540
	z_2	−1.6221	0.5089
YR = 1987	$\hat{c}$	6.4436	1.0244
$n = 212$	p_k	−1.4911	0.8709
	v	7.0126	0.9576
	w	−1.9427	0.2904
	z_2	−1.5865	0.4604

Note: $\hat{c}$, p_k, v, w, and z_2 are respectively the total cost, capital price, physical output, labour price (average total wage income), and bonus share in total wage income in natural logs.

the bonus ratio grew at an annual rate of about 5% in the period 1983–87, the statistical effect was to raise the p.a. growth rate by 0.3% points in the short run, and by 0.75% points in the longer run. This represents a very substantial productivity gain, and emphasizes the key role of bonus payments in stimulating efficiency in the reform period. Improvements in the quality of the labour force had no immediate impact on the growth rate, but an effect was apparent over a three-year growth period: a mean growth in the ratio of 12.6% over three years, contributed 2% to the growth of value added, and about 1% to the growth of output.

(c) *Characteristic variables*

Initially, the equations were run with dummy variables for location. There were few significant coefficients, and these variables were not included in the regressions reported in Tables 5.3 to 5.7. The implication is that the growth process was not affected by where the firm was located, contrary to our expectation that growth in output would be faster, all other things equal, in the coastal region. Any regional effects have been picked up in terms of the other variables.

The industry dummies pick up shifts in the production function that are industry-specific, and are broadly interpreted as reflecting 'technical progress'. Given the general linear model framework adopted, the coefficients are to be interpreted as deviation from the contribution to 'technical progress' in industry 8 (engineering and electrical). The results show that the contribution to growth was greater in this sector than in any other. An interesting pattern emerges: for annual and two-year growth rates, all other industries experienced a contribution 6–10 percentage points less per annum than in industry 8. However, when the three-year growth rates are considered, which include the period 1980–83, the differentials are no longer statistically significant, though still negative. The implication is that 'technical progress' was particularly rapid in industry 8 in the later period 1983–87, but not in the early period of reform.

The effect of technical advance incorporated in new plant and machinery is captured by the *AGE* dummy. The dummy takes the unit value for plants built before 1980. The coefficient is significant for annual and two-year growth rates, indicating a negative contribution to growth of about 4% points p.a. However, this variable is not significant for the three-year growth equations which again includes the 1980–83 period. One interpretation is that older capital stock is relatively inflexible and of poor quality, and presents an obstacle to short-run improvements to productivity; but in the longer run, it can be replaced or reorganized to permit efficiency gains.

The year dummies pick up cyclical exogenous effects on productivity and growth. The main feature of the results is the strongly positive contribution in the period 1983–85, when compared both to 1980–83 and 1985–87. It added 20% points to the growth in value added over the two years.

TABLE 5.17. Elasticity of output with respect to scale

Equation	Annual	Two-year	Three-year
$\dot{v}$	0.52	0.71	1.04
$\dot{s}$	0.85	0.88	1.11
$\dot{v} - \dot{n}$	0.77	0.96	1.30
$\dot{s} - \dot{n}$	0.97	1.00	1.25

Note: calculated from Tables 5.11 to 5.14.

(d) Economies of scale

As indicated above, the elasticities on capital, labour, and materials can be summed to give the elasticity of output with respect to scale. The scale coefficients implicit in the regression analysis are shown in Table 5.17.

The pattern of these coefficients is consistent: in the short run (one year), the firm experienced diseconomies of scale as output expanded, and the same was probably true, though it is less marked, over two years. By contrast, over the longer run, and when the period 1980–83 is included, there were marked scale economies. The implication is that the firms found growth difficult over short time-periods. This may have reflected difficulties in materials supplies, or just the relative inflexibility of the firms in organizing new factors of production.

The growth experiences in the reform period can be divided into three phases: 1980–83, 1983–85, and 1985–87. It was in the second phase that the firms experienced rapid growth in efficiency, no doubt related to the quickening pace of reform, and the rapid expansion of the macroeconomy. There were notable improvements in growth and efficiency related both to improvements in the quality of the labour force and to increase in the bonus/wage ratio. There were also marked differences in 'technical progress' in different sectors. In particular, the engineering and electrical industry experienced more rapid growth in the efficiency of factor use. There were not, however, differences between location, as might have been expected.

4. Determinants of Production Cost

4.1 Introduction

Duality theory suggests that a production function which treats output as a dependent variable can be converted to a cost function where output is treated as an exogenous variable. A necessary but not sufficient condition for such a conversion is that output is predetermined. Sufficient conditions also require input prices to be exogenous to the firms. Thus if both the output and the prices of input and output are set outside the firms, then it is possible to construct an equivalent cost function to reflect the production function. One advantage of a cost function is that it is possible to deduce profit from a production and cost system without estimating a profit function, since profit by definition is the difference between revenue and total cost.

The analysis follows the framework developed by Nerlove (1965) who used the Cobb–Douglas production function to derive an estimable cost function for a firm producing a predetermined output with inputs the prices of which are determined exogenously.

The question is how appropriate is this framework for the analysis of state-owned firms in the reform period. The reforms were aimed at changing the conventional model of mandatory planning to a more market-orientated mechanism. Part of output was transferred to the control of individual enterprises. Incentive schemes were introduced to raise the morale of workers. Enterprises were granted more autonomy not only in terms of output planning, but also in terms of investment, wage payments, and various other decisions. The principle of the reform was to link rewards and performance more closely in the hope that overall efficiency could be increased. In the situation created by the reforms, it seems more appropriate to assume that firms are behaving rationally, or at least they should have been able to show a more rational response to various market signals including output and prices. Moreover, because the output plan is still controlled or influenced by the planning mechanism, at least for the state sector, and input prices such as wages and capital costs were largely determined by the government or through market regulation, it may still be plausible to treat output and prices as exogenous variables. This would enable us to construct a cost function according to the principle of cost minimization.

These ideas are the basis for the empirical cost function. The expectation of cost minimization can be tested through empirical estimation once an appropriate model is established. However, the assumption of exogenous output and prices may not be completely realistic. First, output is likely to be price-responsive under the new economic environment. In particular, firms are now able to adjust output levels to a certain extent. Second, the introduction of the internal wage system suggests that the former unified wage scales may well have been violated and the setting of wage income (labour cost) may not be entirely exogenous given that managers have the tendency to satisfy their workers by paying higher wages and/or bonus. In the long term firms must try to become cost-effective in order to maintain a stronger competitive position. Thus greater autonomy should induce firms to increase productivity to compensate for the higher outlays on wages. If this happens, then the principle of cost-effectiveness will become valid. Whether firms are cost-effective can be tested by using the same framework developed by Nerlove for cost minimization.

4.2 The cost function

It is assumed that the production function of the firm has the Cobb–Douglas form, that there are only two inputs, i.e. capital and labour, and that the quantity of output and the prices of capital and labour are exogenous to the firms.

The notation is as follows:

V = quantity of physical output
K = capital input
N = labour input
P_k = capital price
W = wage
A = constant term
α = output elasticity with respect to capital
β = output elasticity with respect to labour
$\gamma = \alpha + \beta$
$\hat{C}$ = total variable cost
$\hat{W}$ = total basic wages
$\hat{B}$ = total bonus
$\hat{\pi}$ = total fulfilled profit
V = total real value added
P = price per unit of output

The Cobb–Douglas production function is written as follows:

$$V = AK^{\alpha}N^{\beta}Z_2^{\theta}. \tag{5.18}$$

Total variable cost is the sum of capital cost and labour cost

$$\hat{C} = P_kK + WN. \tag{5.19}$$

Equation (5.19) indicates that variable cost is the function of capital and labour inputs because P_k and W are treated as exogenous variables. To produce a certain amount of output the firm can manipulate the amounts of capital and labour inputs to minimize the total variable cost. This requires two preconditions: capital and labour are substitutable, and firms have the freedom to employ as much capital and labour as they wish. This is equivalent to saying that firms can cut down labour input and employ more capital if labour becomes more expensive, or vice versa. These two conditions are unlikely to be satisfied in the short run. Both labour and capital are very difficult to reduce either due to worker resistance or the slow process of scrapping capital. However, long-run adjustment of capital and labour is more likely provided the management has the freedom and the competence to adjust.

These two conditions may be less than realistic in the Chinese economy: even with economic reforms managers are still very restricted in their ability to fire workers and capital cost is difficult to measure and often undervalued deliberately by the government. The substitution of bank loans for government funds for investment may have helped ease this problem. Because bank loans bear interest while government funds do not, the capital cost has inevitably increased, inducing managers to use capital more effectively. Notwithstanding this, the impact of this system may be limited and remains to be tested.

The lack of freedom to fire workers and the distorted signals in relation to capital may be treated as extra constraints when the cost function is constructed; but because economic reforms have been targeted to reduce or even eliminate these constraints by granting more power to the managers, it will be worth while to test how effective these reform measures are. In addition, where firms cannot reduce employment on the production line, it is sometimes possible for the managers to find alternative employment opportunities to absorb redundant labour, and this is behaviour consistent with cost minimization.

To derive an estimable cost function, it is necessary to eliminate capital and labour from equation (5.19). Capital and labour inputs can be treated as a function of their prices. If they can be derived from the production function, then equation (5.19) can be reformulated so that all the right-hand-side variables are prices. To obtain this, a Lagrangean function is needed first:

$$P_k K + WN + \lambda(V - AK^{\alpha}N^{\beta}Z_2^{\theta}). \tag{5.20}$$

Taking the first-order conditions of (5.20) and setting them to zero,

$$\frac{\partial L}{\partial K} = P_k - \lambda\alpha\frac{V}{K} = 0 \tag{5.21a}$$

$$\frac{\partial L}{\partial N} = W - \lambda\beta\frac{V}{N} = 0 \tag{5.21b}$$

$$\frac{\partial L}{\partial \lambda} = V - AK^{\alpha}N^{\beta}Z_2^{\theta} = 0. \tag{5.21c}$$

By solving equation (5.21), the derived demand equations of labour and capital are obtained,

$$K = \left(\frac{V}{A}\right)^{1/(\alpha+\beta)}\left(\frac{\beta}{\alpha}\frac{P_k}{W}\right)^{-\beta/(\alpha+\beta)} \tag{5.22a}$$

$$N = \left(\frac{V}{A}\right)^{1/(\alpha+\beta)}\left(\frac{\alpha}{\beta}\cdot\frac{W}{P_k}\right)^{-\alpha/(\alpha+\beta)} \tag{5.22b}$$

Equations (5.22) are conditional demand functions for capital and labour. They are conditional because they are derived from the Lagrangean function under the condition of producing quantity V minimizing total variable cost given fixed capital and labour prices of P_k and W.

Substituting (5.22) into (5.19) and manipulating,

$$\hat{C} = \hat{A}V^{1/\gamma}P_k^{\alpha/\gamma}W^{\beta/\gamma}Z_2^{-\theta/\gamma}, \tag{5.23}$$

where

$$\gamma = \alpha + \beta$$

and

$$\hat{A} = \left\{A^{-1/\gamma}\left[\left(\frac{\alpha}{\beta}\right)^{-\alpha/\gamma} + \left(\frac{\alpha}{\beta}\right)^{-\beta/\gamma}\right]\right\}.$$

Thus, total cost is expressed in terms of physical output V and the prices of inputs P_k and W. It is interesting that the elasticities of total cost with respect to output and input prices in equation (5.23) are simply combinations of capital and labour elasticities with respect to output in equation (5.18).

The fundamental duality between cost and production function, demonstrated by Shephard (1953), ensures that the relation between the cost function, obtained empirically, and the underlying production function is unique. Under the cost-minimization assumption, which has been embodied in the way the demand functions for inputs are derived, they are just two different but equivalent ways of looking at the same thing.

The Cobb–Douglas function presented in equation (5.23) is attractive for two reasons. First, it leads to a cost function that is linear in the logarithms of the variables:

$$\hat{c} = \hat{a} + \frac{1}{\gamma}v + \frac{\alpha}{\gamma}P_k + \frac{\beta}{\gamma}w, \tag{5.24}$$

where lower-case symbols denote natural logarithms. The linearity of (5.24) makes it especially easy to estimate. Second, a single estimate of return to scale is possible and returns to scale do not depend on output or factor prices.

However, this function is not readily applicable using the present data-set. The difficulty arises from the lack of physical output and capital cost data. To overcome this, indirect estimates have to be made.

(i) *Deriving capital cost.* The problem is to identify those costs which are perceived by the managers of the enterprise to arise from the use of capital, given that the capital is owned by the state and used by the firm without an explicit charge. Interest payments and taxes which are implicitly levied on the use of capital are obvious candidates. Given some uncertainty about the identification of the appropriate items to be included, the problem was resolved by identifying non-capital costs such as bonus, wages, and fulfilled profit. These were then subtracted from value added to leave a residue which is identified as capital costs:

$$P_k = (V - \hat{W} - \hat{B} - \hat{\pi})/K. \tag{5.25}$$

This is at best a crude approximation to capital cost. (More sophisticated estimates are presented in Chapter 8 for use in the investment functions.) Two aspects require further comment. The first is the deduction of fulfilled profit ($\hat{\pi}$). The explanation is that fulfilled profit represents a charge on the activity of the enterprise which prior to reform was remitted in its entirety to the authorities. It therefore represented a fixed cost unrelated to the use of factors of production or material inputs. Even though the reform gave the firm the right to retain some of the fulfilled profit for its own uses, it remained a target which the firm had to meet, so its fixed-cost nature was essentially unchanged. The second aspect is the absence of depreciation charges in the definition of capital costs. Depreciation is regarded, in Chinese accounting, as part of the material inputs to production, and hence is netted out of value added. It is not included in the definition of production costs used in this section, and it would be inappropriate therefore to include it in our definition of capital costs. All variables are deflated to give values in 1980 prices. Capital stock is deflated by a capital price index: all other variables by the price index implicit in the data. (See Appendices 5.1 and 5.2 for details.)

(ii) *Deriving physical output*. There are two problems here. The first is that the data give the value of output (in constant 1980 prices fortunately) rather than a direct measure of physical output. However, given heterogeneity of outputs across the enterprises, even within the same sector, these constant-price output measures are the best that could be expected. The second problem is that actual output may deviate *ex post facto* from planned output, but only actual output is recorded. The procedure adopted here is to use the production function derived in Section 1 of this chapter to calculate 'planned' outputs on the basis of actual factor use. Thus the estimated version of equation (5.6) was used to generate fitted values of output per worker and hence of output. This procedure may also help with the first problem if within a sector inter-firm variations in prices emerge as residuals in what is basically a physical production function. The procedure is equivalent to estimating the cost function with instrumental variables to deal with the endogeneity of realized output, and the error with which output is measured.

The empirical equation for the cost function assumes the following form:

$$\hat{c} = d_0 + \sum_j d_j LC_j + \sum_t d_t YR_t + \delta_0 v + \delta_1 p_k + \delta_2 w + \delta_3 z_2. \tag{5.26}$$

d_0, d_j, and d_t are the intercept and coefficients for the dummy variables of location ($j = 2, 3, 4, 5$) and year ($t = 2, 3, 4, 5$); δ_0 to δ_3 are the elasticities of total variable cost with respect to output, prices, and the bonus variable. Location dummies enter the equation because there is significant variation of the constant terms among different localities. The year dummies are used to detect whether there is a pattern of change of cost-effectiveness over time. δ_0 is by definition equal to the inverse of the returns to scale. If it is less than one, there are economies of scale; if it is greater than one, there are diseconomies.

4.3 Estimated results and interpretations

Equation (5.26) was estimated with aggregated data (1,029 observations over 5 years). The data for 1980 are not used and a substantial number of observations in the remaining 5 years are excluded from

TABLE 5.18. Estimated results with aggregated data ($\hat{c}$) (N = 1029)

Variables	Model 1	Model 2	Model 3	Model 4	Model 5
Intercept	0.9238**	0.6924**	0.8920**	0.7002**	0.5186**
v	0.9468**	0.9825**	0.9474**	0.9828**	1.0263**
w	0.4975**	0.5697**	0.4842**	0.5830**	0.5926**
z_2	−0.2568**	−0.2477**	−0.2597**	−0.2470**	−0.2493**
p_k	0.3772**	0.3902**	0.3778**	0.3899**	0.4381**
LC2	—	0.3132**	—	0.3153**	0.3086**
LC3	—	0.0689**	—	0.0707**	0.1049**
LC4	—	0.2742**	—	0.2766**	0.3198**
LC5	—	0.3146**	—	0.2177**	0.4035**
YR2	—	—	−0.0259	0.0230	0.0230
YR3	—	—	−0.0066	0.0176	0.0161
YR4	—	—	0.0090	0.0369†	0.0253
YR5	—	—	0.0001	0.0098	0.0012
ID1	—	—	—	—	0.4915**
ID2	—	—	—	—	−0.0251
ID3	—	—	—	—	−0.2266**
ID4	—	—	—	—	0.1219**
ID5	—	—	—	—	0.1906**
ID6	—	—	—	—	−0.1713**
ID7	—	—	—	—	−0.0577**
ID8	—	—	—	—	−0.1327**
ε	1.0562	1.0178	1.0555	1.0175	0.9744
A − R^2	0.9424	0.9572	0.9423	0.9572	0.9741

Note: The intercept is for location 1, year 6, and ID0 which is a non-classified sector. $\hat{c}$, v, w, z_2, and p_k are defined on page 192.

LC2–LC5 are location dummy variables of the intercept for locations 2 to 5, YR2–YR5 are year dummies for years 2 to 5, and ID1–ID8 are industry dummies for industries 1 to 8.

** denotes significant level of 1%, * 5% and † 10%.

ε = economies of scale $\varepsilon = 1/\gamma_0$, γ_0 = coefficient for q.

the estimation due to data errors or extreme values which make estimations unstable and inconsistent. Five models are tested and each model has different dummy variables to capture the variations in the intercepts (Table 5.18). The coefficients are very stable and consistent under different specifications and the *t*-tests are highly significant. The adjusted R^2s are also high. There are a number of interesting results. The impact of the bonus variable is significantly negative on the total cost, indicating that a higher percentage of bonus payment in total wage income is associated with a reduction in the total cost outlay. It is also interesting to notice that the size of the negative effect on cost of the bonus variable is very similar to the size of the positive effect on output (see Section 1.2 above). Cost-effectiveness varies substantially among different locations. The intercepts for both locations 1 and 3 (model 2) are much lower than those of other locations, suggesting that the coastal regions are more cost-effective than the inland regions. The large coastal cities (location 1) are the most efficient. There are no significant changes over time in cost efficiency (model 3). Variations in cost-effectiveness across industries are very significant. Industries 3 (textiles) and 6 (chemicals) are the most efficient while industries 1 (extractive), 5 (energy), and 4 (light industry) are the least efficient. There are signs of economies of scale in the first four models, ranging from 1.7% to 5.6%. However, if industry dummies are included, there is a diseconomy of 2.6% as indicated in model 5. The inclusion of industry dummies may be inappropriate in the sense that all the variation across industries has to be restricted to the intercept and this can bias the estimates of the critical coefficients.

The cost function is also estimated using data disaggregated according to years, industries, and locations (Table 5.19). The coefficients for v, w, z_2, and p_k are all consistent in different years, sectors, and locations except in a few groupings such as industry 5. However, the inconsistent estimates for industry 5 have been observed previously. The bonus share shows a consistent and significantly negative effect on cost in every year, industry, and location although the degree of impact differs significantly among industries and locations. Bonus share seems to have greater effects in industries 4 (light), 5 (energy), 6 (chemicals), and 7 (building materials) than in other sectors. The bonus effect in location 1 (large coastal cities) is smaller than elsewhere; it is greatest in location 3 (medium and small coastal cities).

Cross-sectionally, there are always economies of scale, ranging from 3.5% in 1983 to the maximum of 7.3% in 1987. Both 1985 and 1987 had greater economies of scale than the other years. Economies of scale have much wider variations among industries, from negative 10% in industry 5 (energy) to almost 8% in industry 2 (food). Economies of scale are less impressive when the estimation is made using data disaggregated by location. They vary from negative 2.1% in location 3 (medium and small coastal cities) to 5% in location 2 (large inland cities). It is surprising that there are no economies of scale in the coastal regions while the opposite finding is observed in all inland cities.

These estimated results strongly support the hypothesis that economic reforms have induced enterprises to be more concerned about minimizing production costs. The theoretical model is derived under the condition of cost minimization subject to the production constraint assuming a Cobb–Douglas function. The results are consistent with

TABLE 5.19. Estimated results by year, industry and location (dependent variable: $\hat{c}$)

Groups	Intercept	v	w	z_2	p_k	N	R^2	prob > F	ε
YR = 1983	0.9939**	0.9659**	0.5782**	−0.2558**	0.3939**	182	0.9308	0.0001	1.0353
YR = 1984	1.0768**	0.9481**	0.6019**	−0.2595**	0.3401**	214	0.9458	0.0001	1.0547
YR = 1985	0.7393**	0.9427**	0.3901**	−0.2556**	0.3773**	210	0.9457	0.0001	1.0608
YR = 1986	0.7003**	0.9603**	0.4256**	−0.2538**	0.3813**	212	0.9420	0.0001	1.0413
YR = 1987	0.9670**	0.9321**	0.4482**	−0.2811**	0.4262**	211	0.9410	0.0001	1.0728
ID1	1.1485**	1.0061**	0.5401**	−0.1879**	0.3444**	42	0.9752	0.0001	0.9939
ID2	0.8879**	0.9268**	0.2764**	−0.1926**	0.5697**	77	0.8990	0.0001	1.0790
ID3	0.1236**	1.0008**	0.3100**	−0.1892**	0.3886**	91	0.9730	0.0001	0.9992
ID4	1.0423**	0.9684**	0.6267**	−0.3202**	0.3706**	116	0.9547	0.0001	1.0326
ID5	−0.6862**	1.1081**	−0.0876	−0.4432**	1.0253**	33	0.9819	0.0001	0.9024
ID6	0.8816**	0.9520**	0.5234**	−0.3270**	0.4841**	154	0.9605	0.0001	1.0504
ID7	0.8342**	0.9832**	0.6571**	−0.3816**	0.3816**	170	0.9715	0.0001	1.0171
ID8	0.9881**	0.9550**	0.4838**	−0.1966**	0.4384**	201	0.9566	0.0001	1.0471
LC1	0.5386**	0.9919**	0.4363**	−0.1642**	0.4478**	232	0.9419	0.0001	1.0082
LC2	1.2911**	0.9507**	0.6248**	−0.2832**	0.3943**	252	0.9421	0.0001	1.0519
LC3	0.3795**	1.0216**	0.5641**	−0.3300**	0.4039**	144	0.9463	0.0001	0.9789
LC4	1.1368**	0.9632**	0.6223**	−0.2311**	0.3313**	213	0.9721	0.0001	1.0382
LC5	1.0094**	0.9765**	0.5885**	−0.2753**	0.3772**	99	0.9828	0.0001	1.0241

Note: ID1–ID8 denote industries 1 to 8 respectively; LC1–LC5 denote locations 1 to 5 respectively.
$\hat{c}$ = total cost in logarithms; v, w, z_2, and p_k are defined on page 192.
ε = economies of scale, $\varepsilon = 1/\gamma_0$, γ_0 = coefficient for q.
** denotes significance level of 1%.

those found in our previous analysis of productive efficiency, i.e. with an unrestricted Cobb–Douglas production function, in that the values of the coefficients of output and input prices are as expected from the original production function.

The results also suggest that input prices and output can be treated as exogenous variables without causing noticeable errors even after the economic reforms which allowed output and prices to be determined by individual enterprises to a certain degree. Bonus share has exactly the opposite effect on cost as was found for output. It stimulated productive efficiency on the production side but encouraged cost saving on the cost side. Significant economies of scale are present in the modelling results although wide variations are observed among industrial sectors. Location is a significant determinant of costs with firms in coastal cities enjoying substantial cost advantages.

5. Conclusions

The objective of this chapter has been to explore the determinants of productivity levels, output growth, and costs in the sample of state-owned firms. Our particular interest has been in discerning the impact of the reform programme.

Fairly extensive experimentation with other functional forms, including the CES function, convinced us that we would not lose a great deal of information if we used the Cobb–Douglas production function as the basis for analysis. It also has the additional advantage of simplicity, and transparency in interpretation of the results. In the circumstances it fitted the data remarkably well. The same can be said of the cost function, where the additional assumptions of given outputs, and exogenously determined input prices, are required. There is nothing in our results to suggest that either these assumptions, or the hypothesis of cost minimization is misleading.

The fitted coefficients of the production functions and the cost functions gave no surprises in terms of the underlying technology. Economies of scale were present in virtually all industry sectors, more so for firms in small and medium-sized cities. Firms in larger cities appear to have exhausted scale economies, being on average much larger. Light industry uses capital more efficiently than heavy industry, reflecting perhaps years of planners' bias towards investment in heavy industry regardless of the returns. Labour quality, measured by the educational attainments of the work-force, only has an impact on productivity in the more capital-intensive sectors. Location is very important, with firms located in the coastal cities exhibiting much higher productivity and lower costs. These differences persist even when the functions are adjusted for labour quality, capital intensity, and scale. They must therefore reflect the long industrial history of the coastal zone.

One particularly important result is that there is no evidence of a steady improvement in total factor productivity, or reduction in costs over time, such as might be attributed to technical progress. In the production function analysis a cyclical pattern emerges. Total factor productivity fell in the period 1980–83, probably due to too rapid growth of capital and the work-force relative to required industrial output. Thereafter it recovered to a peak in 1985 before falling back in 1986–87. A similar story arises from the analysis of growth in output and productivity. Given the pattern, it is appropriate to identify these movements as reflecting short-term developments in the Chinese economy rather than technical progress.

The growth analysis suggested that the industrial economy suffered from diseconomies in the short run, which possibly arose from the constraints of materials shortages, but also from rapid investment which would not be fully integrated into production immediately. Over longer time-periods (three years or more) these effects disappear. Interestingly, the growth analysis detects no major differences in the experience of firms in different locations.

We now turn to the policy variables. Only two were found to be significant: contract form, and, above all, incentive wages. The results for the contract-responsibility firms, in comparison with the director-responsibility firms, are very interesting given that these two systems were only introduced at the *end* of our period of analysis. It appears that the contract-responsibility system was subsequently applied particularly to those firms, whose initial performance was weak. Director-responsibility firms experienced a fall in total factor productivity over the period, but the performance of contract-responsibility firms improved, though not much. The quality of labour was important for director-responsibility firms, but not for contract-responsibility firms. Contract-responsibility firms grew faster due to faster growth in labour and value added per worker, but without a higher investment rate.

The second policy variable which emerges strongly as a significant and quantitatively important variable is the proportion of bonus payments in the wage total. The interpretation in this chapter has been that bonus incentives had a dramatic effect on productivity, costs, and output growth, particularly in the period 1980–85 when they were introduced. If this interpretation can be sustained, then the payment of bonus was probably the single most important reform affecting the performance of these enterprises. There is, however, one important reservation about this interpretation. Causation could run from efficiency to profits to bonus payments rather than the other way round. This possibility is explored in the next chapter.

APPENDIX 5.1
The Data

Our data-set consists of 386 observations in six different years, 1980, 1983 to 1987. Each observation represents a state-owned manufacturing enterprise. The qualitative and quantitative questionnaires provide more than 200 items for every observation. These items cover all the variables needed to estimate the equations in the text in terms of quantitative indicators but they do not provide adequate information about inflation and prices. The definitions of industrial sectors, firms' locations, and firms' contract forms are provided in Chapter 3. However, in order to make our presentation clearer, we repeat the definition of these characteristic variables.

(i) Year ⇒ YR(t), t = 1, 2, 3, 4, 5, 6.
1 = 1980, 2 = 1983, 3 = 1984, . . . , 6 = 1987
(ii) Contract Form ⇒ CF1 = contract form 1, the contract responsibility.
⇒ CF2 = contract form 2, the director responsibility.
(iii) Industries ⇒ ID(j), j = 1, 2, 3, 4, 5, 6, 7, 8.
1 = Extractive; 2 = Food and drink
3 = Textiles; 4 = Light and craft
5 = Energy; 6 = Chemical and medicine
7 = Building materials and metals; 8 = Electronic and engineering.
(iv) Location ⇒ LC(r), r = 1, 2, 3, 4, 5.
1 = Large coastal city;
2 = Large inland city with reform experiments;
3 = Medium and small-sized coastal and economically more advanced city;
4 = Medium-sized inland city;
5 = Small inland city.

In fitting the production function, we need to estimate real value added as the dependent variable. Real capital stock and labour inputs must also be estimated. Data for the average total number of workers of each enterprise in each year are readily available in the data-set. For labour quality, we calculate the share of labour force with higher education and senior-middle schooling in the total labour force in each firm each year. There are no direct price indexes for value added or for capital stock in the data. However, we can derive a price index for the total industrial output for each firm in each year because total output is measured in current prices and in 1980 constant prices. A price index generated for total industrial output may not be the same as the 'true' index for value added or for material consumption. However the index for total output is considered to be a good proxy for the index of value added.

The price index can be written as:

$$IDX_{it} = \frac{G02_{it}}{G01_{it}}, \quad i = 1, \ldots, n. \quad t = 1, \ldots, 6. \tag{A5.1}$$

where IDX_{it} = price index for gross industrial output for firm i in year t,
$G02_{it}$ = gross industrial output for firm i in year t, measured in current prices,
$G01_{it}$ = gross industrial output for firm i in year t, measured in constant 1980 price.

We deflated the value added by IDX_{it} as follows

$$VA_{it} = \frac{OVA_{it}}{IDX_{it}}, \quad i = 1, \ldots, n. \quad t = 1, \ldots, 6. \tag{A5.2}$$

where VA_{it} = value added in real terms for firm i in year t,
OVA_{it} = value added measured in current prices for firm i in year t.

It is more complicated to estimate the real net assets or capital stock with the available data. If it is a reasonable approximation to use IDX_{it} to deflate the value added for the firms, it is much less reasonable to use IDX_{it} to deflate the capital stock. There are at least two reasons to argue against its use:

(i) Except in the base year (in our case, 1980), capital stock could not simply be deflated by a single index even if the index was exactly the same as the inflation rate of capital stock. For the Chinese state-owned enterprises an index can only be used to deflate the residual portion of capital stocks between different time-periods, i.e. only the differential of capital stock between two different periods, say, t and $t + 1$, can be deflated. This is because the book value of capital stock which already exists in year t will have the same book value in year $t + 1$, etc. even though the same piece of machinery or equipment, in year t may cost more (or less) in year $t + 1$. This is due to the Chinese accounting system which does not revalue when an asset is carried over to a new time-period.

(ii) The price index generated by equation (A5.1) is not an appropriate index to deflate capital stock. It may increase over time for some firms but it may also decline over time for some other firms. However, it may be appropriate to assume that the price for capital stocks will increase monotonically over time and different firms will have a similar price index for capital stock.

Based upon the above assumptions, we derived the index for capital stocks as follows:

$$\overline{IDX_t} = \frac{1}{S}\sum_{i=1}^{S} IDX_{it}^{*} \tag{A5.3}$$

where $\overline{IDX_t}$ is the average price index estimated for capital stock in year t, $IDX_{it}^{*} \equiv IDX_{it}$ if $IDX_{it} > 1.0$.
$S \subset N$ is the number of firms in year t whose $IDX_{it} > 1.0$ and N is the total number of firms in year t, in the capital-goods sector.

The average price index estimated for capital stock for all years is as follows:

Year	1980 $\overline{IDX}_{80}$	1983 $\overline{IDX}_{83}$	1984 $\overline{IDX}_{84}$	1985 $\overline{IDX}_{85}$	1986 $\overline{IDX}_{86}$	1987 $\overline{IDX}_{87}$
Value	1	1.0971	1.1241	1.1900	1.2314	1.3016

In a large data-set, errors are almost inevitable. Of course there are many ways of detecting data reliability. One important way of checking data consistency is to look at logical relationships between data items. We have done the basic data check with the quantitative data and the results are presented in Appendix I: the general reliability of the data-set does not deter us from estimating a reasonable production function. However, this does not mean that we do not need to look at the data in more detail in order to exclude those 'extreme' or 'unreasonable' observations from our analysis.

With the pooled panel data of six years and 386 firms we have a total number of 2,316 observations. When the missing observations are discounted, there still remain some 1,800 usable observations. Then, we set the following two criteria to exclude the 'extreme' observations before any estimation:

(i) If total capital stock for any observation is equal or greater than 1.33 billion yuan, the observation will be excluded. We set this condition because we found that some firms in some years had very large capital stocks which were apparently data errors.

(ii) If the growth rates of capital stock, total number of workers and value added are greater than 130% between 1980 and 1983, and if the same indicators are greater than 100% on an annual basis after 1983, then the corresponding observations will be dropped from the analysis. If we find the capital stock, total number of workers or value added drop by more than 50% within one year the corresponding observations will be excluded.

By imposing these two criteria, the number of observations is cut by about 20% from 1,800 to 1,466. Such a number of observations is still adequate to carry out the estimations in the text. Summary statistics and the number of observations after data trimming for each variable used in our models are presented in Table 5.A1

TABLE 5.A1. Summary statistics of variables used

Variables	N	Mean	Standard deviation	Variables	N	Mean	Standard deviation
Total data				$YR = 6$			
q	1643	−0.5826	0.9182	q	261	−0.4518	0.8901
$k - n$	1660	−0.3932	0.7108	$k - n$	269	−0.0873	0.6213
n	1668	7.3833	0.9516	n	273	7.4580	0.9740
z_0	1565	−1.2896	0.6043	z_0	265	−1.1139	0.4647
Z_2	1568	0.1789	0.0921	Z_2	257	0.2292	0.0963
$YR = 1$				$ID = 1$			
q	307	−0.7478	0.9880	q	94	−1.4361	0.7882
$k - n$	312	−0.6984	0.7673	$k - n$	95	0.1569	0.7602
n	314	7.2165	0.9612	n	95	7.7694	1.3227
z_0	278	−1.4702	0.7504	z_0	87	−1.3612	0.6854
Z_2	284	0.1329	0.0620	Z_2	94	0.1670	0.0935
$YR = 2$				$ID = 2$			
q	243	−0.6977	0.8975	q	220	0.1044	1.1381
$k - n$	245	−0.5097	0.6797	$k - n$	221	−0.5167	0.6861
n	245	7.4092	0.9744	n	223	7.0276	0.8269
z_0	221	−1.4689	0.6644	z_0	209	−1.2885	0.6352
Z_2	232	0.1474	0.0669	Z_2	208	0.1863	0.0910
$YR = 3$				$ID = 3$			
q	277	−0.5719	0.9359	q	172	−0.7546	0.7088
$k - n$	277	−0.4478	0.6766	$k - n$	178	−0.9695	0.7011
n	277	7.3807	0.9303	n	178	7.2776	0.7837
z_0	259	−1.3288	0.5785	z_0	173	−1.4103	0.7867
Z_2	265	0.1817	0.0790	Z_2	160	0.1559	0.0853
$YR = 4$				$ID = 4$			
q	273	−0.4787	0.8806	q	214	−0.9284	0.6433
$k - n$	273	−0.3416	0.6588	$k - n$	218	−0.5059	0.5566
n	274	7.4286	0.9295	n	218	6.8239	0.6793
z_0	266	−1.2296	0.5184	z_0	190	−1.4690	0.6201
Z_2	261	0.1791	0.0738	Z_2	196	0.1618	0.0835
$YR = 5$				$ID = 5$			
q	282	−0.5354	0.8689	q	77	0.5889	1.2013
$k - n$	284	−0.2430	0.6746	$k - n$	74	0.8041	0.7718
n	285	7.4324	0.9267	n	79	7.7048	0.6632
z_0	276	−1.1538	0.5134	z_0	73	−0.9953	0.2883
Z_2	269	0.2034	0.1233	Z_2	79	0.2103	0.0723
$ID = 6$				$LCC = 4$			
q	283	−0.3581	0.7289	q	387	−0.7535	0.8993
$k - n$	287	−0.3174	0.5949	$k - n$	387	−0.5381	0.7359
n	288	7.1641	0.7844	n	392	7.3416	0.9477
z_0	261	−1.26476	0.5965	z_0	374	−1.0361	0.3989
Z_2	278	0.1931	0.1124	Z_2	380	0.1559	0.0734

TABLE 5.A1 (*cont.*)

Variables	N	Mean	Standard deviation	Variables	N	Mean	Standard deviation
$ID = 7$				$LCC = 5$			
q	280	−0.8202	0.5200	q	149	−0.9099	0.8721
$k - n$	283	−0.3553	0.6411	$k - n$	150	−0.4434	0.7816
n	283	7.7317	1.1268	n	150	6.8003	0.8603
z_0	277	−1.3131	0.5590	z_0	143	−1.5194	0.5686
Z_2	275	0.1844	0.0873	Z_2	135	0.1420	0.1048
$ID = 8$				$CF = 1$			
q	303	−0.7623	0.7830	q	967	−0.6679	0.8181
$k - n$	304	−0.4549	0.4523	$k - n$	978	−0.4318	0.6332
n	304	7.7864	0.8062	n	979	7.3691	0.9357
z_0	295	−1.1557	0.4583	z_0	936	−1.3336	0.6216
Z_2	278	0.1740	0.0834	Z_2	906	0.1756	0.0972
$LCC = 1$				$CF = 2$			
q	412	−0.2337	0.9182	q	676	−0.4604	1.0332
$k - n$	418	−0.3788	0.7670	$k - n$	682	−0.3376	0.8064
n	418	7.5482	0.8523	n	689	7.4035	0.9739
z_0	377	−1.3553	0.6689	z_0	629	−1.2242	0.5716
Z_2	410	0.2034	0.0881	Z_2	662	0.1834	0.0844
$LCC = 2$				$DD = 1$			
q	482	−0.6997	0.8725	q	606	−0.5041	0.9863
$k - n$	490	−0.2995	0.6590	$k - n$	617	−0.6435	0.6795
n	491	7.6229	1.0238	n	619	7.0278	0.7850
z_0	470	−1.3633	0.6597	z_0	572	−1.3853	0.6831
Z_2	437	0.1726	0.0774	Z_2	564	0.1692	0.0877
$LCC = 3$				$DD = 2$			
q	213	−0.4527	0.8663	q	1037	−0.6284	0.8731
$k - n$	215	−0.3381	0.5585	$k - n$	1043	−0.2440	0.6872
n	217	7.0018	0.7089	n	1049	7.5931	0.9788
z_0	201	−1.3023	0.5363	z_0	993	−1.2345	0.5465
Z_2	206	0.2099	0.1236	Z_2	1004	0.1843	0.0940

Note: q, $k - n$, and n are respectively per worker value added, per worker net capital, and total number of workers in natural logarithms.

$v - n$ = ln(V/N) real value added per worker;
$k - n$ = ln(K/N) real capital stock per worker;
n = ln(N) total number of workers,
z_0 = ln(Z_0) ratio of workers with higher education and senior-middle schooling to total number of workers,
Z_2 = direct bonus/total incomes (20/17),
YR = years (1 = 1980, 2 = 1983, . . . , 6 = 1987),
ID = industries (1, 2, . . . , 8),
LC = locations (1, 2, . . . , 5),
CF = contract forms (1, 2).

APPENDIX 5.2

Calculating the Growth of Net Capital Stock

Define for each firm:

NK_t net value of capital stock in year t,
OK_t original value of capital stock in year t, which is the sum of all previous capital expenditures without depreciation and without revaluation, but with scrapping subtracted,
DP_t accumulated depreciation on all the previous capital expenditures,
IK_t capital investment completed during year t,
TK_t capital transferred in from another state enterprise in year t,
SK_t capital scrapped during year t.

Then by definition:

$$NK_t = OK_t - DP_t \tag{5.A1}$$

$$OK_t = OK_{t-1} + IK_t + TK_t - SK_t. \tag{5.A2}$$

We note that the *change* in NK between $t - 1$ and t is precisely the addition to capital stock net of depreciation and scrapping during the year. However, the accounting conventions give all these variables at current prices. To build up a real series, we require a price index for capital goods. Unfortunately this is not available for Chinese manufacturing, and we have to make do with a capital-goods sector output price index, IDX.

Suppose that the enterprise was founded in period 0: then using the price index based on period 0 prices, we may calculate:

$$NK_0 = IK_0 + TK_0,$$
$$NK_1 = NK_0 + (NK_1 - NK_0)/IDX_1,$$
$$NK_2 = NK_1 + (NK_2 - NK_1)/IDX_2,$$
etc.

If the firm existed prior to period 0 (1980 in our data), then we have to assume that the initial $NK_0 = OK_0 - DP_0$ in the accounts is a reasonable estimate of the true net capital stock. There will be substantial errors if the price of capital goods has changed rapidly in the periods before period 0 when the firm was accumulating capital stock. It is worth noting that there was little overt price inflation in the 1970s.

Two other sources of errors should be noted. The first is that the rate of depreciation adopted in accounting conventions need not bear any relation to true economic depreciation. The second is that some reported capital stock may be non-productive.

NOTE

1. The measured fluctuation of factor productivity over time may be partly due to data error caused by the very rough approximation of an index to deflate capital stock. The Chinese method of calculating capital stock tends to underestimate the real value of capital in the relatively earlier years or exaggerate the capital value in the relatively later years. However, as long as the data-set is large and observations purely random, the bias induced by a time-dimension can be minimized and it can be captured by a time-trend variable.

6

Profits and Profit Margins

1. Introduction

In this chapter we trace the relation between efficiency and profits. The focus on profit is taken from the reform programme itself, where retention of profit to pay bonuses, and to invest in welfare and physical capital, has been a major feature of the incentives given to state-owned firms. Profit is defined as the difference between revenue and costs; or, netting out material costs, between value added and production costs which conventionally include labour and identifiable capital costs.

This chapter incorporates two distinct approaches to the problem. In the first part, the duality between production and cost functions is exploited to link value added revenue and costs. On the one hand productive inputs generate value added output, which, given prices net of sales taxes, generates revenues for the firm; on the other hand, the use of inputs generates costs. Some labour costs, especially the payment of bonuses, are endogenous to the system, as they also depend on realized profits. This feature is explicitly modelled below.

In the second half of the chapter, the focus is on the profit margins of the firms. The pre-tax profit margin is expressed as the ratio of price to average or marginal cost. It depends on the price elasticity of demand, on the objectives of the firms (or their bureaucratic supervisors) in fixing prices, and on the efficiency with which firms produce. How much of that pre-tax profit margin rewards the firm depends on the level of sales taxes.

2. A Model of Output, Cost, and Profits

In the previous chapter, a detailed discussion of the determination of productivity and output was presented. Within a neoclassical framework, a firm which maximizes profitability should simultaneously minimize cost. Under conditions of perfect competition in both factor and product markets, each firm attempts to maximize its profits by employing optimal quantities of inputs and producing an optimal quantity of output. Each firm can assume that its purchases of factors and the quantity of output which it supplies will not affect prices; hence, the price of the product and the prices of the factors are taken as given in the maximization of profit.

In a pure planned economy, the prices of output and inputs are all determined by the planners rather than the market, but firms can still theoretically maximize their profit within a given price framework. The question is whether they are willing or able to maximize profits. This depends on the incentives and constraints which they face. If they are given adequate incentives, they should be willing to promote productive efficiency, save production costs, and eventually maximize profit, subject to any constraints on their operations. In that sense, output, cost, and profit are interactive and can be estimated in a simultaneous system. This is the main objective of this analysis which seeks to establish a model for the simultaneous estimation of production, cost, and profit.

The aim is to fit the Chinese state-owned enterprise into the framework of profit maximization, and to examine its behaviour within that framework. Economic reforms have introduced various incentives for individual enterprises and their employees. The schemes of profit retention, enlarged autonomy in marketing, and the use of retained funds for welfare, investment, and bonus, should encourage firms and their workers to promote productivity, to save costs, and, above all, to increase profit. If bonus has played an important role in stimulating productive efficiency (Chapter 5, Section 1), it is also expected to have played an important role in reducing costs. In Chapter 4, the wage-bill quota was identified as a constraint on the employment and wage behaviour of the enterprises, and this constraint needs to be made explicit in the analysis.

The model begins with the production function using the classical Cobb–Douglas form. The cost function is derived from the basic production function under the condition of cost minimization. The profit function is simply an identity, i.e. it is the difference between revenue and cost. Labour cost is divided into basic wages and bonus, and both of these cost elements are treated as endogenous variables whereas capital cost is treated as exogenous. The bonus variable enters both the production and the cost functions. A detailed description of the model will be presented next. The estimated results and interpretations are discussed at the end of this Section. Two of the more important findings are that the model performs very well producing results that are consistent over time, across industry, location, and scale, and that the bonus variable plays a significant and positive role in production and a significant but negative role in cost, indicating that bonus (and thus implicitly profit retention) have a positive impact on the generation of profit. These findings suggest that enterprises have responded positively to the reforms and that the principles of profit maximization and cost minimization are of relevance to the enterprises even though they are still operating under many state-imposed restrictions, in particular the wage-bill quota.

The model consists of five simultaneously determined equations, and an identity. In this section, the specifications of each of these different equations are discussed in turn.

(*a*) *Net revenue (value added) function*

Because the sample data cover enterprises in different industries producing different products, outputs are all given in value terms rather than quantity terms. The dependent variable in this equation is the net revenue of each enterprise defined as value added. The structure of the equation is derived from the preceding analysis on productive efficiency (Chapter 5, Section 1). The main difference is that the variable representing labour quality and the year dummy variables are deleted. Thus, the net revenue equation has the following form:

$$V = A_0 A_i A_j K^{\alpha} N^{\beta} (B/W)^{\theta}, \qquad (6.1)$$

where V = value added in constant prices,
$A_0 = e^{a_0}$ is a firm-specific constant term, indicating input productivity at the firm level,
$A_i = e^{\Sigma a_i ID_i}$ for all i, $i = 1, 2, \ldots, 8$, dummy variables for industrial sectors ID_i,
$A_j = e^{\Sigma a_j LC_j}$ for all j, $j = 1, 2, \ldots, 5$, dummy variables for locations LC_j,
K = total capital stock in terms of real net assets in each firm,
N = average numbers of workers during the corresponding year in each firm,
W = wage,
B = bonus per worker,
ϕ = B/W, and
α, β, and θ are the elasticities of output with respect to capital, labour, and the bonus incentive.

For the purposes of estimating the whole system of equations, lagged adjustment in production is assumed, and this is incorporated by including the lagged dependent variable as an explanatory variable. The location dummy variables are dropped, as it is expected that location effects will be picked up by the lagged dependent variable. Capital and labour inputs are adjusted for capacity utilization. Taking logs, the production function equation becomes (where lower case indicates natural logarithms):

$$v_t = \eta_0 + \eta_1 k_t + \eta_2 n_t + \eta_3(b_t - w_t) + \eta_4 v_{t-1} + \eta_j \Sigma ID_j. \quad (6.2)$$

The η coefficients are related to the underlying coefficients of the production function by $\alpha = \eta_1(1 - \eta_4)$, $\beta = \eta_2(1 - \eta_4)$, and $\theta = \eta_3(1 - \eta_4)$. $(1 - \eta_4)$ gives the rate at which production adjusts to desired output.

(*b*) *The basic wage plus welfare equation*

As explained in Chapter 4, in a socialist economy, workers in the state-owned sector are state employees. According to socialist economic principles, they have obligations to generate a surplus both for the enterprise and for the state, and in return they are entitled to various benefits, including welfare and job security. The state also has a commitment to guarantee a minimum wage income for the workers when their firms get into financial difficulties. Applied to individual employees, it takes the form of job security and an income cushion. In the pre-reform era, this gave little incentive to workers since wage incomes were largely set by the state regardless of the actual performance of enterprises. The reforms have introduced a more flexible remuneration system and wage incomes are more closely associated with economic efficiency. However, this flexibility in wage payments is mainly reflected by the discrepancy in bonus payments among different enterprises. Basic wages and welfare are still protected by state policies to guarantee a certain living standard for all employees although these basic incomes may be somewhat affected by economic efficiency.

The wage equation developed in Chapter 4 indicates that the basic wage is determined mainly by the state wages policy, and is only slightly affected by the productivity of the workers within the enterprise. The equation is:

$$w_t = \varphi_0 + \varphi_1(v_t - n_t) + \varphi_2 w_{t-1} + \varphi_3 \bar{w}_{jt} + \varphi_t \Sigma YR_t, \quad (6.3)$$

where the lower-case symbols indicate natural logarithms, and $\bar{w}_{jt}$ is the mean wage in the sector to which the firm belongs. Lagged adjustment is again introduced via the lagged dependent variable.

(c) *Bonus equation*

Unlike basic wages plus welfare, bonus is more likely to be determined by performance. However, a lagged dependent variable is also likely to be important in the sense that once a certain level of bonus has been given in a previous year, workers will expect to have similar current bonus payments from the retained funds accumulated in previous years. During the reform period, bonus payments have been directly linked to the retained profits of the enterprise. If enterprises are able to secure a larger retained profit, they should be able to pay more bonus to their employees. Because retained profit is also linked to total profits achieved, we choose realized profit per worker to be the explanatory variable for bonus per worker.

There are however two factors external to the firm to take into account in explaining the bonus paid by the enterprise. One is that the enterprise will not allow or be allowed to let its bonus payments get out of line with the average bonus paid by other firms in the same location. The second is that the wage-bill quota, which covers all wage and bonus payments by the firm, may be a constraint on the freedom of the enterprise to raise bonuses as much as it would like. The analysis of Chapter 4 suggested that while the wage-bill quota is determined by bargaining between the firm and the local authorities, it does have an impact on the firm. Thus following the analysis in Chapter 4, the bonus equation is specified as:

$$b_t = \theta_0 + \theta_1((fp_t) - n_t) + \theta_2(y_t - y_{t-1}) + \theta_3 b_{t-1} + \theta_4 \bar{b}_t, \quad (6.4)$$

where fp is the log of realized profit, y is the wage-bill quota, and $\bar{b}$ is the local average bonus rate. This specification departs from that in Chapter 4 in that it substitutes profit per worker (FP/N) for output per worker.

(d) *Wage-bill equation*

The specification follows that of Chapter 4. The logic of the specification is that the starting-point for negotiations between the enterprise and the authorities is a forecast of the employment of the firm based on expected output growth, and the local wage and bonus/wage ratios adjusted partially for the particular circumstances of the firm. The partial adjustment is a carry-forward of some, but not all, of the wage and bonus differentials of the previous period. The equation is:

$$\begin{aligned} y_t = \omega_0 &+ \omega_1(v_t - v_{t-1}) + \omega_2 n_{t-1} + \omega_3 \bar{\phi}_{t-1} + \omega_4(\phi_{t-1} - \bar{\phi}_{t-1}) \\ &+ \omega_5 \bar{w}_{t-1} + \omega_6(w_{t-1} - \bar{w}_{t-1}) + \omega_t \Sigma YR_t, \quad (6.5) \end{aligned}$$

where ϕ is the bonus/wage ratio of the firm, and $\bar{\phi}$ is the mean bonus/wage ratio of all firms in the same location. The estimates of Chapter 4 suggested that the wage-bill growth over the period under consideration was determined more by general policy than by factors specific to the firm, and that the authorities expected a rapid growth in bonuses while basic wages were squeezed. These estimates indicate very clearly that the wage bill remained a policy instrument in this period, and that the wage and employment behaviour of the firm was thereby affected. In turn, this had its implications for the cost performance of the firms.

(e) *Total cost equation*

The total cost equation of Chapter 5 was derived by solving the following cost-minimization problem:

$$\min \hat{C} = P_k K + WN,$$

where P_k is the unit cost of capital and W is the wage.

subject to $$V = AK^{\alpha}N^{\beta}\phi^{\theta}$$

to give a total cost function of the form

$$\hat{C} = hV^{1/v}P_k^{\alpha/v}W^{\beta/v-\theta/v},$$

where $v = \alpha + \beta$ and h is a function of A and the α, β, and θ_2. For the analysis of this chapter, a further constraint is required: that wage and bonus payments should not exceed the wage-bill quota,

$$WN + BN = WN(1 + \phi) \leqslant Y.$$

Adding this constraint to the cost-minimization problem gives rise to a cost function of the following form:

$$\hat{C} = A^{-1/u}V^{1/u}P_k^{\alpha/u}W^{\beta/u}Y^{1/u}[G(\phi)]^{-1/u},$$

where $G(\phi)$ is a complex function of ϕ, which includes the Lagrange multiplier on the wage-bill quota constraint, and $u = \alpha + \beta + 1$. For the estimation purposes of this chapter, it is assumed that $G(\phi)$ can be approximated by the log-linear form $G\phi^{\gamma}$ where G is a constant. Assuming that G is subsumed in the constant A, the total cost function can be written:

$$\hat{C} = A^{-1/u}V^{1/u}P_k^{\alpha/u}W^{\beta/u}\phi^{-\gamma/u}Y^{1/u}, \quad (6.6)$$

or in log-linear form:

$$\hat{c} = \delta_0 + \delta_1 v + \delta_2 p_k + \delta_3 w + \delta_4(b - w) + \delta_5 y. \quad (6.7)$$

There is however a difficulty in using (6.7) for econometric estimation. It is evident that δ_0 will be firm-specific. In Chapter 5 this difficulty was reduced by the introduction of characteristics variables (location, industry, year). Here the problem is more acute because A in equation (6.6) subsumes G, which includes the Lagrange multiplier on the wage-bill quota constraint. To avoid estimation bias, it is necessary to rewrite (6.7) in first-difference form,

$$\hat{c}_t = \delta_0^* + \delta_1(v_t - v_{t-1}) + \delta_2(p_{kt} - p_{kt-1}) + \delta_3(w_t - w_{t-1}) \\ + \delta_4(b_t - w_t - \phi_{t-1}) + \delta_5(y_t - y_{t-1}) + \delta_6\hat{c}_{t-1}, \quad (6.8)$$

where δ_0^* is now purged of firm-specific effects, and the coefficient δ_6 should be equal to unity. The other coefficients are related to the underlying coefficients of the production as follows:

$$\delta_1 = \delta_5 = \frac{1}{\alpha + \beta + 1}, \quad \delta_2 = \frac{\alpha}{\alpha + \beta + 1}, \quad \delta_3 = \frac{\beta}{\alpha + \alpha + 1}.$$

The degree of consistency of the estimated coefficients with estimates based on α and β derived from the production function constitutes an important indicator of the extent of cost-minimization behaviour by the enterprises. The coefficient on the bonus/wage ratio is expected to be negative, if the firm is using the bonus to stimulate efficiency rather than just sharing the retained profits with the workers. The intercept, δ_0^* picks up autonomous movements in costs over time, due to general improvements in efficiency, related, for example, to technical progress.

(*f*) *The complete system*

Equations (6.2), (6.3), (6.4), (6.5), and (6.8), augmented by the profit identity given below (6.9), form a complete system, which is summarized here for convenience:

$$v_t = \eta_0 + \eta_1 k_t + \eta_2 n_t + \eta_3(b_t - w_t) + \eta_4 v_{t-1} + \eta_j \Sigma ID_j. \quad (6.2)$$

$$w_t = \varphi_0 + \varphi_1(v_t - n_t) + \varphi_2 w_{t-1} + \varphi_3 \bar{w}_{jt} + \varphi_t \Sigma YR_t. \quad (6.3)$$

$$b_t = \theta_0 + \theta_1(\ln(FP_t) - n_t) + \theta_2(y_t - y_{t-1}) + \theta_3 b_{t-1} + \theta_4 \bar{b}_t. \quad (6.4)$$

$$y_t = \omega_0 + \omega_1(v_t - v_{t-1}) + \omega_2 n_{t-1} + \omega_3\bar{\phi}_{t-1} + \omega_4(\phi_{t-1} - \bar{\phi}_{t-1}) \\ + \omega_5\bar{w}_{t-1} + \omega_6(w_{t-1} - \bar{w}_{t-1}) + \omega_t \Sigma YR_t. \quad (6.5)$$

$$\hat{c}_t = \delta_0^* + \delta_1(v_t - v_{t-1}) + \delta_2(p_{kt} - p_{kt-1}) + \delta_3(w_t - w_{t-1}) \\ + \delta_4(b_t - w_t - \phi_{t-1}) + \delta_5(y_t - y_{t-1}) + \delta_6\hat{c}_{t-1}. \quad (6.8)$$

$$FP_t = \exp(v_t)(1 - \tau_t) - \exp(\hat{c}_t). \quad (6.9)$$

In the profit identity (6.9), τ_t is the sales tax rate paid by the firm in period t. Note that in writing out this system, the firm-specific identifier, i, has been suppressed for the sake of clarity. The subscript j identifies variables relating to the *industry* to which firm i belongs, and variables with a bar relating to the *location* of the firm i. Value added (v_t), basic wage (w_t), bonus rate (b_t), total costs ($\hat{c}_t$), and profit (FP_t) enter the system as endogenous variables. Capital (k_t), labour (n_t), capital cost (P_{kt}), industry (ID_j), year (YR_t), sector- or location-specific variables, and lagged dependent variables are exogenous.

It has already been noted that the coefficients of the wage and cost functions are related to those of the production function, assuming that the firms are behaving in a cost-minimizing manner. Whether these relationships are found empirically is therefore an indirect test of the hypothesis of cost minimization. However, the main objective of the analysis in this chapter is to unravel the feedbacks from profit (defined as the difference between value added and cost) to bonus, and from bonus to efficiency in both production and cost functions, and hence to profits.

The model was run as a simultaneous system using 2SLS and 3SLS techniques, to obtain the fitted coefficients. This fitted model was then used to simulate the model to obtain predicted values of the endogenous variables. The regression results are given in Table 6.1.

The equations for the basic wage and wage bill show no major differences from the analysis of Chapter 4. The bonus equation is specified in a slightly different manner, with profit per worker instead

TABLE 6.1. Estimation results for the equation system for the generation of profits

	2SLS	3SLS
(1) Bonus (b_t)		
Intercept	−0.312 (−1.3)	−0.697 (−2.4)
$(fp_t - n_t)$	0.129 (4.2)	0.129 (4.2)
$y_t - y_{t-1}$	0.597 (2.7)	0.520 (2.6)
b_{t-1}	0.640 (21.8)	0.632 (21.7)
$\bar{b}_t$	0.229 (3.5)	0.142 (1.9)
$\bar{R}^2$	0.61	0.61
N	550	550
(2) Basic wage (w_t)		
Intercept	−0.611 (−4.9)	−0.649 (−5.6)
$(v_t - n_t)$	0.108 (5.4)	0.058 (3.1)
w_{t-1}	0.628 (18.9)	0.652 (20.1)
$\bar{w}_{jt}$	0.089 (1.9)	0.042 (1.0)
$\bar{R}^2$	0.56	0.54
N	550	551

TABLE 6.1 (*cont.*)

	2SLS	3SLS
(3) Wage bill (y_t)		
Intercept	−1.241 (−5.9)	−0.701 (−4.5)
$(v_t - v_{t-1})$	0.326 (4.3)	0.238 (2.4)
n_{t-1}	1.029 (115)	1.021 (123)
$\bar{\phi}_{t-1}$	0.976 (6.7)	0.868 (6.6)
$(\phi_{t-1} - \bar{\phi}_{t-1})$	0.609 (10.4)	0.534 (9.7)
$\bar{w}_{t-1}$	0.568 (7.6)	0.730 (13.3)
$w_{t-1} - \bar{w}_{t-1}$	0.603 (23.3)	0.602 (23.3)
$\bar{R}^2$	0.96	0.96
N	550	548
(4) Production (v_t)		
Intercept	0.293 (2.9)	0.320 (3.3)
k_t [α]	0.065 (3.9) [0.26]	0.070 (4.2) [0.28]
n_t [β]	0.173 [0.69]	0.166 [0.66]
ϕ_t [θ]	0.062 (2.9) [0.25]	0.058 (2.8) [0.23]
v_{t-1} [λ]	0.75 [0.25]	0.750 [0.25]
n_{t-1}	0.049 (2.1)	0.043 (2.1)
ind1	−0.229 (−4.1)	−0.238 (−4.4)
ind2	−0.095 (−2.9)	−0.086 (−2.6)
ind3	−0.031 (−1.0)	−0.023 (−0.8)
ind4	−0.139 (−4.5)	−0.128 (−4.2)
ind5	0.023 (0.4)	0.034 (0.6)
ind6	−0.005 (−0.2)	0.005 (0.2)
ind7	−0.080 (−2.9)	−0.068 (−2.5)
$\bar{R}^2$	0.91	0.91
N	543	543
(5) Cost equation ($\hat{c}_t$)		
Intercept	0.133 (4.3)	0.105 (3.8)
Δv_t	0.236 (6.4)	0.227 (6.1)
Δw_t	0.230 (3.5)	0.213 (4.7)
Δr_t	0.115 (6.0)	0.118 (6.3)
$\Delta \phi_t$	−0.101 (−2.3)	−0.124 (−2.3)
Δy_t	0.498 (7.6)	0.549 (3.2)
$\hat{c}_{t-1}$	0.976 (114)	0.975 (112)
$\bar{R}^2$	0.96	0.96
N	547	543

of output per worker being used as an independent variable. The fitted coefficient implies that an additional profit of 1,000 yuan per worker will generate additional bonus payments of 129 yuan per worker. The production function equation differs from that of Chapter 5 in two respects. First, lagged output is introduced as an explanatory variable, reflecting lags in the adjustment of output to inputs. After experimentation, the coefficient on lagged output was set at 0.75, suggesting fairly rapid adjustment to current inputs. Secondly, it should also be noted that the dependent variable used is output rather than output per worker as in Chapter 5. Taking these features into account, the results are broadly the same as those in Chapter 5. Most importantly, the bonus/wage ratio remains highly significant as a determinant of output, though the fitted coefficient is rather lower than that of Chapter 5 (0.25 rather than 0.36). The implication is that the causation runs in both directions between bonuses on the one hand and efficiency and profits on the other. The cost equation differs from that of Chapter 5 in that the wage bill has been introduced as an independent variable, and that the equation is written in first-difference form, for reasons already discussed. The role of the bonus/wage ratio in reducing costs is evident, and parallels the results of Chapter 5. Comparisons of the coefficients on capital and labour in the production function with the coefficients on cost of capital and wage costs in the cost function show that the theoretical cross-equation relationships held more or less precisely for the case of capital, but that the weight on labour costs in the cost function is a bit lower than would be predicted from the production function (0.23 compared to 0.35 predicted). This suggests that the firms conform to cost minimization with respect to capital usage, but less so in the use of labour, where external constraints on the firm are likely to have greater impact.

The fitted model was used to simulate the predicted levels of value added, total cost, and profit of the firms, both for the complete sample and for subsamples according to location and industry, over the three years 1985–87. The results are given in Table 6.2. The accuracy of the model's predictions is indicated by the mean error of the prediction compared to the actual realization, and by the correlation of predicted and actual values. Not all the 'error' arises from imperfections in the model: at least part of it can be attributed to unidentifiable data errors affecting the measurement of actual values. Inspection of Table 6.2 suggests that the fit of the model is generally good, across years and subsamples, with mean errors usually less than 10%, and R^2 usually greater than 0.8. One feature of the results is that the model tends to over-predict profits in 1985, but under-predict them in 1987. This suggests that the model is failing to pick up some short-run cyclical effects: 1985 was a cyclical peak, and the level of activity then fell up until 1987. One possibility is that costs were more volatile than the model predicts, with higher costs in 1985 and lower costs in 1987.

To conclude, the purpose of this section has been to explore the determinants of the profits of the sample firms within a framework where production, labour costs, and total costs are simultaneously determined. The simultaneous model has integrated the previously separated analyses of Chapters 4 and 5, enabling more attention to be paid to potential feedback effects. One key question has been the extent to which the behaviour of the firms is consistent with cost minimization. The results suggest that the firms are responsive to the prices of factors of production in determining their capital/labour ratios. A second question concerns the role of the bonus which is endogenous depending on the profits of the firm. The analysis of Chapter 5 suggested a key role for the bonus/wage ratio in increasing

TABLE 6.2. Actual and predicted mean values of profit, costs, and output by locations and industries

		1985			1986			1987		
		FP	*V*	$\hat{C}$	*FP*	*V*	$\hat{C}$	*FP*	*V*	$\hat{C}$
Total sample	*P*	637.7	6.87	5.88	626.2	6.94	6.01	660.9	6.91	6.09
	A	613.6	6.88	5.89	616.5	6.94	6.04	671.9	6.92	6.08
	ME	23.0	−0.01	−0.01	9.7	0.0	−0.03	−11.0	−0.01	0.01
	R^2	0.89	0.96	0.95	0.87	0.95	0.94	0.87	0.96	0.94
	N	197	197	197	173	173	173	162	162	162
Locations (1)	*P*	857.3	7.12	6.00	681.8	7.14	6.13	766.2	7.07	6.16
	A	804.2	7.16	6.09	720.2	7.15	6.16	762.1	7.02	6.06
	ME	53.0	−0.04	−0.09	−38.4	−0.03	−0.03	4.0	0.05	0.10
	R^2	0.86	0.95	0.96	0.70	0.91	0.89	0.91	0.94	0.92
	N	45	45	45	36	36	36	34	34	34
(2)	*P*	672.6	7.04	6.04	636.5	7.06	6.09	566.2	6.93	6.13
	A	658.3	7.05	6.06	608.4	7.05	6.14	611.7	6.98	6.16
	ME	14.3	−0.01	−0.02	28.1	0.01	−0.04	−45.5	−0.05	−0.03
	R^2	0.91	0.96	0.92	0.76	0.94	0.92	0.80	0.95	0.91
	N	56	56	56	48	48	48	48	48	48
(3)	*P*	562.9	6.84	5.72	717.3	7.01	5.93	730.7	6.96	6.06
	A	552.0	6.84	5.72	647.5	6.95	5.97	759.8	6.97	6.02
	ME	10.9	0.00	0.00	67.8	0.06	−0.04	−29.1	−0.01	0.04
	R^2	0.86	0.96	0.94	0.91	0.95	0.94	0.89	0.99	0.95
	N	30	30	30	31	31	31	28	28	28
(4)	*P*	620.3	6.76	5.87	695.8	6.87	6.06	793.2	6.89	6.12
	A	619.7	6.75	5.84	708.6	6.88	6.05	780.5	6.89	6.14
	ME	0.6	0.01	0.03	−12.8	−0.01	0.01	12.6	0.00	−0.02
	R^2	0.90	0.97	0.95	0.94	0.98	0.97	0.87	0.97	0.97
	N	45	45	45	38	38	38	35	35	35
(5)	*P*	208.7	6.20	5.43	227.6	6.27	5.59	330.4	6.54	5.81
	A	161.3	6.11	5.38	222.9	6.33	5.64	293.4	6.47	5.81
	ME	47.4	0.09	0.05	4.6	−0.06	−0.06	37.0	0.07	0.00
	R^2	0.18	0.93	0.95	0.58	0.90	0.95	0.37	0.95	0.96
	N	21	21	21	20	20	20	17	17	17

TABLE 6.2 (*cont.*)

		1985			1986			1987		
		FP	*V*	$\hat{C}$	*FP*	*V*	$\hat{C}$	*FP*	*V*	$\hat{C}$
Industries (2)	*P*	472.6	6.51	5.30	504.2	6.83	5.47	419.6	6.73	5.85
	A	417.7	6.50	5.34	505.9	6.84	5.78	509.4	6.79	5.76
	ME	54.9	0.01	−0.04	−1.7	−0.01	−0.01	−89.8	−0.06	0.09
	R^2	0.81	0.97	0.93	0.79	0.96	0.96	0.78	0.95	0.87
	N	22	22	22	15	15	15	18	18	18
(3)	*P*	495.9	6.94	5.89	575.6	7.01	6.05	855.1	7.15	6.23
	A	436.6	6.93	5.95	555.6	7.04	6.11	688.4	7.12	6.35
	ME	59.4	0.01	−0.06	20.0	−0.03	−0.06	166.7	0.03	−0.12
	R^2	0.73	0.97	0.95	0.71	0.93	0.91	0.79	0.97	0.90
	N	25	25	25	26	26	26	23	23	23
(4)	*P*	274.0	6.21	5.35	403.2	6.48	5.57	264.4	6.11	5.36
	A	255.4	6.24	5.33	361.5	6.43	5.57	308.2	6.13	5.33
	ME	18.6	−0.03	0.02	41.7	0.05	−0.00	−43.8	−0.02	0.03
	R^2	0.72	0.89	0.92	0.88	0.94	0.95	0.89	0.94	0.95
	N	25	25	25	21	21	21	22	22	22
(6)	*P*	795.5	7.08	5.96	949.5	7.08	6.09	546.9	6.89	6.06
	A	646.6	7.06	6.07	611.6	7.08	6.14	675.6	6.92	6.05
	ME	112.9	0.02	−0.11	38.0	0.00	−0.05	−128.6	−0.04	0.01
	R^2	0.87	0.96	0.94	0.89	0.97	0.96	0.79	0.96	0.95
	N	35	35	35	33	33	33	30	30	30
(7)	*P*	822.5	7.11	6.13	627.6	7.00	6.14	758.4	7.20	6.40
	A	822.4	7.08	6.08	653.3	7.01	6.15	757.5	7.14	6.32
	ME	0.09	0.03	0.05	−25.7	−0.01	−0.01	0.93	0.06	0.08
	R^2	0.86	0.97	0.95	0.86	0.95	0.94	0.86	0.95	0.94
	N	38	38	38	33	33	33	32	32	32
(8)	*P*	761.8	7.05	6.17	850.0	7.11	6.19	887.9	7.23	6.41
	A	817.6	7.09	6.17	851.6	7.10	6.24	853.8	7.21	6.42
	ME	−55.8	−0.05	0.00	−1.5	0.01	−0.05	34.1	0.01	−0.01
	R^2	0.95	0.95	0.95	0.87	0.91	0.89	0.87	0.94	0.93
	N	45	45	45	37	37	37	29	29	29

Notes: *FP* = Profit
V = Value added
$\hat{C}$ = Total costs
P = Predicted mean value
A = Actual mean value
ME = Mean error between prediction and actual
R^2 = Goodness of fit
N = No. of firms

productivity and reducing total costs, via a presumed incentive effect for workers. But that analysis was not able to eliminate the possibility that the causation is in the other direction, from exogenous efficiency to profits, enabling the firm to pay higher bonus. The analysis of this section has addressed this possibility by explicitly modelling all the links between profits and bonus. While the size of the incentive effect in the production function is somewhat reduced, it still makes an important contribution to efficiency, confirming the presumptions of Chapter 5.

3. A Model of Profit Margins

3.1 Introduction

In this section we report the results of an analysis of profit margins in the sample of firms over the period 1980–87. The use of panel data enables us to explore not only how these margins vary cross-sectionally across industry groups, locations, and firm-size, but also the variation in margins over time. A key element in the analysis is the impact of turnover tax, which is levied on firms' revenues at rates that vary substantially according to product type, and even at the product level. In particular we examine pre- and post-tax profit margins, and the incidence of the turnover tax on the pre-tax profit.

The stylized history of pricing reforms, as outlined in Chapter 1, shows that in 1980, although a process of liberalization of prices had already begun, most prices were still being set by the authorities for implementation by the firms. By 1984, enterprises were permitted to vary the prices of non-quota outputs in a range of ±20% of the official plan prices; this freedom, however, was rescinded to some extent in 1985. At the end of the survey period in 1987, the 'dual-track' pricing system was prevalent. Plan outputs had to be sold at plan prices, and were supported by the supply of planned inputs at (generally favourable) plan prices. Non-plan outputs were not subject to the same degree of control in pricing, but neither did they attract subsidized inputs for their production. Some evidence on the pricing behaviour of firms under the dual-track system is presented in Chapter 2, which analyses the responses of managers to a qualitative questionnaire. The evidence is that products outside the plan quota are not generally sold at plan prices. More than a third of the enterprises charged a price based on their production costs. Some firms looked to see what prices were being charged by other firms in the same markets. Only a minority made an independent assessment of what they thought the market would bear. We cannot be sure exactly how the balance was struck between the plan and non-plan outputs in the case of any particular firm. However we do know (from Chapter 3) that planned allocations as a proportion of total output fell in the period 1985–87 for our sample, and it is generally believed that the proportion had already fallen up to 1985.

Our existing knowledge provides little guidance as to the appropriate theoretical framework for the exploration of these issues. At one extreme we could imagine prices being set by the planning authorities with varying degrees of rationality. The supposition that prices might be set by a mark-up on costs without reference to 'market conditions' is likely to be implausible. This follows from the fact that the turnover tax was a major revenue source for the authorities, and that they were thus presumably interested in some kind of maximization of revenues. Elementary tax theory tells us that they were therefore likely to take *some* account of the price elasticity of demand in deciding both prices and tax rates. A slight variation of this model would involve the authorities in different locations having regard to local conditions in fixing prices, including the costs achievable by firms under their jurisdiction. There would not, in this case, be a single uniform price for a particular output, but a range of prices. This version is closer to the other extreme, where firms are free to set prices (at least for a substantial proportion of their output) with regard to their own perception of costs and market conditions. This is, of course, the market-economy model, and conventionally the outcome will vary depending on the market structure assumed. The implications of these theoretical variants for margins will be explored in the next section of this chapter to give some structure to the empirical work which follows.

In the empirical work, particular attention is paid to the effects of the turnover tax on the profit margin which actually accrues to the firm. The margin is defined as the ratio of profit (revenue less variable costs of both labour and materials) to sales in each firm. Our expectation is that analysis of the determinants of the margin will also give some clues as to the actual pricing behaviour of the enterprises, though the evidence can be interpreted to be consistent with a number of hypotheses about behaviour.

3.2 Some models of the price–cost margin

There are four uncertainties about how to model pricing behaviour. The first is that we cannot be sure about the objective of the actors in the situation: the authorities and the enterprises. The authorities clearly use the firms as a major source of (tax) revenue. What we do not know is whether they are single-minded in their pursuit of tax revenue, setting tax rates (imperfectly, no doubt) to maximize that revenue, or whether they temper their behaviour with regard to the effect on consumers' welfare (e.g. given a revenue target, they fix rates to minimize the loss of consumer surplus), or whether they are concerned about the risk of unpopularity arising from high prices. Similarly, we do not know whether the behaviour of the firms is motivated by compliance with externally determined norms with little economic rationality or by profit maximization. It is quite probable that their motivations changed from compliance with norms/targets to a greater emphasis on profits over the period we are analysing.

This brings us to our second uncertainty: we cannot be sure that we can gauge accurately the relationships between the authorities and the enterprise. Both quantitative indicators, and casual observation, suggest that the autonomy of the enterprises increased over the period. Perhaps the best way to characterize developments is to describe it as a bargaining game between the authorities and enterprises, in which the balance of bargaining strength was wholly in favour of the authorities at the beginning of the period, but progressively moved in favour of the firms as the reforms unfolded.

The third uncertainty concerns the degree to which the conditions in 'markets' affected pricing behaviour. Any attempts to maximize profits and/or tax revenues would, of course, have to take account of demand elasticities, at least implicitly. What is not clear is whether there was any attempt to set prices and outputs to ensure that markets cleared: the extent of rationing and/or stockpiling of unwanted output is not documented, though it was widely reported. Nor do we know whether there was any awareness of competition from other producers, particularly under the jurisdiction of other local or provincial authorities. How far, for example, were industrial producers in Jiangsu province constrained in their pricing behaviour (whether determined by the authorities or by the enterprise) by the prices set by Shanghai producers. The fourth uncertainty is related to this last point. We do not know to what extent prices for products were set for a whole 'market', be it national, provincial, or local, rather than set at the firm level with regard to the circumstances of each firm, especially its costs.

The existence of these uncertainties about pricing behaviour makes modelling difficult. The following analysis is intended to be illustrative rather than exhaustive. To structure the analysis we examine two polar cases. In the first, the enterprise plays no part in pricing/output decisions, but is a passive executive for the authorities (planners). We can thus explore the consequences of different objectives by the authorities. The characterization of the enterprise as a passive executive is certainly too simple. Principal–agent theory reminds us that agents have their own agendas. In a certain world, that does not matter, as the authorities can determine from easily observable outcomes whether their orders have been obeyed. In an uncertain world, monitoring is harder, and the managers of the firms have more scope to pursue their own goals and to avoid detection. Much will then depend on the nature of the 'contract' between the authorities and the firm: what incentives are given for compliance with instructions, and what punishments are available to the authorities if 'disobedience' is detected.

In the second polar case, we look at the behaviour of the authorities and the enterprises in the case where the authorities restrict their role to setting tax rates (and possibly 'targets') and the firm is then free to pursue its own goals within the parameters set for it. The authorities then have to use their own understanding of the behaviour of the firm to set tax rates and other parameters to constrain the outcomes in ways favourable to the authorities' goals.

(a) *Authorities fix prices and tax rates*

Assume initially that the authorities wish to maximize their tax revenue:

$$\tau p q,$$

where τ is turnover or sales tax rate, p is price, and q is level of output.

The constraint is that the firm has to be allowed to meet the zero-profit constraint:

$$pq(1 - \tau) - c(q) - F = 0,$$

where F is fixed cost, $c(q)$ is variable cost or

$$\tau = \frac{pq - c(q) - F}{pq}.$$

Substituting gives tax revenue as:

$$pq - c(q) - F,$$

i.e. the whole of profit. So maximization of tax revenue requires maximization of profit, and the price–cost margins are:

$$\text{pre-tax} \qquad \frac{p - c'(q)}{p} = \frac{1}{\varepsilon},$$

where ε is the demand elasticity,

$$\text{post-tax} \qquad \frac{p(1 - \tau) - c'(q)}{p} = \frac{F}{pq},$$

since the tax absorbs all the profit, in the case where marginal cost is equal to average variable cost.

An alternative assumption is that the authorities wish to raise a certain amount of tax from the enterprises under their control. The tax target is given by how much they have to remit to a higher authority, and by their own expenditure 'needs'. We also assume that the authorities are concerned about the effects of high prices on consumers, though the motivation is possibly as much a concern for political stability as a desire to protect the consumer.

These assumptions give rise to a standard second-best problem in the optimal tax literature:

Goods $j = 1 \ldots n$, with outputs q_j, prices p_j, marginal costs c_j, and per unit tax $\tau_j = p_j - c_j$.

The authorities' tax revenue constraint is in the form

$$\sum_j (p_j - c_j)q_j = R_0.$$

Their concerns about the effects of high prices are given by a social benefit function, which focuses on *quantities* of goods and ignores distributional effects:

$$B(q_1 \ldots q_n).$$

The problem to be solved is to maximize B less the costs of production, subject to meeting the revenue constraint.

$$B(q_1 \ldots q_n) - \sum_j c_j q_j + \phi\left[\sum_j (p_j - c_j)q_j - R_0\right].$$

The appropriate conditions are:

$$\left[\frac{\partial B}{\partial q_1}\cdot\frac{\partial q_1}{\partial p_1} - c_1\frac{\partial q_1}{\partial p_1}\right] + \phi\left[\sum_j (p_j - c_j)\frac{\partial q_j}{\partial p_1} + q_1\right] = 0.$$

$$\vdots$$

$$\left[\frac{\partial B}{\partial q_n}\cdot\frac{\partial q_n}{\partial p_n} - c_n\frac{\partial q_n}{\partial p_n}\right] + \phi\left[\sum_j (p_j - c_j)\frac{\partial q_j}{\partial p_n} + q_n\right] = 0.$$

Two further assumptions are required to interpret these conditions easily: (*a*) that cross-effects can be ignored or just simply *are* ignored by the authorities, so that $\partial q_j/\partial p_i = 0$ when the pricing of good i is under consideration; and (*b*) that at the margin the price of good i is an adequate indicator of benefit to the consumer, $\partial B/\partial q_i = p_i$.

With these assumptions we can interpret the conditions for a representative good i. First, we note that the terms in the first square brackets represent marginal net social benefit (*NSB*), and those in the second square brackets represent the marginal contribution to revenue of a small change in price i (and therefore implicitly the tax rate τ_i).

So for each good i:

$$\frac{\partial NSB/\partial p_i}{\partial R/\partial p_i} = -\phi$$

and

$$\frac{p_i - c_i}{p_i} = \frac{\tau_i}{p_i} = -\frac{\phi}{1+\phi}\frac{q_i}{p_i}\cdot\frac{\partial p_i}{\partial q_i} = \frac{\phi}{1+\phi}\frac{1}{\varepsilon_i},$$

i.e. if cross-effects are ignored, then the proportional tax rate on a good should be inversely proportional to its elasticity of demand. Goods in inelastic demand are 'good' sources of tax revenue for the authorities.

(*b*) *Authorities fix tax rates, firms fix prices*

In this case, the firms accept the tax rates set by the authorities, and are assumed to maximize profits given the constraint. The authorities adjust tax rates, given the presumed responses of the firms, either to maximize tax revenues, or to maximize net social benefit while satisfying a minimum tax-revenue constraint.

(i) The pricing behaviour of the firm

The firm is maximizing:

$$pq(1-\tau) - c(q) - F$$

and sets the price:

$$p = \frac{c'}{(1-1/\varepsilon)(1-\tau)}.$$

The pre-tax profit margin is:

$$\frac{p-c'}{p} = 1 - (1-\tau)(1-1/\varepsilon)$$
$$= (1-\tau)1/\varepsilon + \tau.$$

The post-tax margin is:

$$\frac{p(1-\tau) - c'}{p} = (1-\tau)1/\varepsilon.$$

(ii) The tax-setting behaviour of the authorities

The tax revenue accruing to the authorities is

$$R = \tau p q.$$

Using the previous results, writing the demand function as $q = f(p)$, and defining $k = c'/(1 - 1/\varepsilon)$,

$$R = \tau \frac{k}{1 - \tau} \mathrm{f}\left(\frac{k}{1 - \tau}\right).$$

There are then two possibilities:

(1) The authorities fix τ to maximize revenue, given the pricing behaviour of the firm, i.e. they maximize R. Inspection of the expression for R shows that as τ increases so $\tau/(1 - \tau)$ increases, but the demand for the good decreases. So a value of τ to maximize revenue exists within the range $\tau = \{0, 1\}$. The key question is how optimal τ^* varies with the demand function, and with the parameters underlying k, c', and ε. Inspection of the expression for R shows that a high elasticity of demand implies that increases in tax rate will drive down tax revenue rapidly. The unsurprising result is that the authorities will tend to load tax more heavily on inelastic goods.

(2) The authorities fix τ to generate sufficient revenue (R_0) across a range of taxed goods, but arrange the incidence to limit the impact on welfare. For goods $j = 1 \ldots n$ the objective function is the same as before:

$$B(q_1 \ldots q_n) - \sum_j c_j q_j + \phi\left[\sum_j (p_j - c_j) q_j - R_0\right].$$

Given the prices fixed by the firms as a function of τ_j, the demand functions $q_j = f_j(p_j)$, and the assumption that $\partial B/\partial q_j = p_j$ is an adequate indicator of welfare, it is possible to derive optimal τ_j^* as solutions to this problem. This is not pursued here. But we note that a low elasticity of demand, *ceteris paribus*, implies both greater effectiveness in generating tax revenue, and less adverse effects on welfare (indicated by real consumption).

These analytic exercises are not by any means exhaustive, but they point to the key role of the *industry* price elasticity of demand in determining the tax rates and the price–cost margins. The *location* of the enterprise may be important for two different reasons. First, it may affect the price elasticity of demand if location determines the degree to which a particular enterprise is competing with firms in other locations. Second, the tax revenue budget constraint may vary between authorities in different locations: even if tax rates nominally are uniform across all regions, the rigour and precision of implementation may well vary according to local conditions.

(*c*) *The level at which prices are fixed*

We have assumed up to now that prices are fixed at the level of the firm, with respect to the costs and demands faced by that firm. However, it is possible that prices are fixed at the level of the industry rather than the enterprise, at least within a particular region. For example, the authorities may determine a higher output price for firms within their jurisdiction. Alternatively, where firms fix their own prices, they may be constrained by the 'market' price of other firms in the locality, or the price of inputs from other regions. These possibilities may be explored, though not differentiated from each other, by including the determinants of productive efficiency in the empirical analysis of price–cost margins. Thus if prices are 'given' to the firm, then we might expect economies of scale and other determinants of higher productive efficiency to emerge as significant determinants of the price–cost margin, through their effects on costs.

(*d*) *The effect of the dual-track system*

One aspect of reform in the period since 1984 has been the emergence of the dual-track system for prices. In order to contain inflationary pressures in the economy, enterprises are required to sell plan output at state prices (and are supplied with the inputs for these outputs at state prices); non-plan output can be sold at prices determined by the enterprise. If the authorities succeed in separating plan and non-plan production, then the effect on the average price–cost margin of the firm is ambiguous. The margin on the plan output could be either favourable or unfavourable to the enterprise, given that price control affects *both* inputs and outputs.

The impact of the system is rendered even more ambiguous by the fact that it is not in practice effectively administered. For example, the enterprise may find it difficult to acquire the inputs promised under the plan at favourable prices: supplies may be siphoned off to the open market. In this case, the overall effect on profit margins is likely to be unfavourable. Alternatively, the firm may be able to acquire more inputs than it really needs under the plan, and then divert these either to the market for inputs or to non-plan production. The effect on profit margins is favourable. Naturally firms will complain about shortages of materials, but are likely to conceal excess supplies. So it is difficult to pursue the issue empirically. However, we need to be aware that such factors may have a substantial impact on reported profit margins.

3.3 Empirical specification

Following the analysis of Section 3.2 we work with the following definitions:

- Original (or pre-tax) profit margin (*OM*): the ratio of gross revenue, minus identifiable costs, to gross revenue.
- Tax rate (τ): the ratio of turnover tax to gross revenue.
- Final (or post-tax) profit margin (*FM*): the ratio of gross revenue, net of turnover tax and identifiable costs, to gross revenue.
- Identifiable costs: include all labour and materials costs, and an estimate of capital costs.

The explanatory variables include year (*YR*), industry (*ID*), scale (*SC*), location (*LC*), capital/labour ratio (*K*/*N*), labour quality (Z_0), and labour incentives (Z_2), all of which have been previously defined. Additional variables are:

(i) Age of capital stock (*QTC*): Each firm was required to give the approximate date of installation of its major equipment. *QTC* was used as a dummy variable equal to unity for major equipment of 1980's vintage.

(ii) Provenance of capital stock (*QMC*): A dummy variable set equal to unity if more than 10% of the firm's equipment was imported. Like *QTC*, the assumption is that such equipment will raise margins due to improved product quality and lower costs.

(iii) Selling cost ratio (*SCR*): Gives the ratio of selling expenses to total costs. In so far as selling costs represent greater efforts by the firm to sell its output by shifting its demand curve, then the expectation is that margins will be higher.

(iv) Material cost ratio (*MCR*): Indicates the share of material costs in gross output value. Given the difficulties faced by enterprises in securing material supplies, a higher *MCR* is likely to constrain the firm and reduce its overall profit margin.

The variables listed above are available for a large sample of firms in most years: for additional variables the sample is smaller.

(v) Non-plan shares of inputs (*IS*) and outputs (*OS*): Greater freedom in buying inputs and selling outputs is expected to enable firms to improve profit margins, subject to the caveats expressed in the discussion of the dual-track system above.

(vi) R & D expenditure as a share of total costs (*RDR*): Although the expenditure itself raises costs, there should be offsetting gains in terms of higher margins and/or lower costs.

(vii) Product innovation (*VR*): This is the ratio of the number of new varieties put into production to the total number of varieties produced. The expectation is that new varieties will generate higher margins, though this may be offset to some extent by the launch costs.

(viii) Advertising cost ratio (*ACR*): The ratio of advertising cost to total selling costs, which is expected to be associated with higher margins.

Among the explanatory variables, some (*YR*, *ID*, *SC*, *LOC*, *SCR*, *IS*, *OS*, *RDR*, *VR*, and *ACR*) are identified as relating mainly to the demand side, and can therefore be interpreted as determinants of the price–cost margins and tax rates as outlined above. Other explanatory variables, such as K/N, Z_0, Z_2, *QTC*, *QMC*, *MCR*, and *RDR*, will have their primary impact on costs. Their presence in the regression equations can therefore be regarded as a crude test of the hypothesis, that prices are fixed (or 'market-determined') at a level outside that of the individual firm and hence increased productive efficiency will improve margins.

However the distinction between 'demand-side' and 'cost-side' variables cannot be too rigorously maintained: as already noted, some variables can be interpreted as affecting the margin in more than one way. The influence of these independent variables is tested in a general linear model. We make no attempt to test for feedback from profit margins or tax rates to variables on the right-hand side, though it is quite possible that such feedback does exist.

3.4 Results and discussion

Tables 6.3, 6.4, and 6.5 give mean values for pre-tax margins, turnover tax rates, and post-tax margins by years, by categories of firms (*IND*, *SC*, *LOC*), and by original pre-tax profit margins. Pre-tax profit margins fell on average over the period 1980–87, while the tax take rose slightly: the combined effect was a fall in post-tax margins from 20% to 14%. This pattern was repeated in most industries. Comparing industries, the most striking feature is the high incidence of tax on the food and drink sector. The pre-tax margin exceeded 50% throughout the period, but the tax virtually wiped out the profit margin (it was at its highest in 1984 at 6%). Differences between the other sectors are nothing like as marked. Pre-tax profit margins

TABLE 6.3. Pre-tax profit margins (*OM*): mean values

		1980	1983	1984	1985	1986	1987
Entire sample	%	35.96	32.86	33.17	31.47	31.71	30.31
	N	366	367	372	377	379	381
By industry							
1. Extracting	%	27.59	24.94	24.65	16.19	5.28	13.50
	N	20	19	19	20	19	20
2. Food and drink	%	62.29	54.78	57.20	51.37	51.86	51.3
	N	42	42	43	44	45	45
3. Textiles	%	26.55	18.59	18.23	19.10	17.07	15.66
	N	32	34	34	34	33	34
4. Light and craft	%	31.15	28.07	24.07	26.98	24.54	21.67
	N	40	40	39	40	40	40
5. Energy	%	36.86	37.11	37.31	37.71	35.20	43.55
	N	11	12	12	13	13	13
6. Chemicals	%	32.12	28.48	28.66	29.00	25.74	24.87
	N	56	57	57	59	60	60
7. Building materials	%	33.41	33.15	32.49	34.17	30.65	28.82
	N	52	52	53	52	52	53
8. Engineering and electrical	%	23.55	21.14	22.22	22.20	19.61	17.63
	N	58	58	58	58	59	59
By original profitability							
1. Loss	%	−36.71	−8.05	−1.73	−55.37	−23.70	−12.87
	N	13	6	6	9	9	9
2. Low	%	9.39	9.55	10.25	9.91	9.37	9.59
	N	68	102	91	86	107	129
3. Medium	%	20.24	20.41	21.06	19.77	20.20	19.43
	N	114	123	142	143	146	140
4. High	%	42.92	40.73	42.88	40.96	40.71	42.22
	N	171	136	133	139	117	103
By scale							
1. Large	%	39.00	34.72	35.44	34.49	33.21	31.83
	N	135	134	136	139	141	141
2. Medium	%	25.92	26.86	25.19	23.91	23.08	20.97
	N	123	124	124	124	125	126
3. Small	%	15.37	16.60	17.57	18.65	14.69	28.54
	N	53	55	55	57	56	57
By location							
1. Large coastal city	%	33.85	31.73	33.68	32.28	32.82	31.90
	N	85	85	87	88	88	89
2. Large inland city	%	32.51	33.47	32.81	33.21	29.90	28.17
	N	90	92	93	93	93	94
3. Medium coastal city	%	28.80	24.69	23.18	23.09	21.15	22.53
	N	47	46	45	49	49	49
4. Medium inland city	%	36.20	38.41	35.79	34.50	34.55	32.17
	N	75	77	77	77	78	78
5. Small city	%	35.79	36.44	40.61	29.48	28.66	27.12
	N	34	34	34	34	35	35

Note: *N* = number of observations

TABLE 6.4. Turnover tax rates (τ): mean values

		1980	1983	1984	1985	1986	1987
Entire sample	%	15.74	13.69	14.10	13.76	16.61	16.27
	N	366	367	372	377	379	381
By industry							
1. Extracting	%	5.83	8.10	6.55	3.04	2.97	4.35
	N	20	19	19	20	19	20
2. Food and drink	%	57.36	50.12	51.25	46.08	48.05	48.22
	N	42	42	43	44	45	45
3. Textiles	%	10.45	8.27	8.50	9.73	7.64	4.87
	N	32	34	34	34	35	34
4. Light and craft	%	8.63	8.49	7.85	9.27	9.54	8.89
	N	40	40	39	40	40	40
5. Energy	%	12.64	10.83	11.65	12.60	18.48	27.58
	N	11	12	12	13	13	13
6. Chemicals	%	6.70	6.82	7.82	8.74	8.71	8.52
	N	56	57	57	59	60	60
7. Building materials	%	8.16	8.89	8.75	12.89	12.34	12.27
	N	52	52	53	52	52	53
8. Engineering and electrical	%	6.81	6.35	6.53	7.32	7.07	7.03
	N	58	58	58	58	59	59
By original profitability							
1. Loss	%	−26.41	0.44	1.08	−49.8	−13.63	1.33
	N	13	6	6	9	9	9
2. Low	%	3.58	4.51	4.58	4.14	3.93	3.81
	N	68	102	91	86	107	129
3. Medium	%	7.04	7.11	7.74	4.75	8.96	9.04
	N	114	123	142	143	146	140
4. High	%	19.29	17.21	18.38	19.97	22.08	23.58
	N	171	136	133	139	117	103
By scale							
1. Large	%	17.77	14.40	15.34	15.65	18.09	17.78
	N	135	134	136	139	141	141
2. Medium	%	11.32	15.43	13.38	13.81	13.59	12.91
	N	123	124	124	124	125	126
3. Small	%	8.07	7.84	7.63	8.82	6.76	22.44
	N	53	55	55	57	56	57
By location							
1. Large coastal city	%	11.32	12.43	13.97	14.01	17.28	17.62
	N	85	85	87	88	88	89
2. Large inland city	%	10.39	12.54	12.33	15.43	14.99	14.46
	N	90	92	93	93	93	94
3. Medium coastal city	%	11.23	10.15	9.39	10.61	9.22	9.98
	N	47	46	45	49	49	49
4. Medium inland city	%	20.32	25.21	23.77	17.28	24.31	23.38
	N	75	77	77	77	78	78
5. Small city	%	25.80	27.88	32.98	24.67	23.39	22.12
	N	34	34	34	34	35	35

Note: *N* = number of observations

TABLE 6.5. Post-tax profit margins (*FM*): mean values

		1980	1983	1984	1985	1986	1987
Entire sample	%	20.21	19.25	19.06	17.79	5.09	14.03
	N	366	367	372	377	379	381
By industry							
1. Extracting	%	21.77	18.25	18.07	13.15	2.28	9.13
	N	20	19	19	20	19	20
2. Food and drink	%	4.93	4.67	5.94	5.27	3.79	3.10
	N	42	42	43	44	45	45
3. Textiles	%	16.08	10.31	9.74	9.36	9.42	10.76
	N	32	34	34	34	33	34
4. Light and craft	%	22.44	19.58	16.15	17.66	15.00	12.73
	N	40	40	39	40	40	40
5. Energy	%	24.21	26.28	25.66	25.11	19.38	15.97
	N	11	12	12	13	13	13
6. Chemicals	%	25.40	21.66	20.84	20.26	17.01	16.36
	N	56	57	57	59	60	60
7. Building materials	%	25.24	24.25	23.74	22.41	18.29	16.55
	N	52	52	53	52	52	53
8. Engineering and electrical	%	16.74	14.76	15.67	14.88	12.52	10.59
	N	58	58	58	58	59	59
By original profitability							
1. Loss	%	−10.12	−9.30	−2.84	−0.55	−10.02	−14.20
	N	13	6	6	9	9	9
2. Low	%	5.78	5.02	5.67	5.77	5.44	5.77
	N	68	102	91	86	107	129
3. Medium	%	13.17	13.29	13.32	15.01	11.23	10.37
	N	114	123	142	143	146	140
4. High	%	23.63	23.52	23.88	21.27	18.63	18.64
	N	171	136	133	139	117	103
By scale							
1. Large	%	21.22	20.57	20.09	18.84	15.11	14.05
	N	135	134	136	139	141	141
2. Medium	%	14.56	11.43	11.81	11.26	9.46	8.05
	N	123	124	124	124	125	126
3. Small	%	7.30	8.75	9.94	9.73	7.85	6.10
	N	53	55	55	57	56	57
By location							
1. Large coastal city	%	22.52	19.68	19.69	18.27	15.53	14.27
	N	85	85	87	88	88	89
2. Large inland city	%	22.11	20.93	20.48	17.77	14.91	13.70
	N	90	92	93	93	93	94
3. Medium coastal city	%	17.53	14.51	13.78	12.45	11.91	12.55
	N	47	46	45	49	49	49
4. Medium inland city	%	15.88	13.18	12.52	17.21	10.24	8.78
	N	75	77	77	77	78	78
5. Small city	%	9.94	8.51	7.62	5.47	5.27	4.99
	N	34	34	34	34	35	35

Note: *N* = number of observations

were in the range 20–33% in 1983, and 14–29% in 1987. Tax rates remained fairly stable over time: their net effect was to (slightly) reduce the range of after-tax margins. The profit margins and tax rates on large and medium-scale enterprises remained fairly stable, with large enterprises enjoying higher pre-tax margins on average, and paying more tax which reduced but did not eliminate the differences after tax. Small enterprises experienced some improvement in margins up to 1986, with a sudden jump in 1987, offset by a sharp increase in the average tax rate.

The variation between locations is also interesting. Tax rates are

TABLE 6.6. Determinants of pre-tax profit margins (*OM*)

Variables	Coefficients version 1	Coefficients version 2
Intercept	0.5618**	0.5308**
YR1	0.0223**	0.0410**
YR2	0.0223**	0.0379**
YR3	0.0270**	0.0322**
YR4	0.0270**	0.0330**
YR5	0.0074	0.0134*
ID1	−0.0823**	−0.0819
ID2	0.0981**	0.0911**
ID3	0.0281**	0.0252**
ID4	0.0234**	0.0240**
ID5	0.0194	0.0130
ID6	0.0458**	0.0397**
ID7	0.0297**	0.0220**
SC1	0.0573**	0.0581**
SC2	0.0388**	0.0407**
LOC1	0.0190†	0.0073
LOC2	−0.0014	−0.0067
LOC3	0.0285**	0.0183†
LOC4	0.0214*	0.0223*
QTC	0.0094	0.0093
QMC	−0.0116†	−0.0148*
K/N	0.0120	0.0084**
Z0	−0.0611**	−0.0744**
Z2	—	0.2440**
SCR	−0.1001	−0.1121
MCR	−0.6065**	−0.6126**
N	1 760	1 695
R^2	0.5291	0.5638
F-value	81.29**	86.33**
OM Mean	0.2369	0.2354

Notes: The intercept is for year 6, industry 8, scale 3, location 5.
† denotes significance at 10%, * 5%, and ** 1%.

substantially higher in locations 4 and 5 (medium and small inland cities), more than offsetting the higher pre-tax profits in these locations. Post-tax margins are therefore substantially higher in the coastal cities, and in the large inland cities (locations 1–3). This pattern may reflect less 'competition' in locations 4 and 5 permitting the authorities to insist on high margins which can then be milked for tax revenue. Finally, the relationship between profitability and tax emerges clearly from the analysis of firms classified by original (pre-tax) profit margins: loss-making firms are subsidized, and tax rates are progressive (but do not by any means equalize post-tax margins).

Detailed results on the determinants of pre-tax profits are given in Tables 6.6–6.9. The regressions are quite effective in explaining the variation in cross-section and over time ($\bar{R}^2$ usually in excess of 0.5). On the 'demand' side, margins appear to have declined over time, but particularly in 1986–87. The higher margins in industry 2 (food,

TABLE 6.7. Determinants of pre-tax profit margins (*OM*) by year

Variables	Coefficients and significance levels					
	1980	1983	1984	1985	1986	1987
Intercept	0.4240**	0.5639**	0.6217**	0.5949**	0.6391**	0.5961**
ID1	−0.0448	−0.0944**	−0.0546*	−0.1916**	−0.1285**	−0.0946**
ID2	0.1007**	0.1251**	0.0691**	0.0686**	0.0698**	0.0896**
ID3	0.0310	0.0459*	0.0411*	0.0428*	−0.0013	0.0089
ID4	0.0360	0.0538**	0.0362*	0.0031	0.0133	0.0134
ID5	0.0053	0.0091	−0.0124	0.0008	−0.0085	0.0476
ID6	0.4400†	0.0586**	0.0556**	0.0162	0.0153	0.0529**
ID7	−0.0051	0.0495**	0.0198	0.0220	0.0098	0.0294
SC1	0.1058**	0.0578**	0.0818**	0.0231	0.0368*	0.0428*
SC2	0.0860**	0.0416*	0.0442**	0.0269†	0.0292†	0.0253
LOC1	−0.0221	0.0168	−0.0045	0.0275	0.0304	0.0001
LOC2	−0.0342	0.0304	−0.0116	0.0104	0.0081	−0.0321
LOC3	0.0126	0.0433†	−0.0075	0.0042	0.0152	0.0444
LOC4	0.0071	0.0389†	0.0256	0.0220	0.0436†	−0.0000
QTC	0.0198	0.0080	0.0270	0.0050	0.0034	0.0193
QMC	−0.0124	−0.0038	−0.0519**	−0.0151	−0.0238†	0.0006
K/N	0.0093	0.0239*	−0.0008	0.0104	0.0071	0.0073
Z0	−0.0747†	−0.0729*	−0.0486	−0.0925**	−0.1322*	−0.0529
Z2	0.3086**	0.2716**	0.3223**	0.3363**	0.2349**	0.1355*
SCR	0.7035	0.1017	0.3057	−0.0708	−0.03651	−0.3645
MCR	−0.4378**	−0.6874**	−0.7288**	−0.6416**	−0.6812**	−0.6570**
N	271	277	282	287	280	293
R^2	0.4654	0.6440	0.7370	0.5837	0.5993	0.5321
F-value	10.92**	23.24**	36.71**	18.72**	19.86**	15.54**
OM Mean	0.2565	0.2455	0.2440	0.2404	0.2214	0.2064

Notes: The intercept is for industry 8, scale 3, location 5.
† denotes significance at 10% level, * 5%, and ** 1%.

TABLE 6.8. Determinants of pre-tax profit margins (*OM*) by industry

Variables	Coefficients and significance levels							
	ID1	ID2	ID3	ID4	ID5	ID6	ID7	ID8
Intercept	0.6480**	0.4029**	0.4319**	0.2897**	0.4027**	0.4298**	0.2950**	0.3761**
YR1	0.0738†	−0.0089	0.0451†	0.0877**	0.0576	0.0547**	0.0366†	0.0524*
YR2	0.0276	0.0169	0.0287	0.0663**	0.0198	0.0291	0.0560**	0.0208
YR3	0.0754†	−0.0073	0.0280	0.0465**	−0.0185	0.0268	0.0387*	0.0335†
YR4	0.0231	0.0139	0.0582**	0.0412**	0.0309	0.0116	0.0491**	0.466**
YR5	−0.0086	0.0112	0.0085	0.0333*	0.0026	−0.0023	0.0293	0.0249
SC1	0.1316**	0.0456*	0.0122	0.0086	0.1201**	0.0552**	0.1436**	0.0498*
SC2	0.2760**	0.0481*	−0.0246	−0.0081	0.0480	0.0385**	0.0935**	0.0181
LOC1	−0.0938†	−0.0378	0.0732**	0.0984**	0.0519	0.0092	0.0187	0.0314
LOC2	−0.1118**	−0.0301	0.0583*	0.0257	0.0632	0.0075	−0.0586**	0.0134
LOC3	−0.1007**	−0.0360	0.857**	0.1096**	−0.0286	0.0453*	0.1232**	0.0614*
LOC4	—	0.0044	0.0209	0.0212	—	0.0068	−0.0111	0.0608*
QTC	0.1273**	−0.221	−0.0042	0.0363**	−0.0897*	0.0098	0.0022	−0.0209
QMC	−0.0094	−0.0306*	−0.0042	−0.0145	−0.1958**	−0.0142	0.0079	0.0006
K/N	0.0166	0.0225†	0.0048	−0.0175*	0.0062	−0.0067	0.0003	0.0122
Z0	−0.5501**	−0.1204**	0.0479	−0.0037	0.0610	−0.0159	−0.113**	−0.0354
Z2	0.0729	0.1149	0.0827	0.3668**	0.3065	0.2821**	0.2538**	0.2079**
SCR	−0.6617*	−0.6582	−0.8353	−0.9727	8.8589**	0.8978	0.5235*	1.0238
MCR	−0.7944**	−0.9188**	−0.4635**	−0.3090**	−0.5870**	−0.4445**	−0.2915**	−0.4374**
N	111	241	175	206	72	320	261	302
R^2	0.7272	0.8639	0.4759	0.6233	0.7974	0.3584	0.4827	0.4051
F-value	14.74**	78.66**	7.92**	17.28**	12.73**	9.37**	12.60**	10.74**
OM Mean	0.1642	0.3561	0.1958	0.2154	0.2397	0.2144	0.2485	0.2118

Notes: The intercept is for industry 8, scale 3, location 5.
† denotes significance at 10% level, * 5%, and ** 1%.

TABLE 6.9. Additional determinants of pre-tax profit margins (*OM*)

Variables*	Equation with IS and OS	Equation with RDR and VR	Equation with ACR
Intercept	0.4884**	0.5269**	0.5225**
QTC1	0.0031	0.0107	0.0063
QMC1	−0.0178*	−0.0167**	−0.0094
K/N	0.0044	0.0084**	0.0089**
Z0	−0.0430*	−0.0835**	−0.0793**
Z2	0.2727**	0.2518**	0.2462**
SCR	0.0346	−0.1218	−0.1034
MCR	−0.5782**	−0.6047**	−0.6060**
IS	0.0231*	—	—
OS	−0.0089	—	—
RDR	—	0.0766	—
VR	—	−0.0011	—
ACR	—	—	1.3043
N	1 058	1 567	1 518
R^2	0.6110	0.5586	0.5541
F-value	59.99**	72.19**	71.32**
OM Mean	0.2552	0.2381	0.2351

Notes: The intercept is for industry 8, scale 3, location 5.
† denotes significance at 10% level, * 5%, and ** 1%.

drink, and tobacco) are very evident, while locations 3 (medium/small coastal cities) and 4 (medium inland cities) have the highest margins. None of the additional 'demand'-side variables (selling cost ratio (*SCR*), R & D ratio (*RDR*), non-plan output share (*OS*), new varieties (*VR*), and advertising ratio (*ACR*) is significant.

On the 'cost' side a number of variables are significant. The capital/labour ratio (*K/N*), and the bonus/wage ratio (Z_2) are highly significant, and have strongly positive effects on the margin (see Table 6.9). Scale of enterprise also improves the margin substantially. The non-plan share of inputs (*IS*) has a positive sign and is weakly significant. By contrast, labour quality (Z_0) and the materials cost ratio (*MCR*) have negative effects on the margin. These results suggest that prices are determined at the industry level rather than firm by firm. Efficient operation therefore improves profitability.

Regression results on the determinants of tax rates are given in Tables 6.10–6.13. On the 'demand' side they mirror the results for the pre-tax margin, and confirm the hypothesis that higher tax rates are generally closely correlated with higher margins. This does not, of course, necessarily mean that the authorities are pursuing optimal tax policies: however it is not altogether implausible that the higher

TABLE 6.10. Determinants of turnover tax rates (τ)

Variables	Coefficients version 1	Coefficients version 2
Intercept	0.3611**	0.3702**
YR1	−0.0315**	−0.0303**
YR2	−0.0190*	−0.0177*
YR3	−0.0198*	−0.0198*
YR4	−0.0059	−0.0083
YR5	−0.0062	−0.0056
ID1	−0.0423**	−0.0483**
ID2	0.1681**	0.1622**
ID3	0.0382**	0.0338**
ID4	0.0191*	0.0152†
ID5	0.0308*	0.0252†
ID6	0.0501**	0.0467**
ID7	0.0184*	0.0140†
SC1	0.0330**	0.0367**
SC2	0.0251**	0.0275**
LOC1	−0.0410**	−0.0424**
LOC2	−0.0275**	−0.0246**
LOC3	−0.0277**	−0.0278**
LOC4	−0.0057*	−0.0036
QTC	−0.0099	−0.0086
QMC	−0.0048	−0.0057
K/N	−0.0020	−0.0021
Z0	−0.0335*	−0.0406**
Z2	—	0.0295
SCR	−0.4769**	−0.4817**
MCR	−0.3854**	−0.4017**
N	1760	1695
R^2	0.4533	0.4714
F-value	59.97**	59.57**
τ mean	0.1065	0.1062

Notes: see Table 6.6.

margins and tax rates in industries 2 (food, drink, and tobacco), 3 (textiles and clothing), and 6 (chemicals, medicines, plastics) reflect lower elasticities of demand than in other sectors. Tax rates are also significantly higher in medium inland and small city locations, suggesting greater exploitation by the authorities of the tax-generating capacity of enterprises. More surprising is the significance of both the selling cost ratio (*SCR*), and the non-plan share of sales (*OS*) in reducing the effective tax rate. One explanation is that these variables might be linked to sales on which tax is evaded.

On the supply or cost side, the most distinctive feature is that

TABLE 6.11. Determinants of turnover tax rates (τ) by year

Variables	Coefficients and significance levels					
	1980	1983	1984	1985	1986	1987
Intercept	0.2329**	0.3914**	0.3898**	0.3975**	0.4213**	0.4437**
ID1	−0.0328	−0.0580*	−0.0529†	−0.0368	−0.0512*	−0.0606*
ID2	0.1812**	0.1858**	0.1600**	0.1455**	0.1412**	0.1431**
ID3	0.0374	0.0335	0.0690**	0.0684**	0.0209	−0.0104
ID4	0.0074	0.0227	0.0397*	0.0118	0.0116	0.0006
ID5	0.0477	0.0475	0.0046	0.0164	0.0126	0.0321
ID6	0.0473*	0.0424*	0.0592**	0.0591**	0.0439**	0.0374†
ID7	0.0220	0.0227	0.0158	0.0223	−0.0094	0.0043
SC1	0.0652**	0.0225	0.0515**	0.0243	0.0329*	0.0247
SC2	0.0418*	0.0266	0.0321*	0.0261	0.0238	0.0179
LOC1	−0.0599*	−0.0372	−0.0544**	−0.0348	−0.0269	−0.0346
LOC2	−0.0326	−0.0031	−0.0382†	−0.0108	−0.0103	−0.0339
LOC3	−0.0107	−0.0163	−0.0560*	−0.0427	−0.0317	−0.0103
LOC4	−0.0015	0.0048	−0.0009	−0.0139	0.0099	−0.0203
QTC	−0.0027	0.0075	0.0030	−0.0131	−0.0185†	−0.0049
QMC	−0.0029	−0.0062	−0.0356*	−0.0040	−0.0119	0.0075
K/N	−0.0052	−0.0007	−0.0038	−0.0181*	−0.0002	0.0038
Z0	−0.0792*	−0.0444	−0.0543	−0.0490	−0.0378	−0.0026
Z2	−0.0194	−0.1511	0.1038	0.1271	0.1001†	−0.0359
SCR	0.1738	−0.3624	−0.3119	−0.4699	−0.7366**	−0.6398*
MCR	−0.2409**	−0.4360**	−0.4776**	−0.4502**	−0.4921**	−0.4859**
N	271	277	282	287	280	293
R^2	0.4364	0.5239	0.5883	0.4573	0.5821	0.4479
F-value	9.72**	14.14**	18.72**	11.25**	18.11**	11.07**
τ mean	0.1045	0.1077	0.1032	0.1009	0.1083	0.1065

Notes: see Table 6.7.

neither the capital/labour ratio (K/N) nor the bonus/wage ratio (Z_2) are significant determinants of the tax rate. This strengthens our interpretation of these variables in the explanation of the pre-tax margins: lower costs improve margins, but do not increase tax rates. Labour quality (Z_0) by contrast *is* significant and negative; it does nothing, apparently, to improve efficiency, but it does enable the enterprise to reduce turnover tax. Exactly how this happens is unclear. The materials cost ratio (*MCR*) is again significant and negative: one explanation is that a high ratio implies high implicit carrying costs for materials, and this is reflected in a lower tax rate.

In summary the results on the determinants of post-tax profits (Tables 6.14–6.17) are a 'linear combination' of the results discussed above. The equalizing impact of the tax system is very evident in the results for the industry dummies (see Table 6.14). Industries 1 (extractive) and 2 (food, drink, and tobacco) emerge with the lowest

TABLE 6.12. Determinants of turnover tax rates (τ) by industry

Variables	Coefficients and significance levels							
	ID1	*ID2*	*ID3*	*ID4*	*ID5*	*ID6*	*ID7*	*ID8*
Intercept	0.0831**	0.9396**	0.1865**	0.1635**	0.3672**	0.2194**	0.1012**	0.1598**
YR1	−0.0134	−0.1328**	0.0160	−0.0265**	−0.0376	−0.0110	0.0006	−0.0394**
YR2	−0.0004	−0.0853**	0.0191	−0.0152	−0.0480	−0.0480	−0.0237†	−0.0384**
YR3	0.0007	−0.1003**	0.0264†	−0.0120†	−0.0751	−0.0184	−0.0089*	−0.0360**
YR4	−0.0081	−0.0535†	0.0514**	−0.0012	−0.0786†	0.0022	0.0039**	−0.0113
YR5	0.0016	−0.0217	0.0177	0.0034	−0.0228	0.0040	−0.0047	−0.0097
SC1	0.0148	0.0842**	−0.0029	−0.0074	0.0344	0.0083	0.0511**	0.0386*
SC2	0.0154	0.0565*	−0.0282*	−0.0173†	0.0690	0.0173	0.0599**	0.0278
LOC1	0.0072	−0.0763*	0.0179	0.0486**	0.0672	−0.0098	−0.0470**	−0.0118
LOC2	−0.0079	−0.0315	0.0310	0.0174	0.0802	0.0033	−0.0301*	−0.0118
LOC3	−0.0454**	−0.0469	0.0359*	0.0417**	0.0337	0.0195	0.0052**	0.0132
LOC4	—	0.0441	−0.0102	0.0433**	—	0.0063	−0.0375**	0.0190
QTC	−0.0088	−0.0334	−0.0007	−0.0128†	0.0001	−0.0026	0.0098	−0.0451**
QMC	−0.0035	−0.0229	0.0004	−0.0378**	−0.0520	−0.0129	0.0173	0.0300**
K/N	−0.0091*	−0.0615**	0.0042	−0.0068	−0.0002	−0.0057	−0.0007	0.0188†
Z0	−0.0030	−0.1110*	0.0228	0.0005	−0.1009	−0.0264	−0.0644*	−0.0683*
Z2	0.0068	0.0923	−0.0055	−0.0041	0.0618	0.0351	−0.0054	−0.0631
SCR	−0.1520†	−1.6009**	−1.1942	−0.0719	−0.0595	0.9114†	−0.0290*	0.3498
MCR	−0.0336	−0.9155**	−0.1855**	−0.1187**	−0.4153**	−0.1732**	−0.0096**	−0.1172**
N	111	241	175	206	72	320	261	302
R^2	0.3311	0.7793	0.2779	0.3459	0.3561	0.1272	0.1050	0.1917
F-value	2.74**	43.74**	3.36**	5.52**	1.79*	2.44**	1.58†	3.87**
τ mean	0.0389	0.2657	0.0812	0.0752	0.0866	0.0908	0.0932	0.0715

Notes: See Table 6.8.

TABLE 6.13. Additional determinants of turnover tax rates (τ)

Variables*	Equation with IS and OS	Equation with RDR and VR	Equation with ACR
Intercept	0.4381**	0.3693**	0.3756**
QTC	−0.0156†	−0.0098	−0.0119†
QMC	−0.0048	−0.0051	−0.0021
K/N	−0.0049	−0.0028	−0.0028
Z0	−0.0620**	−0.0480**	−0.0428**
Z2	0.0328	0.0360	0.0279
SCR	−0.6248**	−0.4834**	−0.5025**
MCR	−0.4001**	−0.4012**	−0.4053**
IS	0.0174*	—	—
OS	−0.0333**	—	—
RDR	—	−0.1299	—
VR	—	0.077†	—
ACR	—	—	−1.9302
N	1058	1567	1518
R^2	0.5757	0.4804	0.4757
F-value	51.982**	52.78**	52.07**
τ mean	0.1237	0.1084	0.1077

Notes: see Table 6.9.

TABLE 6.14. Determinants of post-tax profit margins (*FM*)

Variables	Coefficients version 1	Coefficients version 2
Intercept	0.2007**	0.7605**
YR1	0.0538**	0.0555**
YR2	0.0413**	0.0555**
YR3	0.0468**	0.0520**
YR4	0.0329**	0.0414**
YR5	0.0136*	0.0189**
ID1	−0.0400**	−0.0336**
ID2	−0.0700**	−0.0711**
ID3	−0.0101	−0.0086
ID4	0.0043	0.0088
ID5	−0.0113	−0.0122
ID6	−0.0043	−0.0069
ID7	0.0113	0.0080
SC1	0.0243**	0.0214**
SC2	0.0137**	0.0132**
LOC1	0.0600**	0.0497**
LOC2	0.0261**	0.0179*
LOC3	0.0562**	0.0461**
LOC4	0.0271**	0.0259**

TABLE 6.14 (*cont.*)

Variables	Coefficients version 1	Coefficients version 2
QTC	0.0194**	0.0179**
QMC	−0.0068	−0.0091†
K/N	0.0139**	0.0104**
Z0	−0.0276*	−0.0338**
Z2	—	0.2145**
SCR	0.3768**	0.3696**
MCR	−0.2211**	−0.2110**
N	1760	1695
R^2	0.2566	0.2839
F-value	24.97**	26.48**
FM mean	0.1303	0.1292

Notes: see Table 6.6.

TABLE 6.15. Determinants of post-tax profit margins (*FM*) by year

Variables	Coefficients and significance levels					
	1980	1983	1984	1985	1986	1987
Intercept	0.1910**	0.1725**	0.2319**	0.1975**	0.2179**	0.1523**
ID1	−0.0120	−0.0304	−0.0017	−0.0548*	−0.0772**	−0.0339
ID2	−0.0805*	−0.0607**	−0.0909**	−0.0769**	−0.0714**	−0.0535**
ID3	−0.0064	0.0124	−0.0279	−0.0255	−0.0222	0.0193
ID4	0.0285	0.0311	−0.0034	−0.0087	0.0018	0.0128
ID5	−0.0424	−0.0385	−0.0170	−0.0156	−0.0211	0.0155
ID6	−0.0033	0.0162	−0.0037	−0.0430**	−0.0286	0.0154
ID7	−0.0270	0.0268	0.0040	−0.0003	0.0192	0.0253
SC1	0.0407*	0.0353*	0.0302*	−0.0012	0.0039	0.0074
SC2	0.0442*	0.0149	0.0121	0.0008	0.0055	0.0074
LCC1	0.0378	0.0539**	0.0498**	0.0623**	0.0573**	0.0347*
LCC2	−0.0016	0.0335*	0.0266	0.0213	0.0184	0.0018
LCC3	0.0233	0.0606**	0.0485**	0.0469*	0.0469*	0.0547**
LCC4	0.0086	0.0341†	0.0265	0.0359†	0.0336	0.0203
QTC	0.0226	0.0005	0.0240	0.0181†	0.0219*	0.0242**
QMC	0.0105	0.0024	−0.0164	−0.0111	−0.0119	−0.0069
K/N	0.0145	0.0246**	0.0030	0.0285**	0.0073	0.0036
Z0	0.0045	−0.0285	0.0057	−0.0435	−0.0943**	−0.0503†
Z2	0.3280**	0.4226**	0.2184**	0.2092**	0.1349*	0.1714**
SCR	0.5297	0.4640	0.6176*	0.3991	0.37161	0.2753
MCR	−0.1969**	−0.2515**	−0.2514**	−0.1914**	−0.1891**	−0.1711**
N	271	277	282	287	280	293
R^2	0.2533	0.3701	0.3637	0.2958	0.2777	0.2844
F-value	4.26**	7.55**	7.49**	5.61**	5.00**	5.42**
FM mean	0.1520	0.1379	0.1408	0.1335	0.1131	0.0999

Notes: see Table 6.7.

TABLE 6.16. Determinants of post-tax profit margins (*FM*) by industry

Variables	Coefficients and significance levels							
	ID1	*ID2*	*ID3*	*ID4*	*ID5*	*ID6*	*ID7*	*ID8*
Intercept	0.5649**	−0.0368	0.2455**	0.1262**	0.0356	0.2104**	0.1938**	0.2163**
YR1	0.0872*	0.1239**	0.0290*	0.1142**	0.0952†	0.0658**	0.0360*	0.0918**
YR2	0.0281	0.1022**	0.0096	0.0816**	0.0678	0.0528**	0.0521**	0.0591**
YR3	0.0747†	0.0930**	0.0016	0.0635**	0.0566	0.0452**	0.0474**	0.0695**
YR4	0.0312	0.0674**	0.0068	0.0425**	0.1094**	0.0094	0.0452**	0.0579**
YR5	−0.0102	0.0329*	−0.0092	0.0299†	0.0255	−0.0063	0.0339*	0.0346**
SC1	0.1168**	−0.0386*	0.0151	0.0160	0.0857	0.0468**	0.0928**	0.0112
SC2	0.2606**	−0.0084	0.0036	0.0092	−0.0210	0.0212*	0.0335*	−0.0098
LCC1	−0.1009†	0.0385*	0.0553**	0.0498*	−0.0153	0.0190	0.0657**	0.0432*
LCC2	−0.1039**	0.0014	0.0273	0.0083	−0.0170	0.0042	−0.0284†	0.0252
LCC3	−0.0553	0.0109	0.0497**	0.0679**	−0.0623	0.0258*	0.1179**	0.0482**
LCC4	—	−0.0397*	0.0310*	−0.0221	—	0.0004	0.0263*	0.0417*
QTC1	0.1361**	0.0113	−0.0035	0.0491**	−0.0898	0.0123	−0.0075	0.0241*
QMC1	−0.0059	−0.0077	−0.0046	0.0234†	−0.1438**	−0.0012	−0.0095	−0.0294**
K/N	0.0257*	0.0840**	0.0006	−0.0107	0.0063	−0.0010	0.0010	−0.0066
Z0	−0.5470**	−0.0094	0.0251	−0.0042	0.1619	0.0105	−0.0468*	0.0329
Z2	0.0661	0.0226	0.0882**	0.3709**	0.2447	0.2470**	0.2592**	0.2709
SCR	−0.5096†	0.9427**	0.3589	−0.9008	8.9184*	−0.0137	0.5525**	0.6740
MCR	−0.7607**	−0.0033	−0.2780**	−0.1903**	−0.1716	−0.2713**	−0.2819**	−0.3203**
N	111	241	175	206	72	320	261	302
R^2	0.7157	0.3448	0.5391	0.5867	0.4584	0.4562	0.5909	0.4225
F-value	13.92**	6.52**	10.20**	14.83**	2.74**	14.07**	19.50**	11.54**
FM mean	0.1253	0.0904	0.1146	0.1402	0.1530	0.1236	0.1552	0.1403

Notes: see Table 6.8.

TABLE 6.17. Additional determinants of post-tax profit margins (*FM*)

Variables*	Equation with IS and OS	Equation with RDR and VR	Equation with ACR
Intercept	0.0503**	0.1576**	0.1469**
QTC	0.0187**	0.0205**	0.0182**
QMC	−0.0130*	−0.0116*	−0.0073
K/N	0.0093**	0.0111**	0.0117**
Z0	0.0190	−0.0355**	−0.0365**
Z2	0.2399**	0.2158**	0.2183**
SCR	0.6594**	0.3616**	0.3992**
MCR	−0.1781**	−0.2035**	−0.2007**
IS	0.0057	—	—
OS	0.0245**	—	—
RDR	—	0.2065*	—
VR	—	−0.0288*	—
ACR	—	—	3.2245**
N	1 058	1 567	1 518
R^2	0.3378	0.2801	0.2761
F-value	19.48**	22.19**	21.89**
FM mean	0.1315	0.1296	0.1275

Notes: see Table 6.9.

TABLE 6.18. Contributions of independent variables to profit margins and turnover tax rates at mean levels

Variable names	(1) Coefficients	(2) Mean value of variables	(3) = (1) * (2) Coefficients multiplied by mean values	(4) (3)/Mean value of dependent variables * 100%
1. Contribution to pre-tax profitability				
OM	—	0.2354	—	—
K/N	0.0084**	0.9253	0.0078	3.31
Z0	−0.0744**	0.3069	−0.0228	−9.69
Z2	0.2440**	0.1775	0.0433	18.39
SCR	−0.1121	0.0066	−0.0007	−0.30
MCR	−0.6126**	0.6895	−0.4224	−179.44
Total	—	—	—	—

TABLE 6.18 (*cont.*)

Variable names	(1) Coefficients	(2) Mean value of variables	(3) = (1) * (2) Coefficients multiplied by mean values	(4) (3)/Mean value of dependent variables * 100%
2. Contribution to post-tax profitability				
FM	—	0.1292	—	—
K/N	0.0104**	0.9253	0.0096	7.43
Z0	−0.0338**	0.3069	−0.0104	−8.05
Z2	0.2145**	0.1775	0.0381	29.49
SCR	0.3696**	0.0066	0.0024	1.86
MCR	−0.2110**	0.6895	−0.1455	−112.62
Total	—	—	—	—
3. Contribution to turnover tax rate				
τ	—	0.1062	—	—
K/N	−0.0021	0.9253	−0.0019	−1.79
Z0	−0.0406**	0.3069	−0.0125	−11.77
Z2	0.0295	0.1775	0.0052	4.90
SCR	−0.4817**	0.0066	−0.0032	−3.01
MCR	−0.4017**	0.6895	−0.2770	−260.83
Total	—	—	—	—

Notes: *OM*, τ, *FM* are original profitability, turnover tax rate and sales profitability respectively. *K/N* = capital per worker, *Z0* = labour quality, *Z2* = bonus/wage income, *SCR* = sales cost/sales, *MCR* = material cost/sales.

Sources: from Tables 6.6, 6.10, 6.14, and 6.19.

margins. Industry 1 starts as the least profitable before tax, and even a lower tax rate fails to bring it into line. Industry 2, by contrast, starts as the most profitable sector, by a considerable margin, and is reduced, by taxation, to a post-tax margin 7% below average. The decline in profit margins over time is very evident, and particularly in 1986–87. Lower tax rates in locations 1 (large coastal cities) and 3 (medium/small coastal cities) significantly enhance the post-tax margins enjoyed by enterprises located in the coastal zone. The selling cost ratio (*SCR*) and the non-plan sales share (*OS*) also contribute to post-tax margins, though the reason appears to be tax evasion rather

TABLE 6.19. Summary statistics for dependent and independent variables

Variables	N	Mean	Standard deviation
6 years' data			
OM	2064	0.2348	0.1521
τ	2064	0.1045	0.1330
FM	2064	0.1302	0.1011
Z2	1973	0.1775	0.0907
Z0	2064	0.3069	0.1720
K/N	2064	0.9253	0.8934
MCR	2047	0.6895	0.1552
SCR	2064	0.0066	0.0173
ACR	1800	0.0005	0.0020
RDR	1879	0.0025	0.0192
VR	2064	0.1066	0.1600
IS	1838	0.1993	0.2739
OS	1436	0.1950	0.3002
Year 1, 1980			
OM	338	0.2580	0.1614
τ	338	0.1025	0.1339
FM	338	0.1555	0.114000
Z2	318	0.1322	0.0688
Z0	338	0.2579	0.1818
K/N	338	0.6247	0.6320
MCR	338	0.6598	0.1930
SCR	338	0.0020	0.0116
ACR	287	0.0001	0.0006
RDR	300	0.0016	0.0084
VR	338	0.0769	0.1450
IS	297	0.1272	0.2300
OS	245	0.1437	0.2826
Year 2, 1983			
OM	337	0.2446	0.1581
τ	337	0.1077	0.1389
FM	337	0.1368	0.1020
Z2	324	0.1434	0.0695
Z0	337	0.2670	0.1713
K/N	337	0.7637	0.7089
MCR	333	0.6831	0.1474
SCR	337	0.0059	0.0164
ACR	293	0.0002	0.0014
RDR	304	0.0025	0.0187
VR	337	0.1203	0.1692
IS	295	0.1413	0.2323
OS	239	0.1422	0.2683
Year 3, 1984			
OM	347	0.2406	0.1487
τ	347	0.1012	0.1351
FM	347	0.1393	0.0922
Z2	331	0.1833	0.0838
Z0	347	0.2900	0.1657
K/N	347	0.8271	0.7601
MCR	345	0.6924	0.1535
SCR	347	0.0062	0.0147
ACR	300	0.0005	0.0020
RDR	315	0.0021	0.0086
VR	347	0.1071	0.1641
IS	304	0.1663	0.2497
OS	245	0.1809	0.3022
Year 4, 1985			
OM	348	0.2409	0.1429
τ	348	0.1078	0.1322
FM	348	0.1331	0.1015
Z2	334	0.1792	0.0799
Z0	348	0.3240	0.1593
K/N	348	0.9650	0.8870
MCR	347	0.6932	0.1423
SCR	348	0.0076	0.0154
ACR	308	0.0007	0.0024
RDR	320	0.0019	0.0065
VR	348	0.1082	0.1606
IS	314	0.2167	0.2788
OS	236	0.2148	0.3061
Year 5, 1986			
OM	340	0.2214	0.1444
τ	340	0.1061	0.1211
FM	340	0.1153	0.0981
Z2	325	0.1078	0.0978
Z0	340	0.3401	0.1637
K/N	340	1.072	1.0548
MCR	339	0.6979	0.1417
SCR	340	0.0083	0.0205
ACR	299	0.0008	0.0023
RDR	312	0.0049	0.0404
VR	340	0.1142	0.1606
IS	307	0.2402	0.2838
OS	231	0.2313	0.3011
Year 6, 1987			
OM	354	0.2045	0.1514
τ	354	0.1019	0.1367
FM	354	0.1026	0.0896
Z2	341	0.2255	0.1038
Z0	354	0.3595	0.1658
K/N	354	1.2483	1.0665
MCR	353	0.7085	0.1453
SCR	354	0.0093	0.0222
ACR	313	0.0009	0.0025
RDR	328	0.0021	0.0075
VR	354	0.1122	0.1573
IS	321	0.2943	0.3167
OS	240	0.2598	0.3219

than improved prices for output. On the supply side, larger scale, higher capital per worker (KN), greater bonus incentives (Z_2), and the R & D ratio (RDR) push up margins as firms enjoy lower costs. The quality of labour (Z_0) and the materials cost ratio (MCR) are on balance negative factors in the determination of post-tax profit margins, despite the fact that both are associated with lower implicit tax rates.

4. Conclusions

Profits are the difference between revenues and costs. Given that firms have incentives to increase profits, to pay bonuses, and to invest, they can seek either to enhance revenues or to reduce costs. The evidence presented in this chapter suggests that the firms in the sample have relied mainly on cost reduction. This conclusion is based mainly on the analysis of the determinants of pre-tax profit margins and tax rates. Profit margins have declined over time, suggesting that firms have not used their new market freedoms, under the reform, to raise prices. In cross-section none of the 'demand' side variables, e.g. proportion of sales marketed by the firm and selling expenditures, had any discernible effect on margins. Taxes tended to equalize post-tax margins. More efficient firms had higher margins. This evidence is consistent with a situation in which prices are for the most part set by the authorities with a view to milking the tax revenue. Firms accept those prices (and tax rates), but try to improve their efficiency.

The impact of efficiency on profits is clear from both the analyses in this chapter. Thus the four-equation model of Section 1 identifies the particular role of the bonus ratio and of economies of scale in increasing output and decreasing costs: given output prices these have an impact on profits which feeds back via retentions to the payment of bonus. Despite the restrictions on the payment of bonus, the impact on efficiency is evident. The same story emerges from the study of profit margins. Economies of scale, greater capital intensity, and the bonus ratio are correlated with higher pre-tax and post-tax margins, but not with tax rates. This is consistent with the hypothesis that firms are targeting costs rather than revenues to increase their profits.

Two other conclusions can be drawn. The first is that the authorities use sales taxes as a source of revenue, and that the tax rates are adjusted to increase revenues. The high tax rate on food, drink, and tobacco is clear evidence of this. The second is that a fairly simple model of the firm can adequately capture the process of generation of profits. The model presumes that the firm has little discretion over output prices, sales tax rates, basic wage rates, and capital costs. These are all presumed determined outside the firm. Given the incentive of being able to retain profits and pay bonuses, the firm concentrates on increasing output and reducing costs. The neoclassical model based on a production function (even the simplified, though analytically convenient, Cobb–Douglas function) fits the data well, and can simulate the actual outcomes without major error.

7

Flow of Funds Analysis

1. Introduction

Previous empirical chapters have looked at the employment, production, and profit elements of the behaviour and performance of large Chinese state-owned enterprises. In order to complete the picture of their economic activities we now need to explore their financing and investment. In simple schematic terms we may think of labour, which we have examined, combining with existing capital stock to generate output, as indicated by our production function analysis, generating profits. The determinants of retained profit have also been explored, mainly in terms of overall profit and capital requirements. In this chapter and the next two we look at external sources of finance, the determinants of investment expenditure on new capital equipment and their interrelation with each other, and with internal financial flows. This then provides a basis for constructing a fully integrated model of the behaviour of such enterprises.

The essential starting-point for exploring economic behaviour in these areas is *flow of funds* analysis. Within the present Chinese economic system and indeed more generally, this is a pivotal form of analysis. It allows us to identify all sources and uses of funds, examine the relative magnitudes of the components of each, and see how these change over time and as between categories of enterprise. At a later stage it can give us some insights into how managers control enterprises, how external agencies influence their behaviour, and how incentives, risk, budget constraints, and the like affect such enterprises.

The basic flow of funds accounts presented below represent a major reconstruction of the quantitative database described in Chapter 2. A major problem in using this database for flow of funds analysis is that it is based on Chinese accounting procedures, which are not only quite different from those in the West, but unlike the latter are not readily transferable into flow of funds statements. It is therefore necessary to make a number of transformations in order to achieve this. A further problem is that errors in the data and/or omissions can undermine the validity of the identities which should hold in flow of funds analysis of sources and uses. Against this, the fact that certain relationships *should* hold between various transformations of the data does allow us to carry out some substantial checks on the accuracy of the data involved, and of the likely consequences of any errors that do exist.

The chapter proceeds as follows. In Section 2 we present the conceptual basis of Western flow of funds statements. Section 3 presents Chinese accounting items from the quantitative questionnaire in a flow of funds format, identifying the problems that arise in this process and the way in which we have handled these. Section 4 then quantifies the flow of funds on the basis of that format, for all enterprises and various groupings of them. Finally Section 5 outlines a number of ways in which these data are used subsequently.

2. *Flow of Funds Accounts*

Figure 7.1 gives a highly simplified picture of the flow of funds through a typical Western enterprise. Most of it is self-explanatory, but certain notes may be useful.

1. An increase in stocks and work-in-progress is shown as a use of funds because the 'current costs of production' item only includes expenditure incurred in producing goods actually sold in the relevant time-period.

2. Creditors are regarded as a source of funds because they have provided goods and/or services but not yet received payment. They are therefore regarded as having received the payment and lent it back again to the company. Thus trade credit received is, like a loan from a bank, a source of funds. In a similar way debtors are a use of funds.

3. The distinction between short- and long-term loans is in practice blurred but usually dealt with by adopting an arbitrary period for delineating the two (often one year, as that is the normal period covered by company accounts). The distinction is none the less vital, not only because the company must stand ready at all times to cover short-term liabilities, but also because companies are often assessed by their record of performance in using profitably the long-term funds made available to them by shareholders and suppliers of long-term debt finance.

4. Any funds flowing into the 'funds available' box flow out to the right as a use of those funds or remain as cash. But such cash is, like other financial assets, a current asset. As such it is regarded as flowing into the 'cash balance' box and is therefore treated as a use of funds.

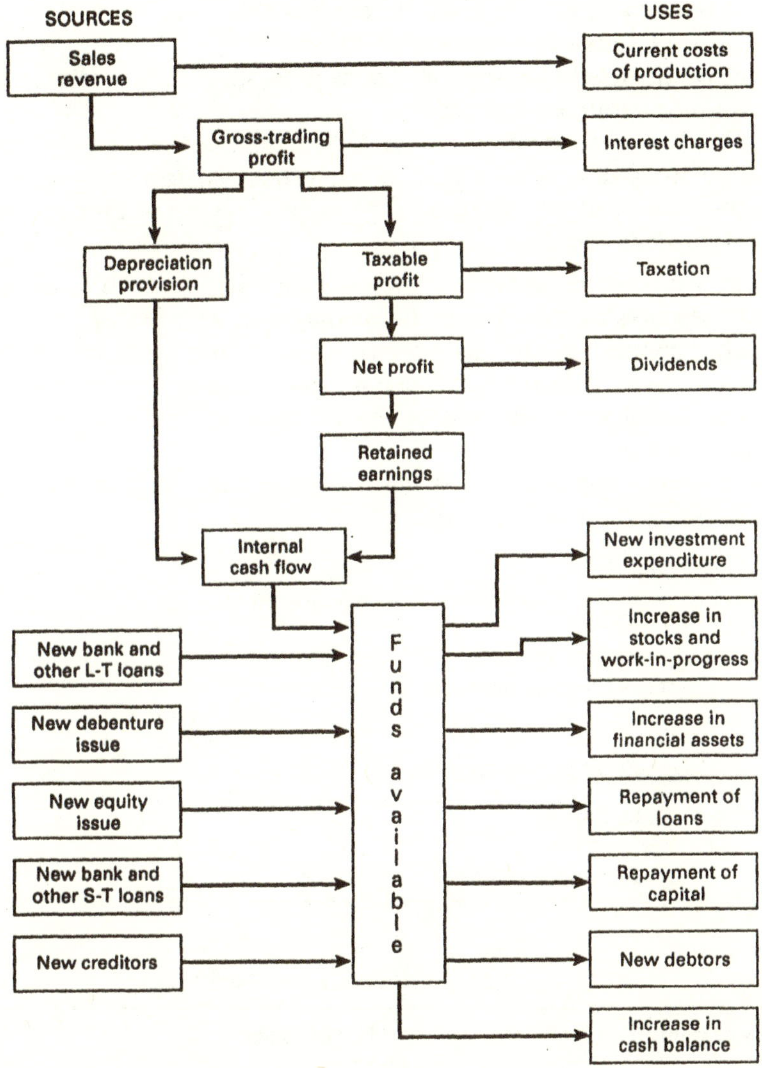

FIG. 7.1. Flow of funds through a typical Western enterprise

If other uses of funds exceeded all the sources shown then this would be a negative flow and the reduction in current assets resulting from the depletion of cash balances would be the additional source of funds, but shown as a negative use of funds. At its simplest the planning of cash flow requires first that for any time-period the sources, including any run-down of cash, are sufficient for all planned uses, particularly those legally required such as payment of suppliers, interest payments, etc. Second, it requires that over the longer term the supply of funds is adequate to meet the uses. Variations in the amount of cash held clearly only deal with short-term discrepancies between other sources and uses.

5. Clearly the delineation of 'funds available' as being after paying out some items but before paying out others is, from an economic point of view, arbitrary. Figure 7.1 is so constructed in order to assist with subsequent accounts analysis.

There are three main types of accounting document which describe different aspects of this flow of funds diagram. The first, in the West normally required in law to be published annually, is the familiar 'Profit and Loss Account' or 'Income and Appropriation Account'. This is essentially a statement of the top half of Fig. 7.1. Its typical form is shown in Table 7.1.

There is one important distinction between the cash flows of Fig. 7.1 and the accounting terms of Table 7.1.

TABLE 7.1. Profit and loss account

Sales revenue	
Gross trading profit	
	– Depreciation – Interest charges
= Profit before taxation	
	– Taxation
= Net profit	
	– Dividends
= Retained earnings	

TABLE 7.2. Sources and uses of funds

Sources of funds	Uses of funds
Gross trading profit after depreciation	Interest paid
Depreciation provision	Tax paid
New long-term loans (net)	Dividends paid
New bond issues (net)	Investment expenditure
New equity issues (net)	Increase in net current assets
	= Increase in stocks
	Financial assets
	Debtors
	Cash
	– Increase in creditors and short-term loans

In order that the figure for net profit in the profit and loss account should indicate the increase in owners' wealth net of all costs and liabilities, the tax figure is the tax liability incurred on the profit made. This may be different from the actual tax payment outflow of Fig. 7.1 because, where tax is paid one year in arrears, the current year's tax payment will be last year's tax liability. If tax paid is less than the current tax liability (as would normally be the case if taxable profits are on a rising trend) then part of taxable profits becomes a tax provision which is in the short term a source of funds over and above retained profit net of tax liability.

The second statement required by law is a balance sheet. However, it is more sensible next to consider the 'Flow of Funds Account' or 'Sources and Uses of Funds Statement'. By no means all companies provide this but it is a useful format. Essentially it is a more general summary of Fig. 7.1. Its typical format is shown in Table 7.2. It follows directly from Fig. 7.1 except that

(i) Sales revenue minus costs of production is shown as gross trading profit net of depreciation.
(ii) New long-term loans, debenture (bond) and equity issues are shown net of repayments.
(iii) Increases in short-term loans and creditors are subtracted from both sides and hence show up as negative uses of funds.
(iv) Increases in stocks, financial assets, debtors, and cash are all uses which increase the company's current assets. Increases in creditors and short-term loans are sources (negative uses) which increase the company's current liabilities. The former minus the latter is then the increase in net current assets for the year and is given this title in Table 7.2.

Both statements presented so far are flow statements, showing various financial flows occurring during the course of one year. The third statement is the balance sheet and is a stock concept. It shows the value of various company assets and liabilities outstanding at the end of each financial year and is, like the profit and loss account or balance sheet, legally required to be published as summary measures of a company's performance. To obtain this we first subtract depreciation, interest, tax, and dividends from both sides of Table 7.2. This is shown in Table 7.3. As the two columns in Table 7.3 give the same total in any given time-period, the sum of each for all time periods in the past up to the date of the balance sheet will also be equal. The sum of all previous earnings is termed the reserves. They do not of course constitute a reserve in the sense of a fund that can be drawn

TABLE 7.3. Depreciation, interest, tax, and dividends subtracted

Sources	Uses
Retained earnings	Investment expenditure
New long-term loans (net)	− depreciation
New bond issues (net)	Increase in net current assets
New equity issues (net)	

on, all these earnings having previously been used in one or more of the ways described under 'uses'. The sum of all periods' new long-term net loans is the total outstanding long-term loans on the date specified. Similarly the sum of all net new bond issues is the total bonds outstanding. The total outstanding equity issue is generally split into two parts. The first, the share issue at par value is the nominal or face value of the shares issued, while the other, the share premium, is the difference between the par value and the funds actually received when the shares were issued. This depends on the price at which the shares were actually sold and is generally positive.

On the right-hand side, the totals are, first, the total expenditure on

TABLE 7.4. Balance sheet

Share issue (par value)	Fixed assets (book value)
Share premium	Current assets
Reserves	Stocks
Bonds	Debtors
Other long-term loans	Financial assets
Tax provision[a]	Cash
Minority interest in subsidiaries[b]	− Current liabilities
	Creditors
	Short-term loans
	Dividends, interest and tax currently due[c]
Capital employed[d]	Capital employed

[a] See above for explanation of this item.

[b] This shows that part of the aggregate capital employed which is in the form of assets in other non-controlled companies. These assets being included in the 'uses' side as part of fixed assets, net current assets, etc., the corresponding liabilities must be added to the 'sources' side to achieve balance.

[c] These are liabilities already incurred but not yet paid.

[d] By adding current liabilities to both sides, an older but still used form of balance sheet is obtained. The 'uses' side is then known as 'assets' and the 'sources' side as 'liabilities'. The share and reserves items are liabilities of the company, as a legal entity, to its owners. The other items are all different types of liability to lenders of funds.

capital minus the accumulated depreciation. This is the current 'written-down' book value of the company's fixed assets. Second, the total of all increases in net current assets is total net current assets, i.e. current assets minus current liabilities. The total of either column is known as capital employed and is the most common measure of the resources available to the company over the long term with which to earn profit. Table 7.4 then gives the typical format of the balance sheet.

Economic analysis of an enterprise is more easily carried out on the basis of flow of funds accounts than the profit and loss account or balance sheet, even though the latter two are the key accounting statements. This is because the profit and loss account deals with only some of the financial transactions involved, while the balance sheet includes cumulative historical data which have no current relevance, e.g. reserves, share issue, and share premium. Current financing may bear no relation to past patterns of financing. The flow of funds account in contrast is a comprehensive statement for the year in which it is drawn up. Thus, while some important items, primarily sales revenue and capital employed, are only available from other statements, a series of annual flow of funds accounts is a good starting-point for analysing enterprises' financial behaviour, particularly as many items in these accounts themselves can be disaggregated back to the sources and uses that determine them.

For many Western firms only the profit and loss account and the balance sheet are available. Large-scale questionnaires designed to obtain standardized information from a large sample of companies typically has to rely on only these two documents or on collecting data that are readily available from their formats. It is important therefore to be able to derive flow of funds accounts from the balance sheet and profit and loss account. The above description of how the balance sheet can, at a conceptual level, be derived from the flow of funds statement provides the basis for the reverse derivation. Re-examination of Table 7.2 shows that, on both the sources and uses side, flow of funds accounts are a combination of certain items from the profit and loss account and changes over the year in question in certain items from the balance sheet. In essence, the sources side is (*a*) gross trading profit after depreciation, (*b*) depreciation, and (*c*) the changes in sources of long-term finance in the balance sheet. The uses side contains (*a*) interest, tax, and dividends, (*b*) investment expenditure, and (*c*) the change in net current assets on the balance sheet. Thus, while some companies may provide accounting information in flow of funds format, where it is not available it can in principle be derived.

3. Chinese Flow of Funds Accounts

There are a number of significant differences between Chinese and Western accounting conventions, the result of which is to alter the manner in which flow of funds accounts are derived. Here we first identify the differences, then present a flow of funds statement, and, third, point out the differences from a Western flow of funds statement and their origin.

The main differences are as follows:

1. Chinese balance sheets are, on both sides, split into three sections: long-term finance, short-term finance, and special funds. Normally each section balances. While superficially this is radically different from Western accounts, in practice it means, first, that in many cases a source of funds is, in effect, for a specific type of use and only available for that use. Second, it means that where an enterprise uses its own resources for short- or long-term uses, accounting procedures ensure that the sums involved are shown as corresponding short- or long-term sources.

2. Grants or subsidies from one or more state authorities may be an important source of funds for some enterprises, and need to be included and classified according to the term structure of their use.

3. Chinese accounts include an item known as the 'firm's own sources'. In principle, a firm's own sources represents the funds available for investment from the enterprise's own cash assets. In any year it is made up as follows:

(i) *Current retained profit after payment of bonuses*. The enterprise is not required to spend all of this on new capital. Some of these retentions may therefore be spent on (*a*) welfare payments, for example to help out low-income workers and their families with living expenses, or to purchase some goods for workers, (*b*) business expenses not recorded within standard state accounting rules and conventions, for example unrecorded business travel, entertainment, gifts etc., or (*c*) investment in other enterprises. It cannot therefore be assumed that all retained profit other than that paid out as bonuses will in fact be part of a firm's own sources.

(ii) *Current retained depreciation*. It should be noted that, unlike in the West, not all of the depreciation provision is necessarily retained, especially in the earlier part of the reform period. In addition, as with retained profit, it cannot be assumed that all retained depreciation will end up as a part of a firm's own resources. Some may be channelled to bonus payments if the latter are well below the maximum limit set by the authorities, and some may find its way into expenditure on technical innovation and the like.

(iii) *Previous savings held over.* This item means that sources may be larger than the sum of retained profit after bonus payments and retained depreciation.

(iv) *Short-term liabilities* in the form of traders' deposits balanced by short-term cash holdings.

These provide an interest-free source of funds that can be included in a firm's own resources, provided that the enterprise has good relationships with the trader or, perhaps, provides various goods or services in kind in return.

(v) *Loss-making contracts* with the relevant higher authority.

In such a contract the enterprise agrees with the authorities a certain maximum-loss figure for future periods. Typically this occurs where intervention or control of prices by the authorities makes it impossible for the enterprise to make a positive profit, but the authorities wish to maintain employment or output without creating an open-ended commitment to subsidize the enterprise irrespective of its behaviour or efficiency. The funds provided by the authorities within such contracts become part of the firm's own resources, and usually can be kept by the enterprise even if losses are smaller than envisaged. Other subsidies may on occasion also appear under this item rather than explicitly as subsidies.

It is not possible, from the accounting information available, to identify the magnitude of each of these components of a firm's own sources. There may also be other sources of funds from the authorities or other enterprises of an otherwise off-budget nature that appear as part of a firm's own sources. The only information available is (*a*) firm's own sources, (*b*) retained profit after payment of bonuses, and (*c*) total depreciation. The difference between firms' own sources on the one hand, and the sum of retained profit after bonuses and depreciation on the other will equal:

Loss-contracts and other subsidies
plus increases in traders' deposits
plus previous resources held over
minus welfare and business payments not recorded elsewhere
minus cross-investment in other enterprises
minus depreciation not retained.

We term this total amount 'other' funds and would expect it typically to be negative for most profitable enterprises, because the first three

TABLE 7.5. Scheme of set of accounts

Sources	Uses
Revenue	Costs
Subsidies	Other uses
Additional inflows	

TABLE 7.6. Adapted scheme of accounts: I

Sources	Uses
Revenue	Costs
Subsidies	Other uses
Firm's own sources	
– Retained depreciation	
– Retained profit after paying bonuses	

components will generally be approximately zero, while the three subsequent deductions will make the total negative. But for some enterprises, subsidies under this heading may be significant, making 'other' funds positive.

To see how this is tackled in accounting terms for the moment we make the simplifying assumption that there are no changes in short-term asset or liability positions to complicate the flow of funds analysis. (This is easily added back in later.) Then, ideally we would wish to have a set of accounts which schematically looked as shown in Table 7.5.

We do not however have the third item on the sources side as such, but only 'firm's own sources', which includes retained profits after payment of bonuses. As this is generated from revenue, inclusion of revenue *and* firm's own sources would involve double-counting of retained profit after bonuses. In addition, firm's own sources will also include retained depreciation, which would be double-counted as well. The basic scheme therefore needs to be adapted (see Table 7.6).

We do not however have figures on the proportion of depreciation which is retained, even though we know that this has changed significantly over time. We can however deal with this as follows. First, we split costs and 'other uses' into their main components, i.e. materials and fuel, wages (involving bonuses), interest, tax, non-retained depreciation, and investment. Second, we add retained depreciation and, for convenience, retained profit minus bonuses to both sides (see Table 7.7). The two depreciation items may then be added together. We then have a format where all items are identifiable.

TABLE 7.7. Adapted scheme of accounts: II

Sources	Uses
Revenue	Materials and fuel
Subsidies	Wages (including bonuses)
Firm's own sources	Interest payments
	Tax
	Investment
	Non-retained depreciation
	Retained depreciation
	Retained profit after bonuses

There is still an element of double-counting in that retained profit after payment of bonuses comes through the revenue item *and* is part of firm's own sources, balanced on the uses side by the inclusion of both retained profit after bonuses *and* the uses to which this is put. In principle this could be dealt with by simply subtracting retained profit after bonuses from both sides. In fact we do not do this for three reasons. First, even then neither the sources nor uses side would be absolutely 'pure' in the sense of no double-counting, because there would still be double-counting of retained depreciation. Second, it somewhat complicates the format to have a negative amount on the sources side. Third, given that retained profit after bonuses is in practice very small in comparison to total sources or total uses, very little distortion, and no systematic distortion is introduced by expressing individual flows as percentages of the total with this small element of double-counting rather than the pure sources figure.

Having noted these points we may now proceed to consider Table 7.8 which gives a Chinese sources and uses statement. We may first note that the basic method for deriving it is that described above for Western firms. The accounts are largely comprised of certain items from the profit and loss account, together with changes over the year in certain items in the balance sheet. There are however two main differences.

1. New long-term finance cannot easily be derived in a useful form from considerations of changes in relevant balance sheet items on the sources side. We only have a four-way split into state-owned assets, enterprise-owned assets, investment by other enterprises, and borrowing. These could be used and should correspond to the accumulated totals of the items actually shown in Table 7.8, but do not distinguish different types of borrowing (from banks, other firms, bond issues),

TABLE 7.8. Flow of funds format for Chinese state-owned enterprises

Sources	Uses
Long-term finance	*Long-term finance*
New LT funds from central govt.	Investment in fixed capital
New LT funds from local authority	Investment in other enterprises
New LT bank loans	
Borrowing from other enterprises	
Investment by other enterprises	
Firm's own sources	
Share issue	
Bond issue	
Foreign investment	
Short-term finance	*Short-term finance*
New ST funds from State	Change in stocks
New ST bank loans	Funds used in instalment system
Firm's own sources	Change in goods supplied
Funds received through instalment system	Change in other debtors
Change in materials supplied	Change in cash and deposits
Change in other creditors	
Delivered profits due	
Tax due	
Special finance	*Special finance*
New sources of special funds	New uses of special funds
Operational finance	*Operational finance*
Sales revenue	Purchases of materials
Net profit from other business*	Purchases of power and fuel
	Depreciation
	Repair expenditure
	Interest payments
	Wage payments
	Other payments
	Selling expenditure
	Loan repayments
	Tax payment
	Training expenditure
	R & D expenditure
	Welfare payments
	Retained profits

* Includes commercial and welfare flows to and from subsidiaries.

different types of enterprise assets (shares, retained earnings, additional inflows), or sources of other firms' investment.

2. Because of the Chinese convention of balancing all three elements of the balance sheet, the net-current-assets term of Western accounts is in China necessarily zero and therefore uninformative. It is therefore more logical, and more convenient, to put the change in

short-term liabilities items (essentially creditors and short-term loans of various sorts) as positive sources rather than as negative uses.

The second set of points to note is that Table 7.8 reflects the different aspects of Chinese accounting conventions identified at the beginning of Section 7.3.

1. The long-term, short-term, and special funding sections all balance. This results from four main features

(*a*) Long-term sources include 'firm's own sources' for long-term purposes, to ensure that long-term sources and uses balance;
(*b*) short-term sources include 'firm's own sources' for short-term purposes, to ensure that short-term sources and uses balance;
(*c*) retained profits are shown as a use of funds; and
(*d*) special funding sources and uses are separately identified and are in principle equal.

2. Central and local government funds for short- and long-term uses are separately identified as short- and long-term sources. The former is the change in a balance sheet item, the latter a flow variable separately identified.

3. Depreciation is shown as a use of funds.

We then have a flow of funds set of accounts, drawn up at the greatest degree of disaggregation possible, the items of which can be read off from the accounting data questionnaire, which should in principle be internally consistent.

4. *Data-Checking*

The purpose of this section is to use flow of funds accounts as a check on the reliability of the data available in the questionnaire. To put this in context, there are three types of data check possible on the sort of database we have.

(i) Checking that certain components add up to the correct aggregate.
(ii) Checking that the balance sheet and its subgroupings balance.
(iii) Checking that the flow of funds account balances.

The first two have been addressed in Appendix I and are not considered here. The third is by far the strictest test. Not only must the balance sheet balance every year, so that changes in it and changes in its subgroupings balance, but the profit and loss account data, which are not subject to a purely internal checking procedure, must be

TABLE 7.9. Deviation of sources from uses of funds

Class	Deviation	1984 obs	%	1985 obs	%	1986 obs	%	1987 obs	%
1	<5%	173	45	179	46	181	47	174	45
2	5–10%	82	21	93	24	79	21	94	24
3	10–20%	68	18	62	16	72	19	63	16
4	20–30%	25	7	20	5	20	5	25	7
5	>30%	38	10	32	8	34	9	30	7
TOTAL		386	100	386	100	386	100	386	100

accurate and therefore be consistent with the annual changes in the balance sheet. For the sort of database with which we are working it is the only check that can guarantee the reliability of the financial flows data.

We have therefore calculated Table 7.8 for every enterprise for each year. If the accounting interpretations are correct and if the enterprises have provided accurate data, then the totals on the left-hand and right-hand sides will be equal. In fact this is rarely precisely the case in the sample. This is perhaps not surprising given the difference between the format used for the questionnaire and the flow of funds rules that assume that sources and uses must sum to the same figures. But the degree of accuracy is, in the circumstances, quite good. Table 7.9 shows the number of enterprises classified by different degrees of accuracy. The latter is measured by the error between total sources and uses as a percentage of the smaller. This is therefore a measurement which cannot understate, and may overstate the degree of error.

The table illustrates that between 66% and 70% of all enterprises are correct to within 10%. This is a provisional conclusion to be reconfirmed later, but provides us with around 250 enterprises in any year where the data are sufficiently reliable to make financial analysis worth while. Appendices 7.1 to 7.3 give equivalent tables for the different locations, industries, and contract forms. In addition nearly half the sample is accurate to within 5% in any year. This is still a sufficiently large sample for analysis and econometric work.

There are two ways of gaining some insight into the extent to which misinterpretation of accounting conventions or errors in the data supplied are the main cause of discrepancy in the sources and uses tables. First, if it is predominantly the latter then we would expect the mean error for the aggregate of enterprises to stay low as less accurate firms are added. This would not be the case for systematic account-

TABLE 7.10. Structure of financial flows for Chinese state-owned enterprises (sample averages; 10,000 yuan)

No. of observations (% of whole sample)	Group 1 172	(45%)	Group 2 348	(91%)	Group 1 180	(47%)	Group 2 354	(92%)	Group 1 181	(47%)	Group 2 352	(92%)	Group 1 173	(45%)	Group 2 356	(92%)
Sources of funds during year	1984		1984		1985		1985		1986		1986		1987		1987	
LT funds from central government	223.5	3.7%	145.3	1.8%	252.1	2.6%	228.1	2.1%	339.3	2.6%	243.7	1.8%	162.9	1.3%	261.5	1.6%
LT funds from local authority	32.7	0.5%	29	0.4%	108.9	1.1%	74	0.7%	52.9	0.4%	45.1	0.3%	58.3	0.5%	57	0.4%
LT bank loans	88.6	1.5%	145.4	1.8%	170.4	1.8%	247.2	2.2%	351.5	2.7%	344.5	2.6%	327.8	2.6%	484.7	3.0%
Borrowing from other enterprises	1.6	0.0%	1.9	0.0%	0.4	0.0%	6.6	0.1%	4.6	0.0%	4.4	0.0%	2.9	0.0%	3.5	0.0%
Investment by other enterprises	3	0.0%	1.9	0.0%	3	0.0%	2.1	0.0%	0.8	0.0%	4.2	0.0%	4.5	0.0%	5.1	0.0%
LT firm's own sources	140	2.3%	234	2.9%	202.5	2.1%	468.9	4.2%	445.7	3.4%	725.7	5.4%	442.2	3.5%	1052.8	6.6%
Share issues	0	0.0%	0	0.0%	0	0.0%	0	0.0%	0	0.0%	0	0.0%	0	0.0%	0.1	0.0%
Bond issues	0	0.0%	0.1	0.0%	0.1	0.0%	1.8	0.0%	69.1	0.5%	36	0.3%	1.8	0.0%	2.9	0.0%
Foreign investment	0	0.0%	28	0.3%	0.7	0.0%	5.9	0.1%	0.1	0.0%	2.1	0.0%	0.1	0.0%	24.2	0.2%
ST funds from the state	11.4	0.2%	20.9	0.3%	12.6	0.1%	7.8	0.1%	17.5	0.1%	36	0.3%	10.8	0.1%	7.3	0.0%
ST firm's own sources	1.7	0.0%	1.6	0.0%	7.3	0.1%	14.2	0.1%	22.6	0.2%	34.2	0.3%	20.6	0.2%	33.6	0.2%
ST bank borrowing	99.9	1.7%	227.8	2.8%	262.2	2.7%	229	2.1%	554.9	4.2%	517.8	3.9%	285.1	2.2%	422.7	2.7%
Receipts from instalment system	0.4	0.0%	0.2	0.0%	0.2	0.0%	3.7	0.0%	−2.1	−0.0%	0.1	0.0%	−5.5	−0.0%	−2.6	−0.0%
Credit for materials supplied	29.3	0.5%	60.9	0.8%	64	0.7%	98	0.9%	94.8	0.7%	51.8	0.4%	125.8	1.0%	136.7	0.9%
Other creditors	20.9	0.3%	16.8	0.2%	50	0.5%	68.2	0.6%	4.6	0.0%	78.4	0.6%	28.3	0.2%	28.8	0.2%
Delivered profits due	−2.3	−0.0%	−0.3	−0.0%	18	0.2%	9.6	0.1%	−4.4	−0.0%	−9.3	−0.1%	−0.9	−0.0%	−1	−0.0%
Tax due	5.2	0.1%	19.6	0.2%	16.1	0.2%	35.5	0.3%	13.6	0.1%	8.3	0.1%	−9.5	−0.1%	−10.3	−0.1%
Special funds	138.4	2.3%	254.4	3.2%	270.8	2.8%	463.5	4.2%	653.8	5.0%	790.8	4.9%	628.6	4.9%	715.3	4.5%
Revenue from sale of products	5261.9	87.4%	6938.6	85.9%	8224.8	85.5%	9226.8	83.0%	10627.5	80.7%	10628.5	79.1%	10795.1	84.4%	12836.6	80.6%
Net profits from other businesses	−33	−0.5%	−50.4	−0.6%	−45	−0.8%	−80.8	−0.7%	−90.9	−0.7%	−105.9	−0.8%	−95.4	−0.7%	−142.9	−0.9%
Total inflow of funds during year	6023.2	100.0%	8075.8	100.0%	9620	100.0%	11110.8	100.0%	13439.9	100.0%	13439.9	100.0%	12783.8	100.0%	15916.9	100.0%
Uses of funds during year																
Investment	491.6	8.2%	595.1	7.7%	758.9	7.9%	1047.3	9.5%	1126.2	8.6%	1327.9	10.2%	935.9	7.3%	1915.5	12.4%
Stocks	85.7	1.4%	197.9	2.5%	370.7	3.9%	405.4	3.7%	444.3	3.4%	424.5	3.3%	211.1	1.7%	272.2	1.8%
Payments under instalment system	5.3	0.1%	11.4	0.1%	5.8	0.1%	6.4	0.1%	12.3	0.1%	28.0	0.2%	30.3	0.2%	16.7	0.1%
Cash and deposits	−9.9	−0.2%	35.8	0.5%	16.9	0.2%	1.8	0.0%	54.5	0.4%	53.8	0.4%	20.9	0.2%	65.3	0.4%
Debts for goods supplied	43.8	0.7%	38.6	0.5%	20.5	0.2%	21.5	0.2%	82.2	0.6%	57.0	0.4%	102.6	0.8%	106.5	0.7%
Other debtors	26.2	0.4%	36.6	0.5%	26.3	0.3%	36.8	0.3%	58.4	0.4%	54.6	0.4%	21.0	0.2%	78.9	0.5%
Special expenditure	141.6	2.4%	235.8	3.0%	226.8	2.4%	392.9	3.6%	638.7	4.9%	795.2	6.1%	638.0	5.0%	694.8	4.5%
Materials	2929.7	48.7%	3468.9	44.7%	4369.2	45.4%	4215.2	38.3%	5350.2	40.9%	4730.8	36.3%	5864.5	46.0%	5832.0	37.6%
Power and fuel	341.8	5.7%	329.6	4.2%	331.8	3.4%	658.8	6.0%	626.7	4.8%	819.7	6.3%	648.0	5.1%	943.4	6.1%
Depreciation	138.5	2.3%	190.3	2.5%	194.8	2.0%	352.8	3.2%	304.3	2.3%	390.8	3.0%	319.3	2.5%	494.6	3.2%
Repairs	85.1	1.4%	123.3	1.6%	110.6	0.1%	14.2	0.1%	22.6	0.2%	34.2	0.3%	20.6	0.2%	33.6	0.2%
Interest payments	43.9	0.7%	49.1	0.6%	67.8	0.7%	70.9	0.6%	108.3	0.8%	107.0	0.8%	141.1	1.1%	139.4	0.9%
Wages	288.5	4.8%	335.6	4.3%	314.8	3.3%	515.9	4.7%	530.3	4.1%	593.2	4.5%	506.7	4.0%	743.4	4.8%
Other payments	92.3	1.5%	119.7	1.5%	133.9	1.4%	253.3	2.3%	258.6	2.0%	271.8	2.1%	280.3	2.2%	334.5	2.2%
Selling expenditure	15.8	0.3%	22.7	0.3%	30.9	0.3%	30.9	0.3%	37.9	0.3%	36.8	0.3%	46.3	0.4%	53.5	0.3%
Repayment of loans	69.3	1.2%	75.9	1.0%	121.9	1.3%	137.5	1.3%	174.1	1.3%	145.4	1.1%	209.3	1.6%	215.7	1.4%
Tax payments	1060.3	17.6%	1666.3	21.5%	2259.3	23.5%	2151.1	19.6%	2709.4	20.7%	2365.7	18.1%	2199.8	17.2%	2595.3	16.7%
Retained profit	139.9	2.3%	194.9	2.5%	216.4	2.2%	457.6	4.2%	307.5	2.4%	555.3	4.3%	355.7	2.8%	652.3	4.2%
R & D expenditure	6.6	0.1%	9.3	0.1%	14	0.1%	10.7	0.1%	38.1	0.3%	30.4	0.2%	20.5	0.2%	34.0	0.2%
Training costs	3.2	0.1%	3.4	0.0%	4.6	0.0%	5.9	0.1%	6.2	0.0%	5.9	0.0%	5.3	0.0%	7.5	0.0%
Welfare expenditure	18.8	0.3%	21.7	0.3%	21.4	0.2%	31.4	0.3%	37.7	0.3%	44.3	0.3%	35.9	0.3%	45.4	0.3%
Total outflow of funds during year	6018.0	100.0%	7762.0	100.0%	9617.3	100.0%	10996.0	100.0%	13081.5	100.0%	13041.1	100.0%	12755.4	100.0%	15504.5	100.0%
Difference in sources and uses	4.8		313.4		2.1		114.3		78.5		396.9		28.2		409.9	

Note: Group 1 = observations accurate to within 5%; Group 2 = observations accurate to within 30%

TABLE 7.11. Negative and positive deviations of sources from uses of funds

Group		Deviation	1984 obs	1984 %	1985 obs	1985 %	1986 obs	1986 %	1987 obs	1987 %
Negative sign	1	<5%	90	47.3	96	43.6	100	47.2	79	40.7
	2	5–10%	40	21.0	61	27.7	42	19.8	50	25.8
	3	10–20%	30	15.8	32	14.5	36	17.0	32	16.5
	4	20–30%	11	5.8	13	5.9	13	6.1	11	5.6
	5	>30%	19	10.0	18	8.2	21	9.9	22	11.3
		Subtotal	190	100	220	100	212	100	194	100
Positive sign	1	<5%	83	42.3	83	50.0	81	46.6	95	49.5
	2	5–10%	42	21.4	32	19.3	37	21.3	44	22.9
	3	10–20%	38	19.4	30	18.1	36	20.7	31	16.1
	4	20–30%	14	7.1	7	4.2	7	4.0	14	7.3
	5	>30%	19	9.7	14	8.4	13	7.5	8	4.2
		Subtotal	196	100	166	100	174	100	192	100

Notes: Negative sign = uses of funds > sources of funds; positive sign = sources of funds > uses of funds.

ing convention errors. Table 7.10 shows the aggregate value of each flow of funds item for two levels of accuracy for each year and for the totals. In each year Group 1 contains only those enterprises which exhibit less than a 5% error. Group 2 contain nearly all enterprises, omitting only those with more than 30% error. As can be seen the aggregate flow of funds error for Group 1 is extremely small, having an average value of 0.3% and a peak value of 0.6%, in 1986. The aggregate error for Group 2 (where the weighted average individual error is 7.9%) is 2.6%, with a peak value of 4%, in 1984. These figures suggest little if any systematic error.

The second approach is to see whether there is a systematic pattern of sources or uses being the higher amount, and, if so, how the size of the error relates to this. Table 7.11 provides information on this. As can be seen both the number of positive and negative errors, and the accuracy within each group are very similar, suggesting few if any systematic errors and certainly no sizeable ones in the flow of funds accounts.

5. *Basic Flow of Funds Data for Chinese Enterprises*

The basic data are provided in Table 7.10. Table 7.12 re-presents the data in percentage form only, giving the average of the percentages for Groups 1 and 2. This is a means of including most of the enterprises in the sample but giving greater weight to those which are accurate to within 5%. Tables 7.14 to 7.17 give equivalent data for individual locations, industries, scales of enterprise, and contract forms. The data are however aggregated up to some extent as indicated in Table 7.13 for ease of presentation. Looking over the years 1984 to 1987 certain changes are clear. Flows explicitly identified as from the state fell significantly from 3.3% to 2.0%. These were replaced partly by bank loans, partly by the retained-profit element in firm's own resources and partly by the depreciation element in the latter. Together these three rose from 8.6% to 11.5%. More generally

TABLE 7.12. Developments in the structure of finance for state-owned enterprises over the reform years, 1984–87

Sources of funds during year	1984	1985	1986	1987
Long-term finance				
LT funds from central government	2.8%	2.3%	2.2%	1.5%
LT funds from local authority	0.5%	0.9%	0.4%	0.4%
LT bank loans	1.6%	2.0%	2.6%	2.8%
Borrowing from other enterprises	0.0%	0.0%	0.0%	0.0%
Investment by other enterprises	0.0%	0.0%	0.0%	0.0%
LT firm's own sources	2.6%	3.2%	4.4%	5.0%
Share issues	0.0%	0.0%	0.0%	0.0%
Bond issues	0.0%	0.0%	0.0%	0.0%
Foreign investment	0.2%	0.0%	0.0%	0.1%
Subtotal	7.7%	8.5%	10.0%	9.9%
Short-term finance				
ST funds from State	0.2%	0.1%	0.2%	0.1%
ST firm's own sources	0.0%	0.1%	0.2%	0.2%
ST bank borrowing	2.2%	2.4%	4.0%	2.4%
Receipts from instalment system	0.0%	0.0%	−0.0%	−0.0%
Credit for materials supplied	0.6%	0.8%	0.6%	0.9%
Other creditors	0.3%	0.6%	−0.1%	−0.0%
Delivered profits due	−0.0%	0.1%	−0.1%	−0.0%
Tax due	0.2%	0.2%	0.1%	−0.1%
Subtotal	3.5%	4.3%	5.4%	3.7%
Special finance				
Special funds	2.7%	3.5%	5.4%	4.7%
Operational finance				
Revenue from sale of products	86.6%	84.3%	79.9%	82.5%
Net profit from other businesses	−0.6%	−0.6%	−0.7%	−0.8%
Subtotal	86.1%	83.7%	79.2%	81.7%
Total inflow of funds during year	100.0%	100.0%	100.0%	100.0%

TABLE 7.12 (*cont.*)

Uses of funds during year	1984	1985	1986	1987
Long-term uses				
Investment	7.9%	8.7%	9.4%	9.8%
Short-term uses				
Stocks	2.0%	3.8%	3.3%	1.7%
Payments under instalment system	0.1%	0.1%	0.2%	0.2%
Cash and deposits	0.1%	0.1%	0.4%	0.3%
Debts for goods supplied	0.6%	0.2%	0.5%	0.7%
Other debtors	0.5%	0.3%	0.4%	0.3%
Subtotal	3.3%	4.4%	4.9%	3.3%
Special uses				
Special expenditure	2.7%	3.0%	5.5%	4.7%
Operational uses				
Materials	46.7%	41.9%	38.6%	41.8%
Power and fuel	5.0%	4.7%	5.5%	5.6%
Depreciation	2.4%	2.6%	2.7%	2.8%
Repairs	1.5%	1.5%	1.4%	1.5%
Interest payments	0.7%	0.7%	0.8%	1.0%
Wages	4.6%	4.0%	4.3%	4.4%
Other payments	1.5%	1.8%	2.0%	2.2%
Selling expenditure	0.3%	0.3%	0.3%	0.4%
Repayment of loans	1.1%	1.3%	1.2%	1.5%
Tax payment	19.5%	21.5%	19.4%	17.0%
Retained profit	2.4%	3.2%	3.3%	3.5%
R & D expenditure	0.1%	0.1%	0.3%	0.2%
Training costs	0.0%	0.1%	0.0%	0.0%
Welfare expenditure	0.3%	0.3%	0.3%	0.3%
Subtotal	86.1%	83.9%	80.2%	82.2%
Total inflow of funds during year	100.0%	100.0%	100.0%	100.0%

we can calculate the proportion of long- and short-term sources, i.e. excluding special funds and operational revenues, which was generated internally. This rose continuously from 33% in 1984 to 50.5%.

Investment increased as a percentage of uses by 24%, and investment net of depreciation by over 27%. The main counterpart to this was a significant fall in operational costs. In fact operational uses minus depreciation and minus retained profits fell from 81.3% to 75.9%. This is a fairly extraordinary shift in just 3 years and a clear financial reflection of the efficiency improvements that occurred through this period.

It is also of interest to look at the proportion of wage costs in the total of wages plus retained profit. This fell from 65.7% to 55.6%,

TABLE 7.13. Aggregation of items in flow of funds tables for subsamples of enterprises

Government sources	long-term and short-term central and local government funds
External sources	bank loans and other borrowing, plus investment by other domestic and foreign firms, plus bond and share issues
Operational sources	business and non-business revenues, plus changes in short-term liabilities
Special funds	long- and short-term special funds
Firm's own sources	long- and short-term firm's own sources
Labour and overhead costs	wages, plus depreciation, repairs, interest, plus welfare, training, and R & D expenses
Inputs and associated costs	materials, energy, plus changes in short-term assets
Investment expenditures	investment in the enterprise and in other businesses
Special expenses	long- and short-term special expenditures
Tax payments	total tax payments
Retentions	retained profit

indicating that a significant part of the growth of value added in the period was retained for investment and related uses rather than paid out as labour income. In keeping with this the ratio of wage costs to investment expenditure fell continuously from 58.2% to 44.9%.

These figures give a reasonably clear picture of what was happening in terms of these enterprises' financial positions during the period 1984–87. They were reducing costs relative to revenue, generating more retained profit and, more generally, higher internal cash flow. Their dependence on external finance and in particular on government sources was falling and they were directing more of their finances to investment. Virtually all the observations made show continuous improvement throughout the period.

Unfortunately the time-span of four years is rather short for determining to what extent these changes reflect a temporary or cyclical upswing in the economy or more fundamental changes resulting from various reform measures designed to increase autonomy and accountability. However, the size of the changes, over a four-year period, suggests that at least some of these effects were the result of reform, especially given that in a still heavily controlled and largely state-owned economy we would expect cyclical effects of the type seen regularly in the West to be rather muted.

Looking at the subsamples, certain conclusions emerge. Enterprises in large inland cities have a very different financial profile, exhibiting significantly lower operational finance, offset by high government

TABLE 7.14. Comparison of locations using flow of funds data (unit: 10,000 yuan)

	1984					1985				
Locations No. of observations	loc1 (52)	loc2 (61)	loc3 (29)	loc4 (53)	loc5 (17)	loc1 (60)	loc2 (61)	loc3 (35)	loc4 (58)	loc5 (19)
Government sources	194	563	43	128	14	271	984	107	82	47
	1.8%	6.7%	1.0%	2.4%	0.5%	1.8%	5.0%	2.1%	1.0%	1.1%
External sources	278	229	194	267	75	719	724	294	380	243
	2.6%	2.7%	4.5%	5.1%	2.9%	4.9%	3.7%	5.7%	4.7%	5.9%
Operational sources	9944	7017	3830	4609	2397	13082	15936	4455	7077	3603
	91%	84%	90%	88%	92%	88%	81%	87%	88%	87%
Special funds	305	212	103	119	75	467	811	161	277	188
	2.8%	2.5%	2.4%	2.3%	2.9%	3.2%	4.1%	3.1%	3.5%	4.5%
Firms' own sources	150	339	108	126	51	258	1139	119	205	61
	1.4%	4.1%	2.5%	2.4%	2.0%	1.7%	5.8%	2.3%	2.6%	1.5%
Subtotal	10871	8360	4278	5249	2612	14797	19594	5136	8021	4142
	100%	100%	100%	100%	100%	100%	100%	100%	100%	100%
Labour and overhead costs	1068	1379	481	765	245	1483	3306	733	1048	515
	10%	16%	11%	15%	10%	10%	17%	14%	13%	12%
Inputs and associated costs	6119	4174	2585	2657	1215	8088	7804	3035	4177	2040
	58%	49%	61%	51%	48%	55%	41%	60%	52%	48%
Investment expenditure	377	999	269	295	99	824	2443	313	507	239
	3.6%	11.8%	6.3%	5.6%	3.9%	5.6%	12.7%	6.2%	6.3%	5.7%
Special expenses	254	216	124	128	82	394	725	96	199	198
	2.4%	2.6%	2.9%	2.4%	3.2%	2.7%	3.8%	1.9%	2.5%	4.7%
Tax payments	2504	1436	719	1266	873	3645	4119	797	1877	1022
	24%	17%	17%	24%	34%	25%	21%	16%	23%	24%
Retentions	196	239	79	141	33	396	833	111	210	196
	1.9%	2.8%	1.9%	1.9%	1.3%	2.7%	4.3%	2.2%	2.6%	4.7%
Subtotal	10518	8443	4257	5252	2547	14830	19230	5085	8018	4210
	100%	100%	100%	100%	100%	100%	100%	100%	100%	100%
Difference between sources and uses	353	−83	21	−3	65	−33	364	51	3	−68
Deviation	3.4%	−1.0%	0.5%	−0.1%	2.6%	−0.2%	1.9%	1.0%	0.0%	−1.6%

TABLE 7.14 (*cont.*)

	1986					1987				
Locations No. of observations	loc1 (54)	loc2 (64)	loc3 (30)	loc4 (57)	loc5 (20)	loc1 (60)	loc2 (69)	loc3 (27)	loc4 (53)	loc5 (17)
Government sources	347	956	111	102	165	372	641	50	215	218
	2.1%	3.8%	1.8%	1.0%	3.4%	2.1%	2.4%	0.6%	1.9%	3.6%
External sources	936	1 451	377	990	346	589	1 354	461	1 003	425
	5.6%	5.8%	6.0%	9.6%	7.4%	3.3%	5.1%	5.8%	8.6%	7.0%
Operational sources	14 556	19 202	5 297	8 455	3 975	16 064	20 028	6 745	9 447	4 923
	88%	76%	84%	82%	85%	90%	75%	85%	81%	81%
Special funds	394	1 415	316	541	63	318	1 826	416	486	298
	2.4%	5.6%	5.0%	5.2%	1.3%	1.8%	6.9%	5.3%	4.2%	4.9%
Firms' own sources	343	2 106	203	269	148	448	2 755	239	459	19
	2.1%	8.4%	3.2%	2.6%	3.2%	2.5%	10.4%	3.0%	4.0%	3.2%
Subtotal	16 576	25 130	6 304	10 357	4 697	17 791	26 604	7 911	11 610	6 056
	100%	100%	100%	100%	100%	100%	100%	100%	100%	100%
Labour and overhead costs	1 763	4 566	933	1 285	621	2 013	4 977	1 135	1 765	795
	11%	19%	15%	12%	13%	11%	19%	14%	15%	14%
Inputs and associated costs	9 162	9 435	3 806	5 207	2 459	10 002	9 893	4 915	5 822	2 937
	55%	39%	60%	50%	53%	57%	38%	61%	49%	50%
Investment expenditure	1 063	3 353	370	710	246	1 109	4 091	454	1 133	390
	6.4%	13.8%	5.9%	6.9%	5.3%	6.3%	15.9%	5.7%	9.6%	6.6%
Special expenses	331	1 576	254	531	50	323	1 736	376	582	293
	2.0%	6.5%	4.0%	5.1%	1.1%	1.8%	6.7%	4.7%	4.9%	5.0%
Tax payments	3 919	4 463	748	2 367	1 081	3 627	4 134	852	2 183	1 256
	24%	18%	12%	23%	23%	21%	16%	11%	18%	21%
Retentions	419	857	184	262	172	495	916	261	323	197
	2.5%	3.5%	2.9%	2.5%	3.7%	2.8%	3.6%	3.3%	2.7%	3.4%
Subtotal	16 657	24 250	6 295	10 362	4 629	17 569	25 747	7 993	11 808	5 868
	100%	100%	100%	100%	100%	100%	100%	100%	100%	100%
Difference between sources and uses	−81	880	9	−5	68	222	857	−82	−198	188
Deviation	−0.5%	3.6%	0.1%	−0.0%	1.5%	1.3%	3.3%	−1.0%	−1.7%	3.2%

Notes: Only enterprises with a 10% level of deviation or less between sources and uses are included.
Locations are as follows: 1: large coastal cities; 2: large inland cities; 3: medium and small coastal cities; 4: medium-sized inland cities; 5: small inland cities.

TABLE 7.15. Comparison of industries using flow of funds data (10,000 yuan)

	1984								1985							
Industries No. of observations	Ind1 (10)	Ind2 (27)	Ind3 (25)	Ind4 (29)	Ind5 (9)	Ind6 (38)	Ind7 (35)	Ind8 (39)	Ind1 (9)	Ind2 (37)	Ind3 (27)	Ind4 (29)	Ind5 (9)	Ind6 (41)	Ind7 (41)	Ind8 (40)
Government sources	3162	18	5	60	68	179	206	105	3879	2	15	77	2458	121	318	199
	34.7%	0.2%	0.1%	3.2%	0.2%	3.3%	2.2%	1.6%	34.4%	0.0%	0.3%	2.4%	6.0%	1.7%	1.3%	2.2%
External sources	111	138	180	150	302	283	339	268	201	484	636	169	218	363	1043	575
	1.3%	1.8%	4.3%	8.0%	1.0%	5.2%	3.6%	4.0%	1.8%	4.0%	11.3%	5.3%	0.5%	5.2%	4.3%	6.2%
Operational sources	5362	7191	3933	1181	28711	4653	8111	5968	5942	11340	4796	2599	36690	6199	19814	7933
	59%	95%	93%	80%	96%	86%	85%	90%	53%	93%	85%	82%	90%	88%	82%	86%
Special funds	271	134	5	119	281	183	510	197	330	220	114	187	551	214	1404	298
	3.0%	1.8%	0.1%	6.4%	0.9%	3.4%	5.4%	3.0%	2.9%	1.8%	2.0%	5.9%	1.3%	3.0%	5.8%	3.2%
Firms' own sources	746	88	87	53	571	100	358	108	931	113	85	144	993	130	1479	210
	8.2%	1.2%	2.1%	2.8%	1.9%	1.9%	3.8%	1.6%	8.3%	0.9%	1.5%	4.5%	2.4%	1.9%	6.1%	2.3%
Subtotal	9110	7572	4210	1866	29966	5398	9524	6646	11283	12159	5646	3176	40910	7027	24058	9215
	100%	100%	100%	100%	100%	100%	100%	100%	100%	100%	100%	100%	100%	100%	100%	100%
Labour and overhead costs	2139	528	530	289	2177	612	1712	906	3245	691	668	504	2893	1076	4462	1160
	27%	7%	13%	16%	8%	11%	18%	14%	30%	6%	12%	16%	7%	15%	19%	13%
Inputs and associated costs	1816	3661	2818	971	15677	3154	5070	3954	2169	5469	3955	1568	21427	4118	9297	5794
	20%	50%	67%	53%	55%	59%	52%	61%	20%	45%	69%	50%	53%	58%	39%	63%
Investment expenditure	3801	237	189	229	786	287	595	286	4665	350	286	311	3491	354	2528	555
	41.5%	3.2%	4.5%	12.4%	2.7%	5.4%	6.1%	4.4%	42.7%	2.9%	5.0%	9.9%	8.7%	5.0%	10.7%	6.0%
Special expenses	166	157	6	117	170	191	481	167	389	165	90	173	130	160	1211	305
	1.8%	2.1%	0.1%	6.3%	0.6%	3.6%	4.9%	2.6%	3.6%	1.3%	1.6%	5.5%	0.3%	2.3%	5.1%	3.3%
Tax payments	1158	2702	596	192	9207	987	1581	1022	332	5376	639	478	11474	1141	4876	1082
	13%	37%	14%	10%	32%	18%	16%	16%	3%	44%	11%	15%	29%	16%	21%	12%
Retentions	81	79	61	50	657	116	340	179	124	210	84	108	707	195	1319	290
	0.9%	1.1%	1.4%	2.7%	2.3%	2.2%	3.5%	2.7%	1.1%	1.7%	1.5%	3.4%	1.8%	2.8%	5.6%	3.2%
Subtotal	9159	7364	4230	1848	28674	5347	9779	6514	10924	12261	5722	3142	40122	7044	23693	9186
	100%	100%	100%	100%	100%	100%	100%	100%	100%	100%	100%	100%	100%	100%	100%	100%
Difference between sources and uses	50	207	21	17	1291	51	255	132	359	102	76	34	788	17	365	29
Deviation	0.5%	2.8%	0.5%	0.9%	4.5%	1.0%	2.6%	2.0%	3.3%	0.8%	1.3%	1.1%	2.0%	0.2%	1.5%	0.3%

TABLE 7.15 (*cont.*)

	1986								1987							
Industries No. of observations	Ind1 (11)	Ind2 (36)	Ind3 (24)	Ind4 (28)	Ind5 (10)	Ind6 (45)	Ind7 (38)	Ind8 (33)	Ind1 (11)	Ind2 (33)	Ind3 (24)	Ind4 (31)	Ind5 (8)	Ind6 (43)	Ind7 (35)	Ind8 (41)
Government sources	4198	140	20	74	876	174	485	113	2706	57	21	125	2026	177	472	162
	34.8%	0.9%	0.3%	2.1%	2.5%	2.3%	1.3%	1.1%	25.2%	0.4%	0.3%	4.2%	4.2%	2.0%	1.0%	1.1%
External sources	83	810	1110	386	732	550	2515	661	51	1297	−260	290	1283	505	2369	990
	0.7%	5.4%	14.6%	14.2%	2.1%	7.1%	6.8%	6.3%	0.5%	8.5%	3.9%	9.7%	2.7%	5.6%	5.1%	7.0%
Operational sources	6015	13456	6104	1986	30812	6401	28636	9040	6611	13331	6286	2384	41922	7641	34659	12145
	50%	91%	80%	73%	89%	83%	77%	87%	62%	87%	95%	79%	88%	85%	75%	85.7%
Special funds	478	369	238	156	1285	372	2234	316	223	375	466	87	893	394	3384	390
	4.0%	2.5%	3.1%	5.8%	3.7%	4.8%	6.0%	3.0%	2.1%	2.5%	7.0%	2.9%	1.9%	4.4%	7.3%	2.8%
Firms' own sources	1290	92	122	111	914	201	3323	287	1154	183	121	117	1603	241	3221	484
	10.7%	0.6%	1.6%	4.1%	2.7%	2.6%	8.9%	2.8%	10.7%	1.2%	1.8%	3.9%	3.4%	2.7%	11.3%	3.4%
Subtotal	12064	14867	7594	2713	34649	7698	37223	10417	10745	15243	6634	3003	47727	8958	46105	14170
	100%	100%	100%	100%	100%	100%	100%	100%	100%	100%	100%	100%	100%	100%	100%	100%
Labour and overhead costs	3780	800	922	438	3081	1254	6895	1425	3739	1095	1056	504	4156	1440	8635	2102
	31%	5%	12%	16%	9%	16%	19%	14%	36%	7%	16%	17%	9%	16%	19%	15%
Inputs and associated costs	2440	6406	5372	1329	18588	4383	14249	6383	2257	6608	3947	1659	24690	5273	16914	8992
	20%	43%	71%	50%	53%	57%	40%	63%	22%	44%	59%	56%	52%	59%	38%	64%
Investment expenditure	5161	663	307	368	1918	537	4351	656	3620	586	385	360	4713	665	6938	955
	42.9%	4.9%	4.0%	13.7%	5.5%	6.9%	12.1%	6.4%	35.2%	3.9%	5.8%	12.2%	10.0%	7.4%	15.5%	6.8%
Special expenses	283	294	188	144	1363	363	2546	266	215	403	529	84	1154	327	3291	386
	2.4%	2.0%	2.5%	5.4%	3.9%	4.7%	7.1%	2.6%	2.1%	2.7%	7.9%	2.8%	2.4%	3.6%	7.4%	2.7%
Tax payments	314	6573	634	325	9356	981	6231	1131	307	6197	547	263	11718	991	7149	1151
	3%	44%	8%	12%	27%	13%	17%	11%	3%	41%	8%	9%	25%	11%	16%	8%
Retentions	39	241	164	78	651	212	1554	333	151	204	231	91	933	308	1819	472
	0.3%	1.6%	2.2%	2.9%	1.9%	2.7%	4.3%	3.3%	1.5%	1.4%	3.5%	3.1%	2.0%	3.4%	4.1%	3.4%
Subtotal	12017	14977	7587	2682	7730	35826	10197	10197	10289	15093	6695	2961	47364	9004	44746	14058
	100%	100%	100%	100%	100%	100%	100%	100%	100%	100%	100%	100%	100%	100%	100%	100%
Difference between sources and uses	47	110	7	31	308	32	1397	220	456	150	−61	42	363	−46	1359	112
Deviation	0.4%	0.7%	0.1%	1.2%	0.9%	0.4%	3.9%	2.2%	4.4%	1.0%	0.9%	1.4%	0.8%	0.5%	3.9%	0.3%

Notes: Only enterprises with a 10% deviation or less between sources and uses are included. Industry locations are as follows: 1. Extractive; 2. Food, drink, tobacco; 3. Textiles etc.; 4. Light industry and craft; 5. Energy; 6. Chemicals etc.; 7. Building materials and metals; 8. Engineering and electrical.

TABLE 7.16. Comparison of scales of industry using flow of funds data (unit: 10,000 yuan)

	1984			1985			1986			1987		
Scales No. of observations	Scale 1 (93)	Scale 2 (88)	Scale 3 (31)	Scale 1 (106)	Scale 2 (88)	Scale 3 (37)	Scale 1 (103)	Scale 2 (87)	Scale 3 (35)	Scale 1 (106)	Scale 2 (87)	Scale 3 (33)
Government sources	494 3.8%	49 1.5%	80 6.8%	670 3.1%	29 0.6%	327 19.9%	806 3.0%	79 1.3%	77 4.3%	680 2.2%	72 1.1%	143 7.9%
External sources	311 2.4%	222 7.0%	33 2.8%	805 3.7%	393 8.3%	100 6.1%	1442 5.3%	742 12.5%	144 8.0%	1676 5.5%	242 3.9%	103 5.7%
Operational sources	11500 89%	2750 86%	963 82%	18762 86%	4030 85%	1092 66%	22038 81%	4790 81%	1390 77%	24485 80%	5447 87%	1305 72%
Special funds	338 2.6%	79 2.5%	33 2.8%	785 3.6%	181 3.8%	90 5.5%	1310 4.8%	179 3.0%	88 4.9%	1486 4.5%	284 4.5%	147 8.1%
Firms' own sources	311 2.4%	91 2.9%	72 6.1%	853 3.9%	118 2.5%	34 2.1%	1568 5.8%	148 2.5%	96 5.3%	2149 7.1%	221 3.5%	120 6.6%
Subtotal	12954 100%	3191 100%	1181 100%	21875 100%	4751 100%	1643 100%	27164 100%	5938 100%	1795 100%	30471 100%	6266 100%	1818 100%
Labour and overhead costs	1606 13%	461 14%	274 23%	3040 14%	628 13%	220 13%	4078 15%	760 13%	427 23%	4740 16%	972 16%	451 24%
Inputs and associated costs	6706 52%	1905 59%	580 49%	10002 46%	2888 60%	773 47%	11772 44%	3586 60%	981 54%	13668 46%	3418 55%	839 45%
Investment expenditure	860 6.7%	244 7.6%	140 11.8%	1877 8.7%	326 6.7%	408 24.9%	2799 10.5%	385 6.4%	197 10.8%	3560 11.9%	479 7.7%	269 14.5%
Special expenses	322 2.5%	83 2.6%	33 2.8%	678 3.1%	130 2.7%	81 4.0%	1338 5.0%	199 3.3%	73 4.0%	1462 4.9%	287 4.6%	160 8.6%
Tax payments	2992 23%	434 14%	131 11%	5276 24%	694 14%	123 7%	5787 22%	876 15%	114 6%	5503 18%	878 14%	96 5%
Retentions	292 2.3%	79 2.5%	33 2.8%	737 3.4%	165 3.4%	36 2.2%	831 3.1%	166 2.8%	36 2.0%	965 3.2%	195 3.1%	39 2.1%
Subtotal	12778 100%	3206 100%	1191 100%	21610 100%	4831 100%	1641 100%	26605 100%	5972 100%	1828 100%	29898 100%	6229 100%	1854 100%
Difference between sources and uses	176	−15	−10	265	−80	2	559	−34	−33	573	37	−36
Deviation	1.4%	−0.5%	−0.8%	1.2%	−1.7%	0.1%	2.1%	−0.6%	−1.8%	1.9%	0.6%	−1.9%

Notes: Only enterprises with a 10% level of deviation or less between sources and uses are included.
Scales are as follows: Scale 1—Large scale; Scale 2—Medium scale; Scale 3—Small scale.

TABLE 7.17. Comparison of contract forms using flow of funds data (10,000 yuan)

	Contract form classified by profit incentives								Contract form classified by assets incentives							
	1984		1985		1986		1987		1984		1985		1986		1987	
Contract form No. of observations	cf1 (123)	cf2 (89)	cf1 (136)	cf2 (97)	cf1 (134)	cf2 (91)	cf1 (131)	cf2 (95)	cf1 (107)	cf2 (105)	cf1 (121)	cf2 (112)	cf1 (117)	cf2 (108)	cf1 (113)	cf2 (113)
Government sources	331	134	460	239	544	214	405	315	379	116	515	208	622	183	466	269
	5.1%	1.6%	3.8%	2.0%	3.5%	1.5%	2.4%	2.0%	5.5%	1.6%	3.9%	1.9%	3.6%	1.5%	2.4%	1.9%
External sources	246	216	588	458	886	1 090	1 045	681	250	216	617	444	950	990	1 132	652
	3.8%	2.6%	4.9%	3.8%	5.6%	7.8%	5.9%	4.3%	3.6%	2.9%	4.7%	4.0%	5.5%	8.0%	5.8%	4.6%
Operational sources	5 404	7 603	9 951	10 707	12 569	11 550	13 974	13 492	5 822	6 842	10 798	9 692	13 909	10 260	15 431	12 112
	84%	93%	83%	88%	80%	83%	79%	85%	84%	92%	83%	88%	80%	83%	79%	85%
Special funds	254	92	476	392	673	697	897	734	282	89	532	344	756	603	1 019	638
	4.0%	1.1%	4.0%	3.2%	4.3%	5.0%	5.1%	4.6%	4.1%	1.2%	4.1%	3.1%	4.3%	4.8%	5.2%	4.5%
Firms' own sources	193	174	525	318	1 021	449	1 403	707	212	157	581	286	1 153	397	1 593	629
	3.0%	2.1%	4.4%	2.6%	6.5%	3.2%	7.9%	4.4%	3.1%	2.1%	4.5%	2.6%	6.6%	3.2%	8.1%	4.4%
Subtotal	6 428	8 219	12 000	12 114	15 693	14 000	17 724	15 929	6 945	7 420	13 043	10 974	17 390	12 433	19 641	14 300
	100%	100%	100%	100%	100%	100%	100%	100%	100%	100%	100%	100%	100%	100%	100%	100%
Labour and overhead costs	954	911	1 866	1 373	2 671	1 574	3 112	2 045	1 039	831	2 029	1 263	2 957	1 436	3 454	1 872
	15%	11%	16%	11%	17%	11%	18%	13%	15%	11%	16%	11%	17%	12%	18%	13%
Inputs and associated costs	3 348	4 466	5 222	6 582	6 779	7 149	7 441	8 413	3 577	4 061	5 593	6 000	7 407	6 409	8 075	7 623
	52%	56%	44%	54%	44%	52%	43%	53%	51%	56%	44%	54%	44%	52%	42%	53%
Investment expenditure	587	378	1 261	742	1 817	936	2 211	1 454	648	346	1 379	683	2 037	836	2 488	1 298
	9.1%	4.7%	10.7%	6.1%	11.8%	6.7%	12.8%	9.1%	9.3%	4.8%	10.8%	6.2%	12.0%	6.8%	13.0%	9.1%
Special expenses	250	84	422	301	662	758	943	649	278	80	475	260	742	656	1 074	565
	3.9%	1.0%	3.6%	2.5%	4.3%	5.5%	5.5%	4.1%	4.0%	1.1%	3.7%	2.4%	4.4%	5.3%	5.6%	4.0%
Tax payments	1 142	2 023	2 923	2 893	3 172	2 906	2 970	876	1 240	1 789	2 769	2 599	3 252	2 738	3 280	2 586
	18%	25%	21%	24%	19%	17%	19%	15%	18%	25%	22%	24%	19%	22%	17%	18%
Retentions	166	165	498	275	560	289	655	365	184	147	550	248	626	260	732	334
	2.6%	2.1%	4.2%	2.3%	3.6%	2.1%	3.8%	2.3%	2.6%	2.0%	4.3%	2.2%	3.7%	2.1%	3.8%	2.3%
Subtotal	6 447	8 027	11 789	12 196	15 382	13 878	17 268	15 896	6 966	7 254	12 795	11 053	17 021	12 335	19 103	14 278
	100%	100%	100%	100%	100%	100%	100%	100%	100%	100%	100%	100%	100%	100%	100%	100%
Difference between sources and uses	−20	191	210	−83	310	121	455	32	−22	165	247	−80	368	97	537	21
Deviation	−0.3%	2.4%	1.8%	−0.7%	2.0%	0.9%	2.6%	0.2%	−0.3%	2.3%	1.9%	−0.7%	2.2%	0.8%	2.8%	0.1%

Notes: Only enterprises with a 10% deviation or less between sources and uses are included.
Contract forms are as follows:

Grouped by profit incentives		Grouped by asset incentives	
cf1	Contract responsibility	cf1	Contract responsibility
	Share capital		Share capital
	Asset management		Asset management
	Leasing	cf2	Leasing
cf2	Director responsibility		Director responsibility

funding, higher special funds, and higher firm's own sources. The last of these is to only a very limited extent the result of higher retentions, indicating that a considerable subsidy component is involved (see Chapter 10). The poor financial performance of enterprises in this location group is further seen on the uses side, where they exhibit significantly higher wage and overhead costs, low input expenditures, high special expenditure, and lower tax payments. Despite this they exhibit uniquely high investment expenditure as a proportion of total uses, illustrating the extent to which various types of subsidy are used to maintain or expand production despite a weak financial position. This need not imply absolutely higher wage and investment expenditure because such enterprises may be experiencing substantially lower sales revenue inflows as a result of price controls and/or low capacity utilization, but in either case these expenditures are high relative to the inflows received. Other points to note are the low contribution from firm's own sources in large coastal and small inland cities, the high input costs and low taxation in medium and small coastal cities, and the greater use of external funds in medium-sized inland cities.

Turning to industrial sectors, two stand out as quite distinctive. Enterprises involved in mining and other extractive processes generate a much lower proportion of their financial flows from revenue, presumably because of the severe price constraints in this sector. As a result, subsidies play a major role, be these explicit or via firms' own sources other than retentions. Taxation is, predictably, much lower. Investment is a much higher proportion of total inflows as a result of subsidies. Labour and overhead costs are a much higher proportion and inputs and associated costs a much lower one, but this will predominantly reflect the unique nature of the industrial processes involved.

The other quite distinctive sector is building materials and metals. This has significantly higher retentions and firms' own sources, and also higher investment expenditure, suggesting that it has experienced particularly buoyant financial conditions. In addition it has uniquely higher levels of special expenditure financed by special funding. We do not know the nature of these amounts, but they suggest that at least some elements of production in this sector have a particularly high priority attached to them with their activities guaranteed by project-specific funding. The only other distinctive characteristics are the particularly high external funding in textiles and in light industry and craft, the high level of investment in the latter, and the predictably high level of tax payments in food, drink and tobacco, and in energy.

It is possible in theory that these results are distorted by the presence in the sample of a few large enterprises with distinctive characteristics. In particular a few large-scale loss-makers in certain industries and locations could statistically bias the observed profiles described above. The disaggregated analysis for locations and industries was therefore repeated excluding all enterprises making aggregate losses over the period 1984–87. These results (not shown) closely match those for the whole sample. None of the specific results described above is invalidated and this suggests that they genuinely are associated with industry and location.

Turning to the financial performance of enterprises of differing scale, a very clear pattern emerges. Small-scale enterprises have the weakest financial performance. They have less retentions despite paying much less in tax, have the highest wage and overhead costs as a percentage of all financial uses, and rely least on operational sources of finance and most on government funding. In most respects large-scale enterprises come out best on these measures and medium-scale enterprises in between. But in two related ways this monotonic relation breaks down. First, large-scale enterprises, like small ones, have the highest levels of firms' own sources, but this may well reflect their profitability; in the small-scale ones it will frequently reflect subsidies, explicit or otherwise. Mirroring this, medium-scale enterprises have the most recourse to external sources of commercial funds, the more profitable larger-scale enterprises not requiring so much and the less profitable smaller-scale ones unable to raise such funds.

Finally we look at the significance of contract form, bearing in mind that, because of the timing of the introduction of the contract-responsibility system, any distinctive pattern is likely to indicate the financial performance which *led* to the decisions on contract form, rather than the form of contract determining financial performance. Here again the pattern is very clear. Whether the incentive systems are grouped by their profit characteristics or their asset characteristics, those enterprises which were switched to the contract-responsibility system were for the most part exhibiting higher wage and overhead costs, and covering less of their financial needs from operational revenues. They did manage to retain somewhat more, but this was only after paying significantly lower taxes, and does not fully account for the higher level of firms' own sources. Subsidies, both explicit and otherwise, were higher as for the most part was special funding. In what we can now see as a familiar pattern for financially weak enterprises, subsidies allowed them to maintain substantially higher levels of investment out of total funding. At a later date it will be of the utmost interest to see to what extent the financial performance of the enterprises which switched to the contract-responsibility system subsequently changed their financial performance relative to other enterprises.

6. Conclusions

In this chapter we have attempted to establish a conceptually appropriate and applicable format for identifying the flow of funds through Chinese state-owned enterprises. Despite some obstacles in terms of how certain flows are treated and accounted for, we have been able to construct flow of funds accounts from our basic database. These allow us to carry out quite powerful checks on the reliability of the data. It emerges that for a substantial subsample the data are reasonably accurate, and that there are few if any systematic errors.

Average flow of funds accounts can then be constructed for all enterprises where the data are sufficiently accurate and for subsamples of these grouped by location, industry, scale, and contract form. The overall tables indicate substantial and continuous improvement in financial performance over the period 1984–87. This is seen primarily in the reduction in operating costs as a percentage of financial outflows, but also in terms of taxation, retentions, and investment.

The subsamples show a much more varied picture, with large inland cities, small-scale enterprises, and the mining and extractive sectors exhibiting much the weakest performance. In each case a very similar pattern is observed. Wages and overhead costs represent a particularly high proportion of financial flows, due either to inefficiencies or price controls or both. The consequences are lower retention and taxation, but investment in each case is maintained at a high level through the provision of subsidies, explicit or otherwise.

Analysis of financial flows can serve several purposes. In the present context and in the light of the initial results described above, three in particular should be emphasized. First, the flow of funds through an enterprise, the financial constraints under which it operates, and the way it responds to, or loosens, those constraints are all key factors in determining behaviour and performance. While there are some clues to these issues in the results so far presented, the latter are not by themselves sufficient to identify the interlinkages between different flows, nor the extent to which outflows have been constrained, in economically rational ways or otherwise. To examine this we need to establish a simultaneous system in which the interactions can be modelled and estimated. This is the prime purpose of Chapter 9. A key feature in such a system however is investment expenditure. It is therefore important to analyse the determinants of investment expenditure first, and this is carried out in Chapter 8.

The second use of flow of funds analysis stems from the observation that certain locations, sectors, and scales of operation are associated with distinctively weak financial behaviour and the existence of substantial subsidies of various kinds. This goes directly to the question of the soft budget constraint which has existed in many planned economies in modern times. The results above suggest that this is likely to be a substantial problem in itself, and we therefore devote Chapter 10 to a more detailed examination of 'soft' budget constraint mechanisms.

Finally, one of the crucial elements in assessing ownership reform proposals is the likely effect of different ownership, control, and incentives on the flow of funds. While this area is inevitably more speculative, the flow of funds analysis above provides a picture of the position from which any ownership reform changes must start, and gives a good indication of the financial problems which will need to be addressed in any such reform programme. These issues are addressed in Chapter 12.

APPENDIX 7.1

TABLE 7.A1. Accuracy of data by location

	Class	Degree of inaccuracy as percentage	1984 obs	1984 %	1985 obs	1985 %	1986 obs	1986 %	1987 obs	1987 %
Large coastal cities	1	<5	40	44.9	46	51.7	45	50.6	43	48.3
	2	5–10	15	16.9	19	21.3	12	13.5	20	22.4
	3	10–20	17	19.1	15	16.9	19	21.3	16	18.0
	4	20–30	8	9.0	4	4.5	6	6.7	5	5.6
	5	>30	9	10.0	5	5.6	7	7.9	5	5.6
Subtotal			89	100	89	100	89	100	89	100
Large inland cities	1	<5	51	44.0	49	42.2	52	44.8	49	42.2
	2	5–10	26	22.4	26	22.4	27	23.2	35	30.2
	3	10–20	22	19.0	20	17.2	24	20.7	20	17.2
	4	20–30	4	3.4	8	6.8	1	0.9	4	3.4
	5	>30	13	11.2	13	11.2	12	10.3	8	6.8
Subtotal			116	100	116	100	116	100	116	100

TABLE 7.A1 (*cont.*)

	Class	Degree of inaccuracy as percentage	1984 obs	%	1985 obs	%	1986 obs	%	1987 obs	%
Medium and small coastal cities	1	<5	24	49.0	28	57.1	26	53.1	23	46.9
	2	5–10	12	24.5	14	28.6	9	18.4	9	18.4
	3	10–20	5	10.2	6	12.3	10	20.4	7	14.3
	4	20–30	4	8.2	1	2.0	2	4.1	9	18.4
	5	>30	4	8.2	0	0.0	2	4.1	1	2.0
Subtotal			49	100	49	100	49	100	49	100
Medium-sized inland cities	1	<5	43	54.4	40	50.6	33	41.8	36	45.6
	2	5–10	12	15.2	18	22.8	24	30.4	18	22.8
	3	10–20	11	13.9	13	16.5	14	17.7	14	17.7
	4	20–30	7	8.9	2	2.5	4	5.1	4	5.1
	5	>30	6	7.6	6	7.6	4	5.1	7	8.9
Subtotal			79	100	79	100	79	100	79	100
Small inland cities	1	<5	15	28.3	16	30.2	25	47.2	23	43.4
	2	5–10	17	32.1	16	30.2	7	13.2	12	22.6
	3	10–20	13	24.5	8	15.1	5	9.4	6	11.3
	4	20–30	2	3.8	5	9.4	7	13.2	3	5.7
	5	>30	6	11.3	8	15.1	9	17.0	9	17.0
Subtotal			53	100	53	100	53	100	53	100

APPENDIX 7.2

TABLE 7.A2. Accuracy of data by industry

	Class	Degree of inaccuracy as percentage	1984 obs	%	1985 obs	%	1986 obs	%	1987 obs	%
Extractive	1	<5	11	47.8	6	26.1	4	17.4	7	30.4
	2	5–10	2	8.7	7	30.4	8	34.8	5	21.7
	3	10–20	3	13.0	6	26.1	4	17.4	4	17.4
	4	20–30	3	13.0	3	13.0	1	4.3	3	13.0
	5	>30	4	17.4	1	4.3	6	26.1	4	17.4
Subtotal			23	100	23	100	23	100	23	100
Food, drink, and tobacco	1	<5	23	42.6	32	59.2	31	57.4	21	38.9
	2	5–10	10	18.5	10	18.5	11	20.4	20	37.0
	3	10–20	12	22.2	6	11.1	9	16.7	9	16.7
	4	20–30	5	9.3	2	3.7	1	1.9	1	1.9
	5	>30	4	7.4	4	7.4	2	3.7	3	5.6
Subtotal			54	100	54	100	54	100	54	100

TABLE 7.A2 (*cont.*)

	Class	Degree of inaccuracy as percentage	1984 obs	%	1985 obs	%	1986 obs	%	1987 obs	%
Textiles	1	<5	25	55.6	21	46.7	25	55.6	21	46.7
	2	5–10	6	13.3	14	31.2	3	6.6	11	24.4
	3	10–20	7	15.6	7	15.6	9	20.0	8	17.8
	4	20–30	6	13.3	1	2.2	6	13.3	4	8.9
	5	>30	1	2.2	2	4.4	2	4.4	1	2.2
Subtotal			45	100	45	100	45	100	45	100
Light industry and craft	1	<5	22	50.0	22	50.0	19	43.2	25	56.8
	2	5–10	11	25.0	11	25.0	13	29.5	8	24.4
	3	10–20	4	9.1	9	20.5	7	15.9	7	17.8
	4	20–30	3	6.8	1	2.3	1	2.3	1	8.9
	5	>30	4	9.1	1	2.3	4	2.3	3	2.2
Subtotal			44	100	44	100	44	100	44	100
Energy	1	<5	8	42.1	8	42.1	8	42.1	7	36.8
	2	5–10	4	21.0	2	10.5	5	26.3	4	21.0
	3	10–20	2	10.5	3	15.8	0	0.0	1	5.3
	4	20–30	1	5.3	1	5.3	0	0.0	2	10.5
	5	>30	4	21.0	5	26.3	6	31.6	5	26.3
Subtotal			19	100	19	100	19	100	19	100
Chemicals etc.	1	<5	30	42.3	36	50.7	41	57.7	37	52.1
	2	5–10	18	25.3	14	19.7	13	18.3	14	19.7
	3	10–20	13	18.3	11	15.5	9	12.7	14	19.7
	4	20–30	4	56.3	3	4.2	3	4.2	3	4.2
	5	>30	6	8.4	7	9.9	5	7.0	3	4.2
Subtotal			71	100	71	100	71	100	71	100
Building materials and metals	1	<5	24	40.0	25	41.7	29	48.3	23	38.3
	2	5–10	14	23.3	17	28.3	13	21.7	17	28.3
	3	10–20	15	25.0	9	15.0	13	21.7	11	18.3
	4	20–30	2	3.3	4	6.6	2	3.3	4	6.6
	5	>30	5	8.3	5	8.3	3	5.0	5	8.3
Subtotal			60	100	60	100	60	100	60	100
Engineering and electrical	1	<5	30	42.9	29	41.4	24	34.3	33	47.1
	2	5–10	17	24.3	18	25.7	13	18.6	15	21.4
	3	10–20	12	17.1	11	15.7	21	30.0	9	12.9
	4	20–30	1	1.4	5	7.1	6	8.6	7	10.0
	5	>30	10	14.3	7	10.0	6	8.6	6	8.6
Subtotal			70	100	70	100	70	100	70	100

APPENDIX 7.3

TABLE 7.A3. Accuracy of data by contract form

	Class	Degree of inaccuracy as percentage	1984 obs	1984 %	1985 obs	1985 %	1986 obs	1986 %	1987 obs	1987 %
Contract-responsibility system	1	<5	95	49.7	97	50.8	97	50.8	97	50.8
	2	5–10	41	21.5	47	24.6	42	22.0	42	22.0
	3	10–20	26	13.6	27	14.1	32	16.8	28	14.7
	4	20–30	15	7.9	10	5.2	8	4.2	14	7.3
	5	>30	14	7.3	10	5.2	12	6.3	10	5.2
Subtotal			191	100	191	100	191	100	191	100
Director-responsibility system	1	<5	57	42.6	64	47.8	63	47.0	60	44.8
	2	5–10	30	22.4	32	23.9	29	21.6	34	25.4
	3	10–20	32	23.4	29	21.6	30	22.4	28	20.9
	4	20–30	6	4.5	1	0.7	4	3.0	4	3.0
	5	>30	9	6.7	8	6.0	8	6.0	8	6.0
Subtotal			134	100	134	100	134	100	134	100

8

Investment Behaviour

1. Introduction

Investment decisions represent a crucial, some would say overriding element in the behaviour of enterprises. The quantity and quality of new capital installed are the prime determinants of the growth of enterprises and the scope for efficient production in the future. Investment is the main variable through which good performance in one period feeds through to good performance subsequently, but can also be the means through which lack of proper financial disciplines generates inefficiency and resource misallocation. It is therefore important to start by looking at the setting within which investment decisions have been taken during the reform years of the 1980s.

We have seen that, during this period, economic reform in China, previously restricted largely to the agricultural sector, began to transform the economic environment within which industrial enterprises operated. Price reform was carried out gradually via the dual system, whereby many products were produced and traded both as part of the state plan and within a market mechanism simultaneously at different prices. But in a relatively short period this led to a huge reduction in the scope of the plan, largely confining it by the late 1980s to strategically important and/or export-related products and commodities. Internal reform of enterprises and the way they operated was equally dramatic with the introduction of a number of new forms of relationship between enterprise managers and local industrial bureaux, all of which created much greater incentives for managers to operate their enterprises efficiently and profitably, and all of which gave much greater discretion to managers in their day-to-day operation of enterprises.

In other areas, however, the extent of reform was more limited or, indeed, virtually non-existent. Relatively little liberalization occurred as far as the interaction of the supply and demand for labour was concerned, with enterprises having little or no discretion over the size or structure of their work-force, and with employees being heavily dependent on their workplace for social support, housing, and education. Most industrial enterprises, and all large ones, remained fully in public ownership, with industrial bureaux therefore remaining responsible for, and ultimately in complete control of, industrial enterprises. Not unrelated to this, all external financing of enterprises remained, effectively, in the hands of the industrial bureaux. Though in practice enterprises would typically deal directly with banks, this was within the framework, control, and permissions of the industrial bureaux concerned. Similarly most investment expenditure and all medium- or large-scale investment projects remained subject to state approval, both at an early planning stage and at the later project approval stage. The requisition and sale of land also remained heavily circumscribed. In short, while the *process* of production—obtaining supplies, carrying out operations, setting prices, and selling—became heavily decentralized, increasingly carried out in a market environment and as a result of profit, or profit-related incentives, the control of the main factors of production—capital, labour, and land—remained, and continues to remain, very largely within the control and direction of the State.

As far as finance and investment are concerned, large state-owned enterprises in China are in some respects rather like the divisions of many typical Western corporations. They are responsible for day-to-day operations, largely determine their own prices, and take decisions in the light of a number of internal incentive mechanisms; but to obtain any significant amount of funding or to embark on any sizeable investment programme they need approval, through a number of stages, of higher authorities which indirectly represent the ultimate owners. The latter are of course quite different in China, and there may be differences in the extent to which the objective of the owners are articulated, accurately interpreted, or actually pursued. But the instruments and mechanisms of control are not so very different, and there is no reason in principle why an industrial bureau might not try to enforce types and levels of performance which are similar or indeed identical to those which the board of a Western corporation might try to impose.

The way in which the state operates its powers over financing and investment are crucial in determining how state-owned enterprises perform and hence how the industrial sector performs. The longer-term production possibilities, level, type and age of equipment, and general economic development of enterprises are all determined by these decisions. With the liberalization of pricing and incentives there is clearly scope to enforce tight financial and profitability rules of the type that many companies in the West would adopt. Alternatively quite different priorities and criteria may be adopted. A third possibility is that investment and financing are controlled in quite arbitrary or perhaps even random ways, at least as far as economic priorities are concerned. Just how tight, rational, or efficient the policies adopted by industrial bureaux might have been during the reform period of the 1980s is difficult to identify, partly of course because all sorts of additional elements determine *ex post* performance, but also because there are necessarily no observations of rejected or abandoned projects. There are none the less ways in which some insight can be gained into this central question.

The main objective of this chapter is to explore the extent to which the very different institutional environment within which investment decisions are taken in China generates behaviour different from that exhibited within a framework of capitalist institutions. While there is no reason necessarily to expect the same behaviour, this gives us a benchmark against which to identify differences. They can then be viewed in the context of the different institutional arrangements and economic mechanisms which Chinese state-owned enterprises face. The basic approach therefore is to take a generalized neoclassical model of investment behaviour that has been of some interest and use in analysing investment behaviour in the West, make some amendments where necessary in order to fit it to the behaviour of Chinese state-owned enterprises, utilize current best-practice econometric techniques, and explore the extent to which Chinese investment behaviour is consistent with such a model, and hence with the motivational assumptions explicit in it. This can then be used, first, to provide an equation to describe investment behaviour in China at the enterprise level and, second, to permit investigation of the extent to which in practice enterprises have pursued, or have been allowed to pursue, profit-maximizing strategies by the banks and industrial bureaux which control them. It can also provide a basis for simulation exercises designed to explore the likely consequences of alternative regimes. Section 2 looks at basic theory, Section 3 at econometric considerations, Section 4 at data, Section 5 at results, and Section 6 at implications.

2. *The Generalized Neoclassical Investment Function*

In broad terms this section follows the neoclassical approach to investment functions pioneered by Jorgenson (1963: 247–59; also Jorgenson and Siebert 1968: 681–712) but in certain respects follows the more general formulation used by Feldstein and Flemming (1971: 415–34), in particular in not restricting the elasticity of substitution to unity but allowing its value to be determined by the data.

Profit maximization requires that the addition to total revenue from employing one more unit of capital be equal to the cost of so doing, i.e.

$$P_{jt}\mathrm{d}Q_{jt} = C_{jt}\mathrm{d}K_{jt}, \tag{8.1}$$

where P_{jt} is the price of products, denoted by Q, produced by enterprise j in time t,

$\mathrm{d}Q_{jt}$ is the incremental production by enterprise j in time t as a result of its incremental increase in capital stock, $\mathrm{d}K_{jt}$, and

C_{jt} is the user cost of that capital for enterprise j in time t.

With a Cobb–Douglas production function $Q = \mathrm{A}K^{\alpha}L^{\beta}$

$$\frac{\mathrm{d}Q}{\mathrm{d}K} = \mathrm{A}\alpha K^{\alpha-1}L^{\beta} = \frac{\alpha Q}{K}. \tag{8.2}$$

With appropriate suffixes and utilizing (8.1) and (8.2),

$$\alpha_j \frac{Q_{jt}}{K_{jt}} = \frac{C_{jt}}{P_{jt}}. \tag{8.3}$$

The optimal capital stock, i.e. that which satisfies this equation is given by

$$K^*_{jt} = \alpha_j \frac{Q_{jt}P_{jt}}{C_{jt}}. \tag{8.4}$$

Thus the desired capital stock is a function of output, prices, the user cost of capital, and α_j, the elasticity of capital with respect to output.[1]

This formulation, based on a strict Cobb–Douglas formulation, automatically restricts the elasticity of the desired capital stock with respect to both relative prices and output to unity. There seems no particular reason why either restriction should be valid, and we here add separate elasticity parameters to both terms in order to generalize the formulation, i.e.

$$K^*_{jt} = \alpha_j^{\sigma_1} Q_{jt}^{\sigma_1} \left(\frac{P_{jt}}{C_{jt}}\right)^{\sigma_2}. \tag{8.5}$$

The user cost of capital is normally given by the price of capital goods, multiplied by the interest rate plus depreciation rate minus any appreciation in capital prices. Here we ignore the final term because, in the Chinese context, any such gains are rarely if ever realizable. Thus

$$C_{jt} = P^k_{jt}(i_{jt} + \delta_{jt}), \tag{8.6}$$

where P^k is the price of capital goods, i is the interest rate, δ is the depreciation rate, and suffixes have the same meaning as before. In principle therefore we allow for each enterprise to have its own relevant interest rate and depreciation rate each period.

Equation (8.6) ignores taxation. This is a complex matter, the details of which we do not address here. But for each enterprise there will be an overall marginal incidence of taxation on profits which we regard as constant for any given enterprise in any given year over the relevant range of profitability, designated $\bar{t}_{\pi_{jt}}$ for the jth enterprise in period t. Hence the effective user cost of capital is given by

$$C_{jt} = \frac{P^k_{jt}(i_{jt} + \delta_{jt})}{(1 - \bar{t}_{\pi_{jt}})}$$

and so

$$\frac{C_{jt}}{P_{jt}} = \frac{P^k_{jt}(i_{jt} + \delta_{jt})}{P_{jt}(1 - \bar{t}_{\pi_{jt}})}. \tag{8.7}$$

We now proceed to generalize equation (8.7) in two ways. First, the perceived impact of taxation on the user cost of capital may be different from that of the interest rate and depreciation rate. To deal with this, separate elasticity parameters β_1 and β_2 are introduced. Second, equation (8.7), in keeping with the neoclassical approach, presumes that there is no distinction *per se* between internal and external financing. In practice, enterprises may well perceive these differently. With regard to commercial funds, there are likely to be constraints, sometimes prohibitive ones, on the use of external funds, whatever their user cost in relation to returns on investment, which do not apply either to the same extent or, perhaps, at all to internal sources of funds. To allow for this we introduce a term F^{λ} multiplicatively into the equation where F is the level of internal funds available and λ is a parameter. If, therefore, λ equals zero, there is no effect on investment of the availability of internal funds *per se*. A negative value indicates that increased availability of internal finance effectively reduces the user cost of capital relative to product prices and results in higher investment expenditure than otherwise. In practice there are some problems of interpretation (see below) which reduce what can be learnt from this variable, but its inclusion can still help to improve the results obtained for the other determinants.

We need also to consider external funds supplied on a non-commercial basis, that is, subsidies of one form or another supplied at zero cost. Some investment prospects may occur only if subsidies are available, either because they would not be commercially viable at prevailing rates of interest or because no other finance, internal or external is available. In principle this could be taken into account by introducing a further multiplicative term reflecting such subsidies. In practice this is problematic from an econometric perspective because our database includes only a very small number of enterprises in receipt of long-term subsidies, but these enterprises tend to have very distinct characteristics (see Chapter 10). We therefore proceed as follows. In this chapter we exclude the enterprises in receipt of large long-term subsidies for investment, so that we can focus on the investment behaviour of profitable and generally unsubsidized enterprises. This gives us the clearest possible picture of what might be regarded as normal responses in relation to investment behaviour. Subsequently in Chapter 10 we focus specifically on loss-making enterprises, examining the extent to which they are subsidized and what use they make of the funds available to them, including investment uses. In this way we try to separate out the economic behaviour of enterprises in response to constraints and incentives on the one hand and the economic environment within which they operate on the other.

Restricting our data-set to exclude enterprises in receipt of long-term subsidies for investment we may reflect financial constraints through the F^{λ} term alone. Equation (8.7) therefore becomes

$$\frac{C_{jt}}{P_{jt}} = \frac{P^k_{jt}}{P_{jt}}(i_{jt} + \delta_{jt})^{\beta_1}(1 - \bar{t}_{\pi_{jt}})^{-\beta_2}F^{\lambda}_{jt}. \tag{8.8}$$

Substituting this into equation (8.5) gives

$$K^*_{jt} = \alpha_j^{\sigma_1} Q_{jt}^{\sigma_1}\left(\frac{P^k_{jt}}{P_{jt}}(i_{jt} + \delta_{jt})^{\beta_1}(1 - \bar{t}_{\pi_{jt}})^{-\beta_2}F^{\lambda}_{jt}\right)^{-\sigma_2}. \tag{8.9}$$

This is the basic formulation for the desired capital stock with which we will work.

In general, investment in any period will be a partial response to the discrepancy between the actual capital stock that would result in that period after allowing for depreciation in the absence of any investment, and the desired capital stock for that period, i.e.

$$I_{jt} = \gamma_j[K^*_{jt} - K_{jt-1}(1 - \delta_{jt})]. \tag{8.10}$$

γ_j may be interpreted as a traditional speed-of-adjustment parameter, reflecting planning and construction lags, bottlenecks, and the like. In the Chinese context, however, it may also reflect multiple levels of administrative intervention that, irrespective of availability of funds, may restrict investment below that necessary for profit maximization, or lead to excessive investment because of non-economic objectives of the intervening state authority. There may also be welfare and other non-commercial investments in the investment data which drive a wedge between the actual capital stock as measured, and the optimal capital stock as determined in equation (8.9) above. Finally following both the managerialist literature in the West and Kornai in the East (Kornai 1982: 26 ff.), enterprises may try to pursue growth strategies which lead to 'excessive' investment, i.e. more than is necessary to bring the existing capital stock up to the profit-maximizing level.

In addition K^*_{jt} has to be estimated by managers on the basis of relevant past information concerning the determinants of the optimal capital stock. In general this implies that

$$K^*_{jt} = \sum_{x=1}^{\infty} W_{t-x} K^*_{t-x}, \tag{8.11}$$

where W represents a weighting function. Empirically it is not possible to take account of all the factors involved, which primarily relate to timing and lag structure. We only have annual data for a relatively short run of years, and there are too many factors involved to permit them all to be distinguished. Instead we adopt two approaches. One simply assumes a one-year lag and full adjustment in that year. The second identifies the estimated value of next period's optimal capital stock on the basis of the trend values of the determinants over previous years. This latter formulation then subsumes both the lags in identifying the optimal capital stock and lags in adjusting to it, as well as any of the other forces described above which may prevent full adjustment within one year.

Rearranging equation (8.10), substituting equation (8.9) into it, assuming a one-year lag and putting the result into logs, the basic format of the equation to be estimated is

$$\begin{aligned}\ln[I_{jt} + (1 - \delta_{jt})K_{jt-1}] = {} & \sigma_1 \ln_j + \sigma_1 \ln Q_{jt-1} - \sigma_2 \ln \frac{P^k_{jt-1}}{P_{jt-1}} \\ & - \sigma_2 \beta_1 \ln(i_{jt-1} + \delta_{jt-1}) \\ & + \sigma_2 \beta_2 \ln(1 - \bar{t}_{\pi_{jt-1}}) - \sigma_2 \lambda \ln F_{jt-1}.\end{aligned} \tag{8.12}$$

3. Econometric Considerations

Typically equation (8.12) would be estimated in the form:

$$\begin{aligned}\ln[I_{jt} + (1 - \delta_{jt})K_{jt-1}] = a_0 + a_1 \ln Q_{jt-1} + a_2 \ln \frac{P^k_{jt-1}}{P_{jt-1}} \\ + a_3 \ln(i_{jt-1} + \delta_{jt-1}) \\ + a_4 \ln(1 - \bar{t}_{\pi_{jt-1}}) \\ + a_5 \ln F_{jt-1} + u_{jt},\end{aligned} \tag{8.13}$$

where $a_0 = \sigma_1 \log \alpha_j \quad a_3 = -\sigma_2\beta_1$
$a_1 = \sigma_1 \quad a_4 = \sigma_2\beta_2$
$a_2 = -\sigma_2 \quad a_5 = -\sigma_2\lambda.$

This constrains α_j to be constant for all j, and u_t is an error term.

This would permit estimation of all the parameter values in which we are interested. The parameter estimates may however be inefficient if there are enterprise-specific factors at play and/or time-series effects in the panel data which generate some autocorrelation. Evidence that such effects are present is provided later. It is therefore necessary to transform equation (8.13) in order to try to eliminate any such effects.

There are two ways in which this might be done. In the first, we divide the stochastic effects represented by u_{jt} into two; a component e_j which reflects firm-specific and other autocorrelated effects, and e_{jt} which is pure white noise.

Hence equation (8.13) becomes

$$\begin{aligned}\ln[I_{jt} + (1 - \delta_{jt})K_{jt-1}] = a_0 + a_1 \ln Q_{jt-1} + a_2 \ln \frac{P^k_{jt-1}}{P_{jt-1}} \\ + a_3 \ln(i_{t-1} + \delta_{jt-1}) \\ + a_4 \ln(1 - \bar{t}_{\pi_{jt-1}}) \\ + a_5 \ln F_{jt-1} + e_j + e_{jt}.\end{aligned} \tag{8.14}$$

Writing the equivalent equation for period $t-1$ and subtracting from equation (8.14) gives

$$\begin{aligned}\Delta\ln[I_{jt} + (1 - \delta_{jt})K_{jt-1}] = a_1 \Delta\ln Q_{jt-1} + a_2 \Delta\ln \frac{P^k_{jt-1}}{P_{jt-1}} \\ + a_3 \Delta\ln(i_{jt-1} + \delta_{jt-1}) \\ + a_4 \Delta\ln(1 - \bar{t}_{\pi_{jt-1}}) \\ + a_5 \Delta\ln F_{jt-1} + \Delta e_{jt}.\end{aligned} \tag{8.15}$$

This first-difference formulation then eliminates any enterprise-specific or other autocorrelated elements.

This approach assumes that the vector of explanatory variables, $\mathbf{X}_{jt}$, is uncorrelated with e_{jt-1}. If this assumption is incorrect then the estimation of parameter values will be inefficient. Arellano and Bond (1988) have proposed a dynamic panel data (DPD) method for dealing with this problem. This recognizes that the vector $\mathbf{X}_{jt}$ may be correlated with $e_{j,t}$ and/or $e_{j,t-1}$ and makes only the much weaker assumption that it is not correlated with $e_{j,t+1}$. In this case each explanatory variable is regressed on all its previous values except that in period $t-1$, and the estimated value of each based on these instruments then used in the main regression, i.e.

$$\begin{aligned}\Delta\ln[I_{jt} + (1-\delta_{jt})K_{jt-1}] = {} & a_1\Delta\hat{\ln}Q_{jt-1} + a_2\Delta\hat{\ln}\frac{P^k_{jt-1}}{P_{jt-1}} \\ & + a_3\Delta\hat{\ln}(i_{jt-1} + \delta_{jt-1}) \\ & + a_4\Delta\hat{\ln}(1 - \bar{t}_{\pi_{jt-1}}) \\ & + a_5\Delta\hat{\ln}F_{jt-1} + \Delta e_{jt},\end{aligned} \tag{8.16}$$

where

$$\begin{aligned}\Delta\hat{\ln}Q_{j,t-1} &= \mathrm{f}(\ln Q_{j,t-2}, \ln Q_{j,t-3} \ldots \ln Q_{j,t-n}) \\ \Delta\left(\hat{\ln}\frac{P^k_{j,t-1}}{P_{j,t-1}}\right) &= \mathrm{f}\left(\ln\frac{P^k_{j,t-2}}{P_{j,t-2}}, \ln\frac{P^k_{j,t-3}}{P_{j,t-3}}, \ldots \ln\frac{P^k_{j,t-n}}{P_{j,t-n}}\right) \\ \Delta\hat{\ln}(i_{j,t-1} + \delta_{j,t-1}) &= \mathrm{f}(\ln(i_{j,t-2} + \delta_{j,t-2}), \ln(i_{j,t-3} + \delta_{j,t-3}), \\ & \quad \ldots \ln(i_{j,t-n} + \delta_{j,t-n})) \\ \Delta\hat{\ln}(1 - t_{\pi_{j,t-1}}) &= \mathrm{f}(\ln(1 - \bar{t}_{\pi_{j,t-2}}), \ln(1 - \bar{t}_{\pi_{j,t-3}}), \\ & \quad \ldots \ln(1 - \bar{t}_{\pi_{j,t-n}})) \\ \Delta\hat{\ln}F_{j,t-1} &= \mathrm{f}(\ln F_{j,t-2}, \ln F_{j,t-3}, \ldots \ln F_{j,t-n})\end{aligned}$$

with in our case, $2 \leqslant n \leqslant (t - 1983)$.

We therefore use this as a check on the assumption in the main regression that the vector $\mathbf{X}_{jt}$ is uncorrelated with e_{jt} and e_{jt-1}.

An alternative procedure is to carry out a dynamic transformation of equation (8.13). Suppose that

$$u_{jt} = e_j \cdot u_{jt-1} + e_{jt}, \tag{8.17}$$

where e_j is the coefficient of correlation between successive error terms as a result of enterprise-specific and other serial effects and e_{jt} is white noise. u_{jt-1} can be written as

$$\begin{aligned} u_{jt-1} = \ln(I_{jt-1} + (1 - \delta_{jt-1})K_{jt-2}) - a_0 - a_1\ln Q_{jt-2} \\ -a_2\ln\frac{P^k_{jt-2}}{P_{jt-2}} - a_3\ln(i_{jt-2} + \delta_{jt-2}) \\ - a_4\ln(1 - \bar{t}_{\pi_{jt-2}}) - a_5\ln F_{jt-2}. \end{aligned} \tag{8.18}$$

Multiplying equation (8.18) by e_j and combining it with (8.13) and (8.17), gives

$$\begin{aligned} \ln(I_{jt} + (1 - \delta_{jt})K_{jt-1}) = {} & a_0 - e_j a_0 + e_j\ln(I_{jt-1} + (1 - \delta_{jt-1})K_{jt-2}) \\ & + a_1\ln Q_{jt-1} - e_j a_1\ln Q_{jt-2} \\ & + a_2\ln\frac{P^k_{jt-1}}{P_{jt-1}} - e_j a_2\ln\frac{P^k_{jt-2}}{P_{jt-2}} \\ & + a_3\ln(i_{jt-1} + \delta_{jt-1}) - e_j a_3\ln(i_{jt-2} + \delta_{jt-2}) \\ & + a_4\ln(1 - \bar{t}_{\pi_{jt-1}}) - e_j a_4\ln(1 - \bar{t}_{\pi_{jt-2}}) \\ & + a_5\ln F_{jt-1} - e_j a_5\ln F_{jt-2} + e_{jt}. \end{aligned} \tag{8.19}$$

This then embodies the set of restrictions that the coefficient on a two-period lag variable equals that on the corresponding one-period lag variable multiplied (negatively) by e_j. Subsequently $\ln Q_{jt}$ and $\ln Q_{jt-1}$ were dropped in the fully dynamic specification because of their high multicollinearity with $\ln K_{jt}$ and $\ln K_{jt-1}$. Statistical results based on the original estimating equation suggest that this is acceptable. Equation (8.19) is then the dynamic specification of equation (8.13) when autocorrelation may be present. Overall therefore we have a basic specification and two variants, a first-difference and a dynamic specification to allow for possible autocorrelation in the panel data.

4. Data

The basic data-set is all compiled from our quantitative survey for the years 1983 to 1987. For the regressions, out of the total of 386 enterprises the sample typically varied between 200 and 350 enterprises once data omissions, data inconsistencies, lag-structure, and other considerations had been allowed for. Specifically an enterprise, for inclusion in the regressions, must have the necessary observations for at least 3 consecutive years. Outliers were also eliminated, as follows

(i) Investment in any year must be positive but less than 40 million yuan. This is because investment greater than this, which is relatively rare, is likely to involve major projects which would be the subject of direct administrative controls by the State rather than the enterprise itself.

(ii) The gross nominal user cost of capital should be positive but less than 30%.

(iii) The net rate of return on capital should be less than 100%.

(iv) The index of relative capital prices for the enterprise (see below) should not move outside the range 0.01 to 2, i.e. capital prices do not rise less than 1% or more than 200% of the rise in general prices over the same period.

The data for each variable are as follows:

I_{jt} Annual real value of total new capital investment, covering replacement and expansion in relation to construction, machinery equipment, and tools that have an economic life in excess of 2 years and nominal value over 36,000 yuan. Welfare investment is also included in the aggregate. Regressions were also run for various subcategories of investment, namely, productive investment, construction investment, and equipment investment.

The real value is obtained by deflating the nominal values obtained from the questionnaire by the price index for capital goods for the enterprise. This index is constructed as follows:

$$P^k_{jt} = \left(\frac{C}{I}\right)_{jt} \cdot Cp_t + \left(\frac{E}{I}\right) \cdot Ep_t,$$

where C_{jt} is total investment expenditure by enterprise j in time period t in buildings and construction,

E_{jt} is total investment expenditure by enterprise j in time period t in equipment,

Cp_t is the average price index of capital construction per annum in China in period t, and

Ep_t is the average price index of industrial equipment in China in period t.

Cp_t and Ep_t are taken from the *China Quarterly*.[2] The capital price index for each enterprise is therefore a weighted sum of the national construction and equipment indices where the weights are those appropriate to the individual enterprise for the relevant year. $(1 - \delta_{jt})K_{jt-1}$ is the written down value in period t of the capital stock in existence in period $t - 1$. This is in practice derived from the formula

$$K_{jt} = BK_{j0}(1 - \delta_{j0})^n + \sum_{t=1}^{n} \frac{(BK_{jt} - BK_{jt-1})(1 - \delta_{jt})^{n-t}}{P^k_{jt}}$$

$$(t = 1, 2, 3, \ldots n)$$

(If $\Delta BK_{jt} < 0$, $P^k_{jt} = 1$ and $(1 - \delta_{j0}) = 1$)

where BK_{j0} is the book value of capital assets in year 0;

δ_{j0} is the depreciation rate in year 0;

K_{jt} is the real value of capital assets after depreciation (see the reference in note 2 for further elaboration of this formula);

Q_{jt} is net output of the enterprise deflated by an enterprise-specific price index of output, P_{jt};

P_{jt} is the ratio of the nominal value of gross output to the real value of gross output, both of which are available from the enterprise data-set;

i_{jt} is the interest rate for enterprise j in period t and is found by dividing the total interest paid in period t by the total loans outstanding in the balance sheet drawn up in period t;

δ_{jt} is the depreciation rate for enterprise j in period t and is found by dividing the annual depreciation for period t by the total book value of capital assets in period t (*Chinese Accountancy Manual* 1984);

$\bar{t}_{\pi_{jt}}$ is the rate of tax on the profits of enterprise j in period t, calculated as the sum of income and adjustment taxes divided by total gross realized profits (it is therefore an average rather than marginal tax rate for the relevant year);

F_{jt} is the total value of an enterprise's own sources of long-term finance deflated by the capital price index. This includes retained profit, retained depreciation, and other sources.

5. *Results*

Equation 8.13 was the first to be estimated. Year, location, and industry dummies were included and a number of variants tried as follows. First, a simple one-period lag was used (Code 1) and then regressions carried out in which current values of explanatory variables were replaced by estimated values taken from time-trends fitted to the previous value of those variables (Code 2). Regressions were run for aggregate investment (Agg), as well as productive (P), construction (C), equipment (E), and welfare (W) investment; for different scales of enterprises (Scale 1, large; Scale 2, medium; Scale 3, small);

for different stages of the reform years (Ref. 1, 1984–85; Ref. 2, 1986–87); for alternative contract forms (cf1, the contract-responsibility system; cf2, the director-responsibility system);[3] and for two different measures of financial autonomy, F_1, level of internal funds available; F_2, proportion of state-controlled (plan) output in the enterprise's total output.

The rationale for the latter proxy is that, apart from the term F_{jt-1} in equation (8.13) the investment equations are derived from clear, albeit generalized, neoclassical behaviour. The F_{jt-1} term introduces the possibility of deviations from such behaviour. F1 is a standard way of incorporating imperfections and constraints in the capital market; F2 indicates the extent to which enterprises are required to incorporate non-profit maximizing considerations. This is not a good proxy but there are few alternatives with a natural metric.

There are, as indicated above, a large number of results. Rather than reproduce them all we first reproduce the full results for two basic cases (see Table 8.1) and then look at more summary results for a number of the more interesting variants (Table 8.2). Points of interest from other regressions are noted in the commentary.

Table 8.1 gives parameter estimates and *t*-values (in brackets) for aggregate investment, with internal finance used for F_j. Column 1 uses actual annual data, column 2 uses estimated values derived from time-series regressions. The parameter values derived from the two approaches are generally similar indicating that, although the simple one-period lag structure is very crude, it is a reasonable approximation to a more sophisticated one.

The value of the intercept does not fit the basic equation in that it should equal $\sigma_1 \ln\alpha_j$ which should be negative. However, this is of no great consequence because the specification includes a number of dummies, which will distort the intercept value, and because there will typically be some level of investment that may occur independent of the considerations involved in the specification.

With regard to the dummies, there is clear evidence of an investment boom in the period 1984–87 over and above what can be explained by the main independent variables. The location dummies offer strong confirmation of a result which we have previously noted in the flow of funds data, namely that enterprises in large inland cities, that is to say enterprises in large conurbations other than in the coastal zones, have *ceteris paribus* exhibited substantially and statistically significant higher levels of investment than in other locations. Enterprises in coastal cities, on the other hand, whatever the size of the conurbation, tend to invest less. We cannot of course say whether

TABLE 8.1. Determinants of aggregate investment expenditure by large-scale Chinese enterprises 1983–1987

	Equation 1 One-period lag	Equation 2 Multi-period lag
Intercept	1.865 (9.1)	2.048 (8.2)
Coefficients on		
P_k/P	−0.627 (7.1)	−0.754 (5.9)
$i + \delta$	−0.353 (7.7)	−0.326 (4.2)
$1 - t_\pi$	0.083 (1.9)	0.065 (3.6)
F	0.128 (6.8)	0.149 (2.4)
Q	0.610 (22.7)	0.678 (24.7)
Dummies		
Years (vs 1987)		
1984	−0.222 (3.3)	
1985	−0.137 (2.2)	
1986	−0.087 (1.5)	−0.114 (2.1)
Contract form (vs cf2)		
cf1	−0.016 (0.4)	0.041 (0.7)
Locations (vs small inland cities)		
Large coastal	−0.139 (1.5)	−0.132 (1.1)
Large inland	0.238 (2.7)	0.252 (2.2)
Small/Medium coastal	−0.151 (1.6)	−0.056 (0.5)
Medium inland	0.018 (0.2)	0.012 (0.1)
Industries (vs. light industry and craft)		
Extractive	0.502 (2.1)	0.908 (4.2)
Food, drink, tobacco	−0.331 (6.6)	−0.548 (6.5)
Textiles, tailoring, leather	−0.222 (5.0)	−0.283 (3.6)
Energy	0.250 (1.0)	0.129 (0.2)
Chemicals/medium/plastics	−0.213 (5.8)	−0.045 (1.4)
Building materials/metals	0.011 (2.4)	0.001 (0.8)
Engineering and electrical	0.180 (2.2)	0.081 (0.8)
$\bar{R}^2$	0.73	0.70
N	677	468

any enterprises were over- or under-investing relative to the profit-maximizing level because the dummies only pick up investment levels in different locations relative to each other. But it is significant that much the highest levels of investment occur in the locations where, as we shall see later, subsidies of various forms are also highest.

Turning to the industry dummies, here also we obtain useful confirmation of earlier observations, namely that enterprises in the extractive industry were investing significantly more than elsewhere. Here again these are enterprises where subsidies are also higher.

TABLE 8.2. Estimation results for aggregate investment, investment by scale of enterprise and by stage of the reform process

	1 Agg F_1	2 Agg F_1	1 Scale 1 F_1	1 Scale 2 F_1	1 Scale 3 F_1	1 Ref 1 F_1	1 Ref 2 F_1
P_k/P	−0.627 (7.1)	−0.754 (5.9)	−0.609 (6.3)	−0.564 (2.8)	−0.846 (2.8)	−0.512 (3.7)	−0.745 (6.1)
$i+\delta$	−0.353 (7.1)	−0.326 (4.2)	−0.271 (4.5)	−0.415 (5.8)	−0.198 (1.9)	−0.406 (5.0)	−0.319 (5.6)
$1-t_\pi$	0.083 (1.9)	0.054 (3.6)	0.068 (1.3)	0.220 (3.1)	0.373 (2.9)	0.048 (0.7)	0.109 (1.8)
F	0.128 (6.8)	0.149 (2.4)	0.127 (4.8)	0.076 (2.7)	0.140 (2.9)	0.134 (5.1)	0.127 (4.6)
Q	0.610 (22.7)	0.678 (24.7)	0.371 (9.4)	0.535 (11.7)	0.777 (7.3)	0.598 (14.8)	0.621 (16.7)
σ_1	0.610	0.678	0.371	0.535	0.777	0.512	0.745
σ_2	0.627	0.754	0.609	0.564	0.846		
β_1	0.563	0.432	0.445	0.736	0.234	0.793	0.428
β_2	0.132	0.072	0.117	0.390	0.441	0.094	0.146
λ	−0.204	−0.198	−0.208	−0.135	−0.165	−0.261	−0.169
$\bar{R}^2$	0.73	0.70	0.57	0.64	0.81	0.72	0.74

Notes: Scale 1, Large; Scale 2, Medium; Scale 3, Small. Ref 1 84–85; Ref 2 86–87.

However, this result may reflect no more than that price controls substantially reduced revenue in this sector, which was then made up in other ways. In other words we cannot reject the hypothesis that investment in this sector was at the level which would have been generated by a profit-maximising enterprise operating without price constraints. It is also noteworthy that investment tended to be higher than elsewhere in energy, building materials and metals, and engineering and electrical, though results elsewhere suggest that this may be due more to price controls and/or subsidies in the first but superior performance or expectations in the latter two.

The contract-form dummy is clearly insignificant. At one level this is unsurprising. The contract-responsibility system was introduced towards the end of the period covered and there would therefore appear to be little reason to expect investment behaviour during the period to be associated with contract form. It is worth recalling however (see Chapter 7, Section 5) that financial performance was found to be statistically correlated, implying that enterprises characterized by a certain type of financial performance were systematically more likely to be switched to the contract-responsibility system. The result here therefore is informative in that it suggests that it genuinely was differences in existing financial performance rather than related investment behaviour which was important in influencing decisions on the implementation of new organizational control mechanisms.

Turning to the main parameters of interest, all coefficients are significant and of the right sign. Using these results we may calculate values for the various parameters of interest. σ_1, the elasticity of capital with respect to output, is 0.678 in equation (8.2) (Table 8.1) which is not dissimilar from typical values found in the West. σ_2 needs careful interpretation. In the basic equation it is the elasticity with respect to the real user cost of capital. However, in the more general specification adopted here we can estimate the elasticity with respect to the real price of capital goods, the interest-plus-depreciation cost of capital and profits tax separately, with σ_2 equal only to the first. The value of σ_2 is quite similar to σ_1, suggesting that the elasticity of capital with respect to the ratio of sales revenues to capital prices is constant irrespective of which component of sales revenue, i.e. prices or output changes.

In a pure neoclassical model, the values of β_1 and β_2 should both be unity. In fact they are typically around 0.5 and 0.1 respectively. As a result the elasticity on the cost of funds is approximately 0.33. The fact that this is considerably lower than the elasticity on output again parallels results in the West and is indicative of putty-clay technology.

The overall elasticity with respect to profits taxation is typically less that 0.1 in the aggregate analysis. Overall, real capital prices are significantly more important than interests rates and depreciation, which in turn are significantly more important than tax effects in determining investment behaviour.

Of particular interest is the value of λ. Under perfect capital market conditions this will equal zero. In fact it has a value of approximately -0.2, suggesting that there is a statistically significant finance constraint linking enterprise investment to purely internally generated funds. On the other hand this value is not at all high. It is quite likely that Western companies would exhibit similar values if not higher values. In the West however this would probably reflect investment autonomy coupled with a preference for internal funding, partly to reduce transactions costs but also to reduce the impact of financial market scrutiny. In China, quite different considerations are likely to apply. First, the constraint on the use of external funds will frequently arise not because enterprises are more reluctant to use external funds, nor necessarily because a financial institution would not itself wish to lend, though both effects may occur. Rather it will be the relevant higher authority which decides explicitly whether investment projects, particularly large ones, can proceed and this also determines whether the necessary funding will be made available. By itself this mechanism might be expected to give a rather high (negative) value of λ. The value revealed by our results at least suggests that the constraints imposed by higher authorities on enterprises' investment did not in practice greatly restrict or distort overall expenditure levels.

Against this, the higher authority may also restrict some investment prospects which, were they to go ahead, might be financed partly or completely from internal funds. This would tend to weaken the link between investment and internal funding, thereby biasing the value of λ towards zero. While therefore the value of λ is of some interest, we cannot directly infer the extent of external constraints on enterprises' investment, because of the scope for the higher authority to regulate both externally and internally financed investment. We utilize different methods in the next chapter to explore the issue further. However, given that in this period there was considerably increased emphasis on granting enterprises greater autonomy in the use of their own funds, albeit approval for larger-scale investment funded internally would still be required, the extent of the bias may not be great, and we can still take the value of λ, and variations in it across subsamples, as a rough indication of external constraints.

Overall the aggregate results are reasonably satisfactory, being plausible, consistent across different specifications, and fairly robust. $\bar{R}^2$s are around 0.7, which, for an adjustment variable like investment is high. While we can say relatively little about external constraints, and nothing about externally provided subsidies, we are able to infer that investment behaviour on the part of the enterprises involved is reasonably predictable and in large measure consistent with profit-maximizing principles. Both demand and all the major components of the cost of capital have statistically significant predicted effects. The signals given by these demand and supply variables may of course themselves be distorted. Revenues may be affected by price and/or quantity restrictions, interest rates may be artificially low, capital prices subsidized or otherwise distorted, and taxation determined by a range of other considerations. But the response of investment to those signals indicates quite strong neoclassical patterns, and this allows us to be reasonably confident about predicting the effects on investment of changes in the determinants, be these changes the general result of the path of macroeconomy or some specific consequences of further economic reform measures.

Turning to the subsamples, there are several main points of interest. First, the equation has considerably more explanatory power the smaller the scale of the enterprise. This is an interesting if not unexpected result because it indicates that it is the larger-scale enterprises that are more subject to other considerations or constraints arising out of the objectives and operations of higher authorities, in particular the industrial bureaux. Second, and consistent with this, the value of λ is nearer zero for smaller-scale enterprises, though the change is neither large nor monotonic. Also consistent, the impact of taxation is noticeably higher for smaller-scale operations. Third, the elasticity with respect to output is strongly related inversely to size, though this is not surprising or very interesting given the greater scope for variations in capital-intensity in larger enterprises in pooled data. We return to this below when we allow for firm-specific effects. Fourth, the effect of the cost of capital is always significant but appears to be noticeably more important for medium-size enterprises. The reason for this is not clear, unless it is that constraints override the effect for large-scale enterprises and greater availability of internal finance or subsidies in relation to investment plans reduces its importance in smallscale enterprises.

With regard to a comparison of earlier and later years of reform within the sample period, while the results are slightly stronger overall for the latter period, the differences, in terms of elasticities, statistical significance, and correlation coefficients, are all very small. The value of λ does however fall significantly in the latter period, and this is consistent with the reform process leading to less imperfections in the provision of capital.

Replacing F_1 by F_2, the ratio of state to total output, which is a totally different measure of imperfection or constraint, gives similar results (not shown) in that coefficients are of the right sign and statistically significant. Parameter values are typically only about 0.04 however, suggesting that qualitatively the effect, or at least the effect as measured by this particular proxy, is not very strong. Finally, the regressions for different subcategories for investment, i.e. production, construction, equipment, and welfare-related investment, do not reveal any significant variations from the aggregate results.

As indicated earlier there is a potentially serious problem with panel data of the type used here, namely that the results may reflect firm-specific attributes. In order to address this we ran the following tests. The basic equations were re-estimated, (*a*) in first differences but without instruments, (*b*) in first differences using instruments as explained earlier, and (*c*) with a fully dynamic specification. These were run without dummies as these would no longer be appropriate. The results are given without an F variable in Table 8.3 and with F_1 in Table 8.4.

The results of these alternative specifications are mixed. All parameter signs remain the same and nearly all remain statistically significant. First-difference specifications naturally have very much lower correlation coefficients, but overall these results suggest that the earlier

TABLE 8.3. Estimates of parameters with different specification methods but excluding firm's internal finance

Equation	Levels Static	First differences Non-instrumented	First differences Instrumented	Levels Dynamic
Intercept	0.660 (2.4)	0.125 (10.4)	0.138 (6.6)	0.457 (6.6)
L_nK_{-1}	—	—	—	0.949 (92.1)
$L_n(P_K/P)$	−0.742 (5.8)	−0.158 (1.8)	−0.505 (1.8)	−0.119 (1.5)
$L_n(i+\delta)$	−0.532 (6.6)	−0.260 (7.0)	−0.176 (1.4)	−0.246 (6.5)
$L_n(1-t_n)$	0.021 (0.4)	0.039 (1.8)	0.003 (0.1)	0.046 (2.1)
L_nQ	0.783 (31.5)	0.079 (1.9)	0.176 (0.9)	—
R^2	0.66	0.10	0.05	0.94
DW	1.0	2.2	2.0	—
N	530	530	530	526
No. of firms	218	218	218	218

Note: Constraints:
(1) $\theta_2 = 0.949 \cdot (-0.246) = 0.233$
(2) $\lambda_2 = 0.949 \cdot (-0.119) = 0.113$
(3) $\delta_2 = -0.949 \cdot 0.046 = -0.044$

TABLE 8.4. Estimates of parameters with different specification methods but including firm's internal finance

Methods	Levels Static	First differences Non-instrumented	First differences Instrumented	Level Dynamic
Intercept	1.232 (8.2)	0.115 (9.1)	0.144 (4.2)	0.458 (6.4)
L_nK_{-1}	—	—	—	0.945 (84.9)
$L_n(P_K/P)$	−0.692 (5.4)	−0.006 (0.1)	−0.866 (1.8)	−0.003 (0.1)
$L_n(i+\delta)$	−0.503 (6.2)	−0.291 (7.8)	−0.276 (1.5)	−0.280 (7.5)
$L_n(1-t_\pi)$	0.028 (0.5)	0.032 (1.5)	0.005 (0.1)	0.036 (1.7)
L_nF	0.196 (7.8)	0.034 (3.4)	0.067 (1.2)	0.038 (3.7)
L_nQ	0.591 (16.7)	0.020 (0.4)	0.085 (0.5)	—
R^2	0.69	0.15	0.02	0.95
DW	1.1	2.1	2.1	—
N	448	448	448	443
No. of firms	190	190	190	190

Note: Constraints:
(1) $\theta_2 = -0.945 \cdot (-0.280) = 0.2656$
(2) $\lambda_2 = -0.945 \cdot (-0.003) = 0.003$
(3) $\delta_2 = -0.945 \cdot (0.036) = -0.034$
(4) $\omega_2 = -0.945 \cdot (0.038) = -0.036$

estimates are reasonably robust in the face of firm-specific effects. Against this there are two concerns. First, some parameters do become insignificant in certain specifications, most notably that on output, indicating substantial firm-specific effects in certain areas. Second, actual parameter estimates do change substantially from those obtained in the basic case, even though the derivations are such that they should not. However, with the exception of the coefficient on output the general pattern of values across the independent variables is fairly similar, particularly if we restrict observation to those values which are statistically significant.

Overall these further tests give fairly solid qualitative support for the basic approach and results, but are quantitatively more erratic. Given the demanding nature of the first-difference and dynamic formulations this may not be of too much concern, though that is a matter for judgement. The main substantive implication is that there are powerful firm-specific effects in the panel data in relation to output effects.

6. Conclusions

The first main conclusion of the above analyses is that a generalized neoclassical approach, allowing for financial constraints, is not inappropriate for analysing and explaining investment expenditure in China despite the very different circumstances within which the relevant decisions are taken. Indeed it is unlikely that, just looking at the econometric results, one could distinguish the underlying investment performance from that which would be expected in any developed industrial country. This has two opposing but not necessarily incompatible implications. The first is that the process of economic reform in China, involving the gradual but largely complete transfer to market prices, the decentralization of financial decisions, and the institution of profit-related controls which to some extent mirror the effects of private ownership, has gone sufficiently far for investment behaviour to reflect essentially the same sorts of considerations as in the West. Certainly it seems unlikely that a similar analysis, were it to be repeated for the 1960s or 1970s, would have generated the same results, though we are unable to test this.

Second, however, it may be that specifications of the sort used, though testable given the data available, are not sufficiently detailed to enable us to identify certain unique or at least distinguishing features of the economic environment within which Chinese investment decisions are taken. In particular we cannot determine the extent to which departures from pure neoclassical behaviour reflect imperfections and/or constraints peculiar to Chinese industry. Do they reflect familiar financial constraints and associated rationing effects, or more arbitrary direct restraints and controls that arise from the ownership and authority structure within which investment decisions are made? In particular we cannot say to what extent the composition of investment, as opposed to its total level, is determined by standard profit or sales-maximizing objectives or by other considerations, be these more social in nature, or private but none the less alternative objectives on the part of enterprises or industrial bureaux. This is not surprising given the absence of data across alternative ownership and authority forms but is none the less a significant limitation. Be this as it may, we can still use equations based on the above analysis as part of an overall model of enterprise behaviour, employing simulation techniques to determine how alternative economic environments might be expected to modify enterprise performance.

A similar point applies to the overall quality or success of the investment carried out. Even where we estimate that investment is guided by profit-maximizing considerations, this does not tell us whether the investment achieved the intended results, nor indeed what percentage was even completed and made operational. This type of issue requires a different approach which focuses on the profitability actually achieved by enterprises in relation to the cost-of-capital considerations described earlier.

The second main inference derives from the first. We should not expect even quite substantial further reform, in terms of ownership, control, or incentive structures, to lead to major changes in the investment *behaviour* of profitable enterprises. The quite different framework that exists in the West generates similar types of investment behaviour in these enterprises. Overall investment *performance*, in terms of appropriate levels, composition, and efficiency may well be influenced, but this is likely to be through changes in the external environment, in particular through changes in the direct and/or financial controls exercised by higher authorities and in subsidy behaviour, rather than through further internal reforms designed to make enterprise decision-making more economically rational.

A final conclusion relates to the relative significance of macroeconomic effects and reform effects in influencing investment expenditure. For example, a more restrictive macroeconomic stance, in terms of both fiscal and monetary policy, would, given the elasticity estimates derived, have a significant impact. Assuming average values of interest rates and depreciation, a 1% rise in the former would, on the basis of the analysis, result in a fall in aggregate investment of approximately $3\frac{1}{2}$%, though this needs to be compared to equivalent estimates from aggregate time-series regressions. This may be contrasted with an illustrative but rather speculative estimate that, if all of the differences between the implied finance constraint on large enterprises and small ones is due to the greater control by higher authorities that occur in the former, then relaxation of that control would have increased investment by about 10% in the companies concerned. Such issues really require a more elaborate simultaneous framework in which account is taken of the repercussions of all the major financial and expenditure decisions of an enterprise on each other. This is taken up in the next chapter. But such calculations are enough to show that investment may be quite sensitive to both the macroeconomic environment and to further reform measures.

NOTES

1. Strictly Q_{jt} should be formulated in terms of P_{jt}, thereby dropping out of the equation.
2. For a detailed discussion and assessment of the construction of these price indices see Liu and Morris (1991).
3. In fact the distinction is considerably more complex than this allows for (see definitions of cf1 and cf2 in Table 7.17) and the results indicated that the contract form dummy was not significant.

9

The Interaction of Financial and Expenditure Decisions

1. Introduction

Previous chapters have looked at a range of financial and expenditure characteristics of Chinese state-owned enterprises. In particular we have looked at the pattern of inflows and outflows of funds (Chapter 7), identified the role of bonus payments in determining efficiency (Chapter 4), and examined the determinants of investment expenditure (Chapter 8). Bonus payments appear to be particularly important in influencing efficiency in the short term, and investment is likely to be the main determinant of longer-term development. Both must compete with other claims on finance and both ultimately depend on the availability of funds, internally generated and externally available. The main purpose of this chapter is to take some first steps towards understanding the pattern of interactions of financing and expenditure occurring in Chinese enterprises.

We will primarily be concerned with two questions. First, to what extent are there identifiable links between various financial inflows and outflows from which systematic financial behaviour by enterprises can be inferred. At one extreme there may be clear one-to-one relationships between particular inflows and outflows and specific trade-offs between different sources or between different uses. At the other extreme there may be a largely random pattern over time and across enterprises as each responds in an *ad hoc* manner to its internal financial position and in relation to the external bodies with which it has financial connections. Here we seek to understand the systematic elements, ultimately as a basis for predicting how alternative control mechanisms might affect financial flows.

Second, we need to know to what extent enterprises are financially constrained and how this affects behaviour. Later we shall seek to relate these to performance characteristics but for the present confine ourselves to the issue of the financial constraint itself. We have seen that enterprises behave in reasonably predictable and essentially profit-maximizing ways in terms of the investment they aim to carry out. But to what extent are they able to carry out this investment, or other expenditures which they view as desirable, and to what extent do financial constraints prevent them? Finally, we also take the opportunity to make preliminary inspections of the impact of non-financial variables on financial decisions.

To examine these issues we employ simultaneous econometric estimation techniques. Section 2 outlines the basic rationale for simultaneous testing of enterprise financial behaviour, the testing format, and some initial considerations concerning how to interpret patterns of results. Section 3 discusses the data and details of equation specification. Section 4 presents initial results and interpretation. Section 5 reviews what can be learnt about enterprise financial behaviour from the analysis and points to further elaboration in the development of a full, simultaneous simulation of Chinese enterprise behaviour.

2. *Simultaneous Analysis of Financial Decisions*

Enterprises are continuously concerned with a vast array of financial and expenditure decisions. It is therefore necessary to construct a framework for analysing those decisions which is sufficiently simplified as to be tractable but which none the less allows insight into this behaviour. Starting therefore from the detailed structure of inflows and outflows described in Chapter 7 we first identify a simplified pattern of inflows and outflows which will meet these criteria. Essentially enterprises may be viewed as having two main sources of funds: first short-term cash flow generated by current operations, equal to profit plus retained depreciation, and second generally longer-term external sources, comprising those directly from the state in the form of grants, subsidies etc. and those from banks and other financial institutions generally in the form of loans. This classification does not however include 'other' components of a firm's own sources (see Chapter 7, Section 3). For the great majority of enterprises in our sample this is not a significant source of funds; indeed overall it is typically negative as a result of some leakage of funds to welfare expenditure, investment in other businesses etc. But for a small number of enterprises with very low or, in particular, negative profitability it may include sizeable short- or long-term subsidy inflows. Overall therefore this item includes a mixture of flows. In the econometric analysis we exclude loss-making enterprises, examining them separately in the next chapter and, for the rest, include 'other' elements of a firm's own sources with the cash-flow variable, partly because for profitable enterprises, the 'other' flows tend to be shorter-term ones, and partly because for the great majority of these enterprises, these flows, like profits and depreciation, will reflect production decisions and activity and hence will be prior exogenous decisions as far as financial flow analysis is concerned. On the uses side, enterprises have three main uses of the funds available. These are remittances of various kinds to the state, primarily tax and profit delivery; investment expenditures; and payments to the work-force in the form of bonuses, welfare payments etc., which are discretionary payments over and above the basic wages paid as part of current productive activity.

Price, production, and sales decisions in conjunction with market conditions determine profitability and depreciation which, from a flow of funds perspective, are therefore exogenous. The three main uses decisions and the external-sourcing decision are then constrained by the fact that external funding added to internal cash flow must equal the sum of the three uses. Thus at most, only three of the four financial-flow variables are independent. The fourth must be a residual with a value predetermined by the other three.

In addressing the question of which should be regarded for analytical purposes as a residual we need first to consider the position with regard to remittances to the state, which are in a somewhat unique position. At one extreme these might be determined entirely by the state with or without overall reference to profitability or cash flow. In this case taxes and delivered profit would become exogenous to the financial decisions of the exterprise, the item should be dropped from analysis, and we would be left with only two independent financial decisions. At the other extreme the level of funds remitted to the State may be a matter for bargaining between the enterprise and the state (see Chapter 4), with the eventual level being heavily dependent on the overall financial position of the enterprise. In this case remittance would be an important financial-decision variable, determined in part at least by the level of other financial flows. As such it would need to be included as a potential dependent variable, though it might in some circumstances be the residual variable in the system.

Because the degree of exogeneity of the value of total remittance to the state is one of the key issues of interest, we need to conduct the analysis described below on two bases: first, with remittance treated as an exogenous constraint on financial decisions and, second, with remittance as a separate dependent variable reflecting a distinct financial decision. In principle the pattern of results can then indicate whether and to what extent remittance is within the influence or control of the enterprise. The results can then be compared to those on autonomy derived in Chapter 3. In order to avoid loss of generality we treat remittance as endogenous in the following description of the analysis.

In the absence of strong prior reasons for treating any one of the four main financial flows as the residual, all in principle could be. At one extreme, external sources could be raised to whatever extent the three independent decisions on uses of funds required. More realistically perhaps, investment, perhaps bonuses, or even remittance may be the residual in that, given internal and external sources and prior independent decisions on other uses, one use is the residual claimant on funds and determined by the value of the residual funds. This is in rather sharp contrast to the position in most large publicly quoted companies in the West where, over the long term, independent decisions tend to be made on a variety of uses and external borrowing, up to the prudential borrowing limits, with new equity finance as the cumulative long-term residual. Thus for Chinese enterprises we need to test for this facet of the linkages between different financial flows by carrying out the analysis on the basis of different assumptions about residual flows.

On the basis of these preliminaries we may now present a simplified view of the format of analysis. Each independent financial decision can in principle be influenced by all the other financial flows involved. We therefore need an econometric equation for each independent decision which can then be aggregated up into simultaneous-equation blocks reflecting the dual directions of causality that can run between two financial variables. With remittance endogenous any block will have three equations; with remittance exogenous any block will have two. But we can greatly shorten the basic presentation by forming a single four-equation block from which any two or any three equations can be extracted for a particular simultaneous system test. Table 9.1 presents the four-equation block in outline, the details of which we now consider.

The basic pattern has two elements. First, each financial variable is in principle a function of all the others. Second, each may be a function of certain predetermined variables. Here we hypothesize that remittance may be a function of liquidity, investment a function of growth and profitability, the latter lagged to reflect decision lags. External sources may be constrained by existing debt ratios. Finance for bonuses and welfare payments may depend in part on profitability and liquidity.

TABLE 9.1. Simultaneous equation format

	R	*I*	*E*	*BW*	*FP/KL*	*GRT*	*LA/K*	*SD/K*
R		*	*	*			*	
I	*		*	*	*	*		
E	*	*		*				*
BW	*	*	*		*		*	

Definitions:
- *R* — Remittance of all kinds to the state
- *I* — Investment expenditure
- *E* — External funds, including both bank and state sources
- *BW* — This variable may be *B*, bonuses, or *W*, welfare payments, or their sum, *BW*
- *FP/KL* — Return of fulfilled profit on capital, the *L* indicating a one-period lag
- *GRT* — Growth rate
- *LA/K* — Ratio of liquid assets to capital employed
- *SD/K* — Ratio of debt to capital employed

Before discussing this format and its interpretation in more detail, it is worth making one basic observation. In general, as between any two statistically related variables we may infer causality in one direction, causality in the other direction, or mutual dependence on some other variable. Each line in Table 9.1 hypothesizes a causal relation running from the variables listed across the top to the dependent variable on the left-hand side. Simultaneous testing means that we should be able to ignore reverse causality, because that is picked up elsewhere in the system. But robust statistical results from estimating such systems are none the less in general capable of two possible interpretations, namely the hypothesized causality or mutual dependence on unobserved variables. We can however inspect results for this and indeed use it to make inferences about financial behaviour.

We shall be concerned with the extent to which enterprises' decisions on the expenditure items in the system are constrained by internal and external financial flows. We can get some insight into the effect of the latter by observing the extent to which each individual expenditure item is correlated with external finance. Internal constraints are more difficult to identify because internal finance available for these outflows is not directly observable, but they can none the less be inferred from the pattern of coefficient signs. For example, leaving aside the predetermined variables, which have been referred to above, the remittance equation hypothesizes that, *ceteris paribus*, investment, bonuses, and welfare expenditure will reduce remittances while increased external financing would permit greater remittances. More realistically it would reduce the financial incentive or the financial pressure to reduce remittances in bargaining with the state over delivered profit, adjustment taxes, etc. The signs on investment, external financing, and bonuses etc. would be negative, positive, and negative respectively. The *ceteris paribus* assumption implies that these variations occur for a given level of internal finance, and hence are not constrained by the latter. An alternative situation would be if remittance was determined jointly with the three other items in the light of variations, that is the tightness or otherwise, in the enterprise's internal cash flow. In this case, if the latter were tight, remittance, investment, and bonuses would all be lower than otherwise and external financing higher. If internal cash flow were buoyant then all these flows would move the other way. In this case these flows would be constrained by internal funds and the signs on the endogenous variables in the remittance equation would all be reversed, i.e. positive on investment, negative on external financing, and positive on bonuses and welfare.

In similar fashion in the investment equation, a causal relation would imply a positive coefficient on external funding, indicating partial dependence of investment on the external finance available. Negative coefficients on remittance and bonuses would indicate the trade-off that exists with these alternative uses of funds. If, on the other hand, the various financial flows are all mainly constrained by internal cash-flow considerations then the pattern of parameter signs would be reversed.

The external sources equation suggests that external funding is determined by the need for it as reflected in the main three uses. An overriding internal finance constraint would mean that as the constraint varied, e.g. tightened, so uses would contract and external financing increase, giving a pattern of negative coefficients. Using the same logic, bonuses and welfare would be related positively to external funding and negatively to remittance and investment if bonus decisions were taken within a given internal cash-flow constraint, but in the opposite direction if bonuses were mainly constrained by internal cash flow.

Overall we will be interested in four types of results. First, how do the results compare as between including and not including remittance in the system? Second, do we find a set of significant parameter values which indicate systematic linkages between various financial decisions? Third, does the pattern of parameter signs conform to one or other of the predicted patterns, dependent on the extent to which financial decisions on external funding and internal uses can be varied independent of internal cash-flow considerations? Finally, what can be learnt from the role of the predetermined variables and the values of the set of parameter estimates generated?

3. Data and Specification

The data used are derived from the detailed quantitative questionnaire responses. The specific variables are constructed as shown in Table 9.2.

Two remittance variables were constructed and tested; a narrow definition including only income tax or profit delivery, adjustment tax, and other charges; and a broader definition comprising all payments to the state, including not only income tax and adjustment tax but sales tax, revenue taxes, and other charges. The rationale for the former is that it is essentially the total of income tax and adjustment tax that enterprises primarily bargain over and in the light of which

TABLE 9.2. Definition of variables used

Variables	Definitions of variables
R/S	$\frac{\text{Broad definition of remittance}}{\text{Sale revenue}}$
RI/S	$\frac{\text{Narrow definition of remittance}}{\text{Sale revenue}}$
E/S	$\frac{\text{External sources of finance}}{\text{Sale revenue}}$
I/S	$\frac{\text{Investment expenditure}}{\text{Sales}}$
WF/S	$\frac{\text{Uses for welfare}}{\text{Sale revenue}}$
BO/S	$\frac{\text{Various kinds of bonus}}{\text{Sale revenue}}$
BW/S	$\frac{\text{Welfare + Bonus}}{\text{Sale revenue}}$
FP/KL	$\frac{\text{Lagged fulfilled profit}}{\text{Capital}}$
GRT	Growth rate of sales revenue
LA/K	$\frac{\text{Liquid assets}}{\text{Capital}}$
SD/K	$\frac{\text{Stock of debts at the end of the year}}{\text{Capital}}$

other financial decisions are made. The presumption is that the other major payment, namely sales tax, is regarded purely as an automatic payment from gross revenue. The rationale for the broad definition is that all such financial flows are potentially relevant and that some of the other payments to the state may in part be bargainable. We believe the former to be the appropriate measure but for completeness use both.

External sources have two main components, state subsidies and bank credit. In principle this variable could be split into its two component parts and four-equation blocks run. In practice we have too few observations of sizeable state subsidies for simultaneous econometric purposes. We therefore leave this issue to the next chapter where the role of subsidies is explicitly examined.

The bonuses and welfare payments variable clearly also has two components. In principle we are interested in what we may term discretionary wage bonuses, but we cannot exclude the possibility that, to some extent, welfare payments are determined in the same way. Hence we use both variables, first separately and then together.

The other variables are reasonably straightforward, in particular investment expenditure, growth, and profitability. Growth should be measured in real terms ideally but at present is measured in terms of nominal sales growth. To the extent that inflation varies over time and across sectors or indeed enterprises this will reduce the statistical significance of this variable. As we shall see, the results were generally rather poor but this may well reflect the inadequate current price specification.

Various alternative current and lagged measures of the return on capital were used. For the most part this made little difference but, in order to pick up the incentive and signalling effects of profitability rather than a financial-flows effect (which in the above framework would introduce spurious correlation), we prefer and generally use a simple one-period lag. Finally, two variables are constructed as shown in Table 9.2 to reflect liquidity and debt structure.

Turning to specification there are two main problems. First all correlations would, if carried out exactly as shown in Table 9.1, be heavily dominated by pure size considerations; all sources and uses will normally be proportionately larger in a larger company. To deal with this we normalize all endogenous variables by enterprise size, as measured by sales. In principle the capital base could be used for this purpose but this would set up spurious correlations with some of the predetermined variables.

Second, simultaneous systems need to meet certain criteria if they are to avoid specification problems, primarily of under- or over-determination. In the present case this resolves itself into three requirements: first, that no two equations in a system have entirely common predetermined variables; second, that the number of predetermined variables in any equation is not less than the number of endogenous variables; and, third, that there are sufficient observations to satisfy the degrees-of-freedom constraint. The pattern of variables included on purely a priori economic grounds meets the first of these requirements but not the second. In specific block regressions therefore, when necessary, another of the predetermined variables is included, or if more appropriate, lagged external financing is introduced as a new predetermined variable.

As far as the number of observations is concerned, the requirement is satisfied. We use pooled time-series and cross-sectional data from the years 1984–87 inclusive. The restriction to this period is caused by the need to have lagged values, which are not available from 1982 for 1983 data. In terms of the enterprises included from the full data-set we operate with a large sample and a small sample. The former comprises all observations where the flow of funds data are accurate to within 10% as identified in Chapter 7. The latter utilizes only those enterprises for which the data are accurate to within 10% for each year in the sample. This has 525 observations and is generally to be preferred. However, the large sample tests, using approximately 950 observations, generally give similar results.

Finally, we add a constant to each equation. In an ideal system there should not be a significant constant or intercept term in any of the equations but in practice it is important to include them. An insignificant coefficient is one additional indicator of a properly specified equation and a significant one at least indicates some element of the dependent variable which is independent of the hypothesized determinants. As it turns out a gratifyingly large number of the constants do turn out to be insignificant, but there are some important cases where this is not so.

4. *Summary of Main Results*

Given the number of variables involved, the different specifications in which we have an interest, and the alternative possible samples, the simultaneous-system approach which we have employed generates a very large set of results, certainly too large to reproduce in full in the text. Fortunately this is not necessary. Many specifications are fairly

TABLE 9.3. Simultaneous equation block 1d.RS1.(S). Bonuses omitted. Narrow definition of remittance. Lagged rate of return variable. Small sample (*t*-statistics in brackets)

$$\frac{RS1}{S_t} = \underset{(0.28)}{-0.004} + \underset{(2.72)}{0.906}\frac{I}{S_t} - \underset{(2.67)}{0.952}\frac{E}{S_t} + \underset{(12.6)}{0.135}\frac{FP}{K_{t-1}} + \underset{(2.89)}{0.099}\frac{LA}{K_t} \qquad \bar{R}^2 = 0.27$$

$$\frac{I}{S_t} = \underset{(3.94)}{0.023} + \underset{(2.10)}{0.320}\frac{RS1}{S_t} + \underset{(63.6)}{1.070}\frac{E}{S_t} - \underset{(2.36)}{0.024}\,GRT_t - \underset{(2.98)}{0.061}\frac{FP}{K_{t-1}} \qquad \bar{R}^2 = 0.89$$

$$\frac{E}{S_t} = \underset{(7.71)}{-0.053} + \underset{(61.3)}{0.945}\frac{I}{S_t} + \underset{(4.02)}{0.215}\frac{RS1}{S_t} + \underset{(1.07)}{0.010}\,GRT_t + \underset{(3.97)}{0.050}\frac{SD}{K_{t-1}} \qquad \bar{R}^2 = 0.88$$

Symbols:

RS1	Narrow definition of remittance
I	Investment expenditure
E	External finance
S	Sales revenue
FP/K	Return on capital
LA/K	Ratio of liquid assets to capital
GRT	Growth rate
SD/K	Ratio of debt finance to capital

Notes: System estimated using two-stage least squares.
Small sample comprises 525 observations pooled cross-section and time-series. Includes only those enterprises for which flow of funds data are correct to within 10% in all 4 years.

minor versions of each other for which, as it happens, the results are little changed. Our approach therefore is to start by taking one major illustrative block and discussing the results, noting in passing alternatives which have only minor, if any, effects on the results. Then we go on to consider other blocks which illustrate important differences. In this way it is possible to summarize all the results while keeping the number of tables manageable.

Table 9.3 gives the results for one of the central cases. Bonuses and/or welfare payment have been omitted as the residual, the preferred definitions of remittance (narrow) and return on capital (lagged one period) have been used and the equations estimated by two-stage least squares on the smaller (most reliable) data-set. The variables are as identified in Table 9.2.

Looking at the remittance equation first, the constant is, as expected, insignificant. Both the endogenous finance variables are significant, investment expenditure being positively correlated, external financing negatively related. As we saw in Section 9.2, if enterprises were able to vary sources and uses for given internal cash flow in essentially an unconstrained way, then we should expect the opposite signs on these two variables. The fact that we have two uses significantly and positively correlated, and a source and a use significantly and negatively correlated, in a simultaneous system which allows elsewhere for reverse causalities, is an indicator that all three variables are linked by their dependence on internal finance. More buoyant cash flow (probably associated with higher current profitability) is associated with higher remittance, higher investment, and less external financing. By itself the result is suggestive rather than definitive; we will need to consider it as but one element in the context of the results as a whole, but it is an important finding none the less.

Turning to the predetermined variables we find that both last year's return on capital and liquidity are positively and significantly correlated with remittance. If remittances were entirely non-discretionary (in the sense defined above) then it is not clear that either variable should be significant, though current liquidity may be related to current profits and the latter may be related not only to remittance but to last year's return on capital as well. We infer from these results that last year's return on capital and the current year's liquidity are significant (negative) determinants of relative strength in bargaining over remittance. It may be that a higher remittance commitment engenders higher average liquidity as enterprises prepare to meet it. However, alternative specifications which include lagged liquidity also give a significant positive coefficient, and this supports the view that bargaining strength is important in determining remittance. This also supports the result found, by quite different methods in Chapter 3, that there is an important discretionary element in the payment required by and paid to the state.

The correlation coefficient is 0.27. This is a fairly typical value for such an analysis. It is however quite low by comparison with that of some of the other equations. This is not surprising however given that remittance must to some considerable degree be beyond the influence of the enterprise.

The investment expenditure equation has a significant constant, which is an undesirable property of the equation. However, the coefficient is small, equal to only 22% of the mean value of the dependent variable, and probably reflects some general underlying level of investment, primarily basic replacement expenditures and the like which enterprises need to carry out independent of their performance or financial positions. It is also worth adding that several other specifications, although less preferred on other grounds, give an insignificant constant. With regard to the endogenous flow variables both external finance and remittance are significant (external financing extremely so) and positive. These two findings are the first indication of what subsequently turns out to be a central result. The positive correlation between two uses of funds underlines the existence of an internal cash-flow constraint and is completely consistent with the previous remittance equation. But the positive correlation between investment and external financing is an indication that external finance is a determinant of investment expenditure independent of internal financial constraints. This is not a sign that planned investment requires appropriate external finance to carry it out—that relationship is picked up in the next equation; rather it is an indication that, when external finance becomes available it is systematically utilized for investment purposes. We will see later a clear and generally consistent pattern emerging along these lines.

The coefficients on both growth and lagged return on capital appear perverse, though these are atypical results. Whether investment responds in lagged fashion to the previous year's growth and profitability, or enterprises use them as signals of current or future growth and profitability, the signs should be positive. They are also both significant. In the case of growth it may be due to the effect of current sales appearing in the numerator of the predetermined variable and the denominator of the dependent variable, or may be distorted by the use of nominal sales figures. Alternatively there may be some significant negative autocorrelation in industry performance and this might explain both perverse signs. Alternative specifications generally give positive but insignificant coefficients, and in fact only three cases of a significant perverse coefficient (one on profitability, two on growth) occur in the whole set of results. The correlation coefficient is remarkably high at 0.89. This derives from the strong correlation with the external financing variable.

The external-finance equation has a significant negative constant which indicates some misspecification but which probably reflects the extent to which investment expenditure and remittances can be made before there is a need to resort to external finance. Both investment expenditure and remittance coefficients are positive and significant. The effect of investment is very strong, indicating that external funds are primarily raised for this purpose. Higher remittances also lead to higher levels of external finance and both indicate how the demand for external finance is generated. The growth rate, though having the expected sign, is insignificant, probably for reasons given above. Finally the effect of the pre-existing debt/capital ratio is significant and positive. In a situation where enterprises were free to find their own equilibrium level of leverage we would expect this coefficient to be negative. The positive coefficient suggests, first, that enterprises are constrained to a disequilibrium point and, second, that there is persistence through time of an enterprise's ability to negotiate new loans. *Ceteris paribus*, those with a history of raising more debt finance in the past appear, if only to a relatively small extent, to be better placed to raise new external finance. The correlation coefficient is again high at 0.88 suggesting that the equation gives a reasonably powerful explanation of external financing.

We may summarize the basic picture that emerges as follows. First, there is some indication that remittance is, from the enterprise's point of view, a financial decision over which it can exert some influence through bargaining on the basis of its financial position. This is consistent with our results in Chapter 3 where financial variables were added to single-equation explanations of remittances. Second, the results indicate that enterprises typically are internally finance-constrained, with remittance, investment, and external financing all responding, the first two positively, the third negatively, to that constraint. Third, and consistent with this, external finance is strongly responsive to financing requirements for investment, and to a lesser extent if high remittance levels reduce available finance. This is not of course to say that virtually all investment is financed externally. We know from the flow of funds data that on average nearly half is not. Rather it shows that changes in investment are highly dependent on external finance being available and this is consistent with the evidence above that there is a strong internal finance constraint.

Before commenting on the wider significance of these results we go on to explore other simultaneous blocks. Tables 9.4, 9.5, and 9.6 give illustrative results for the small sample, still using the narrow definition of remittance where it is included but for different three-equation blocks. We do not go through these results in the same detail as above. Rather we bring out some of the main inferences.

First, it is clear that the investment–external finance relation dominates. As in Table 9.3, the parameters on these two are always highly significant and close to unity. When only one is present in an equation block, the explanatory power of the block falls substantially.

Second, in general the coefficients on the financial variables in the remittance equations support the interpretation of Table 9.3. All are significant, the sources variable is negatively correlated, and two of the three uses variables are positively correlated. The only exception is the negative coefficient on investment expenditure in the remittance equation in Table 9.5. This result tends to persist through various specifications (Table 9.3 being one of the exceptions) and, to the extent that external finance is the residual (i.e. missing equation) variable, higher investment expenditure is associated with lower

TABLE 9.4. Simultaneous equation block 1b.RS1.(S). Investment omitted. Narrow definition of remittance. Lagged rate of return variable. Lagged liquidity variable. Small sample (t-statistics in brackets)

$$\frac{RS1}{S_t} = \underset{(1.87)}{-0.029} - \underset{(2.08)}{0.141}\frac{E}{S_t} + \underset{(4.10)}{5.46}\frac{B}{S_t} + \underset{(12.6)}{0.146}\, FPK_{t-1} \qquad \bar{R}^2 = 0.26$$

$$+ \underset{(1.86)}{0.053}\, LAK_{t-1} - \underset{(0.42)}{0.008}\frac{\varepsilon}{S_{t-1}}$$

$$\frac{E}{S_t} = \underset{(2.58)}{-0.594} + \underset{(0.10)}{0.329}\frac{RS1}{S_t} + \underset{(6.78)}{40.69}\frac{B}{S_t} + \underset{(0.59)}{0.220}\, FPK_{t-1} \qquad \bar{R}^2 = 0.10$$

$$- \underset{(0.48)}{0.052}\, GRT_t + \underset{(1.80)}{0.536}\, SDK_{t-1}$$

$$\frac{B}{S_t} = \underset{(4.17)}{0.006} + \underset{(4.17)}{0.178}\frac{RS1}{S_t} + \underset{(5.73)}{0.026}\frac{E}{S_t} \underset{(4.75)}{-0.027}\, FPK_{t-1} \qquad \bar{R}^2 = 0.12$$

$$- \underset{(1.41)}{0.004}\, GRT_t - \underset{(1.95)}{0.011}\, LAK_{t-1}$$

Symbols:

RS1	Narrow definition of remittance
I	Investment expenditure
E	External finance
S	Sales revenue
FPK	Return on capital
LAK	Ratio of liquid assets to capital
GRT	Growth rate
SDK	Ratio of debt finance to capital

Notes: System estimated using two-stage least squares.
Small sample comprises 525 observations pooled cross-section and time-series. Includes only those enterprises for which flow of funds data are correct to within 10% in all 4 years.

remittance, the coefficient only turning significantly positive when, as in Table 9.3, an external-finance equation is included.

It may be that we should disregard the evidence of a negative coefficient on the grounds that the simultaneous systems without endogenous external-finance equations are misspecified and that the result is inconsistent with the other evidence available on the existence of internal financial constraints. Against this, it is not obvious that external finance is not the proper residual variable in the system, and it may be that the particular relation picked up by this coefficient *is* an exception to the internal-constraint characteristic. Even though all other sources and uses variables in the remittance equations have coefficient signs which indicate the operation of a significant internal-finance constraint, the coefficient on investment generally suggests otherwise; which is to say that with regard to this one element in the endogenous component of the remittance equation, there is some

TABLE 9.5. Simultaneous equation block 1c.RS1.(S). External finance omitted. Narrow definition of remittance. Lagged rate of return variable. Lagged liquidity variable. Small sample (t-statistics in brackets)

$$\underset{}{\frac{RS1}{S_t}} = \underset{(1.86)}{-0.030} - \underset{(3.06)}{0.148}\frac{I}{S_t} + \underset{(4.00)}{6.04}\frac{B}{S_t} + \underset{(12.1)}{0.148}\,FPK_{t-1} + \underset{(1.55)}{0.046}\,LAK_{t-1} - \underset{(0.29)}{0.006}\frac{E}{S_{t-1}} \qquad \bar{R}^2 = 0.26$$

$$\frac{I}{S_t} = \underset{(2.20)}{-0.513} + \underset{(0.27)}{0.864}\frac{RS1}{S_t} + \underset{(7.00)}{42.54}\frac{B}{S_t} + \underset{(0.38)}{0.042}\,GRT - \underset{(0.92)}{0.348}\,FPK_{t-1} + \underset{(1.44)}{0.436}\,SDK_{t-1} \qquad \bar{R}^2 = 0.12$$

$$\frac{B}{S_t} = \underset{(3.82)}{0.006} + \underset{(4.03)}{0.165}\frac{RS1}{S_t} + \underset{(6.01)}{0.025}\frac{I}{S_t} - \underset{(1.15)}{0.003}\,FPK_t - \underset{(4.55)}{0.025}\,FPK_{t-1} - \underset{(1.61)}{0.009}\,LAK_{t-1} \qquad \bar{R}^2 = 0.13$$

Symbols:

RS1	Narrow definition of remittance
I	Investment expenditure
E	External finance
S	Sales revenue
FPK	Return on capital
LAK	Ratio of liquid assets to capital
GRT	Growth rate
SDK	Ratio of debt finance to capital

Notes: System estimated using two-stage least squares.
Small sample comprises 525 observations pooled cross-section and time-series. Includes only those enterprises for which flow of funds data are correct to within 10% in all 4 years.

room for escape from that constraint, some flexibility to vary these payments within a given cash-flow position, and hence some ability to reduce remittance *ceteris paribus* if investment expenditure is high. This may well occur in some cases fairly automatically if the higher authority concerned operates rules on remittances which take account of investment demands on finance. The same would happen in the West under any of a number of tax-based incentive schemes for investment. Alternatively it may be the result of individual bargaining over the appropriate remittance to be paid. But in either case it suggests scope for a trade-off which statistically offsets the positive relation we would otherwise predict on the basis of the internal financial constraints that the other results consistently indicate. Consistent with this and with the results in Table 9.3, the coefficients on the predetermined variables in the remittance equations also indicate a bargaining or discretionary element in the determination of remittances.

TABLE 9.6. Simultaneous equation block 1a.RS1.(S). Remittance omitted. Lagged rate of return variable. Lagged liquidity variable. Small sample (*t*-statistics in brackets)

$$\frac{I}{S_t} = \underset{(0.90)}{0.009} - \underset{(32.83)}{0.983}\frac{E}{S_t} + \underset{(3.48)}{3.050}\frac{B}{S_t} + \underset{(2.37)}{0.023}\, GRT_t - \underset{(0.19)}{0.002}\, FPK_{t-1} - \underset{(3.11)}{0.060}\, LAK_{t-1} \qquad \bar{R}^2 = 0.89$$

$$\frac{E}{S_t} = \underset{(1.28)}{0.019} + \underset{(26.82)}{1.050}\frac{I}{S_t} - \underset{(3.46)}{4.55}\frac{B}{S_t} + \underset{(1.85)}{0.022}\, GRT_t - \underset{(1.08)}{0.019}\, SDK_{t-1} - \underset{(1.13)}{0.017}\, SDK_{t-1} \qquad \bar{R}^2 = 0.83$$

$$\frac{B}{S_t} = \underset{(3.69)}{0.018} + \underset{(0.60)}{0.055}\frac{I}{S_t} + \underset{(0.84)}{0.081}\frac{E}{S_t} - \underset{(3.32)}{0.007}\, FPK_{t-1} - \underset{(3.30)}{0.016}\, SDK_{t-1} - \underset{(1.23)}{0.009}\, LAK_{t-1} \qquad \bar{R}^2 = 0.20$$

Symbols:
- *RS1* Narrow definition of remittance
- *I* Investment expenditure
- *E* External finance
- *S* Sales revenue
- *FPK* Return on capital
- *LAK* Ratio of liquid assets to capital
- *GRT* Growth rate
- *SDK* Ratio of debt finance to capital

Notes: System estimated using two-stage least squares.
Small sample comprises 525 observations pooled cross-section and time-series. Includes only those enterprises for which flow of funds data are correct to within 10% in all 4 years.

The third main issue concerns bonuses. Overall the bonus equations do not have great explanatory power and have significant constant terms, suggesting that bonuses are not only set by reference to other considerations, such as profitability, contract fulfilment etc., but that they are not particularly circumscribed by financial considerations. (There is evidence however that the data are particularly unreliable in this area. In only 18% of observations was the sum of different types of wage and bonus within 10% of the aggregate figure supplied in the questionnaire.)

Where statistically significant, bonuses are always positively correlated with other uses, confirming the general picture of an internal financial constraint. On the sources side, bonuses are negatively correlated with external finance in Table 9.6, which is consistent, but positively in Table 9.4, which is not. However investment expenditure is omitted from Table 9.4 and so the latter result is probably just picking up the fact that higher production boosts both bonuses and investment, and hence external finance. What is at first sight surprising is that bonus payments regularly and systematically bear an inverse relation to both lagged profitability and liquidity. Unless there is strong negative autocorrelation in both the profit and liquidity series, which would be unusual to say the least, this result is implausible. It is in sharp contrast to the significant coefficients on these two variables in remittance equations, where they regularly have their predicted positive value.

Almost certainly this arises from a misspecification. As far as the endogenous flow variables are concerned, they directly and mutually determine each other, so that absolute current size-deflated variables are appropriate. However, the predetermined profit and liquidity variables in the bonus equations are hypothesized causal variables where adjustment mechanisms may well be appropriate. If for example the change in bonuses is a partial adjustment function of the change in profits (and up to an externally determined limit we have seen that this is quite likely), then for a given level of current profit and past bonuses, neither of which appears in the simultaneous system, current bonuses will be a negative function of past profits. This does not invalidate the system in that the latter explores the constraints on being able to pay the bonuses determined this way. But it does mean that given our specification we should not be surprised at a negative coefficient in these cases. Similar comments may apply to a negative value on profitability in the investment equation in Table 9.3 and another on liquidity in the investment equation in Table 9.6.

Overall it is clear that the investment and external-funds equations are powerful ones in the analysis of financial flows, with financial uses generally and investment expenditure in particular being subject to strong external financial constraints. The overall pattern of coefficients in most other respects tends to support the view that there are strong internal finance constraints and the remittance equations indicate that there is some scope for bargaining in the light of investment expenditure and financial position. Bonuses tend not to be explicable to any great degree by financial considerations but respond, along with other uses, to variations in the internal financial position of enterprises.

As mentioned earlier a large number of alternative specifications were also run, though most were relatively minor modifications, testing as much for robustness of results as alternative financial behaviour. A series of different lag structures on predetermined variables were tried but in all cases the results were similar and marginally less explanatory. All equation blocks were repeated with the larger sample of 952 observations. While this changed some coefficient values by small amounts and also *t* values, there were few critical value changes and the general picture described above is equally well supported. In view of the results on bonuses, the basic blocks were rerun using the sum of bonuses and welfare payments in case there was some financial constraint on the total of these but some differences across enterprises in how benefits were distributed to the work-force. However a very similar set of results emerged. In a block of the form shown in Table 9.6, the aggregate bonus and welfare equation contained insignificant coefficients on investment and external finance; but positive significant ones on investment, remittance, and external finance in equation blocks of the form shown in Tables 9.4 and 9.5. The negative correlations with profitability and liquidity also persisted.

The one test change that did make a difference was substituting the broader definition of remittance. This systematically changed the sign of the financial-flow variable coefficients in the remittance equations and the sign on remittance in the investment and bonuses equations. These changes persisted irrespective of lag structure, sample, or definition of the bonus variable, and are perverse in that, to the extent that sales tax acts as anything more than an automatic flow-through of funds from customer to the state, other uses would, on these results, be higher and external sources lower in years when sales tax payments were higher. If correct this would imply a very strong cash-flow constraint. Almost certainly though these results should be ignored. The equations are almost certainly misspecified if total remittance is included because of the inclusion of sales tax. This is directly correlated with sales revenue which is used as the deflator in the equations. For this reason the narrow definition is our preferred one.

The final variation was to test some two-equation simultaneous blocks. If remittances are regarded as largely exogenously determined and bonuses as a residual then we have a two-equation block in investment expenditure and external financing. The results are largely consistent with what has been found already, namely highly significant positive coefficients between investment and external funds, positive coefficients on profitability, liquidity and debt structure as far as external finance is concerned, and negative ones on profitability and debt structure as far as investment expenditure is concerned. The explanatory power is high, suggesting that any bargaining effect, though it may have a significant effect on remittance, does not have any very pronounced effect on other financial flows. Alternative two-equation blocks are generally less informative but regularly give the same pattern of results as the three-equations blocks.

5. Conclusions

It should be stressed that the results above are very preliminary. They are the outcome of a first attempt to apply a potentially quite powerful econometric technique to Chinese manufacturing enterprises to obtain some initial insight into the main financial relationships and dependencies. There are problems with some variables, notably that for growth; some of the results for lagged predetermined variables look odd and require further analysis; and there are numerous extensions that need to be tried, primarily decomposing external funds into bank credit, state subsidies, and other sources, and repeating the analysis for subsamples determined by contract form and by commercial performance levels. But some inferences can none the less be drawn.

The main results are the clear evidence of significant internal finance constraints on nearly all the main expenditures identified, of significant external constraints on investment, and of some limited scope for bargaining by enterprises, or discretion on the part of the higher authorities in determining remittances. The existence of tight financial constraints is not surprising given two characteristics of the economic behaviour and environment of Chinese state-owned enterprises during the mid-1980s. These are first the tendency towards rational profit-maximizing behaviour in investment decisions which emerged from the analysis of the previous chapter, including in particular the powerful effects stemming from demand growth and the cost of funds. Second, the period was characterized by rapid growth and very low real interest rates. Together these conditions were likely to ensure very strong investment demand which would then be beyond the capacity of most individual enterprises to finance, generating strong internal financial constraints. The total level of investment for each enterprise would then become heavily dependent on the availability of external finance, with investment needs being a prime determinant of the demand for external finance and the availability of the latter being the key determinant of overall investment. It is perhaps worth noting that virtually none of this picture would be altered as a result of reform of the internal allocation mechanisms or external control mechanisms towards greater autonomy or incentive-driven systems.

A further interesting conclusion is that bonuses and welfare payments, while having clear financial effects, do not for the most part seem very dependent on the financial flows involved. Instead they appear primarily determined elsewhere, and hence are largely exogenous to the simultaneous system used here. They then contribute to the internal finance constraint but are not to any appreciable degree financially constrained themselves. There is therefore an important sense in which, after payment of bonuses and remittance, the latter being to some degree flexible in the light of financial position and investment needs, capital expenditure is the residual claim on internal funds, the latter being supplemented as far as possible through external sources.

Ironically, therefore, in the light of the simultaneous approach adopted, there is at least on the uses side only very limited interdependence, though only a simultaneous technique can provide evidence for this. Instead there appears to be more of a priority ranking with bonuses determined largely independent of financial considerations, remittances partially bargainable and investment as the residual use. The total level of investment then becomes crucially dependent on external funding, which implies that, despite the thrust of economic reform towards greater autonomy, in production, pricing, sales, and remuneration, there remains little effective autonomy in practice in relation to the level of investment, and hence growth and development of enterprises. The overall shortage of finance, stemming largely from the macroeconomic environment of the time, still makes the various sources and uses highly interdependent; but there appears to be a fairly clear priority ordering for dealing with this, rather than the simultaneously constraining trade-off decisions which would emerge from a traditional approach of optimizing a continuous utility function under constraints. If enterprises' financial behaviour were to be interpreted in terms of an overall utility function then the above results suggest at least a partial lexicographic ordering.

Two further inferences may be made. First, we can in principle use expenditure and external finance equations as part of a larger simultaneous system enhancing the production and employment side as well. This is carried out in Chapter 11. Second, proposals for further reform, in incentive or control mechanisms or in ownership, need to be formulated in the light of what our results reveal about financial behaviour, priorities, and financial shortage. That is to say, we need to be clear whether suggested reforms are likely to *alter* any or all of these, or whether they involve other changes the consequences of which must be estimated *given* these characteristics. We shall return to this in Chapter 12.

10

The Soft Budget Constraint

1. Introduction

One of the most important questions in identifying the behaviour and performance of enterprises in any economy is that of what happens when they veer towards financial insolvency. Even if few enterprises actually face this situation and even for enterprises that have never faced it, their views on the consequences of insolvency may act as powerful incentive mechanisms. So far we have said virtually nothing about this, for two reasons. On the empirical side, our basic data-set is not particularly suitable for exploring this issue. On the methodological side, it is important to try to identify and understand the economic behaviour of Chinese state-owned enterprises under what might be termed 'normal' conditions. This is not just because we need some benchmark against which we may evaluate behaviour in or near insolvency, though that is important. It is also because nearly all our estimation procedures are linear. While this traditional assumption may be acceptable for exploring behaviour under normal conditions—on the grounds that the potential gains from using non-linear methods are unlikely to justify the increased complexity and loss of rigour—it is very unlikely to be acceptable for exploring behaviour in or near insolvency, because enterprises in the latter condition may well show quite significant departures from behaviour in non-solvency states. Indeed it would be surprising if it were otherwise. We have therefore preferred to conduct most of our analysis excluding enterprises that are financially very weak and so far without regard to the behaviour of the latter or the problems they pose. It is the purpose of this chapter, in contrast, to look specifically at the issue of financial weakness in Chinese state-owned enterprises and its consequences.

In the context of state-owned enterprises, this issue revolves around the concept of the soft budget constraint. This term is used to cover a whole range of mechanisms whereby an enterprise in financial difficulty may experience some reduction in the financial constraints on behaviour which would otherwise operate. The phenomenon of a soft budget constraint is observed by many to be very widespread in socialist countries generally, with China being no exception. Here we use such data as we have to see what light can be thrown on the mechanism in as far as it operates on enterprises in our sample.

Before proceeding, it is necessary to take note of an important distinction. The soft budget constraint can be conceived of either from a macroeconomic or a microeconomic perspective. At the macroeconomic level, governments may, through design or default, reduce or remove financial constraints on an economy, if necessary by creating and supplying whatever funds are necessary to maintain solvency, with the consequence that enterprises become limited by physical constraints—a so-called 'shortage' economy. But, irrespective of whether there is a soft budget constraint of this macroeconomic sort, there may be a microeconomic one in that individual enterprises may, to a greater or lesser extent, find that their own financial constraint does not reflect either their profitability or their operating financial position because of intervention, for whatever purpose, by the state. Given our disaggregated enterprise database, it is the latter with which we will be concerned.

This distinction is particularly important in the context of the Chinese economy. Granick has argued that the Chinese economy, unlike those of Eastern Europe, contains some enterprises controlled from the centre by various organs of the central government bureaucracy, and others controlled by lower-level provincial authorities (Granick 1990). Given that the latter cannot print money, and indeed typically face quite tight constraints on the tax which they must remit to the central authorities, Granick argued that the enterprises controlled at the provincial level would face hard budget constraints. Only centrally controlled enterprises could reckon to be able to receive whatever funding was necessary to keep them afloat. The two-tier control mechanism, unique to China, therefore gives a different pattern and extent of soft budget constraints to that observed in other socialist economies.

There seems no reason to dispute this, and Granick offered some evidence in support of his contention. But it must be stressed that this only refers to the conventional macroeconomic sense of the soft budget constraint. However constrained the public finances of a particular province, if state authorities intervene in the finances of enterprises so that there are only weak or perhaps no clear linkages between the performance of an enterprise and its control over financial resources then a soft budget constraint in the microeconomic sense can and typically will operate.

Our primary aim therefore in this chapter is to examine the extent to which individual enterprises in our data-set were able, when necessary to escape the full consequences of poor financial performance and how this affected their behaviour. Our evidence indicates that such phenomena affect both centrally and provincially controlled enterprises.

Having clarified the nature of the soft budget constraint concept with which we will be concerned, it is worth making a number of initial observations on the concept. First, while the soft budget constraint is generally discussed in the context of state-owned enterprises in socialist economies, and is generally seen as one of the dominant characteristics of such economies, the problem is restricted neither in theory nor in practice to such settings. As is well known, many state-owned companies in a number of essentially capitalist Western nations have operated to a greater or lesser degree under such a constraint. Less widely recognized but much more important, some privately owned companies have from time to time experienced a soft budget constraint as governments sought to maintain employment, modernize, re-equip, and overcome perceived inadequacies in the ability of the capital market adequately to finance longer-term development. This is important because it illustrates that the soft budget constraint is not purely a function of ownership, even though the extent of it, the motives for it, and the way it operates may all reflect ownership.

The second introductory point to note is that, in the context of the performance of socialist economies in recent years and the proposals for systemic reform, the soft budget constraint has almost universally been seen as a major cause of inefficiency and a significant, if not the overriding obstacle to reform initiatives. This breaks down into three related issues:

(i) that the 'soft' budget constraint weakens or even eliminates the incentives for enterprises to operate efficiently, because jobs and income are to a considerable extent secured against poor performance as a result of the soft budget constraint;

(ii) that this in turn weakens the impact of market signals, where these exist, because the penalties attached to paying too much or receiving too little, for goods, inputs, finance etc., are attenuated; and

(iii) that the political and bureaucratic, as opposed to market-determined, methods through which the soft budget constraint operates provides a fertile area for both petty and major corruption, using financial relaxation as a lever to pursue personal goals, reward associates etc.

Such problems are almost certainly endemic in socialist economies. Indeed much of the vigour for reform stems from recognition of these problems and a desire to remove them. One of the key elements in the very topical 'big bang' reform programmes being introduced in a number of Eastern European economies at the present time is the wish to reduce or eliminate the soft budget constraint, through privatization and creation of effective capital markets, thereby not only improving incentives and efficiency but also helping to underpin the momentum towards the use of market mechanisms and the reduction of corruption. In China, reform has been going on longer and in more gradual fashion. But while the shift from centralized planning to market-determined prices has gone further, changes which might eliminate the soft budget constraint have been more muted. Collectives have developed some greater autonomy, joint ventures generally face more stringent financial constraints, and banks have played an increasing role in the financing of state-owned enterprises, but the first two of these have had little quantitative impact and the banks remain not only state-owned but generally under very close control of the provincial authorities.

Given this, it is important to stress that the notion of a soft budget constraint in the general sense of publicly owned financial resources being supplied to enterprises with inadequate financial resources of their own is not universally detrimental. In the absence of an effective capital market, in an economy undergoing major expansion, structural development, and reform, there can be a number of quite sound reasons for government authorities, directly or indirectly, to relax financial constraints. These may include the need for investment required to develop away from depressed markets, for major re-equipping, avoiding higher costs of social security spending arising from bankruptcy etc. The problem therefore is not one of a soft budget constraint *per se* but of the criteria behind its use, its prevalence, objectives, and implementation. It may of course be that desirable economic and social objectives can be achieved in other ways, or that government financial help of one sort or another can be provided to enterprises in a manner and on such terms that it does not constitute a relaxation of the budget constraint. Or it may be that there are advantages which can be achieved only through a soft budget constraint but that their magnitude falls so far short of the disadvantages that it is still optimal to remove the scope for such activities completely. It is nevertheless worth noting that there may in some situations be benefits, not least because if those reasons are strong enough then governments may seek to reintroduce elements of a soft budget constraint whatever the reform of institutions, ownership, or economic mechanisms introduced to eliminate it.

In this context we may add that, for state-owned enterprises, we cannot automatically assume that all state funding represents subsidization of losses. The equity of such enterprises is owned by the state, and the only way in which that equity can be increased, except from retentions of earnings, is through new government funding. In some cases this may represent commercially sound financing of profitable investment opportunities, with the return to the government received in the form of the higher profits tax which will eventually accrue. In principle it is possible to measure the return to the government on such equity investment, though we cannot do it here with the database available. However, as much of the state funds paid to enterprises in our sample went to loss-making enterprises, we will view such payments as subsidies rather than equity investments.

The third point to note is that the soft budget constraint, though in essence an economic mechanism, exists within, and may well reflect, strong political and cultural considerations. At one very obvious level, if the state owns enterprises and feels responsible for them, then assisting those in difficulty may well have a political or indeed moral imperative attached that would not exist for a bank making an arms'-length financial transaction. At a deeper level, if state-owned enterprises represent, as in China, not only an organizational form of production but a key institution in society for providing income, security and insurance, education, housing, and pensions, then the reduction of incentives resulting from the soft budget constraint may well not be a prime consideration for those in authority. While for many this naturally leads on to proposals for reform which would jettison all these other functions, and while this may well be very sound policy advice, it remains true that, until this happens, both the existence of the soft budget constraint, the extent of its use and the way in which it is operated will all reflect the considerations that derive from the many non-economic functions of state-owned enterprises. More generally, reforms designed to remove the soft budget constraint will be neither well founded nor practical unless they go hand-in-hand with reforms designed to relocate these other responsibilities.

At a still more fundamental, if rather intangible level, the operation of the soft budget constraint has to be seen in the context of views about human responsibility. Much of the rationale for state intervention in the financial position of enterprises arises from the fact that the latter is often outside the control or responsibility of the enterprise concerned. Thus, while the notion that the state should step in to relieve individuals of the consequences of their own inefficiencies or mistakes is often seen in the West as very damaging, the view that individuals should suffer the consequences of economic conditions entirely outside their control, as is the case in capitalist economies, looks no less odd. Our purpose here is less to debate the moral or philosophical pros and cons of these sorts of views than to point out that unless analysis and proposals for reform take account of such considerations as they exist in society, then such reforms may easily prove quite ineffective.

An interesting and apposite illustration is the new bankruptcy laws in China. Despite their existence, virtually no bankruptcies have resulted. This is primarily because, in many cases, the reasons for insolvency are partly or even totally outside enterprises' control. More recent attempts to enforce local bankruptcy 'quotas' may quite possibly make matters worse, depending on the selection criteria used. More generally, whatever the incentive mechanisms, patterns of ownership or even legal bankruptcy provisions, if there is more at stake than just a production process and if financial pressures are seen to have been unavoidable, then the soft budget constraint will almost certainly continue, by one means or another, in a society whose philosophical stance on responsibilities and justice attaches considerable importance to the problem of undue losses.

Given the importance of the issue and the considerations outlined above, it is clearly important to try to examine the workings of the soft budget constraint, using our database on large state-owned enterprises during the period 1984–87. There is, however, an immediate problem. The enterprises were selected by the Chinese authorities from amongst large state-owned enterprises (LSOEs) across numerous provinces in China and from different types of region. They were not systematically selected to be representative of different performance levels. It is not clear that the authorities would have any great interest in selecting financially very weak or potentially (still less actually) insolvent enterprises, and any such enterprises selected initially might well have had strong reasons, both in terms of demand on resources and in terms of what such detailed information might reveal, for avoiding the task. Be that as it may, an initial inspection of the data reveals that very few of the enterprises made a loss in any of the years involved. Given that severe financial constraints might well not appear unless an enterprise continued to make losses, it is unlikely that our sample, useful as it is for other issues, can throw a lot of light on the soft budget constraint problem.

None the less there are a few enterprises that were probably in severe financial difficulty in the sample; and there are a much larger number which were probably feeling some financial pressure, for one reason or another. Given this, it is in principle possible to look at how behaviour varies as these pressures build up in order to get some feel for the likely dimensions of the problem. We therefore use the database to explore the matter as best we can, but recognizing from the beginning that we are mainly concerned merely with identifying some possible factors involved and that we are unlikely with this data-set to be able to establish the forces at work or their magnitude with any confidence.

Against this background, our data allow at least two types of observation or analysis of the operation of the 'soft' budget constraint.

1. Chapter 7 presented a picture of the flow of funds through Chinese LSOEs for the years 1984–87. It is therefore possible to examine the flow of funds for enterprises in a weak financial position and/or making losses to see how, if at all, these flows differ as between this group and the rest. An examination based on this approach is pursued in Section 2.

2. It is possible to identify various indicators of financial difficulty and examine how these may be related to mechanisms through which a 'soft' budget constraint may operate. This is carried out in Sections 3 and 4. Section 3 provides some descriptive statistics and charts while Section 4 uses regression analysis to explore the links between financial distress and methods of loosening financial constraints. We also use statistical analysis to try to identify systematic deviations of behaviour in financially weak enterprises. Implications and conclusions are presented in Section 5.

2. *Flow of Funds Analysis of Financially Weak Enterprises*

Our first observations on financially weak enterprises are summarized in Tables 10.1 to 10.4. Each shows selected sources and uses which are of interest, as a percentage of total sources or uses respectively for long-term loss-makers, defined as those making a loss not only in the year in question but for at least two years or more in the sample period (column 1); for short-term loss-makers, defined as those making a loss in the year in question alone (column 2); for the fifty least profitable enterprises making a positive return on capital, grouped in tens (columns 3–7) and in aggregate (column 8); and for all profitable

TABLE 10.1. 1984 Flow of funds for enterprises classified by return on capital employed (selected items, percentage of total sources, and uses)

		LT Loss-makers	ST Loss-makers	Lowest positive profit enterprises						Profitable firms
				Level 1 (1–10)	Level 2 (11–20)	Level 3 (21–30)	Level 4 (31–40)	Level 5 (41–50)	Average 50 firms	
Sources										
1	LT government subsidies	16.0	0.0	2.0	1.4	1.7	0.7	3.6	1.9	1.0
2	LT bank loans	1.7	0.0	3.2	1.0	1.5	2.5	0.9	1.8	1.4
3	Firms' own sources	27.3	0.0	3.7	2.6	4.1	1.6	2.0	2.8	1.8
4	ST bank loans	2.0	17.5	1.7	1.0	1.9	2.7	2.8	2.0	1.9
5	Creditors	2.2	−39.2	0.3	1.6	2.4	0.4	−1.7	0.6	0.8
6	Sales revenue	56.5	109.0	87.4	94.7	81.5	90.8	88.1	88.5	90.2
7	Net flows from other business	−5.5	−2.3	−0.8	−0.8	−0.5	−1.1	0.0	−0.6	−0.4
Uses										
8	Investment	33.2	0.0	9.7	5.5	5.8	4.4	6.4	6.4	4.4
9	Stock in trade	1.9	−47.2	0.9	0.2	2.6	1.9	1.4	1.4	2.3
10	Debtors	0.0	27.8	−0.3	0.2	2.0	0.8	3.0	1.1	0.4
11	Materials	13.1	50.1	42.8	53.3	34.9	52.1	37.4	44.1	53.6
12	Power and fuel	6.7	19.6	13.9	9.6	7.3	3.7	10.9	9.1	3.1
13	Capital payments	12.2	11.8	6.1	6.2	8.2	6.0	5.8	6.5	3.4
14	depreciation	7.0	6.4	3.6	3.3	5.1	2.7	3.1	3.6	1.7
15	repairing funds	4.9	3.5	2.0	1.7	2.4	1.6	2.1	1.9	1.1
16	interest payment	0.3	1.0	0.5	1.2	0.8	1.7	0.6	1.0	0.6
17	Wage payments	22.4	16.3	6.1	7.9	5.9	6.0	5.2	6.2	3.3
18	Selling expenditure	0.0	0.1	1.2	0.7	0.1	0.1	0.4	0.5	0.3
19	Total taxation	3.3	9.4	8.4	11.1	20.5	17.0	23.8	16.2	21.5
20	income tax	0.0	0.0	1.5	5.8	4.8	4.3	9.5	5.2	9.7
21	sales tax	3.3	9.4	7.0	5.3	15.8	12.6	14.3	11.0	11.8
22	Retained profit	1.7	1.6	1.6	2.2	3.5	3.2	2.5	2.6	2.5
23	R & D expenditure	0.0	0.0	0.0	0.1	0.1	0.2	0.2	0.1	0.2
24	Training expenditure	0.1	0.0	0.1	0.1	0.0	0.1	0.1	0.0	0.0
25	Welfare expenditure	1.9	1.4	0.5	0.6	0.2	0.4	0.4	0.4	0.2

TABLE 10.2. 1985 Flow of funds for enterprises classified by return on capital employed (selected items, percentage of total sources, and uses)

		LT Loss-makers	ST Loss-makers	Lowest positive profit enterprises						Profitable firms
				Level 1 (1–10)	Level 2 (11–20)	Level 3 (21–30)	Level 4 (31–40)	Level 5 (41–50)	Average 50 firms	
Sources										
1	LT government subsidies	5.5	5.2	0.9	2.6	2.8	1.2	1.1	1.7	1.3
2	LT bank loans	0.5	0.4	1.5	3.1	3.2	4.2	2.1	2.8	2.2
3	Firms' own sources	9.7	6.0	2.6	2.1	3.3	2.6	2.4	2.6	3.2
4	ST bank loans	0.9	0.1	4.0	1.4	1.1	1.6	2.4	2.1	2.2
5	Creditors	3.5	1.6	0.8	2.9	1.9	3.3	2.2	2.2	1.4
6	Sales revenue	84.1	81.5	83.3	86.8	82.6	85.0	87.3	85.0	86.0
7	Net flows from other business	−4.7	−3.9	−0.3	−0.8	−0.9	−0.7	−0.8	−0.7	−0.6
Uses										
8	Investment	14.5	10.3	5.3	7.8	9.4	9.0	5.4	7.4	7.2
9	Stock in trade	8.6	−1.4	5.1	2.5	3.4	4.1	4.6	3.9	3.3
10	Debtors	0.2	0.8	1.3	0.5	0.8	0.7	0.5	0.8	0.3
11	Materials	36.1	26.6	40.0	40.5	52.5	40.6	53.3	45.4	40.9
12	Power and fuel	9.7	1.0	10.0	9.1	5.4	11.4	5.3	8.2	5.2
13	Capital payments	9.5	9.9	5.0	5.8	4.6	6.8	4.9	5.4	4.8
14	depreciation	4.7	6.5	2.8	3.3	2.4	4.0	2.3	2.9	2.7
15	repairing funds	4.4	2.6	1.5	1.8	1.3	2.1	1.6	1.7	1.4
16	interest payment	0.4	0.9	0.6	0.7	0.9	0.7	1.1	0.8	0.6
17	Wage payments	7.6	18.5	4.7	5.4	4.9	5.6	5.4	5.2	3.4
18	Selling expenditure	0.3	0.1	0.5	0.7	0.4	0.4	0.3	0.5	0.3
19	Total taxation	4.8	22.1	17.6	18.9	10.5	14.4	11.4	14.6	24.8
20	income tax	0.0	0.1	1.2	4.2	2.7	8.5	4.8	4.2	9.4
21	sales tax	4.8	22.0	16.5	14.7	7.8	5.9	6.7	10.3	15.4
22	Retained profit	5.8	0.9	3.6	2.7	1.7	2.6	4.4	3.0	3.8
23	R & D expenditure	0.0	0.0	0.0	0.0	0.0	0.1	0.1	0.1	0.1
24	Training expenditure	0.0	0.3	0.1	0.1	0.0	0.1	0.1	0.1	0.0
25	Welfare expenditure	0.5	1.1	0.3	0.4	0.4	0.4	0.4	0.4	0.2

TABLE 10.3. 1986 Flow of funds for enterprises classified by return on capital employed (selected items, percentage of total sources, and uses)

		LT Loss-makers	ST Loss-makers	Lowest positive profit enterprises						Profitable firms
				Level 1 (1–10)	Level 2 (11–20)	Level 3 (21–30)	Level 4 (31–40)	Level 5 (41–50)	Average 50 firms	
Sources										
1	LT government subsidies	21.9	0.9	4.0	1.9	2.2	0.8	0.7	1.9	0.8
2	LT bank loans	0.0	0.0	1.1	1.9	4.0	4.4	5.3	3.3	2.3
3	Firms' own sources	26.9	5.1	2.4	7.2	5.1	1.7	3.7	4.0	4.8
4	ST bank loans	0.7	8.1	8.6	5.2	4.3	2.4	4.7	5.0	3.3
5	Creditors	4.1	7.6	0.1	1.6	−0.9	0.7	1.0	0.5	1.5
6	Sales revenue	46.8	85.2	79.4	66.2	81.2	85.2	80.7	78.5	83.2
7	Net flows from other business	−3.9	−3.3	0.0	−1.1	−0.9	−0.7	−0.9	−0.7	−0.7
Uses										
8	Investment	30.1	6.0	6.6	11.6	9.5	7.3	10.0	9.0	8.4
9	Stock in trade	4.7	−2.4	5.1	2.6	2.4	3.1	2.6	3.1	3.7
10	Debtors	1.0	7.6	2.0	0.0	0.4	0.3	0.0	0.5	1.2
11	Materials	15.9	49.5	38.3	28.9	31.4	39.9	51.4	38.0	38.1
12	Power and fuel	4.9	4.3	9.1	10.2	8.8	4.0	4.4	7.3	6.2
13	Capital payments	10.4	6.4	5.1	5.6	6.2	3.7	5.0	5.1	5.2
14	depreciation	6.4	2.5	2.6	2.8	3.3	1.9	2.4	2.6	2.9
15	repairing funds	3.9	1.1	1.3	2.0	1.9	0.9	1.5	1.5	1.5
16	interest payment	0.1	2.8	1.2	0.8	1.0	0.9	1.1	1.0	0.7
17	Wage payments	25.2	8.3	4.7	5.3	4.7	3.6	5.3	4.7	3.7
18	Selling expenditure	0.0	0.2	0.3	0.5	0.1	0.2	0.6	0.3	0.2
19	Total taxation	1.0	13.8	16.1	14.8	24.1	28.3	8.8	18.4	22.0
20	income tax	0.0	0.0	0.3	3.0	3.0	1.5	2.8	2.1	8.0
21	sales tax	1.0	13.8	15.9	11.8	21.1	26.8	6.1	16.3	14.0
22	Retained profit	0.3	0.3	3.0	2.3	2.6	2.1	2.5	2.5	3.6
23	R & D expenditure	0.0	0.2	0.2	0.1	0.4	0.0	0.4	0.2	0.1
24	Training expenditure	0.2	0.0	0.0	0.1	0.0	0.0	0.1	0.0	0.0
25	Welfare expenditure	1.5	0.6	0.3	0.4	0.3	0.3	0.4	0.3	0.4

TABLE 10.4. 1987 Flow of funds for enterprises classified by return on capital employed (selected items, percentage of total sources, and uses)

		LT Loss-makers	ST Loss-makers	Lowest positive profit enterprises						Profitable firms
				Level 1 (1–10)	Level 2 (11–20)	Level 3 (21–30)	Level 4 (31–40)	Level 5 (41–50)	Average 50 firms	
Sources										
1	LT government subsidies	16.5	6.2	2.8	0.9	2.2	1.7	1.4	1.8	0.6
2	LT bank loans	0.0	1.3	2.2	1.7	2.2	3.2	2.6	2.4	2.9
3	Firms' own sources	22.1	1.3	3.3	10.7	2.1	4.8	4.4	5.1	7.2
4	ST bank loans	0.1	4.7	4.1	2.5	7.6	1.7	4.6	4.1	2.2
5	Creditors	−1.0	−1.0	0.3	−0.8	−0.9	1.5	1.0	0.2	1.3
6	Sales revenue	62.7	85.3	86.7	76.1	86.5	77.2	79.0	81.1	82.1
7	Net flows from other business	−4.7	−0.7	−0.5	−1.4	−0.7	−0.9	−0.7	−0.8	−0.9
Uses										
8	Investment	26.7	9.4	7.6	16.4	6.9	8.4	8.4	9.5	11.4
9	Stock in trade	−2.2	1.8	2.7	2.2	−0.1	1.9	3.3	2.0	1.8
10	Debtors	−0.3	0.0	0.4	1.0	3.1	1.2	1.8	1.5	1.4
11	Materials	28.9	36.6	38.8	39.1	44.8	33.1	31.7	37.5	40.2
12	Power and fuel	6.3	3.8	8.9	8.8	4.1	8.1	8.3	7.6	6.8
13	Capital payments	7.6	3.5	4.8	6.3	4.5	6.6	4.9	5.4	6.2
14	depreciation	4.6	1.5	0.0	2.9	2.7	3.6	2.4	2.3	3.5
15	repairing funds	2.4	0.7	0.9	2.3	0.0	1.9	1.4	1.3	1.8
16	interest payment	0.6	1.3	1.6	1.1	0.8	1.1	1.1	1.1	0.9
17	Wage payments	19.8	3.8	4.4	5.8	4.4	4.5	4.0	4.6	4.4
18	Selling expenditure	0.4	0.1	0.4	0.2	0.7	0.2	0.3	0.4	0.3
19	Total taxation	2.3	33.6	25.3	8.9	26.0	18.5	23.8	20.5	15.1
20	income tax	0.0	0.0	0.6	1.4	1.7	2.7	4.5	2.2	6.2
21	sales tax	2.3	33.8	24.7	7.5	24.2	15.8	19.3	18.3	8.9
22	Retained profit	0.2	1.1	2.1	1.4	1.6	2.2	2.6	2.0	4.3
23	R & D expenditure	0.0	0.1	0.0	0.1	0.0	0.1	0.1	0.0	0.2
24	Training expenditure	0.2	0.0	0.0	0.1	0.1	0.0	0.1	0.1	0.0
25	Welfare expenditure	2.1	0.3	0.3	0.4	0.3	0.2	0.3	0.3	0.3

TABLE 10.5. Distribution of short-run and long-run loss-making enterprises across industries

	Short	Long
1. Extracting	3	3
2. Food and drink	5	1
3. Textiles	1	
4. Light and craft	3	2
5. Energy		
6. Chemicals	1	
7. Building materials	2	
8. Engineering and electrical	2	
TOTAL	17	6

Note: Profit is defined as total sales revenue plus non-traded income minus total cost of sales minus non-traded expenditure minus total sales tax.

companies (column 9). Tables 10.1 to 10.4 refer to 1984 to 1987 respectively. Because we are using flow of funds analysis, we restrict the sample to those enterprises showing reasonable consistency in their financial data (within 10% accuracy, as explained in Chapter 7).

Below we identify the broad differences that low or negative profitability appears to make. We then note some additional but less significant differences. We then try to interpret the findings to give a stylized picture of financially weak enterprises, to the extent that the data allow this.

There is, however, one preliminary empirical point to be made. There is a significant difference in the sectoral pattern as between short-term and long-term loss-makers. Table 10.5 shows the number of short- and long-term loss-makers in each sector. This shows that the short-run loss-makers are distributed across almost the whole spectrum of industry sectors, whereas long-term ones are mainly light industry and craft, which includes paper and pulp, and extracting (mining), though energy would also have appeared but for the criterion of data consistency applied in the selection of the sample. The former group will largely correspond to enterprises that have for one reason or another in the normal course of activity run into a period of loss-making, and are in fact commonly referred to as 'normal loss' enterprises. The latter will tend to be enterprises occupying commanding positions in the chain of production or in the economy of the region where the persistent losses made may well have resulted from direct intervention to control prices. These are commonly referred to as 'policy-loss' enterprises. We explore the distinction in more detail below.

Reviewing Tables 10.1 to 10.4, three main features stand out on the sources side and three on the uses.

1. Revenue from the sale of products is a significantly lower proportion of total sources for long-term loss-making enterprises. Across all four tables it is on average 62.5% as against 85.4% for profitable enterprises, 83.3% for the 50 lowest-profit enterprises, and 84.0% for short-term unprofitable enterprises.[1]

2. Subsidies from central government are very much higher for loss-makers, being 15.0% for long-term unprofitable enterprises, and 4.1% for short-term ones, as against 0.9% for profitable enterprises. Low-profit enterprises receive bigger subsidies than more profitable ones but, at an average of 1.8%, are only slightly more subsidized in this way. The overwhelming bulk of such subsidies, equal to about 4% of the total inflow of funds to the whole sample of approximately 250 enterprises, goes to the handful actually making losses. Funds defined as provincial subsidies are in contrast very small, do not appear to differ significantly as between loss-making and other enterprises, and are not therefore included in the tables. As we shall see, however, this is largely because subsidization at the provincial level occurs in other ways.

3. The third main difference on the sources side, and the most problematic is the item known as the 'firm's own resources'. For profitable firms it is 4.2% of total sources. For the fifty least profitable firms it falls to 3.6%. For short-term loss-makers it rises to 4.1%. But for long-term loss-makers it is 21.5%. It is clearly a very important source of funds for long-term loss-makers and we therefore need to investigate it in more detail. It may be recalled from Chapter 7 that this item comprises:

(i) current retained profit after payment of bonuses minus certain welfare payments, business expenses and investment in other enterprises which enterprises may choose to make out of those retained profits;
(ii) current retained depreciation minus any payments on technical innovation or further bonuses that may come from this source;
(iii) plus previous sources held over;
(iv) plus short-term cash holdings balancing traders' deposits and other short-term liabilities;
(v) plus finance from loss-making contracts.

It should also be recalled that from the accounting information available it is not possible to identify the magnitude of each of these components of a firm's own sources. Instead we distinguish (*a*) retained profit after payment of bonuses, (*b*) total depreciation, and (*c*) 'other' firm's own sources (which is the difference between firm's own sources on the one hand, and the sum of retained profit after bonuses and depreciation on the other).

We would expect the third typically to be negative for most profitable enterprises (see Chapter 7, Section 3). This is borne out by the data, which show that, of long-term profitable enterprises, 85.5% on average across the period 1983–87 exhibited negative values. Over the period the figure fell from 88.0% to 81.0%, but this is likely to reflect the shift away from depreciation funds having to be paid over to the authorities.

Table 10.6 shows how the composition of firm's own sources varies as between different categories of enterprise. This indicates clearly not only the big increase in the total of a firm's own sources when it is making losses but also how significant the 'other' item is in the total. As a purely illustrative exercise, if we were to assume that, *apart from subsidies*, the components of the 'other' financial flows were the same for both profitable and loss-making enterprises (and this is not entirely implausible) then subsidies of one form or another would constitute around 1.2% of short-term loss-makers' and 16% of long-term loss-making enterprises' total financial sources *under this heading*. This is

TABLE 10.6. Firm's own sources in different categories of enterprise (% of total sources of funds)

	Long-term loss-makers	Short-term loss-makers	Low-profit enterprises	Profitable enterprises
Retained profit after bonus	0.2[a]	0.8	2.5	3.6
Depreciation	5.7	4.2	2.9	2.7
Other	15.6[a]	−0.9	−1.8	−2.1
Total firm's own sources	21.5	4.1	3.6	4.2

Note: [a] The crude figure for retained profit after bonus for long-term loss-makers was 2.0% and the 'other' figure 13.8%, but both were heavily influenced by an anomalous figure for one enterprise in 1985, which records very large retained profit despite negative profitability overall. The explanation appears to be that payments received from the state for having successfully reduced losses were treated as part of retained profit rather than a separate item of the firm's own resources coming under the 'other' heading. This figure therefore overstates the retained profit figure and understates the 'other' item. Excluding this enterprise the retained profit figure is 0.2% and 'other' 15.6%.

in addition to approximately another 4% provided explicitly as subsidies to short-term loss-makers and 15% to long-term ones (see above), so that it is not unreasonable to believe that up to one-third of long-term loss-making enterprises' financial inflows on average come from subsidies in one way or another.

4. Turning to the uses-of-funds side, the first main difference is the much lower expenditure on materials, with a figure of 23.5% for long-term loss-makers, as against 37.5% for short-term loss-makers, 41.3% for low profit enterprises, and 43.2% for all profitable enterprises. That the purchase of materials would be lower as a percentage of uses of funds for long-term loss-making enterprises facing substantial reductions in sales revenue as a proportion of financial sources is not surprising, but the size of the reduction in expenditure on materials in relation to the reduction in revenue, on the crude figures an average 45% reduction as against a 27% reduction in sales revenue, is at first sight unexpectedly large. One possible explanation is the sectoral distribution of loss-making enterprises, i.e. if light industries and extractive industries have low material input ratios. For short-term loss-makers the falls in revenue and materials, at 2% and 5% respectively, are much more modest.

5. Expenditure on wages as a percentage of total usage of funds runs from 3.7% for all profitable enterprises to 5.2% for the least profitable fifty, to 10.2% for short-term unprofitable enterprises and 18.8% for long-term unprofitable ones. To what extent this reflects the inability of enterprises to reduce their wage bill in the face of losses caused by a reduction in sales revenue is examined below, but this is clearly likely to be one element contributing to the rise. To some extent however the causality may be somewhat different, with enterprises going into losses partly *because* of their employment and associated wage-bill commitments.

6. The final main distinction lies in the percentage use of funds for investment, with figures of 7.9% for all profitable enterprises, 8.1% for low-profit ones, 8.6% for short-term unprofitable, and 26.1% for long-term unprofitable enterprises. This strongly suggests that enterprises become committed to investment projects, either physically in the sense that, once under construction they need to be completed, or financially in the sense that external or internal funds become earmarked for projects so that there would be no financial saving from cessation of construction, or politically in the sense that projects have been approved by higher authorities and will not or cannot then be terminated as a result of weakening profitability or a deteriorating financial position.

Before trying to interpret these figures we next comment briefly on some other more minor points of interest arising from Tables 10.1 to 10.4. On the sources side, first, it is noteworthy that bank loans represent a much *lower* percentage of total sources of long-term loss-making enterprises (1.5%) than for profitable companies (4.6%) or for short-term loss-makers (4.9%) indicating that the mechanisms by which long-term loss-making enterprises are kept afloat do not to any appreciable extent involve additional bank loans,[2] at least for the period 1984–87. Second (not included in the tables), neither borrowing from other enterprises nor investment by other enterprises are quantitatively important or significantly different as between loss-making and profitable enterprises. Third, losses on ancillary (i.e. non-production) activities contribute significantly to loss-making enterprises' poor performance. For profitable enterprises this represented a drain of 0.7% of their total financial sources, but 2.6% in the case of short-term unprofitable and 4.7% in the case of long-term unprofitable ones. To put this in context the latter figures may be compared to the 4.1% of funds used on average by profitable enterprises to pay wages.

On the uses side there are a number of further points of interest. Expenditure on power and fuel is approximately 43% lower (3.0% as opposed to 5.3%) for short-term loss-making enterprises as against a reduction in expenditure on materials of 13%. If we were to take the energy figures as a proxy for production activity then it would appear that short-term losses are associated with significant reductions in activity, with the financial consequences to some extent reflecting an increase in material stockholding. Similar calculations are not appropriate for long-term loss-makers as the figures will to a considerable extent reflect the very sector-specific utilization of inputs exhibited by those enterprises.

Another indication of the financial squeeze on short-term loss-making enterprises can be observed directly from the figures for stocks and debtors. Changes in these two main elements of the short-term current assets position reveal that they were responsible for 3.6% of profitable enterprises' use of funds, but only 2.1% of short-term loss-makers' uses with stock changes going negative in two years. Selling expenditure is also reduced heavily, from 0.3% for profitable companies to 0.1% for unprofitable ones. R & D expenditure, only 0.1% for profitable firms, effectively disappears in loss-making enterprises. A number of other items however appear less readily adjustable downwards, or actually increase in long-term loss-makers, hence exhibiting higher percentages where substantially lower revenues have generated losses. These include expenditure on repairs, up from 1.4% to 3.9%; on welfare[3], up from 0.3% to 1.5%; and on training, which is 0.15% for long-term loss-makers but surprisingly negligible for profitable enterprises and short-term loss-makers. Depreciation is also much higher at 5.7% as opposed to 2.7%, presumably reflecting both greater obsolescence and financial shortage.

Interest payments represent a higher percentage of outflows for short-term unprofitable enterprises (1.5%) than for profitable ones (0.7%) but are a lower percentage for long-term unprofitable ones (0.35%). We can be reasonably confident therefore that the financial position of short-term loss-makers is not eased by subsidization via interest relief from the bank. For long-term loss-makers, we cannot make any clear inference. Interest payments appear to be lower, but, as we have seen, bank loans to long-term loss-makers might also be lower. The repayment of loans (not shown) is, if anything, slightly higher as a percentage for long-term unprofitable enterprises. But it must be remembered that the total figure on which this percentage is based is typically substantially reduced in long-term loss-making enterprises, so that it is still possible that there is some element of interest or loan repayment relief wrapped up in these figures. More direct observations on interest charges are provided later.

Finally, we look at retained profit and taxation. The former drops from 3.6% to 0.8% for short-term loss-makers. The crude figure for long-term loss-makers is higher at 2.0%, but this heavily reflects one major anomaly in the data (see notes to Table 10.6). Apart from this the figure drops to 0.2%. Taxation falls from 20.9% to 19.8% for short-term unprofitable enterprises but to only 2.9% for long-term unprofitable ones. These figures however combine both income tax and sales tax. Table 10.7 splits these out and from this it is clear that loss-making enterprises, as one would expect, pay virtually no tax on profits. In addition sales tax is very much lower for long-term loss-makers, partly reflecting the lower sales tax rates in the sectors concerned. The table also indicates that income tax for the least profitable enterprises making positive profits typically lie about half way between those for loss-making and profitable enterprises.

Putting all the above together, we may loosely characterize loss-

TABLE 10.7. Taxation of profitable and unprofitable enterprises (% of uses)

	Long-term loss-makers	Short-term loss-makers	Low-profit enterprises	Profitable enterprises
Sales tax	2.9	19.8	14.0	12.5
Income tax	0.0	0.0	3.4	8.3
TOTAL	2.9	19.8	17.4	20.9

making enterprises as follows. First, there are short-term loss-makers experiencing a reduction in retained profit after payment of bonuses. They maintain the level of their own sources however, partly through higher depreciation charges and partly through an increase in 'other' contributory elements. In addition they may receive direct subsidies from the state and together on average these elements contribute nearly 7% of total financial inflows. The pressure of losses results, as we would expect, in reductions in expenditure on materials, fuel and power, and stockholding, but these are insufficient by themselves to offset the drain on cash flow. In addition, expenditure is maintained on investment and is significantly higher on wages. The squeeze on funds is not to any appreciable extent relaxed by reductions in interest commitments, new bank lending, or lower repayments, though some rollover provision may be exercised. In this sense, banks do not assist in easing the position of short-term loss-makers. (They may of course, quite separately, be the vehicle by which state subsidies are made available to enterprises.) Income tax liabilities however disappear as a result of the losses made.

In many respects the position for long-term loss-makers is quite different. Sales revenue as a proportion of total inflows is about 30% lower than for profitable firms while, at the same time, expenditure on investment and wages is very much higher. Expenditure on some smaller items such as repairs, training, and welfare is also higher than in profitable enterprises. The resulting severe shortage of funds is met in three ways.

First, profits tax of course disappears. Second, very substantial subsidies, equal on average to about 15% of total inflows, are paid to such enterprises to keep them in operation. Third, further subsidization occurs through a boost to the firm's own resources, equal on average to over 20%, so that over one-third of long-term loss-makers' funds come, via one means or another, from subsidies.

Table 10.8 provides some summary statistics of selected key items, and some ratios based on them.[4] The last three rows show (*a*) the proportion of revenue after payment of taxes and for inputs of materials and power that goes on wages and capital investment, (*b*) the ratio of subsidies, either explicit or under 'other' in firm's own resources, to revenue minus tax and inputs of materials and power, and (*c*) the proportion of wages and capital expenditure met by those subsidies. This last line brings out clearly how significant subsidies are for unprofitable enterprises, but in particular for the long-term loss-making ones, with nearly 70% of these expenditures matched by subsidies.

TABLE 10.8. Selected financial flow figures for profitable and unprofitable enterprises and summary ratios (percentages of sources or uses unless otherwise specified)

	Profitable enterprises	Low-profit enterprises	Short-term unprofitable enterprises	Long-term unprofitable enterprises
Sources				
Sales revenue	85.4	83.2	84.0	62.5
Subsidies	0.9	1.8	4.1	15.0
Firms' own sources				
Retained profit	3.6	2.5	0.8	0.2
Depreciation	2.7	2.9	4.2	5.7
Other	−2.1	−1.8	−0.9	15.6
Uses				
Materials and fuel	48.5	49.3	40.5	30.4
Wages	3.7	5.2	10.2	18.8
Investment	7.9	8.1	8.6	26.1
Tax	20.9	17.4	19.8	2.9
Revenue − tax − Materials and fuel	16.0	16.5	23.7	29.2
$\frac{\text{Wages + Investment}}{\text{Revenue − Tax − Materials and Fuel}}$	72.5%	80.6%	79.3%	153.8%
$\frac{\text{Subsidies + 'other' items in firm's own resources}}{\text{Revenue − Tax − Materials and Fuel}}$	−7.5%	0.0%	13.5%	104.7%
$\frac{\text{Subsidies + 'other' items}}{\text{Wages + investment}}$	−10.3%	0.0%	17.0%	68.1%

3. The Budget Constraint and Enterprise Performance: Preliminary Evidence

There are a number of different ways through which an enterprise might get into difficulty and a number of ways in which the budget constraint experienced as a result might be loosened. The previous section provides some important clues in relation to both of these but utilizing only flow of funds data. In this section we broaden the analysis in two ways. First, we look at a wider range of measures of performance and of the budget constraint; second, we look at classes of enterprise across the whole range rather than focusing specifically on the least profitable. In addition we use our whole sample of enterprises rather than the more restricted one exhibiting a high degree of consistency of financial data which we used for the flow of funds analysis. In practice, with one exception the results and inferences are consistent as between the two modes of analysis. Some basic data are provided in graphical form in Figs. 10.1 to 10.15 each of which shows average values of a relevant variable for each of six groups of enterprises for each of the years 1984–87. The six groups comprise three categories of loss-making enterprises, namely long-term loss-makers (loss made in all four years); medium-term loss-makers (losses made in two or three of the years 1984–87), and short-term loss-makers (losses made in the one year alone). The three other categories comprise low-, medium-, and high-profit enterprises respectively in the year concerned.

Inspection of these charts suggests the following main results. First, long-term state subsidies are, as expected, massively concentrated on loss-making enterprises but, in particular, and except for 1987, on long-term loss-making ones (Fig. 10.1). Such funding is not therefore primarily a mechanism for dealing with short-term problems, giving an enterprise time to re-establish profitability. Such support as there is for short- and medium-term loss-makers is in fact heavily concentrated in one year, namely 1987. But continuing losses lead to very substantial reliance on state funding. The budget constraint is therefore much weaker than one would predict purely from observation of the response to an enterprise going into losses for the first time, though it is plausible to assume that it is tighter for enterprises experiencing declining activity than for those forced to operate under tight price controls.

At first sight this sits oddly with the evidence from Fig. 10.2 that state financing of short-term working capital ('circulating capital') is

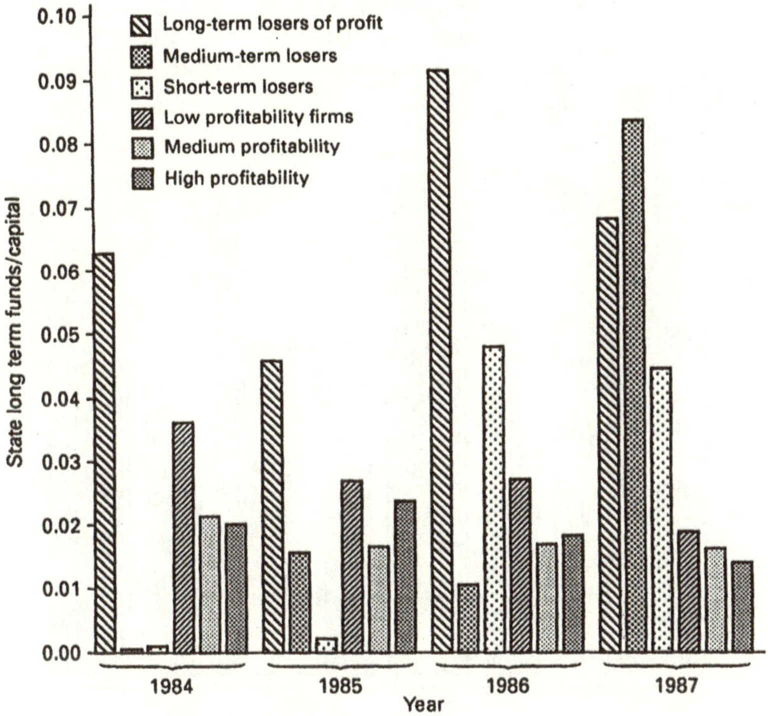

FIG. 10.1. Budget constraint on firms according to performance (long-term state funds)

significantly lower for long-term loss-makers. However, examination of Fig. 10.3, which shows state funding of working capital as a proportion of total working capital, indicates that it is once again the long-term loss-makers which have much higher support from the state. Figure 10.2 is then explained by the fact that total working capital is much lower in the long-term loss-makers, primarily because they are in sectors which, by the nature of the product involved, have lower working capital.

Second, and in keeping with both the above and the flow of funds analysis, firms' own sources, mainly comprising retained profit net of bonuses, retained depreciation and subsidies, and other inflows resulting from loss-making and related contracts, are considerably higher *both* for medium- and long-term loss-makers *and* for enterprises with high profitability. This twin-peaked distribution, which is very clear in Fig. 10.4 for all four years, reflects the higher retained profits associated with higher profitability and the higher subsidies via contractual

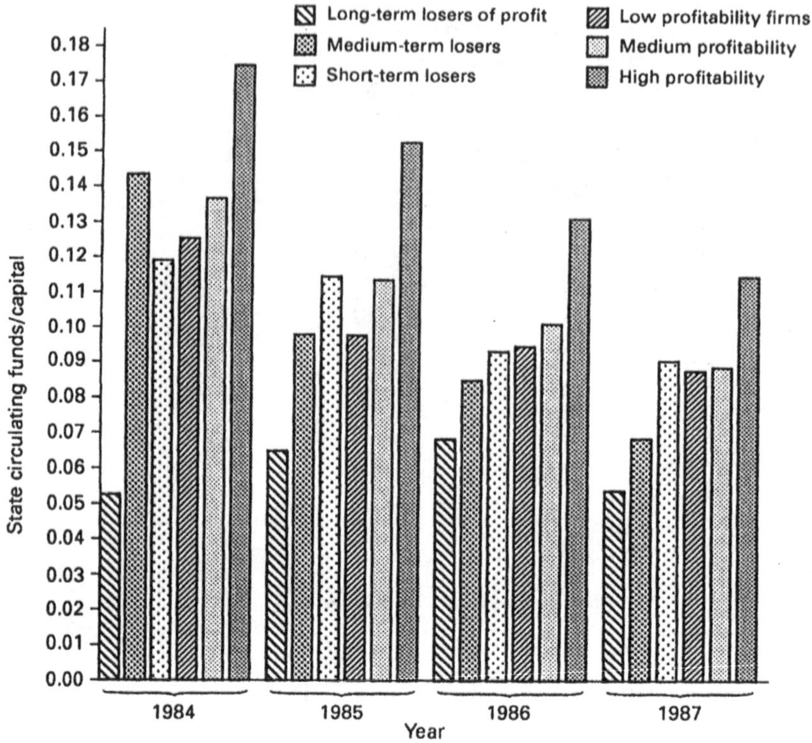

FIG. 10.2. Budget constraint on firms according to performance (state funds for circulating capital)

payments paid to medium- and long-term loss-makers. Figure 10.4 is therefore a particularly graphic representation of the 'soft' budget constraint. As with specified central government subsidies, a move into short-term losses brings little if any support, with firms' own sources going to their lowest level. But, unlike central government subsidies, the support provided via firms' own sources grows strongly for medium-term loss-makers, indicating that this tends to be the first line of budget-constraint relaxation, with persistence of losses into the long term generally providing little further increase in this form of support. Rather, as we have seen above, for persistent loss-makers in particular sectors explicit central subsidization becomes the main form of support.

Our third observation concerns borrowing, repayments, and interest rates. Figure 10.5 shows that short- and medium-term loss-makers can generally still carry out new borrowing (particularly so in 1986) but that long-term loss-makers can raise virtually no new loan

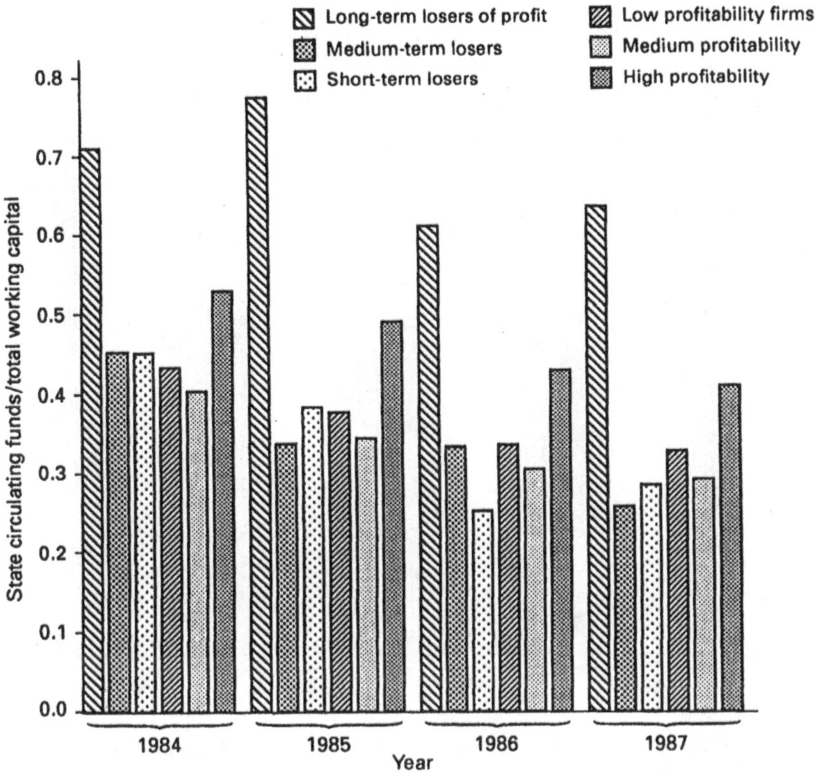

FIG. 10.3. Budget constraint on firms according to performance (proportion of circulating capital financed by state subsidies)

finance. The latter is consistent with what we observed from the flow of funds analysis, and is of course to be expected, but the former is more surprising, suggesting a significant time-lag before accumulating losses have a strong impact on external borrowing. This almost certainly arises from the fact that external borrowing is primarily for investment purposes; that such expenditure typically has a long gestation period; and that it cannot normally be embarked upon without agreement on the funding of projects over the years of construction. A deterioration in current profits may not then have any great impact on investment or borrowing, a point noted in the flow of funds analysis, either because it would be more costly to halt projects than complete them, or because of bureaucratic inertia which prevents decisions being reassessed or reversed.

Consistent with this, enterprise debt positions (Fig. 10.6) generally indicate a slight increase as profits rise but in most years it is noticeable

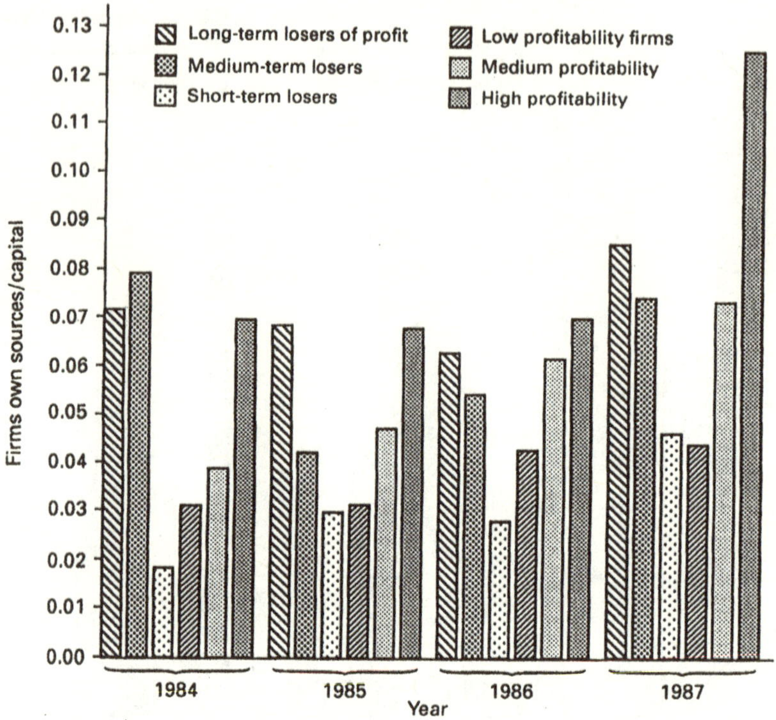

FIG. 10.4. Budget constraint on firms' according to performance (firms' own sources of finance)

how the debt position of medium- and long-term loss-makers has been reduced whereas short-term loss-makers often have very much higher debt ratios. This indicates that enterprises may use debt, or roll-over debt, to tide them over short-term losses, but that, unless actually written off, they have to correct the position and adjust to their very limited debt-capacity position if they make persistent losses. A similar sort of position applies to creditors as well (Fig. 10.7). Repayment of loans as shown in Fig. 10.8, also generally continues in short and medium loss-makers at much the same rate as in low-profits enterprises, though, as expected medium- and high-profit enterprises have progressively higher repayment rates. Long-term loss-makers, on the other hand, repay no loans at all. As can be seen however in Fig. 10.9, this clear pattern of external financial flows has relatively little effect on the *ex post* interest rate paid. The rate is typically a little lower for loss-makers, a result echoed in the flow of funds analysis, and given the reduced creditworthiness of such enterprises we might

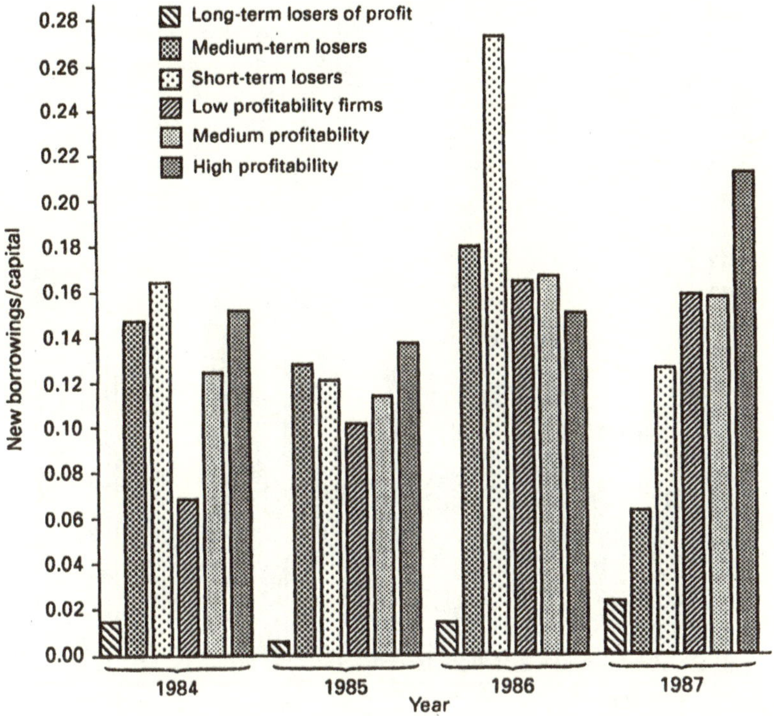

FIG. 10.5. Budget constraint on firms according to performance (total new borrowings)

have expected to see a higher rate being paid, so that there is probably some further element of subsidization here. But the effect is clearly not marked. Thus the banks are in some ways isolated from the effects of negative profit or effective insolvency. The two main effects on bank flows are, non-repayment of loans by long-term loss-makers, and second, signs of roll-over of loans by low-profit and short- or medium-term loss-makers, as opposed to substantially higher repayment by high-profit enterprises.

Turning to taxation, two points stand out. First, Fig. 10.10 indicates the highly progressive nature of the tax on profits, the generally high figure on short-term loss-makers in the otherwise smooth trend reflecting lags in the structure of tax payments. Medium- and long-term loss-makers typically pay very little if any tax on income, as is to be expected. Second, the sales-tax rate, shown in Fig. 10.11, is often higher and sometimes much higher, on loss-making enterprises. It is this factor which keeps overall taxation so high as a proportion of the

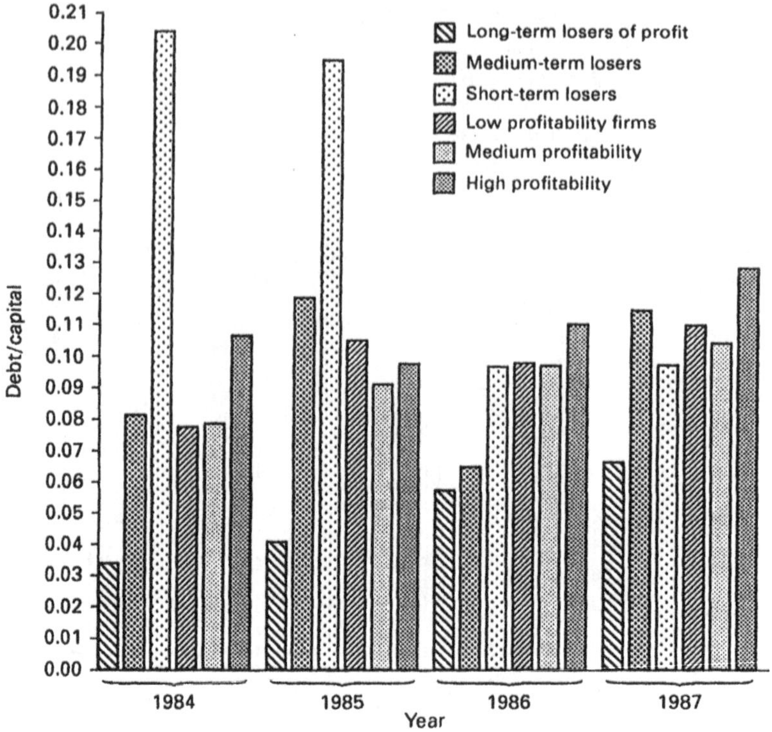

FIG. 10.6. Budget constraint on firms according to performance (debt ratios)

overall flow of funds. To a considerable extent this is a sectoral phenomenon, with the sales-tax rate varying across sectors, but this does not fully explain the quite high rates for long-term loss-makers, because the light industry and craft sector and in particular the extraction industries have lower than average sales-tax rates. This result is however at variance with that found in the flow of funds analysis, and in practice the only such inconsistency. It may be therefore that this reflects unreliability of the data in our larger sample.

Next we look at depreciation. Figure 10.12 shows that the depreciation rate is fairly constant across profitable enterprises, which is not surprising, but falls somewhat for loss-making ones, primarily medium- and long-term loss-makers. This is at first sight surprising. We would expect capital to become obsolescent faster in long-term loss-making enterprises and managers to write down equipment as quickly as possible to reduce the size of accounting losses. In addition the flow of funds analysis indicated somewhat higher depreciation

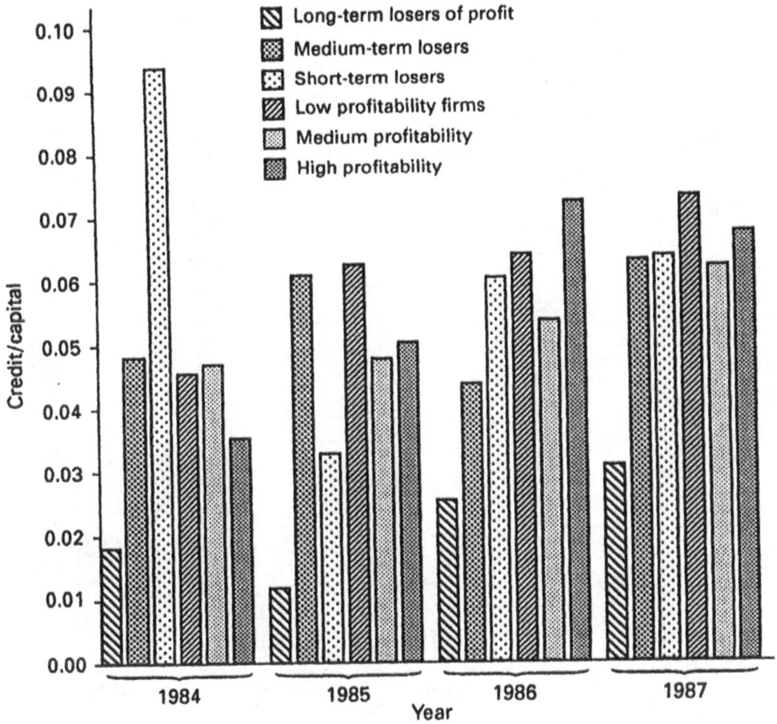

FIG. 10.7. Budget constraint on firms according to performance (credit ratios)

provision as a proportion of total funding. There is however no inconsistency if loss-making enterprises typically have more durable capital, in particular in extraction and utilities, but are experiencing substantial reductions in revenue. Depreciation provision would then be a smaller proportion of the capital stock but a higher proportion of the total inflow of funds. The differences in depreciation rates are in practice however relatively small.

As expected, long-term loss-making enterprises have much lower retention reserves (Fig. 10.13), highly profitable enterprises strikingly high ones. But cash reserve positions (Fig. 10.14) are much more variable, apart from the high cash reserves of the most profitable enterprises. Finally, as background information, Fig. 10.15 looks at growth rates of output across the different categories of performance. This shows a tendency for loss-makers to grow more slowly but the pattern is neither clear, monotonic, nor persistent. But given that normal losses may reflect poor sales growth or excessive expansion,

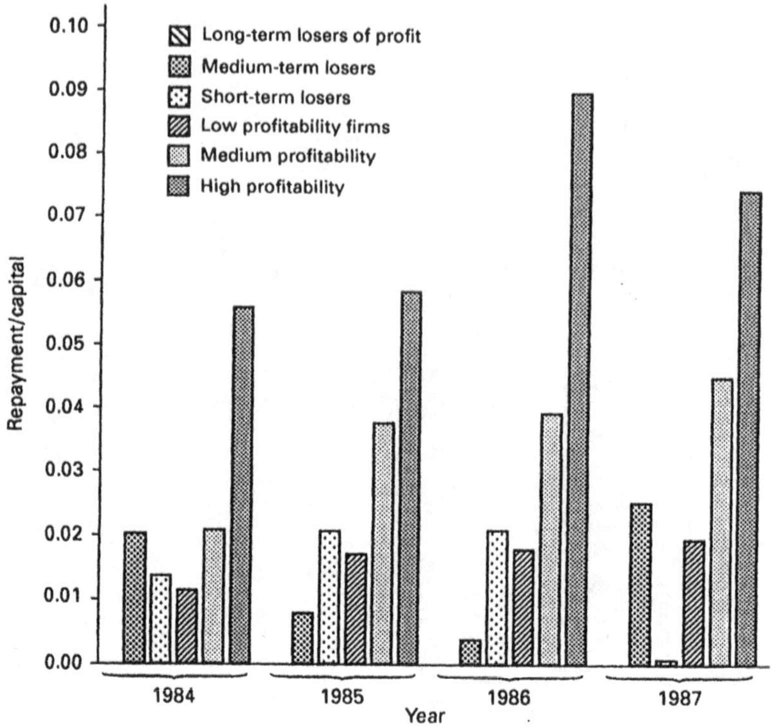

FIG. 10.8. Budget constraint on firms according to performance (repayment of loans)

and that policy losses may bear no relation to output growth, this is not necessarily surprising.

Looking across these data as a whole, it is clear that, for persistent loss-making enterprises, the state provides large-scale subsidization in one form or another. While previously agreed borrowing may continue for some time after an enterprise starts to make losses, the banks' own finances are generally not the main vehicle for softening the budget constraint, though roll-over of loans will occur in some cases and some loans to long-term loss-makers may be written off. The figures are also influenced by the sectoral distribution of the loss-making enterprises and perhaps the age and durability of their capital.

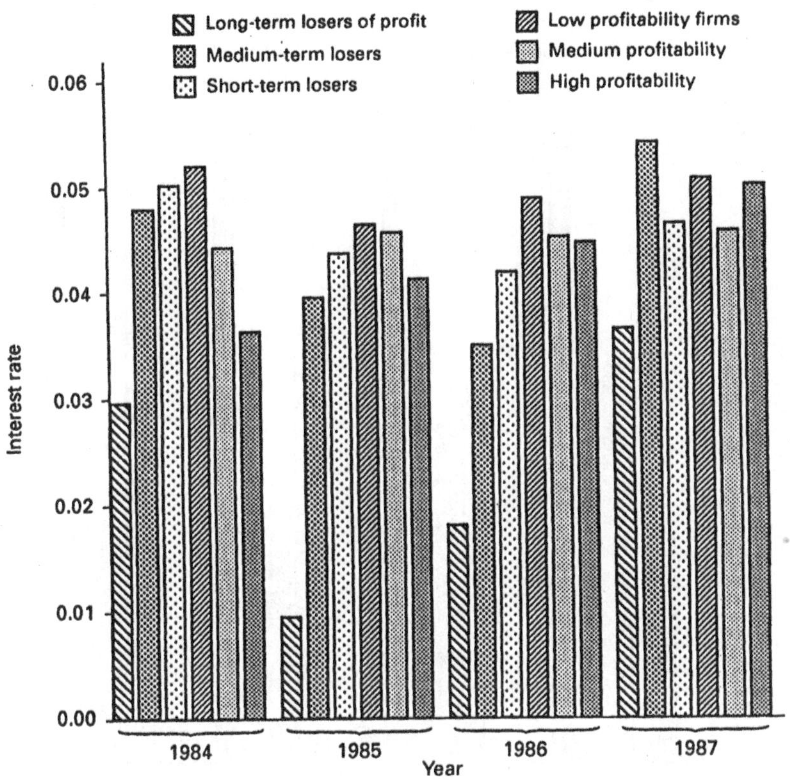

FIG. 10.9. Budget constraint on firms according to performance (interest rates)

4. *The Budget Constraint and Enterprise Performance: Statistical Analysis*

The previous section took a preliminary look at the data on possible indicators of a soft budget constraint in relation to enterprise profitability. This section systematically regresses the various indicators on measures of profitability and other performance variables which might reflect weak or deteriorating financial positions. We first outline the measures to be used and the general procedures followed, and then discuss results.

We first identify four separate measures of financial difficulty. These are:

(i) low or negative profitability,
(ii) a substantial fall in the value of output,

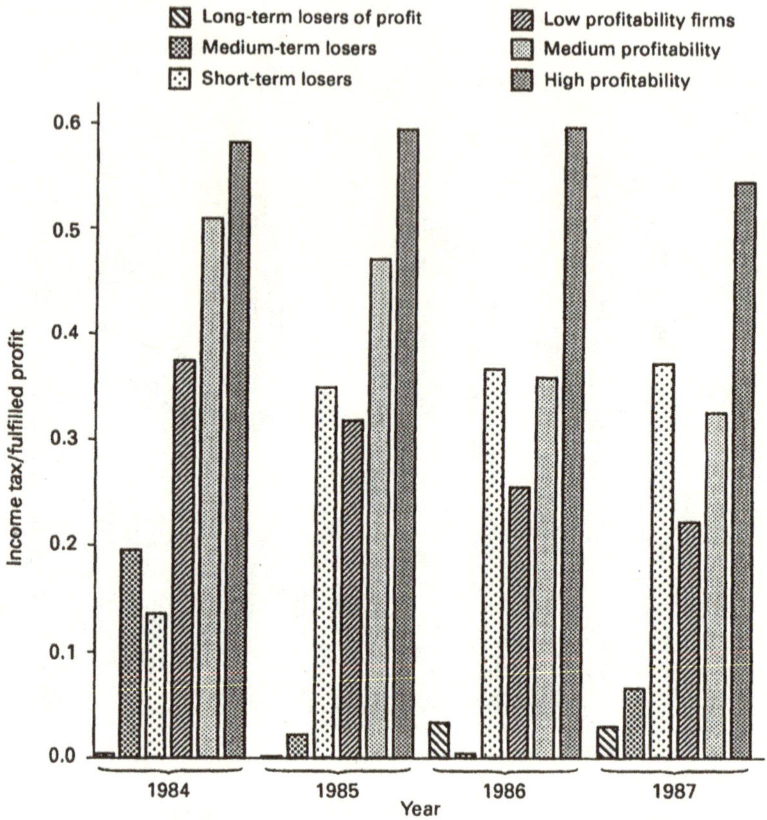

FIG. 10.10. Budget constraint on firms according to performance (income-tax rates)

(iii) low or negative net current assets, and
(iv) low retentions.

Next we identify five possible indicators of soft budget constraint, namely:

(i) reduced interest rate,
(ii) increase in subsidies,
(iii) increase in loans/borrowing,
(iv) lower repayment of loans, and
(v) reduction in taxation.

In some cases where relevant item (ii) is also split into short-term and long-term subsidies. Items (ii) to (v) are all deflated by capital employed to eliminate size effects.

In addition we need to consider firms' own sources. This may be a

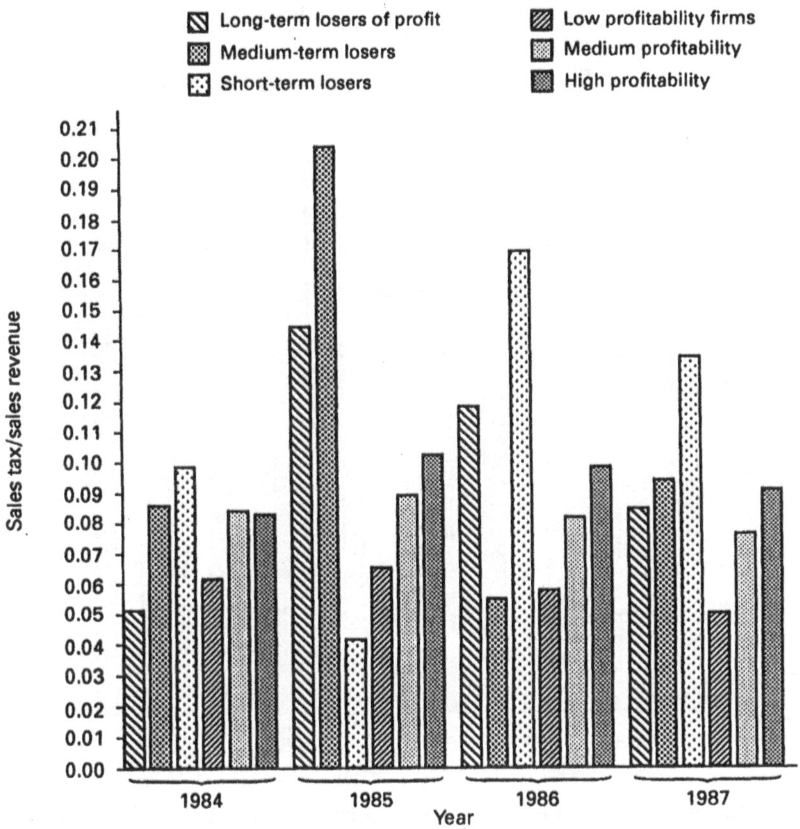

FIG. 10.11. Budget constraint on firms according to performance (sales-tax rates)

measure of financial performance, with low or negative profit enterprises having very low figures for this item. At the same time it may well, as we have seen, be a measure of the soft budget constraint, with poorly performing enterprises receiving substantial injections of funds from external sources into their own resources. In our initial regressions therefore we use only retained profit plus depreciation as the performance measure (noting that not all depreciation is necessarily retained), and firms' own sources minus retained profit and depreciation as the budget constraint indicator.

Armed with the resulting five performance and six constraint measures we then run five-times-six simple regressions, first across all enterprises and second across only the weakest 15% in terms of the performance measure used. We also calculate the mean residuals for the weakest 15% in the all-enterprise regressions. Our purpose in

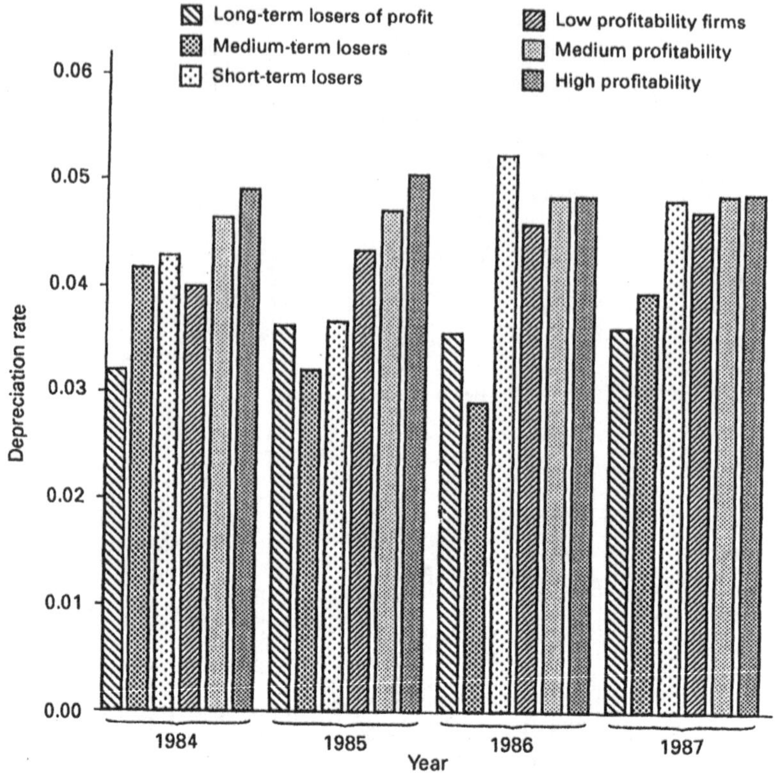

FIG. 10.12. Budget constraint on firms according to performance (depreciation rates)

each case is the same, namely to explore the extent, if at all, to which the budget constraint faced by the weaker enterprises differed systematically from that faced by the rest of the sample. Schematically, in Figs. 10.16 and 10.17 we wish to identify cases where the budget-constraint measure changes disproportionately at low levels of performance. Thus Fig. 10.16 might illustrate such variables as taxation, interest rates, or repayment of loans falling disproportionately fast for low-profit enterprises, identified both by the lower intercept and higher gradient in the 15% regression than in the all-enterprise regression, and by the non-zero mean residuals for the bottom 15% in relation to the all-enterprise regressions, indicated by the shaded area. Figure 10.17 shows a similar picture but for constraint variables such as subsidies or borrowing.

The regression results of the exercise are given in Table 10.9. In the matrix, each column corresponds to one performance measure, each

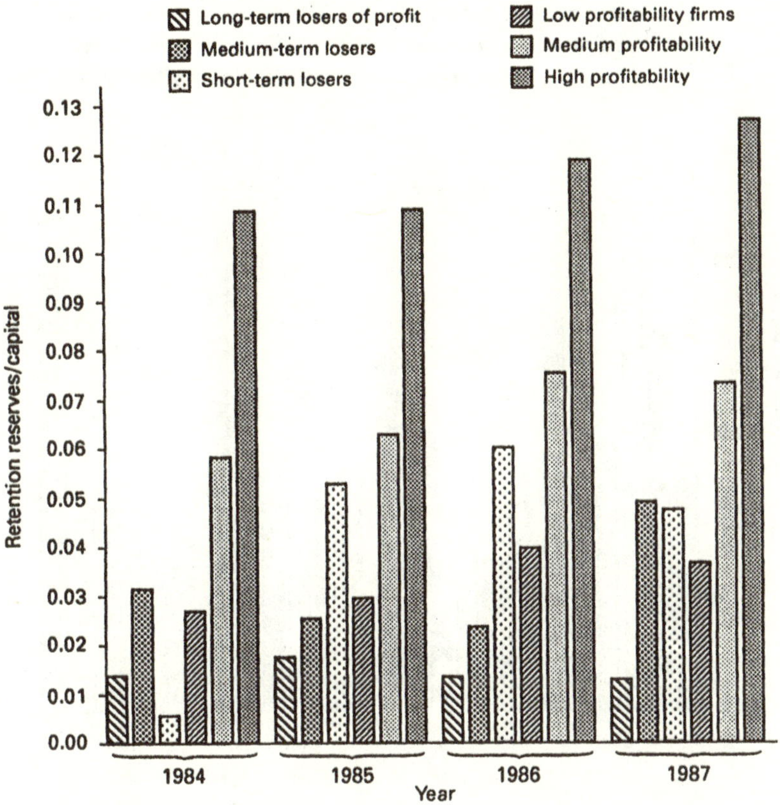

FIG. 10.13. Budget constraint on firms according to performance (retention reserves)

row to one possible soft budget constraint mechanism. Each cell in the matrix gives four coefficients: first the intercept and second the performance measure coefficient, together with their *t*-statistics, for the whole sample; and below the equivalent figures for the weakest 15% of the sample as measured by the relevant performance variable. We summarize the information provided in Table 10.10. For each constraint variable and each performance variable we indicate wherever the predicted pattern (as in Figs. 10.16 and 10.17) emerges by a tick; a cross indicates a pattern consistent with no significant deviation for weak enterprises, i.e. a 'hard' constraint, e.g. higher interest rates for financially weak enterprises. No entry indicates that neither pattern emerged. Whether the slope regression coefficients are significant (at 10% level) is indicated by one or two asterisks (virtually all intercept

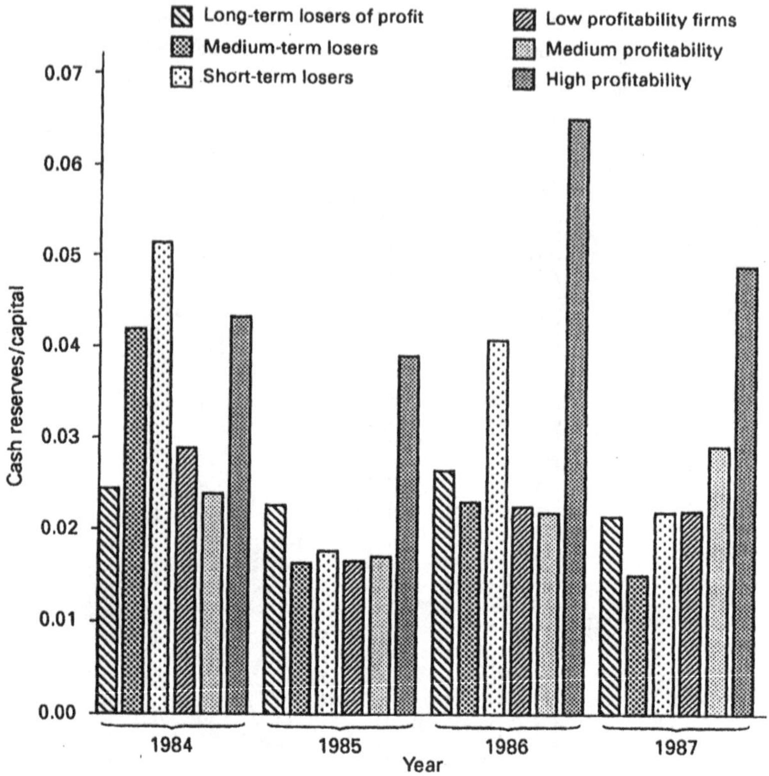

FIG. 10.14. Budget constraint on firms according to performance (cash reserves)

coefficients are statistically significant); the mean residual values of the weakest 15% from the all-enterprises regression line are also given. In all cases these are in the same metric as the dependent variable and therefore, apart from interest rates, these figures are percentages of capital employed.

The first point to note when considering Table 10.10 is that variations in the interest rate do not appear to be related significantly to any of the performance variables in the manner hypothesized apart from net current assets. Bearing in mind that our measure of the interest rate is an *ex post* one, indicating the effective interest rate actually paid on borrowing, we conclude that reductions in interest payments are generally not a means by which the position of financially weak enterprises is eased, and we do not consider this further. Second, while long-term subsidies appear to be important (see below), short-term ones generally are not, and so we do not consider these any

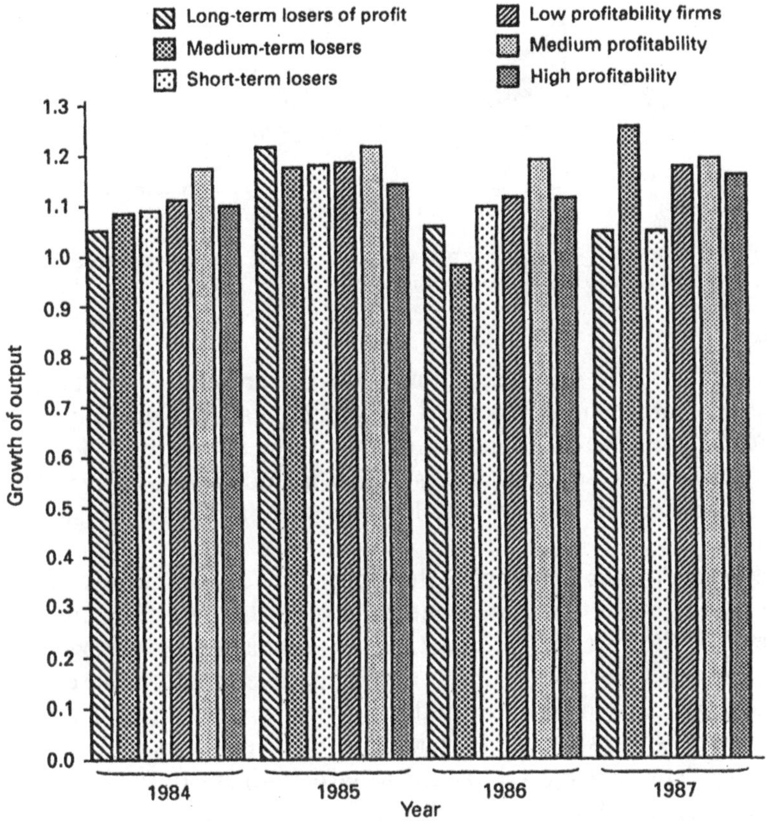

FIG. 10.15. Budget constraint on firms according to performance (growth of output)

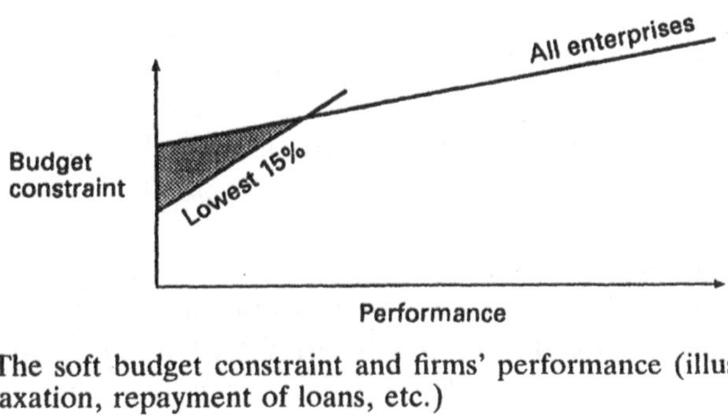

FIG. 10.16. The soft budget constraint and firms' performance (illustrating such variables as taxation, repayment of loans, etc.)

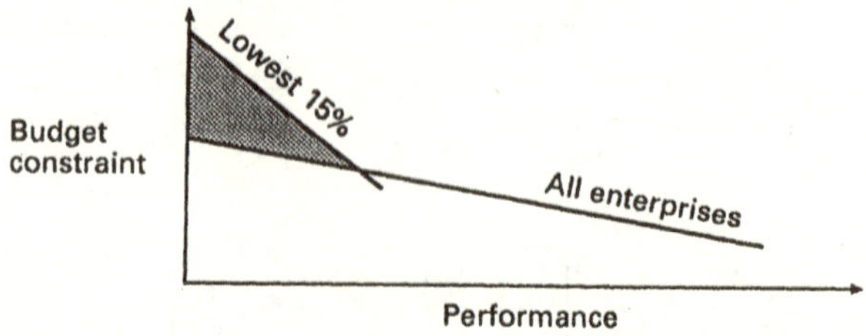

FIG. 10.17. The soft budget constraint and firms' performance (illustrating variables such as subsidies or borrowing)

further either. The only exception is for the growth-of-output performance measure, where it is short-term and total subsidies rather than long-term ones which exhibit the hypothesized pattern. Note that regressions on net current assets which include short-term liabilities are disregarded, in view of the likelihood that reverse causality will exist.

The more striking evidence is that, of the remaining twenty-five cells in the matrix, no fewer than nineteen exhibit the pattern predicted on the basis of the soft budget constraint mechanism hypothesized. Only one rejects this pattern, with the remaining five indeterminate. Of the nineteen which confirm the pattern, both gradient coefficients are significant in six cases, one is significant in seven cases and neither in six cases. (The single example of a hard budget constraint pattern, namely loans as a function of retained profit and depreciation has one gradient coefficient significant.) Given the potential problems described earlier in using this particular data-set to explore the soft budget constraint, this is surprisingly strong confirmation for the workings of the soft budget constraint and for the particular mechanisms identified through which it operates. Loans and long-term subsidies are clearly important, but the strongest evidence relates to firms' own resources other than retained profit and depreciation where for four of the five performance measures the hypothesized pattern appears with all but one gradient significant. Indeed the evidence is probably stronger still, in that the results for the fifth performance measure, profitability, are close to the hypothesized pattern but exhibit a gradient for the weakest 15% which is insignificantly different from zero rather than negative. In terms of performance, it is clear from the table that, as we would expect, profitability and profitability-related measures are very important indicators of financial weakness. But a substantial fall in output is also very significant and, to a somewhat lesser extent, low net current assets. Two anomalies in

TABLE 10.9. Performance measures and the 'soft' budget constraint: regression estimates

	Profitability		Growth of output		Net current assets		Retention reserves		Retained profit and depreciation	
Interest rate	0.052	−0.005	0.056	−0.008	0.032	0.038	0.048	−0.002	0.044	0.019
	(23.6)	(2.58)	(13.5)	(2.18)	(15.6)	(8.17)	(37.6)	(0.11)	(27.9)	(1.89)
	0.054	−0.011	0.058	−0.007	0.016	0.119	0.045	0.467	0.054	−0.077
	(12.1)	(0.99)	(4.52)	(0.45)	(1.91)	(2.28)	(8.34)	(0.78)	(8.21)	(1.59)
LT subsidies	0.049	−0.019	0.025	−0.004	0.049	−0.070	0.020	−0.004	0.020	−0.009
	(7.08)	(1.91)	(2.70)	(0.57)	(10.7)	(6.89)	(7.15)	(0.12)	(5.98)	(0.65)
	0.117	−0.492	−0.038	0.027	0.097	−0.335	0.023	0.857	0.044	−0.169
	(2.64)	(1.34)	(0.13)	(0.81)	(4.02)	(2.30)	(3.64)	(1.22)	(2.79)	(1.42)
ST subsidies	0.091	−0.006	0.146	−0.030			0.102	0.150	0.097	0.075
	(8.18)	(1.02)	(13.0)	(3.23)			(30.3)	(3.41)	(22.3)	(4.34)
	0.016	0.025	0.159	−0.048			0.093	0.254	0.077	0.148
	(3.76)	(0.18)	(4.50)	(1.18)			(9.59)	(0.24)	(5.19)	(1.32)
Total subsidies	0.150	−0.016	0.193	−0.049			0.127	0.131	0.117	0.066
	(17.6)	(2.11)	(12.4)	(3.78)			(27.9)	(2.22)	(21.6)	(3.05)
	0.134	−0.021	0.271	−0.145			0.119	−0.387	0.135	0.933
	(7.7)	(0.03)	(5.10)	(2.37)			(10.5)	(0.31)	(2.62)	(2.41)
Loans	0.233	−0.013	0.131	0.075	0.113	0.268	0.207	0.115	0.175	0.162
	(9.79)	(0.58)	(3.02)	(2.06)	(5.10)	(5.29)	(17.8)	(0.76)	(9.25)	(2.14)
	0.259	−0.023	0.383	−0.206	0.052	0.490	0.229	−2.68	0.135	0.736
	(4.64)	(0.17)	(3.10)	(1.75)	(1.09)	(1.71)	(5.80)	(0.61)	(1.80)	(1.32)
Repayment of loans	0.017	0.017	0.002	0.028	0.033	0.002	0.026	0.126	0.268	0.040
	(2.76)	(3.12)	(0.18)	(3.14)	(6.25)	(0.89)	(8.04)	(2.98)	(8.09)	(2.93)
	0.007	0.032	−0.008	0.035	0.008	0.114	0.030	−0.677	0.004	0.063
	(0.82)	(1.57)	(0.52)	(1.91)	(0.67)	(1.55)	(3.81)	(0.76)	(0.53)	(1.15)

TABLE 10.9 (*cont.*)

	Profitability		Growth of output		Net current assets		Retention reserves		Retained profit and depreciation	
Taxation	0.413	−0.014	0.455	−0.064	0.383	−0.008	0.404	−0.161	0.422	−0.063
	(16.6)	(0.63)	(10.1)	(1.68)	(16.6)	(0.15)	(30.1)	(0.93)	(24.3)	(0.92)
	0.224	0.382	0.205	0.191	0.352	0.223	0.292	4.38	0.014	1.41
	(3.89)	(2.73)	(1.33)	(1.08)	(4.12)	(0.50)	(5.70)	(0.77)	(0.21)	(2.69)
Firm's own sources minus retained profit and depreciation	−0.001	−0.022	0.014	−0.043	−0.032	0.032	−0.009	−0.476	0.025	−0.200
	(0.05)	(3.85)	(0.72)	(3.55)	(2.33)	(1.98)	(0.69)	(10.2)	(0.91)	(11.5)
	0.023	0.031	0.041	−0.098	−0.065	−0.21	0.032	−1.07	0.084	−0.721
	(1.09)	(1.24)	(0.71)	(2.03)	(0.23)	(1.84)	(1.61)	(0.98)	(3.05)	(2.36)

Note: Each cell shows the intercept and slope coefficient values for the whole sample and, below, the equivalent figures for the weakest 15% of the sample.

TABLE 10.10. Performance measures and the 'soft' budget constraint: summary results

	Profitability	Change in output	Net current assets	Retentions	Retained profit and depreciation
Interest rate	X * 0.2%	* 0.3%	√ *° −0.3%	√ 0.1%	X * −0.3%
LT subsidies	√ * 1.5%	0.9%	√ *° 0.5%	−0.3%	√ 1.1%
ST subsidies	X *° 0.4%	√ *°	N/A	X *° −0.9%	X *° −0.3%
Total subsidies	√ 2.0%	√ ° −3.7%	N/A	−1.2%	° 2.3%
Loans	√ 1.0%	√ *° 0.9%	*° −2.6%	√ 0.04%	X * 0.4%
Repayments of loans	√ * −1.3%	√ *° −0.4%	√ −0.7%	* −2.0%	√ * 0.6%
Taxation	√ ° −3.2%	√ * −3.1%	√ 0.6%	√ −1.5%	√ ° −3.4%
Firm's own resources minus retained profit and depreciation	* 2.3%	√ *° 0.9%	√ *° 0.1%	√ * 1.0%	√ *° 1.4%

Notes: √ = 'soft' budget constraint; X = 'hard' budget constraint; * = slope coefficient significant for whole sample; ° = slope coefficient significant for weakest 15% of sample; % figures are mean residuals of weakest 15% from the all-enterprises regression line.

the table should be noted. In the cases of subsidies in response to falls in output, and loans in response to low net current assets, the soft budget constraint pattern of regression results emerges but the sign of the residual mean is negative rather than positive. While this is statistically quite explicable it is not clear what economic interpretation, if any, can be attached to this, though it suggests that, for example, while subsidies are disproportionately higher for enterprises with very large falls in output, others in the bottom 15% have disproportionately lower subsidies.

We can obtain some grasp of the dimensions of the soft budget constraint by aggregating (with appropriate signs) the mean residuals for the various soft budget constraint mechanisms for any given performance measure (ignoring interest-rate and short-term subsidy variations). This suggests that an enterprise in the bottom 15% of profitability will on average find its financial position improved disproportionately to the extent of 9.3% of its capital employed. It should be noted that in the regressions all of the mechanisms contribute to this aggregate whereas in practice any individual enterprise may well be assisted very largely through one particular mechanism or another. (The equivalent figures for depressed retained profits and depreciation alone is 6.9% and for retention reserves, 3.3%.) This may be put in perspective by noting that the average return on capital employed for the whole sample is 39.2% and for the bottom 15% it is 5.1%. It should however be recalled from the earlier data on financial flows that this support is likely to be heavily concentrated on the enterprises actually making losses.

5. Conclusions

It is important to recall that our database contains relatively few loss-making enterprises, and is therefore not well suited to examine the operation of a soft budget constraint in Chinese enterprises. In particular it does not permit any substantial statistical analysis of the sort that would be possible and potentially very illuminating if we had a substantial number of unprofitable enterprises in a still larger sample of enterprises generally. Against this, the data we have are quite detailed, the loss-makers that are contained in the sample are for the most part substantially different from the rest in terms of a number of variables, and this does allow us to carry out some quite detailed descriptive work which permits a number of interesting observations on the behaviour of such enterprises and on the workings of the soft budget constraint.

It is clear that it is important to distinguish persistent or long-term loss-making enterprises and those making shorter-term losses. Within our sample the former are almost entirely in the light industry and craft and extractive industries, which may be subject to sector-specific output price restrictions. The losses of these enterprises therefore may not necessarily indicate anything about either the state of demand facing them, their efficiency, or their levels of activity. They are also large and may well play a crucial role in their provincial economy. If so, then irrespective of whether their prices have been used as a significant element in macroeconomic management, be this for anti-inflationary, growth, or distributional objectives, government may well not permit these enterprises to collapse. This does not of course mean that either their ownership or control are irrelevant—indeed these are probably more crucial in such key enterprises than elsewhere. But it does mean that the impact of the losses made, how we interpret them, and what the impact would be of alternative forms of ownership and control are all likely to be quite different from their counterparts in other less significant enterprises. In particular, although the size of the losses, the consequences of them, and the manner and efficiency of operation of the enterprises concerned may all differ under different control mechanisms, the soft budget constraint may to some degree be inevitable in the sense that both the state and the enterprises know that they will not be allowed to suspend operations. To the extent that the State, sensibly or otherwise, uses control of the prices set by such enterprises as a tool of macroeconomic management, this merely exacerbates such a consequence. Thus, while decontrol of prices, managerial incentive mechanisms, and perhaps even privatization may all have a role to play in the improvement of the economic performance of these enterprises, it is important to note that their continued operation is assured, and from the perspective of the enterprises' financial position there is not a great deal of difference between price controls offset by subsidies or the absence of both, even though in terms of profitability this is a major distinction.

When we turn to medium- and short-term loss-making enterprises the situation is quite different. These, though still small in number in our sample, span all the broadly defined sectors. Some elements of the type of soft budget constraint facing extractive and light industry sector enterprises may exist here in that, given the state's objective of providing employment and associated social benefits to all, such enterprises cannot be allowed to fail. There is nevertheless considerably more discretion available in deciding how to respond to such enterprises, in part at least because the consequences of substantial contraction or collapse may be much more localized. In comparison with extractive (and energy) sector enterprises it is likely to be the potential loss of employment income rather than the loss of production itself, with all the knock-on effects which the latter would have in 'commanding' sectors, which softens the constraints, and this is both more flexible and less vital.

Our results show reasonably systematic features in terms of the response to such losses. Material and energy inputs are reduced but wage payments and investment expenditure are both typically very insensitive to deteriorating financial conditions. The former are largely fixed by relatively rigid wage-rate and employment constraints. The latter may in part reflect quite rational economic behaviour. The profitability of long-term investment currently under consideration is not necessarily undermined by a downturn in current profits. Even if it is, it may be more profitable to complete half-finished projects than not, even though losses will result in either case. But there may also be long time-lags in the bureaucracy of the process for deciding on and financing capital expenditure, and there may be extraneous factors, political or otherwise, which result in investment projects becoming to some extent independent of purely commercial considerations.

The resulting financial pressures have a number of predictable consequences in terms of profits, taxation, stocks, borrowing, etc. But the most interesting consequences are the ways in which loss-making enterprises are kept afloat financially. Short-term loss-makers on average have higher depreciation charges, receive some explicit subsidies, and obtain further financial support via inflows to their own resources. Together these constitute over 7% of total flows, which in many cases will be greater than either their wage bill or the profits they make in other years. Long-term loss-makers on average obtain around a third of their total inflows via subsidies. Combined with less expenditure on fuel and materials and with low tax payments this permits very high proportionate levels of expenditure on wages and new capital. With regard to borrowing, interest payments, and repayment of loans, the evidence suggests little subsidization from bank finance. Both short- and long-term loss-makers find financial support from state sources albeit to quantitatively very different degrees.

With regard to borrowing and repayment of loans, two points stand out. First, across all loss-makers a fairly clear soft budget constraint pattern emerges from such statistical analysis as we have been able to carry out. Second, when we focus only on short- and medium-term loss-makers, we find that new borrowing is generally not greatly affected, in terms of either amount or cost, and repayment of loans is not greatly different from that of many profitable enterprises. These two findings are not inconsistent. They indicate that enterprises going into losses can expect to maintain both wage and investment expenditure and the external financial flows associated with the latter, with remaining shortfalls met by inflows to the firm's own sources. Persistent losses result in more explicit and more permanent arrangements to subsidize enterprises including renegotiation of loan contracts, but given our sample we are not able to say to what extent this is explicitly associated with price controls, and not therefore available in other circumstances.

Having identified some of the characteristics of the soft budget constraint, it is equally important to remember the dimensions of the effects involved within our sample. Adding together the long-term subsidies and unspecified 'other' elements in firms' own sources for the loss-making enterprises, the total is over twice the total retained profit of the profitable enterprises. These two sources on average account for 17% of the total inflow of funds of loss-making enterprises, which may be contrasted with the 3.5% of the total inflow of funds to profitable enterprises which ends up as retained profit.

Our main interest in the soft budget constraint lies in trying to identify what would happen to behaviour and performance if it ceased to operate. This cannot be done on the basis of the above. Rather it requires simulation exercises to be run on a set of equations which represent the main behavioural relationships operating within enterprises, and this we are not yet in a position to carry out. But what the above analysis enables us to do is to identify the main characteristics of enterprises running into financial difficulty and the main mechanisms by which the soft budget constraint operates. This indicates that while much of the *behaviour* of Chinese state-owned enterprises both real and financial, can readily be understood in terms of neoclassical formulations more usually associated with enterprises in the West, the institutional *environment* in which they operate is quite different, potentially giving rise to quite different economic decisions in responses to that environment. Our results suggest that at the microeconomic level, the scope for such effects is very large indeed.

NOTES

1. The figures for short-term loss-makers have been calculated on the basis of 1985–87 only as there was a uniquely large set of stocks, loans, and creditors movements in 1984 in one firm which distorts all the percentage calculations.
2. Banks may of course write off past loans. The format of the database does not allow us to derive reliable estimates of this, but to the extent that it occurs, the soft budget constraint faced by enterprises will in the long term be magnified beyond that evidenced here.
3. Some potentially large welfare payments are also included in 'net profits from other businesses' but cannot be separated out from other flows to or from subsidiaries.
4. Note that the figures for firm's own resources in long-term loss-makers are adjusted for one firm accounting subsidy payments as retained profit. See note to Table 10.6.

11

A Complete Model of the Firms and Policy Simulations

1. Introduction

In previous chapters different aspects of firms' behaviour during the reform period have been analysed. In Chapter 4 a model of the employment and wage decisions of the firm was presented, in which the constraints of the wage bill imposed by the labour bureau were found to be significant. An important feature of that analysis was the relation of the bonus to the efficiency of the firm as measured indirectly by value added per worker. The policy mechanism behind this is that firms are permitted to retain some profits for the payment of bonuses.

In Chapter 5, the production and cost behaviour of the firm was explored within a production function framework. The major impact of the bonus/wage ratio on efficiency was identified. However, other policy variables, such as measures of firm autonomy in input and product markets, appeared to have no discernible effects.

In Chapter 6, the determinants of profits were analysed. In the absence of data on actual quantities and prices, the analysis focused on profits as the difference between total revenues and total costs, and on the overall profit margin over costs thus identified. The significance of profits as far as enterprises are concerned is that in the reform period firms have been allowed to retain a proportion of profits, and have been given the right to spend the retentions on bonuses, welfare investment, and physical investment. The details of the development of the profit-(income-)tax system, and the consequences for the retention of profits by the firm were explored in Chapter 3. The allocation of retained profits to different uses is in principle based on rules, but it is evident that there was some scope for adjusting the proportions, at least in the short term. The allocation to bonus was analysed in Chapter 4, as noted above. Retained profits were also an important component of the internal sources of funds available to the firms.

External and internal finance, and the expenditures on investment are the subjects of Chapters 7–9. Key findings are that the firms' investment behaviour was affected by the variables identified in neoclassical investment theory, and that firms' investment was generally finance-constrained throughout the reform period. The main policy variables are the level of retentions, the flow of investment grants and subsidies (which declined substantially in this period), the interest rate charged on bank loans, and controls on the quantity of funds available to the firm.

In this chapter, all the elements previously described and analysed are integrated into a single model of the firm. The structure of the model is given by the flow chart in Fig. 11.1. There are four major sections in the chart, corresponding to four areas where the firm has to take decisions: wages, bonus, and employment; investment and finance; production; and the generation of profits. What Fig. 11.1 makes clear is that these areas are behaviourally interdependent: analysing one without reference to the others (or presuming that decisions in other areas are 'given') will give rise to bias, particularly in the context of econometric modelling. Moreover, it is only in a full model that the impact of policy measures can be made clear. For example, a change in the rules on the taxation of profit will affect payment of bonus, and hence the quantity of labour employed and the efficiency with which production is undertaken; and it will affect the supply of internal funds, leading to a change in investment behaviour. These in turn will feed back to production and profits. To evaluate policy impacts, the econometric model is used to simulate the effects of changes in policy parameters. This method also permits an examination of policy variants, within the same model structure.

2. *The Equation System and Econometric Specification*

The complete equation system for the model of the firm is given in Table 11.1. It consists of nine behavioural equations and three identities. Detailed descriptions of the equations are given in previous chapters. So only a general description is required here.

The first four equations, relating to employment and wages, are taken from Chapter 4. In that chapter, we found that employment is positively related to the ratio of value added to the basic wage, negatively related to the bonus/wage ratio, and constrained by the wage-bill quota. The basic wage is largely determined outside the firm, and the wage bill is only partially adjusted to the particular

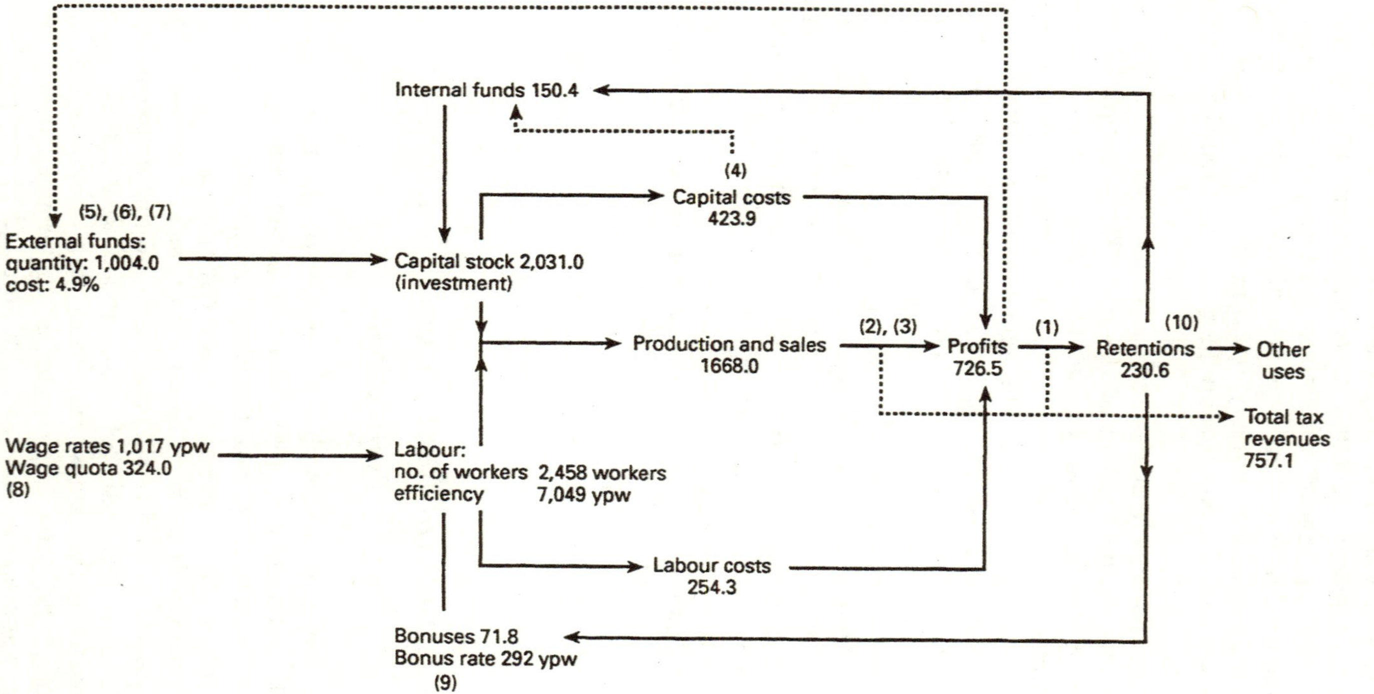

Policy Instruments: 1. Profit-retention rate; 2. Sales-tax rate; 3. Price; 4. The depreciation rate; 5. The interest rate; 6. State subsidies; 7. Credit control; 8. Wage-bill quota; 9. Ceiling on bonus rate; 10. Division of retentions

Note: units are 10,000 yuan except where indicated; ypw = yuan per worker.

FIG. 11.1. Flow chart of complete model of the firm (simulation sample mean values)

circumstances of the firm. The bonus, although constrained by the wage bill, is related to efficiency as indicated by output per worker. In the simultaneous system of this chapter, the bonus equation specifies retained profits per worker, in place of value added per worker, in order to capture the feedbacks from profits to bonus allowed by the economic reform programme. The lagged dependent value is included in the equations for bonus and basic wage to allow for lagged adjustment. The mean bonus in the locality and mean wage in the industry are also added to the bonus and wage equations to capture labour-

TABLE 11.1. Specification of equations and identities in the complete model of the firm

1. *Employment and wages*

Bonuses $$b_{it} = \theta_0 + \theta_1(rp_{it} - n_{it}) + \theta_2 y_{it} + \theta_3 b_{it-1} + \theta_4 \bar{b}_t + \theta_5 YR_{85} + \varepsilon_{bt}. \quad (11.1)$$

Basic wage $$w_{it} = \vartheta_0 + \vartheta_1(q_{it} - n_{it}) + \vartheta_2 w_{it-1} + \vartheta_3 \bar{w}_{jt} + \Sigma YR_t + \varepsilon_{wt}. \quad (11.2)$$

Employment $$n_{it} = \beta_0 + \beta_1(q_{it} - w_{it}) + \beta_2 y_{it} + \beta_3 \phi_{t-1} + \beta_t \Sigma YR_t + \beta_4 SC + \varepsilon_{nt}. \quad (11.3)$$

Wage bill $$y_{it} = \omega_0 + \omega_1(q_{it} - q_{it-1}) + \omega_2 n_{it-1} + \omega_3 \bar{\phi}_{t-1} + \omega_4(\phi_{it-1} - \bar{\phi}_{t-1}) + \omega_5 \bar{w}_{kt-1} + \omega_6(w_{it-1} - \bar{w}_{kt-1}) + \omega_t \Sigma YR_t + \varepsilon_{wbt}. \quad (11.4)$$

2. *Production*

Production $$q_{it} = \eta_0 + \eta_1(k_{it} + u_{it}) + \eta_2(n_{it} + u_{it}) + \eta_3(b_{it} - w_{it}) + \eta_4 q_{it-1} + \eta_j \Sigma IND_j + \varepsilon_{qt}. \quad (11.5)$$

3. *Capital and finance*

Capital stock $$k_{it} = \delta_0 + \delta_1 q_{it-1} + \delta_2 pk_{it} + \delta_3 \log(IR + DR)_{it} + \delta_4 \log(1 - T_{it}^{\pi}) + \delta_5 \log(F^I + F^S) + \delta_6 f^{\chi} + \delta_7 k_{it-1} + \delta_t \Sigma YR_t + \varepsilon_{kt}. \quad (11.6)$$

External funds $$F_{it}{}^{\chi} = \rho_0 + \rho_1 IR_{it} + \rho_2(K_{it} - K_{it-1}) + \rho_3 FP_{it} + \rho_4 F_{it}^S + \rho_5 F_{it-1}^{\chi} + \varepsilon_{\chi t}. \quad (11.7)$$

Internal funds $$F_{it}^I = \alpha_0 + \alpha_1(RP_{it} - B_{it}N_{it}) + \alpha_2 DP_{it} + \alpha_3 F_{it-1}^I + \alpha_t \Sigma_t YR + \varepsilon_{it}. \quad (11.8)$$

4. *Profit and retentions*

Retained profit $$RP_{it} = \mu_0 + \mu_1 FP_{it} + \mu_2(K_{it} - K_{it-1}) + \mu TX_{it-1} + \mu_4 RP_{it-1} + \mu_t \Sigma YR_t + \varepsilon_{rt}. \quad (11.9)$$

Interest-paid identity $$IP_{it} = IR_{it}(F_{it}^{\chi} + F_{it}^{0}). \quad (11.10)$$

Depreciation identity $$DP_{it} = 1.04\, K_{it}\, DR_{it}/(1 - DR_{it}). \quad (11.11)$$

Profit identity $$FP_{it} = Q_{it}(1 - T_{it}^{\tau}) - (IP_{it} + DP_{it} + REPF_{it} + OTHP_{it}) - W_{it}N_{it}. \quad (11.12)$$

Note: Lower-case symbol indicates variable in natural logs.

Notes to Table 11.1: (i indexes the firm)

- Q_{it} — Real value added during year t, which is defined as sales revenue net of material costs.
- N_{it} — Average number of workers concerned with production during the year.
- W_{it} — Real basic wage rate.
- B_{it} — Real bonus rate.
- Y_{it} — Real annual wage-bill of a firm.
- $\bar{B}_t$ — Average bonus rate in the locality of the firm in year t.
- $\bar{w}_t$ — Average basic wage rate in the locality of the firm in year t.
- $\bar{w}_{jt}$ — Average basic wage rate in a sector j in year t.
- ϕ_{it} — Ratio of bonus to basic wage in year t.
- $\bar{\phi}_t$ — Average ratio of bonus to basic wage in the locality of the firm.
- K_{it} — Real value of capital assets after depreciation.
- U_{it} — Utilization of factor inputs which is the annual ratio of actual working hours to regulated work hours.
- PK_{it} — Relative price index for capital goods, which is the ratio of price index of capital goods to price index of output.
- IR_{it} — Interest rate in year t: the total interest paid in year t divided by the total loans outstanding.
- DR_{it} — Depreciation rate in year t: annual depreciation divided by the book value of capital.
- T^{π}_{it} — The rate of tax on the profit of firm i in year t, calculated as the sum of income and adjustment taxes divided by total fulfilled profits.
- F^{I}_{it} — The total value of a firm's own sources of long-term finance deflated by the capital price index. This may consist of retained profit after bonus payment, retained depreciation and other sources.
- F^{χ}_{it} — The total value of a firm's external finance including both long-term and short-term finance, deflated by capital price index.
- F^{s}_{it} — The total value of a firm's state subsidies, deflated by capital price index.
- RP_{it} — Real retained profit in year t.
- I_{it} — Annual real value of total capital investment, covering replacement and net investment in construction, machinery, equipment, and tools that have an economic life in excess of 2 years and nominal value over 36 yuan. Welfare investment is included. I_{it} is deflated by the capital price index.
- TX_{it} — Total real value of income and adjustment taxes paid in year t.
- F^{O}_{it} — The total value of firms' other borrowings including special borrowings listed in balance sheet drawn up in year t, and is deflated by the price index of output.
- DP_{it} — Annual depreciation withdrawing from the revenue deflated by the output price index.
- T^{τ}_{it} — The rate of value added tax calculated as total tax payment divided by total revenue.
- $REPF_{it}$ — The total value of repairing funds in year t.
- $OTHP_{it}$ — Other charges and fixed payments from the revenue, deflated by the price index of output.
- idk_{it} — The price index of output at firm i level.
- idx_{it} — The price index of capital goods.
- YR_t — Year dummy.
- IND_j — Industry dummy.
- FP_{it} — Fulfilled profit after sales tax remittance.
- SC — Dummy for light industry (0) and heavy industry (1).

market effects. In the basic wage equation, and the employment equation, Cobb–Douglas technology is assumed, with an elasticity of output with respect to labour of 0.657 (based on previous estimation) imposed. The Cobb–Douglas form also gives rise to constraints on the values of the constants in these equations, which constraints are imposed in the estimation procedures.

The production equation builds on the empirical work reported in Chapter 5, in particular the use of the Cobb–Douglas form of the function. A number of new features should be noted. First, the dependent variable is output (measured by value added at constant prices) rather than output per worker. A potential multicolinearity problem is dealt with in the normal manner by dividing by lagged employment, which generates an additional term among the independent variables (n_{it-1}). Second, the inputs of capital and labour are adjusted for capacity utilization, an effect which in the previous work was captured by year dummies. Third, lagged output is included to improve the fit of the equation for prediction and simulation purposes. The natural interpretation of the coefficient is that it equals $(1 - \lambda)$, where λ is the partial adjustment coefficient. However, the fitted coefficient value ($\lambda = 0.25$) suggests an implausibly slow adjustment, even given the impediments to adjustment arising from the residual planning system, and firm inertia.

The capital stock equation (11.6), the external funds equation (11.7), and the internal funds equation (11.8) are essentially those developed in Chapters 7, 8, 9. Multicollinearity is also a problem in equation (11.6), so once again the variables have been divided by employment in the previous period. In principle, the inclusion of all three equations should leave the system overdetermined, via the sources and uses-of-funds identity. However, some retained profits may be directed to other (current) uses within the firm, and there may be other sources not accounted for. So all three equations are retained for estimation purposes. Note that the internal funds equation includes two sources of funds: retained profits net of bonus payments, and depreciation. The lagged dependent variable picks up the accounting process by which those sources are passed through reserve accounts. The same feature appears in the external funds equation. For simultaneous estimation it was necessary in the internal fund equation to fix the coefficient on the lagged dependent variables at a level (0.8) previously established by single-equation estimation.

The final set of equations includes one behavioural equation (for retained profits) and three identities (for interest payments, depreciation, and gross profits). The profit-retention equation is that presented in Chapter 3, based on bargaining between the enterprise and the authorities, and only imperfectly related to the rules of the tax- and profit-retention system. It is estimated in levels rather than as a ratio of current fulfilled profit, as in Chapter 3. The interest identity calculates the payment by multiplying external borrowings for investment, and for all other uses, by the interest rate applied in a given year. Depreciation is calculated in Chinese accounts on the book value of assets.[1]

The profit identity is given by subtracting wage costs (not bonus), interest, depreciation, and some other categories of cost from the post-tax values of value-added sales. This formula conforms to that used to calculate profit in Chinese accounts with the exception of the deduction of selling expenses, which is omitted from the identity. The validity of the identity was examined by comparing the values it generates with those reported in the accounts, and it was found to predict the actual values very closely in the majority of firms.

3. Results

The model was estimated using data for the period 1983–87. After deleting firms which failed the profit identity test described in the previous section, and those which were outliers in the data which might have affected the stability of the estimates, about 200 firms had data which were consistent and continuous in this period. The outliers were identified by running the equations as a simultaneous system, and then inspecting the residuals. The model was estimated by OLS, 2SLS, and 3SLS, and the full results are presented in Table 11.2. The 3SLS method minimizes the covariance matrix across the system allowing for the possibility that shocks are correlated across the equations. A potential drawback of 3SLS is that major data errors in one part of the system can generate substantial distortions in the fitted coefficients. In practice, comparisons of 2SLS and 3SLS results suggest that there are no problems of this kind.

Before turning to simulation, the structure of relationships within the model can be explored by evaluating quantitative partial impacts of changes at the sample means. While these impacts can give an indication of the strength of relationships between the different elements of the model, they cannot take into account the full impact within the model once all feedbacks have occurred. This should be borne in mind when the following description of the system is considered.

TABLE 11.2. Estimation of the complete model

	OLS	2SLS	3SLS	Original estimations (single equations)
Employment and wages				
(1) *Bonus equation*				
Intercept	−0.492 (−2.5)	−0.613 (−2.9)	−0.846 (−4.1)	0.175 (0.91)
$rp_t - n_t$	0.122 (7.6)	0.142 (5.6)	0.132 (5.5)	0.157 (5.7)[a]
y_t	1.173 (10.9)	0.683 (2.6)	0.694 (2.8)	0.646 (9.8)
b_{t-1}	0.639 (27.1)	0.617 (23.1)	0.659 (25.2)	0.467 (19.6)
$\bar{b}_t$	0.156 (2.8)	0.113 (1.9)	0.008 (0.1)	0.166 (3.6)
YR85	−0.037 (−1.0)	−0.086 (−2.0)	−0.110 (−2.6)	−0.116 (−3.5)
$\bar{R}^2$	0.62	0.61	0.60	0.63
				$N = 847$
(2) *Basic wage equation*				
Intercept ⟨1⟩	−0.037	−0.025	−0.021	−0.038 (−6.3)
$(q_t - n_t)$	0.088 (6.2)	0.059 (4.0)	0.050 (3.9)	0.079 (6.3)
w_{t-1}	0.703 (27.3)	0.730 (28.1)	0.750 (31.8)	0.653 (27.1)
$\bar{w}_{jt}$	0.244 (9.6)	0.233 (9.1)	0.211 (9.0)	0.300 (17.0)
YR85	−0.019 (−1.1)	−0.015 (−0.8)	−0.010 (−0.5)	0.014 (0.7)
YR86	0.029 (1.6)	0.032 (1.7)	0.039 (2.2)	0.052 (2.8)
YR87	−0.019 (−1.0)	−0.017 (−0.9)	−0.007 (−0.4)	0.009 (0.3)
$\bar{R}^2$	0.56	0.55	0.55	0.54
				$N = 840$

TABLE 11.2 (*cont.*)

	OLS	2SLS	3SLS	Original estimations (single equations)
(3) *Employment equation*				
Intercept ⟨2⟩	−0.122	−0.118	−0.097	
$(q_t - w_t)$	0.291 (27.2)	0.281 (24.5)	0.230 (27.6)	0.211 (18.3)
y_t	0.708 (46.8)	0.727 (44.9)	0.804 (55.0)	0.818 (51.2)
ϕ_{t-1}	−0.243 (−27.9)	−0.249 (−27.7)	−0.260 (−30.9)	−0.298 (−33.3)
YR85	0.086 (4.3)	0.087 (4.4)	0.076 (4.0)	0.102 (4.4)
YR86	0.074 (3.6)	0.064 (3.1)	0.039 (2.1)	0.059 (2.6)
YR87	0.086 (4.1)	0.076 (3.6)	0.045 (2.4)	0.068 (2.9)
SC	0.055 (3.7)	0.047 (3.2)	0.014 (1.3)	0.081 (2.3)
R^2	0.93	0.93	0.92	0.93
				$N = 839$
(4) *Wage-bill equation*				
Intercept	−1.278 (−7.1)	−1.294 (−7.2)	−1.021 (−7.9)	−0.879 (−7.2)
$(q_t - q_{t-1})$	0.205 (7.5)	0.160 (4.9)	0.240 (11.0)	0.164 (5.9)
$\underline{n}_{t-1}$	1.029 (143.1)	1.029 (143.5)	1.006 (167.0)	1.019 (136)
$\bar{\phi}_{t-1}$	0.943 (7.9)	0.926 (7.7)	0.716 (8.1)	1.395 (8.4)
$(\phi_{t-1} - \bar{\phi}_{t-1})$	0.629 (12.8)	0.625 (12.7)	0.741 (18.5)	0.589 (5.6)
$\bar{w}_{t-1}$	0.516 (8.1)	0.506 (7.9)	0.531 (11.7)	0.668 (17.3)
$(w_{t-1} - \bar{w}_{t-1})$	0.600 (28.0)	0.600 (27.90)	0.561 (32.2)	0.541 (23.6)
YR85	−0.069 (−3.5)	−0.065 (−3.6)	−0.064 (−3.8)	−0.009 (−0.5)
YR86	0.038 (1.7)	0.041 (1.8)	0.040 (2.1)	0.072 (3.9)
YR87	−0.004 (−0.2)	−0.002 (−0.1)	0.004 (0.2)	0.017 (0.9)
R^2	0.96	0.96	0.96	0.96
				$N = 837$

Production					
(5) *Production equation*					
Intercept	η_0	0.189 (2.4)	0.271 (3.2)	0.593 (8.2)	−0.507
$(k_t + u_t)$	η_1 $\boxed{\alpha}$	0.070 (5.2) [0.280]	0.056 (3.9) [0.224]	0.060 (2.0) [0.240]	0.368
$(n_t + u_t)$ ⟨3⟩	η_2 $\boxed{\beta}$	0.170 [0.680]	0.184 [0.736]	0.149 [0.596]	0.702
ϕ_t	η_3 $\boxed{\theta}$	0.069 (5.8) [0.276]	0.109 (5.3) [0.436]	0.187 (11.2) [0.748]	0.222[b]
q_{t-1} ⟨4⟩	η_4 [λ]	0.750 [0.250]	0.750 [0.250]	0.750 [0.250]	—
n_{t-1} ⟨5⟩	η_5	0.060 (3.9)	0.109 (5.3)	0.146 (7.7)	—
IND1		−0.194 (−4.3)	−0.171 (−3.7)	−0.129 (−3.4)	−0.532
IND2		−0.070 (−2.6)	−0.071 (−2.6)	−0.082 (−3.5)	0.079
IND3		−0.060 (−2.3)	−0.052 (−2.0)	−0.042 (−1.9)	0.262
IND4		−0.152 (−5.7)	−0.152 (−5.6)	−0.108 (−4.8)	−0.2279
IND5		−0.005 (−0.1)	−0.009 (−0.2)	−0.044 (−1.1)	0.1779
IND6		−0.027 (−1.1)	−0.028 (−1.2)	−0.051 (−2.6)	0.437
IND7		−0.095 (−4.1)	−0.102 (−4.3)	−0.075 (−3.7)	0.059
YR5		0.058 (3.6)	0.045 (3.8)	0.062 (3.8)	(*IND8*) 0.115
$\bar{R}^2$		0.91	0.91	0.89	0.80
					$N = 464$
Capital and finances					
(6) *Capital stock equation*					
Intercept	δ_0	0.938 (14.6)	0.961 (14.7)	0.927 (14.3)	
q_{t-1}	δ_1 $\boxed{\delta_1}$	0.159 (16.5) [0.642]	0.158 (13.9) [0.638]	0.157 (14.4) [0.654]	
pk_t	δ_2 $\boxed{\delta_2}$	−0.159 (−4.7) [0.663]	−0.146 (−4.2) [0.608]	−0.183 (−5.4) [−0.762]	
$(IR + DR)_t$	δ_3 $\boxed{\delta_3}$	−0.253 (−11.1) [−0.979]	−0.229 (−10.7) [−0.954]	−0.224 (−10.5) [−0.933]	
$\log(1 - T^{\pi}_{t-1})$	δ_4 $\boxed{\delta_4}$	0.029 (3.2) [0.121]	0.027 (2.9) [0.112]	0.028 (2.8) [0.117]	
$\log(F^I + F^S)_t$	δ_5 $\boxed{\delta_5}$	0.011 (3.9) [0.050]	0.020 (4.7) [0.083]	0.020 (4.8) [0.088]	
f^{χ}_t	δ_6 $\boxed{\delta}$	0.045 (6.0) [0.188]	0.034 (3.6) [0.141]	0.034 (3.5) [0.141]	
k_{t-1} ⟨6⟩	δ_7 [λ]	0.760 [0.240]	0.760 [0.240]	0.760 [0.240]	
n_{t-1} ⟨7⟩	δ_8	−0.789	−0.793	−0.789	
YR85		0.069 (4.0)	0.069 (3.9)	0.070 (4.1)	
YR86		0.033 (1.9)	0.034 (1.9)	0.037 (2.1)	
YR87		0.104 (5.6)	0.107 (5.7)	0.107 (5.7)	
$\bar{R}^2$		0.94	0.94	0.94	

TABLE 11.2 (*cont.*)

		OLS	2SLS	3SLS	Original estimations (single equations)
(7) *External funds equation*					
Intercept		3.821 (2.9)	3.698 (2.8)	3.843 (2.9)	
IR_t	[ρ_1]	−0.249 (−2.0) [−1.960]	−0.281 (−2.0) [−2.322]	−0.231 (−1.7) [−1.925]	
$(K_t - K_{t-1})$	[ρ_2]	0.387 (8.5) [3.047]	0.321 (2.9) [2.653]	0.343 (3.2) [2.858]	
FP_t	[ρ_3]	0.130 (4.5) [1.024]	0.141 (4.8) [1.165]	0.137 (4.7) [1.142]	
F^x_{t-1}	[λ^x]	0.873 (35.2) [0.127]	0.879 (31.5) [0.121]	0.880 (32.0) [0.120]	
F^s_t		−0.344 (−2.7) [−2.708]	−0.303 (−2.1) [−2.504]	−0.308 (−2.3) [−2.567]	
YR85		0.139 (0.8)	0.258 (0.3)	0.271 (0.3)	
YR86		0.659 (0.9)	0.744 (1.0)	0.685 (0.9)	
YR87		−1.191 (−1.5)	−0.046 (−1.3)	−1.025 (−1.3)	
$\bar{R}^2$		0.73	0.73	0.73	
(8) *Internal funds equation*					
Intercept		0.275 (0.9)	0.438 (1.0)	0.482 (1.3)	
$(RP - B{\cdot}N)_t$	[α_1]	0.105 (3.8) [0.648]	0.102 (2.8) [0.650]	0.076 (2.1) [0.494]	
DP_t	[α_2]	0.130 (2.2) [0.802]	0.091 (1.4) [0.580]	0.094 (1.4) [0.610]	
F^I_{t-1}	[λ^I]	0.838 (29.7) [0.162]	0.843 (29.4) [0.157]	0.84 (29.8) [0.154]	
YR85		0.015 (0.1)	0.017 (0.1)	0.049 (0.2)	
YR86		−0.067 (−0.3)	−0.063 (−0.3)	−0.039 (−0.2)	
YR87		0.347 (1.5)	0.358 (1.5)	0.408 (1.8)	
$\bar{R}^2$		0.60	0.60	0.60	

(9) *Retained profit equation*						
Intercept		0.015 (2.1)	0.016 (2.2)	0.016 (2.1)		0.63 (17.2)
FP_t	[γ_1]	0.123 (12.7) [0.392]	0.121 (13.4) [0.378]	0.116 (11.9) [0.372]		—
$(K_t - K_{t-1})$	[γ_3]	−0.006 (−0.6) [0.019]	0.019 (1.0) [0.059]	0.019 (1.1) [0.061]		−0.0061 (−1.9)
TX_{t-1}	[γ_4]	−0.028 (−3.3) [−0.089]	−0.028 (−3.3) [−0.088]	−0.027 (−3.2) [−0.087]		0.115 (−4.4)
RP_{t-1}	[γ^1]	0.686 (22.1) [0.314]	0.680 (21.6) [0.320]	0.688 (22.1) [0.312]		—
YR85		0.020 (4.6)	0.010 (4.2)	0.019 (4.2)		−0.10
YR86		0.002 (0.4)	0.001 (0.3)	0.001 (0.2)	[*YR84*]	−0.05
YR87		0.007 (1.5)	0.005 (1.1)	0.006 (1.1)	[*YR85*]	−0.007
$\bar{R}^2$		0.69	0.69	0.68	[*YR86*]	
No. of pooled observations		796	796	796	R^2 0.27	$N = 525$

Notes:

[a] The variable for this coefficient is output.

[b] Log [Bonus/(Bonus + Basic wages)], see Table 5.2.

Numbers in ( ) brackets are t-test values.

Numbers in [ ] brackets are the implied Cobb–Douglas elasticities in the production-function equation (11.5), and the capital-stock equation (11.6), and the long-run retention elasticities in the retained-profit equation (11.9).

⟨1⟩ Imposed constraint $\vartheta_0 = \vartheta_1 \log(\bar{\beta})$, where $\bar{\beta}$ is the labour elasticity (0.657) based on previous estimations of the production function.

⟨2⟩ Imposed constraint $\beta_0 = \beta_1 \log(\bar{\beta})$, where $\bar{\beta}$ is the labour elasticity (0.657) based on previous production function estimates.

⟨3⟩ Calculated according to the formula $1 - \eta_1 - \eta_2 - \eta_3 - \eta_4$.

⟨4⟩ Coefficient is $(1 - \lambda)$, where λ is the lagged adjustment coefficient for output.

⟨5⟩ The n_{t-1} term arises from the adjustment of the equation for multicolinearity.

⟨6⟩ Coefficient is $(1 - \lambda)$ where λ is the lagged adjustment coefficient for capital stock.

⟨7⟩ The n_{it} term arises from the adjustment of the equation for multicolinearity.

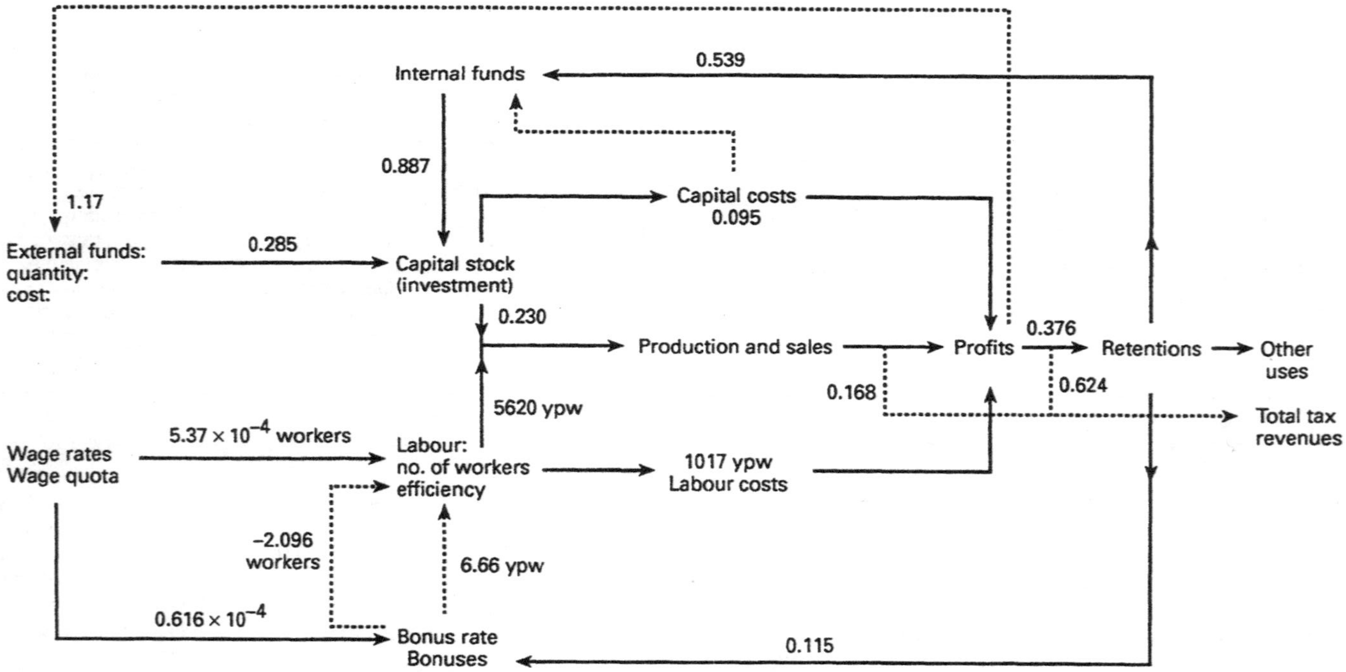

Note: Coefficients give change in dependent variable for a one-yuan change in the originating variable, e.g. one additional yuan of retentions gives 0.115 additional yuan to bonuses, *ceteris paribus*.

Units are yuan values unless otherwise noted: ypw = yuan per worker.

FIG. 11.2. Partial equilibrium impacts (at simulation sample means)

The estimated impacts based on the 2SLS estimates are given in Fig. 11.2. The coefficients generally indicate the impact of a one yuan change in a given variable on the other variables to which it is linked by arrows. (In Fig. 11.1, the sample mean values for each of the variables are given.)

Beginning with the retained-profits equation (11.9), we note that the short-run coefficient on profits (FP_t) is 0.12 and the implied long-run coefficient is 0.38. The profits-tax rate at the end of the period was 55%, and firms had to pay some other profit-related local taxes or adjustment taxes, so the long-run coefficient is consistent with the tax 'rules'. These retained profits are allocated by the firm to bonus payments, physical investment, and welfare investment.

Looking first at the bonus equation (11.1), the short-run elasticity response of bonus rate to retained profits per worker is 0.142 (in the 3SLS version), and the long-run coefficient (taking into account adjustment captured by the lagged bonus variable) is 0.44. At the sample means, this implies that an additional yuan of retained profit will increase the bonus fund by 0.115 yuan. Equations (11.1) and (11.9) together imply that an additional 100 yuan of profit generates an additional 4.4 yuan of bonus payments.

The partial nature of this impact is emphasized if it is noted that it does not consider the constraint of the wage quota on additional bonus payments, and the adjustment of the productive labour force by the firm in response to higher labour costs. An addition of 10,000 yuan to the wage-bill quota gives increased employment of 5.37 workers. The nature of the causation here is not clear. One possibility is that the quota is a constraint on the firm, and that relaxing the constraint permits the firm to increase its labour force to the desired level. The alternative explanation is that an increase in quota is equivalent to requiring the firm to take on more workers. The same increases in the wage bill also enables the firm to pay higher bonuses at the rate of 0.616 yuan per worker (or 1,514 additional yuan in bonuses across an average labour force of 2,458 workers). The additional 5.37 workers are paid 7,034 yuan in total (293 yuan per worker in bonus and 1,017 yuan per worker in basic wages), giving a total additional expenditure on wages and bonus of about 8,600 yuan from the additional wage-bill injection of 10,000 yuan. An increase in the bonus rate also has a slight effect on the employment of productive workers: an increase of one yuan per worker (2,458 yuan in total) leads to a reduction in the production work-force of 2.1 workers (a saving of 2,751 yuan of expenditure on wages), possibly due to the wage-bill constraint.

An increase in the bonus rate apparently has a major effect on workers' efficiency. At the sample mean, a one yuan increase in the bonus rate generates additional output worth 6.66 yuan per worker. This is a very powerful effect, and illustrates the contention of Chapter 5 that bonus was a major force for improving efficiency in the reform period.

The route from profits to investment runs directly via retentions and internal funds, and indirectly via the effect on the supply of external funds. The internal funds equation (11.8) has a short-run coefficient on retained profits, after bonus payments, of about 0.10, and the implied long-run coefficient is 0.61. The expectation is that the long-run coefficient should be close to unity, since retained profits not allocated to bonuses should all be added to internal funds. The coefficient therefore implies considerable 'leakages' to other uses. Taking equations (11.1), (11.9), and (11.8) together, the implication is that one yuan of additional profit generates about 0.203 yuan of additional internal funds for investment. A similar problem of 'leakages' is also implied by the coefficient on depreciation in the internal-funds equation (11.8): the short-run coefficient is 0.091, the long-run coefficient is 0.58. A much stronger feedback from profits occurs in the equation for external funds (11.7). Profits (FP_t) are included as a shift variable in the supply-of-funds equation: the short-run coefficient is 0.14 and the long-run coefficient about 1.17 implying that one yuan of additional profit enables the firm to raise 1.17 yuan of additional finance.

The effect of internal and external finance on the capital stock is captured in equation (11.6). The interpretation of this equation is given in Chapter 8. The important point to note is that the flow of funds is modelled as having its impact via the cost of capital, as a constraint on capital stock. The coefficients on internal and external funds suggest that both are constraints on the demand for capital stock, with external funds being a stronger constraint. The long-run elasticity of capital stock with respect to external funds is 0.14, and with respect to internal funds, 0.08.

An additional yuan of internal finance generates an additional 0.887 yuan of capital stock, the remaining 0.113 presumably being dissipated without adding to real assets. External funds include both long-term and short-term finance: one additional yuan of external funds generates 0.285 yuan of additional real assets. In 1987, for example, about 37% of the firms' borrowing was for long-term finance: if we assume an investment 'efficiency' of 0.887, the expectation is that one yuan of additional external funds in that year would have generated 0.328

additional assets, which is quite close to the proportion predicted by the equation.

Additions to the capital stock and to the labour force generate additions to output, costs, and profit via the value-added production function (11.5) and the profit identity (11.12). An additional yuan of real assets raises output by 0.230 yuan and capital costs by 0.095 yuan implying an incremental profit rate of about 13.5%. An additional worker, with the bonus incentive, and given the capital stock, raises output by 5,620 yuan, compared to an average productivity of 7,049 yuan. The direct cost to the firm of an additional worker is 1,017 yuan per worker in wages and bonus. There will, of course, be additional housing and welfare costs. Even so, it is likely that the returns to additional workers exceed the employment costs by a large margin.

4. *Policy simulations*

A second way of looking at the results is to explore the policy variables in the system. In the set of equations relating to employment and wages, the key policy variables are the retention ratio (since bonuses are paid from retained profits), the level of bonus permitted to be paid by the firm, the basic wage rate (which is largely fixed outside the firm), and the wage bill. The coefficient on retained profit per worker in the bonus-rate equation (11.1) has a long-run value of about 0.37. This suggests that the firms are up against a constraint on bonus payments from retentions, and that relaxation of the policy rule would lead to higher payments. Equations (11.1) and (11.3) suggest that the wage-bill quota is a constraint on both bonus payments and employment. The elasticity of the bonus rate with respect to the wage bill is about 0.63, and the elasticity of employment is about 0.71. Note that there is an additional negative feedback from a higher bonus: employment falls as the bonus increases, given that the wage-bill quota is a constraint.

In the set of equations relating to capital stock and finance (equations (11.6)–(11.9)) a number of potential policy variables can be identified. In equation (11.6), the price of capital goods, the interest rate on loans, the profit-tax rate, and the level of investment subsidies are all policy instruments with significant impacts on the demand for capital stock. The interest rate appears as a significant variable in the external-funds equation (11.7). Another policy variable in this part of the equation system is the retention ratio in (11.9): a lower profit-tax rate would generate a higher supply of internal funds for both bonus payments and for investment.

TABLE 11.3(*a*). Characteristics of the simulation sample: Industrial distribution

	Simulation sample		Model sample	
Industrial code	No. of observations	% share	No. of observations	% share
1	—	—	24	3.0
2	48	12.9	90	11.2
3	48	12.9	106	13.2
4	32	8.6	103	12.8
5	16	4.3	20	2.5
6	56	15.1	145	18.1
7	88	23.7	147	18.3
8	84	22.6	168	20.9
TOTAL	372	100%	803	100%

TABLE 11.3(*b*). Characteristics of the simulation sample: Firm characteristics (sample averages)

	Simulation sample	Model sample
Fixed capital (10 000 yuan)	2 031	1 966
Workers (number)	2 458	2 034
Output (10 000 yuan)	1 668	1 516
Bonus rate (yuan per worker)	301	292
Wage bill (10 000 yuan)	324	278

Alternatively the authorities can affect the supply of funds directly by changing the level of investment subsidies paid.

The sample used for the simulation exercises is ninety-three firms, slightly less than half the complete sample used for estimation. The characteristics and industrial distribution of the simulation sample are given in Table 11.3. The firms in the simulation sample are slightly larger on average than those in the estimation sample, but otherwise there is little difference. The main criterion for choosing the simulation sample was that the firms should have complete data for the period 1983–87. But the sample had to be further narrowed to exclude firms that generated instability in the dynamic simulation, or caused the simulation to fail (e.g. by generating negative values for a variable that is entered in log form in one part of the system, or by endogenous variables violating some other constraint within the system).

The ability of the model to predict the values of endogenous variables is an important test of the degree to which it fits the data. The equation system may be written in matrix form as:

$$\mathbf{Y} = \mathbf{A} + \mathbf{BX} + \mathbf{CY} + \mathbf{DY}_{-1}$$

where $\mathbf{Y}$ is the vector of endogenous variables, $\mathbf{X}$ is the vector of exogenous variables, and $\mathbf{Y}_{-1}$ are the lagged values of the endogenous variables. **A**, **B**, **C**, **D** are coefficient vectors. The solution to the system is given by:

$$\mathbf{Y} = [1 - \mathbf{C}]^{-1}\mathbf{A} + [1 - \mathbf{C}]^{-1}\mathbf{BX} + [1 - \mathbf{C}]^{-1}\mathbf{DY}_{-1}.$$

This system is solved for each year for each firm, using the actual values of the lagged endogenous variables for 1984, and predicted values for subsequent years. The results are given in Table 11.4 for each year 1984–87. These show that the system predicts well, though its precision decreases over time (as shown by the correlation between actual and predicted values). We conclude that the model is sufficiently accurate to be used for simulation of policy changes.

TABLE 11.4. Actual and predicted values of endogenous variables (93-firm sample used for simulation)

		1984	1985	1986	1987
No. of firms		93	93	93	93
Output	Predicted	1316.0	1454.0	1548.0	1668.0
	Actual	1368.0	1494.0	1615.0	1696.0
	Margin of error	−52.1	−40.0	−66.8	−27.8
	MABS	164.48	250.2	287.3	374.0
	R^2	0.94	0.90	0.88	0.85
Workers	Predicted	2086.0	2177.0	2341.0	2458.0
	Actual	2109.0	2146.0	2202.0	2264.0
	Margin of error	−23.26	31.0	139.0	194.0
	MABS	242.37	370.2	435.8	497.0
	R^2	0.95	0.88	0.84	0.82
Capital	Predicted	1413.0	1590.0	1749.0	2031.0
	Actual	1404.0	1587.0	1759.0	1953.0
	Margin of error	9.63	3.0	−10.0	78.0
	MABS	141.87	220.9	317.3	395.0
	R^2	0.97	0.95	0.91	0.85
Wage-bill	Predicted	228.0	237.7	283.5	323.9
	Actual	230.3	251.3	287.1	312.4
	Margin of error	−2.3	−13.5	−3.6	11.6
	MABS	28.20	49.4	72.3	86.6
	R^2	0.95	0.88	0.81	0.75
Wage rate	Predicted	775.0	849.0	961.0	1017.0
	Actual	786.0	874.0	995.0	1056.0
	Margin of error	11.3	24.4	−34.2	−38.6
	MABS	102.0	176.0	165.0	103.0
	R^2	0.33	0.12	0.22	0.12

TABLE 11.4 (*cont.*)

		1984	1985	1986	1987
Bonus rate	Predicted	176.0	190.0	249.0	292.0
	Actual	196.0	219.0	262.0	316.0
	Margin of error	−20.3	−29.1	−12.5	−23.4
	MABS	63.2	75.5	90.1	103.0
	R^2	0.27	0.03	0.06	0.06
Value added per worker	Predicted	6414.0	6820.0	6822.0	7049.0
	Actual	6825.0	7281.0	7497.0	7706.0
	Margin of error	−411.0	−462.0	−675.0	−657.0
	MABS	1212.0	1706.0	1946.0	2108.0
	R^2	0.69	0.43	0.26	0.23
Fufilled profit	Predicted	615.34	619.8	659.2	726.5
	Actual	600.98	600.5	669.1	729.4
	Margin of error	14.36	19.2	−9.8	−3.0
	MABS	124.77	173.9	214.7	271.0
	R^2	0.84	0.75	0.73	0.64
Internal funds	Predicted	87.19	103.5	116.6	150.4
	Actual	90.71	100.0	107.4	142.1
	Margin of error	−3.51	3.5	9.2	8.4
	MABS	52.30	59.2	65.3	94.1
	R^2	0.42	0.48	0.43	0.39
External funds	Predicted	627.0	772.4	942.1	1004.0
	Actual	631.9	776.8	943.9	986.9
	Margin of error	−4.9	−4.4	−1.7	17.4
	MABS	179.8	290.2	410.9	435.9
	R^2	0.80	0.67	0.58	0.49
Retained profit	Predicted	122.8	186.6	215.3	230.6
	Actual	116.6	177.4	204.7	222.9
	Margin of error	6.2	9.1	10.6	7.6
	MABS	49.7	87.4	96.4	94.5
	R^2	0.54	0.37	0.47	0.59
Interest paid	Predicted	41.5	52.5	65.7	80.3
	Actual	41.0	53.9	69.5	85.1
	Margin of error	0.5	−1.4	−3.7	−4.8
	MABS	9.4	15.6	22.8	25.6
	R^2	0.86	0.80	0.74	0.78
Depreciation	Predicted	75.8	93.0	109.9	137.3
	Actual	94.0	106.1	115.7	123.1
	Margin of error	−18.0	−13.1	−5.8	14.2
	MABS	19.8	17.9	19.8	26.8
	R^2	0.81	0.86	0.88	0.87
Tax revenues	Predicted	775.1	756.9	744.4	757.1
	Actual	782.2	758.1	784.0	777.4
	Margin of error	−7.0	−1.2	−39.4	−20.3
	MABS	158.2	206.8	223.6	281.3
	R^2	0.86	0.80	0.77	0.68

TABLE 11.5. Simulating effects of adjustment of the retention rate and wage-bill

	Labour and wage-bill endogenous			Labour exogenous		Wage-bill exogenous		
	Initial	Retentions alone	Retentions + wage-bill	Initial	Adjustment	Initial	Retentions + wage-bill	Wage-bill alone
Control variables								
Retention rate	37%	39.36% (+4.75%)	39.32% (+4.58%)	37.6% (0.0)	39.39% (+4.75%)	37.6%	39.39% (+4.75%)	37.6% (+0.0)
Wage-bill	324.0	—	325.0 (+0.3)	322.7	325.9 (+1%)	324.0	334.0 (+10.0)	334.0 (+10.0)
Labour force	2458.0	—	—	2458	2458	—	—	—
Endogenous elements								
No. of workers	2458.0	2455.0 (−3.0)	2472.5 (14.5)	—	—	2432.3	2487.5 (55.2)	2493.0 (60.7)
Wage-bill	324.0	324.35 (0.35)	—	322.7	—	—	—	—
Wage rate*	1017.1 (0.1)	1017.1 (0.1)	1016.7 (−0.3)	1013.9	1014.1 (0.2)	1016.1	1014.0 (−2.0)	1014.0 (−2.1)
Output/worker*	7049.0	7070.2 (21.2)	7041.0 (−8.0)	6928.7	6948.3 (19.6)	7096.5	6948.2 (−148.3)	6933.0 (−163.5)
Output	1668.0	1670.9 (2.9)	1676.1 (8.1)	1647.5	1652.1 (4.6)	1645.7	1667.5 (21.8)	1667.0 (21.3)
Capital	2031.0	2032.6 (1.6)	2034.0 (3.0)	2024.9	2027.5 (2.6)	2018.9	2026.9 (8.0)	2026.4 (7.5)
Internal funds	150.4	152.7 (2.3)	152.7 (2.3)	150.8	152.7 (2.1)	150.2	153.1 (2.9)	151.1 (0.9)
External funds	1004.0	1005.6 (1.6)	1007.1 (3.1)	1000.9	1002.8 (1.9)	996.5	1004.4 (7.9)	1004.7 (8.2)
Fulfilled π	726.5	729.0 (2.5)	731.5 (5.0)	720.0	723.7 (3.7)	714.4	726.6 (12.2)	725.7 (11.3)
Retained π	230.6	240.6 (10.0)	240.8 (10.2)	229.4	239.6 (10.2)	228.4	240.6 (12.2)	231.0 (2.6)
Net π	654.7	654.9 (0.2)	656.8 (2.1)	648.0	650.7 (2.7)	642.5	651.9 (9.4)	651.9 (9.4)
Bonus rate*	292.0	296.0 (4.0)	296.3 (4.3)	294.0	299.0 (5.0)	293.3	300.0 (6.7)	295.0 (1.7)
Capital costs	423.9	424.1 (0.2)	424.3 (0.4)	423.5	423.8 (0.3)	423.7	424.7 (1.0)	424.7 (1.0)
Labour costs	254.3	254.0 (−0.3)	255.8 (1.5)	253.1	253.2 (0.1)	252.2	257.5 (5.3)	258.1 (5.9)
Tax revenues	757.1	750.1 (−7.0)	753.4 (−3.7)	739.2	733.4 (−5.8)	738.6	742.6 (4.0)	751.2 (12.6)
No. of firms	93	93	93	93	93	93	93	93

Notes: Figures in brackets show the difference between values in the initial column and in the corresponding column.
* = yuan per worker, otherwise 10,000 yuan.
Making the labour force exogenous required a re-estimation of the system with that constraint: hence the slight variation in initial numbers.

In Table 11.5, policy simulations relating to retentions and the wage bill are tabulated and the results are presented in Figs. 11.3 to 11.6. These simulations give the long-run average responses of the firms to a particular policy change, after all the feedbacks in the system have been accounted for and after lagged adjustment has been completed. The policy changes to be illustrated are well within the variance of experience of the firms in the sample, and one can be confident that the effects identified are of the right order of magnitude, as well as having appropriate signs.

The simulations in Figs. 11.3, 11.4, and 11.5 focus on the effect on bonus rates, employment, and efficiency of an increase in retentions brought about by a slight adjustment in the profit-retention rates (i.e. lower taxes). In Fig. 11.3 the main effects are an increase in the bonus rate by 4 yuan per worker, and an increase in efficiency of 21.2 yuan per worker. But higher bonuses are paid at the expense of employment of productive workers, given the wage-bill quota constraint. In Fig. 11.4, this constraint is relaxed by adjusting the quota upwards in line with the bonus. This permits an increase in production workers, with a correspondingly greater increase in sales and profits but a decline in productivity. In Fig. 11.5, the wage-bill quota is again increased in line with retained profits, but the impact on employment is removed by holding the labour force constant. The objective is to isolate the 'pure' effect of increased retentions on bonus and output. In this simulation, the retention rate is increased by 1.8 percentage points (to increase the average retention by 100,000 yuan), and the wage quota is increased by 1% (32,000 yuan). The bonus is increased by 5 yuan per worker, labour efficiency increases by 19.6 yuan per worker, and there is an entirely beneficial effect on output. The total tax revenues of the authorities fall (by 58,000 yuan).

In Fig. 11.6 attention switches to the role of the wage quota. An increase in the wage quota generates a sharp increase in employment, with a fall in output per worker. Workers are paid more or less the same as before, but now more of them are employed. It is evident that this is a profitable move for the firm: profits increase because the cost of employing workers at the margin is so much lower than the value of additional output they generate, despite the decline in labour productivity which results. The authorities benefit from additional tax revenues.

Figures 11.7 and 11.8 (Table 11.6) sharpen the focus on the effects of the bonus rate by considering increases/decreases of 100 yuan from the average of 292 yuan per worker p.a. Once again two effects dominate the results. One is the impact on efficiency, and the other is

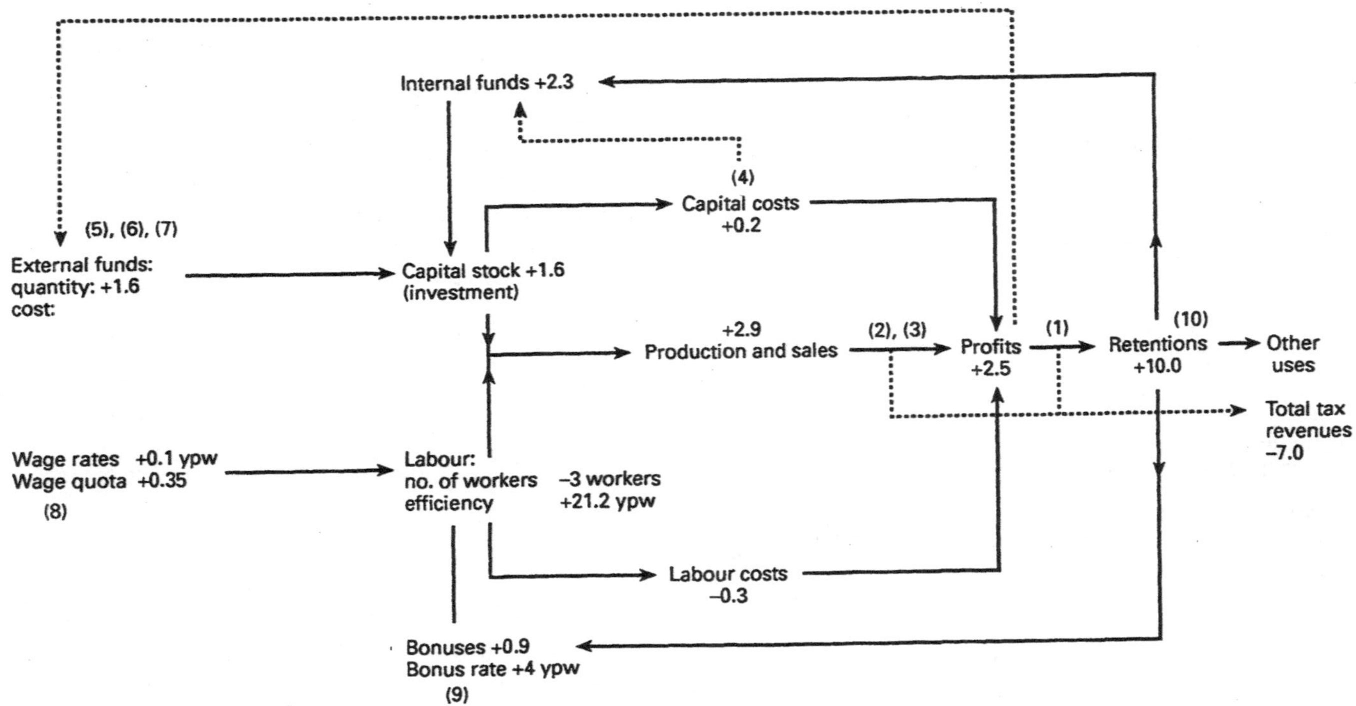

Policy instruments: 1. Profit-retention rate; 2. Sales-tax rate; 3. Price; 4. Depreciation rate; 5. Interest rate; 6. State subsidies; 7. Credit control; 8. Wage-bill quota; 9. Ceiling on bonus rate; 10. Division of retentions
Policy: adjust retention ratio to increase retentions by 10: see Table 11.5 (col. 2)

Note: units are 10,000 yuan except where indicated; ypw = yuan per worker.

FIG. 11.3. Policy simulation (1)

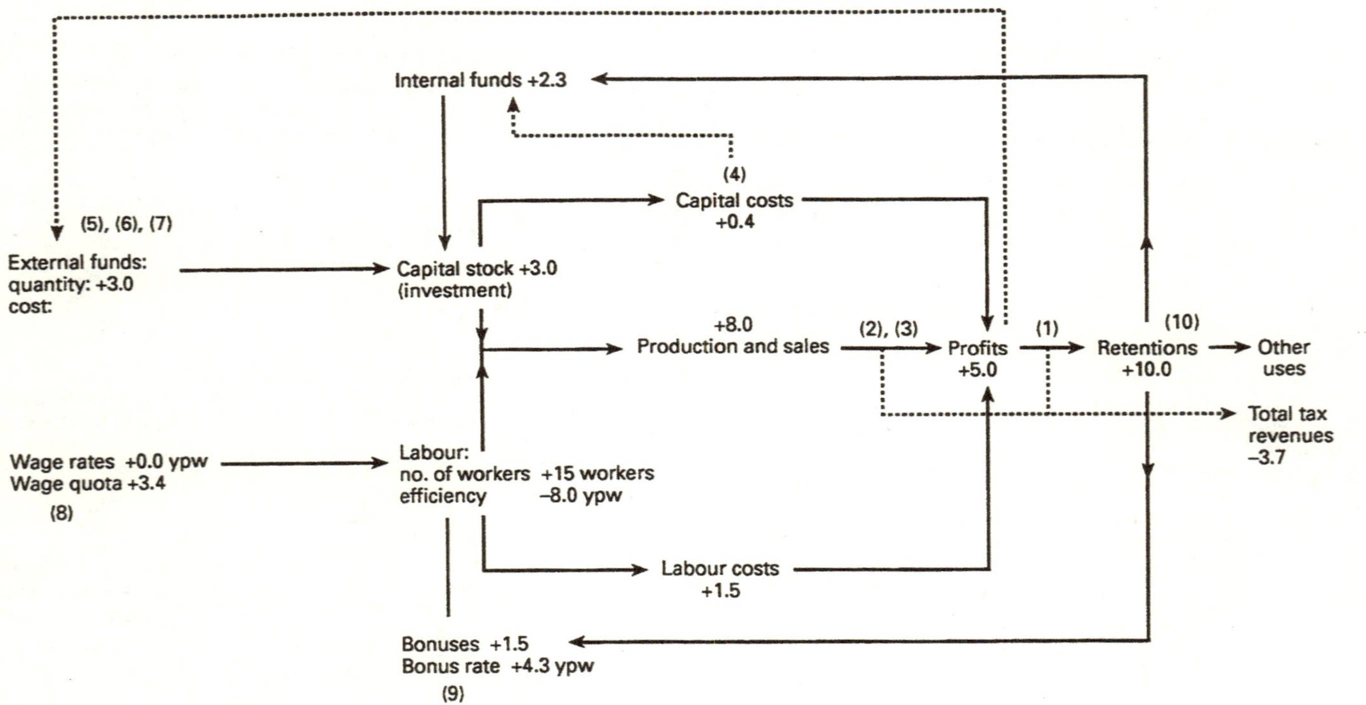

Policy instruments: 1. Profit-retention rate; 2. Sales-tax rate; 3. Price; 4. Depreciation rate; 5. Interest rate; 6. State subsidies; 7. Credit control; 8. Wage-bill quota; 9. Ceiling on bonus rate; 10. Division of retentions

Policy: retention ratio increased to give retention +10: wage bill increased in line with additional bonus: see Table 11.5 (col. 3)

Note: units are 10,000 yuan except where indicated; ypw = yuan per worker.

FIG. 11.4. Policy simulation (2)

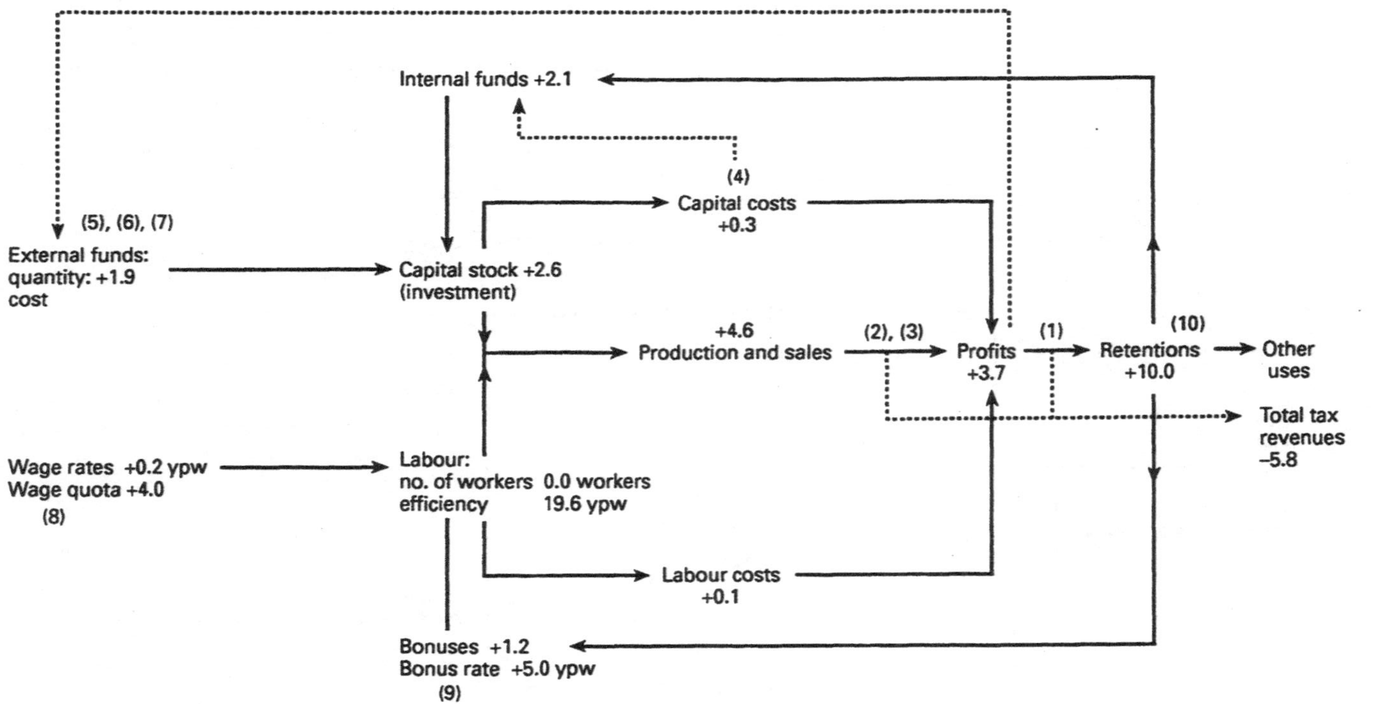

Policy instruments: 1. Profit-retention rate; 2. Sales-tax rate; 3. Price; 4. Depreciation rate; 5. Interest rate; 6. State subsidies; 7. Credit control; 8. Wage-bill quota; 9. Ceiling on bonus rate; 10. Division of retentions

Policy: retention ratio increased to give retention +10, and wage bill increased by 1%, with holding no. of workers as constant.

Note: units are 10,000 yuan except where indicated; ypw = yuan per worker.

FIG. 11.5. Policy simulation (3)

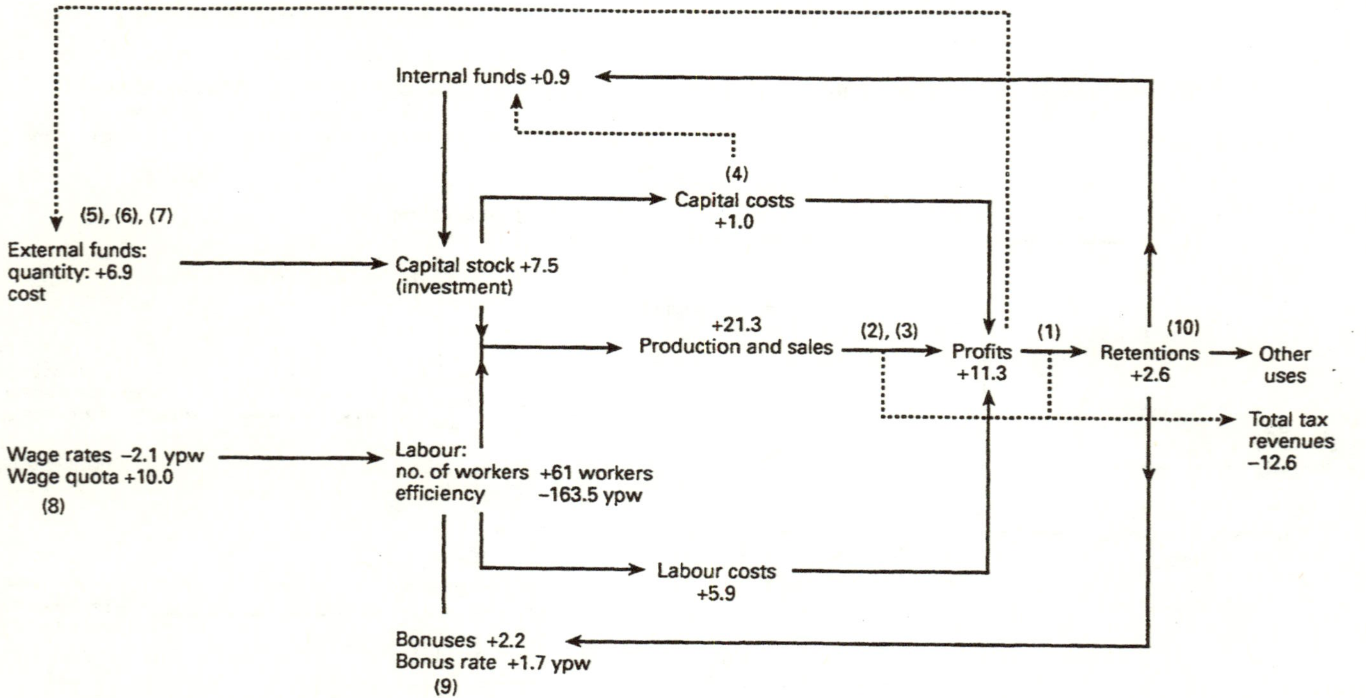

Policy instruments: 1. Profit-retention rate; 2. Sales-tax rate; 3. Price; 4. Depreciation rate; 5. Interest rate; 6. State subsidies; 7. Credit control; 8. Wage-bill quota; 9. Ceiling on bonus rate; 10. Division of retentions
Policy: wage quota +10: see Table 11.5 (col. 8)

Note: units are 10,000 yuan except where indicated; ypw = yuan per worker.

FIG. 11.6. Policy simulation (4)

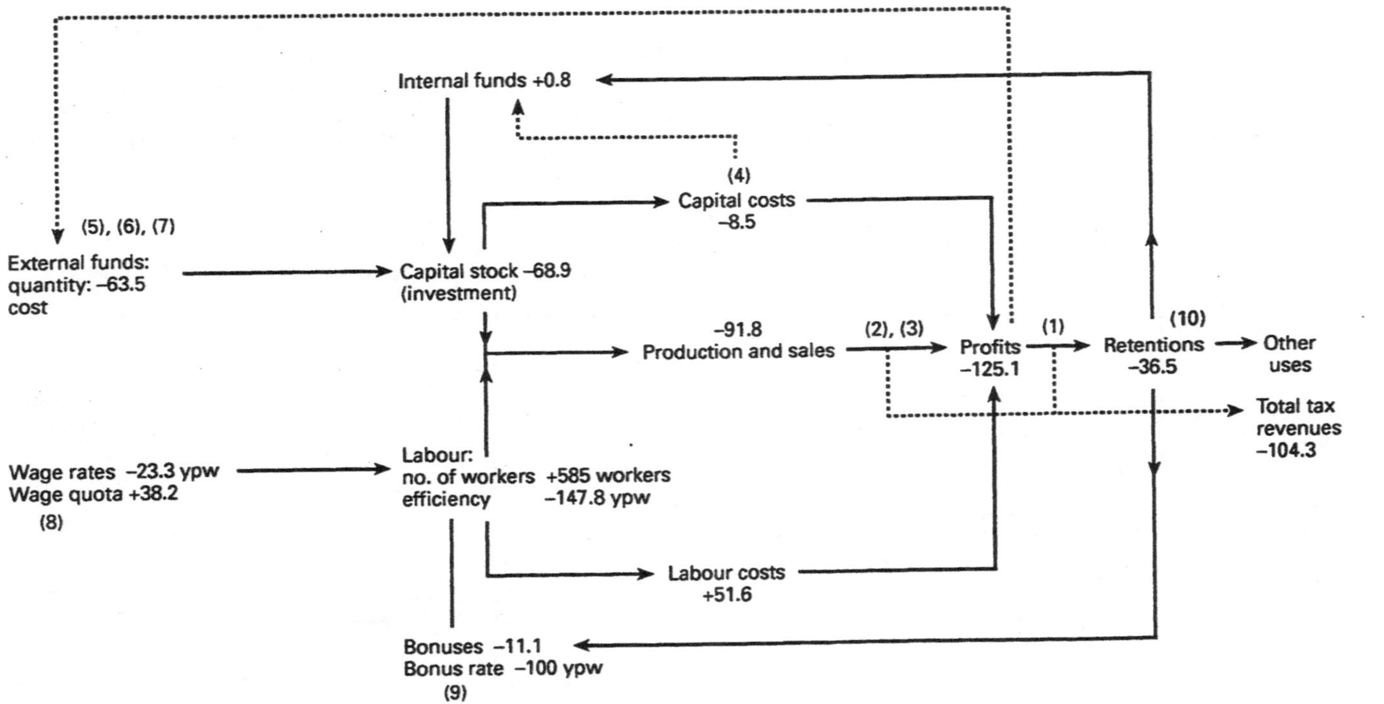

Policy instruments: 1. Profit-retention rate; 2. Sales-tax rate; 3. Price; 4. Depreciation rate; 5. Interest rate; 6. State subsidies; 7. Credit control; 8. Wage-bill quota; 9. Ceiling on bonus rate; 10. Division of retentions
Policy change: bonus decreased by 100 yuan per worker: see Table 11.6.

Note: units are 10,000 yuan except where indicated; ypw = yuan per worker.

Fig. 11.7. Policy simulation (5)

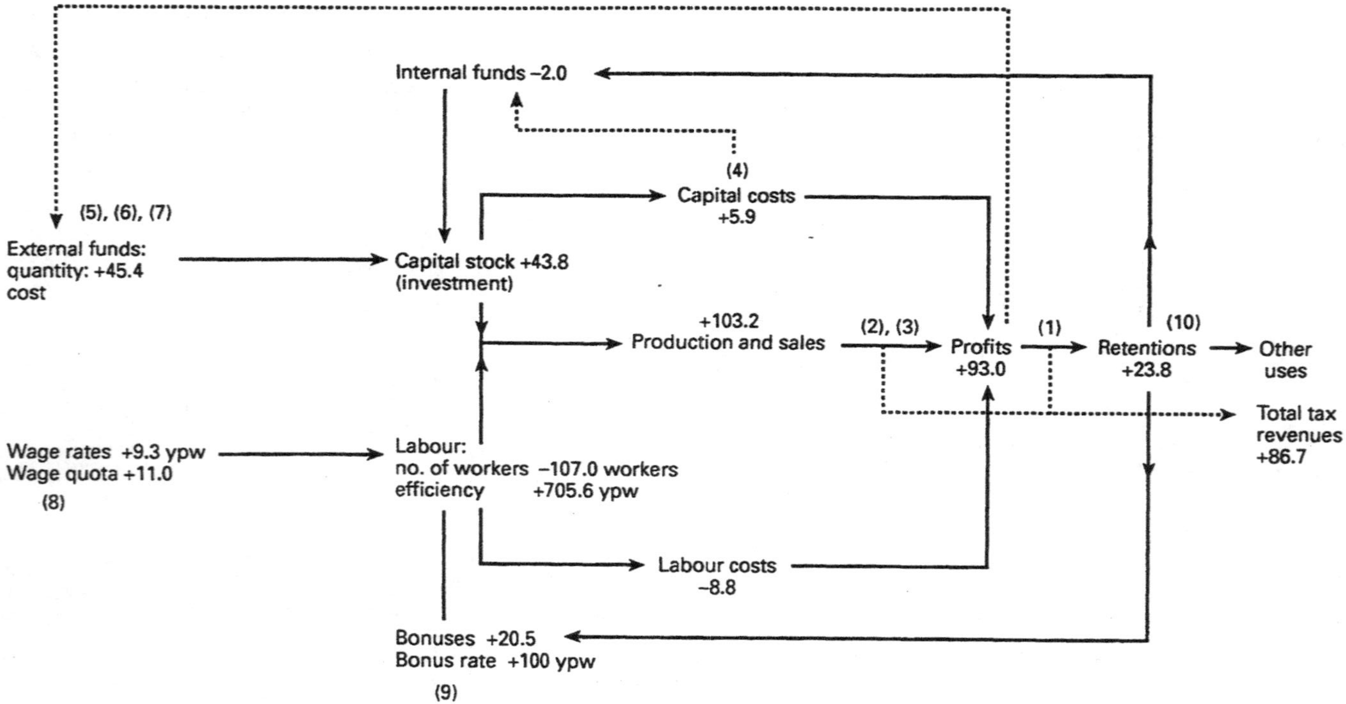

Policy instruments: 1. Profit-retention rate; 2. Sales-tax rate; 3. Price; 4. Depreciation rate; 5. Interest rate; 6. State subsidies; 7. Credit control; 8. Wage-bill quota; 9. Ceiling on bonus rate; 10. Division of retentions
Policy: bonus increased by 100 ypw: see Table 11.6

Note: units are 10,000 yuan except where indicated; ypw = yuan per worker.

FIG. 11.8. Policy simulation (6)

TABLE 11.6. Simulating effects of adjustment of the bonus rate

	Initial level	Cutting bonus	Raising bonus
Control variable			
Bonus rate*	342.2	242.2 (−100)	442.2 (+100)
Endogenous variables			
No. of workers	2524.0	3109.2 (585.2)	2417.5 (−106.5)
Wage-bill	334.8	373.0 (38.2)	345.8 (11.0)
Wage rate*	1023.8	999.5 (−23.3)	1033.1 (9.3)
Output/worker*	7416.9	5949.1 (−1467.8)	8122.5 (705.6)
Output	1768.9	1677.1 (−91.8)	1872.1 (103.2)
Capital	2142.7	2073.8 (−68.9)	2186.5 (43.8)
Internal funds	157.8	158.6 (0.80)	155.8 (−2.0)
External funds	1062.4	998.9 (−63.5)	1107.8 (45.4)
Fulfilled π	793.2	668.1 (−125.1)	886.2 (93.0)
Retained π	252.0	215.5 (−36.5)	275.8 (23.8)
Net π	708.4	597.6 (−110.8)	780.3 (71.9)
Bonus rate	—	—	—
Capital costs	452.1	443.6 (−8.5)	458.0 (5.9)
Labour costs	262.1	313.7 (51.6)	253.3 (−8.8)
Tax revenues	800.4	696.1 (−104.3)	287.1 (86.7)
No. of firms	75	75	75

Notes: Figures in brackets show the differences between values in column (1) and in the corresponding column.
* = yuan per worker, otherwise all values in 10,000 yuan.

the impact on employment via the wage-bill quota. The latter adds to the efficiency effect via changes in the capital/labour ratio. The simulated effects on both efficiency and employment are large. In the case of a bonus decrease, an increase of employment, at the mean, of about one-quarter generates a fall in output, due to the offsetting fall in efficiency. Labour costs rise (basic wages) and profits fall. The fall in profits generates negative feedbacks to external funds and capital stock. In the case of a bonus increase, employment in production drops sharply, but efficiency gains more than compensate, so there is a net rise in production. Labour costs fall, and profit rises. The feedback effects to funds and capital stock are positive, increasing the capital stock yet further.

Further simulations were run to explore the effect of much larger increases in bonus payments per worker. These took the simulation outside the range of the experience of the firms in the sample, so the results cannot be regarded as reliable predictions. However they suggest that very large increases in bonus rates (up to four or five times the sample mean value) would generate substantial increases in

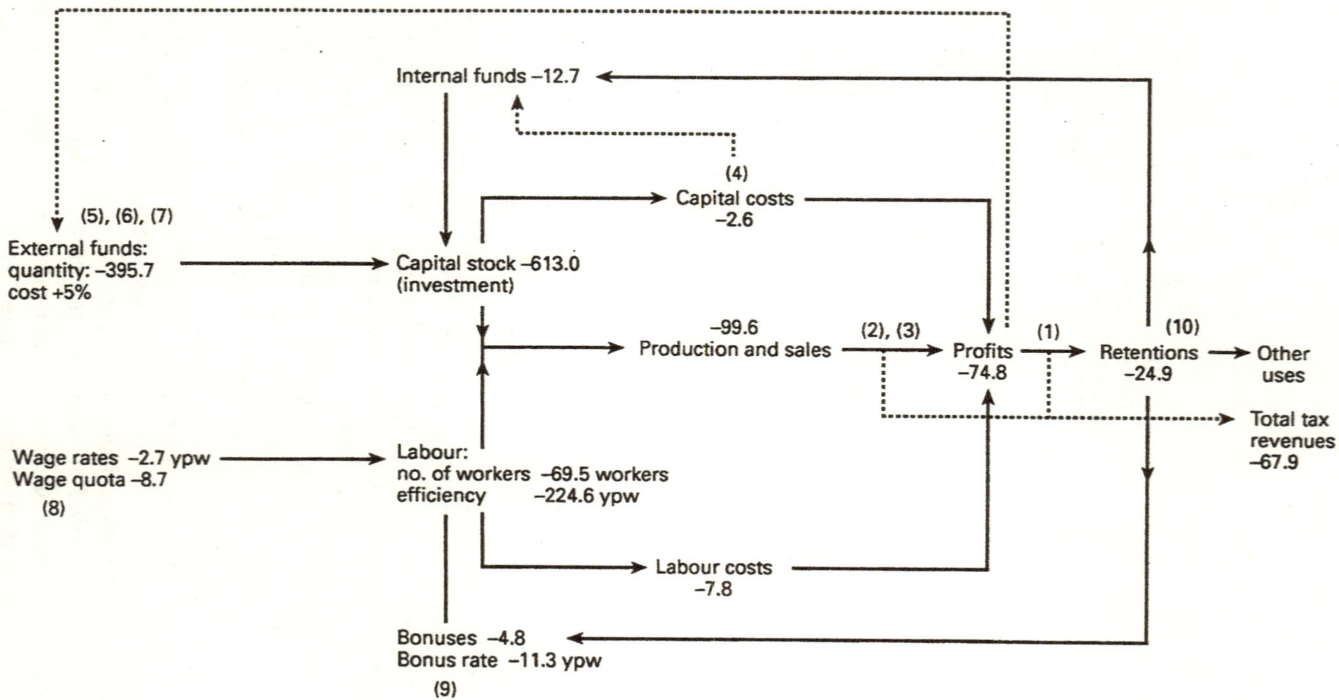

Policy instruments: 1. Profit-retention rate; 2. Sales-tax rate; 3. Price; 4. Depreciation rate; 5. Interest rate; 6. State subsidies; 7. Credit control; 8. Wage-bill quota; 9. Ceiling on bonus rate; 10. Division of retentions
Policy change: interest rate increased by 5% points: see Table 11.7.

Note: units are 10,000 yuan except where indicated; ypw = yuan per worker.

FIG. 11.9. Policy simulation (7)

output, though at the expense of employment. These results reflect the high elasticity of output with respect to the bonus/wage ratio incorporated in the production equation. This elasticity has been interpreted as reflecting incentive effects. There is no means of knowing whether those incentive effects would be sustained for much larger bonus rates.

The simulations in Figs. 11.3 and 11.8 trace the effects of policy changes on finance and investment. Figure 11.3 explores the case of an increase in retentions (reduction in profit tax). The expected effects are increased internal funds and capital stock giving higher production and sales, with additional feedbacks from profits to external funds and capital stock. In Fig. 11.9 and Table 11.7 the effects of a 5 percentage point increase in interest rate (from a mean value of about 4.9%) are simulated. The long-run equilibrium impact on the capital stock is substantial, a reduction of about 30%. Short-run impacts would be much smaller, suggesting that a high interest policy has to be sustained for some time if it is to be effective in squeezing investment and economic activity. The fall in investment is accompanied by a decline in external funds taken up by the firm. As the capital/labour ratio worsens, productivity falls, and employment declines, giving a fall in output.

Figure 11.10 summarizes the information from the simulation of the

TABLE 11.7. Simulating effects of adjustment of the interest rate

	Initial Level	Reduction	Increase	Large Increase
Control variable				
Interest rate	4.786%	0.0% (−4.786%)	7.286% (+2.5%)	9.786% (+5.0%)
Endogenous variables				
No. of workers	2551.6	2661.7 (110.1)	2512.8 (−38.8)	2482.1 (−69.5)
Wage-bill	336.6	349.9 (13.3)	331.8 (−4.8)	327.9 (−8.7)
Wage rate*	1019.3	1023.3 (4.0)	1017.8 (−1.5)	1016.6 (−2.7)
Output/worker*	7121.2	7456.3 (335.1)	6997.4 (−123.8)	6896.6 (−224.6)
Output	1739.4	1900.0 (160.6)	1683.8 (−55.6)	1639.8 (−99.6)
Capital	2084.7	3452.5 (1367.8)	1720.4 (−364.3)	1471.6 (−613.1)
Internal funds	155.2	179.4 (24.2)	147.8 (−7.40)	142.5 (−12.7)
External funds	1053.2	1661.5 (608.3)	837.6 (−215.6)	657.5 (−395.7)
Fulfilled π	755.2	870.9 (115.7)	711.7 (−43.5)	680.4 (−74.8)
Retained π	240.3	283.4 (43.1)	225.9 (−14.4)	215.4 (−24.9)
Net π	678.8	786.8 (108.8)	638.1 (−40.7)	608.9 (−69.9)
Bonus rate*	294.9	312.0 (17.1)	288.6 (−6.3)	283.6 (−11.3)
Capital costs	440.4	448.2 (7.8)	440.6 (+0.20)	437.8 (−2.6)
Labour costs	264.6	277.2 (12.6)	260.2 (−4.4)	256.8 (−7.8)
Tax revenues	795.7	898.4 (102.7)	756.7 (−39.0)	727.8 (−67.9)
No. of firms	86	86	86	86

Notes: Figures in brackets show the differences between values in column (1) and in the corresponding column.

* indicates that the unit is yuan per worker, otherwise all values in 10,000 yuan.

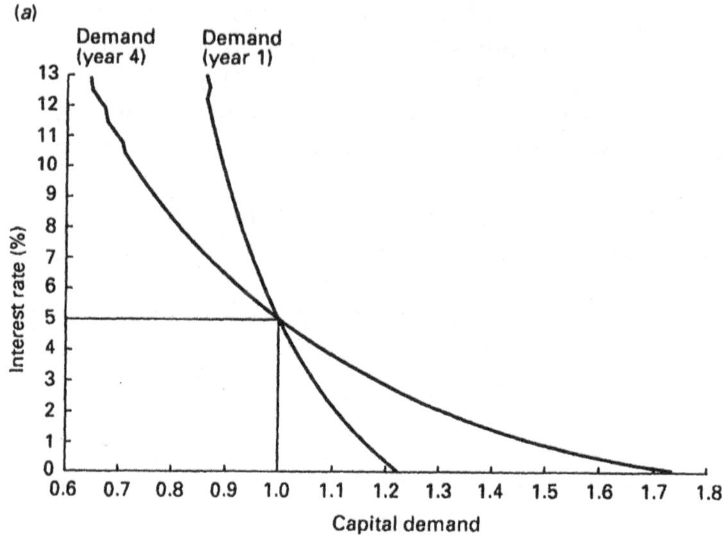

Notes: Capital stock normalized on the initial stock at 5% interest rate.
Sample size: YR1(79), YR4(79).

FIG. 11.10. (*a*) Demand for capital stock in both the short run and long run

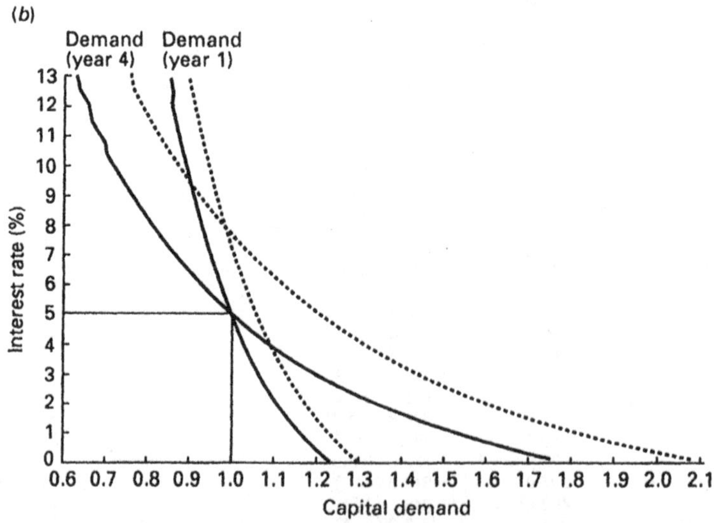

Notes: ---- demand curve with output price increased by 30%
Capital stock normalized on the initial stock at 5% interest rate.
Sample size: YR1(79), YR4(79).

FIG. 11.10. (*b*) Demand for capital stock with output price increased by 30 per cent equilibrium capital stock for a range of interest rates. The figure distinguishes the relatively small short-run effects from the long-run effects, given that adjustment of the capital stock is subject to considerable lags. In the long run a reduction in the interest rate to near zero would generate a 70% increase in the capital stock. It is evident from these graphs that the demand for capital stock with respect to the interest rate is quite elastic.

5. Conclusions

The purpose of this chapter has been to integrate the separate analyses of the previous chapters in a single model of the Chinese state-owned enterprise. The four main elements of the model are employment and worker remuneration, investment and finance, production, and the generation and uses of profits. The complete model can be used in two ways. The first is to see whether the conclusions of the previous chapters concerning the determinants of firms' behaviour hold up in a model where all the feedbacks between different aspects of the firms' operations are allowed for. The second is to get quantitative assessments of the impact of different policy variables on the behaviour of the enterprises, for example the responses to changes in bonuses, wage-bill quotas, tax rates, and interest rates.

The estimation of the complete model gives results which are entirely consistent with those derived from the separate analyses. For example, there was some doubt in earlier discussions as to the causal mechanism which was generating the large impact of the bonus/wage variable on productivity. The full model indicates that, even taking into account feedback from profits to bonus, there remains a strong positive effect of bonus on productivity. It is not the case that high bonuses are paid by firms that happen (for some other reason) to be more efficient, and therefore generate higher profits. Thc results also confirm the previous conclusions that the enterprises during the period of reform began to behave in a 'neoclassical' manner, within the constraints that continued to be imposed on them. The model in particular allows an examination of responses to prices in factor use. Thus the employment equation shows firms increasing employment with respect to the productivity/basic wage variable, and decreasing employment with respect to the bonus/wage ratio, but within the continuing constraint of the externally imposed wage-bill quota. Similarly, the demand for capital stock is quite responsive (especially in the long run) to changes in the interest rate, within the constraints on internal funds implied in the tax system, and the limits on external funds implying some degree of credit rationing. The ability of firms to retain some profits—a key feature of this reform programme—is behaviourally very important within the model, despite some restrictions on how these retentions may be spent. The model is able to trace the flows into the payment of bonuses, and into capital expenditures.

The second use of the model is to assess the quantitative impacts of policy instruments on the operations of the firms, given that their behaviour is reflected, at least on average, in the parameters of the model. The main policy variables explored are the taxation system (retention ratios) on profits, the wage-bill quota, the rates at which profit-related bonuses are paid, and the interest rate on firms' borrowings.

As far as productive efficiency is concerned, the main effects are related to the payment of bonuses from retentions. It remains a moot point whether further increases in bonus payments would generate equally dramatic improvements.

Relaxing the wage-bill quota on the firm would certainly give the enterprises scope for increasing payments to workers. The analysis also indicates that it would have an employment effect. This is puzzling given that most enterprises indicated that they had excess workers in this period. The equation system may therefore be reflecting a different causal mechanism, whereby increased wage-bill quota is associated with a requirement on the enterprise to take on more labour. The other explanation is that the firms would indeed like to take on more workers with production skills, the system parameters suggesting that the value of marginal product greatly exceeds the additional wage costs for production workers, but that the firms have an excess of non-production (low-skilled) workers.

Simulations with the interest-rate variable suggest that investment and long-run capital stock are quite sensitive to sustained changes in the cost of capital, though the short-run effects are quite small. These simulations, and the evidence that the firms were credit-constrained, imply that monetary policy instruments could be used very effectively to control the investment and financial behaviour of the state-owned enterprise sector.

There are a number of further policy issues which cannot however be addressed within the model. Some major issues concern the continuation of intervention by the enterprise's 'higher authorities' in all aspects of the operations of the firm. Although the planning system has been largely dismantled as a mechanism for directing the activities of the enterprises, the enterprise still has to agree its plans with the relevant industry bureau, not least plans for investment. Another issue is the choice of outputs, pricing, and marketing by the enterprise. We have not been able, with the data available, to analyse price formation and the ways in which the firm responds to shifts in demand. We do know, however, that the enterprises have increasingly been given autonomy in selling their products, so the issues are very important. From the standpoint of policy, the authorities need to give attention to competition. The danger is that some state-owned enterprises will have effective monopolies in their markets, and others may find it convenient to enter informal collusive agreements to share markets and to prevent competition.

These conclusions, from the complete model and policy simulations, imply that the reforms have gone a long way to inducing the state-owned enterprises in China to be more responsive to price signals in a manner which is consistent with a degree of profit-maximizing, cost-minimizing behaviour. By the same token, it is plausible to argue that the authorities could effectively influence the state-owned sector via the traditional Western policy instruments of monetary policy, taxation rules, and competition policy, diminishing yet further direct intervention in the affairs of individual enterprises. The question to be addressed is how much further progress can be made along these lines if the enterprises remain state-owned. In the next chapter, the continuing constraints arising from state-ownership are analysed, and the options for private ownership are discussed.

NOTE

1. Define: depreciation (DP), book value of assets (BK), and depreciation rate (DR). The book value in a given year includes both current capital stock (K) and depreciation: $BK = K + DP$. Depreciation is calculated as a proportion of book capital: so

$$BK = K + DR \cdot BK \quad \text{or} \quad BK = \frac{K}{1 - DR}$$

$$\therefore \quad DP = \frac{DR}{1 - DR} K.$$

However, application of this formula systematically underestimates the value of depreciation given in the accounts. In fact actual depreciation is on average 4% higher. To compensate for this a factor of 1.04 is introduced into the formula:

$$DP = 1.04K\left(\frac{DR}{1 - DR}\right).$$

PART III
Options for Reform

12

Ownership Reform Issues

1. Introduction

In the preceding chapters of this book we have looked in some detail at the functioning and performance of Chinese state-owned industrial enterprises. This is of interest in its own right, and throws light on some of the impact and repercussions of the economic reform programme pursued in China in the middle years of the 1980s. But the analysis naturally leads on to the questions of the future of economic reform. How should it evolve from here and at what pace? Is further change necessary or desirable? Indeed, have some of the developments in recent years gone too far? These are controversial and very far-reaching questions which cannot be answered solely by reference to empirical analysis of recent enterprise performance, important though that is. The purpose of this chapter is to examine some of the considerations involved, as a basis for making suggestions for the future. A complementary purpose is to place what has been achieved in the present stage of economic reform in context, the better to see how such suggestions fit with the evolution of reform and of the Chinese economy more generally. This in turn forms a backcloth for examining more specific enterprise reform proposals which have been put forward in recent years.

Debate on ownership of an economy's assets has a very long ancestry. Both in the nineteenth century and for much of the twentieth century it has been seen by many as a fundamental, if not *the* fundamental issue in political economy, being central to the structure of social and political relations, to production efficiency, distribution, and accumulation of wealth. This debate has been given a new impetus and added urgency as a result of the collapse of the former Soviet Union and the search by the countries of Eastern Europe previously controlled by the Soviet Union for new economic structures within which new forms of economic behaviour can develop. Nearly all the former socialist economies of Eastern Europe have since 1989 embarked on major transformation of their economies, including price decontrol, monetary and fiscal reform, and programmes of wholesale privatization. So rapid have these events been that in many cases policy decisions have quite outstripped adequate analysis of economic reform or its likely consequences.

Much of the recent debate on the reform of socialist economies has, unsurprisingly given the events of 1989–92 in Eastern Europe, started from the perspective of a centrally planned command economy and the desirability of, and means by which such an economy can be converted to a Western-style market economy. Key characteristics of these socialist economies were the organization of production by highly centralized state planning, operating across the whole region; prices which were heavily controlled and rarely bore any relation to resource costs even supposing that the latter could be identified; the virtual absence in most of the industrial sector of any kind of efficiency or profitability incentives; very rigid employment practices; limited private ownership particularly in the industrial sector; and, permeating all these areas, virtually no effective market mechanisms for determining the allocation of resources.

In each of these respects, the contrast with the West was stark. The economies of OECD are characterized by private ownership, free prices, market mechanisms and the associated incentives, and limited state control of resources or production. It is perhaps understandable therefore, in the turbulent times which followed the end of Soviet control and the establishment, virtually overnight in some cases, of democratic processes, that economic policy in Eastern Europe should have been directed towards achieving a massive restructuring of all these elements as fast as possible. The apparatus of state planning disappeared remarkably rapidly; the almost instantaneous abolition of price controls which had been in place for generations (the so called 'big bang' approach); the setting-up of a programme of rapid privatization; the end of disguised unemployment; and a commitment to let markets determine resource allocation have all occurred in less than two years. To the extent that the extraordinary political developments of this period have allowed any proper reflection of the economic issues involved—and this may not be great—the dominant strategy appears to have been one of establishing the main economic mechanisms observed in the West as fast as possible in the hope that this would accelerate the move to Western style efficiency gains and associated improvements in living standards.[1]

In this process the question of enterprise reform has not played a large part (see Sadowski 1991 and Mayhew and Seabright 1992). There has been a widespread presumption that privatization of most industrial assets is an integral part of the transformation process, the only significant limitation—one which except in the former GDR is proving severe—being the availability of saleable businesses or assets and of interested buyers. Basic questions such as *whether* full-scale privatization is desirable, what alternatives might exist, whether the internal organizational skills and the external financial structures necessary for successful privatization exist or can be developed have largely been bypassed. Equally fundamental issues concerning the *forms* of ownership and control in a privatized system, the different risk, incentive, and efficiency characteristics which are associated with different types of private ownership have barely been considered at all. Even the question of how to sequence different stages of reform, which has received rather more attention in the academic literature, has had little if any discernible influence on policy decisions (see Rybczynski 1991).

This is important background in considering enterprise reform in China. Superficially at least, it is easy to view China in similar terms to Eastern Europe, a state-owned socialist economy now trying, indeed for considerably longer than Eastern Europe to move towards a more Western-style economy, and one in which a switch to private ownership has played an important part. It is therefore important to recognize and stress that the position of the Chinese economy is radically different. In addition to very different culture and social structures, and a much more decentralized system of political control, its historical experience of economic reform has been quite different. Unlike in Eastern Europe, reform was initiated under relatively stable political conditions and without the major changes in the location or methods of political control which accompanied reform in Eastern Europe. This meant that the process has been more deliberate, more controlled, and more gradual. Even after the politically more unstable period since 1989, and after a consequent halt to the reform process, it now seems likely that reform will recommence in a gradual manner and without major disruption.

As China's experience demonstrates, the 'big bang' approach to price decontrol is not an essential component of economic reform, nor does it have any strong theoretical underpinning. It is usually argued that it is necessary to get a strong supply response early on in the reform process, and freeing prices will not only quickly signal shortages but encourage rapid output increases. However, in an economy in which production has not normally been determined by prices but where instead the structure and level of production has been planned, such effects may be rapidly undermined by the wage–price inflation spiral that tends to develop; the distortions that occur as suppliers, particularly of primary products, respond to rising prices by hoarding;

and by the deflationary consequences of government trying through monetary, fiscal, and exchange rate policy to control inflation. The resultant sharp falls in activity such as those witnessed in Poland and the former Soviet Union then start to undermine the tax base, exacerbating the problems considerably. This sequence of events has very largely been avoided in China. Extensive price reform has been achieved without reductions in output and living standards and, indeed, in a period of rapid growth.

This in turn has permitted extensive reform of enterprises in the context of reasonably stable conditions and increasingly effective market signals. Managers have obtained considerable experience in responding to these and operating in a quasi-Western manner, pursuing profit targets, responding to incentives linked to performance, and exercising considerable autonomy to make decisions. As a corollary, very different financing arrangements to those in Eastern Europe have evolved.

The countries of Eastern Europe may in practice have had little effective discretion over the pace or sequencing of reform. The manner and speed of political reform following the removal of the former Soviet Union's restraining grip may have created political imperatives that made slower, more ordered, or differently structured reform impossible. Advice from some in the West encouraging rapid replication of Western economic structures was, understandably in the circumstances, likely to be readily adopted. Yet it must be pointed out that such pressures do not predetermine the course of reform nor make privatization inevitable. The different experiences of different countries in Eastern Europe suggest that there was some scope for alternative reform programmes (see, for a succinct summary, Fry and Nuti 1992, esp. Table 2), and it is arguable that the severe economic problems now affecting many of these countries are to some extent a consequence rather than a cause of the reform programmes pursued. In any event, the Chinese economic reform process is not constrained in this way. It has time and the scope to analyse, choose, and plan further steps in the reform process in a coherent and theoretically sound manner; it can pursue enterprise reform in the light of the likely consequences of different strategies and it can hope to implement further change without the damaging consequences that have arisen within the quite different transition dynamics of Eastern Europe.

Against this background, Section 2 looks briefly at economic reform in China to date and reviews some of the more important aspects of the economic performance of large state-owned enterprises as identified in earlier chapters. This serves to illustrate how far China has already come from the centrally planned system which most of Eastern Europe faced in 1989. This is also an important element in identifying which facets of enterprise reform are critical to economic efficiency. Section 3 then briefly discusses the argument for further enterprise reform.

Sections 4 to 6 consider possible future reforms and the rationale for them. These sections do not seek to go through the many proposals for reform that have been developed both within China and elsewhere. Our main concern is with the critical issue of private ownership. Our approach is as follows: Section 4 reviews an important and fairly typical type of proposal for enterprise reform which retains public ownership of large-scale enterprises, together with comments. Section 5 is a more theoretical section exploring the efficiency characteristics of ownership and what differences a switch to private ownership might make. In these sections, we largely restrict ourselves to economic issues of incentives and efficiency with only passing reference to the arguments of various political theorists since Marx who, based on societal considerations, have seen public ownership as an end in itself. Section 6 then looks at different institutional forms of private ownership and their impact. Section 7 looks briefly at the principal–agent problem and Section 8 at a series of consequences of ownership reform. Section 9 summarizes our analysis and tries to draw out a number of conclusions concerning the future of enterprise reform.

2. *Large State-Owned Enterprises in China in the Process of Economic Reform*

The changes that have occurred in the functioning of the Chinese economy in the last 15–20 years are enormous and profound. Reform in the agricultural sector, through changes in both incentive structures and property rights, has transformed the economic arrangements for producing food, greatly expanded agricultural production and productivity, and underpinned the economic reform process more generally by ensuring a secure and adequate supply of this most basic commodity.[2] In the industrial sector as a whole, change has been equally dramatic. Approaching half of industrial production is generated in enterprises that exhibit new ownership patterns, be this private or collective.[3] Productivity in these sectors has increased dramatically, making an important contribution to the rapid growth of real output in China throughout most of the 1980s.[4]

Turning to the sector with which the analysis of this book is concerned—large state-owned industrial enterprises—reform, though less far-reaching, has none the less been striking. First, and most obviously, a large proportion of the inputs and outputs of these enterprises has gradually come, via the dual-track system, to be supplied at or near to market-determined prices. The exceptions still controlled by plan quotas have largely been reduced to a number of key commodities and production related to export requirements (see Chapters 1 and 2). Second, and also extremely important, these enterprises have been given very considerable autonomy in their production operations, and a number of control systems have been introduced with the clear and specific purpose of generating powerful incentives for managers to pursue efficient, profit-maximizing strategies in their production and distribution activities. These include the contract-, director- (or management-), and asset-responsibility systems, the profit-related contracts and profit-delivery mechanisms which they incorporate, and the widespread availability of bonuses for managers and operatives. These can be quite substantial in relation to basic earnings and are usually linked directly to performance, in particular profitability (see Chapter 4). In many respects we have found that the process of reform has gone far enough both for behaviour to be substantially 'Western' and for us to be able to detect this in the data on enterprise activity. The incentive effect of bonus payments appears very strong (see Chapter 5); investment is substantially neoclassical in general form (see Chapter 8); despite substantial constraints, employment decisions appear to reflect similar motivation (see Chapter 4). Thus pay, productivity, employment, and investment are all reasonably predictable on the basis of our analysis given any particular set of constraints.

The one exception is the narrowing of pay differentials as a result of greater autonomy in the setting of pay plus bonuses. It would have been natural to expect increasing differentials, partly because of the relatively high degree of equality of incomes as between different classes of worker initially and because of the increased discretion accruing to those on higher incomes. In fact it appears that there have been only rather small increases in the absolute value of the bonuses paid, leading to a *narrowing* of differentials, and suggesting a significant element of collectivism in the determination of bonuses. In terms of their incentive effects, such systems are typically viewed as being subject to a serious free-rider problem, i.e. why should any individual respond to a bonus incentive if the level of the latter is largely determined by the joint effort of all one's co-workers? But in some circumstances, most notably production in small groups or even many small groups, the free-rider problem may not materialize, and cultural values developed over long periods may make it less prominent in certain societies. In any event, despite the narrowing of differentials, bonuses have been sufficiently sizeable, widespread, and powerful to have had a strong effect on both productivity and output.

Consistent with this, as explained in Chapter 1, the centralized planning system is no longer functioning in China. This fact was reflected in the responses of enterprise managers to the qualitative questionnaire described in Chapter 2. What exists is closer to an 'indicative' plan. Firms make plans in consultation with their immediate supervisory authority, and those plans are then consolidated at provincial, industrial, and national levels. These consolidated plans are scrutinized for their aggregate impact on the economy, and adjustments made which are then transmitted back down the hierarchy to the enterprises. However, enterprises have considerable freedom to produce and sell outside the planned system. So the impact of the planning system on their operations is quite limited, though in terms of major investment projects and finance, and in supply of materials and energy, the firms may still be significantly restrained (see below).

The effect of this system is to enhance the role of the local authorities (county, city, or province) in the direction and monitoring of the activities of the firm. They have targets, which they are required to meet, for tax revenues (profit delivery) to be passed up to their higher authorities. Excess of tax revenues over the targets can be retained wholly or in part by the local authorities for expenditure on local projects, and to enhance their lifestyle. Enterprises are the major source of this tax revenue. This gives strong incentives for local authorities to ensure that the local enterprises do well and this interest is pursued by the local industry bureau on behalf of the local authority. Thus the local authorities will be interested in creating favourable conditions for their enterprises, in the procurement of materials and energy, and in the allocation of investment funds by the bank. They will also be concerned to see effective management. Loss-making enterprises are a drain on local tax revenues, and there will be incentives to improve their performance.

Local control of enterprises does however have disadvantages. One is that it will frequently be hard to close down operations even if they are completely uneconomic. Local political considerations may require that loss-making enterprises continue in operation indefinitely. Part of the difficulty is that the enterprises have a dual function as producers and as providers of social security: the natural local concern for the latter can override considerations of productive efficiency or commercial realities. A second disadvantage is that the local authority may adversely affect the long-run performance of a successful enterprise by syphoning off higher tax revenues in the short run (particularly if revenue is required to subsidize other loss-making firms). A third disadvantage is that enterprise 'success' may come to depend more on the manager's skill in handling the local bureaucracy (the use of 'contacts' and 'relationships') than on productive efficiency or marketing skills. A fourth disadvantage is that the local authorities will have incentives to block entry into the local markets of efficient new producers which are not state-owned, or of low-cost products from other provinces, since competition will have adverse effects on the local state-owned firms which are major sources of tax revenue. Similarly, a local authority may block the sale outside its area of materials that are required for local production, even though higher prices for those materials could be obtained from enterprises elsewhere.

Other aspects of state-owned enterprise activity have seen only modest change. There have been some experiments to improve the levels of manning and disposition of the work-force and, more generally, a growing recognition of the need for greater autonomy on the part of enterprise managers to determine their employment needs in the light of their production requirements, a flexibility which is now sufficiently large to be empirically identifiable in our employment equations. But there are still very considerable constraints on this, severe obstacles to the laying off of surplus labour and little overt unemployment. Given the dependence of many workers on their enterprise for social security benefits, including health, pensions, and educational facilities, as well as income security, there are clear restrictions on how far such changes can go at the present time.

Financing of industry is another area which has seen only modest change. Bank finance is crucial for much enterprise investment and as we have seen (see Chapters 8 and 10) in many cases this is provided on a reasonably arms'-length commercial basis as would be the case in the West. This looks quite different from the arrangements which have typically been observed in socialist economies, where state bureaucracies make all such decisions and use this as a main way of controlling the allocation of resources. In practice, the changes are much less significant. Most financial allocations and all major ones must still be approved by the relevant industrial bureau or other state agency, the banks remain largely subservient to these institutions and are themselves state-owned. Subsidies in one form or another remain substantial. Most enterprises facing a deteriorating financial position can expect to see their budget constraint softened in one way or another. Bankruptcy remains rare and, where enforced, generally rather arbitrary. Investment decisions appear to respond in largely neoclassical manner to the main determinants, but in a world of rapid growth of demand and negative real interest rates, the consequent high demand for investment can rarely be fully financed, so that financial constraints give a substantial measure of control over investment, even if the formal controls on investment authorization have relatively little effect (see Chapters 3 and 8). Land transactions also remain heavily controlled. In short, the Chinese state-owned enterprise sector is evolving into one in which the production and distribution *process* is increasingly at the discretion of enterprise managers but the allocation of the factors of production, labour, capital, land, and finance, is still heavily controlled, predominantly by local authorities.

There has been least reform in the large state-owned enterprise sector with respect to enterprise *ownership*. Despite the substantial changes in agriculture and in small industrial enterprises, and despite a smattering of experimental changes in one or two areas, large enterprises remain overwhelmingly state-owned. Much of this chapter will be concerned with this controversial topic; what difference, if any, ownership makes, whether private sector allocation mechanisms can operate in the case of publicly owned assets, and what the consequences for the rest of the reform process might be. In general the question of ownership relates to all the main attributes which determine the efficiency of production and distribution processes—control, incentives, risk-bearing, and finance—and is bound therefore, along with the issue of competition, to be a central consideration in any economic assessment of the future of reform.

In summary, while large-scale enterprises in China have remained almost entirely publicly owned they have achieved a significant measure of autonomy in the control of the production processes for which they are responsible; they face quite well-developed market signalling mechanisms in relation to much of their production and sales activity; their managers and their work-force are faced with quite powerful incentives to be efficient and to be profitable; and the state apparatus which ultimately controls them contains significant incentives to assist and promote their efficiency. Clear problems remain, in relation to employment and financing, the social roles that such enterprises have to fulfil, and the impact of the local state bureaucracies which control key inputs, investment, and managerial appointments. But in some ways the economic system within which they operate is closer to that facing many Western firms, particularly in countries with strong actively interventionist industrial policies, than the centralized systems which have been the starting-point for economic transition in most other socialist or once socialist economies. China therefore has experience of gradual but largely successful reform, and an institutional and political environment within which it can pursue further properly constructed gradualist policies. Unlike Eastern Europe it has the opportunity to choose from alternative reform strategies, but it also has current systems of operation and control which it will not lightly wish to jeopardize. It is within this context that proposals for further reform must be located.

3. *Extending the Reform Process in Large State-Owned Enterprises*

While reform of large state-owned enterprises has been considerable in the last 10 years, few observers believe that the process has now ceased, despite the halt that occurred for two years after the events of June 1989 in Beijing and elsewhere. Many of the changes in the allocation of responsibility that have occurred, though introduced widely, have in many respects been experimental. Even where successful in terms of efficiency, profitability, and growth, much has been learnt about how large enterprises respond to various incentives and control mechanisms which suggests further reform. A large number of such developments are actively being discussed both within and outside China, and it is to this, in the context of the present stage of reform, that we now turn.

There are, it must be said, cogent arguments for being cautious about further enterprise reform in China at the present time. First, the reforms of the 1980s have themselves been sufficient to achieve a dramatic improvement in economic growth. Chinese GDP grew at an average annual rate of 10.6% in the 1980s (SYC 1991: 27). The state-owned industrial sector grew at over 8% p.a. and in the main reform years 1983–88 at nearly 12% p.a. all in real terms.[5] Thus liberalization of prices and the introduction of powerful incentive mechanisms in the operation and control of enterprises appear to have been remarkably successful. Second, although we have argued that the experience of Eastern Europe may have little direct relevance, the attempts by the countries concerned to concentrate the process of reform into a very short time-span provide a stark lesson in the dangers of too rapid a transition.

In particular, attempts to impose harder budget constraints and/or introduce extensive private ownership into large enterprises, both of which are very much to the forefront of much policy discussion in China at present have proved very difficult to implement elsewhere, and might well jeopardize the maintenance of output, employment, and living standards in China if introduced into an economic system still adjusting to the major changes of the 1980s.

Third, although there are still problems in the functioning of the state-owned industrial sector in China, these to some extent arise not from enterprise behaviour but from other policies of the state which arguably should be addressed first. In many cases, persistent losses and the budgetary and control problems which arise from this are largely due to severe price controls on certain key products. Monetary policy has generated substantially negative real interest rates even in periods of rapid growth, generating excessive investment demand, rationing of finance, and inefficiency in the allocation of investment funds. Reduction of funding for poorly performing enterprises, more forceful implementation of existing bankruptcy provisions, and greater autonomy in investment and financing could all be achieved without any change in the ownership or control structures under which enterprises currently operate.

A case may therefore be made that further major reform of state enterprises in China is not necessary. Existing reforms have met with considerable success; more far-reaching reforms elsewhere have not; many existing problems require correction elsewhere in the economic system; and much could be done to improve the workings of the present control system. Powerful as these arguments are, we none the less believe that there is a case for further reform. Perhaps the most immediate reason for believing that enterprise reform, not excluding ownership reform, must remain a priority in China is the evidence that performance in state-owned industrial enterprises has not matched that in firms where alternative ownership patterns have been introduced. Productivity growth in collectively owned enterprises rose at nearly twice the rate as in state-owned industries in the 1980s, and since 1985 productivity in privately owned enterprises has risen at 12.8% p.a. as against 4.3% in state-owned ones (SYC 1991).[6] We cannot automatically assume that such differences purely reflect ownership differences; sectoral composition and scale factors may be important and the impact of taxation and interest rates, industrial policy, and bankruptcy provisions may vary across different types of enterprise. But such comparisons none the less offer prima-facie evidence that there may be scope for markedly better performance from state-owned industrial enterprises. If so, the size of this sector is such that improvements in productivity, profitability, investment, and remuneration could have very powerful effects on growth and living standards in China.

Second, although various managerial-responsibility systems and the incentive mechanisms associated with them only emerged in the 1980s, there is now sufficiently widespread experience of decentralization, managerial discretion, and/or autonomy in the face of decontrolled prices to make further gradual evolution a feasible option. The possibility that this might generate too *rapid* a transition is likely to be less important than securing the appropriate *sequencing* of changes, in particular as between further reform of managerial decision-taking procedures on the one hand and new institutional arrangements for financing enterprises and transferring the non-commercial responsibilities of enterprises on the other.

The third reason for pursuing enterprise reform, and the one which in practice is generating much of the momentum for further change at the policy level is the continued existence of a number of clear constraints on enterprises' performance. Four in particular are a cause for concern.

1. State bureaucracies at the local level (province, county, or city) retain very considerable power over the allocation of funds, investment programmes, employment levels, key inputs, taxation, and managerial appointments. As we have seen, there are quite strong incentives for local and state institutions to use these powers to promote enterprise efficiency, but this does not ensure the most effective use of such power. The authorities have other responsibilities relating to employment, social security, public investment, short-term tax revenue requirements, and the like which, though legitimate considerations, may lead to allocation and control decisions that inhibit the most effective use of resources. The very bureaucracy of the machinery necessary to control all the major resource decisions of a large number of enterprises and the need to determine priorities between many competing claims on resources exacerbates the problem. In some cases, the authorities may engage in direct intervention and/or discriminatory action towards or against particular enterprises in the light of non-commercial considerations, personal connections, party ties, associated side-payments, etc. Decisions may become divorced from any clear market test of priorities.

2. The existence of a soft budget constraint, particularly for large-scale enterprises remains an enormous problem (see Chapter 10),

absorbing resources on a large scale, inhibiting the effectiveness of market signals and incentives, and distorting resource-allocation decisions at the levels of the state, the enterprise, and the consumer. In many cases this problem stems directly from the position of the local state authorities and the use of their powers over finance and taxation.

3. The control structure for any particular enterprise remains dangerously monolithic. When a relevant authority makes a decision—on funding, investment, etc.—then no alternative course of action is possible. An enterprise cannot seek out alternative sources of finance, or even apply its own funds for an investment project which has failed to obtain approval. No competitive mechanism exists which could put the decisions of the authorities to a full market test, even though there are incentives for them to try to mimic the results of such a process.

4. Finally, many enterprises are to a considerable extent in a position to exercise a significant degree of monopoly power in their product markets, generally on the basis of geographical monopoly, coupled with cost-based or institutionally imposed barriers to transportation. The creation of such positions is of course an activity pursued by enterprises throughout the world. Typically it leads to misallocation of resources and exploitation of customers, leading in turn to attempts by governments to prohibit such activities. But in the current Chinese economic structure, the authorities have strong incentives to maintain or encourage such monopoly power because it generates greater control and greater potential for taxable profits. This is not a problem in a fully centralized system because prices are then controlled, nor in the market economies of the West where government does not have extensive ownership interests. But the combination of relatively free prices and operational autonomy for enterprises, coupled with local public ownership and tax commitments to Beijing generates a strong incentive to maintain monopoly positions, thereby inhibiting incentives for efficiency.

These four problems, which are clearly interrelated, are the primary reasons for the continuing debate on enterprise reform, and it is these which must be addressed in any major proposals in this field. There is however a further reason for pursuing enterprise reform which may eventually turn out to be the most important. It may be argued that ownership *per se* is not necessarily very significant from an economic perspective; that with ingenuity virtually all the incentive and efficiency effects associated with private ownership can be replicated in a world of public ownership, and that the internal mechanisms now operating in most Chinese state-owned enterprises can achieve this (see Vickers and Yarrow 1988, ch. 4 for a discussion of this point). In particular, contracts can be constructed between enterprises and the state based on profitability, asset values, and bonus arrangements which mimic the operation of private ownership based on shareholdings and dividend payments and which generate the same incentives to maximize profits and efficiency. On this view it is only government interventions and constraints that inhibit the mechanism from being fully effective, and therefore these which need to be addressed, rather than further reform of enterprises themselves or of their ownership. Some would add that while ownership *per se* need not be crucial to economic performance it clearly matters from a political perspective. If efficient allocation mechanisms can be devised which operate in the context of public ownership in a socialist economy then there are clear advantages in avoiding unnecessary political conflict which might arise from moves towards privatization.

Against this others have argued, not least in China, that many of the problems of enterprise performance and control in the state-owned sector are, directly or indirectly, the result of state ownership *per se*; that there are quite severe limits to the extent to which rules, contracts, and internal incentive mechanisms can ever replicate Western-style behaviour and efficiency in the context of public ownership; and that, as a result, China's long-term prospects crucially depend on reform of enterprise ownership.[7] This line of argument implies that most if not all of the problems previously identified—lack of autonomy over factors of production, *ad hoc* intervention in enterprise activities, control of finance, soft budget constraints, and ineffective bankruptcy threats—in one way or another ultimately depend on the *ownership* structure of enterprises. There has been little chance in the immediate turmoil following the collapse of the Soviet Union for such reasoning to be examined carefully in Eastern Europe. But China still has clear options in this regard and the opportunity to explore such arguments before making far-reaching policy decisions.

In summary, we believe that the enterprise-reform process in China can and will continue in the coming decade, and that a proper assessment of the role of ownership must be an integral part of this. To address these issues we first consider how reform might proceed within the context of continuing public ownership. This is covered in Section 4. We then explore in two further sections what difference ownership changes might make to enterprise behaviour and efficiency and the implications of this for future reform.

4. *Reform of State Ownership in Large Industrial Enterprises*

There exist a number of proposals for institutional reform within the framework of continuing state ownership designed to build further on the advances already made and we do not seek to repeat or add to them here. Rather we focus on one major and fairly typical such proposal, originally made by the World Bank in 1985, developed by the same institution in 1989, and recently elaborated upon by Adrian Wood (1990). The essence of this proposal is a reallocation of existing ownership rights. At present these are mainly vested in the provincial, city, or county authorities to which an enterprise is responsible, though some more strategically important enterprises come under the control of the relevant central ministry. The proposed reform would reconstitute enterprises as joint-stock companies with the shares then being held by a much more diffused set of public institutions, including state-owned banks, pension funds and insurance companies, and a number of state asset-management bureaux some based within the enterprise's county, city, or province but others not. An enterprise would therefore remain publicly owned, but ownership would be quite widely dispersed among a number of institutions, in sharp contrast to the present position in which an enterprise belongs to only one local state organization. The share-owning agencies of the state would, in these proposals, be 'interested predominantly in profits', where this is taken to mean that these institutions would be responsible for their profits and losses.

The main advantage sought from this reform is a very substantial diminution in the power of the local authority to direct or control an enterprise in any manner which would inhibit its efficiency or profit-seeking activities. Other objectives, short-term expedients, self-serving interventions, etc., would all be resisted because they would not be in the interests of the other public bodies which owned and controlled the enterprise. Ownership would be less monolithic and there would be more resistance to large-scale subsidies. A number of the social objectives currently carried out by enterprises, in particular housing, pensions, and social security could be reallocated to the relevant publicly owned parent institutions, with appropriate adjustment of the financial flows from enterprises. Thus most of the current problems of large state-owned enterprises would in some measure be addressed.

As Wood emphasizes, these proposals would be subject to three important caveats. First, there would be some exceptions to the reform, primarily in key utilities and defence-related industries. Second, and more problematic, the institutions would need to be geared to medium- or long-term profits. Otherwise the maintenance of an enterprise's capital base and its longer-term investment and expansion could be threatened. This implies the need for some mechanism to generate incentives for the institutions to pursue longer-term objectives, and this may not be easy. Third, further price reform and increased competition would be necessary to ensure that profits were a reasonable indicator of efficiency rather than of a monopolistic position. This is particularly difficult given, as we have already noted, that the institutions which own enterprises have a clear interest in the maintenance of local or more widely held monopoly positions. Dealing with this would almost certainly require action by the central government to generate more competition, provide safeguards for it, and break down existing barriers to trade between different regions.

The essence therefore of the proposal lies in the existence of multiple institutions, with the ownership of any one enterprise spread across several institutions of different types and from different regions, thereby weakening the link between the interests of any particular state agency and the enterprises in which it held a stake. This is coupled with the idea that the investing institutions would operate in competition with each other, thus increasing the motivation of the institutions to require and assist improvements in efficiency within the enterprises in which they hold a stake. The full proposal then goes on to look at the financial dynamics involved including, in particular, provisions for financial institutions to trade shareholdings in individual enterprises with each other.

This type of proposal represents an ingenious and useful way of moving enterprises forward in China while retaining full public ownership. It increases incentives for efficiency, increases enterprise autonomy, and addresses, in some cases very neatly, the main problems still facing the large state-owned enterprise sector in China. There is no insuperable hurdle to its introduction, particularly if, as has been suggested, it is initially operated on an experimental basis in selected regions. None the less there may be difficulties over and above those already noted.

The first concerns profit taxation. This currently is a major source of a local government's revenue which it must raise to meet local expenditure requirements and tax targets laid down by the central government. It is at best unclear how the authorities would ensure sufficient revenue under such a system or how they would respond if they seemed likely to fall short of their requirements. If, as seems likely, enterprises still faced a major owner in the shape of their own local government and its dependencies, then the role of the other owners in bringing about the hoped-for behavioural changes might well be quite small. The local authorities and the enterprises responsible to them would be subject to many of the same pressures as at present with, in practice, relatively little change in the existing power structure. But a more fundamental change, with no one institution having significant discretionary powers to direct, control, or intervene in the operations of the enterprises in which it held a stake would create major difficulties for authorities' financial planning. More generally, different institutions would frequently have very different interests, generating considerable tension between them both within and between regions. For example, should the tax-revenue requirements of one locality take priority over the investment needs of an enterprise in another locality? Should debt repayment to one financial institution take precedence over maintaining production and employment of a major enterprise? Should an enterprise use local component supplies or cheaper sources in another province? All these dilemmas and many others face the authorities under present arrangements, but the latter provide a mechanism, however faulty it may be at times, for resolving them. No clear alternative exists under genuine multiple ownership and, while it is possible to theorize on a set of rules for determining priorities, in practice this is likely to be difficult. Indeed, many of the present problems identified earlier arise precisely because of the difficulty within the Chinese system of delineating and enforcing clear, consistent, and transparent rules for determining enterprises' appointments, decisions, and financial flows. This is not to say that some such arrangements would be unworkable; rather that in practice the dispersion of ownership and control would tend to be limited, with minority stockholders exerting only modest constraints on the principal stockholders.

The second problem is more political. Let us imagine for the moment that the scheme was completely effective, with the ownership institutions being largely in the position of financial intermediaries in the West. There would be substantial managerial autonomy, and owning institutions would receive fixed or variable returns; there might be some scope for institutions to dispose of underperforming shares, funding of weak enterprises could also be cut, and in more extreme circumstances the institutions acting in concert could replace the management of an enterprise or force it into liquidation. The question then arises whether the *authorities* would retain any effective control of enterprises. It is quite possible that in such circumstances they would to a considerable extent come to occupy a similar position to investors in the USA or the UK acting as a source of funds but exercising relatively little if any effective control.

This might not be undesirable, and could be seen as one of the aims of this type of proposal but it implies state ownership without effective state control. It is quite likely that a structure deemed to be a public ownership system, with the power, authority, and responsibility of the state which that implies, but with little practical content to that title would be potentially unstable. A substantial amount of economic power would pass to the institutions even though responsibility for economic performance would still lie with state authorities. In the event of the latter being unable to meet its economic and social objectives there would be strong incentives for the state to intervene and a potentially volatile situation if the multiple-ownership structure made this ineffective. In practice, the possibility of such problems may generate strong resistance to any such reform.

Again, we do not discount such proposals on this account. Similar, if less strong objections could have been made in relation to a number of the managerial incentive mechanisms which were none the less introduced in the second half of the 1980s and which have achieved some considerable measure of success; though the experience of 1989–92 illustrates how severe the conflict between even modest managerial autonomy and the perceived responsibilities of the state authorities can be. Rather it suggests that ownership *per se* may be of significance and that proposals designed to produce incentive mechanisms and managerial autonomy normally associated with Western private capitalism within a state-ownership system may face greater difficulties than has sometimes been thought. In order to examine this it is necessary to be clear precisely what function ownership itself provides and whether there is some binding relationship between any particular type of ownership and the economic mechanisms which influence enterprise behaviour. It is to this that we now turn.

5. *The Enterprise: Ownership, Control, Risks, and Incentives*

5.1 The functions of ownership

At first sight the notion of 'an enterprise', be this in the context of the capitalist system in the West or in the socialist system in China, seems quite straightforward. We observe many thousands of them and can readily identify their main characteristics as entities for carrying out the economic transformation and distribution of resources, goods, and services. They all have owners, who are generally private shareholders in the West and generally the state in China; they all have managerial decision-takers responsible for the day-to-day decisions which determine their operation; and they all have employees who carry out operations. In particular cases any two or even all three of these individuals or groups within an enterprise may be one and the same.

It does not, however, require a great deal of curiosity to find some vagueness and perhaps some confusion in this basic picture. To see this we may use Hess's example of an individual who, seeing an unfulfilled demand for leather shoes advertises for people who can prepare leather hides, and for others who can cut, shape, and sew them into shoes (Hess 1983: 2–3). He then rents a building, buys hides for them with which to work, pays those who turn up in the building to work per hide or per pair of shoes, and sells the finished articles to salesmen. Any net gains from these transactions he keeps, and any net losses he bears. This looks very like a conventional enterprise involving the obtaining of inputs, which combine to produce outputs which are then sold. But no 'enterprise' as such exists. The individual who took the initiative has, as an individual, merely entered into four different types of market transaction, namely buying hides, paying labour, renting property, and selling shoes. He is certainly not an 'owner' of an enterprise, not just because he does not own one but because there is no enterprise to own. He is not a manager in any ordinary sense because he is merely making a series of deals all of which are spot-market transactions at market-determined prices for cash. In other words, he may be described as a trader but not a manager. He is not an operative in any sense as he carries out no production-line work and he certainly is not an employee of anyone.

To have a clear picture of the essential nature of an enterprise we must ask how the above example needs to be altered in order for us to conclude that an enterprise exists. The answer can be derived directly from Coase's seminal work on the nature of the firm where he asked why there are 'islands of conscious power in a sea of market transactions' (Coase 1937). The essence of that 'conscious power' is that *it*, rather than prices, acts as the mechanism which co-ordinates economic resource-allocation decisions. The reason that no enterprise exists in the foregoing example is precisely that all the transactions are price-dependent with price alone determining, for example, whether hides are delivered, whether anyone will manufacture shoes, etc. The instigator of all the activities becomes the co-ordinating mechanism, and the operations involved become part of an enterprise, only when his contracts with the processing and sales people involves a *grant of authority* by the latter to the former such that they agree, within certain specified or understood limits, to carry out activities as directed by the co-ordinator. There is now considerable literature on the characteristics and circumstances of transactions which result in this grant of authority generating greater efficiency than market transactions, leading to the existence of enterprises and higher remuneration for the contracting parties (see e.g. Hess 1983; Alchian and Demsetz 1972; Williamson 1975, 1981).

Let us imagine therefore that the initiator now recruits people to work for him and co-ordinates their activities by direction. Some buy hides, others process and sell them. The initiator still rents the building and pays each worker a predetermined wage. There is now an enterprise in existence. In comparing this with the original situation, three points are important. First, if all goes well there is still a surplus which, except in so far as the contracts involve profit-related bonuses or profit-sharing, accrue to the initiator of the operations. If the residual is negative then he bears this loss. Second, the initiator, by virtue of his now acting as the co-ordinating mechanism, becomes a *manager* of resources. Third, there is still no enterprise in the sense of a collection of assets but there is in the sense of a *set of contracts* between the interested parties. At first sight it makes little sense to say that anyone 'owns' a set of contracts but the initiator is the owner of the enterprise in two senses. First, he owns *the right to receive or dispose of the surpluses* that occur and the obligation to bear any losses. It is important to describe what is owned in these terms because the initiator may decide to draw up another contract passing all such surpluses to another individual, his family, a trust, or a charity. (Contracts may also determine that someone else bears any losses.) This does not confer ownership on the latter body, because the initiator of the operations retains the right, subject to the contracts he has freely entered into, to determine the destination of the surpluses. If on the other hand he drew up a contract which ceded to others in perpetuity the right to determine the use of the surpluses then at that point ownership in this first sense would pass to the other parties to the contract.

The second element of ownership is more problematic. Even if the initiator disposes of the residual rights, he is still the common party to the set of contracts, can negotiate and renegotiate any or all of them, as a result can determine who will be parties to the contract and who therefore will participate in the enterprise. By these means he can determine its objectives, functions, and operations, and whether it will continue to exist or not. This element of ownership could in principle continue independent of the allocation of residual returns and residual, i.e. non-insurable, risk.

At first sight this second aspect of ownership serves to blur the concepts of ownership and management. In many Western firms it is the *management* which is the common party to all contracts, including those with the owners; it is the management that negotiates most contracts, hires and fires, thereby determining participation in the enterprise, and generally controls its operations. The ownership function of shareholders typically appears to be purely that of residual risk-bearing. In some cases it can easily seem that effectively the senior managers of a firm are functionally even though not legally the owners, with the residual risk-bearing function having been contracted out to shareholders. But this would be to ignore a crucial element in the nexus of contracts, namely that ultimately only the owners can make the ultimate decisions as to *who the managers will be*. Suppose in our illustrative example above the initiator draws up contracts which hire managers to carry out all the resource-co-ordinating activities involved. For the sake of argument, let us suppose that he also draws up other contracts which permanently cede the right to dispose of residual returns or bear residual losses to some other party or parties. He none the less, even in these extreme circumstances, still retains an ownership function, namely the right to determine who the managers will be and how much they are paid. In practice this right may exert considerable influence on how the enterprise is managed as managers seek to retain their positions and income, and an extensive literature has built up on the nature of the owner–manager relationship and the problems of communication, incentive-compatibility, and risk-sharing between them that emerges. One main strand of this, the principal–agent literature, is addressed in more detail in Section 7. For the moment we need stress only the fundamental point that ownership in an enterprise crucially involves the right to appoint and dismiss the managers and set the terms on which they are employed. In addition ownership is normally associated with the residual risk-bearing function and often equated with it, but this, at least in principle, is a separate function.

To summarize, an enterprise is essentially a set of co-ordinating contracts which embody grants of authority and which act as an alternative resource-allocation mechanism to spot market contracts. These contracts identify the interested parties, specify the relations that exist between them, and determine who will do what and what each will receive. The defining characteristic of management is that it co-ordinates the contracts and the activities they specify, hence management is the immediate manifestation of the 'conscious power' which determines resource allocation, production, and distribution. The defining characteristic of ownership is the contractual power to determine who will comprise the management and their remuneration, and the right to determine the allocation of residual gains and losses. This latter right is in theory permanently alienable but is rarely, if ever, so in practice. We will therefore assume both ownership functions operate though there may be contracts in which the owner, for a period at least, assigns the potential residual gains and losses to another party.

Before proceeding, two caveats should be added. First, owners need to recruit and monitor managers and these functions may themselves be delegated, typically to a board of directors (though the directors may retain managerial co-ordination functions as well). This, however, does not transfer ownership because the owners still retain the right to appoint the board. Ownership and resource co-ordination become more removed from each other and we need to distinguish ownership, control of managers, and management decision-taking itself, but the nature and location of the ownership function remain unchanged.

Second, though non-voting shares are currently out of favour, they have frequently traded in the past at very little if any discount to their voting equivalent.[8] Non-voting shares typically have exactly the same residual risk characteristics as their voting counterparts, the only difference therefore being the absence of any right to determine who the managers will be. It would therefore seem as if investors place little or no value on what we have argued is the defining characteristic of ownership. However, non-voting shares are often issued in order to secure a different division of a company's profits to that represented by ownership shares. In such cases the market in non-voting shares may in practice be formed largely by voting shareholders, resulting in little discount. In addition where product-market competition or stock markets are effective in generating managerial efficiency, non-voting shareholders may free-ride on the control function exercised by voting shareholders, again reducing or eliminating the discount. Alternatively, where there are significant constraints on dispersed shareholders exercising their ownership function, the present value of the probability that this function will be exercised may be very low. In neither case does it follow that the ownership function as defined above is not valuable where it can be exercised.

5.2 *Control, risks, and incentives*

Within this framework we now look at the link between the control and risk-bearing aspects of ownership, and their relationship to incentives in organizations. Specifically, we argue that the residual risk-bearer must *either* have effective control of managerial decision-taking, which in the present context means direct power to appoint, dismiss, and set remuneration, *or* be able to sell the right to be the residual risk-bearer, or both.[9] This is based on the idea that no individual or group will normally be prepared to bear such risks if there is neither the possibility of escaping them through a sale of the rights and obligations involved, nor any power to influence the decisions which determine whether the residual is positive or negative or its size. This point is important in explaining why companies which are unlisted on a stock exchange are typically managed or closely controlled by their shareholders (see Hay and Morris 1984). In such companies there is typically some difficulty in selling shares, and as a result the owners need to exercise direct control. Small shareholdings in unquoted companies held outside the managerial group are usually the result of gifts, trusts, or inheritance. Typically in the West therefore the bearers of residual risk must either have direct control of management, as in virtually all unquoted companies, or, where that control function is weakened as in the typical quoted company, they must have a market for that residual risk, provided by a stock market.[10]

This analysis can be formulated in terms of incentives. If residual gains or losses accrue to one or more individuals who can neither escape these consequences nor exert any control over the managers whose decisions determine those gains or losses, then incentives for enterprise efficiency will be weakened. They are irrelevant to the residual risk-bearers because, *ex-hypothesi*, the latter have no discretion to influence decisions. But the impact of incentives on the individual or group who exercises control is also reduced because the consequences of better or worse performance can be shifted to the residual risk-bearers. The owner, whether this is the management, other individuals or institutions, or the state, may choose to set up incentive mechanisms which relate managerial positions and pay to performance with greater or lesser success; but with residual losses transferable elsewhere there is no necessity to do this, no binding reason to maintain such mechanisms in operation and no automatic penalty for failure to do so.

These problems clearly do not occur if the residual risk-bearers have control. Discretion lies with the risk-bearers and the consequences of their decisions accrue to them, creating a strong incentive to achieve maximum performance. If the residual risk-bearers do not exercise direct control but can trade in residual risk, incentives will again be important. The risk-bearers have a direct incentive to acquire such rights in better-performing enterprises and to obtain rising values of those rights through improving performance. Those exercising direct control have incentives to respond because, if performance is inadequate then it will not be possible to find or retain residual risk-bearers. This may lead to bankruptcy of the enterprise, loss of control, or the transfer of residual risk to those exercising control, depending on the legal, financial, and institutional arrangements in force. Thus, if the defining characteristics of ownership is control then it follows that efficiency requires either (*a*) that owners bear the residual risk or (*b*) there is a market for residual risk.

We now consider the case of state ownership. We must first distinguish between the population as a whole, in whose name at least state-owned assets are notionally held, and the institutions of the state which actually appoint and direct the managers of state-owned enterprises. Given this distinction and given the arguments above it is clear that in practice the ownership of enterprises is in the hands of the institutions of the state. It is they which control managers through powers of appointment, dismissal, and the power to set remuneration, and it is they which allocate residual risk. They can in principle allocate it to other enterprises via the allocation of investment funds or higher taxation, or to the population more generally via higher or lower public expenditures resulting from higher- or lower-profit delivery. But in neither of these cases does the institution, as owner, itself bear residual risk nor is there any market in residual risk for those who bear it. In other words, neither of the conditions necessary for incentive efficiency established above holds.

This in essence is the argument for supposing that public ownership must be inefficient. Neither the institutions which effectively exercise the ownership function nor the managers of the enterprises they own have sufficient incentive to be efficient because residual risk lies elsewhere. That the bearers of residual risk none the less provide this function despite having neither control *nor* a market in residual risk occurs only because it is imposed upon them by the state as a result of power relations rather than individual preferences. There are numerous reasons why the state might choose such arrangements. The ability to assign residual risk can be used to influence income distribution, while control of enterprises via control of their managers can be used directly to secure various economic and social objectives.

Those responsible for the state institutions which carry ownership rights in principle and often in practice have considerable powers and wide discretion over how to use them. There may be some externalities deriving from state ownership, though it is not clear that ownership rights, as opposed to regulatory and tax powers, are necessary to achieve them. There may also be political objections to private ownership and significant costs associated with a transfer to private ownership and the setting-up of institutional arrangements necessary to make it effective. But these do not alter the basic inference that state ownership does not in principle generate a set of efficient incentive relations between risk and control in enterprises.

The central questions then are whether the largely decentralized nature of state control that exists in China at the present time or proposals for multiple state-ownership institutions such as that described in the previous section can overcome this problem.

5.3 Single-agency state ownership in China

With regard to the current institutional arrangements in China, there can be little doubt that the degree of decentralization of state powers and the key role of local authorities have important incentive advantages. Profit delivery or tax revenue will be heavily dependent on enterprise performance and efficiency, and as these authorities themselves face tax delivery targets set by central government which need to be met first if local expenditure plans are to be funded, this creates incentives for them to facilitate performance improvements by enterprises. Indeed this may have been a significant element in the development of the enterprise reform movement in many parts of China in the 1980s, and in some of the consequent improvements in efficiency.

In terms of the analysis above this can be interpreted as a mechanism whereby the owners come to bear at least some of the residual risk and as a result use their control to set up incentive mechanisms for managers such that they and/or their enterprises also bear some of the risk. This occurs through the financial rewards, investment funds, security, and promotion attached to successful completion of profit contracts.

There are however reasons stemming from our analysis of the links between ownership control and risk to expect significant limitations on these efficiency incentives. First, the incentive effects operating on local state authorities are at best partial. While there may be some advantages from increased tax revenue as a result of superior enterprise performance, the consequences for the responsible individuals within the local state institution may be relatively small, and there may be little or no repercussion on individual wealth or income if enterprise performance is below the maximum. There is no necessary reason for the authorities to respond to lower local revenues given that they can effectively insulate their own position from such fluctuations, with the costs being borne by the local population at large. In other words, although the decentralized structure creates some pressures on local authorities, *residual* risk can still be allocated to the population irrespective of the latter's preferences and with no scope for them to divest themselves of that risk. In addition the incentive effect of having to meet central tax targets and of increased local revenues once these are met is reduced where, over a period, tax targets are set in the light of the tax revenues raised in the past. In such circumstances higher-profit delivery one year carries the likelihood of higher tax commitments in future years.

Second, the control exercised by the authorities coupled with the ability to avoid much of the residual risk function means that there is considerable scope for other objectives, be these social ones stemming from other responsibilities of the state, or private ones stemming from the individual interests of those in control, to play an important role in determining how the control function is exercised. For example, sales tax, employment, and even social stability are all more closely related to the level of enterprise *activity* and output than efficiency, profitability, or solvency. The external costs of business failures in terms of unemployment and social security costs are reasons for supporting inefficient enterprises and, while in some situations this may represent a rational assessment by the authorities of the costs of subsidies as against the costs of business failure, it none the less weakens the incentive mechanism operating on managers. In addition, most if not all of the costs of making a wrong calculation on such matters fall not on the owners who control the enterprises but on the population as residual risk-bearers. Personal connection, political advantage, or career plans may also play important roles in the control of managers given that purely commercial incentives or remuneration considerations are relatively weak.

The third limitation on incentive efficiency relates to the consequences for the financing of enterprises of residual risk being borne by the population at large. The latter notionally hold the equity in state-owned enterprises. If an insolvent enterprise is allowed to fail, then loss of assets and funds invested constitute a loss of public finance and are borne by the community. By the same token, enterprises' equity can be increased only through retained profit or injections of new public funds. If, as is often the case, the former is inadequate fully to finance expansion, and the latter carries the risk of creating a soft budget constraint then, as was seen in Chapter 9, enterprises come to depend heavily on debt finance from state-owned banks. Enterprises will then tend systematically to become overgeared because, while some may be able to achieve an optimal balance of debt and equity in the light of the commercial risks they face, the restrictions on equity will prevent some, and perhaps most, from doing so. This increases the riskiness of enterprises' financial structure, which makes it more likely, even if they have sound long-term prospects, that they will become insolvent in a business downturn. The state, even if viewed purely in its role as the owner of the enterprise (and therefore ignoring the wider costs to the state of insolvency), has an incentive to prevent this, but such action exacerbates the problem of enforcing hard budget constraints on enterprises. It is not difficult to design equity instruments which would reflect the residual risks involved, but this would not make much difference under present institutional arrangements. This is because they could not be sold to the bearers of the residual risk to raise new equity while at the same time preserving full state ownership. Nor of course could there be a market in such rights.[11]

Overall therefore there are quite important limitations on the efficiency of present institutions of state ownership in China resulting from the risk and control characteristics which they embody. We have examined these in terms of the nature of ownership and the way in which efficiency relates to risk-bearing and control. But the consequences may be seen empirically in a number of ways. The continuing problems of so-called 'policy losses' (see Chapter 10, Section 2) and 'soft' budget constraints are one measure. The evidence referred to earlier (see Chapter 12, Section 3) that state-owned enterprises continue to be out-performed by other types of enterprise is another indication. As our interview and questionnaire results indicated, managerial autonomy is still to some degree circumscribed by direct intervention and control from the higher authorities, particularly if short-term revenue or output priorities prevail. Equally if not more significant than all of these was the ease with which, under the present ownership structure, the activities and priorities of enterprises could be redirected in the aftermath of the social unrest in 1989 in order to meet political objectives, irrespective of their consequences for the efficiency of enterprises, their financial performance, or the economic costs to the community. This illustrates both the rather fragile nature of the incentive relations and efficiency gains achieved by the enterprise reform of the mid-1980s and the potential weakness of ownership structures which do not meet the underlying requirements laid out above.

5.4 Multiple-agency state-ownership in China

Using the same perspective we now consider multiple state-ownership as outlined in Section 4 above. The advantages of this approach have been spelt out previously. The scope for interventions which inhibit efficiency would be reduced; key decisions through which control is exercised would be less monolithic; subsidization would be more constrained; and an institutional framework for separating off the non-commercial responsibilities of enterprises would be created. In other words a number of the drawbacks of the current arrangements would be reduced, perhaps substantially.

Ownership control, while clearly being more dispersed would still reside with the state institutions which appointed or dismissed managers. Residual risk would still be borne by the population, but with the potentially important difference that to some degree this role could be, if not marketable, at least transferable. This is because in principle different state institutions, each with different segments of the population dependent on it, could to some extent choose enterprises in which to take stakes. While it is not realistic to imagine that this discretion would be unfettered—a local authority would be unlikely or unable to dispense with holding a major ownership stake in the key enterprises in its locality—there would be some scope for residual risk obligations to be reallocated in the light of enterprise performance. It cannot be ruled out that an actual market might develop between various state institutions for the buying and selling of ownership rights in state-owned enterprises where those rights conveyed both control and the power to assign residual risk.

All this is consistent with the view that such a multiple-ownership scheme would offer advantages. There would none the less be limitations on the extent to which these arrangements would meet the criteria established above. We consider this under three headings: the location of residual risk, transferability of residual risk, and ownership control of enterprises.

With regard to the first, the location of residual risk would in principle be the same as at present. Some of the gains and losses of enterprises would accrue to the owning agency, be this in pecuniary or non-pecuniary form, but the main residual risk-bearer would still be one or more sections of the population, namely those who would gain or lose as a result of higher or lower accruals of income to any particular owning agency. While the distribution of gains and losses across the population might change there would still be no scope for any of those affected either to shift the residual risk or to exercise any control on enterprises. As at present, they would exercise no effective ownership right and no incentive effects would emanate from their notional ownership. In other words, the fundamental characteristic of public ownership, namely the lack of either control or incentive mechanisms running from the primary bearers of residual risk to enterprises, would remain largely unchanged.

Turning to transferability of residual risk, there are clear advantages to multiple-agency ownership. Equity stakes in enterprises could in principle be bought and sold, either in bilateral trades between agencies or even in a quasi-market. Ideally this would be associated with a high degree of autonomy of the agencies involved, with their financial resources dependent on the performance of the enterprises in which they held stakes. This would create strong incentives to identify, finance, and promote efficient enterprises and, as a consequence, economic pressure on enterprises to operate efficiently. But there are two major obstacles to this. First, local authorities would still have discretion to supplement and/or redirect enterprise funds to some degree independent of enterprise performance. Loss-making enterprises could continue to be funded, whether as part of an overall economic or social policy, or in the light of party or other non-commercial criteria, and profit delivery could be adjusted in the light of all manner of economic and non-economic objectives. These considerations would not in general apply to other state-ownership agencies, for example banks and other financial institutions, but here the second obstacle arises, namely the extent to which the latter would in practice be given autonomy in the financing of enterprises. As we have seen, at present banks have virtually no such autonomy for any significant funding. It is unlikely that the state at either central or local level would relinquish the power to use the banking system to achieve both economic and other objectives while the banks or the financial institutions continued to be owned by them. Furthermore, such power would, under multiple ownership, be likely to embrace decisions on equity transfer. While dispersed ownership might raise the cost of intervention and/or reduce its effectiveness, it is not clear that the scope for intervention would be significantly weakened while such institutions remained state-owned. Above all, the penalty for failure by the institutions—to maximize enterprise efficiency, to direct funding to the most efficient ones within an institution's portfolio, or to build up equity stakes in more efficient enterprises at the expense of less efficient ones—in all cases remains attenuated because of the scope for shifting much of the cost to the community at large.

In practice the main thrust of multiple ownership is not in fact relocation of residual risk, nor even transferability of risk, but a shift in effective decision-taking powers from agencies of the state to managers of enterprises. The desirability of this rests on the belief that the latter will be concerned only with enterprise performance and that dispersed state-ownership will substantially reduce the scope for intervention by any of the agencies involved. The evidence of Western economies, examined in more detail in the next section, illustrates that dispersed equity holdings tend to put more decision-taking power in the hands of managers and reduce the scope for any one stakeholder to intervene. The two main issues here are, first, whether the pursuit of managerial objectives, largely unfettered by ownership control, is advantageous from the standpoint of economic welfare. This is the focus of the next section. Second, this loss of ownership control is only likely to be feasible even in principle if a genuine market in equity stakes emerges. Without this the stakeholding institutions would *ex-hypothesi* have neither direct control nor the ability readily to transfer residual risk. This does not mean that ownership would *de facto* pass completely to the managers themselves because, at least in extreme circumstances and given collective action, the state equity-holding institutions would still retain the power to appoint or dismiss the managers. The issue is more whether local authorities would be prepared to accept a substantial diminution of ownership control unless the associated financial and social obligations were equally reduced. This could happen because, unlike the position in the West, the ultimate providers of the finance have no discretion to accept or avoid these consequences. This places the local authorities in a quite different position from that of an investing financial institution in the West. None the less the dispersion of ownership rights would for most local authorities represent a clear loss of ownership control with no obvious benefit to them to offset it.

None of this implies that there would be no advantages in such arrangements, only that the disposition of the residual risk and control functions would be likely to remain significantly less than optimal from the point of view of incentives and efficiency. Control, whether retained by state agencies or to some extent ceded to managers, would remain substantially divorced from the main residual risk-bearers and, even if a market came to be created in risky equity stakes, the participants in the market would not be the main bearers of the risk involved.

The question remains as to whether the rewards and penalties accruing specifically to those managing the equity-owning institutions in a multiple ownership structure could be tied sufficiently strongly and directly to their financial performance to make the latter their overriding objective, even though most of the residual risk would still lie elsewhere. This, after all, is the position of investing institutions in the West. In practice this would require at least two conditions. First, financial institutions would have to be given effective financial and decision-taking autonomy. They would monitor and invest in enterprises as they thought best, utilizing state funds on which a fixed or variable return would be paid. Unsuccessful financial institutions would be cut off from funding and ultimately taken over or left to go bankrupt, while successful ones would be able to generate more internal funds and obtain more state funding on commercial terms. Similar conditions would then apply to enterprises themselves.

Second, local authorities would have to withdraw completely from the direct ownership or funding of enterprises because the first condition above could not apply to such bodies. State ownership of enterprises would exist only by virtue of the ownership of the financial institutions which held the equity of enterprises. Local authorities would also need to bind themselves in some credible manner not to intervene, nor to make institutional appointments on other than financial performance grounds.

Such arrangements are unlikely to be feasible. It is not clear that such commitments by local authorities could be made credible given that the financial institutions would be owned by those authorities and would determine enterprise behaviour and performance. If they were made credible then the loss of ownership control would be considerable, and exacerbated by the dispersion of ownership at the level both of financial institutions and enterprises. It is quite possible that such arrangements could then become politically unstable. This is because they imply that agencies of the state with overall ownership responsibilities for industrial enterprises would be unable to exercise this responsibility as they saw fit, even though most of the costs or benefits of enterprises' performance fell on the population represented by the local authority.

In summary, multiple state-ownership offers some clear advantages in terms of enterprise autonomy, the implementation of efficiency criteria, and some limited transferability of risk. But it is unlikely to relocate risk, permit principal risk-bearers discretion to shift risk, or integrate ownership control with residual risk. The conditions necessary to generate pure efficiency incentives by allocating sufficient residual risk to those exercising the control function are unlikely to be feasible because they imply a substantial loss of ownership control by the local authorities but with no reduction in their responsibilities.

5.5 Private ownership

At heart, the fundamental problem in both current or reformed state ownership is that it locates ultimate control in individuals who to a great extent can avoid the residual risk inherent in enterprise operation, allocating the latter to others who can neither exercise control nor themselves transfer the residual risk. As a result, incentives to efficiency for the owning institutions are reduced and for the main risk-bearers are irrelevant. Reform of decision-taking structures may well be able to reduce the costs involved but are unlikely to eliminate them.

The essential difference with private ownership is that in principle it solves this problem. There are of course many different institutional forms of private ownership some of which, as indicated above, look very similar at an institutional level to the multiple state-ownership structure described previously. But the crucial distinction is that, directly or indirectly, the ownership control function lies with the residual risk-bearer, or the latter function is transferable at the discretion of the risk-bearer himself. Whether equity stakes are held directly in enterprises or via investing institutions, whether control is direct or risk is marketable, mechanisms exist whereby residual risk-bearers can influence enterprise managers and in which they have clear incentives to do so purely in the light of performance criteria. While institutions may stand as intermediaries between risk-bearer and enterprise, these institutions depend only on their own ability to invest and/or influence enterprise performance and hence on their ability to retain the financial support of the risk-bearers. Poor enterprise performance generates clear incentives for residual risk-bearers to take action to improve it. Alternatively they may escape this burden but only through a voluntary transaction at a market-determined price. As with state ownership so with private ownership there are different institutional arrangements that can embody these relationships, some of which may be more effective or less costly than others (see next section). But the fundamental characteristic remains that residual risk-bearers face incentive mechanisms directly related to enterprise performance, and the position and rewards of enterprise managers are influenced by ownership control or transfer exercised in the light of those incentives. Ownership *per se* is thus a determinant of performance even though there is scope under state ownership to design mechanisms which to some extent replicate those operating under private ownership.

6. *Control and Behaviour of Enterprises under Private Ownership*

Given the above, it is not surprising that, in the period since 1989, a hallmark of almost all policies designed to transform socialist economies has been large-scale privatization of industrial assets. In many cases this has been seen as an essential element of the process, without which a switch to an effective market-based economy is either very difficult or impossible. Numerous schemes for bringing about the privatization of industrial assets have been proposed and a number implemented in Eastern Europe and China, but most have entailed distributing shares in some way to sections of the population, thus mirroring the private ownership of companies in the West. Such approaches usually, though not always, entail the development of a stockmarket on which equity stakes can be traded. However, just as quite different forms of state ownership are possible, with potentially quite different characteristics in terms of risks, incentives, and efficiency, so a number of different structures of private ownership are possible, also with different such characteristics. It is to this that we now turn.

If we wish to examine the introduction of private capital then we have to envisage institutional arrangements which either provide easy access to an active stockmarket, or ones which provide private equity-owners with effective control of the enterprises in which they take such stakes. As far as small enterprises are concerned, the latter solution is usually adopted and is in practice the only feasible one. One or more individuals own the small enterprise, manage it, and bear the residual risk associated with their ownership. Such arrangements are not difficult to set up, nor are they particularly controversial. It is understandable that in many socialist economies both past and present, such arrangements have been the first used to introduce private ownership and to date the ones in which most progress has been made. A significant proportion of the Chinese economy reflects this type of arrangement.

For larger enterprises there is generally an irreconcilability between the size of the equity stakes that an individual or group of individuals could normally amass and the stake it would be necessary to hold in order to exercise effective control of management, and it is this which leads on to the need for a market in equity instruments. There are exceptions. A joint venture between a state-owned enterprise and a privately owned foreign one can introduce private capital into large-scale operations with the foreign enterprise having certain control rights but without any market for the equity stake which it holds. However, any large foreign enterprise involved in such a joint venture will itself typically be a joint-stock company with dispersed private shareholding and an active market in its equity stock. The exercise of effective control by its management in the joint venture is only acceptable to the ultimate owners because there is such a market.

It is not difficult therefore to understand why the creation and development of stockmarkets might be seen as a precondition for achieving any significant degree of privatization of large state-owned enterprises if the latter is not to result largely in foreign acquisition. A stockmarket provides for transferability of, and exit from, the residual risk-bearing function, and permits ownership of an enterprise to pass from one group of owners to another through the mechanism of take-overs. Equally important, in the process, managerial control of an enterprise can and frequently will pass from one group of managers to another. In principle this constitutes a powerful mechanism for shifting responsibility for the use of resources from less efficient to more efficient management teams.

The problem with this is that although, as we have seen, private ownership in principle meets the criteria necessary to generate effective efficiency incentives, the last twenty years or so have seen an accumulation of evidence in the West that a stockmarket may well not act as an efficient mechanism for allocating enterprise control. On the theoretical side, Grossman and Hart amongst others have demonstrated that the stockmarket may fail to act efficiently because of the existence of a free-rider problem (Grossman and Hart 1980). If a take-over is thought likely to occur which will replace inefficient management and improve performance then each individual shareholder has an incentive to hold on to his shares in order to gain from the improvement. If all do this the take-over will fail.

There are a number of factors which may mitigate this problem; in particular the free-rider problem will tend to disappear if there is uncertainty about the *motive* for the take-over. If some firms, in pursuit of growth, are prepared to pay more than the present value of future profits, then those who hold on to the shares might not realize a higher value eventually. They then have an incentive to sell rather than free-ride. Other ways of circumventing the free-rider problem, including mechanisms which penalize free-riders, compulsory acquisition legislation, and the use of 'toe-hold' stakes in prospective target companies have been suggested, and the use of unconditional bids or the activities of risk arbitrageurs can also reduce its impact, but none of these will necessarily eliminate it (see Hay and Morris 1991: 513–16 for an elaboration of these points).

On the empirical side there have been at least three types of evidence in support of the view that the stockmarket is not efficient in allocating control of resources. First, post-merger performance has tended to be less good than pre-merger performance or the performance of enterprises not involved in merger (see e.g. Meeks 1977; Ravenscraft and Scherer 1987). Again there are caveats. The evidence does not preclude the possibility that the prospect of deteriorating performance is what led to the merger in the first place. Efficiency gains from the merger can then be quite consistent with lower performance post-merger. But this is unlikely fully to explain the bulk of the evidence.

Second, several studies have found that the net gain in the value of the shares of a victim company in a take-over is no greater than and may be less than the loss of value of the raider's shares, suggesting a negative-sum outcome of the merger (see Firth 1979). However, one might expect stockmarkets to learn from this and more recent evidence suggests that this result may no longer hold (see Franks *et al.* 1987; Jensen and Ruback 1983; Jarnell *et al.* 1988).

Third, a number of studies examine the characteristics of raiders and victims and find little support for the view that take-overs predominantly involve more profitable or higher-valued enterprises taking over less profitable or lower-valued ones (see Singh 1975; Kuehn 1975). Primarily they involve larger companies taking over smaller ones, notwithstanding that there have in recent years been a number of attempts, though rarely successful, to take over large companies. This evidence is of some significance, though not conclusive. Much of the rationale for take-overs may lie in current or prospective characteristics of the market, competitive pressures within it, product or process rationalization or development, technological considerations or geographical factors, which do not have any simple relation to, or any direct reflection in current or past returns on capital. A high valuation ratio may reflect only that the stockmarket views an enterprise as having scope to utilize its assets more effectively or in different ways such that the assets will increase in value, a subsequent take-over being the mechanism by which these changes are achieved. The tendency for raiders to be larger may reflect the relatively large fixed costs, financial and otherwise, of engaging in merger, so that only a subset of all desirable mergers, namely those where the raider is large, actually occur. The stockmarket is then inefficient as a mechanism due to transaction costs but the mergers which *do* occur are not themselves inefficient. It can be seen therefore that there may be exceptions to most or all of the evidence demonstrating stockmarket inefficiency. None the less the general thrust of all these different approaches suggests clear limitations on the effectiveness of the stockmarket as a mechanism for allocating corporate control.

There is however a further line of argument which though again not conclusive is of great relevance to the issue of private ownership in China. Indeed arguably it is fundamental to the whole question of what type of institutional reforms would be desirable in the Chinese economy in order to promote further efficiency gains via improvements in monitoring, control, and risk-allocating mechanisms. It starts with the controversial but inconclusive debate as to whether stockmarkets are *myopic*. Many industrialists have absolutely no doubt that stockmarket investors, not least institutional ones, adopt damagingly short-time horizons in assessing financial investment opportunities, often quoting the very short intervals, typically 3 months but sometimes less, between each performance review of those responsible for investment decisions in financial institutions. Hard evidence for myopia is however hard to find and, if anything at first sight rather against such a conclusion (see Marsh 1991; Chan *et al.* 1990; Pakes 1985). Empirically, stockmarkets appear quite good at anticipating not only future dividends and/or profitability more generally but also the value-increasing repercussions of investment expenditure, research and development, new products, etc., all of which are primarily long-term profit-generating activities (for a summary of the evidence see Camerer 1989; Morris 1994). Short performance review intervals are irrelevant because, if longer-term gains are properly anticipated then this will show up straight away in capital appreciation, and even an analyst assessed quarterly on his investment performance will want to acquire such shares at an early date. More generally, systematic myopia seems to many implausible. If investors really are missing out on long-term profit opportunities in a systematic manner, then *someone* is likely to notice, come in and pick up neglected stocks cheaply, hold them for the long term and out-perform the market.

Yet the view that joint-stock companies quoted on active stock exchanges such as those in the USA and the UK are thereby constrained to adopt unnecessarily short business horizons is widely held by those involved. One possible reconciliation of these views starts from the Marris model of the managerially controlled enterprise (Marris 1963).[12] This presumes that managers of an enterprise will mainly pursue growth rather than profitability because their basic objectives, the pursuit of greater remuneration, status, power, and security, all typically depend on size rather more than profitability. The model then implies that an enterprise will grow faster but generate lower profitability the more growth-orientated its managers and the weaker the stockmarket discipline on its share price. Using this model, Odagiri argued that, in the industrial sector of an economy containing both profit-maximizing and growth-maximizing enterprises, the latter will come to predominate, because, in the limit a growth-maximizer will always be prepared to invest more, or pay more for another enterprise than a profit-maximizer (Odagiri 1981). This is because the growth-maximizer achieves more size from such activities. Increased size is a part of its utility function but not part of that of a profit-maximizer. Eventually therefore the industrial sector of a capitalist economy (and, we will argue later, in some circumstances in a socialist one as well) can be characterized as growth-maximizing subject to a finance constraint, with the growth rate of the *economy* then determined by the extent of managers' growth motivation and the extent to which this is constrained by the stockmarket or, we might add, any other institutional arrangements which determine managerial discretion. Where managerial labour mobility is weak, and therefore the pursuit of power, prestige, large salary, and security has to be pursued via growth of a manager's existing enterprise (rather than through periodic transfer to progressively larger enterprises) and where the stockmarket is relatively underdeveloped (both of which conditions were and to some extent still are characteristic of the Japanese economy) growth will be rapid. Where both conditions are reversed, as for example in the USA and the UK, growth will be much lower.

A potentially far-reaching inference may be drawn from this. Traditionally it has been thought that the more nearly perfect are markets the higher the level of economic welfare attainable, and this is a standard result of welfare economics viewed from a microeconomic perspective. But the above argument suggests that it is *ineffective* markets, for managerial labour and for enterprise assets respectively, that maximize growth and hence in a *macroeconomic* perspective maximize economic welfare.

The implications for the myopia debate are striking. On the one hand, stockmarket investors are, in this picture, quite rational and do not in the usual sense at least suffer from myopia. They assess opportunities along profit-maximizing lines and their failure to support a number of projects, new investments, and R & D which enterprise managers would like them to support stems not from myopia on *their* part but from the pursuit of growth *on the part of the managers* in excess of that which could be justified purely by reference to standard profitability calculations. On the other hand the growth objective and freedom to pursue it is what, across the industrial sector as a whole and over the long term, generates faster growth of the economy, and with it more rapidly rising living standards and higher economic welfare. Managers may correctly sense that the longer-term health and prospects for an economy will be better if the workings of the stockmarket are restrained and the threat of take-over reduced, even though the benefits cannot simply be attributed to some systematic blind spot on the part of the individual investors who comprise the stockmarket. It is not some failure of the latter group to pursue maximization of profits that is the problem but the effect of the stockmarket itself in restraining enterprise growth.

This line of argument is largely theoretical. But two types of evidence are consistent with it. First, as many have noted, the performance of the Japanese and German economies, where there is relatively little effective stockmarket activity and virtually no hostile take-overs, has been superior to that of the US and UK economies where stockmarkets are very active and take-over common. This of course is hardly conclusive given the number of observations and the many other factors relevant to the performance of these economies. But more detailed analyses, particularly of Japanese business operations, suggests more solid support (Odagiri 1992). Japanese companies have typically seen market share as the key criterion in their business plans and investment decisions, often using extremely short product life-cycles to maintain market share even though this can be relatively unprofitable. The intense competition which these strategies generate has often squeezed profitability further, and by international standards Japanese profitability has been quite low (Odagiri 1992, ch. 8). But in such circumstances survival has often been dependent on new products, cost-cutting investment, and the fruits of research and development. It is therefore not surprising that investment, provided it passes some rather low minimum cost of capital or payback threshold, is determined primarily by whether it is necessary for market growth or leadership, developing new business opportunities, or maintaining the momentum of new product development rather than by detailed DCF calculations. Contrary to much of the best accounting practice in the USA and UK many Japanese firms do not have detailed figures for individual product line profitability even *ex post*, let alone *ex ante*. While all this is primarily true of the large conglomerate enterprises for which Japan is famous, it has similar repercussions on the very sizeable small-firm sector in Japan which supplies many of the large companies. It would be surprising if the ability to conduct business in this manner, with direct consequences for competition, efficiency, and growth, were unrelated to the *keiretsu* system in which only a minority of shares are held at arms' length by individuals or financial institutions; in which therefore active share trading generally has little repercussion on management discretion or control; and in which hostile take-overs are therefore very rare.

The second type of evidence is quite different. Hay and Morris have compared the behaviour and performance of companies listed on the UK stock exchange with that of UK companies that are unquoted (Hay and Morris 1984; Hay *et al.* 1991). In the 1970s unquoted companies, typically family businesses in which the senior management owned or controlled, directly or indirectly, the great majority of the shares, exhibited superior growth, profitability, and productivity performance, even allowing for industry and size differences. In the 1980s these differences were much less marked, with unquoted companies performing better in the first half, quoted companies in the latter half. But, strikingly, quoted companies responded much more to immediate profit opportunities, doing disproportionately well in business upswings and disproportionately badly in recession. Unquoted companies, largely free of any pressure from external owners or other providers of risk capital to maximize short-term profit, followed a much more stable trajectory of production, investment, and profitability through the cycle, a characteristic also noted in many Japanese companies, and overall generated better performance from this longer-term strategy. As the only difference between the two samples not otherwise allowed for was whether their shares were quoted and therefore tradable on the stock exchange or not, it is difficult to escape the conclusion that readily marketable equity does tend to inhibit economic performance and welfare.

Though this analysis stems from the myopia debate it is not this debate which is our main concern here. Rather it is the theoretical argument and evidence that the existence of equity investments which are held because they are marketable is not particularly conducive to economic welfare, and that reforms in socialist economies which place a high priority on their creation may be misplaced. The alternative, as exemplified in the Japanese and German economies, has several main characteristics. First, the equity capital of most enterprises is held mainly by a relatively small number of *other* enterprises, including parent companies, affiliates, customers and suppliers, banks, and other domestic financial institutions. For the most part these do not actively trade in the equity. Though there may be active trading by other shareholders, and share prices can be quite volatile, this rarely creates the prospect of hostile take-over. As a result the stockmarket is a weak disciplinary force on management decision-taking. This is quite different from the UK and the USA where, although a majority of shares are held by financial institutions, these holdings tend to be highly dispersed, with each institution holding only a very small proportion of the shares of any one enterprise. In these circumstances the most effective response to the prospect of deteriorating conditions, as far as the shareholder is concerned, is to sell the shares. This in turn reinforces the importance of maintaining relatively small shareholdings in any one enterprise.

Second, the industrial and financial institutions which hold most of the shares generally have direct representation on company boards by virtue of their ownership, and exercise direct 'insider' control via those representations. This type of control has several advantages. It is generally more fully and immediately informed than the indirect control which comes from the potential take-over threat if 'outsider' owners become dissatisfied and sell their holdings. It is a form of control that can exercise itself progressively if performance deteriorates, utilizing loss of bonuses, demotions, business reorganization, and even agreed restructuring of companies if required, rather than the much more abrupt discontinuities often associated with take-over, and also with the defensive efforts sometimes made to stave off take-over as a result of loss of investor confidence. In some circumstances it can also help to avoid unnecessary bankruptcy by generating a greater mutuality of interest between suppliers of debt and equity finance, not least when they are one and the same. The main consequence of this ownership-management structure is that the more long-term orientated investment, R & D-intensive and market-expanding strategies of management can more readily be pursued and this generates faster economic growth, higher living standards, and in some cases, ironically, better domestic profit opportunities than would otherwise have existed. Growth and market-penetration criteria also make export markets natural targets even though they may offer only limited profit opportunities, at least initially, whereas more short-term profit-orientated companies would tend to see such export opportunities as subsidiary to their main operations.

Third, insider control requires an appropriate set of financial intermediaries. Given that individual wealth is much more widely dispersed than corporate assets, insider control of enterprises requires financial institutions that can take in funds from a large number of dispersed individuals and aggregate these up into blocks of finance sufficiently large to take the major stakes in corporate enterprises which individually or jointly confer direct control.[13] More specifically these institutions must be identified or created; their ownership must be determined; their methods of operation and control must be made explicit and their relationship to market mechanisms specified; and the means by which they channel the economy's savings to enterprises made clear. These are all major issues in their own right, but ones which need to be clarified *prior* to any process of reform of ownership of industrial enterprises if the benefits of insider control are to be established. However resolved, this type of control emphasizes the role of financial intermediaries rather than the stockmarket.

There are a large number of ways in which investors might hold debt or equity investments in financial intermediaries. Debt holdings may be non-marketable as in the case of deposits, or marketable as in the case of certificates of deposit or holdings of bonds issued by the intermediary. Equity holdings similarly may be non-marketable as with pension funds, or marketable as with various types of trust investments or holdings of the equity of the intermediaries themselves. Intermediaries may then take marketable debt or equity positions in enterprises, make non-marketable loans, or provide equity capital in cases where no market exists for the equity.

Insider control is consistent with any of these instruments provided that the role of marketable enterprise equity is not significant. A whole range of financial intermediaries, primarily banks, savings and loans institutions, investment banks or pension funds can take in funds on either a debt or equity basis, marketable or otherwise and use these to take both debt and equity stakes in industrial enterprises and obtain the incentive and efficiency effects of insider control, provided that the debt and equity stakes in any given enterprise are concentrated in the hands of a relatively small number of institutions.[14]

It may be questioned whether the existence of dispersed holdings of equity of the financial intermediaries themselves might undermine effective insider control by virtue of the fact that it would require a market in this equity. This could generate the weaker and less efficient exercise of control that we have argued arises with marketable ownership. The problems associated with markets for enterprise equity, i.e. the informational deficiencies, lack of progressive constraints, problems of achieving smooth restructuring and of dealing with potential bankruptcy, together with those stemming from the shorter time-horizons associated with market-orientated control, will then in principle apply to the holding by individuals of marketable equity in financial institutions. However, these problems may be less severe in relation to financial institutions. Provision of information to investors is generally more straightforward because the activities of financial intermediaries, namely receiving and determining the disposition of funds, are more readily conveyed; restructuring of financial holdings is typically easier than is the case with more integrated industrial enterprises; and financial intermediaries are typically highly diversified in terms of the businesses in which they have capital at risk, which reduces the threat of bankruptcy. These will appreciably lessen the problems.

More important, as already noted, there is a mismatch between the concentration of asset-holding necessary for insider control of larger enterprises and the dispersed distribution of wealth held by the population in a system of private ownership. At *some* point in the financial system therefore it is necessary to have dispersed holdings in a relatively small number of institutions and, as a consequence, a market in these assets. Any adverse consequences of this will be attenuated if the dispersed holdings are in financial intermediaries which can hold block stakes in enterprises rather than in enterprises direct. We may also add that the scope for appropriate prudential regulation is greater because of the limited number of financial intermediaries in relation to the number of enterprises. In essence therefore, the implementation of efficient insider control under a private-ownership regime in China would require the following: (*a*) creation of a number of joint-stock privately owned financial institutions able to accept funds by way of deposits or through the issue of marketable certificates of deposit, and by way of financial investment by individuals either in non-marketable claims such as insurance and pension rights, or in marketable ones such as investment trust holdings, property bonds, etc.; (*b*) the conversion of industrial enterprises to joint-stock status with equity participation available to financial institutions in minimum-sized block holdings; and (*c*) the establishment of a regulatory regime for financial institutions for normal prudential reasons but the abandonment of direct public controls on the provision of finance to enterprises.

There are of course a large number of problems, legal, social, and economic, involved in achieving this type of systemic reform. In particular there are questions of valuation of the property rights distributed, the time-scale for achieving this redistribution and the wider consequences of creating private channels of funding from individuals to enterprises rather than the existing public ones. Our purpose here however is not to provide a blueprint for such a transition, which would be a major undertaking in its own right. Rather it is to bring out the requirements for systemic and institutional change which stem from a consideration of the nature of ownership, the associated incentives, risks, and financial flows, and hence the requirements for efficiency gains associated with ownership reform.

Such a structure does not preclude individual holdings in enterprises, by managers, workers, or investors unrelated to the enterprise in question. Nor does it preclude direct funding by the state in particular circumstances, or the existence of a market in equity. But it suggests that these types of holdings will be marginal from an ownership and control perspective, though they may be of great financial importance to the individual investor. It means that any equity market would effectively exist for only a small minority of the capital outstanding. This need not appreciably weaken the insider-control structure that stems from the majority of an enterprise's capital being held by a relatively small number of investing institutions.

Having looked at alternative forms of private ownership and their characteristics it is important to contrast this with our earlier assessment of state-ownership structures. Two major conclusions emerge. First, the institutional framework described above as necessary to generate effective insider control looks very similar to that which would emerge under multiple state-ownership. Each envisages a relatively small number of institutions providing debt and equity finance to enterprises and making financial decisions on the basis of enterprise performance. As we have seen, however, the incentive mechanisms inherent in private ownership are likely to be more effective because of the different location of residual risk and control and the different linkages it generates between them.

Second, the fact that private ownership may in principle generate superior incentive mechanisms does not mean that outsider-control mechanisms under private ownership will necessarily be preferable to the insider-control mechanisms under state ownership which multiple agencies would generate. We are unable to say with any certainty whether the potential advantages of private ownership would outweigh the problems associated with outsider control or not. If they do then privatization of any form will be preferable to state ownership, but if not, then multiple state-ownership would be preferable to the introduction of dispersed private shareholdings and the creation of active stockmarkets such as has been sought in Eastern Europe and attempted in some parts of China. On the basis of our arguments above, however, insider control by privately owned financial institutions would be preferable to either. Whether this objective would be pursued better by creating the institutions first, with privatization coming subsequently, or by first creating widespread private ownership of large enterprises with the requisite institutions coming into existence and amassing block holdings later is not clear and may in practice represent a false dichotomy. In practice private insider-control requires the creation of joint-stock enterprises and financial intermediaries and suitable provisions or regulations to ensure concentrated holdings of enterprise equity. There is no fundamental hurdle to such reforms being implemented simultaneously.

To summarize, we believe that a particular institutionalized form of private ownership which generates an insider form of control is likely to be superior to either continued state ownership or to the dispersed type of privatization of enterprise assets currently being pursued as part of the transitional process in some socialist economies. This does not mean that there could not be efficiency gains from these other types of reform. Rather it is the case that no other approach provides both optimal ownership *and* institutional structures. They should therefore at best be seen as no more than transitional phases on the road to full enterprise reform.

7. The Principal–Agent Issue

The previous sections have looked at the issues of ownership and control virtually without reference to the principal–agent problem. This may at first sight appear surprising, given that this problem has been at the very centre of much recent theorizing about the relationship between owners of enterprises on the one hand and agents such as managers whom they recruit to act for them. One reason for this omission is that this type of problem (described below) and the inefficiencies which stem from it are to be found in *all* forms of large-enterprise ownership. A second reason is that the problem identified in principal–agent analysis may not be particularly significant in comparison with the other problems which exist in current arrangements in Chinese enterprises, and in any process of transition to private ownership. Third, there are theoretical solutions to the problem, which can in practice be implemented and which therefore go a long way towards alleviating the concerns. We now go on briefly to explore these issues.

The essence of the principal–agent problem is straightforward (for a simple formal derivation see Hay and Morris 1991: 312–17). In the present context a shareholder is a principal who recruits a manager to act as his agent. The agent has a different utility function from the principal and his actions or effort cannot be directly observed. The only circumstances in which the agent will act as the principal wishes, i.e. will replicate what the principal would do if the principal were acting himself, is if the agent obtains the same marginal benefit for each increment of effort as the principal would have done. If the principal's concern is purely profit then the agent must receive a pound for each extra pound he earns, just as the principal would have done. The only solution for this is if the principal takes a lump sum from the agent consistent with the agent still being willing to act as an agent, and then lets the agent keep everything he can earn. This, however, loads all the risk on the agent, the principal having a certain guaranteed sum in all states of the world. If the principal is risk-neutral because he holds a diversified portfolio of shares, and the agent is risk-averse because all his remuneration is dependent on his position as agent, then all the risk has been loaded on to the transactor least prepared to bear it, and so risk is not optimally distributed. A profit-sharing scheme between the principal and agent could achieve an optimal distribution of risk but then the incentives to the agent to act in the interests of the principal are reduced. No contract embracing optimal incentives and optimal risk-sharing is then possible. A number of rather trivial exceptions, e.g. where agents are risk-neutral, where no disutility of effort enters the agent's utility function, and where there is *ex post* observability of the agent's effort have been explored.

Though this type of problem has received a lot of attention, there are reasons for thinking that in practice, both in China and the West, the problem which it describes is not particularly crucial. This is because there is a particular type of remuneration schedule that can solve the principal–agent problem. The problem arises partly because only the outcome is observable. This is dependent on the agent's action and the state of the world, both of which are unobservable. However, if there are many agents facing the *same* state of the world in each time-period then the variation in agents' action or effort can be inferred (Hay and Morris 1991: 312–17). If the outcome of one agent's actions is poor at a time when that of all other agents facing the same state of the world is good, it can be inferred that the first agent's effort was low. In order to reflect this it is necessary to establish a *relative* performance-related remuneration schedule, in which each agent is remunerated not in terms of the outcome of his actions but in terms of the relative outcome. The highest rewards go to those generating the *best* outcome, irrespective of the absolute level of the outcome.

Three important characteristics of this type of remuneration schedule are that it gives optimal incentives to agents to act as the principal would have done, that the remuneration actually paid is not influenced by the exogenous and uncontrollable state of the world, and that the principal therefore bears the risks inherent in the states of the world. In addition the schedule does not need revising in the light of changes in the state of the world, as would be the case in an absolute performance-related remuneration schedule.

It might be thought that this extension of the principal–agent problem is little more than a theoretical curiosum in that relative performance-related pay schedules rarely if ever are implemented and, indeed, are very likely to be strongly resisted by the agents concerned. It is certainly true that established pay scales in the West rarely if ever incorporate such schedules. This, however, ignores two facts. First, there are a number of examples of such remuneration in the West, the most widespread being the regular bonuses and prizes awarded by, for example, car manufacturers to those franchisees who sell most cars in an area in a given period, these prizes often including family holidays abroad and the like, the value of which is sizeable in relation to annual overall income. 'Salesman of the month' awards and similar schemes have the same effect. Second, and much more significant, promotion is likely to be very largely determined by relative performance with the amount of future remuneration at stake far exceeding any current income received. Whatever the state of the world and the consequent general level of performance, it is the better-performing agents who tend to get promoted and hence gain access to the higher incomes associated with higher positions. In theory, the existence of multiple agents and promotion opportunities eliminate the standard principal–agent problem.

Two problems remain. First, the analysis does require that agents genuinely face the same states of the world. Rarely is this completely the case, if only because agents transact with different customers, are responsible for different work-forces, and work with different capital. Nevertheless, in many real world situations these differences are not sufficiently important to undermine the use of promotion as part of an optimal remuneration system. The second problem is more serious. The promotion mechanism may work very well within the typical management structure, where the outcome of each agent's effort is reasonably observable by his immediate superior, be this defined in terms of profit or in terms of input to a team's contribution towards profit. This is unlikely to be the case however as between the most senior managers of an enterprise and the shareholders. While overall performance of the management group may be easily seen, the contribution of each individual manager may be difficult to identify. In addition there is no more senior post to which the most successful managers would be promoted.

The principal–agent problem can none the less still be largely overcome in the context of an insider-control structure. First, the crucial elements in the problem are the asymmetry of information between principal and agent and the non-observability of agents' effort. Where the principals are a small number of equity-holding institutions, they will typically be represented directly on the board of the enterprise, and this will substantially reduce or even in some cases eliminate both problems. Second, to the extent that such problems remain the principals will be able to implement a relative remuneration system in that they will influence or determine promotion opportunities within the senior management positions.

In addition, the financial resources allocated by the equity-owning institutions to each enterprise, and hence the status, power, and security accruing to its managers, will in part depend on the relative performance of the different enterprises in which they hold equity stakes. An outsider-control system operating via dispersed equity holdings in a stockmarket has some similarities but is likely to be weaker, first because the use of internally generated funds is less likely to be scrutinized closely by the principals and second the latter will typically have much less good information on the opportunities, decisions, and abilities of the managerial group.

It may be added that the principal–agent problem is more readily overcome where companies adopt a so-called M (or multidivisional) structure internally rather than a U (unitary) structure (see Williamson 1971). Williamson has argued that if firms adopt the former, as increasingly has occurred in the West, then control by the board must predominantly be exercised by the setting of performance targets formulated largely in terms of profitability, the monitoring of these, and adjustment of the targets in the light of performance over time. This mechanism can generate behaviour similar to profit maximization over time but, equally important, constitute an organizational structure within which relative performance-related rewards can easily be implemented.

Principal–agent problems also arise in financial relationships, generating agency costs. A number of such costs can occur (see Jensen and Meckling 1976). Here we highlight two fairly typical ones. First, debt finance is in principle an optimal incentive contract in that it involves a fixed return to the lender, with all gains in excess of this being retained by the company. It does not of course share risk optimally. But, in addition there is an agency cost of debt in that it creates an incentive for managers, if they are acting entirely in the interests of existing shareholders, systematically to adopt more risky projects. This is because such projects systematically increase the likelihood of particularly high or particularly low returns. The former increases returns on equity but not on debt. The latter reduces debt-holders' expected returns through insolvency but not the equity-holders', due to limited liability. The net result is an unambiguous shift of wealth from bondholders to equity-holders. This agency cost may occur either because control mechanisms ensure that managers operate purely in the interests of shareholders, or because they hold shares themselves.

Second, there is an agency cost of equity, namely the incentive which managers have to spend resources on their own perquisites, where the marginal return to them is 100% of the funds used, rather than pay dividends to equity-holders where their marginal return is only equal to the (possibly very small) fraction of all the equity which the managers own.

Both types of agency cost are likely to be prevalent in state-owned enterprises. Managers have an incentive to dissipate profits in the form of perquisites rather than remit them to the state, and an incentive to adopt excessively risky projects financed by debt. They will obtain rewards and status if the risks pay off but the state will lose if they do not succeed. However, similar effects operate under private ownership and were originally identified in that context. In the present context the main implication lies elsewhere, namely in relation to control form. With insider control both types of cost are likely to be reduced, primarily because both equity- and debt-holders will be present on the boards that make investment decisions and determine managerial expenditure. There may on occasion be conflict *between* principals over exposure to risk, but the agency costs associated with the principal–agent relationship can largely be overcome.

We conclude that the type of principal–agent problem which has attracted considerable attention in recent years is not central to our present concern. Not only do such problems exist under state ownership as well as private ownership but scope exists for solving them, particularly when insider-control methods are available. This is true whether we have in mind private ownership or the type of reorganized public ownership described in the previous section. It is not the question of whether agents can in practice be controlled under conditions of uncertainty, information asymmetry, and divergence of objectives that is crucial; rather it is the extent of marketability of residual risk and the location and effectiveness of control, as elaborated in Sections 5 and 6, which are the key determinants of efficiency.

8. Some Implications of Enterprise Reform

We have in this chapter been mainly concerned with the economic characteristics of ownership and its functions at the level of the industrial enterprise. We do not seek here to elaborate on the detailed steps which would be necessary in order to implement an enterprise-reform programme of the type introduced above. But there are some additional changes which, whether or not they are desirable in isolation, would need to be implemented if such a programme were to be successfully introduced.

First, such reform cannot be fully effective unless market signals are reasonably accurate indicators of resource costs. This implies continuation of price reform and the effective elimination of state-planned quotas and price controls. So called loss-contracts remain appropriate where there are externality effects, relating for example to congestion, pollution, and health and safety and in some circumstances in the light of the shadow price of foreign exchange, but not otherwise. Second, there is a need for greater tax transparency, such that all enterprises can know clearly and *ex ante* the likely tax implications of their decisions. This does not of course rule out changes to the structure of taxation but does imply that all enterprises face the same taxation schedules and hence the same incidence of taxation in equivalent financial positions. Failure to complete these reforms would to some degree inhibit investors from taking stakes in enterprises likely to be affected and could seriously weaken the incentive linkages between enterprise performance and investment risk.

Third, it must be recognized that further private ownership will tend to generate greater inequality of wealth in the economy. The extent of this will tend to be less under the insider control structure described here than under an outsider system based primarily on a stockmarket, because in general the financial structure associated with the former permits smaller, more dispersed investment by individuals and access for them to diversified portfolios. But there will still be gainers and losers, differences in the extent to which individuals are prepared to bear risk, and different preferences as between expenditure and accumulation of wealth, all of which will generate greater wealth inequalities. However, reduction of state ownership does not necessarily render the state less able to influence inequality. It retains or can establish appropriate tax mechanisms for achieving redistribution, though this itself will require institutional reforms and may be costly and time-consuming to implement.

Fourth, the introduction of private ownership has major implications for the way in which the state discharges its social welfare functions. At present employment policy, health, pensions, education, and housing are all to a greater or lesser extent dependent on and provided through industrial enterprises. With ownership reform, the level of employment would become largely a matter for macroeconomic demand management but there would remain major problems over the mechanisms for providing unemployment benefit, as well as the other benefits noted above. Health insurance, pensions, education, and housing can all be provided publicly or privately, and in the West are mainly provided separately from enterprises, but this does not mean that China could quickly or easily convert to a similar framework. Initially it would probably be necessary for local government to set up new boards to take over these functions from enterprises, thereby reducing enterprise costs, but financing these bodies through higher levels of taxation. (Such bodies might well have ownership functions also in a multiple state-ownership system.) It would be a separate question to what extent these functions were then supplied exclusively by the state or were in some degree available via a private sector, in particular in housing, pensions, and health insurance.

Fifth, the extension of private ownership to larger industrial enterprises would make it essential to generate competition between them, and to maintain and promote this via a powerful competition policy. Without effective competition, enterprises may operate inefficiently without serious penalty and can exploit dominant positions to generate excessive profits. This proposition is also valid in a world of managerial enterprises pursuing growth strategies, where growth of market share and diversification into other markets are crucial driving forces. The intensity of competition may be enhanced by aggressive growth strategies of firms, in both established and new products, in domestic and export markets, but this will not necessarily eliminate all dominant positions.

Generating an increase in competition is not likely to be easy where existing large enterprises have dominant positions in their industry in the province in which they are located. In time better communications, transport, and distribution systems may well increase competition via greater geographical integration, but this is likely to be a slow process. In some cases international trade can offer a powerful source of competition, as can inward investment in new joint ventures. But more generally the only alternative is a policy of progressively breaking up existing enterprises prior to, or in the process of privatization. In many industries this will also be difficult. Large-scale production lines cannot easily be divided and, while there may be scope for splitting enterprises into new individual product line firms, this will frequently make relatively little difference to the market power exercised in relation to any particular product.

In practice the most efficient way to tackle this problem involves concentrating the early stages of privatization in regions and industries where substantial competition already exists or is emerging, and adopting specific measures to make the structure of other industries more competitive prior to privatization. These measures would include incentives for managers to establish new production lines, preferential terms for new enterprises in the provision of finance and contracts, accelerated closure of older production lines where opportunity arises, and where possible the splitting up of production into separate divisions which could then be sold off separately. In most cases fragmentation need not go so far as to inhibit the achievement of economies of scale, though even where it does, the efficiency gains arising from competition may justify this. These relate not only to the direct effects of product-market competition on efficiency but also to the gains from private ownership associated with the greater competition. There would be clear advantages in linking the process of deconcentration to that of privatization, establishing new units of production and the institutional arrangements for the relocation of ownership of them simultaneously.

Sixth, the absence of state ownership of an enterprise, while reducing the likelihood of a 'soft' budget, does not eliminate it. Governments may provide subsidies for many economically sound or unsound reasons to privately owned enterprises in financial difficulty. It would therefore be necessary to establish arrangements which, if not eliminating subsidies, would severely limit them. These would involve five main characteristics: (i) separation of the subsidy function away from provincial government agencies and banks to new bodies charged with industrial policy responsibilities; (ii) transparency of subsidies in the sense that their size, source, and purpose would be clearly accounted; (iii) monitoring of subsidies to ensure that their use was consistent with eventual elimination of the factors that made them necessary in the first place; (iv) conditionality of subsidies on performance improvements over time; and (v) progressive penalties for continuing poor performance. These could involve for example reducing subsidies, making them conditional on managerial changes, arranging for the selling-off of some assets, and eventual take-over. Under a reformed public ownership system, adjustment of bonus arrangements, demotions, and reallocating managerial control would be alternative strategies.

It follows from all the above that the next stages of ownership reform cannot be seen in isolation. Reforms to date, increasing autonomy, the development of contractual arrangements between the authorities and enterprise managers, and establishing incentive mechanisms for managers and workers, have been dependent to some degree on price reform, because the latter determines the signals and rewards in the context of which such reforms operate; and to some extent reform of the tax system has followed on from the managerial contract systems introduced. But existing reforms have not required nor been extensively associated with the development of competition or reform of social security provision. Increasingly however these, together with further price decontrol and additional moves to tax transparency, will become essential if further enterprise reform is to be feasible and capable of generating improvements in economic welfare. It is important therefore that these associated reforms be set in motion as early as possible.

9. Conclusions

The reform of socialist economies around the world has become a major issue of the 1990s. The position of large state-owned enterprises in China is however exceptional in two respects. First, the regionally decentralized structure of state authority coupled with obligations on provincial, city, and county authorities to meet centrally determined tax burdens means that these authorities have incentives to enhance the efficiency and profitability of the enterprises under their control which do not exist in a more centralized system. Second, a decade of reforms has already generated a large measure of price decontrol, limitation of state planning to a largely 'indicative' role, growing enterprise autonomy, and a series of contractual arrangements between the authorities and enterprises which embody significant efficiency incentives. These reforms have contributed to rapid growth in the 1980s and have avoided many of the problems now facing reform in Eastern Europe.

We have none the less argued that further substantial reform is both feasible and desirable. A number of elements in enterprise operations remain heavily controlled by the authorities, most notably employment, investment, and finance. These powers are used to pursue a number of objectives some economically sound, some not, and are also deployed in the light of a range of social welfare responsibilities which state authorities bear. The decision structure which determines all main resource-allocation issues in a region is still essentially monolithic, there is little incentive to create or maintain competition between enterprises and there are indicators that as a result of these features the performance of state-owned enterprises lags behind that of other types of enterprise. The responsibilities of state authorities together with current financing arrangements contribute towards the existence of soft budget constraints which inhibit efficiency incentives and weaken enterprise performance.

Further useful reforms can be achieved within a framework of continuing state ownership of enterprise. Progress could be made by converting more enterprises to joint-stock status, with the equity then held by a number of state institutions including several local authorities, banks, and other financial institutions concerned mainly with profitability. This would increase enterprise autonomy, reduce the monolithic nature of key resource decisions, make intervention on non-commercial grounds more difficult, and reduce the scope for budget constraints to be relaxed. Problems would still exist in relation to profit delivery, the decision criteria adopted, and the promotion of competition between enterprises; mechanisms through which conflict between the various equity-owning institutions could be reduced would need to be established and the diminution of economic power exercised by local authorities might lead to some instability or unwillingness to let such reform work effectively. But such changes would be likely to be beneficial and could fit well into the continuing process of enterprise reform started in the 1980s.

We none the less argue that ownership matters and that without the introduction of private ownership, gains from further reform will necessarily be limited. This is not for the most part based on evidence comparing private and public ownership. It is in principle possible to make such comparisons in the West and, as we have seen, to a limited extent in China; and this evidence is consistent with our views. But such comparisons are in China generally clouded by other differences, in particular industry and scale effects, and the extent of competition. Certainly no direct evidence on private ownership in large industrial enterprises in China is available. Rather we base our argument on the defining functions of ownership and the incentive effects that emerge from different locations of those functions. On this view, an enterprise is a set of contracts which the managers co-ordinate. Ownership consists of the powers to appoint, reward, and dismiss managers and to allocate residual risk. The existence of effective incentives to ensure enterprise efficiency requires either that the residual risk-bearers control enterprises through the power to appoint managers, etc., or that there is a market in residual risk. The fundamental problem with state ownership is that ultimately it is not possible to ensure this condition. Typically ownership control lies with various state institutions and residual risk with some cross-section of the population. The latter have neither control nor marketability of their risk. While some institutional forms of state ownership will be superior to others, with multiple state-ownership offering potential to associate some residual risk with control and to permit some transferability of risk, these basic features are inherent in public ownership. In contrast private ownership prevents those exercising control from unilaterally assigning residual risk elsewhere. Either it is combined with control or is transferable through voluntary trading, in both cases creating efficiency incentives for the enterprise.

We then argue that 'outsider' control, where residual risk is predominantly tradable, is likely to be less efficient than 'insider' control where those bearing residual risk are either directly involved in control or vest these powers in groups who can exercise direct control. They may not necessarily face an effective market for residual risk. This conclusion arises partly because of inefficiences in markets for corporate control but also because of the welfare effects arising from the pursuit of longer-term growth objectives which can be inhibited by too active a market for corporate control. This suggests that attempts to shift from the present structure of state ownership of large industrial enterprises to widely dispersed private shareholdings is unlikely to be optimal. A better strategy for reform would be to establish joint-stock status for enterprises, permit the creation of various types of private financial intermediaries including banks, investment trusts, and pension funds, and then arrange for the sale of enterprise stock to these institutions. These arrangements would not rule out scope for some individual shareholdings in an enterprise, in particular by the managers and work-force of the enterprise, nor would it exclude a continuing public sector stake in some enterprises. Such institutional arrangements might in the first instance be established within a framework of state ownership of the financial institutions involved, with stakes in these subsequently being sold to the public.

Such changes could not occur in isolation. They would gain from continuation of the process of price decontrol and increasing tax transparency. More important they would entail a radical transfer of social security functions away from enterprises, an active programme of deconcentration of production and distribution, and the introduction of a strong competition policy designed to reduce and then remove dominant market positions arising from the legacy of state ownership. While cases will still arise where the authorities would wish to intervene through provision of subsidies, they would not do so as a result of ownership responsibilities but as part of an explicit industrial policy, and such intervention would normally be transparent, temporary, and conditional.

We cannot say whether a substantial shift to private ownership of large enterprises is politically feasible at the present time, or whether it will be in the future. Traditionally it has been argued that a socialist form of organization, in which the people own the means of production, distribution, and exchange, must entail ownership by the state as the representative of the people. Such a view is consistent with a number of alternative forms of public ownership, but would rule out private ownership irrespective of its incentive or efficiency characteristics. Against this it may be argued, on the basis of the functions of ownership examined above, that state ownership constitutes ownership by the institutions of the state rather than by the people, and cannot therefore be justified purely in terms of its representative nature. In practice private ownership has increasingly been introduced in China, suggesting that efficiency criteria are relevant. Whether it can successfully be extended into large industrial enterprises may therefore depend eventually on whether the state can devise the necessary forms of regulation to achieve its economic and social objectives independent of the ownership function which it currently exercises.

Overall, there can be little doubt that economic reform in China in the 1980s has for the most part been immensely successful. The process of enterprise reform has been characterized by highly innovative thinking aimed at bringing Western-style incentives into the management of state-owned enterprises. There is no reason to think that the gains from such a process are at an end and, as we have seen, further reforms are available which will more closely replicate a Western system while none the less maintaining full state ownership. We have argued however that differences of ownership between institutionally similar decision and control structures are not of a minor or technical nature, but ones which *per se* have a significant effect on the existence, impact, and efficiency of the incentive mechanisms involved. This does not, as we have shown, imply that private ownership is a sufficient condition for efficiency. It does suggest that a particular institutional form of private ownership of large industrial enterprises should be a main goal of the next stage of economic reform in China if their full potential for efficiency gains is to be realized.

NOTES

1. The main exception is Hungary, which had a history of growing liberalization on which to build. See Kaser and Allsopp (1992). For arguments in support of the 'big bang' approach see M. Boyko (1991).
2. Agricultural output grew by 85.8% in the 1980s. Labour productivity grew at 4.7% p.a., 1980–84 but then stagnated (SYC 1991: 26, 43, and 44).
3. In 1990, the breakdown of total industry output was as follows: state-owned, 57.1%; collectively owned, 37.3%; privately owned, 5.6% (SYC 1991: 356, 357, and 372).
4. Productivity growth in the 1980s has been as follows: state-owned, 4.4% p.a.; collectively owned, 8.1% p.a.; privately owned (since 1985) 12.8% p.a. (ibid.).
5. Calculated from data on pp. 26, 43–4, 356–7, and 372 of SYC 1991.
6. For specific evidence on the relative performance of state-owned enterprises elsewhere see Boardman and Vining (1989).
7. For a presentation of the theoretical argument against state ownership, see De Alessi (1980: ii. 1–47).
8. Non-voting shares have been subject to increasingly severe restrictions which have made them progressively less attractive.
9. Fama and Jensen (1983) have shown that, if residual risk is separate from managerial decision-taking, then *control* of managers must be separate from the latter. Our argument adds that if control is none the less separate from residual risk then those bearing the risk must be able to trade it.
10. Strictly it is free exit, i.e. the ability to liquidate a risk position rather than marketability that is important, e.g. a holding in an investment trust may not be marketable nor confer any control rights, but is widely accepted because the position can be liquidated within certain rules. For convenience we continue to use the concept of marketability, treating such liquidation as the sale of the financial instrument back to the issuer.
11. A potentially important reform within the context of single-agency state ownership is *leasing*. In principle this transfers both control and residual risk, at least for a period, to those taking on the leasehold of industrial assets, thereby meeting the

incentive and risk conditions specified above. Leasing also has the advantages, first, that it could evolve quite easily out of the contractual arrangements already existing between many enterprises and industrial bureaux; and second, that leases or franchises can be auctioned, thereby increasing competitive pressures to efficiency. Against this there are some familiar problems, in particular the incentive to take short term gains at the expense of assets or returns beyond the lease period, the responsibility on the state to maintain operations if the management group fails (ultimate residual risk), the asymmetric advantages to encumbents when leases come up for renewal, and the difficulties of valuing assets when leases are re-assigned and assets transferred.

12. Other reconciliations are discussed in D. Morris (1994).
13. We address below the outsider control of the intermediaries themselves which this implies.
14. This does not mean that the holdings of any one financial institution could not be quite highly diversified across a number of enterprises, but in general insider-control mechanisms attach much less weight to a portfolio approach, particularly if it leads to too heavily dispersed holdings.

APPENDIX I

Characteristics of the Sample and Data Consistency

1. Introduction

The purpose of this Appendix is to make a comparison between the characteristics of the firms in our sample and the characteristics of the universe of industrial enterprises in China, and to report on some tests of the reliability of the data-set. The nature of the sample is important because we need to know whether conclusions based on the analysis of the sample can be used to make inferences about the sector as a whole, and to make policy recommendations. The reliability of the data will obviously affect both the nature of the statistical analyses, and the degree of confidence in the results. Poor data restrict the range of analyses that can be undertaken, and undermine our confidence in the results.

2. The Characteristics of the Sample

The comparison of the sample with the total universe of industrial enterprises can be made in three ways: the distribution of firms according to size and sector, size characteristics of the firms, and some simple indicators of performance. Comparisons are presented for 1987; similar exercises for earlier years generated similar results, but are not repeated here.

In Table AI.1 the distribution of sample firms by scale and industry is compared to the universe of industrial enterprises in 1987. The identification of firms by scale is based on criteria that vary from sector to sector. However it is evident that the sample is heavily skewed towards large and medium-sized firms. Thus large-scale firms account for 77% of the employment, 83% of the output, and 84% of the fixed assets of the sample firms: the corresponding percentages for the universe of state-owned firms are 19%, 30%, and 45%. The sectoral analysis suggests that the large-scale bias in the sample means that some sectors are under- or over-represented. The major discrepancy arises in the ferrous metal industry, which accounts for 32% of employment and 27% of output value in the sample, compared to 5% and 7% nationally. The main effect of this is to give the appearance that virtually every other sector is under-represented in the sample. However, if ferrous metals firms are excluded, the distribution of the other firms is not far from the national average, though light industry continues to be under-represented (presumably because of smaller-scale operations), notably in food and textiles. Engineering is also under-represented.

TABLE AI.1. Size distribution of sample (S) enterprises and total industry (T) enterprises in 1987

	Firm's number		Proportion of workers		Proportion of gross output		Proportion of fixed assets	
	S	T	S	T	S	T	S	T
I. By scale								
1. Large	142	2888	77.09	18.90	83.36	29.73	83.29	44.85
2. Medium	126	6862	18.03	15.34	14.77	19.35	12.51	20.58
3. Small	56	408154	4.88	65.71	1.87	50.92	2.30	34.56
Total	324	417904	100.00	100.00	100.00	100.00	100.00	100.00
II. By sectors								
1. Coalmining	8	9458	10.94	8.86	1.46	3.26	6.50	8.34
2. Oil	2	29	3.40	1.06	1.28	2.70	5.72	5.89
3. Ferrous material	1	1270	0.04	0.47	0.02	0.21	0.02	0.43
4. Non-ferrous	1		0.10		0.05		0.08	
5. Building materials	4	10092	0.39	1.49	0.08	0.44	0.24	0.63
9. Water	7	2836	0.82	0.35	0.34	0.24	1.45	1.16
Total industry 1								
10. Food	22	43664	2.11	5.53	2.31	7.45	0.97	4.02
11. Drink	16	14706	1.08	1.97	1.39	2.11	0.97	1.64
12. Tobacco	14	304	2.36	0.43	9.70	2.56	1.50	0.49
13. Feed	2	3643	0.01	0.19	0.02	0.47	0.00	0.15
Total industry 2								
14. Textiles	29	23026	5.75	5.53	4.30	12.69	2.33	7.12
15. Sewing	7	18965	0.43	3.48	0.31	2.10	0.11	0.76
16. Leather	9	7990	0.55	1.56	0.28	1.11	0.13	5.04
Total industry 3								

17. Timber	7	10 989	0.95	1.35	0.50	0.74	0.44	0.59
19. Paper	16	9 762	1.34	2.39	0.97	2.11	0.81	1.67
20. Printing	14	10 538	0.74	1.61	0.50	1.03	0.52	0.89
21. Stationery	7	3 943	0.42	0.75	0.43	0.54	0.19	0.25
Total industry 4								
23. Power	7	11 407	0.79	2.18	0.92	3.35	1.93	12.85
24. Oil-processing	8	626	1.47	0.58	8.17	3.13	3.42	1.84
25. Coal-processing	4	2 038	0.73	0.33	1.20	0.30	1.06	0.47
Total industry 5								
26. Chemicals	15	16 228	5.43	6.01	7.85	7.57	11.97	7.53
27. Medicine	14	2 664	2.92	1.16	3.80	1.92	1.84	0.94
28. Fibres	8	435	0.98	0.57	1.13	1.19	1.16	1.78
29. Rubber	18	3 587	2.33	1.30	2.91	1.53	1.19	0.77
30. Plastic	11	13 234	0.71	2.16	0.97	1.92	1.33	1.29
Total industry 6								
31. Building materials	21	55 837	2.99	11.78	1.50	5.48	1.75	6.44
32. Ferrous metal	14	2 766	32.06	4.57	26.70	7.08	40.82	8.80
33. Non-ferrous	13		3.09		6.86		3.13	
34. Metal-processing	12	30 460	1.40	4.62	0.82	3.12	0.65	1.82
Total industry 7								
35. Engineering	25	42 412	5.92	15.30	4.26	11.39	3.38	11.47
36. Transport equipment	15	10 227	3.36	4.72	2.15	3.93	1.93	4.28
37. Electrical	13	14 013	1.72	4.05	2.68	4.44	1.06	2.37
38. Electronics	11	4 043	1.50	2.40	3.68	3.13	1.03	2.02
39. Meters	6	3 434	0.60	1.24	0.42	0.75	0.35	0.79
Total industry 8								
TOTAL	386		100.00	100.00		100.00	100.00	100.00

TABLE AI.2. The fiscal characteristics and performance of sample enterprises (S) and total industry (T) enterprises in 1987

	Workers per firm		Original value of fixed assets per worker		Depreciation rate		Labour productivity		Gross output/ original value of fixed assets	
	S	T	S	T	S	T	S	T	S	T
I. By scale										
1. Large	6831	4674	26274	30428	3.6		45001	21509	275.66	85.8
2. Medium	1800	1550	16985	17727	3.2		27117	17255	225.42	117.9
3. Small	1096	115	11826	6792	3.2		17597	12510	297.93	177.8
Average	3242	2113	18361	16052			29905	17091	266.34	127.2
II. By sectors										
Industry 1										
1. Coalmining	21513	585	14562	13382	6.52	4.50	3883	3746	33.44	30.59
2. Oil	30679	22783	27354	78693	5.61	4.77	15331	27125	114.68	57.5
3. Ferrous metal	567	231	13280	12899	3.98	5.03	8695	6882	116.73	47.4
4. Non-ferrous	1621		22844		4.81		7748	6794	67.51	45.9
5. Building materials	1531	92	15765	5921	4.18	5.06	5333	4865	48.71	45.6
9. Water	1851	78	48721	46614	0.81	3.14	16787	10012	35.23	24.8
Industry 2										
10. Food	1510	79	12570	10963	2.85	4.55	29940	24312	306.98	235.3
11. Drink	1066	84	22515	11755	4.13	4.72	25259	15749	516.38	159.8
12. Tobacco	2557	878	17152	16676	4.77	4.13	100622	84754	790.47	688.0
13. Feed	59	39	3837	11548	7.08	4.68	61415	50950	2576.09	391.25
Industry 3										
14. Textile	3121	150	12065	5795	2.71	4.96	27569	18334	229.71	200.0
15. Sewing	957	115	6557	3100	1.65	6.21	21258	19134	322.89	349.0
16. Leather	958	122	7409	4580	3.06	5.64	14381	14264	244.08	276.1

Industry 4										
17. Timber	2 151	76	11 953	6 339	2.31	5.12	10 620	10 290	142.83	134.35
19. Paper	1 321	153	16 567	10 058	3.15	4.98	16 588	16 450	142.09	158.9
20. Printing	836	96	18 599	7 761	3.58	5.06	17 249	12 270	123.86	145.95
21. Stationery	942	120	10 849	4 674	2.59	5.62	24 422	20 356	309.13	272.77
Industry 5										
23. Power	1 783	120	61 825	84 023	1.0	3.43	28 360	25 547	59.64	33.01
24. Oil-processing	2 897	581	48 967	45 506	4.04	5.29	107 000	80 350	312.47	212.17
25. Coal-processing	2 882	101	43 181	20 523	3.65	3.88	26 808	12 791	142.61	71.24
Industry 6										
26. Chemicals	5 691	231	25 136	17 804	2.45	5.04	25 692	19 872	142.13	114.67
27. Medicine	5 421	272	16 348	11 571	4.34	5.50	43 980	32 430	291.85	256.64
28. Fibres	1 939	790	39 983	44 420	1.27	4.85	52 963	44 760	129.14	29.44
29. Rubber	2 040	226	13 134	8 455	5.25	5.02	35 532	29 136	293.75	253.04
30. Plastic	1 010	102	30 158	8 459	1.80	5.86	39 348	24 328	185.21	153.13
Industry 7										
31. Building materials	2 245	132	15 953	7 417	4.73	5.19	10 768	7 752	111.98	88:94
32. Ferrous metal	36 035	1 032	34 910	27 192	3.86	3.80	21 605	19 976	165.74	93.82
33. Non-ferrous	3 744		23 614		2.64		64 479	26 391	446.48	116.02
34. Metal-processing	1 838	95	12 887	5 561	2.96	5.63	15 875	14 820	172.50	177.03
Industry 8										
35. Engineering	3 725	225	15 531	10 574	3.97	4.57	20 921	12 889	179.04	105.58
36. Transport equipment	3 528	288	12 505	12 719	2.46	4.41	17 249	14 273	185.28	97.10
37. Electrical	2 089	180	16 475	8 283	5.45	5.19	42 799	20 754	269.06	185.22
38. Electronics	2 152	370	17 502	11 976	3.15	6.03	84 468	31 737	315.18	172.33
39. Meters	1 575	226	15 984	8 872	2.05	4.49	37 657	11 228	106.29	94.6

TABLE AI.3. The performance of sample enterprises (S) and total industry (T) enterprises in 1987

	Profit and tax/ original value of fixed assets		Profit and tax per worker		Remittance (profit and tax) per worker		Retained profit per worker	
	S	T	S	T	S	T	S	T
I. By scale								
1. Large	74.59	20.22	14 445	6 152	5 797	5 085	1 558	919
2. Medium	40.83	21.29	5 766	3 774	2 785	2 904	1 006	652
3. Small	37.04	20.90	2 856	1 413	1 127	937	834	321
Average	50.82	20.80	7 689	3 780	3 236	2 975	1 133	631
II. By sectors								
Industry 1								
1. Coalmining	−0.96	−1.40	−60	−105	−151	293	114	22
2. Oil	15.65	10.18	2 803	8 091	1 340	6 677	402	386
3. Ferrous metal	21.78	8.91	2 892	1 350	282	770	794	455
4. Non-ferrous	28.41	7.23	6 490		3 374		242	
5. Building materials	6.28	6.39	815	688	523	410	154	195
9. Water	9.46	6.36	4 347	2 998	1 627	1 520	2 245	1 264
Industry 2								
10. Food	31.11	20.54	3 889	2 108	1 706	1 405	1 112	546
11. Drink	125.14	33.67	11 198	3 596	4 653	3 401	1 341	393
12. Tobacco	459.87	397.39	77 692	65 225	25 695	68 996	1 574	1 309
13. Feed	231.12	30.52	8 839	3 429	2 379	772	6 494	1 870
Industry 3								
14. Textiles	36.47	26.98	4 126	1 691	2 098	1 234	1 027	425
15. Sewing	52.74	31.30	4 233	964	2 883	600	891	198
16. Leather	28.96	27.54	2 259	1 261	505	823	467	256

Industry 4								
17. Timber	14.14	17.94	1 755	1 246	551	830	747	351
19. Paper	20.92	25.00	3 448	2 551	1 977	1 925	516	426
20. Printing	21.40	22.82	4 058	1 771	1 445	971	1 338	509
21. Stationery	102.91	47.92	8 712	2 240	4 814	1 445	1 531	488
Industry 5								
23. Power	−6.87	12.61	−1 053	10 332	5 893	8 948	634	998
24. Oil-processing	77.99	69.25	39 298	31 395	22 906	28 433	2 481	1 507
25. Coal-processing	24.84	7.18	7 866	1 676	5 184	1 624	2 483	894
Industry 6								
26. Chemicals	25.79	22.08	6 674	4 140	3 037	3 043	1 039	695
27. Medicine	54.28	45.26	8 609	5 237	3 331	2 900	2 403	1 312
28. Fibres	24.19	20.23	9 263	8 965	2 804	7 246	1 952	1 009
29. Rubber	51.49	51.88	7 393	3 917	4 651	3 386	548	371
30. Plastic	26.87	21.52	6 722	1 830	2 418	1 076	1 276	307
Industry 7								
31. Building materials	22.62	17.14	3 262	1 245	1 538	889	1 080	275
32. Ferrous metal	30.05	20.94	6 203	5 790	3 181	4 341	1 317	1 434
33. Non-ferrous	27.79	17.11	5 857		2 344		1 344	
34. Metal-processing	35.13	31.31	3 761	1 600	1 733	987	880	343
Industry 8								
35. Engineering	30.40	16.31	4 475	1 959	1 840	1 253	1 108	503
36. Transport equipment	18.44	12.71	2 150	1 907	835	1 228	720	626
37. Electrical	53.57	31.67	11 216	2 860	5 007	1 952	1 159	530
38. Electronics	31.19	21.73	6 160	2 949	2 297	1 633	1 751	661
39. Meters	30.34	18.26	4 941	1 921	1 711	1 204	1 263	466
Average	51.97	34.01	8 268	5 838	3 718	5 069	1 296	657

In Table AI.2, comparisons are made of size, fixed assets per worker, labour productivity, and output per fixed assets. Once again, it is evident that the sample is dominated by large firms. The average size is more than 50% larger than the national average and the discrepancy is most apparent in the small-scale category where the sample firms are larger by a multiple of nine. Furthermore, the larger scale of sample firms is associated with higher physical assets per worker, higher labour productivity, and higher output per fixed assets. While there are some exceptions to this pattern at the sectoral level, the average cannot be attributed to outliers in a few sectors which are distorting the comparisons. In Table AI.3 further comparisons are made on the basis of financial indicators: gross returns (profit plus tax) on fixed assets, gross returns (profit plus tax) per worker, tax and remitted profits per worker, and retentions per worker. Once again there is a consistent pattern across all sectors with the sample firms generally having higher returns, remitting more profit and paying more tax, but still retaining more profit on a per-worker basis.

It is evident that in comparison with firms from the whole industrial sector in China, our sample represents the largest and probably most efficient firms. Unfortunately, the comparison can only be made with the whole sector which includes collective-owned and privately owned enterprises which are relatively small in size. We have no means of comparing our sample with the state-owned sector alone, but we have no reason to believe that it is a biased sample of that sector. Given that the focus of the research is on the state-owned sector, a sample from that sector is obviously the most appropriate. Moreover, from the point of view of the aggregate Chinese industrial sector, it is evident that the state-owned sector makes a major contribution to output and employment.

3. Appraisal of Reliability of the Database

3.1. Introduction

The Chinese Enterprise Database provided by the Chinese Academy of Social Sciences consists of 176 quantitative variables relating to the production and finances of 386 Chinese state-owned manufacturing enterprises in 1980, and for each year between 1983 and 1987. There are more than 400,000 items of information. Before analysis can be undertaken, it is clearly important to appraise the quality and reliability of the data.

The principle of checking for errors is to use the concept of accounting balance and flows. Thus the sum of the assets should equal the sum of the liabilities in the balance sheet; sources of funds should equal uses of funds; value added should equal the sum of its component costs, and should also equal value of output less material inputs; and investment should be equated to the sources of funds for investment.

Failure to add up may indicate either an error in the data, or that the

TABLE AI.4. Structure of the data

Identifiers
Each enterprise is identified by a six-digit number. The first two digits identify the industry (coded 01 to 39), the second two digits identify the location, and the last two digits identify the enterprise at that location.

Production account	1–59		
1–3	Value of output		
4–16	The production costs		
17–56	The work-force: wages and characteristics		
57–59	Working hours, capacity utilization		
Investment and finances	60–76		
60–63	Investment		
64–76	Sources of finance for investment		
R & D, innovation, and training	77–82		
Balance sheet data	83–129		
	Assets		*Liabilities*
Fixed	83–87	Long-term	106–110
Circulating	88–99	Circulating finance	111–123
Special	100–105	Special	124–129
Profits and taxation	130–150		
130–140	Profit from activities		
141–150	Taxation, investment, loan repayments		
Annual changes	151–156		
Allocation of profit	157–170		

accounts represented in the database are incomplete or that we have failed to understand the accounting conventions applied. The last possibility led us to try a number of different specifications of the accounting identities to see which had the highest 'success' rate in encompassing the data. As a working rule we distinguished three categories: those where the values satisfied the presumed accounting identity precisely; those where the error was less than 5% of whichever was the lower total on either side of the accounting identity; and those where the error was larger. We accepted the first two categories as confirming the supposed identity: but errors >5% were identified as 'unknown'. It is our expectation that the data satisfying the first two categories will be satisfactory for further analysis: but the 'unknown' data points should not be used unless the source of the error (or of the misunderstanding of the relevant accounting identity) can be identified.

The data structure is summarized in Table AI.4. The accounts are divided into two groups. The first group consists of production (management) accounts: production in the short run, investment activity, and allocations to R & D and training. The second group comprises accounting data: balance sheets, profits and taxation, and uses of retained profits. Our understanding is that this pattern broadly reflects Chinese accounting practice applied to the state-owned manufacturing enterprises: but they are in an abbreviated form, and this may account for some of the discrepancies reported below.

3.2 Checks for reliability

(i) *Balance sheets*

Our expectation is that the balance sheets will contain the following items:

	Assets		*Liabilities*
Fixed	83 or 87	Long-term finance	106
Circulating	88	Circulating finance	111
Special	100	Special finance	124
	——		——
Total assets		Total liabilities	

Total assets should equal total liabilities. The identification of the correct variable for fixed assets was uncertain. The detailed results of our tests are given in Table AI.5(*a*). The formula which accords best with the data is

$$87 + 88 + 100 = 106 + 111 + 124.$$

If we take the < 5% error criterion as an indicator of acceptability of the data, then 75% of the cases conformed with the formula in 1980, increasing to 89% in 1987. However the proportion for which the formula fitted precisely was only 34.7% in 1980, and this increased by only two percentage points by 1987. A handful of enterprises fitted an alternative formula with 83 replacing 87. The 'unknown' formula group was 20% of the sample in 1980, and was still at about 10% in 1987. As expected there was a statistical improvement in the data quality over the period.

Further tests showed that a considerable number of the 'unknown' cases were the same firms in consecutive years, and that they were clustered in particular industries (see Table AI.5(*b*)). The former might be the result of persistent accounting errors carried forward from year to year, or of persistent adoption of alternative accounting conventions. The incidence was higher in the following industries: water, food, drink, tobacco-processing, food-processing, tailoring, oil-processing, electronics, and telecommunications.

Some of the main sections in the balance sheet listed above are also broken down into their components in the questionnaire. So we carried out further checks to see whether these components added up to the totals given for each section. The results are given in Table AI.5(*c*). These checks reveal two problem areas. The first is 'special assets' where the components do not add to the total for more than half the enterprises over all 6 years. This probably

TABLE AI.5(*a*). Balance sheets: data consistency checks

		1980 No. and % of firms		1983 No. and % of firms		1984 No. and % of firms		1985 No. and % of firms		1986 No. and % of firms		1987 No. and % of firms	
Equation	$d = 0$	134	34.7	160	41.5	154	39.9	155	40.2	149	38.6	142	36.8
(1)	$0 < d < 5\%$	156	40.4	159	41.2	182	47.2	180	46.6	194	50.3	201	52.2
Equation	$d = 0$	4	1.0	3	0.8	2	0.5	3	0.8	2	0.5	2	0.5
(2)	$0 < d < 5\%$	11	2.8	6	1.6	3	0.8	5	1.3	4	1.0	5	1.3
Unknown		81	21.0	58	15.0	45	11.7	43	11.1	37	9.6	36	9.3
TOTAL		386	100	386	100	386	100	386	100	386	100	386	100

Notes: (1) = Equation: 87 + 88 + 100 = 106 + 111 + 124; (2) = Equation: 83 + 88 + 100 = 106 + 111 + 124; d = Deviation: $d\% = d * 100/a$, $(a < b)$ or $d\% = d * 100/b$, $(b < a)$, where $d = a - b$.

TABLE AI.5(*b*). Data consistency checks on balance sheets: firms with $d > 5\%$

Code of industry	No. of firms						Total in 6 yrs	%
	1980	1983	1984	1985	1986	1987		
(1)	1	2	0	0	1	1	5	1.7
(2)	0	0	1	0	1	0	2	0.7
(5)	2	1	1	1	0	0	5	1.7
(9)	2	1	2	1	2	2	10	3.5
(10)	10	8	5	4	3	4	34	11.8
(11)	3	3	2	2	2	1	13	4.5
(12)	5	4	1	1	3	2	16	5.6
(13)	2	2	2	1	1	1	9	3.1
(14)	6	1	0	3	2	2	14	4.9
(15)	3	4	4	3	3	2	19	6.6
(16)	1	1	1	1	1	2	7	2.4
(17)	0	1	0	0	0	0	1	0.3
(19)	3	2	1	0	0	1	7	2.4
(20)	1	1	0	2	0	0	4	1.4
(21)	2	0	1	1	1	1	6	2.1
(23)	2	2	1	1	0	1	7	2.4
(24)	3	0	2	2	1	1	9	3.1
(25)	1	1	1	0	0	0	3	1.0
(26)	2	2	1	1	1	1	8	2.8
(27)	5	3	2	2	2	2	16	5.6
(28)	2	1	2	0	1	1	7	2.4
(29)	2	0	0	1	1	1	5	1.7
(30)	2	4	2	1	1	2	12	4.2
(31)	3	3	2	3	2	1	14	4.9
(32)	2	2	1	0	0	0	5	1.7
(33)	2	0	1	1	1	1	6	2.1
(34)	3	2	1	2	1	1	10	3.5
(35)	1	1	0	0	0	1	3	1.0
(36)	2	2	2	2	2	2	12	4.2
(37)	2	1	1	1	0	0	5	1.7
(38)	4	4	1	1	1	1	12	4.2
(39)	1	0	0	1	0	0	2	0.7
GRAND TOTAL							288	100.0

reflects the absence of some major components from the list given in the questionnaire. The second is 'other circulating capital', where the 'unknown' category is between a third and a half of the enterprises in each year. A particular difficulty is that the increased flexibility in obtaining finance offered to Chinese enterprises under the reform has not been fully reflected in adjustments to accounting procedures.

We also attempted to check the movements in item 87 (net value of fixed assets at the end of the financial year). Our expectation was that this item would be arrived at as follows: net value of fixed assets = net value of fixed

TABLE AI.5(c). Data consistency checks: balance sheet items

		1980 No. and % of firms		1983 No. and % of firms		1984 No. and % of firms		1985 No. and % of firms		1986 No. and % of firms		1987 No. and % of firms	
Equation	$d = 0$	124	32.1	102	26.4	118	30.6	101	26.2	97	25.1	114	29.5
(1)	$0 < d < 5\%$	164	42.5	191	49.5	195	50.5	217	56.2	226	58.5	215	55.7
Unknown		98	25.4	93	24.1	73	18.9	68	17.6	63	16.3	57	14.8
TOTAL		386	100	386	100	386	100	386	100	386	100	386	100
Equation	$d = 0$	275	71.2	189	49.0	152	39.4	117	30.3	103	26.7	96	24.9
(2)	$0 < d < 5\%$	56	14.5	148	38.3	183	47.4	192	49.7	213	55.2	198	51.3
Unknown		55	14.2	49	12.7	51	13.2	77	19.9	70	18.1	92	23.8
TOTAL		386	100	386	100	386	100	386	100	386	100	386	100
Equation	$d = 0$	174	45.1	128	33.2	132	34.2	132	34.2	127	32.9	115	29.8
(3)	$0 < d < 5\%$	79	20.5	74	19.2	80	20.7	72	18.7	79	20.5	76	19.7
Unknown		133	34.5	184	47.7	174	45.1	182	47.2	180	46.6	195	50.5
TOTAL		386	100	386	100	386	100	386	100	386	100	386	100
Equation	$d = 0$	337	87.3	339	87.8	228	59.1	335	86.8	330	85.5	335	86.8
(4)	$0 < d < 5\%$	14	3.6	15	3.9	21	5.4	20	5.2	25	6.5	20	5.2
Unknown		35	9.1	32	8.3	137	35.5	31	8.0	31	8.0	31	8.0
TOTAL		386	100	386	100	386	100	386	100	386	100	386	100
Equation	$d = 0$	108	28.0	43	11.1	39	10.1	32	8.3	33	8.5	33	8.5
(5)	$0 < d < 5\%$	75	19.4	58	15.0	56	14.5	75	19.4	100	25.9	90	23.3
Unknown		203	52.6	285	73.8	291	75.4	279	72.3	253	65.5	263	68.1
TOTAL		386	100	386	100	386	100	386	100	386	100	386	100

TABLE AI.5(*c*) (*cont.*)

		1980 No. and % of firms		1983 No. and % of firms		1984 No. and % of firms		1985 No. and % of firms		1986 No. and % of firms		1987 No. and % of firms	
Equation	$d = 0$	198	51.3	183	47.4	175	54.9	212	54.9	223	57.8	207	53.6
(6)	$0 < d < 5\%$	113	29.3	161	41.7	173	44.8	161	41.7	147	38.1	164	42.5
Unknown		75	19.4	42	10.9	38	9.8	13	3.4	16	4.1	15	3.9
TOTAL		386	100	386	100	386	100	386	100	386	100	386	100
Equation	$d = 0$					11	2.8	11	2.8	15	3.9	16	4.1
(7)	$0 < d < 5\%$					281	72.8	303	78.5	301	78.0	311	80.6
Unknown						94	24.4	72	18.7	70	18.1	59	15.3
TOTAL		386	100	386	100	386	100	386	100	386	100	386	100

Notes:
(1) = Equation: 11 = 112 + 113 + 114 + 115 + 116 + 119 = 120 + 121 + 122 + 123
(2) = Equation: 124 = 125 + 126 + 127 + 128 + 129
(3) = Equation: 93 = 94 + 95 + 97 + 98 + 99
(4) = Equation: 106 = 107 + 108 + 109 + 110
(5) = Equation: 100 = 101 + 103 + 104 + 105
(6) = Equation: 89 = 90 + 91 + 92
(7) = Equation: 087 = 087 (previous year) − 007 + (083 − 083 (previous year))
d = Deviation: $d\% = d * 100/a$, $(a < b)$ or $d\% = d * 100/b$, $(b < a)$, where $d = a - b$.

assets (previous period) *less* depreciation (7) *plus* increase/decrease in net value of fixed assets (revaluation) *plus* additions to fixed assets by investment.

Unfortunately, there is no item in the questionnaire relating to revaluations of existing fixed assets, though it is thought that enterprises do undertake such revaluations in order to calculate their fixed costs appropriately. For additions to fixed assets by investment, we used the change from the previous year in item 83 (original value of fixed assets). This formula fitted 75–85% of the enterprises with deviations of less than 5%.

(ii) *Production accounts*

There are three formulae by which this account may be checked. The first is the general formula giving the gross value of output (2) as the sum of material input costs (4) and value added by the enterprise (11). The second breaks down material input costs (4) into the following components:

Raw materials at market prices	5
Fuel and Energy	6
Depreciation	7
Funds for repairing equipment	8
Value of materials received from buyers of the products	9
Others	10

The third formula breaks down value added (11) into its components:

Profits plus sales taxes	12
Wages	13
Welfare funds	14
Interest payments	15
Others	16

As can be seen from the detailed results in Table AI.6, the second and third formulae conform quite closely to the data, with a success rate of more than 90% if the 5%-error criterion is applied. The general formula is less accurate: it fits precisely in only 11–16% of the cases depending on the year, and the percentage unknown is 23% of the cases in 1980, falling below 10% of the cases in 1987. A number of enterprises are listed in the unknown category in several consecutive years: this suggests that they are using alternative accounting criteria, rather than data errors (unless it be the inability of the enterprise accountants either to identify the right numbers or to add them up!) There was above average incidence of the unknown category in the following sectors: coal mining, drink, food processing, tailoring, printing houses, electric power generation, building materials.

(iii) *Sales revenue and profit*

Two formulae were used to check whether a particular main item in the accounts was the sum of the component items listed with it. The first formula gives sales revenue (130) as a sum of the following items:

TABLE AI.6. Data consistency checks: production account

		1980 No. and % of firms		1983 No. and % of firms		1984 No. and % of firms		1985 No. and % of firms		1986 No. and % of firms		1987 No. and % of firms	
Equation	$d = 0$	44	11.4	62	16.1	43	11.1	40	10.4	61	15.8	62	16.1
(1)	$0 < d < 5\%$	242	62.7	228	59.1	281	72.8	275	71.2	272	70.5	283	73.3
Unknown		0	0.0	0	0.0	0	0.0	0	0.0	0	0.0	0	0.0
(2)	$0 < d < 5\%$	11	2.8	14	3.6	6	1.6	7	1.8	3	0.8	3	0.8
TOTAL		386	100	386	100	386	100	386	100	386	100	386	100
Equation	$d = 0$	241	62.4	278	72.0	262	67.9	260	67.4	278	72.0	283	73.3
(4)	$0 < d < 5\%$	97	25.1	77	19.9	100	25.9	103	26.7	90	23.3	84	21.8
Unknown		48	12.4	31	8.0	24	6.2	23	6.0	18	4.7	19	4.9
TOTAL		386	100	386	100	386	100	386	100	386	100	386	100
Equation	$d = 0$	276	71.5	279	72.3	277	71.8	264	68.4	303	78.5	300	77.7
(6)	$0 < d < 5\%$	92	23.8	89	23.1	96	24.9	108	28.0	71	18.4	76	19.7
Unknown		18	4.7	18	4.7	13	3.4	14	3.6	12	3.1	10	2.6
TOTAL		386	100	386	100	386	100	386	100	386	100	386	100

Notes:
(1) = Equation: 02 = 11 + 04
(2) = Equation: 01 = 11 + 04
(4) = Equation: 04 = 05 + 06 + 07 + 08 + 09 + 10
(6) = Equation: 11 = 12 + 13 + 14 + 15 + 16
d = Deviation: $d\% = d * 100/a$, $(a < b)$ or $d\% = d * 100/b$, $(b < a)$, where $d = a - b$.

TABLE AI.7. Data consistency checks: sales revenue and profits

		1980 No. and % of firms		1983 No. and % of firms		1984 No. and % of firms		1985 No. and % of firms		1986 No. and % of firms		1987 No. and % of firms	
Equation	$d = 0$	153	39.6	147	38.1	132	34.2	111	28.8	53	13.7	20	5.2
(1)	$0 < d < 5\%$	185	47.9	194	50.3	220	57.0	240	62.2	303	78.5	340	88.1
Unknown		48	12.4	46	11.9	34	8.8	34	8.8	30	7.8	26	6.7
TOTAL		386	100	386	100	386	100	386	100	386	100	386	100
Equation	$d = 0$	63	16.3	38	9.8	52	13.5	41	10.6	38	9.8	41	10.6
(2)	$0 < d < 5\%$	219	56.7	184	47.7	190	49.2	210	54.4	198	51.3	177	45.9
Equation	$d = 0$	0	0.0	0	0.0	0	0.0	0	0.0	0	0.0	0	0.0
(3)	$0 < d < 5\%$	22	5.7	48	12.4	36	9.3	33	8.5	30	7.8	28	7.3
Unknown		82	21.2	116	30.1	108	28.0	99	25.6	120	31.1	142	36.8
TOTAL		386	100	386	100	386	100	386	100	386	100	386	100

Notes:
(1) = Equation: 130 = 134 + 135 + 137 + 142 + 143
(2) = Equation: 140 = 137 + 138 − 139
(3) = Equation: 140 = 137 + 138
d = Deviation: $d\% = d * 100/a$, $(a < b)$ or $d\% = d * 100/b$, $(b < a)$, where $d = a - b$.

Production costs	134
Selling costs	135
Profits from sales	137
Sales tax	142
Tax on products	143

The second formula gives fulfilled profit (140) as a sum of profits from sales (137), and non-operating income (138 less 139).

The data were generally consistent with the first formula, but failed to satisfy the second formula in about 37% of cases in 1987 (see Table AI.7).

(iv) *Flow of funds*

Checks on the flow of funds (sources and uses) are reported in Chapter 7, where the discussion forms part of the framework for the analysis of firms' financial and investment behaviour.

References

Alchian, A., and Demsetz, H. (1972), 'Production, Information Costs and Economic Organisation', *American Economic Review*, 62: 777–95.

Arellano, M., and Bond, S. (1988), 'Some Tests of Specification for Panel Data: Monte Carlo Evidence and an Application to Employment Equations', Applied Economics Discussion Paper 55 (Oxford: Institute of Economics and Statistics, Oxford University).

Beijing Review, various dates.

Boardman, A., and Vining, A. (1989), 'Ownership and Performance in Competitive Environments: A Comparison of the Performance of Private, Mixed and State-Owned Enterprise', *Journal of Law and Economics*, 32: 1–33.

Boyko, M. (1991), 'Price Decontrol: The Microeconomic Case for the "Big Bang" Approach', *Oxford Review of Economic Policy*, 7/4: 35–45.

Buchanan, J. M., Tollison, R. D., and Tullock, G. (1980), *Toward a Theory of the Rent-Seeking Society* (College Station, Tex.: Texas A & M University).

Byrd, W. A. (1991), 'Contractual Responsibility Systems in Chinese State-Owned Industry: A Preliminary Assessment', in *Advances in Chinese Industrial Studies*, ii (Greenwich, Conn.: JAI Press).

Camerer, C. (1989), 'Bubbles and Fads in Asset Prices', *Journal of Economic Surveys*, 3: 32–40.

Chan, S., Martin, J., and Kensinger, J. (1990), 'Corporate Research and Development Expenditures and Share Values', *Journal of Financial Economics*, 26: 255–76.

Child, J. (1987), 'Enterprise Reform in China: Progress and Problems', in M. Warner (ed.), *Management Reforms in China* (London: Frances Pinter).

Chen, K., Jefferson, G., Rawski, T. G., Wang, H., and Zheng, Z. (1987), 'Productivity Change in Chinese Industry 1953–85', *Journal of Comparative Economics*, 12: 570–91.

— — — — — (1988), 'New Estimate of Fixed Investment and Capital Stock for Chinese State Industry', *China Quarterly*, 114 (June), 243–60.

Chinese Accountancy Manual (1984) (Shanxi Publishing House), 65.

Coase, R. (1937), 'The Nature of the Firm', *Economica*, NS 4: 386–405.

De Alessi, L. (1980), 'The Economics of Property Rights: A Review of the Evidence', in R. Zerbe (ed.), *Research in Law and Economics*, ii (Greenwich, Conn.: JAI Press).

Dernberger, R. F., and Eckhaus, R. S. (1988), *Analysis II: Financing Asian Development* ii. *China and India* (Lanham, Md.: University Press of America).

Dong, Fureng (1992), 'The Conduct of China's State-Owned Enterprises under a Two-Tier System', mimeo (Beijing: Chinese Academy of Social Science).

Du, Haiyan (1989), 'A Review of the Reform of China's State-Owned Enterprises during the Past Decade (1979–89)', mimeo (Beijing: Chinese Academy of Social Science).

— (1992), 'Contract Responsibility System of State-Owned Enterprises at the Present Stage in China', mimeo (Beijing: Chinese Academy of Social Science).

EEPRC (1988), *Economic Events in the People's Republic of China* (Beijing: Economic Publishing House).

Enterprise Management (1987), 'State Council's Eight Regulations for stimulating Enterprise Autonomy', Editorial article, *Enterprise Management*, Feb. 1987 (Beijing, in Chinese).

Fama, E., and Jensen, M. (1983), 'Separation of Ownership and Control', *Journal of Law and Economics*, 26: 301–25.

Feldstein, M., and Flemming, J. (1971), 'Tax Policy, Corporate Savings and Investment Behaviour in Britain', *Review of Economic Studies*, 38: 415–34.

Firth, M. (1979), 'The Profitability of Takeovers and Mergers', *Economic Journal*, 89: 316–28.

Franks, J., Harris, R., and Mayer, C. (1987), 'Means of Payment in Takeovers: Results for the UK and US', Discussion Paper 200 (London: Centre for Economic Policy Research).

Fry, M., and Nuti, D. (1992), 'Monetary and Exchange-Rate Policies during Eastern Europe's Transition: Some Lessons from Further East', *Oxford Review of Economic Policy*, 8/1: 27–43.

Granick, D. (1990), *Chinese State Enterprises: A Regional Property Rights Analysis* (Chicago University Press).

Grossman, S., and Hart, O. (1980), 'Takeover Bids, the Free-Rider Problem and the Theory of the Corporation', *Bell Journal*, 2: 42–64.

Griliches, Z., and Ringstad, V. (1971), *Economies of Scale and the Form of the Production Function* (Amsterdam: North-Holland).

Hay, D., and Morris, D. (1984), *Unquoted Companies* (London: Macmillan).

— — (1991), *Industrial Economics and Organization* (Oxford University Press).

— — Scott Evans, I., Macey-Dare, R. (1991), 'The Performance of Quoted and Unquoted UK Companies in the 1980s' (Oxford: Institute of Economics).

He, Jianzhang (1982), 'More on Planned Economy and Market Regulation', *Economic Studies* (Beijing: Institute of Economics, Chinese Academy of Social Science).

Hess, J. (1983), *The Economics of Organisation* (Amsterdam: North-Holland).

Hsu, R. (1992), *Economic Theories in China 1979–1988* (Cambridge University Press).

Huang, Yasheng (1990), 'Web of Interests and Patterns of Behaviour of Chinese Local Economic Bureaucracies and Enterprises during Reform', *China Quarterly*, 123 (Sept.).

Jarnell, G., Brickley, J., and Netter, J. (1988), 'The Market for Corporate Control: The Empirical Evidence since 1980', *Journal of Economic Perspectives*, 2: 49–68.

Jensen, M., and Meckling, M. (1976), 'Theory of the Firm, Managerial Behaviour, Agency Costs, and Ownership Structure', *Journal of Financial Economics*, 3: 305–60.

— and Ruback, R. (1983), 'The Market for Corporate Control: The Scientific Evidence', *Journal of Finance and Economics*, 11: 5–50.

Johnson, J. (1960), *Statistical Cost Analysis* (New York: McGraw-Hill).

Jorgenson, D. (1963), 'Capital Theory and Investment Behaviour', *American Economic Review*, 53: 247–59.

— and Siebert, C. (1968), 'A Comparison of Alternative Theories of Corporate Investment Behaviour', *American Economic Review*, 58: 681–712.

Kaser, M., and Allsopp, C. (1992), 'Macroeconomic Transition in Eastern Europe', *Oxford Review of Economic Policy*, 8/1: 1–13.

Kornai, J. (1982), *Growth, Shortage and Efficiency* (Oxford, Blackwell).

Kuehn, D. (1975), *Takeovers and the Theory of the Firm* (London: Macmillan).

Laaksonen, Oliva (1988), *Management in China during and after Mao* (Berlin: Walter de Gruyter).

Lin, C. Z. (1988), 'China's Economic Reforms II'; *Asia-Pacific Economic Literature*, 2/1: 1–25.

Liu, Guy S., and Morris, D. (1991), 'Price Deflators for the Capital Stock of Chinese State-Owned Enterprises', Working Paper, Centre for Modern Chinese Studies, Oxford.

Ma Hong (1983), *New Strategy for China's Economy* (Beijing: New World Press).

Marris, R. (1963), *Economic Theory of Managerial Capitalism* (London: Macmillan).

Marsh, P. (1991), 'Market Assessments of Company Performance', paper at NEDO conference on capital markets and company success, Nov. (1991).

Mayhew, K., and Seabright, P. (1992), 'Incentives and the Management of Enterprises in Economic Transition: Capital Markets are not Enough', *Oxford Review of Economic Policy*, 8/1: 105–29.

Meeks, G. (1977), *Disappointing Marriage: A Study of the Gains from Merger* (University of Cambridge).

Morris, D. (forthcoming), 'The Stock Market and Problems of Corporate Control in the UK' in P. Temple *et al.* (eds.), *British Economic Performance in the 1980s* (Routledge).

Naughton, B. (1985), 'False Starts and Second Wind: Financial Reforms in China's Industrial System', in E. Perry and C. Wong (eds.), *The Political Economy of Reform in Post-Mao China* (Harvard University Press).

Nerlove, M. (1965), *Estimation and Identification of Cobb-Douglas Production Function* (Chicago: Rand McNally).

Odagiri, H. (1981), *The Theory of Growth in a Corporate Economy* (Cambridge University Press).

Odagiri, H. (1992), *Growth through Competition, Competition through Growth* (Oxford University Press).

Pakes, A. (1985), 'On Patents, R & D and the Stock Market Rate of Return', *Journal of Political Economy*, 93: 390–409.

Perkins, D. (1988), 'Reforming China's Economic System', *Journal of Economic Literature*, 26/2.

Ravenscraft, D., and Scherer, F. (1987), *Mergers, Sell-offs and Economic Efficiency* (Washington, DC: Brookings Institution).

Reynolds, Bruce Lloyd (1988), *Chinese Economic Reform: How Far, How Fast?* (Boston, Mass.: Academic Press).

Riskin, C. (1987), *China's Political Economy: The Quest for Development since 1949* (Oxford University Press).

Rybczynski, T. (1991), 'The Sequencing of Reform', *Oxford Review of Economic Policy*, 7/4: 26–34.

Sadowski, Z. (1991), 'Privatisation in Eastern Europe: Goals, Problems, and Implications', *Oxford Review of Economic Policy*, 7/4: 46–56.

Sah, E. K. (1990), 'The System of Contracted Management Responsibility in Mainland China', *Issue and Studies*, 26 (Taipei, Taiwan).

Shephard, R. W. (1953), *Cost and Production Functions* (Princeton University Press).

Singh, A. (1975), 'Takeovers, Economic Natural Selection and the Theory of the Firm', *Economic Journal*, 85: 497–515.

SYC (1984, 1991), *Statistical Year Book of China*, Eng. version (Beijing: Statistical Publishing House).

Taihe, Z. (1984), *Economic Reform in Contemporary China* (Beijing: China's Social Science Publishing House, in Chinese).

Tian, Yun (1982), 'The Sichuan Experiment: More Authority to Enterprises', in Wenming Su (ed.), *Economic Adjustment and Reform* (Sichuan: People's Publishing House of Sichuan).

Vickers, J., and Yarrow, G. (1988), *Privatisation: An Economic Analysis* (Cambridge, Mass.: MIT Press).

Walder, Andrew G. (1987), 'Wage Reform and the Web of Factory Interests', *China Quarterly*, 109: 22–41.

Williamson, O. (1971), 'Managerial Discretion, Organisation Form and the Multi-Division Hypothesis', in R. Marris and A. Wood (eds.), *The Corporate Economy* (London: Macmillan).

— (1975), *Markets and Hierarchies* (New York: Collier Macmillan).

— (1981), 'The Modern Corporation: Origins, Evolution, Attributes', *Journal of Economic Literature*, 19: 1537–68.

Wood, A. (1990), *Joint Stock Companies with Rearranged Public Ownership: Invigoration of China's State Enterprises further Considered*, Discussion Paper CP/11, Suntory-Toyota International Centre for Economics and Related Disciplines (University of London).

World Bank (1989), *China: Finance and Investment* (Washington, DC: World Bank).

— (1990), *China, Macroeconomic Stability and Industrial Growth under Decentralized Socialism* (Washington, DC: World Bank).

Xiao, Suzhu (1989), 'Short-Term Behaviour of Enterprise under Contract Responsibility and the Firm's Collective Consumption', *China's Economic Problems*, Apr. 1989 (Beijing, in Chinese).

Zhang, Zan-Luen (1987), *The Director Responsibility System* (Beijing: Economic Publishing House).

Index

The manufacturer's authorised representative in the EU for product safety is Oxford University Press España S.A. of el Parque Empresarial San Fernando de Henares, Avenida de Castilla, 2 – 28830 Madrid (www.oup.es/en or product.safety@oup.com). OUP España S.A. also acts as importer into Spain of products made by the manufacturer.

www.ingramcontent.com/pod-product-compliance
Lightning Source LLC
LaVergne TN
LVHW102007210926
848483LV00009B/116

* 9 7 8 0 1 9 8 2 8 8 4 5 9 *